Processes, Systems, and Information
An Introduction to MIS

Processes, Systems, and Information

An Introduction to MIS

Second Edition

Earl McKinney Jr.
Bowling Green State University

David M. Kroenke

PEARSON

Boston Columbus Indianapolis New York San Francisco Upper Saddle River
Amsterdam Cape Town Dubai London Madrid Milan Munich Paris Montréal Toronto
Delhi Mexico City São Paulo Sydney Hong Kong Seoul Singapore Taipei Tokyo

Editor-in-Chief: Stephanie Wall
Executive Editor: Bob Horan
Development Editor: Laura Town
Program Manager Team Lead: Ashley Santora
Program Manager: Denise Vaughn
Editorial Assistant: Kaylee Rotella
Director of Marketing: Maggie Moylan
Executive Marketing Manager: Anne Fahlgren
Project Manager Team Lead: Judy Leale
Project Manager: Jane Bonnell
Operations Specialist: Michelle Klein
Creative Director: Blair Brown
Senior Art Director: Janet Slowik

Interior and Cover Designer: Karen Quigley
Interior Illustrations: Simon Alicea
Cover Photo: sopose/Shutterstock
VP, Director of Digital Strategy & Assessment: Paul Gentile
Digital Editor: Brian Surette
Digital Development Manager: Robin Lazrus
Senior Digital Project Manager: Alana Coles
Digital Production Project Manager: Lisa Rinaldi
Full-Service Project Management and Composition:
    Integra
Printer/Binder: Courier/Kendallville
Cover Printer: Lehigh-Phoenix Color/Hagerstown
Text Font: 10/12 Times

Credits and acknowledgments borrowed from other sources and reproduced, with permission, in this textbook appear on the appropriate page within text.

Library of Congress Cataloging-in-Publication Data

McKinney, Earl H., Jr.
    Processes, systems, and information: An introduction to MIS / Earl H. McKinney Jr. and David M. Kroenke.
        pages cm
    Includes index.
    ISBN 978-0-13-354675-0
    1. Management information systems.   I. Kroenke, David M.   II. Title.
    T58.6.K7733 2015
    658.4'038011—dc23

                                                    2013039917

10 9 8 7 6 5 4 3 2 1

ISBN 10:   0-13-354675-6
ISBN 13: 978-0-13-354675-0

Brief Contents

Contents

Preface

Since the emergence of ERP and EAI systems in the early 1990s, the MIS discipline has undergone a slow but persistent change. Whereas the early emphasis of MIS was on the management and use of information systems *per se,* emerging cross-functional systems began to place the focus on processes that utilize such systems. We believe that existing MIS textbooks, particularly those at the introductory level, do not sufficiently recognize this change in emphasis. Hence, we offer this textbook that provides a strong process orientation.

Why This Second Edition?

The changes in this second edition are listed in Table 1. Several major changes led to these modifications. One *major change* was to make the flow of the three chapters on dynamic processes (Chapters 9–11) a single, reusable sequence of questions. We want students to see that a single process-oriented sequence of questions can be applied not only to these three chapters but to any dynamic process.

A second change was to add a question at the end of several chapters that summarizes what we expect to see in the next 10 years. While this simple "2024?" could include many topics, we attempted to limit this discussion to the changes in technology that will have the greatest impact on organizational processes and IS.

This second edition also includes a new SAP tutorial on business intelligence (BI). BI and Big Data are essential topics in business schools today for all students, not just for IS majors. In this tutorial, we give students with no IS background a hands-on experience with several of the BI operations discussed in the chapter.

To satisfy the growing number of schools who are "flipping" their classrooms, this edition includes several new MIS InClass exercises and offers improvements to many other InClass exercises. We have used these exercises for many years and have seen the positive benefits they offer as students become engaged in these active learning exercises.

We have also tried to improve the applicability of the major concepts in the book. We added sections on how students can immediately employ several of the conceptual models that form the textbook's foundation. For example, we have now included sections on the application of the five components of IS, the definition of information, and characteristics of processes.

We also expanded our explanation of the importance of procedures. Procedures are the steps by which an IS is used to support a process activity and are often a key to improving the process. In several of the chapters, we more completely describe procedures and how poorly understood procedures can limit processes.

Chapter 3 has been updated to include discussions of Windows 8, native and thin clients, quality criteria for mobile interface user experiences, and a discussion of the cloud. In this edition, Chapter 4 now includes discussions of NoSQL DBMS products and databases as well as Big Data.

A final major change in this second edition concerns the teaching of ethics. In this edition, every Ethics Guide asks students to apply Immanuel Kant's categorical imperative as well as utilitarianism to the business situation described in the guide.

As shown in Table 1, these broad changes led to many of the changes in the chapters, but there were many other changes as well. Several changes were made to keep the chapters up to date. Events and technology move fast, and to keep the text current, we check every sentence and industry reference for obsolescence.

Importance of MIS

Chapter 1 claims that MIS is the most important class in the business curriculum. That's a bold statement, and every year we ask whether it remains true. Is there any discipline having a greater impact on contemporary business and government than IS? We continue to doubt there is. Every year brings important new technology to organizations, and many of these organizations respond by creating innovative applications that increase productivity and otherwise help them accomplish their strategies. In the past year, cloud-based services have continued to revolutionize the

TABLE 1 Changes in the Second Edition

Chapter	Change
1	Added new employment data
	Updated job requirements based on NBER study
	Included a more complete description of the five forces
	Discussed differences between a business process and an information system
	Presented new data on worldwide Internet growth
	Added discussion about the explosion in data and mobile computing
	Added new Singing Valley Case Study 1
2	Included a more complete explanation of the relationship of procedures to processes
	Added new opening vignette about a fast food restaurant
	Made a comparison of two students' four nonroutine skills
	Changed the MIS InClass exercise to a demonstration of sandwich making
	Added how the five-component model can be applied
	Included discussion on how information definitions can be used
3	Added Windows 8, but reduced the emphasis on Microsoft
	Included Microsoft's CEO change
	Added comparison of native and thin-client applications
	Added discussion of quality mobile UX
	Increased emphasis on cloud
	Updated and adapted InClass exercise
4	Introduced NoSQL
	Introduced Big Data
5	Added new opening vignette about a pizza shop in the student union
	Included an application of the characteristics of processes
	Added new sections on automation and procedures
	Inserted new section on process management techniques
	Added new Case Study 5 on Google Cars
6	Added two key characteristics of ERP systems—a single database and inherent processes that integrate well
	Added new data terms—transactional, master, organizational; included single and multiple instance
	Added discussion on the ERP implementation and upgrade processes
	Added a new MIS InClass exercise demonstrating single source of data
7	Included discussion of the SAP implementation process at CBI
	Reorganized the end of the chapter and included a new 2024 question
8	Added a discussion of Google Adwords and Analytics to e-commerce question
	As in Chapter 7, a reorganization led to a new 2024 question
9	Reduced emphasis on SharePoint, BPMN, and process diagrams
	Added a new section on the five components of a collaboration IS
	Included new discussion of collaboration support of project management
	Added a new question on how students can apply collaboration IS to their teams
	Added a new 2024 question
10	Included the topic of competing social media objectives
	Added descriptions on connection data and hashtags
	Added many new examples of business process use of social media
	Added a new 2024 question

Chapter	Change
11	Included a new three-activity BI process—acquire, analyze, and publish
	Added OLAP slice and dice diagrams and examples
	Included an expanded discussion on visualization with examples
	Added new examples of business processes supported by BI
	Included a new question on Big Data
	Added new appendix with a hands-on tutorial to slice and dice Big Data
	Added a new 2024 question
12	Added a new opening vignette
	Added the scrum development process
	Included a new security scenario with the security discussion
	Added threats of XSS and APT
	Added personal security section
	Included a new chapter case study
All	Used the categorical imperative and utilitarianism in Ethics Guides

economics of server hosting while mobile devices simplify yet enrich user experiences. More sophisticated and demanding users push organizations into a rapidly changing future, one that requires continual adjustments in business planning. To participate, our graduates need to know how to apply emerging technologies to better achieve their organizations' strategies. Knowledge of MIS is critical to this application.

The effects of changing technology and new user demands fall on processes and information systems at all levels—workgroup, organizational, and inter-enterprise. The impact on the latter is especially dramatic because cloud-based hosting and mobile devices enable independent organizations to work together in ways previously unimaginable.

As stated, we continue to believe we can enter the classroom with the confidence that we are teaching the single most important course in the business school—an argument that relies on two observations. First, because of nearly free data storage and data communications, businesses are increasingly finding and, more important, increasingly *required* to find innovative applications for information systems. The incorporation of Facebook and Twitter into marketing systems is an obvious example, but this example is only the tip of the iceberg. For at least the next 10 years, every business professional will, at a minimum, need to assess the efficacy of proposed IS applications. To excel, business professionals will need to not only assess but define innovative IS applications. Further, professionals who want to emerge from the middle ranks of management will, at some point, need to demonstrate the ability to manage projects that develop these innovative information systems.

Such skills will not be optional. Businesses that fail to create systems that take advantage of nearly free data storage and communication will fall prey to the competition that can create such systems. So, too, will business professionals.

The second premise for the singular importance of the MIS class relies on the work of Robert Reich, former Secretary of Labor for the Clinton administration. In *The Work of Nations*,[1] Reich identifies four essential skills for knowledge workers in the 21st century:

- Abstract reasoning
- Systems thinking
- Collaboration
- Experimentation

[1] Robert B. Reich, *The Work of Nations* (New York: Alfred A. Knopf, 1991), p. 229.

For reasons set out in Chapter 1, beginning on page 2, we believe the MIS course is the single best course in the curriculum for learning these four key skills.

While most Introduction to MIS textbooks address technical innovation and nonroutine skills, *Processes, Systems, and Information, Second Edition,* uniquely enables the Intro course to also address business processes. The process view of business is the dominant view of business today; students need a consistent, extended opportunity to master the language and apply it. The Introduction to MIS class that uses this textbook can expose both IS and non-IS students to process concepts and appropriately place IS in its vital role of supporting and improving processes. With this process foundation, students are better able to understand the benefits and challenges of ERP systems.

Background on Processes and IS

The relationship between business processes and information systems is complex. They are not one and the same; a given process might use several different information systems, and, at the same time, a given information system might support many different processes. So, we cannot say that a process encapsulates all of its information systems, nor can we say that an information system encapsulates all of its processes.

In part because of this complex relationship, we define *MIS* as the management and use of *processes, information systems, and information* to help organizations achieve their strategy (Chapter 1). We further define *management* not in the traditional sense of plan, organize, control, and staff, but rather as the *creation, monitoring, and adapting of processes, information systems, and information.* The fabric of this text is woven around and through these definitions.

Potential adopters of this textbook are departments that make business processes a key component or thread throughout their curricula. This group includes all of the universities that are part of the SAP University Alliance, those that are part of the Microsoft Dynamics Academic Alliance, and other institutions for which a business process orientation is important. Chapters 7 and 8 provide specific examples of the use of SAP, and the cases that conclude each of those chapters provide tutorial exercises that use the SAP University Alliance's Global Bikes Inc. (GBI) case. This is the same case and client data used in University Alliance training, so it will be familiar to many instructors.

In our opinion, a text must go beyond the operational processes that comprise Chapters 7 and 8. Of course, operational processes are most important, and five chapters of our text include or are devoted to them. However, other dynamic processes, such as collaboration, project management, problem solving, business intelligence, and social networking, are also important. Hence, we believe that this text should include much more than SAP-oriented processes.

Text Features

A challenge of teaching the Introduction to MIS course from a process orientation is the lack of business knowledge and experience on the part of most students. Many universities offer the Introduction to MIS course at the sophomore and even freshman levels. Most of these students have completed few business courses. Even when this course is taught to higher-level students, however, few of them have significant business or process experience. They have been lifeguards or baristas. When we attempt to talk about, for example, the impact of process change on departmental power, that discussion goes over the heads of students. They may memorize the terms, but they often lose the essence of the discussion. The features of this text are designed, in part, to address this problem.

Question-Based Pedagogy

Research by Marilla Svinicki in the Psychology Department of the University of Texas indicates that today's students need help managing their time. She asserts that we should never give homework assignments such as "read pages 75–95." The problem, she says, is that students will fiddle with those pages for 30 minutes and not know when they're done. Instead, she recommends that we give our students a list of questions and the assignment that they be able to answer those questions. When they can answer the questions, they're done studying. We have used this approach in our classrooms, and we believe that it is most effective. Students like it as well. Hence, we have organized each chapter as a list of questions.

Opening Vignettes

Each chapter opens with a short vignette of a business situation and problem that necessitates knowledge of that chapter. We use two different fictitious organizational settings:

1. Central Colorado State, a university with students engaged in activities similar to the activities of our readers
2. Chuck's Bikes, Inc., a bicycle manufacturer that competes with Global Bikes

Each of these vignettes presents a situation that illustrates the use of the chapter's contents in an applied setting. Most contain a problem that requires knowledge of the chapter to understand and solve.

MIS InClass Exercises

Every chapter includes a student group exercise that is intended to be completed during class. These exercises are designed for teachers who seek to use active learning exercises, also called flipping the classroom. The purpose of the exercise is to engage the student with knowledge gained from the chapter. These exercises are part lab and part case study in nature. In our experience, some of them lead to spirited discussions, and we could have let them run on for two or three class periods, had we had that luxury.

SAP Tutorial Exercises

The appendices to Chapters 7 and 8 contain process exercises that involve the SAP Alliance's Global Bike case. Professors at institutions that are members of the alliance can use these with their students. Because not every department that uses this book is a member of that alliance, we have made these exercises optional appendices. You can omit the exercises without any loss of continuity.

The exercises are, we hope, purposeful yet simple to do. Our goal is to make it possible for them to be conducted by teaching assistants and faculty who have not yet attended the SAP university training. To that end, we provide extensive instructor support materials. Instructors who have had training by the SAP University Alliance will immediately recognize that these tutorials use exactly the same data and screens they used during training.

Earl McKinney, the author of the tutorial exercises, has been teaching SAP for 7 years at Bowling Green State University. The tutorial exercises included in this book have been tested extensively with Introduction to MIS students in a BGSU lab setting. In addition to the exercises, Earl has written a detailed teaching guide on how to best use the exercises as well as tips and pointers about their use and his experience about where students are most likely to struggle.

As mentioned earlier, with this second edition, we've added a BI tutorial after Chapter 11. This tutorial uses Business Objects Explorer from SAP. While a particular set of data is specified in the tutorial, students and instructors can also simply read the tutorial, learn how the operations like slicing and filtering are done, and use these Explorer skills on any dataset.

Over these years, Earl learned that when doing SAP exercises, it is far too easy for students to slip into "monkey-see, monkey-do" mode without any clear understanding of what they are doing or why. Based on this classroom experience, we believe that the setup to procurement and sales in Chapters 7 and 8, together with the exercises themselves, help students move beyond simple copy mode, in which they learn the SAP keystrokes, to learn the nature of process-oriented software and its role in organizations.

Like all who have used the GBI case, we are grateful to the SAP Alliance and to the case's authors. In accordance with both the letter and spirit of the SAP Alliance community's policy, we have placed these exercises on the SAP University Alliance Web site. We hope you will find sufficient value in this text to use it in your classroom, but please feel free to use these exercises even if you do not adopt this text.

By the way, the body of Chapters 7 and 8 uses the example of Chuck's Bikes, Inc., rather than GBI. We made this change at the request of the SAP Alliance. The alliance prefers that authors not add new material to GBI, change any characters, make videos, and so forth. We created CBI so as to comply with that request while at the same time providing more detailed business scenarios that are compatible with GBI.

Ethics Guides

We believe that business ethics are a critically important component of the Introduction to MIS course and that the best way to teach ethics is in the context of case-like situations. We also believe that ethics ought not to be relegated to a single chapter or chapter section. Including ethics in one place leads to the inoculation theory of education: "We don't need to discuss ethics, we've already done that." Accordingly, each chapter contains one two-page spread called an Ethics Guide. They are shown in the table of contents; to sample just one of them, turn to page 20.

In recent years, we believe there has been a shift in students' attitudes about ethics. Many students seem to be increasingly cynical and callous about ethical issues. As a result, when we try to raise interest with them about unethical behavior, we find ourselves interjecting and defending a particular set of values, a role that strikes many students as inappropriate. A common attitude seems to be, "We should think for ourselves, thank you anyway."

In frustration about the situation, we turned to a good friend of many years, Dr. Chuck Yoos, emeritus professor from the U.S. Air Force Academy. We told him our goals for presenting the Ethics Guides and asked him what criteria he would use with his students if he only had 20 minutes per guide. His response was that while there are many ways of addressing ethics in business, Kant's categorical imperative and the utilitarianism of Bentham and Mill would be at the top of his list. We investigated both and decided to use them with this edition.

Our goal in doing so is to ask students, whose ethical standards may be immature, to learn and apply the categorical imperative and utilitarianism perspectives. By doing so, students are asked to "try on" those perspectives and in the process think more deeply about ethical principles than they do when we allow them simply to apply their personal ethical standards.

The Ethics Guide in Chapter 1 introduces the categorical imperative, whereas the Ethics Guide in Chapter 2 introduces utilitarianism. If you choose to use these perspectives, you will need to assign both of those guides.

Collaboration Exercises

As stated in Chapter 1, collaboration is a key skill for today's business professionals. Accordingly, we believe that teaching collaboration, collaboration processes, and collaboration information systems is an important component of this course. To that end, each chapter includes a collaboration exercise to be accomplished by a student team. In our opinion, it is not possible for students to complete all of these in one term. Instead, we recommend using three or four of them throughout the term.

In doing these exercises, we recommend that students not meet face to face, at least not most of the time, but use modern collaboration tools for their meetings. Google Docs and related tools are one possibility. We prefer requiring students to use Office 365 and Microsoft SharePoint.

End-of-Chapter Cases

The chapter-opening vignettes are based on real-life experience, but the organizations they describe are fictitious. We use fictitious companies because we want students to learn from organizational mistakes and, at times, even organizational foolishness. We have not found many real companies that will allow us to share their laundry in this way, and, in any case, it seems unfair to ask for an organization's cooperation and then turn around and publish its problems.

However, we do believe students need to see examples of the role of MIS in actual organizations to help them bridge the chapter content to the real world. Hence, each chapter concludes with a case that illustrates some aspect of the chapter's contents in a real-world company. Unlike the introductory vignettes, the cases all have happy endings.

Active Reviews

Each chapter includes an Active Review at the end. These reviews help students ensure that they have learned the most essential material. They also serve as a list of potential exam questions and thus help students prepare for exams.

Application Exercises

For courses that involve a Microsoft Office component, we have developed a set of Excel and Access exercises for all chapters. These exercises, which assume the student has beginner's level expertise with these products, appear beginning on page 400. They are listed approximately in increasing order of difficulty.

What We Left Out

We chose to keep this book to the traditional 12-chapter length because we find that this number of chapters fits best into the number of class lessons of most courses. Because we are adding substantial process-oriented material, however, that meant we needed to remove some content from the typical Introduction to MIS text.

In this text, we have reduced and simplified the discussions of hardware, software, and data communications to fit into a single chapter. Furthermore, we simplified and shortened the discussion of information systems development. Finally, you will find no mention of IS departmental management in this text. It is not that we believe the shortened and omitted content is unimportant; rather, we think the opportunity cost is the least for these topics.

This text includes some material that has been previously published in David Kroenke's text *Using MIS*. The two texts differ in that *Using MIS* makes information systems primary, whereas this text makes business processes primary. Both texts will continue to be published. Because of this difference, however, every sentence that was brought over was examined from the perspective of business processes and much of that content was changed in both minor and major ways. The discussion of collaboration, for example, is reframed into the context of dynamic business processes. That said, the majority of the material in this text is new.

Chapter Outline

This text is organized into five parts: Introduction, Technology, Structured Processes, Dynamic Processes, and MIS Management.

Introduction

Chapter 1 sets the stage by illustrating the need for this course and especially for the behaviors and skills that students gain in the course. It defines *MIS* and summarizes the means by which organizations obtain goals and objectives. Porter's industry, five forces, and value chain models are presented.

Chapter 2 defines and illustrates processes, information systems, and information. It uses a common fast food restaurant to illustrate the relationship of processes and information systems. It also defines information using the Gregory Bateson definition that *information* is a difference that makes a difference.

Technology

Chapters 3 and 4 address technology. Chapter 3 provides a quick summary of hardware, software, and network products and technologies. Chapter 4 discusses database processing. These chapters serve as a technology platform for the discussions in the remaining chapters.

Structured Processes

Chapters 5 through 8 discuss structured processes and related information systems and information. Chapter 5 provides an overview of the scope and objectives of business processes. It also discusses process adaptation and improvement and the use of process objectives and measures in making process changes. Chapter 6 is a survey of ERP information systems, their benefits, and their challenges.

Chapters 7 and 8 are "applied" chapters. They show how SAP is used in two representative processes: procurement and sales. Two processes were chosen so that students could begin to see what is common to all processes and what might differ between processes. These two processes, buying and selling, are fundamental to business and are widely used. Each chapter includes a student lab exercise appendix that uses the Global Bikes case from the SAP Alliance's curriculum.

Dynamic Processes

Chapters 9 through 11 address what we term *dynamic processes*. Such processes are neither as structured nor as rigid as the more structured operational processes. We dislike the term *unstructured processes* because we believe that such processes do have structure, at least at a meta-level. Each of the three chapters follows a similar flow: The IS that supports each process is discussed first, followed by the activities in the process, and concluding with the business processes supported by the dynamic process.

Chapter 9 discusses collaboration processes for both project management and workflow applications. Chapter 10 addresses the use of social media in organizations. We discuss Lin's theory of social capital, apply that theory to organizational use of social media systems, and survey the processes supported by social media systems. Chapter 11 considers business processes supported by business intelligence (BI) systems and discusses BI systems, data warehouses, data mining, and Big Data.

MIS Management

Part 5 consists of a single chapter, Chapter 12, that addresses MIS management processes. It includes business process management (BPM), the systems development life cycle (SDLC), the scrum development process, and information security. It includes a discussion of processes involved in creating and using an organizational security program.

Supplements

The following supplements are available at the Online Instructor Resource Center, accessible through *www.pearsonhighered.com/kroenke*.

Instructor's Manual

The Instructor's Manual, prepared by Timothy O'Keefe of the University of North Dakota, includes a chapter outline, list of key terms, suggested answers to the MIS InClass questions, and answers to all end-of-chapter questions.

Test Item File

This Test Item File, prepared by ANSR Source, Inc., contains more than 1,500 questions, including multiple-choice, true/false, and essay questions. Each question is followed by the correct answer, the learning objective it ties to, page reference, AACSB category, and difficulty rating.

PowerPoint Presentations

The PowerPoints, prepared by Robert Szymanski of Georgia Southern University, highlight text learning objectives and key topics and serve as an excellent aid for classroom presentations and lectures.

Image Library

This collection of the figures and tables from the text offers another aid for classroom presentations and PowerPoint slides.

TestGen

Pearson Education's test-generating software is available from *www.pearsonhighered.com/irc*. The software is PC/MAC compatible and preloaded with all of the Test Item File questions. You can manually or randomly view test questions and drag and drop to create a test. You can add or modify test bank questions as needed. Our TestGens are converted for use in BlackBoard, WebCT, Moodle, D2L, and Angel. These conversions can be found on the Instructor's Resource Center. The TestGen is also available in Respondus and can be found on *www.respondus.com*.

CourseSmart

CourseSmart eTextbooks were developed for students looking to save on required or recommended textbooks. Students simply select their eText by title or author and purchase immediate access to the content for the duration of the course using any major credit card. With a CourseSmart eText, students can search for specific keywords or page numbers, take notes online, print out reading assignments that incorporate lecture notes, and bookmark important passages for later review. For more information or to purchase a CourseSmart eTextbook, visit *www.coursesmart.com*.

Acknowledgments

First, we thank the numerous fellow-traveler professors and professionals who encouraged the development of this text and who have helped us in many ways along our path. In particular, we thank:

Yvonne Antonucci, *Widener University*

Cynthia Barnes, *Lamar University*

John Baxter, *SAP*

William Cantor, *Pennsylvania State University–York Campus*

Thomas Case, *Georgia Southern University*

Gail Corbitt, *SAP*

Darice Corey, *Albertus Magnus College*

Mike Curry, *Oregon State University*

Heather Czech, *SAP*

Peter Daboul, *Western New England University*

Janelle Daugherty, *Microsoft Dynamics*

Peter DeVries, *University of Houston, Downtown*

Lauren Eder, *Rider University*

Kevin Elder, *Georgia Southern University*

John Erickson, *University of Nebraska at Omaha*

Donna Everett, *Morehead State University*

David Firth, *The University of Montana*

Jerry Flatto, *University of Indianapolis*

Kent Foster, *Microsoft*

Biswadip Ghosh, *Metropolitan State College of Denver*

Bin Gu, *University of Texas at Austin*

William Haseman, *University of Wisconsin–Milwaukee*

Jun He, *University of Michigan–Dearborn*

Mark Hwang, *Central Michigan University*

Gerald Isaacs, *Carroll University*

Stephen Klein, *Ramapo University*

Ben Martz, *University of Northern Kentucky*

William McMillan, *Madonna University*

Natalie Nazarenko, *SUNY College at Fredonia*

Timothy O'Keefe, *University of North Dakota*

Tony Pittarese, *East Tennessee State University*

Martin Ruddy, *Bowling Green State University*

James Sager, *California State University–Chico*

Narcissus Shambare, *College of Saint Mary*

Robert Szymanski, *Georgia Southern University*

Lou Thompson, *University of Texas, Dallas*

Ming Wang, *California State University*

Harold Webb, *University of Tampa*

We wish to thank the unique production team that helped us bring this book into existence. First and foremost, we thank Bob Horan, our editor, for his vision for a process-oriented introductory MIS text and for his untiring support throughout the process. Thanks, too, to Laura Town, our developmental editor, whose direction, guidance, and patient efforts to help us improve the book paid, we believe, great dividends. Everyone should have an opportunity to work with a person like Laura—she's a joy to work with and exceedingly competent. We thank Jane Bonnell who helped us marshal this text and all its supplements through the Pearson production process and Sue Nodine of Integra for her management of the project as well. We also thank Janet Slowik, art director, and her team for designing this book.

We thank our friend and colleague, Chuck Yoos, of Fort Lewis College, for hours and hours and hours of conversation on the meaning of information, the role of information in organizations today, and how to address the instruction of business ethics. Chuck is responsible for the helpful distinction between *perceiving data* and *conceiving information* and many other insights that have shaped this text's material. Chuck's Bikes is named in honor of him.

Finally, we are most grateful to our families, who have lovingly supported us through these processes; to them we dedicate this book.

Earl McKinney Jr.
Bowling Green, Ohio

David Kroenke
Whidbey Island, Washington

About the Authors

Earl McKinney Jr. Teaching the introduction to MIS course has been Earl McKinney's passion for 20 years. He first caught the bug at his alma mater, the U.S. Air Force Academy, and has continued his addiction during his tenure at Bowling Green State University. While teaching that class and other undergraduate and graduate classes, Earl has also introduced a half dozen new courses on security, social media, ERP, and information. He has been awarded a number of department and college teaching awards by students and fellow faculty. His interest in the broader context of the business curriculum is reflected in several of his publications and by the Decision Science Institute's National Instructional Innovation Award.

Earl's research in e-commerce, small team communication during a crisis, and theoretical work on the notion of information has been published in *Behaviour and Information Technology, Human Factors, Information and Management,* and *MIS Quarterly.* He consults with James Hall, the former head of the NTSB for British Petroleum, the U.S. Forest Service, and several Air Force agencies on human factors and aviation communication issues.

He holds an undergraduate economics degree from the Air Force Academy, a Master's of Engineering from Cornell University, and a PhD in MIS from the University of Texas. A former Air Force fighter pilot, Earl lives in Bowling Green with his wife and has two grown sons.

David Kroenke David Kroenke has many years of teaching experience at Colorado State University, Seattle University, and the University of Washington. He has led dozens of seminars for college professors on the teaching of information systems and technology; in 1991 the International Association of Information Systems named him Computer Educator of the Year. In 2009, David was named Educator of the Year by the Association of Information Technology Professionals-Education Special Interest Group (AITP-EDSIG).

David worked for the U.S. Air Force and Boeing Computer Services. He was a principal in the start-up of three companies. He also was vice president of product marketing and development for the Microrim Corporation and was chief of technologies for the database division of Wall Data, Inc. He is the father of the semantic object data model. David's consulting clients have included IBM, Microsoft, and Computer Sciences Corporations, as well as numerous smaller companies. Recently, David has focused on using information systems for collaboration in education and industry.

His text *Database Processing* was first published in 1977 and is now in its 13th edition. He has published many other textbooks, including *Database Concepts,* 6th ed. (2013), *Using MIS,* 7th ed. (2015), *Experiencing MIS,* 5th ed. (2015), *MIS Essentials,* 4th ed. (2015), *SharePoint for Students* (2012), and *Office 365 in Business* (2012). David lives on Whidbey Island, Washington. He has two children and three grandchildren.

Processes, Systems, and Information

An Introduction to MIS

PART 1

WHY MIS?

K nowledge of information systems will be critical to your success in business. If you major in accounting, marketing, management, or another major, you may not yet know how important such knowledge will be to you. The purposes of Part 1 of this textbook are to demonstrate why this subject is so important to every business professional today and to introduce important terms and concepts that you will need to succeed in business.

Chapter 1 lays the foundation. First, we discuss why this course is of critical importance to every business student today. We claim, in fact, that it is the most important course you will take. Then we define *MIS* and explain how organizational strategy determines the structure and functions of MIS components.

In Chapter 2, we will define and illustrate business processes, information systems, and information. As you will see, these three constructs are closely interwoven. Understanding the relationships among them sets the foundation for the rest of this text.

We begin each chapter with a short business vignette to help you relate the chapter's concepts to the business world. Chapter 1 begins with Chuck's Bikes, Inc. (CBI), a bicycle wholesaler that also assembles its own line of bicycles. Throughout the text, we'll meet various employees of CBI; in Chapter 1, we see Kelly terminating an employee, for reasons that you will soon learn.

In Chapter 2, we will investigate the processes of a fast food restaurant near a typical university named Central Colorado State. At the restaurant we'll meet Jake, a student at the university, and see how he puts the ideas of this course to work.

"**F**ired? You're firing me?"

"Well, *fired* is a harsh word, but...well, Chuck's Bikes has no further need for your services."

"But, Kelly, I don't get it. I really don't. I worked hard, and I did everything you told me to do."

"Jennifer, that's just it. You did everything *I* told you to do."

"I put in so many hours. How could you fire me?"

"Your job was to find ways we can generate additional revenue from our existing retailers."

"Right! And I did that."

"No, you didn't. You followed up on ideas *that I gave you*. But we don't need someone who can follow up on my plans. We need someone who can figure out what we need to do, create her own plans, and bring them back to me....and others."

"How could you expect me to do that? I've only been here 4 months!"

"It's called teamwork. Sure, you're just learning our business, but I made sure all of our best salespeople would be available to you..."

"I didn't want to bother them."

"Well, you succeeded. I asked Jason what he thought of the plans you're working on. 'Who's Jennifer?' he asked."

"But doesn't he work out of our other office?"

"Right...and 37 percent of our sales come out of that office. Probably worth talking to him."

"I'll go do that!"

"Jennifer, do you see what just happened? I gave you an idea, and you said you'll do it. That's not what I need. I need you to find solutions on your own."

Q1. Why is Introduction to MIS the most important class in the business school?

Q2. What is MIS?

Q3. How does MIS relate to organizational strategy?

Q4. What five forces determine industry structure?

Q5. What is competitive strategy?

Q6. How does competitive strategy determine value chain structure?

Q7. How does competitive strategy determine business processes and information systems?

"I worked really hard. I put in a lot of hours. I've got all these sales reports written."

"Has anyone seen them?"

"I talked to you about some of them, but I was waiting until I was satisfied with them."

"Right. That's not how we do things here. We develop ideas and then kick them around with each other. Nobody has all the answers. Our plans get better when we discuss and rework them...I think I told you that."

"Maybe you did. But I'm just not comfortable with that."

"Well, it's a required skill here."

"I know I can do this job."

"Jennifer, you've been here almost 4 months; you have a degree in business. Several weeks ago, I asked you for your first idea about how to up-sell our customers. Do you remember what you said?"

"Yes, I wasn't sure how to proceed. I didn't want to just throw something out that might not work."

"But how would you find out if it would work?"

"I don't want to waste money..."

"No, you don't. So, when you didn't get very far with that task, I backed up and asked you to send me a diagram of the life cycle for new clients...how we first contact them, how we make our first sale, how we grow our sales to them..."

"Yes, I sent you that diagram."

"Jennifer, it made no sense. Your diagram had clients talking to Neil in accounts receivable before they were even customers."

"I know that process; I just couldn't put it down on paper. But I'll try again!"

"Well, I appreciate that attitude, but times are tight. We don't have room for trainees. When the economy was strong, I'd have been able to look for a spot for you, see if we can bring you along. But we can't afford to do that now."

"What about my references?"

"I'll be happy to tell anyone that you're reliable, that you work 40 to 45 hours a week, and that you're honest and have integrity."

"Those are important!"

"Yes, they are. But today, they're not enough."

For a similar story, see also *www.youtube.com/watch?v=8UQx-zUuGf4*.

Chapter Preview

"But today, they're not enough."

Do you find that statement sobering? And if timely hard work isn't enough, what is? We will begin this book by discussing the key skills that Jennifer (and you) needs and explain why this course is the single best course in all of the business school for teaching you those key skills.

You may find that last statement surprising. If you are like most students, you have no clear idea what your MIS class will be about. If someone were to ask you, "What do you study in that class?" you might respond that the class has something to do with computers and maybe computer programming. Beyond that, you might be hard-pressed to say more. You might add, "Well, it has something to do with computers in business," or maybe, "We are going to learn to solve business problems with computers using spreadsheets and other programs." So, how could this course be the most important one in the business school?

We begin with that question. Once you have gained an understanding of how important this class will be to your career, we will discuss fundamental concepts.

Q1. Why Is Introduction to MIS the Most Important Class in the Business School?

Introduction to MIS is the most important class in the business school. That statement was not true in 2005, and it may not be true in 2024. But it is true in 2014.

Why?

FIGURE 1-1

Changes in Price/ Performance of Processors

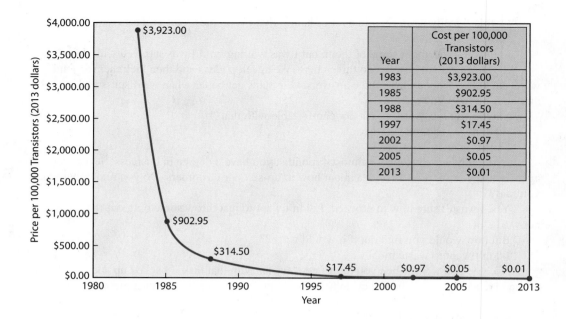

Year	Cost per 100,000 Transistors (2013 dollars)
1983	$3,923.00
1985	$902.95
1988	$314.50
1997	$17.45
2002	$0.97
2005	$0.05
2013	$0.01

The ultimate reason lies in a principle known as **Moore's Law**. In 1965, Gordon Moore, co-founder of Intel Corporation, stated that because of technology improvements in electronic chip design and manufacturing, "The number of transistors per square inch on an integrated chip doubles every 18 months." His statement has been commonly misunderstood to be "The speed of a computer doubles every 18 months," which is incorrect but captures the essence of his principle.

Because of Moore's Law, the ratio of price to performance of computers has fallen from something like $4,000 for a standard computing device to a fraction of a penny for that same computing device.[1] See Figure 1-1.

As a future business professional, however, you needn't care how fast a computer your company can buy for $100. That's not the point. Here's the point:

> **Because of Moore's Law, the cost of data processing, communications, and storage is essentially zero.**

Think about that statement before you hurry to the next paragraph. What happens when those costs are essentially zero? Here are some consequences:

YouTube	Tumblr
Skype	Instagram
Facebook	Google+
Twitter	LinkedIn

In addition to these new apps, Moore's law is also driving several other trends. First, access to the Internet is growing rapidly worldwide, as shown in Figure 1-2. While U.S. growth has slowed, in some countries, access more than doubled over the period of 2008–2012. This growth is expected to continue, because in most of these countries less than half of the population had Internet access in 2012.

Moore's law is also leading to an explosion in data. As shown in Figure 1-3, since 2011, more data is being produced each year than in all the years in human history before 2007 *combined*.

Finally, the most recent significant impact of Moore's law is in mobile platforms. With improved computing performance, mobile device use is expanding rapidly, as shown in Figure 1-4.

These trends of new apps, more access, more data, and greater mobile use are rapidly changing the way businesses use IT. In addition, the opportunities they present to connect to customers throughout the world and improve business activities within the organization mean that

---

[1] These figures represent the cost of 100,000 transistors, which can roughly be translated into a unit of a computing device. For our purposes, the details don't matter. If you doubt any of this, just look at your $49 cell phone and realize that you pay $40 a month to use it.

Country	2008–2012 New Internet Users (millions)	2012 Internet Users (millions)	Growth 2008–2012 (percent)	Population Penetration (percent)
China	264	564	88%	42%
India	88	137	180	11
Indonesia	39	55	244	23
Iran	35	42	500	55
Russia	33	70	89	49
Nigeria	31	48	182	30
Philippines	28	34	467	35
Brazil	27	88	44	45
Mexico	19	42	83	37
USA	18	244	8	78
Argentina	17	28	155	68
Egypt	17	30	131	38
Columbia	13	25	108	54
Turkey	13	35	59	47
Vietnam	12	31	63	35

FIGURE 1-2

Top 15 Countries in New Internet Users

Source: United Nations/International Telecommunications Union, internetworldstats.com

IT is more important to businesses today than any other time in history. This leads us to the first reason Introduction to MIS is the most important course in the business school today:

> **Future business professionals need to be able to assess, evaluate, and apply emerging information technology to business.**

You need the knowledge of this course to attain these skills, and having these skills will lead to greater job security.

How Can I Attain Job Security?

A wise and experienced business executive once said that the only job security that exists is "a marketable skill and the courage to use it." He continued, "There is no security in our company, there is no security in any government program, there is no security in your investments, and there is no security in Social Security." Alas, how right he turned out to be.

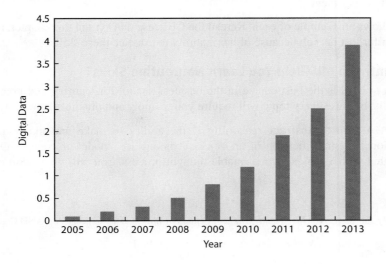

FIGURE 1-3

Global Digital Data Created (in Millions of Petabytes)

Source: Mary Meeker and Liang Wu, "Internet Trends," May 29, 2013, http://www.kpcb.com/insights/2013-internet-trends, slide 11.

FIGURE 1-4
Global Mobile Traffic as Percentage of Total Internet Traffic

Source: Statcounter global stats.
http://gs.statcounter.com/

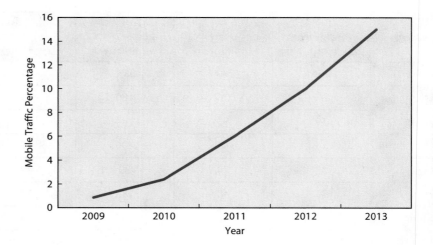

So, what is a marketable skill? Job seekers used to name particular skills, such as computer programming, tax accounting, or marketing. But today, because of Moore's Law, because the cost of data processing, storage, and communications is essentially zero, any routine skill can and will be outsourced to the lowest bidder. And if you live in the United States, Canada, Australia, Europe, and so on, that is unlikely to be you. Numerous organizations and experts have studied the question of what skills will be marketable during your career. Consider two of them.

First, the RAND Corporation, a think tank located in Santa Monica, California, has published innovative and groundbreaking ideas for more than 60 years, including the initial design for the Internet. In 2004, RAND published a description of the skills that workers in the twenty-first century will need:

> Rapid technological change and increased international competition place the spotlight on the skills and preparation of the workforce, particularly the ability to adapt to changing technology and shifting demand. These shifts in the nature of organizations...favor strong nonroutine cognitive skills.[2]

Whether you are majoring in accounting or marketing or finance or information systems, you need to develop strong nonroutine cognitive skills.

A second study by Robert Reich, former Secretary of Labor, enumerates these nonroutine cognitive skills:[3]

- Abstract reasoning
- Systems thinking
- Collaboration
- Ability to experiment

Figure 1-5 shows an example of each. Reread the CBI case that started this chapter, and you will see that Jennifer lost her job because of her inability to practice these skills.

How Can Intro to MIS Help You Learn Nonroutine Skills?

Introduction to MIS is the best course in the business school for learning and practicing these four key skills, because every topic will require you to apply and practice them. Here's how.

ABSTRACT REASONING **Abstract reasoning** is the ability to make and manipulate models. An abstraction is a simplification of an object; it is an idea, model or concept that can then be manipulated with a logical or reasonable thought process. You will work with one or more

---

[2] Lynn A. Karoly and Constantijn W. A. Panis, *The 21st Century at Work* (Santa Monica, CA: RAND Corporation, 2004), p. xiv.
[3] Robert B. Reich, *The Work of Nations* (New York: Alfred A. Knopf, 1991), p. 229.

Skill	Example	Jennifer's Problem
Abstract reasoning	Construct a model or representation.	Confusion about life cycle for new clients.
Systems thinking	Model system components and show how components' inputs and outputs relate to one another.	Confusion about when/how customers contact accounts receivable.
Collaboration	Develop ideas and plans with others. Provide and receive critical feedback.	Unwilling to work with others with work-in-progress.
Experimentation	Create and test promising new alternatives, consistent with available resources.	Fear of failure prohibited discussion of new ideas.

FIGURE 1-5
Need for Reich's Four Critical Skills

models in every course topic and book chapter. For example, in Chapter 2 you will learn ways to *model* business processes, and you will also learn a *model* of the five components of an information system.

In this course, you will not just manipulate models provided in this text or a model that your instructor has developed; you will also be asked to construct models of your own. In Chapter 4, for example, you will learn how to create data models, and in Chapter 5 you will learn how to make process models.

SYSTEMS THINKING Can you go to a grocery store, look at a can of green beans, and connect that can to U.S. immigration policy? Can you watch tractors dig up a forest of pulpwood trees and connect that woody trash to Moore's Law? Do you know why one of the major beneficiaries of YouTube is Cisco Systems? Answers to all of these questions require systems thinking. **Systems thinking** is the ability to model the components of the system and to connect the inputs and outputs among those components into a sensible whole, one that explains the phenomenon observed. For example, how do all of those items get on the shelves at Walmart? It involves the supply chain, business processes, and computer networks, but how?

As you are about to learn, this class is about processes and information *systems.* Processes are parts of systems—the output of one process is the input to another process. For example, the process of acquiring the material to make bicycles is the input to the process of production; and the output of production is the input to the sales process. Systems thinking is also important to information systems. Throughout this book, we will discuss and illustrate systems. You will be asked to critique systems, compare alternative systems, and apply different systems to different situations. All of those tasks will prepare you for systems thinking as a professional.

COLLABORATION Here's a fact that surprises many students: Effective collaboration isn't about being nice. In fact, surveys indicate the single most important skill for effective collaboration is to give and receive critical feedback. Advance a proposal in business that challenges the cherished program of the VP of marketing, and you will quickly learn that effective collaboration skills differ from party manners at the neighborhood barbeque. So, how do you advance your idea in the face of the VP's resistance? And without losing your job?

In this course, you can learn both skills and information systems that will be of use for such collaboration. Even better, you will have many opportunities to practice them. Chapter 9 will teach you collaboration skills and illustrate several sample collaboration information systems. In addition, every chapter of this book includes collaboration exercises that you may be assigned in class or as homework.

ABILITY TO EXPERIMENT

"I've never done this before."

"I don't know how to do it."

"But will it work?"

"Is it too weird for the market?"

The fear of failure is a major stumbling block that paralyzes so many good people and so many good ideas. In the days when business was stable, when new ideas were just different verses of the same song, professionals could allow themselves to be limited by the fear of failure.

But think again about the application of social networking to the oil change business. Is there a legitimate application of social networking there? If so, has anyone ever done it? Is there anyone in the world who can tell you what to do? How to proceed? No. As Reich says, professionals in the twenty-first century need to develop experimentation skills.

Successful experimentation is not throwing buckets of money at every crazy idea that enters your head. **Experimentation** is, however, making a careful and reasoned analysis of an opportunity, envisioning potential products or solutions or applications of technology, and then developing those ideas that seem to have the most promise, consistent with the resources you have. Successful experimentation also means learning from the experience: If it worked, why? If not, why not?

In this course, you will be asked to use products with which you have no familiarity. Those products might be Microsoft Access, Visio, or something called SAP, or they might be features and functions of Blackboard that you have not used. You may be asked to collaborate using Microsoft Office 365 or Google Docs with Google+. Will your instructor explain every feature of those products that you will need? You should hope not. You should hope your instructor will leave it up to you to envision new possibilities on your own and to experiment with those possibilities, consistent with the time you have available.

Jobs

Employment is the third factor that makes the Introduction to MIS course vitally important to you. During most of 2013, the U.S. unemployment rate averaged 7.5 percent over all ages and job categories; but according to the U.S. Bureau of Labor Statistics, unemployment of those ages 20 to 24 averaged over 13 percent. Employment was better for college graduates than for those without degrees, but even college grads had a high rate of unemployment. Hope Yen, writing for the Associated Press, said in April 2012 that one in two college graduates are either unemployed or underemployed.[4] But this is not the case in all job categories.

Spence and Hlatshwayo studied employment in the United States from 1990 to 2008.[5] They defined a *tradable job* as one that was not dependent on a particular location; this distinction is important because such jobs can be outsourced overseas. As shown in Figure 1-6, Computer Systems Design and Related Services had the strongest growth of any tradable job type in the United States. By the way, because this graph shows tradable jobs, it puts an end to the myth that all the good computer jobs have gone overseas. According to their data analysis, sourced from the U.S. Bureau of Labor Statistics, many computer jobs remain in the United States.

The number of jobs in Computer Systems Design dipped substantially after the dot-com bust in 2000; since 2003, however, job growth has not only recovered but accelerated dramatically. While this category includes technical positions such as computer programmer and database administrator, it also includes nontechnical sales, support, and business management jobs.

However, information systems and computer technology provide job and wage benefits beyond just IS professionals. Acemoglu and Autor published an impressive empirical study of job and wages in the United States and parts of Europe from the 1960s to 2010.[6] They found that early in this period, education and industry were the strongest determinants of employment and salary. However, since 1990, the most significant determinant of employment and salary is the nature of work performed. In short, as the price of computer technology plummets, the value of jobs that benefit from it increases dramatically. For example, plentiful, high-paying jobs are available to business professionals who know how to use

---

[4] Hope Yen, "1 in 2 new graduates are jobless or underemployed," Associated Press April 23, 2012, http://news.yahoo.com/1-2-graduates-jobless-underemployed-140300522.html.

[5] Michael Spence and Sandile Hlatshwayo, *The Evolving Structure of the American Economy and the Employment Challenge* (New York: Council on Foreign Relations, 2011).

[6] Daron Acemoglu and David Autor, "Skills, Tasks, and Technologies: Implications for Employment and Earnings" (working paper), National Bureau of Economic Research June 2010, http://www.nber.org/papers/w16082.

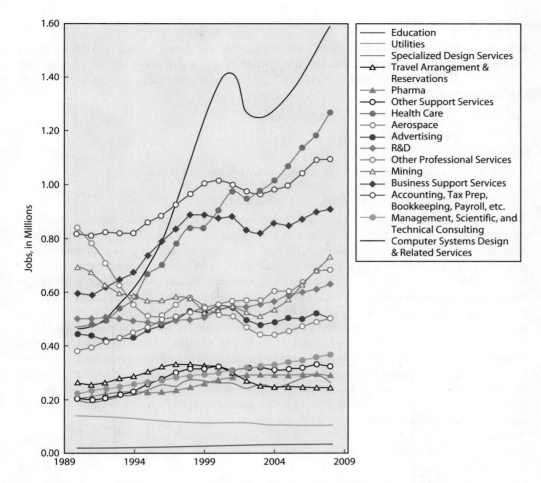

FIGURE 1-6

Growth of Tradable Jobs by Sector over the Past 20 Years

Source: From The Evolving Structure of the American Economy and the Employment Challenge by Michael Spence and Sandile Hlatshwayo. Copyright © 2011 by The Council on Foreign Relations Press. Reprinted with permission.

information systems to improve business process quality, interpret data mining results for improved marketing, or use emerging technology like 3D printing to create new products and address new markets.

What Is the Bottom Line?

The bottom line? This course is the most important course in the business school because:

1. **It will give you the background you need to assess, evaluate, and apply emerging information systems technology to business.**
2. **It can give you the ultimate in job security—marketable skills—by helping you learn abstract reasoning, systems thinking, collaboration, and experimentation.**

Please give this course your best shot; we believe that effort will pay off handsomely. We understand everyone says this about their topic, so ask non-IS friends, teachers, friends of parents, and others how important is it for you to be able to use and understand how technology is employed by businesses. Think of it this way: If you were planning a future in Germany, wouldn't you want to be good with the German language? Same here—you're going into a high-tech business environment...so be good with technology language. With that introduction, let's get started![7]

---

[7] For another perspective on the importance of these skills, read www.nytimes.com/2011/07/13/opinion/13friedman.html?_r=1.

Q2. What Is MIS?

We've used the term *MIS* several times, and you may be wondering what it is. **MIS** stands for **management information systems**, which we define as the management and use of processes, information systems, and information to help organizations achieve their strategies. This definition has three key elements:

- Processes, information systems, and information
- Management and use
- Achieve strategies

Consider each, starting with processes, information systems, and information.

Processes, Information Systems, and Information

Chapter 2 discusses these three terms and their interrelationships in detail. For now, however, consider the following intuitive definitions. A *process,* or, as it is sometimes called, a *business process,* is a way of doing something. CBI has a process for acquiring new customers. The process involves finding potential customers, contacting them, assigning a sales person, and so forth. Because organizations accomplish work via processes, focusing on them is key to improving organizational effectiveness and efficiency, as you will learn throughout this book.

An *information system* is a collection of components, including but not limited to a computer, that stores and retrieves data and produces information. Business processes and information systems are not the same things. A process may use multiple information systems, and an information system may touch many different processes. You can avoid considerable confusion by differentiating between these two concepts. Finally, *information* is a meaningful insight that helps employees do their jobs. But we're getting ahead of the story. In Chapter 2, we will formalize these definitions, explore them in detail, and investigate their relationships. Use these informal definitions as placeholders just to get started.

Management and Use

The next element in our definition of MIS is the management and use of processes, information systems, and information. Here we define **management (of MIS)** as the creation, monitoring, and adapting of processes, information systems, and information. Figure 1-7 shows the scope of MIS, but the cells are blank. One of the major purposes of this text is to help you fill in those cells.

Consider CBI's process for acquiring new customers. That process did not just pop up like a mushroom after a hard rain; it was constructed by someone to meet CBI's needs. Over time, requirements for that process will change; perhaps CBI will introduce a discount for first-time customers. CBI needs to monitor its processes to detect when a new customer places an order. When it does, the process will need to be adapted to meet the new requirements.

Similar statements apply to information systems. Information systems need to be created; computers, programs, databases, and other elements need to be constructed in such a way that they meet the requirements of the business processes that they serve. Like processes, they need to be monitored to ensure that they continue to meet their requirements, and they need to be adapted when they do not.

The same comments pertain to information. For example, managers at CBI have a set of reports that show bike sales. Over time, monitoring of manager decisions about sales may indicate that new information is needed to help managers improve those decisions. If so, the information system will need to be adapted to help managers find more meaningful insights.

FIGURE 1-7
Scope of MIS

	Process	Information Systems	Information
Create			
Monitor			
Adapt			

At this point, you might be saying, "Wait a minute. I'm a finance (or accounting or management) major, not an information systems major. I don't need to know how to build or adapt processes or information systems." If you are saying that, you are like a lamb headed for shearing. Like Jennifer, throughout your career, in whatever field you choose, you will work with processes, information systems, and information. To ensure these elements meet your needs, you need to take an *active role* in their management. Even if you are not a business analyst, a programmer, a database designer, or some other IS professional, you must take an active role in specifying process, system, and information requirements and in helping manage developmental projects to create or adapt them. Without active involvement on your part, it will only be good luck that causes processes, information systems, or information to meet your needs.

In addition to development tasks, you will also have important roles to play in the *use* of MIS. Of course, you will need to learn how to follow processes and employ information systems to accomplish your goals. But you will also have important ancillary functions as well. For example, when using an information system, you will have responsibilities for protecting the security of the system and its data. You may also have tasks for backing up data. When the system fails (most do, at some point), you will have tasks to perform while the system is down as well as tasks to accomplish to help recover the system correctly and quickly.

Achieve Strategies

The last part of the definition of MIS is that MIS exists to help organizations achieve their *strategies*. First, realize that this statement hides an important fact: Businesses themselves do not "do" anything. A business is not alive, and it cannot act. It is the people within a business who sell, buy, design, produce, finance, market, account, and manage. So, MIS exists to help people who work in a business achieve the strategies of that business.

At times, it can be difficult for organizations to stay focused on business strategy because information technology is seductive: "Our competitor is using Twitter to announce products; we better do the same." Because of the rapid pace of technology development, it can be tempting to construct information systems just to be "modern," so that the company can claim to be an "Enterprise 2.0 company," or for some other reason. Constructing systems for such reasons is unwise and wasteful of both time and money. Processes, information systems, and information need to be created for the purpose of achieving the organization's strategy. Period. They are not created because the IS department thinks they need to be created or because the company is "falling behind the technology curve."

This point may seem so obvious that you wonder why we mention it. Every day, however, some business somewhere is developing an information system for the wrong reasons. Right now, somewhere in the world, a company is deciding to create a social networking site for the sole reason that "every other business has one." This company is not asking questions such as:

- "What is the purpose of our Facebook page?"
- "What is it going to do for us?"
- "What is our policy for employees' contributions to the page?"
- "What should we do about critical customer reviews?"
- "Are the costs of maintaining the page sufficiently offset by the benefits?"

Even more serious, somewhere right now an IS manager has been convinced by some vendor's sales team or by an article in a business magazine that his or her company must upgrade to the latest, greatest high-tech gizmo. This IS manager is attempting to convince his or her manager that this expensive upgrade is a good idea. We hope that someone somewhere in the company is asking questions like, "What strategic goal or objective will be served by the investment in the gizmo?"

As a future business professional, you need to learn to look at information systems and technologies only through the lens of *business need*. Learn to ask, "All of this technology may be great, in and of itself, but what will it do for us? What will it do for our business and our particular strategy?"

Because strategy is so important to MIS, we will discuss the relationship between MIS and strategy in the next question and then, in the balance of this chapter, explore the relationship of MIS to value chains and related concepts.

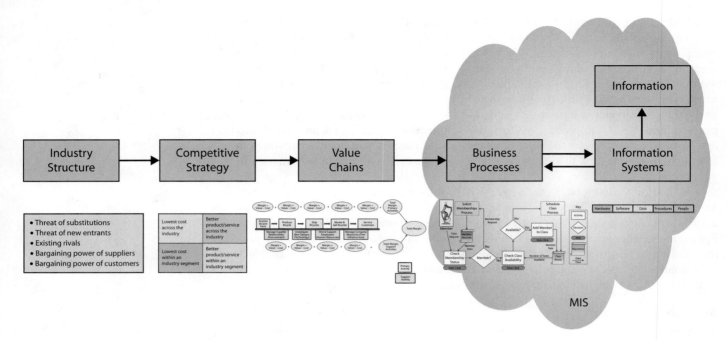

FIGURE 1-8

Organizational Strategy Determines MIS

Q3. How Does MIS Relate to Organizational Strategy?

According to the definition of MIS, information systems exist to help organizations achieve their strategies. As you will learn in your business strategy class, an organization's goals and objectives are determined by its *competitive strategy*. Thus, ultimately, competitive strategy determines the structure, features, and functions of every information system. Business processes can also influence the design of information systems. However, as you will learn in Chapter 2, the relationship between business processes and information systems is complex; in some cases, the information system's capabilities will be constrained. If so, the information system's features and functions may determine the structure of business processes as well. Finally, as shown in Figure 1-8, information systems produce information.

Michael Porter, one of the key researchers and thinkers in competitive analysis, developed three different models that can help you understand the elements in Figure 1-8. To understand this figure, we begin with Porter's five forces model.

Q4. What Five Forces Determine Industry Structure?

Organizational strategy begins with an assessment of the fundamental characteristics and structure of an industry. One model used to assess an industry structure is Porter's **five forces model**,[8] summarized in Figure 1-9. According to this model, five competitive forces determine industry profitability: threat of substitutes, threat of new entrants, existing rivals, bargaining power of suppliers, and bargaining power of customers. The intensity of each of the five forces determines the characteristics of the industry, how profitable it is, and how sustainable that profitability will be.

To understand this model, consider the strong and weak examples for each of the forces in Figure 1-9. A good check on your understanding is to see if you can think of different examples for each category. Also, take a particular industry—say, auto repair—and consider how these five forces determine the competitive landscape of that industry.

Figure 1-10 illustrates how the five forces model can be applied to the retail industry and to Walmart in particular. A **substitute** performs the same or similar function as an industry's product by another means. Examples include email as a substitute for post office mail or ebooks as substitutes for traditional books. Substitutes can also be doing without, buying used, or doing it yourself. The threat of a substitute is stronger if the substitute's

[8] Michael Porter, *Competitive Strategy: Techniques for Analyzing Industries and Competitors* (New York: Free Press, 1980).

Force	Example of Strong Force	Example of Weak Force
Threat of substitutions	Toyota's purchase of auto paint	Your power over the procedures and policies of your university
Threat of new entrants	Frequent traveler's choice of auto rental	Patients using the only drug effective for their type of cancer
Existing rivals	Students purchasing gasoline	Grain farmers in a surplus year
Bargaining power of suppliers	Corner latté stand	Professional football team
Bargaining power of customers	Used car dealers	Internal Revenue Service

FIGURE 1-9
Examples of Five Forces

price is lower, if the benefits of the substitute are similar, and if it is easy for the buyer to switch products. For example, Walmart views e-commerce and used products as substitution threats. Walmart judges the threat from e-commerce to be high because switching costs are low and prices can be low.

The threat from new entrants is based on industry barriers to entry and the reaction new entrants can expect from established companies in the industry. Barriers to entry include high customer switching costs, large financial investments to get started, sales and distribution channels that are not accessible to new entrants, and government policies. Walmart views existing regional retailers that grow to become national retailers as a high new entrant threat because they face few barriers to entry.

The competition from industry rivals, also called copycats, is high when rivals compete with each other using price discounting, new products, and service improvements. Competition from rivals is particularly high when competitors are numerous, when industry growth is slow, and when exit barriers are high. Walmart considers Target, Kmart, and Sears to be rivals and the rivalry force medium.

The last two forces concern bargaining power forces from suppliers or from customers. The strength of these forces depends on the number of available suppliers and buyers, switching costs, the differentiation of the product, and the relative size of the firm (here Walmart) compared to the size of suppliers or customers. Walmart's suppliers include Procter & Gamble, Microsoft, and thousands of smaller players. Because there are many suppliers for Walmart to choose from, low switching costs for Walmart to switch from one to another, limited product differentiation by the suppliers, and the tremendous relative size advantage for Walmart, the bargaining power of suppliers is weak. People like you and me are Walmart's buyers, and because you have many suppliers and low switching costs and Walmart's products are not differentiated from other suppliers' products, you have some buyer power. However, that power is completely overcome by Walmart's size advantage. As a result, Walmart sees the bargaining power of its buyers as weak.

Force	Examples	Strength of Force
Threat of substitutes	e-commerce	Strong
Threat of new entrants	Regional chains that grow	Strong
Existing rivals	Target, Kmart, Sears	Medium
Bargaining power of suppliers	Procter & Gamble, Microsoft	Weak
Bargaining power of customers	You and I	Weak

FIGURE 1-10
Five Forces at Walmart

To summarize, Walmart concludes that its competitive strategy, and the IS that supports that strategy, should address e-commerce, regional threats, and industry rivals. An IS that addresses weak forces and attempts to lock in customers or prevent buyers from switching, while useful, will not be strategically aligned.

Q5. What Is Competitive Strategy?

An organization responds to the structure of its industry by choosing a **competitive strategy**. Porter followed his five forces model with the model of four competitive strategies shown in Figure 1-11.[9] According to Porter, a firm can engage in one of four fundamental competitive strategies. An organization can be the cost leader and provide products at the lowest prices in the industry, or it can focus on adding value to its products to differentiate them from those of the competition. Further, the organization can employ the cost or differentiation strategy across an industry, or it can focus its strategy on a particular industry segment.

The key is for companies to commit to one of the four competitive strategies. It is always wrong to try to do more than one competitive strategy at a time. Too often a company will state a strategy of low cost leadership *and* a differentiation on customer service. The result is typically accomplishing neither, as these goals are often at odds and pursuing both sends mixed messages within the firm about which is most important. A second principle of strategy is that a competitive strategy must be distinctive and maintainable. If competitors are pursuing a similar strategy and do it better, the impact of this strategy on your company may be fatal.

Consider the car rental industry, for example. According to the first column of Figure 1-11, a car rental company can strive to provide the lowest-cost car rentals across the industry, or it can seek to provide the lowest-cost car rentals to a "focused" industry segment—say, U.S. domestic business travelers.

As shown in the second column, a car rental company can instead seek to differentiate its products from the competition. It can do so in various ways—for example, by providing a wide range of high-quality cars, by providing the best reservation system, by having the cleanest cars or the fastest check-in, or by some other means. The company can strive to provide product differentiation across the industry or within particular segments of the industry, such as U.S. domestic business travelers.

According to Porter, to be effective, the organization's goals, objectives, culture, and activities must be consistent with the organization's strategy. To those in the MIS field, this means that all processes, information systems, and information must be constructed to facilitate the organization's competitive strategy.

Consider the competitive strategy at Walmart. Walmart has chosen a low-cost strategy industry-wide. Walmart seeks to fight off threats from e-commerce, regional chains, and industry rivals by having the lowest cost structure in the industry. Keep in mind that cost is not price. Cost is what it takes to produce a product or service, while price is what people are willing to pay for it. You might also be thinking that cost leadership does not sound distinctive—couldn't several firms have this same strategy? Porter tells us that only one company in an industry can actually be the leader. If you attempt this strategy and your costs are actually higher than another firm, this may be your last strategy.

FIGURE 1-11

Porter's Four Competitive Strategies

	Cost	**Differentiation**
Industry-wide	Lowest cost across the industry	Better product/service across the industry
Focus	Lowest cost within an industry segment	Better product/service within an industry segment

[9] Michael Porter, *Competitive Strategy* (New York: Free Press, 1980).

Q6. How Does Competitive Strategy Determine Value Chain Structure?

Organizations analyze the structure of their industry, and using that analysis, they formulate a competitive strategy. They then need to organize and structure the organization to implement that strategy. If, for example, the competitive strategy is to be the *cost leader*, then business activities should be developed to provide essential functions at the lowest possible cost.

A business that selects a *differentiation* strategy would not necessarily structure itself around least-cost activities. Instead, such a business might choose to develop more costly processes, but it would do so only if those processes provided benefits that outweighed their risks.

Porter defined **value** as the amount of money that a customer is willing to pay for a resource, product, or service. The difference between the value that an activity generates and the cost of the activity is called the **margin**. A business with a differentiation strategy will add cost to an activity only as long as the activity has a positive margin.

A **value chain** is a network of value-creating activities. According to Porter, that generic chain consists of five **primary activities** and four **support activities**.

Primary Activities in the Value Chain

Figure 1-12 summarizes the primary activities of the value chain. Raw materials are obtained using inbound logistics activity, products and goods are produced in operations/manufacturing activity, and those products and goods are shipped to customers using outbound logistics activity. Additionally, organizations have sales and marketing as well as customer service activities.

To understand the essence of these activities, consider the bicycle wholesaler CBI (see Figure 1-13). First, CBI acquires bicycle parts (inbound logistics). This activity concerns the receiving and handling of raw materials and other inputs. The accumulation of those materials adds value in the sense that even a pile of unassembled parts is worth something to some customer. A collection of the parts needed to build a bicycle is worth more than an empty space on a shelf. The value is not only the parts themselves, but also the time required to contact vendors for those parts, to maintain business relationships with those vendors, to order the parts, to receive the shipment, and so forth.

In the operations activity labeled Produce Bicycle, the bicycle maker transforms raw materials into a finished bicycle, a process that adds more value. Next, the company ships bicycles (outbound logistics) to customers. Of course, there is no customer to send the bicycle to without the marketing and sales activity. Finally, the customer service activity provides support to the bicycle users.

Each stage of this generic chain accumulates costs and adds value to the product. The net result is the total margin of the chain, which is the difference between the total value added and the total costs incurred.

Primary Activity	Description
Inbound logistics	Receiving, storing, and disseminating inputs to products
Operations/manufacturing	Transforming inputs into final products
Outbound logistics	Collecting, storing, and physically distributing products to buyers
Sales and marketing	Inducing buyers to purchase products and providing a means for them to do so
Customer service	Assisting customers' use of products and thus maintaining and enhancing the products' value

FIGURE 1-12

Primary Activities in the Value Chain

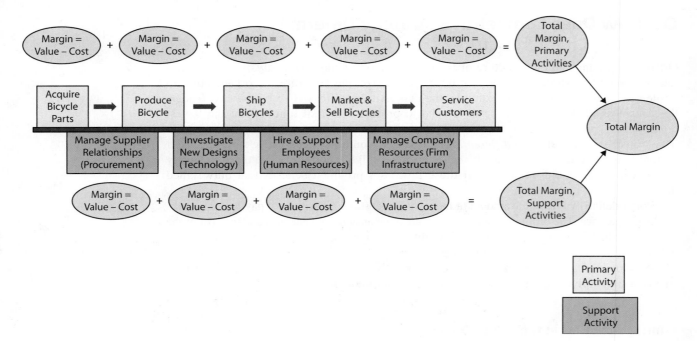

FIGURE 1-13
Bicycle Company's Value Chain

Support Activities in the Value Chain

The support activities in the generic value chain contribute indirectly to all of the primary value chain activities. They include procurement, technology, human resources, and firm infrastructure.

Porter defined *procurement* as the processes of finding vendors, setting up contractual arrangements, and negotiating prices. He defined *technology* broadly. It includes research and development, but it also includes other activities within the firm for developing new techniques, methods, and procedures. He defined *human resources* as recruiting, compensation, evaluation, and training of full- and part-time employees. Finally, *firm infrastructure* includes general management, finance, accounting, legal, and government affairs.

Supporting functions add value, albeit indirectly, and they also have costs. Hence, as shown in Figure 1-13, supporting activities contribute to a margin. In the case of supporting activities, it would be difficult to calculate the margin because the specific value added of, say, the manufacturer's lobbyists in Washington, D.C., is difficult to know. But there is a value added, there are costs, and there is a margin, even if it is only in concept.

Value Chain Linkages

Porter's model of business activities includes **linkages**, which are interactions across value activities. For example, manufacturing systems use linkages to reduce inventory costs. Such a system uses sales forecasts to plan production; it then uses the production plan to determine raw material needs and then uses the material needs to schedule purchases. The end result is just-in-time inventory, which reduces inventory sizes and costs.

By describing value chains and their linkages, Porter started a movement to create integrated, cross-departmental business systems. Over time, Porter's work led to the creation of a new discipline called business process design. The central idea is that organizations should not automate or improve existing functional systems. Rather, they should create new, more efficient business processes that integrate the activities of all departments involved in a value chain. We will revisit this idea of activity integration throughout this book when we examine process improvement.

MIS InClass 1

Industry Structure → Competitive Strategy → Value Chains → Business Processes ↔ Information Systems

As shown in Figure 1-8, information systems requirements are a logical consequence of an organization's analysis of industry structure via the chain of models shown in the title above. Consequently, you should be able to combine your knowledge of an organization's industry, together with observations of the structure and content of its Web storefront, to infer the organization's competitive strategy and possibly make inferences about its activities and business processes. The process you use here can also be useful in preparing for job interviews.

Form a team of three (or as directed by your professor) and perform the following exercises. Divide work, as appropriate, but create common answers for the team.

1. The following pairs of Web storefronts have industry segments that overlap in some way. Briefly visit each site of each pair:

    www.sportsauthority.com vs. www.soccer.com
    www.target.com vs. www.sephora.com
    www.woot.com vs. www.amazon.com
    www.petco.com vs. www.healthyfoodforpets.com
    www.llbean.com vs. www.rei.com

2. Select two pairs from the list in item 1. For each pair of companies, answer the following questions:
    a. How do the companies' markets/market segments differ?
    b. How do their competitive pressures differ?
    c. How do their competitive strategies differ?
    d. How does the "feel" of the content of their Web sites differ?
    e. How does the "feel" of the user interface of their Web sites differ?
    f. How could either company change its Web site to better accomplish its competitive strategy?
    g. Would the change you recommend in item f necessitate a change in one or more of the companies' activities? Explain your answer.

Source: monticello/Shutterstock; Eric Isselée/Shutterstock; Denis Pepin/Shutterstock; gresei/Shutterstock.

3. Use your answers in item 2 to explain the following statement: "The structure of an organization's information system (here, a Web storefront) is determined by its competitive strategy." Structure your answer so that you could use it in a job interview to demonstrate your overall knowledge of business planning.
4. Present your team's answer to the rest of the class.

Competitive Strategy for You

Examine Figure 1-11, but this time consider those elements of competitive advantage as they apply to you personally. As an employee, the skills and abilities you offer are your personal product. Unless you want to be the low-cost employee, you need to differentiate yourself. So, ask yourself, "How can I use my time in school—and in this MIS class, in particular—to create new skills, to enhance those I already have, and to differentiate my skills from the competition?" You might also ask, "What is my long-term competitive strategy? What skills can I develop that will continue to grow after I begin my career?"

Q7. How Does Competitive Strategy Determine Business Processes and Information Systems?

Figure 1-14 shows a business process for renting bicycles. The value-generating activities are shown in the top of the table, and the implementation of those activities for two companies with different competitive strategies is shown in the rows that follow.

The first company has chosen a competitive strategy of low-cost rentals to students. Accordingly, this business implements business processes to minimize costs. The second company has chosen a differentiation strategy. It provides "best-of-breed" rentals to executives at a high-end conference resort. Notice that this business has designed its business processes to ensure superb service. To achieve a positive margin, it must ensure that the value added will exceed the costs of providing the service.

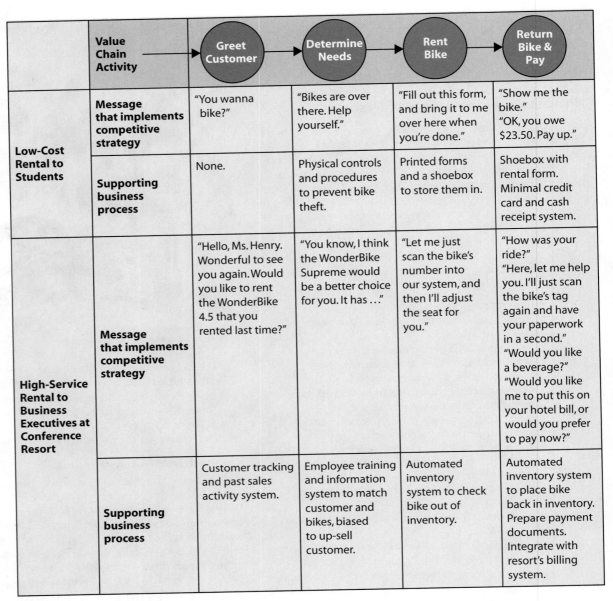

Value Chain Activity		Greet Customer	Determine Needs	Rent Bike	Return Bike & Pay
Low-Cost Rental to Students	**Message that implements competitive strategy**	"You wanna bike?"	"Bikes are over there. Help yourself."	"Fill out this form, and bring it to me over here when you're done."	"Show me the bike." "OK, you owe $23.50. Pay up."
	Supporting business process	None.	Physical controls and procedures to prevent bike theft.	Printed forms and a shoebox to store them in.	Shoebox with rental form. Minimal credit card and cash receipt system.
High-Service Rental to Business Executives at Conference Resort	**Message that implements competitive strategy**	"Hello, Ms. Henry. Wonderful to see you again. Would you like to rent the WonderBike 4.5 that you rented last time?"	"You know, I think the WonderBike Supreme would be a better choice for you. It has ..."	"Let me just scan the bike's number into our system, and then I'll adjust the seat for you."	"How was your ride?" "Here, let me help you. I'll just scan the bike's tag again and have your paperwork in a second." "Would you like a beverage?" "Would you like me to put this on your hotel bill, or would you prefer to pay now?"
	Supporting business process	Customer tracking and past sales activity system.	Employee training and information system to match customer and bikes, biased to up-sell customer.	Automated inventory system to check bike out of inventory.	Automated inventory system to place bike back in inventory. Prepare payment documents. Integrate with resort's billing system.

FIGURE 1-14
Operations Value Chain and Business Processes for Bicycle Rental Companies

Now, consider the information systems required for these business processes. The processes used by the student rental business require minimal information systems support. The only computer/software/data component in its business is the machine provided by its bank for processing credit card transactions.

The high-service business uses processes that require more sophisticated information systems, as shown in Figure 1-15. It has a sales tracking database that tracks past customer rental activity and an inventory database that is used to select and up-sell bicycle rentals as well as control bicycle inventory with a minimum of fuss to its high-end customers.

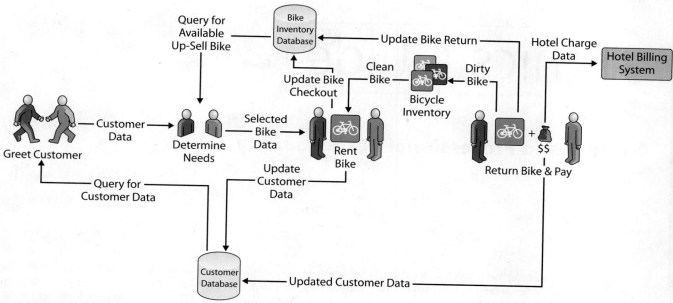

FIGURE 1-15

Business Process and Information Systems for High-Service Bike Rental

To see how competitive strategy affects processes and information at a large firm, once again consider Walmart. Instead of the four simple value chain activities as shown in the top of Figure 1-14, Walmart would have hundreds of activities and hundreds of business processes. To be the low-cost leader in the industry, Walmart uses very sophisticated IS to link its activities and processes together to reduce cost and create value.

So the bottom line is this: Organizations analyze their industry and choose a competitive strategy. Given that strategy, they examine their value chain and design business processes that span value-generating activities. Those processes determine the scope and requirements of each organization's information systems. This textbook's main focus is to help you better understand business processes and the information systems that support them. In our next chapter, we examine processes and information systems in more depth and introduce the topic of information, the final element of Figure 1-8.

Ethics Guide

Ethics and Professional Responsibility

Suppose you're a young marketing professional who has just taken a new promotional campaign to market. The executive committee asks you to present a summary of the sales effect of the campaign, and you produce the graph shown in Figure 1-16. As shown, your campaign was just in the nick of time; sales were starting to fall the moment your campaign kicked in. After that, sales boomed.

But note the vertical axis has no quantitative labels. If you add quantities, as shown in Figure 1-17, the performance is less impressive. It appears that the substantial growth amounts to less than 20 units. Still, the curve of the graph is impressive, and if no one does the arithmetic, your campaign will appear successful.

This impressive shape is only possible, however, because Figure 1-17 is not drawn to scale. If you draw it to scale, as shown in Figure 1-18, your campaign's success is, well, problematic, at least for you.

Which of these graphs do you present to the committee?

Each chapter of this text includes an Ethics Guide that explores ethical and responsible behavior in a variety of MIS-related contexts. In this chapter, we'll examine the ethics of data and information.

Centuries of philosophical thought have addressed the question "What is right behavior?" and we can't begin to discuss all of it here. You will learn much of it, however, in your business ethics class. For our purposes, we'll use two of the major pillars in the philosophy of ethics. We introduce the first one here and the second in Chapter 2.

The German philosopher Immanuel Kant defined the **categorical imperative** as the principle that one should behave only in a way that one would want the behavior to be a universal law. Stealing is not such a behavior because if everyone steals, nothing can be owned. Stealing cannot be a universal law. Similarly, lying cannot be consistent with the categorical imperative because if everyone lies, words are useless.

When you ask whether a behavior is consistent with this principle, a good litmus test is "Are you willing to publish your behavior to the world? Are you willing to put it on your Facebook page? Are you willing to say what you've done to all the players involved?" If not, your behavior is not ethical, at least not in the sense of Kant's categorical imperative.

Kant defined duty as the necessity to act in accordance with the categorical imperative. Perfect duty is behavior that must always be met. Not lying is a perfect duty. Imperfect duty is action that is praiseworthy but not required according to the categorical imperative. Giving to charity is an example of an imperfect duty.

Kant used the example of cultivating one's own talent as an imperfect duty, and we can use that example as a way of defining professional responsibility. One can say that business professionals have an imperfect duty to obtain the skills necessary to accomplish their jobs. We also have an imperfect duty to continue to develop our business skills and abilities throughout our careers.

We will apply these principles in the chapters that follow. For now, use them to assess your beliefs about Figures 1-16 to 1-18 by answering the following questions.

Source: .shock / Fotolia

FIGURE 1-16

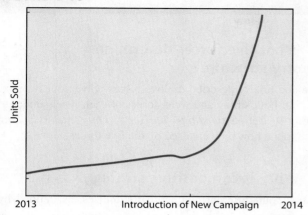

FIGURE 1-17

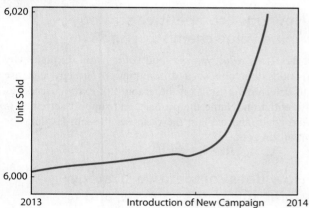

FIGURE 1-18

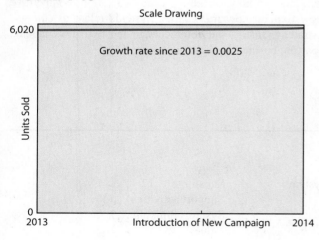

DISCUSSION QUESTIONS

1. Restate Kant's categorical imperative using your own words. Explain why cheating on exams is not consistent with the categorical imperative.

2. While there is some difference of opinion, most scholars believe that the Golden Rule ("Do unto others as you would have them do unto you.") is not as limiting to behavior as Kant's categorical imperative. Justify this belief.

3. Suppose you created Figure 1-16 using Microsoft Excel. To do so, you keyed the data into Excel and clicked the Make Graph button (there is one, though it's not called that). Voilà, Excel created Figure 1-16 without any labels and drawn out of scale as shown. Without further consideration, you put the result into your presentation.
   a. Is your behavior consistent with Kant's categorical imperative? Why or why not?
   b. If Excel automatically produces graphs like Figure 1-16, is Microsoft's behavior consistent with Kant's categorical imperative? Why or why not?

4. Change roles. Assume now you are a member of the executive committee. A junior marketing professional presents Figure 1-16 to the committee and you object to the lack of labels and the scale. In response, the junior marketing professional says, "Sorry, I didn't know. I just put the data into Excel and copied the resulting graph." What conclusions do you, as an executive, make about the junior marketing professional in response to this statement?

5. Is the junior marketing person's response in question 4 a violation of a perfect duty? Of an imperfect duty? Of any duty? Explain your response.

6. As the junior marketing professional, which graph do you present to the committee?

7. According to Kant, lying is not consistent with the categorical imperative. Suppose you are invited to a seasonal BBQ at the department chair's house. You are served a steak that is tough, over-cooked, and so barely edible that you secretly feed it to the department chair's dog (who appears to enjoy it). The chairperson asks you, "How is your steak?" and you respond, "Excellent, thank you."
   a. Is your behavior consistent with Kant's categorical imperative?
   b. The steak seemed to be excellent to the dog. Does that fact change your answer to a?
   c. What conclusions do you draw from this example?

Active Review

Use this Active Review to verify that you understand the material in the chapter. You can read the entire chapter and then perform the tasks in this review, or you can read the text material for just one question and perform the tasks in this review for that question before moving on to the next one.

Q1. Why is Introduction to MIS the most important class in the business school?

Define *Moore's Law* and explain why its consequences are important to business professionals today. Explain the trends in IT being driven by Moore's Law. Give the text's definition of *job security*, and use Reich's enumeration of four key skills to explain how this course will help you attain that security. Summarize IS-related job opportunities.

Q2. What is MIS?

Define *MIS*. Describe, in the intuitive manner used in this chapter, the meaning of processes, information systems, and information. Define the term *management (of MIS)*, and summarize the reasons why this text claims it is important to all businesspeople, not just MIS professionals. Explain the confusion in the statement "organizations achieve their strategies." Summarize why it can be difficult for organizations to focus their MIS on organizational strategy.

Q3. How does MIS relate to organizational strategy?

Summarize the reasons that the Porter models are relevant to MIS. Diagram and explain the relationship among industry structure, competitive strategy, value chains, business processes, information systems, and information.

Q4. What five forces determine industry structure?

Name and briefly describe the five forces. Give your own examples of both strong and weak forces of each type, similar to Figure 1-9. Define *substitute, barrier to entry,* and *switching cost.* Explain how they are used by the five forces.

Q5. What is competitive strategy?

Describe four different competitive strategies, as defined by Porter. Give an example of four different companies that have implemented each of the strategies.

Q6. How does competitive strategy determine value chain structure?

Define the terms *value, margin,* and *value chain.* Explain why organizations that choose a differentiation strategy can use value to determine a limit on the amount of extra cost to pay for differentiation. Name the primary and support activities in the value chain and explain the purpose of each. Explain the concept of linkages.

Q7. How does competitive strategy determine business processes and information systems?

Describe the relationship between a value chain and a business process. Explain how business processes relate to competitive strategy. Explain how information systems relate to competitive strategy. Justify the comments in the two rows labeled "Supporting business process" in Figure 1-14.

Key Terms and Concepts

Using Your Knowledge

1-1. One of life's greatest gifts is to be employed doing work that you love. Reflect for a moment on a job that you would find so exciting that you could hardly wait to get to sleep on Sunday night so that you could wake up and go to work on Monday.

a. Describe that job. Name the industry, the type of company or organization for whom you'd like to work, the products and services it produces, and your specific job duties.

b. Explain what it is about that job that you find so compelling.

c. In what ways will the skills of abstract reasoning, systems thinking, collaboration, and experimentation facilitate your success in that job?

d. Given your answers to parts a–c, define three to five personal goals for this class. None of these goals should include anything about your GPA. Be as specific as possible. Assume that you are going to evaluate yourself on these goals at the end of the quarter or semester. The more specific you make these goals, the easier it will be to perform the evaluation. Use Figure 1-5 for guidance.

1-2. Suppose you decide to start a business that recruits students for summer jobs. You will match available students with available jobs. You need to learn what positions are available and what students are available for filling those positions. In starting your business, you know you will be competing with local newspapers, Craigslist (*www.craigslist.org*), and your college. You will probably have other local competitors as well.

a. Analyze the structure of this industry according to Porter's five forces model.

b. Given your analysis in part a, recommend a competitive strategy.

c. Describe the primary value chain activities as they apply to this business.

d. Describe a business process for recruiting students.

e. Describe information systems that could be used to support the business process in part d.

f. Explain how the process you described in part d and the system you described in part e reflect your competitive strategy.

1-3. Consider the two different bike rental companies in Figure 1-14. Think about the bikes they rent. Clearly, the student bikes will be just about anything that can be ridden out of the shop. The bikes for the business executives, however, must be new, shiny, clean, and in tip-top shape.

a. Compare and contrast the operations value chains of these two businesses as they pertain to the management of bicycles.

b. Describe a business process for maintaining bicycles for both businesses.

c. Describe a business process for acquiring bicycles for both businesses.

d. Describe a business process for disposing of bicycles for both businesses.

e. What roles do you see for information systems in your answers to the earlier questions? The information systems can be those you develop within your company, or they can be those developed by others, such as Craigslist.

1-4. Samantha Green owns and operates Twigs Tree Trimming Service. Samantha graduated from the forestry program of a nearby university and worked for a large landscape design firm performing tree trimming and removal. After several years of experience, she bought her own truck, stump grinder, and other equipment and opened her own business in St. Louis, Missouri. Although many of her jobs are one-time operations to remove a tree or stump, others are recurring, such as trimming a tree or groups of trees every year or every other year. When business is slow, she calls former clients to remind them of her services and of the need to trim their trees on a regular basis. Samantha has never heard of Michael Porter or any of his theories. She operates her business "by the seat of her pants."

a. Explain how an analysis of the five competitive forces could help Samantha.

b. Do you think Samantha has a competitive strategy? What competitive strategy would seem to make sense for her?

c. How would knowledge of her competitive strategy help her sales and marketing efforts?

d. Describe, in general terms, the kind of information system she needs to support sales and marketing efforts.

Collaboration Exercise 1

Collaborate with a group of fellow students to answer the following questions. For this exercise, do not meet face to face. Your task will be easier if you coordinate your work with SharePoint, Office 365, Google Docs with Google+, or equivalent collaboration tools. (See Chapter 9 for a discussion of collaboration tools and processes.) Your answers should reflect the thinking of the entire group, not just that of one or two individuals.

1. Abstract reasoning.

a. Define *abstract reasoning,* and explain why it is an important skill for business professionals.

b. Explain how a list of items in inventory and their quantity on hand is an abstraction of a physical inventory.

c. Give three other examples of abstractions commonly used in business.

d. Explain how Jennifer failed to demonstrate effective abstract reasoning skills.

e. Can people increase their abstract reasoning skills? If so, how? If not, why not?

2. Systems thinking.

a. Define *systems thinking,* and explain why it is an important skill for business professionals.

b. Explain how you would use systems thinking to explain why Moore's Law caused a farmer to dig up a field of pulpwood trees. Name each of the elements in the system, and explain their relationships to each other.

c. Give three other examples of the use of systems thinking with regard to consequences of Moore's Law.

d. Explain how Jennifer failed to demonstrate effective systems-thinking skills.

e. Can people improve their systems-thinking skills? If so, how? If not, why not?

3. Collaboration.

a. Define *collaboration,* and explain why it is an important skill for business professionals.

b. Explain how you are using collaboration to answer these questions. Describe what is working with regard to your group's process and what is not working.

c. Is the work product of your team better than the product any one of you could have produced separately? If not, your collaboration is ineffective. If that is the case, explain why.

d. Does the fact that you cannot meet face to face hamper your ability to collaborate? If so, how?

e. Explain how Jennifer failed to demonstrate effective collaboration skills.

f. Can people increase their collaboration skills? If so, how? If not, why not?

4. Experimentation.

a. Define *experimentation,* and explain why it is an important skill for business professionals.

b. Explain several creative ways you could use experimentation to answer this question.

c. How does the fear of failure influence your willingness to engage in any of the ideas you identified in part b?

d. Explain how Jennifer failed to demonstrate effective experimentation skills.

e. Can people increase their willingness to take risks? If so, how? If not, why not?

f. Do you think IS make experimentation easier or harder?

5. Job security.

a. State the text's definition of *job security.*

b. Evaluate the text's definition of job security. Is it effective? If you think not, offer a better definition of job security.

c. As a team, do you agree that improving your skills on the four dimensions in Collaboration Exercise 1 will increase your job security?

d. Do you think technical skills (accounting proficiency, financial analysis proficiency, and so on) provide job security? Why or why not? Do you think you would have answered this question differently in 1980? Why or why not?

6. Apply the models in Figure 1-8 to a company of your choosing. Specify the strength of each of the five forces, select a competitive strategy, identify value-adding activities, diagram a process, and describe the information system that will support your analysis.

CASE STUDY 1

Singing Valley

Singing Valley Resort is a top-end 50-unit resort located high in the Colorado mountains. Rooms rent for $400 to $4,500 per night, depending on the season and the type of accommodations. Singing Valley's clientele are well to do; many are famous entertainers, sports figures, and business executives. They are accustomed to, and demand, superior service.

Singing Valley resides in a gorgeous mountain valley and is situated a few hundred yards from a serene mountain lake. It prides itself on superior accommodations; tip-top service; delicious, healthy, organic meals; and exceptional wines. Because it has been so successful, Singing Valley is 90 percent occupied except during the "shoulder seasons" (November, after the leaves change and before the snow arrives, and late April, when winter sports are finished but the snow is still on the ground).

Singing Valley's owners want to increase revenue, but because the resort is nearly always full and because its rates are already at the top of the scale, it cannot do so via occupancy revenue. Thus, over the past several years it has focused on up-selling to its clientele activities such as flyfishing, river rafting, cross-country skiing, snowshoeing, art lessons, yoga and other exercise classes, spa services, and the like.

To increase the sales of these optional activities, Singing Valley prepared in-room marketing materials to advertise their availability. Additionally, they trained all registration personnel on techniques of casually and appropriately suggesting such activities to guests on arrival.

The response to these promotions was only mediocre, so Singing Valley's management stepped up its promotions. The first step was to send an email to its clientele advising them of the activities available during their stay. An automated system produced emails personalized with names and personal data.

Unfortunately, the automated email system backfired. Immediately upon its execution, Singing Valley management received numerous complaints. One long-term customer objected that she had been coming to Singing Valley for 7 years and asked if they had yet noticed that she was confined to a wheelchair. If they had noticed, she said, why did they send her a personalized invitation for a hiking trip? The agent of another famous client complained that the personalized email was sent to her client and her husband, when anyone who had turned on a TV in the past 6 months knew the two of them were involved in an exceedingly acrimonious divorce. Yet another customer complained that, indeed, he and his wife had vacationed at Singing Valley 3 years ago, but he had not been there since. To his knowledge, his wife had not been there, either, so he was puzzled as to why the email referred to their visit last winter. He wanted to know if, indeed, his wife had recently been to the resort without him. Of course, Singing Valley had no way of knowing about customers it had insulted who never complained.

During the time the automated email system was operational, sales of extra activities were up 15 percent. However, the strong customer complaints conflicted with its competitive strategy so, in spite of the extra revenue, Singing Valley stopped the automated email system, sacked the vendor who had developed it, and demoted the Singing Valley employee who had brokered the system. Singing Valley was left with the problem of how to increase its revenue.

Questions

1-5. Analyze Singing Valley's strategy and its problem. At the minimum, include the following in your response:
   a. An analysis of the five forces of the Singing Valley market. Make and justify any necessary assumptions about its market.
   b. A statement of Singing Valley's competitive strategy.
   c. A statement of the problem.
   d. Develop two innovative ideas for solving the Singing Valley problem. For each idea, provide:
   - A brief description of the idea.
   - A process diagram (like Figure 1-15) of the idea. Figure 1-15 was produced using Microsoft Visio; if you have access to that product, you'll save time and have a better result if you also use it.
   - A description of the information system needed to implement the idea.

1-6. Explain how each of the four nonroutine skills— abstract reasoning, systems thinking, collaboration, and experimentation—can be used by an employee at Singing Valley to develop solutions for Singing Valley's problem.

Jake is working his last night shift of his summer job at a well-known fast food restaurant.[1] His manager Mary has asked him to show two relatively new hires, Sally and Austin, the ropes.

Jake begins, "I understand Mary wanted you to shadow me to learn my secrets. You've got to promise me you won't tell her exactly how I do things. I've enjoyed letting her think I am some kind of genius. If she asks you how I did it, tell her it's Kaizan. That's what I tell her."

He continues, "At Central Colorado State where I go to school, they preach that we should think about processes all the time. I tried to resist at first, but now I've fallen in the habit of seeing things as processes and how information systems can make processes better. So, all my secrets are just process improvement ideas."

Jake takes the small herd in the back where the burgers are made. "When I put the burgers together as the Assembler, I look at the order screen to tell myself what to do next in order to make the process of assembling go faster. If I see that the next order has a Tripleburger, I look at the rest of the eight orders on the screen to see if there are more orders for Triples coming. If there are, I start cooking all the meat at the same time and get all the buns and toppings ready for when the meat is done. When I first started working here, I just did one order at a time, but by looking at all eight orders I save myself a lot of time and effort."

Sally asks, "I thought everyone just looked at one or two orders at a time. You look at eight?"

Q1. What is a business process?

Q2. What is an information system?

Q3. How do business processes and information systems relate?

Q4. How do structured and dynamic processes vary?

Q5. What is information?

Q6. What are necessary data characteristics?

---

[1] While the characters' names and dialogue are fictitious, this story is based on the experiences of Alex, a student using this textbook in spring 2012.

"Yeah, but I just scan them. I look to see if there are multiple orders for the same burger so I can start them at the same time, or if there are fries on several orders I'll grab all the fries on one trip. I don't look too closely at the other stuff."

Austin chimes in, "Is that it? Is that all you're doing differently?"

"Well, secret number two is that I pay attention to the other processes in the store. There is the Drive-Thru process, the In-Store Order process, the Drink Making process, and the Fry Making process. If I'm not actually assembling at the moment, I observe the other processes to determine which one is running behind. Then I do some activity to help that process—bag some fries, fill some drinks, that sort of thing."

"Here's another example. If you have to empty the outdoor trash cans, take four empty bags and make one circuit, not four separate trips."

"Also, be willing to experiment a bit. I've tried some stuff that didn't work. For example, one night I tried to do the closing process in steps moving clockwise around the store, but that put too many steps in the wrong order; and one time I tried putting a second coffee bag next to the coffee maker so the next person wouldn't have to get the bag…but I found that most people saw the bag lying there and put it away."

"You'll think of stuff. The key is to see the processes. The best way to become skilled at seeing processes is to practice at school or at home, like the steps to get ready for school in the morning, pack a suitcase for a trip, or make a lunch. It becomes a habit and you laugh when you catch yourself thinking about how to make even the most unimportant things better."

"And remember, don't tell Mary. She'll be disappointed that it was so simple."

Chapter Preview

In Chapter 1, we defined MIS as the management and use of business processes, information systems, and information to help organizations achieve their strategies. This chapter extends that initial discussion by defining and describing that definition's three fundamental terms: business process, information system, and information. We begin by describing the features of business processes. Then we will introduce you to the standard way of documenting business processes. Because processes depend on information systems, we follow our discussion of business processes by defining information systems and describing their components. Then we explain how business processes and information systems relate. Next, we present several definitions of information to better understand where and how information is created. Finally, because information depends on data, we discuss factors that influence data quality.

Q1. What Is a Business Process?

A **business process** is a sequence of activities for accomplishing a function. For example, your university has business processes to:

- Add a class to the business curriculum
- Add a new section to a class schedule
- Assign a class to a classroom
- Drop a class section
- Record final grades

An **activity** is a task within a business process. Examples of activities that are part of the record final grades process are:

- Compute final grades
- Fill out grade reporting form
- Submit the grade reporting form to the departmental administrator

Business processes also involve resources, such as people, computers, and data and document collections. To show how resources are connected to business processes, next we explain how processes and resources can be diagrammed using the Drive-Thru process at Jake's fast food restaurant as our example.

An Example Business Process

DOCUMENTING BUSINESS PROCESSES To talk meaningfully about business processes, we need some way of documenting each process and activity. Or, using Reich's term in Chapter 1, we need to create an *abstraction* of business processes. The computer industry has created dozens of techniques for documenting business processes over the years, and this text will use one of them known as the **Business Process Model and Notation (BPMN) standard**. We use this technique because it is a global standard and is widely used in industry. Microsoft Visio Premium,[2] for example, includes templates for creating process drawings using BPMN symbols. We will use BPMN diagrams in many of the upcoming chapters.

Figure 2-1 is a BPMN model of the Drive-Thru process at the fast food restaurant. Each of the long columns is headed by a name such as *Cashier* and *Food Runner*. To begin the process, the *Cashier* greets the customer and asks for his or her order. The cashier records the order in a computer system called the *Order Tracker*. After the customer pays the *Cashier* at the first drive-thru window, the customer pulls forward and is given his or her order by the *Presenter*. The *Food Runner* is directed by the *Presenter* to bag the food items when the runner's assistance would help.

Each of the four columns in Figure 2-1 identifies a **role**, which is a subset of the activities in a business process that is performed by a particular actor. **Actors** can be people; in the opening vignette, Jake is an actor who could play the role of *Food Runner* in the Drive-Thru process. As you will learn, actors can also be computers, such as the *Order Tracker*, but that's getting ahead of the story.

The long columns in Figure 2-1 are called **swimlanes**; each lane contains all the activities for a particular role. Swimlanes make it easy to determine which roles do what. According to the BPMN standard, the process starts at a circle with a narrow border and ends at a circle with a heavy border. Thus, in Figure 2-1, the business process starts at the top of the *Cashier* swimlane and ends at the heavy-bordered circle at the end of the *Presenter* swimlane.

FIGURE 2-1

Fast Food Restaurant Drive-Thru BPMN Diagram

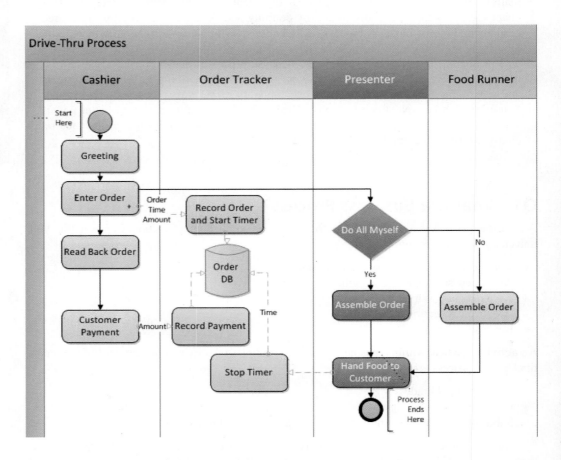

---

[2] Visio is a diagram-drawing product licensed by Microsoft. If your university belongs to the Microsoft Academic Alliance (which is likely), you can obtain a copy of Visio for free. If you want to draw diagrams that use BPMN symbols, be certain that you obtain the Premium version of this product, which is available from the Academic Alliance.

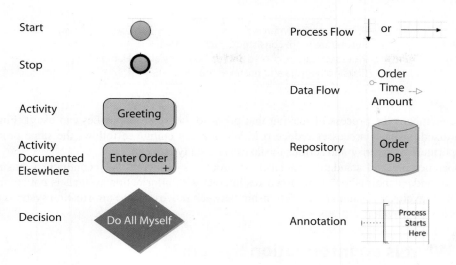

FIGURE 2-2
Summary of BPMN Symbols

The BPMN standard defines dozens of symbols; the symbols we will use in this text are summarized in Figure 2-2. Activities are shown in rectangles with rounded corners, and decisions are shown by diamonds. A solid arrow shows the flow of action; the solid arrow between Read Back Order and Customer Payment in Figure 2-1 means that once the *Cashier* has finished reading back the order to the customer, the next activity in the process is the payment activity. Dotted arrows show the flow of the data named on the arrow. Thus, the dotted arrow between the Customer Payment activity and the Record Payment activity means that the data named on that arrow (Amount) is sent from the Customer Payment activity to the Record Payment activity.

A **repository** is a collection of something, usually a collection of records. In Figure 2-1, the symbol that looks like a small tin can represents a repository. Here we have a repository named *Order DB*. As hinted in that name, a repository is often a database (DB), but it need not be. It might be a cardboard box full of records. And some repositories, like inventories, are collections of things other than data.

HOW MUCH DETAIL IS ENOUGH? As an abstraction, a business process diagram shows some details and omits others. It has to; otherwise it would be hundreds of pages long and include too many obvious details. We don't need to show that the *Cashier* must open the window before exchanging money with the customers or that he or she must turn on a computer before using it. However, we need to show sufficient detail so as to avoid ambiguity. The process with one big activity named Fulfill Drive-Thru Orders leaves out too much detail. Such a diagram would not show, for example, that the *Presenter* must choose to assemble orders himself or ask the *Food Runner* to assemble the order.

To simplify process diagrams, the details of some activities are documented separately. In Figure 2-1, consider the Enter Order activity. The activity is shown with a plus sign, indicating that the details of the Enter Order activity are documented elsewhere. As stated, such external documentation is used to simplify a diagram; it is also used when the details of the subprocess are unknown or unimportant to the process under study or when those details are documented elsewhere. For example, the details of the Enter Order activity such as repeating the order and concluding the exchange with totals and where to drive are unimportant to the overall process.

Why Do Organizations Standardize Business Processes?

Other than very small businesses, most businesses choose to standardize business processes. The benefits of standardizing processes are listed in Figure 2-3. Standardizing processes enables the business to enforce policies. For example, the fast food restaurant has a policy that all customer orders are to be recorded electronically, not just verbally, that customer orders are to be read back to the customer by the cashier, and that timing starts when the order is first recorded. By standardizing the process, these policies can be enforced. Second, standardized business processes produce consistent results. When every employee follows the same process steps, the results will be the same, regardless of who is staffing the cash window or assembling drinks. Third, standardized processes are scalable. If the owner creates a pizza with new toppings, he

FIGURE 2-3

Benefits of Standardizing Processes

> Policies can be enforced.
> Results are more consistent.
> Processes can be copied and reused; they are scalable.
> Risks from errors and mistakes are reduced.

then standardizes the process of making that pizza so the other employees can use it. Finally, standardized business processes reduce risk. When every employee follows the same process, the opportunities for error and serious mistakes are greatly reduced.

Documenting and standardizing business processes is increasingly common in business. However, understanding how these processes interact with information systems is not common. We will more closely examine the relationship between processes and information systems after we discuss information systems.

Q2. What Is an Information System?

A **system** is a group of components that interact to achieve some purpose. As you might guess, an **information system (IS)** is a group of components that interact to produce information. That sentence, although true, raises another question: What are these components that interact to produce information?

Figure 2-4 shows the **five-component framework**—a model of the components of a functioning information system: **computer hardware**, **software**, **data**, **procedures**, and **people**. These five components are present in every information system, from the simplest to the most complex. For example, when you use a computer to write a class report, you are using hardware (the computer, storage disk, keyboard, and monitor), software (Word, WordPerfect, or some other word-processing program), data (the words, sentences, and paragraphs in your report), procedures (the steps you use to start the program, enter your report, print it, and save and back up your file), and people (you).

Consider a more complex example, such as an airline reservation system. It, too, consists of these five components, even though each one is far more complicated. The hardware consists of dozens of computers linked together by data communications hardware. Further, hundreds of different programs coordinate communications among the computers, and still other programs perform the reservations and related services. Additionally, the system must store millions upon millions of characters of data about flights, customers, reservations, and other facts. Hundreds of different procedures—instructions for booking a flight, cancelling a reservation, or selecting a seat—are followed by airline personnel, travel agents, and customers. Finally, the information system includes people, not only the users of the system, but also those who operate and service the computers, those who maintain the data, and those who support the networks of computers.

Notice the symmetry in these five components. Hardware and people do things. Programs and procedures are instructions. Programs tell hardware what to do, and procedures tell people what to do. Data is the bridge between the machine side (hardware and software) and the human side (procedures and people).

The important point here is that the five components in Figure 2-4 are common to all information systems, from the smallest to the largest. As you think about any information system, including the order IS at the fast food restaurant, learn to look for these five components.

Before we move forward, note that we have defined an information system to include a computer. Some people would say that such a system is a **computer-based information system**. They would note that there are information systems that do not include computers, such as a calendar hanging on the wall outside of a conference room that is used to schedule the room's use. Such systems have been used by businesses for centuries. Although this point is true, in this book we focus on computer-based information systems. To simplify and shorten the book, we will use the term *information system* as a synonym for *computer-based information system*. Please also note that not all computers are information systems; for example, robotic computers are not IS.

FIGURE 2-4

Five Components of an Information System

Five-Component Framework

Hardware	Software	Data	Procedures	People

Recognize that you are the key.
Make each component work.
Estimate the scope of new information systems.
Order components by difficulty and disruption.

FIGURE 2-5

How to Apply the Five-Component Model

How Can I Use the Five-Component Model?

Now that you understand the five components better, you're ready to apply your understanding and gain some valuable insights about information systems. To pique your interest, we believe there are at least four helpful ways to apply this idea, and they are listed in Figure 2-5.

RECOGNIZE THAT YOU ARE THE KEY You are part of every information system you use. Indeed, your mind and your thinking are not merely *a* component of the information systems you use; they are the *most important* component. Here's the point: Even if you have the perfect information system, if you do not know what to do with the data that it produces, the other components are a waste of time and money. The quality of your thinking determines in large part the quality of the information system.

MAKE EACH COMPONENT WORK Information systems often encounter problems—despite our best efforts, they don't always work right. All too often in these situations, blame is fixed on the wrong component. You will frequently hear that the culprit is the computer that doesn't work quite right, and certainly at times the hardware or software can be at fault. But with the five-component model, you have more suspects to interrogate. Sometimes the data is not in the right format, the procedures are not clear, or the people using the system are not trained or motivated. By using the five-component model, you can better locate the cause of a problem and pursue smarter solutions.

ESTIMATE THE SCOPE OF NEW INFORMATION SYSTEMS The five-component framework can also be used when assessing the scope of new systems. When a vendor pitches the need for a new technology to you, use the five components to assess how big of an investment that new technology represents. What new hardware will you need? What programs will you need to license? What databases and other data must you create? What procedures will need to be developed for both the use and administration of the information system? And, finally, what will be the impact of the new technology on people? Which jobs will change? Who will need training? How will the new technology affect morale? Will you need to hire new people? Will you need to reorganize? The five-component model helps you think more completely about the impact of new technology.

ORDER COMPONENTS BY DIFFICULTY AND DISRUPTION Finally, as you consider the five components, keep in mind that Figure 2-4 shows them in order of ease of change and the extent of organizational disruption. It is a simple matter to order additional hardware. Obtaining or developing new programs is more difficult. Creating new databases or changing the structure of existing databases is still more difficult. Changing procedures, requiring people to work in new ways, is even more difficult. Finally, changing personnel responsibilities and reporting relationships and hiring and terminating employees are very difficult and very disruptive to the organization.

Not everyone understands information systems this way; most businesspeople think of information systems as computers or applications. By understanding the five components, not only can you apply the lessons just mentioned, you can also apply the most important lesson found in our next topic—procedures link information systems to processes.

Q3. How Do Business Processes and Information Systems Relate?

To understand this crucial question, look again at the Drive-Thru process and information system in Figure 2-1. Who are the actors playing the roles in that process? The *Cashier* role is played by a person, so too the *Presenter* and *Food Runner* roles. The only role performed by a computer-based system is the *Order Tracker* IS. Based on this, we would say that the Drive-Thru process is supported by one IS—the Order Tracker IS.

FIGURE 2-6

Processes and the Two IS at the Fast Food Restaurant

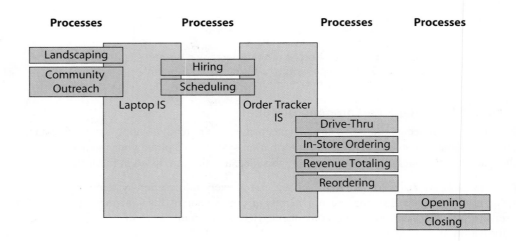

Notice that if a second IS is added to the Drive-Thru process, we then have a process that is supported by two IS. For example, the second IS might use a motion detection system to record traffic patterns of cars that join the drive-thru line. We could continue this example with a third or fourth IS for the Drive-Thru process. In general, we say that a process can be supported by any number of information systems—from zero to many.

Now let's look at it from the IS point of view and ask how many processes one IS can support. The Order Tracker IS supports the Drive-Thru process, but it also supports the process that adds up the revenue for the day and the process to reorder items from the warehouse. So, in this case, we see that one IS can support one or many processes. The relationship between IS and processes at the fast food restaurant is shown in Figure 2-6.

Starting from the right side of Figure 2-6, the processes used to open and close the store do not rely on any IS. These processes are a series of activities performed entirely by human actors. Moving left in the figure, we can see that the Drive-Thru, In-Store Ordering, Revenue Totaling, and Reordering processes are supported by the Order Tracker IS. At the other end of Figure 2-6, another IS, the Laptop IS, is used by the manager to exchange email in the Landscaping process as well as the Community Outreach process. Finally, two processes, Hiring and Scheduling, are supported by both IS. There are many other processes that occur at the restaurant, but you get the idea.

The Role of Procedures

There is one more item to discuss about the relationship between IS and processes—the important role of procedures. Procedures, one of the five components of an IS, anchor an IS to a process. A procedure is a set of instructions for a person to follow when operating an IS. For example, when you create a Facebook account, the Facebook IS gives you a procedure to follow in the form of instructions for filling out the on-screen application.

Each information system has a different procedure for every process the information system supports. The Facebook information system includes a procedure for each of its processes—there is a procedure for creating an account, posting a picture, searching for friends, and setting privacy preferences. Let's return to the fast food example. Figure 2-7 shows the processes supported by the Order Tracker IS. Notice that for each process, the Order Tracker IS has a unique procedure. For the Hiring process, the Hiring procedure is a series of instructions for entering new employee data into the Order Tracker IS. The Drive-Thru procedure is a series of instructions for inputting orders, changing orders, and calculating amount due.

To wrap this up, an IS will have a different procedure for every process, and a process will have a different procedure for every IS that supports it. In many of the chapters that follow, we'll rely on these fundamental ideas about IS, processes, and procedures. But you might already notice a few useful applications of this model. When you think about improving a process, make sure you identify all the IS that support it. When you make changes to an IS, make sure you anticipate all the processes that use that IS. Finally, when either the IS or the process changes, the procedure will also need to change. It might surprise you that many businesspeople are not aware of the distinction between procedures and processes, but Jake knew, and now you do, too.

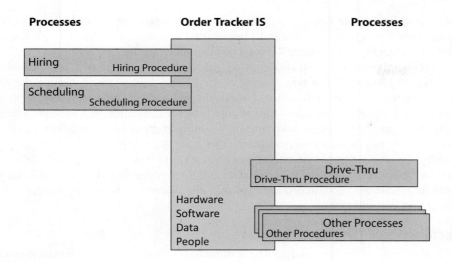

FIGURE 2-7

Procedures, Processes, and the Order Tracker IS

Q4. How Do Structured and Dynamic Processes Vary?

Businesses have dozens, hundreds, even thousands of different processes. Some processes are stable, almost fixed, in the flow among their activities. For example, the daily processes of opening or closing the fast food restaurant are fixed—employees perform the same listed steps in the same order every time. These processes are highly standardized so that the procedures are done the same way each time regardless of who is working.

Other processes are less structured, less rigid, and sometimes creative. For example, how does the restaurant manager decide on landscaping improvements? The manager can look at other restaurants or visit a nursery, but the process for deciding what to do next is not nearly as structured as that for opening or closing the restaurant.

In this text, we divide processes into two broad categories. **Structured processes** are formally defined, standardized processes. Most structured processes support day-to-day operations: scheduling work shifts, calculating daily sales tax totals, and so forth. **Dynamic processes** are less specific, more adaptive, and even intuitive. Deciding whether to open a new store location and how best to solve a problem of poor employee training are examples of dynamic processes.

Characteristics of Structured Processes

Figure 2-8 summarizes the major differences between structured and dynamic processes and gives examples of each from the fast food restaurant. Structured processes are formally defined with specific detailed activities arranged into fixed, predefined sequences, like that shown in the BPMN diagram in Figure 2-1. Changes to structured processes are slow, made with deliberation,

Structured Processes	Dynamic Processes
Formally defined process, activity flow fixed	Informal process
Process change slow and difficult	Process change rapid and expected
Control is critical	Adaptation is critical
Innovation not expected	Innovation required
Efficiency and effectiveness are important	Effectiveness typically more important
Procedures are prescriptive	Procedures are supportive
Examples in this book: Chapter 7 Procurement; Chapter 8 Sales	Examples in this book: Chapter 9 Collaboration; Chapter 10 Social Media; Chapter 11 Business Intelligence
At Fast Food Restaurant: Scheduling, Drive-Thru, In-Store Ordering, Revenue Totaling, Reordering, Opening, Closing	At Fast Food Restaurant: Landscaping, Community Outreach, Hiring

FIGURE 2-8

Differences Between Structured and Dynamic Processes

and difficult to implement. Control is critical in structured processes. Innovation of structured processes is not expected, nor is it generally appreciated or rewarded. "Wow, I've got four different ways of closing the store at night" is not a positive accomplishment.

For structured processes, both efficiency and effectiveness are important, and we will define these aspects in Chapter 5. For now, assume that *efficiency* means accomplishing the process with minimum resources, and *effectiveness* means that the process contributes directly to the organization's strategy. Reducing average drive-thru time for customers by 5 seconds would be a huge efficiency gain. If the competitive strategy is getting every order correct, then a Drive-Thru process that leads to a decrease in errors is effective.

Finally, the procedures for structured processes are prescriptive. They clearly delimit what the users of the system can do and under what conditions they can do it. In Chapters 7 and 8, you will see how procedures occur in procurement and sales. Variations on those procedures will not be tolerated, as you will learn.

Characteristics of Dynamic Processes

The second column of the table in Figure 2-8 summarizes characteristics of dynamic processes. First, such processes tend to be informal. This does not mean that they are unstructured; rather, it means that the process cannot be reduced to fixed activities done the same way every time. Instead, these processes are often created on the fly, their activities are fluid and intermingled with other processes, and they frequently include backtracking and repetition. As a result, BPMN diagrams of dynamic processes are always highly generic. They have activities with generalized names like "gather data," "analyze past sales," and "assess maintenance costs." Human intuition plays a big role in a dynamic process. Examples at the fast food restaurant include hiring, landscaping, and community outreach.

Dynamic processes, as their name implies, change rapidly as requirements and situations change. If structured processes are cast in stone, dynamic processes are written in sand on a windy beach. "We'll try it this way. If it works, great; if not, we'll do something else." A good example is the Community Outreach process at the fast food restaurant. Today, this process involves choosing which youth sports team to support, but tomorrow when an employee asks if the restaurant would like to be a sponsor for a new 5K run, the activities in the process change. Such change is expected. The need to try one method and revise it as needed reinforces the need to experiment—one of the four key skills for success, as discussed in Chapter 1.

Rather than being controlled, dynamic processes are adaptive; they must be so to evolve with experience. Dynamic process actors collaborate. As they give feedback to each other, the process evolves into one that no single person might have envisioned but that works better than anyone could have created on their own ahead of time.

Adaptation requires innovation. Whereas innovation on a structured process like computing sales revenue is likely to get you fired, innovating with Twitter to forecast sales will be highly rewarded.

For the most part, dynamic processes often have fewer well-accepted objectives than structured processes, and these objectives tend to emphasize effectiveness rather than efficiency. Did the process help us accomplish our strategy? This is not to say that efficient use of resources does not matter; rather, dynamic processes change so fast that it is often not possible to measure efficiency over time. Typically, costs are controlled by budget: "Get the best result you can with these resources."

Finally, procedures for dynamic processes are supportive rather than prescriptive. The instructions for using an information system are less rigid. The procedures for using email to coordinate a Landscaping process—the time between emails, the contents of the email, and other procedures—will change each time a Landscaping process is executed.

This structured–dynamic distinction is important. For one, the behavior you choose as a business professional depends on the type of process in which you are involved. Innovation will be expected in dynamic processes but discouraged in structured processes. For information systems, this process distinction is important in the nature and character of the system. As stated, the procedures of an IS used to support structured processes will restrict your behavior and readily (and successfully) frustrate any attempts at innovation. In contrast, an IS that supports a dynamic process supports innovation. For example, using text messaging to support a collaboration process is an open book. Put anything in it you want; control that content in whatever way you think is appropriate. As you learn about information systems this semester, understand that their procedures are a direct reflection of the kind of process they are intended to support.

PART 2

INFORMATION TECHNOLOGY

The two chapters in Part 2 address the information technology that is the foundation for MIS. You may think that such technology is unimportant to you as a business professional. However, today's managers and business professionals work frequently with information technology as purchasers and purchase approvers, if not in more involved ways.

Chapter 3 discusses hardware, software, and computer networks. It defines basic terms and fundamental computing concepts. You will need these terms so that, for example, when we refer to thin-client or native applications later in this text, you will know what those terms mean. Also, you may someday work for (or own!) a small business and have important decisions to make about what computing equipment and software you need.

Chapter 4 describes database processing. You will learn the purpose and roles for databases and database applications. You will also learn how to create simple entity-relationship data models, which are abstractions from which you can create database structure. We will illustrate database modeling and design using the database employed by the intramural sports league.

The purpose of these two chapters is to teach you the basics about technology to enable you to be an effective IT consumer. You will learn basic terms, fundamental concepts, and useful frameworks so that you will have the knowledge to ask good questions and make appropriate requests of the IS professionals who will serve you. Those concepts and frameworks will be far more useful to you than the latest technology trend, which may be outdated by the time you graduate.

Chapter 3   Hardware, Software, and Networks

"... if we don't have an iPad app, we don't have a business."

Chuck's Bikes Inc. (CBI) is a small bicycle manufacturer that buys frames, gears, brakes, tires, and related gear and assembles them into finished bicycles that it sells to retailers. Emily Johnson, CBI's CFO; Lucas Massey, IT director; and Drew Mills, sales manager, are having an impromptu meeting in the company's lunchroom. Drew continues to text while they talk.

"We don't have the resources," Lucas says in response to a question from Drew. Lucas is looking at the top of Drew's head.

"What do you mean?" Drew looks up ... his short response sounds angry.

"As in money, you know. *Dinero.* Budget. Don't have it."

"Emily, is that right?" Drew looks at Emily while he texts.

"Well, this sounds important. We might be able to...." She can't finish her sentence before Lucas jumps back in.

"Wait a minute; weren't we talking about *reducing* expenses last week?" Lucas's face is turning red.

"Lucas, I don't know about budget, but what I'm telling you is that if we don't have an iPad app, we don't have a business." Drew furiously texts on his phone ...

"OK, let's talk about it for a second. You want an Android app, too?" Lucas sounds like he's talking to a 2-year-old.

"Yes." Drew ignores the tone in Lucas's voice.

"OK. How about a Win 8 app?" Lucas continues.

Q1. What do business professionals need to know about computer hardware?

Q2. What do business professionals need to know about software?

Q3. What are the differences between native and thin-client applications?

Q4. What characterizes quality mobile user experiences?

Q5. What do business professionals need to know about data communications?

Q6. What happens on a typical Web server?

Q7. Why is the cloud the future for most organizations?

"I don't know. Not as much as an iPad app, for sure. But why not build one application for all of them?" Drew is getting impatient with all these questions.

"I wish it were that simple. But it just comes down to…" Lucas is trying to stay calm.

"Resources." Drew finishes his sentence for him.

"Yup."

"Look, it's not just me. I was just texting Addison, and she says she's having a hard time with San Diego Sports."

"No! Not San Diego!" Emily jumps in, "We need them. What's going on?" Emily knows San Diego Sports is a key customer in this year's revenue plan.

"Addison says they brought up the iPad issue in her negotiations last week. They said they didn't think we were competitive…because we don't have an iPad app."

"Well, customers can order on Safari." Lucas offers this lamely; by now he knows this issue isn't going away.

"Yeah, they can, Lucas. But they don't want to! They want to use their iPads and their Androids."

There's a pause in the conversation. Then Emily continues, "Lucas, have you looked into international development?" Emily's realizing they have to do something about this, too.

"You mean India?"

"Yeah, or some Asian company somewhere. Jerome over at Pickins.com told me that's what they did."

"We know nothing about it. What are we gonna do, run an ad in a New Delhi newspaper?" Lucas stares at the ceiling.

"No, but I can find out what Jerome did." Emily ignores his sarcasm.

Lucas realizes he needs to chill out. "I was looking into Indian developers last week, Emily…for something else. It's pretty scary."

"Why?"

"Like I said, we don't know what we're doing. We could waste a lot of money and time."

"Well…"

"One site had bad grammar and misspelled words," but as he says this, he's getting more interested.

"Does that matter?"

"Maybe not. It doesn't inspire confidence, though. I wonder about open source…. Nah," Lucas muses.

Emily interrupts him, "I've heard about it, but what exactly is open source?"

"It's when a bunch of amateurs get together over beer and munchies and write computer programs for a hobby." Drew sounds irritated as he puts his phone away. That's more than Lucas can stand.

"Drew, you know that's ludicrous. What about Linux? Huh? Seems to work pretty well for us. But I don't think open source will work here…"

"Linux, Schminix. I've got to go. I'm setting up tomorrow's golf club event…assuming we get the deal. I'm telling you two, you want to stay in business, get us an iPad app…like this week."

Drew strides out of the room, leaving Lucas and Emily staring at one another.

"Lucas, I think we better do something."

"OK, I'll look into it. How much money do you have?"

"Nice try. Send me a proposal and we'll see." Emily didn't get to be a CFO by falling for that question.

"OK, give me a week to look around. Meanwhile, would you find out what Pickins.com did?"

"Sure."

As stated, this chapter presents the minimum essential knowledge you'll need to be an effective decision maker about today's hardware, software, and network technology. You may think, "Well, I don't need to know that, I'll just rely on outside experts to tell me what to do." But that strategy may not work in the twenty-first century. Many of your competitors will be able to effectively collaborate with IT professionals and gain a competitive advantage over you. In fact, today, basic knowledge of technology is a key component of any business professional's toolkit. So, let's get started with hardware.

Chapter Preview

Q1. What Do Business Professionals Need to Know About Computer Hardware?

As discussed in the five-component framework, hardware consists of electronic components and related gadgetry that input, process, output, and store data according to instructions encoded in computer programs or software. All hardware today has, at least to the level that is important to us, more or less the same components. We'll begin with that and then we'll quickly survey basic types of computers.

Hardware Components

Every computer has a **central processing unit (CPU)**, which is sometimes called "the brain" of the computer. Although the design of the CPU has nothing in common with the anatomy of a human brain, this description is helpful because the CPU does have the "smarts" of the machine. The CPU selects instructions, processes them, performs arithmetic and logical comparisons, and stores results of operations in memory. Some computers have two or more CPUs. A computer with two CPUs is called a **dual-processor** computer. **Quad-processor** computers have four CPUs. Some high-end computers have 16 or more CPUs.

CPUs vary in speed, function, and cost. Hardware vendors such as Intel, Advanced Micro Devices, and National Semiconductor continually improve CPU speed and capabilities while reducing CPU costs (as discussed under Moore's Law in Chapter 1). Whether you or your department need the latest, greatest CPU depends on the nature of your work.

The CPU works in conjunction with **main memory**. The CPU reads data and instructions from memory, and it stores results of computations in main memory. Main memory is sometimes called **RAM** for **random access memory**.

All computers include **storage hardware**, which is used to save data and programs. Magnetic disk is by far the most common storage device, although optical disks such as CDs and DVDs are also popular. Thumb drives are small, portable magnetic storage devices that can be used to back up data and transfer it from one computer to another. In large corporate data centers, data is sometimes stored on magnetic tape.

Types of Hardware

Figure 3-1 lists the basic types of hardware. **Personal computers (PC)** are classic computing devices that are used by individuals. As stated in Chapter 1, their price-performance ratio declines every year. The Mac Pro is an example of a modern PC. Apple brought **tablets** (sometimes called **slates**) to prominence with the iPad. In June 2012, Microsoft announced Surface, another tablet. Google and others sell tablets as well. **Smartphones** are cell phones with processing capability; the Motorola (now owned by Google) Droid is a good example. Today, because it's hard to find a cell phone that isn't smart, people often just call them phones.

A **server** is a computer that is designed to support processing from many remote computers and users. You can think of a server as a PC on steroids; a typical example is the Dell PowerEdge server. As a business professional, you probably will not be involved in the choice of server hardware. Finally, a **server farm** is a collection of, typically, thousands of servers. Server farms are often placed in large truck trailers that hold 5,000 servers or more. PCs, tablets, and smartphones that access servers and the cloud are called **clients**.

FIGURE 3-1
Basic Types of Hardware

Hardware Type	Example(s)
Personal Computer (PC) *Including desktops and laptops*	Apple Mac Pro
Tablet *Including ebook readers*	iPad, Microsoft Surface, Google Nexus 7, Kindle Fire
(Smart)Phone	Motorola (Google) Droid
Server	Dell PowerEdge Server
Server Farm	Racks of servers

FIGURE 3-2

Bits Are Easy to Represent Electronically

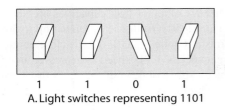

1   1   0   1
A. Light switches representing 1101

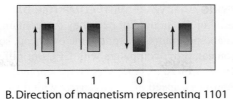

1   1   0   1
B. Direction of magnetism representing 1101

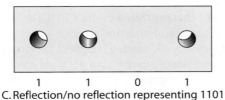

1   1   0   1
C. Reflection/no reflection representing 1101

The capacities of computer hardware are specified according to data units, which we discuss next.

Computer Data

Computers represent data using binary digits, called bits. A bit is either a zero or a one. Bits are used for computer data because they are easy to represent electronically, as illustrated in Figure 3-2. A switch can be either closed or open. A computer can be designed so that an open switch represents zero and a closed switch represents one. Or the orientation of a magnetic field can represent a bit; magnetism in one direction represents a zero, magnetism in the opposite direction represents a one. Or, for optical media, small pits are burned onto the surface of the disk so that they will reflect light. In a given spot, a reflection means a one; no reflection means a zero.

COMPUTER DATA SIZES All computer data are represented by bits. The data can be numbers, characters, currency amounts, photos, recordings, or whatever. All are simply a string of bits. For reasons that interest many but are irrelevant for future managers, bits are grouped into 8-bit chunks called **bytes**. For character data, such as the letters in a person's name, one character will fit into one byte. Thus, when you read a specification that a computing device has 100 million bytes of memory, you know that the device can hold up to 100 million characters.

Bytes are used to measure sizes of noncharacter data as well. Someone might say, for example, that a given picture is 100,000 bytes in size. This statement means the length of the bit string that represents the picture is 100,000 bytes or 800,000 bits (because there are 8 bits per byte).

The specifications for the size of main memory, disk, and other computer devices are expressed in bytes. Figure 3-3 shows the set of abbreviations that are used to represent data storage capacity. A **kilobyte**, abbreviated **K**, is a collection of 1,024 bytes. A **megabyte**, or **MB**, is 1,024 kilobytes. A **gigabyte**, or **GB**, is 1,024 megabytes; a **terabyte**, or **TB**, is 1,024 gigabytes; a **petabyte**, or **PB**, is 1,024 terabytes; and an **exabyte**, or **EB**, is 1,024 petabytes. Sometimes you will see these definitions simplified as 1K equals 1,000 bytes and 1MB equals 1,000K, and so on. Such simplifications are incorrect, but they do ease the math.

FIGURE 3-3

Important Storage-Capacity Terminology

Term	Definition	Abbreviation
Byte	Number of bits to represent one character	
Kilobyte	1,024 bytes	K
Megabyte	1,024 K = 1,048,576 bytes	MB
Gigabyte	1,024 MB = 1,073,741,824 bytes	GB
Terabyte	1,024 GB = 1,099,511,627,776 bytes	TB
Petabyte	1,024 TB = 1,125,899,906,842,624 bytes	PB
Exabyte	1,024 PB = 1,152,921,504,606,846,976 bytes	EB

SPECIFYING HARDWARE WITH COMPUTER DATA SIZES Computer disk capacities are specified according to the amount of data they can contain. Thus, a 500GB disk can contain up to 500GB of data and programs. There is some overhead, so it is not quite 500GB, but it's close enough.

You can order computers with CPUs of different speeds. CPU speed is expressed in cycles called *hertz*. In 2013, a slow personal computer has a speed of 1.5 Gigahertz. A fast personal computer has a speed of 3+ Gigahertz with dual processors. As predicted by Moore's Law, CPU speeds continually increase.

Additionally, CPUs today are classified as 32-bit or 64-bit. Without delving into the particulars, a 32-bit is less capable and cheaper than a 64-bit CPU. The latter can address more main memory; you need a 64-bit processor to effectively utilize more than 4GB of memory. 64-bit processors have other advantages as well, but they are more expensive than 32-bit processors.

An employee who does only simple tasks such as word processing does not need a fast CPU; a 32-bit, 1.5 Gigahertz CPU will be fine. However, an employee who processes large, complicated spreadsheets or who manipulates large database files or edits large picture, sound, or movie files needs a fast computer like a 64-bit, dual processor with 3.5 Gigahertz or more. Employees whose work requires them to use many large applications at the same time need 4 GB or more of RAM. Others can do with less.

One last comment: Main memory is volatile, meaning its contents are lost when power is off. Magnetic and optical disks are nonvolatile, meaning their contents survive when power is off. If you suddenly lose power, the contents of unsaved memory—say, documents that have been altered—will be lost. Therefore, get into the habit of frequently (every few minutes or so) saving documents or files that you are changing.

Q2. What Do Business Professionals Need to Know About Software?

As a future manager or business professional, you need to know the essential terminology and software concepts that will enable you to be an intelligent software consumer. To begin, consider the basic categories of software shown in Figure 3-4.

Every computer has an **operating system (OS)**, which is a program that controls that computer's resources. Some of the functions of an operating system are to read and write data, allocate main memory, perform memory swapping, start and stop programs, respond to error conditions, and facilitate backup and recovery. In addition, the operating system creates and manages the user interface, including the display, keyboard, mouse, and other devices.

Although the operating system makes the computer usable, it does little application-specific work. If you want to check the weather or access a database, you need application programs such as an iPad weather application or Oracle's customer relationship management (CRM) software.

Both client and server computers need an operating system, though they need not be the same. Further, both clients and servers can process application programs. The application's design determines whether the client, the server, or both process it.

We will next consider the operating system and application program categories of software.

What Are the Major Operating Systems?

The major operating systems are listed in Figure 3-5. Consider each.

NONMOBILE CLIENT OPERATING SYSTEMS Nonmobile client operating systems are used on personal computers. The most popular is **Microsoft Windows**. Some version of Windows resides on more than 80 percent of the world's desktops, and if we consider just business users, the figure is more than 90 percent.

FIGURE 3-4

Categories of Computer Software

	Operating System	Application Programs
Client	Programs that control the client computer's resources	Applications that are processed on client computers
Server	Programs that control the server computer's resources	Applications that are processed on server computers

Category	Operating System	Used for	Remarks
Nonmobile Clients	Windows	Personal Computer Clients	Most widely used operating system in business. Current version is Windows 8.1. Metro-style applications provide a touch interface.
	Mac OS	Macintosh Clients	First used by graphic artists and others in arts community; now used more widely. First desktop OS to provide a touch interface. Current version is the Mac OS X Mavericks.
	Unix	Workstation Clients	Popular on powerful client computers used in engineering, computer-assisted design, architecture. Difficult for the nontechnical user. Almost never used by business clients.
	Linux	Just about anything	Open source variant of Unix. Adapted to almost every type of computing device. On a PC, used with Open Office application software. Rarely used by business clients.
Mobile Clients	Symbian	Nokia, Samsung, and other phones	Popular worldwide, but less so in North America.
	BlackBerry OS	Research in Motion BlackBerrys	Device and OS developed for use by business. Very popular in beginning, but strongly challenged by iPhone and others.
	iOS	iPhone, iPod Touch, iPad	Rapidly increasing installed base with success of the iPhone and iPad. Based on Mac OS X.
	Android	T-Mobile and other phones. Tablets and eReaders like the Kindle Fire	Linux-based phone/tablet operating system from Google. Rapidly increasing market share.
	Windows RT	Windows 8 for ARM devices	Windows 8 tailored specifically for ARM devices, mostly tablets, but some PCs, too.
Servers	Windows Server	Servers	Businesses with a strong commitment to Microsoft.
	Unix	Servers	Fading from use. Replaced by Linux.
	Linux	Servers	Very popular. Aggressively pushed by IBM.

FIGURE 3-5
Major Operating Systems

The most recent client version of Windows is Windows 8.1. Windows 8 was, a major rewrite of prior versions that is distinguished by two different user interfaces. One is the classic Windows interface and the second is touch-oriented. Microsoft claims that Windows 8 applications work just as well on portable, mobile devices such as tablets as they do on desktops. One key feature of Windows 8 touch applications is the minimization of menu bars, status lines, and other visual overhead. Figure 3-6 shows an example of a Windows 8 interface for searching images in Windows Explorer.

Apple Computer, Inc. developed its own operating system for the Macintosh, **Mac OS**. The current version is Mac OS X Mavericks. Apple touts it as the world's most advanced desktop operating system, and until Windows 8, it was. Now OS X and Windows 8 compete neck and neck for that title.

Until recently, Mac OS was used primarily by graphic artists and workers in the arts community. But for many reasons, Mac OS has made headway into the traditional Windows market. In 2012, all versions of Windows accounted for 80 percent of the PC market while the Mac OS sales accounted for 15 percent.[1] As many business users replace PCs with tablets, these percentages will change to favor Apple because the iPad has an enormous lead on Microsoft's Surface and Surface Pro and tablets from other vendors.

[1] Greg Sterling, Report: iPhone, iPad Now Drive More Web Traffic Than Mac OS, *Marketing Land,* last modified February 10, 2012, http://marketingland.com/report-iphone-ipad-now-drive-more-web-traffic-than-mac-os-5867.

FIGURE 3-6

Example Windows 8 Touch Interface

Source: Microsoft Corporation.

Mac OS was designed originally to run the line of CPU processors from Motorola, but today a Macintosh with an Intel processor is able to run both Windows and Mac OS.

Unix is an operating system that was developed at Bell Labs in the 1970s. It has been the workhorse of the scientific and engineering communities since then. Unix is generally regarded as being more difficult to use than either Windows or Mac OS. Many Unix users know and employ an arcane language for manipulating files and data. However, once they surmount the rather steep learning curve, most Unix users become fanatic supporters of the system. Sun Microsystems and other vendors of computers for scientific and engineering applications are the major proponents of Unix. In general, Unix is not for the business user.

Linux is a version of Unix that was developed by the open source community (discussed on pages 58–59). This community is a loosely coupled group of programmers who mostly volunteer their time to contribute code to develop and maintain Linux. The open source community owns Linux, and there is no fee to use it. Linux can run on client computers, but usually only when budget is of paramount concern. Linux is by far the most popular as a server OS.

MOBILE CLIENT OPERATING SYSTEMS Figure 3-5 also lists the five principal mobile operating systems. **Symbian** is popular on phones in Europe and the Far East, but less so in North America. **BlackBerry OS** was one of the most successful early mobile operating systems and was used primarily by business users on BlackBerry devices. It is now losing market share to iOS and Android and may soon disappear from the market.

iOS is the operating system used on the iPod Touch, iPhone, and iPad. When first released, it broke new ground with its ease of use and compelling display, features that are now being copied by the Android and Windows 8 tablet devices. With the popularity of the iPhone and iPad, Apple has been increasing its market share of iOS and now claims that it is used on 44 percent of all mobile devices. The current version of iOS is iOS 7.

Android is a mobile operating system licensed by Google. Android devices have a very loyal following, especially among technical users. Recently, Android has been gaining market share over the BlackBerry OS on phones, and it received a big boost when it was selected for the Amazon Kindle Fire. Ebook readers like the Kindle became very popular; as of 2012, one in four Americans owned at least one of these devices.[2] However, their popularity may be threatened by multipurpose tablets.

Most industry observers would agree that Apple has led the way, both with the Mac OS and the iOS, in creating easy-to-use interfaces. Certainly, many innovative ideas have first appeared in a Macintosh or iSomething and then later been added, in one form or another, to Android or Windows. It seems clear that touch-based interfaces are the future for all client devices.

---

[2] Joe Wilcox, "One in four Americans own an e-book reader or tablet," *BetaNews,* accessed September 4, 2013, http://betanews.com/2012/01/23/one-in-four-americans-own-an-e-book-reader-or-tablet/.

Windows RT is a version of Windows 8 designed for use on ARM devices. **ARM** is a power-saving computer architecture that is designed for portable devices such as phones and tablets. Numerous vendors sell Windows RT tablets, including a version of Microsoft Surface. The principal way that Windows RT devices differ from Windows 8 devices (such as the Microsoft Surface Pro) is that with Windows RT, all applications must be purchased from the Microsoft store.

SERVER OPERATING SYSTEMS The last three rows of Figure 3-5 show the three most popular server operating systems. **Windows Server** is a version of Windows that has been specially designed and configured for server use. It has much more stringent and restrictive security procedures than other versions of Windows and is popular on servers in organizations that have made a strong commitment to Microsoft.

Unix can also be used on servers, but it is gradually being replaced by Linux.

Linux is frequently used on servers by organizations that want, for whatever reason, to avoid a server commitment to Microsoft. IBM is the primary proponent of Linux and in the past has used it as a means to better compete against Microsoft. Although IBM does not own Linux, IBM has developed many business systems solutions that use Linux. By using Linux, neither IBM nor its customers have to pay a license fee to Microsoft.

Virtualization

Virtualization is the process by which one computer hosts the appearance of many computers. One operating system, called the **host operating system**, runs one or more operating systems as applications. Those hosted operating systems are called **virtual machines (vm)**. Each virtual machine has disk space and other resources allocated to it. The host operating system controls the activities of the virtual machines it hosts to prevent them from interfering with one another. With virtualization, each vm is able to operate exactly the same as it would if it were operating in a stand-alone, nonvirtual environment.

Three types of virtualization exist:

- PC virtualization
- Server virtualization
- Desktop virtualization

With **PC virtualization**, a personal computer, such as a desktop or portable computer, hosts several different operating systems. Say a user needs, for some reason, to have both Windows 8 and Linux running on his or her computer. In that circumstance, the user can install a virtual host operating system and then install both Windows 8 and Linux on top of it. In that way, the user can have both systems on the same hardware. VMWare Workstation is a popular PC virtualization product that can run both Windows and Linux operating systems.

With **server virtualization**, a server computer hosts one or more other server computers. In Figure 3-7, a Windows Server computer is hosting two virtual machines. Users can log onto either of those virtual machines and they will appear as normal servers. Figure 3-8 shows how virtual machine VM3 appears to a user of that server. Notice that a user of VM3 is running a browser that is accessing SharePoint. In fact, this virtual machine was used to generate many of the SharePoint figures in Chapter 2. Server virtualization plays a key role for cloud vendors, as you'll learn in Chapter 6.

FIGURE 3-7

Windows Server Computer Hosting Two Virtual Machines

Source: Microsoft Corporation.

FIGURE 3-8
Virtual Machine Example

PC virtualization is interesting and sometimes quite useful, and server virtualization is key to cloud economics, as you will learn in Q7. Desktop virtualization, on the other hand, has the potential to be revolutionary. With **desktop virtualization**, a server hosts many versions of desktop operating systems. Each of those desktops has a complete user environment and appears to the user to be just another PC. However, the desktop can be accessed from any computer to which the user has access. Thus, you could be at an airport and go to an airport computer and access your virtualized desktop. To you, it appears as if that airport computer is your own personal computer. Later, you could do the same to a utility computer sitting in your hotel room. Meanwhile, many other users could have accessed the computer in the airport, and each thought he or she had his or her personal computer. IBM offers desktop virtualization for as low as $12 a month per PC.

Desktop virtualization is in its infancy, but it might have a major impact during the early years of your career.

Own Versus License

When you buy a computer program, you are not actually buying that program. Instead, you are buying a **license** to use that program. For example, when you buy a Windows license, Microsoft is selling you the right to use Windows. Microsoft continues to own the Windows program. Large organizations do not buy a license for each computer user. Instead, they negotiate a **site license**, which is a flat fee that authorizes the company to install the product (operating system or application) on all of that company's computers or on all of the computers at a specific site.

In the case of Linux, no company can sell you a license to use it. It is owned by the open source community, which states that Linux has no license fee (with certain reasonable restrictions). Large companies such as IBM and smaller companies such as RedHat can make money by supporting Linux, but no company makes money selling Linux licenses.

What Types of Applications Exist, and How Do Organizations Obtain Them?

Application software performs a service or function. Some application programs are general purpose, such as Microsoft Excel or Word. Other application programs provide specific functions. QuickBooks, for example, is an application program that provides general ledger and other accounting functions. We begin by describing categories of application programs and then describe sources for them.

Horizontal-market application software provides capabilities common across all organizations and industries. Word processors, graphics programs, spreadsheets, and presentation programs are all horizontal-market application software.

Examples of such software are Microsoft Word, Excel, and PowerPoint. Examples from other vendors are Adobe's Acrobat, Photoshop, and PageMaker and Jasc Corporation's Paint Shop Pro. These applications are used in a wide variety of businesses across all industries. They are purchased off-the-shelf, and little customization of features is necessary (or possible).

Vertical-market application software serves the needs of a specific industry. Examples of such programs are those used by dental offices to schedule appointments and bill patients, those used by auto mechanics to keep track of customer data and customers' automobile repairs, and those used by parts warehouses to track inventory, purchases, and sales.

Vertical applications usually can be altered or customized. Typically, the company that sold the application software will provide such services or offer referrals to qualified consultants who can provide this service.

One-of-a-kind application software is developed for a specific, unique need. The IRS develops such software, for example, because it has needs that no other organization has.

You can acquire application software in exactly the same ways that you can buy a new suit. The quickest and least risky option is to buy your suit off-the-rack. With this method, you get your suit immediately, and you know exactly what it will cost. You may not, however, get a good fit. Alternately, you can buy your suit off-the-rack and have it altered. This will take more time, it may cost more, and there's some possibility that the alteration will result in a poor fit. Most likely, however, an altered suit will fit better than an off-the-rack one.

Finally, you can hire a tailor to make a custom suit. In this case, you will have to describe what you want, be available for multiple fittings, and be willing to pay considerably more. Although there is an excellent chance of a great fit, there is also the possibility of a disaster. Still, if you want a yellow and orange polka-dot silk suit with a hissing rattlesnake on the back, tailor-made is the only way to go. You can buy computer software in exactly the same ways: **off-the-shelf software**, **off-the-shelf with alterations software**, or tailor-made. Tailor-made software is called **custom-developed software**.

Organizations develop custom application software themselves or hire a development vendor. Like buying the yellow and orange polka-dot suit, such development is done in situations in which the needs of the organization are so unique that no horizontal or vertical applications are available. By developing custom software, the organization can tailor its application to fit its requirements.

Custom development is difficult and risky. Staffing and managing teams of software developers is challenging. Managing software projects can be daunting. Many organizations have embarked on application development projects only to find that the projects take twice as long—or longer—to finish as planned. Cost overruns of 200 and 300 percent are not uncommon. We will discuss such risks further in Chapter 10.

Every application program needs to be adapted to changing needs and changing technologies. The adaptation costs of horizontal and vertical software are amortized over all of the users of that software, perhaps thousands or millions of customers. For custom-developed software, however, the using organization must pay all of the adaptation costs itself. Over time, this cost burden is heavy.

Because of the risk and expense, custom development is the last-choice alternative and is used only when there is no other option. Figure 3-9 summarizes software sources and types.

	Software Source		
Software Type	Off-the-shelf	Off-the-shelf and then customized	Custom-developed
Horizontal applications			
Vertical applications			
One-of-a-kind applications			

FIGURE 3-9

Software Sources and Types

What Is Firmware?

Firmware is computer software that is installed into devices such as printers, print servers, and various types of communication devices. The software is coded just like other software, but it is installed into special, read-only memory of the printer or other device. In this way, the program becomes part of the device's memory; it is as if the program's logic is designed into the device's circuitry. Users do not need to load firmware into the device's memory.

Firmware can be changed or upgraded, but this is normally a task for IT professionals. The task is easy, but it requires knowledge of special programs and techniques that most business users choose not to learn.

Is Open Source a Viable Alternative?

The term *open source* means that the source code of the program is available to the public. **Source code** is computer code that is written and understood by humans. Figure 3-10 shows a portion of computer code that supports an animation on a Windows 8 phone. Source code is compiled into **machine code** that is processed by a computer. Machine code is, in general, not understandable by humans and cannot be modified. When you access the phone application, the machine code version of the program in Figure 3-10 runs on your computer. We do not show machine code in a figure because it would look like this:

1101001010010111111001110111100100011100000111111011101111100111...

In a **closed source** project, say Microsoft Office, the source code is highly protected and only available to trusted employees and carefully vetted contractors. The source code is protected like gold in a vault. Only those trusted programmers can make changes to a closed source project.

With open source, anyone can obtain the source code from the open source project's Web site. Programmers alter or add to this code depending on their interests and goals. In most cases,

FIGURE 3-10
Source Code Sample

```
/// <summary>
/// Allows the page to draw itself.
/// </summary>
private void OnDraw(object sender, GameTimerEventArgs e)
{
    SharedGraphicsDeviceManager.Current.GraphicsDevice.Clear(Color.CornflowerBlue);

    SharedGraphicsDeviceManager.Current.GraphicsDevice.Clear(Color.Black);

    // Render the Silverlight controls using the UIElementRenderer.
    elementRenderer.Render();

    // Draw the sprite
    spriteBatch.Begin();

    // Draw the rectangle in its new position
    for (int i = 0; i < 3; i++)
    {
        spriteBatch.Draw(texture[i], bikeSpritePosition[i], Color.White);
    }

    // Using the texture from the UIElementRenderer,

    // draw the Silverlight controls to the screen.
    spriteBatch.Draw(elementRenderer.Texture, Vector2.Zero, Color.White);

    spriteBatch.End();
}
```

programmers can incorporate code they find into their own projects. They may be able to resell those projects depending on the type of license agreement the project uses.

Open source succeeds because of collaboration. A programmer examines the source code and identifies a need or project that seems interesting. He or she then creates a new feature, redesigns or reprograms an existing feature, or fixes a known problem. That code is then sent to others in the open source project who then evaluate the quality and merits of the work and add it to the product, if appropriate.

Typically, there is a lot of give and take; there are many cycles of iteration and feedback. Because of this iteration, a well-managed project with strong peer reviews can result in very high-quality code, like that in Linux.

The Internet proved to be a great asset for open source, and many open source projects became successful, including:

- Open Office (a Microsoft Office look-alike)
- Firefox (a browser)
- MySQL (a DBMS, see Chapter 4)
- Apache (a Web server, see Q7)
- Hadoop (see Chapters 4 and 11)
- Android (a mobile device operating system)

WHY DO PROGRAMMERS VOLUNTEER THEIR SERVICES? To anyone who has never enjoyed writing computer programs, it is difficult to understand why anyone would donate their time and skills to contribute to open source projects. Programming is, however, an intense combination of art and logic, and designing and writing a complicated computer program is exceedingly pleasurable (and addictive). If you have an artistic and logical mind, you ought to try it.

The first reason that people contribute to open source is that it is great fun! Additionally, some people contribute to open source because it gives them the freedom to choose the projects on which they work. They may have a programming day job that is not terribly interesting, say, writing a program to manage a computer printer. Their job pays the bills, but it is not fulfilling.

In the 1950s, Hollywood studio musicians suffered as they recorded the same style of music over and over for a long string of uninteresting movies. To keep their sanity, those musicians would gather on Sundays to play jazz, and a number of high-quality jazz clubs resulted. That's what open source is to programmers: A place where they can exercise their creativity while working on projects they find interesting and fulfilling.

Another reason for contributing to open source is to exhibit one's skill, both for pride as well as to find a job or employment as a consultant. A final reason is to start a business selling services to support an open source product.

SO, IS OPEN SOURCE VIABLE? The answer depends on the individual company or business and its needs. Open source has certainly become legitimate. According to *The Economist,* "It is now generally accepted that the future will involve a blend of both proprietary and open-source software."[3] During your career, open source will likely take a greater and greater role in software. However, whether open source works for a particular situation depends on the requirements and constraints of that situation.

Q3. What Are the Differences Between Native and Thin-Client Applications?

Chuck's Bikes has important decisions to make regarding mobile applications. Drew didn't know to use the correct terms, but what he needs to determine is whether CBI needs a native or thin-client application. Everyone in the company would have been better off if he had known to ask the question that way. You might be in a similar situation, so you need to understand those alternatives and how they compare.

Applications can be categorized as **native applications**, which are those that can run on just one operating system, or as **thin-client applications**, which are those that run in browsers on

[3] "Unlocking the Cloud," *The Economist,* last modified May 28, 2009, www.economist.com/node/13740181

MIS InClass 3

3D Print Yourself!

3D printing, also known as **additive manufacturing**, is the process of creating three-dimensional objects by layering two-dimensional printouts. Each pass of the 3D printer adds a new 2D layer and fuses it to the layers below. Both the toys and motorcycle in the photos shown here were entirely produced by 3D printers.

To create an object, engineers construct a three-dimensional data model, using general-purpose design software known as **CAD (computer added design) software**. Product engineers design a new object or manipulate an already existing object to create a model of the item to be printed. That model is input to a 3D printer, which produces an object that conforms to the model using "ink" of plastic, metal, rubber, and even biological material such as cells.

With traditional manufacturing, setup costs normally make the production of one-off (single-unit) items prohibitive. Because there are no setup costs, 3D printing can economically produce single-unit quantities. Even more important, 3D printing can produce items that are impossible to construct using traditional manufacturing methods. Engine manifolds with many intricate tunnels and passageways are an example.

3D printing also has medical applications; cells and even some organs can be constructed using 3D printing technology. Often the tissues are constructed using ink that is made of the patient's own cells. While the technology is some years away, it may be possible to use 3D printing to create replaceable body parts on demand and unique to each person's anatomy.

What does all this mean for industry? Form a team as instructed by your professor and formulate your own conclusions by answering the following questions:

1. Search the Web for the term *3D printing examples* and identify five applications that your team thinks are the most exciting, have the most potential, or represent the greatest opportunity. Explain why you chose each.
2. Search the Web for the term *3D printing vendors* and identify three vendors that your team thinks represent excellent investment opportunities. Explain why you chose each.
3. Explain how 3D printing could be used to enable customers to customize their own products.

Source: © Tobias Hase/dpa/Corbis

Source: © Piero Cruciatti/Demotix/Corbis

4. Explain how 3D printing changes the economics of spare part manufacturing, inventory, and shipping.
5. 3D printing requires a CAD data model, a 3D printer, and appropriate ink. Explain how a 3D printer vendor could use the business model of the Apple iTunes store to facilitate the sales of its printers and ink. Describe opportunities that such a business model creates for product designers.

many different operating systems. In the latter case, browsers provide a more or less consistent environment for the application; the peculiarities of operating systems and hardware are handled by the browser's code and hidden from the thin-client application.

Figure 3-11 contrasts native and thin-client applications on their important characteristics. Consider the native applications column first.

Developing Native Applications

Native applications are developed using serious, heavy-duty, professional programming languages. Mac OS and iOS applications are constructed using Objective-C, Linux (Android) applications are constructed using Java, and Windows applications are constructed using C#, VB.Net, C++, and others. All of these languages are **object-oriented**, which means they can be used to create difficult, complex applications and, if used properly, will result in high-performance code that is easy to alter when requirements change. The particular characteristics of object-oriented languages are beyond the scope of this text.

	Native Applications	Thin-client Applications
Development languages	Objective-C Java C#, VB.net (object-oriented languages)	html5 CSS3 JavaScript (scripting languages)
Developed by	Professional programmer only	Professional programmers and technically oriented Web developers and business professionals
Skill level required	High	Low to high
Difficulty	High	Easy to hard, depending on application requirements
Developer's degree	Computer science	Computer science Information systems Graphics design
User experience	Can be superb, depending on programming quality	Simple to sophisticated, depending on program quality
Possible applications	Whatever you can pay for…	Some limits prohibit very sophisticated applications
Dependency	iOS, Android, Windows	Browser difference only
Cost	High. Difficult work by highly paid employees, multiple versions required	Low to medium … easier work by lesser-paid employees, only multiple browser files necessary. Sophisticated applications may require high skill and pay.
Application distribution	Via application stores (e.g., Apple iTunes store)	Via Web sites
Example	Vanguard iPad application (free in Apple's iTunes store)	Seafood Web site: *www.brownfamilyseafood.com* Picozu editor: *www.picozu.com/editor*

FIGURE 3-11

Characteristics of Native and Thin-Client Applications

Object-oriented languages are used by professional programmers who have devoted years to learning object-oriented design and coding skills. Typically such developers were computer science majors in college.

The benefit of object-oriented languages is that they give programmers close control over the assets of the computing device and enable the creation of sophisticated and complex user interfaces. If the programs are well written, they perform fast and use memory efficiently. The limits on native applications are usually budgetary and not technological. As a businessperson, you can get just about any application you can afford.

The downside of native applications is that they are, well, native. They only run on the operating system for which they are programmed. An iOS application must be completely recoded in order to run on Android and recoded again to run on Windows.[4] Thus, to reach all users, an organization will need to support and maintain three separate versions of the same application. It will also have to staff and manage three different development teams with three different skill sets.

As a general rule, the cost of native applications is high. Many organizations reduce that cost by outsourcing development to India and other countries, but native applications are still expensive relative to thin-client applications. The standard way for distributing native applications is via a company store, such as the Apple iTunes store. An excellent example of a native application is Vanguard's iPad application. It is easy to use, has complex functionality, and is highly secure, as you would expect. Companies such as Vanguard can afford to pay for exceedingly high-quality applications.

---

[4] Not quite true. Much of the design and possibly some of the code can be reused between native applications. But, for your planning, assume that it all must be redone. Not enough will carry over to make it worth considering.

Developing Thin-Client Applications

The third column in Figure 3-11 summarizes thin-client application characteristics. Such applications run inside a browser such as Firefox, Chrome, Opera, Safari, or Internet Explorer (IE). The browser handles the idiosyncrasies of the operating system and underlying hardware. In theory, an organization should be able to develop a single application and have it run flawlessly on all browsers on all devices. Unfortunately, there are some differences in the way that browsers implement the thin-client code and some application features do not work in some browsers.

As shown in the first row of Figure 3-11, thin-client development languages are html5, CSS3, and JavaScript. These are not object-oriented languages and hence are much easier to learn. Html5 is the latest version of html, which you will learn about in Q7. The advantages of this latest version are the support for graphics, animation, 3D drawing, and other sophisticated user experiences. CSS3 is used with html5 to specify the appearance of content coded in html. JavaScript is a scripting programming language that is much easier to learn than object-oriented languages. It is used to provide the underlying logic of the application.

Thin-client applications can be written by professional programmers, and, indeed, most are. However, it is possible for technically oriented Web developers and business professionals to develop them as well. The entry-level technical skill required is low, and simple applications are relatively easy to develop. Sophisticated user experiences are difficult. Thin-client application developers may have degrees in computer science, information systems, or graphic design.

The user experience provided by a thin-client application varies considerably. Some are simply fancy Web-based brochures (*www.brownfamilyseafood.com*); others are quite sophisticated, such as SpiroCanvas in Figure 3-12 (*www.gethugames.in*), or even more impressive, *www.biodigitalhuman.com* in Figure 3-13 (runs in Opera; may not yet work in other browsers).

Thin-client applications are limited by the capabilities of the browser. While browsers are becoming increasingly sophisticated, they cannot offer the full capabilities of the underlying operating system and hardware. Thus, thin-client applications are unable to support specialized and complex applications, though this becomes less true each year.

As stated, the major advantage of thin-client over native applications is that they will run on any operating system and device. While there are some browser differences, these differences are very minor when compared with the differences between iOS, Android, and Windows. In general, unlike native applications, you can assume that a thin-client application has one code base and one development team.

Because thin-client applications can be developed by less-skilled, lesser-paid employees and because only one code base and one development team are necessary, they are

FIGURE 3-12
GetHuGames'
SpiroCanvas

Source: www.gethugames.in/
spirocanvas.

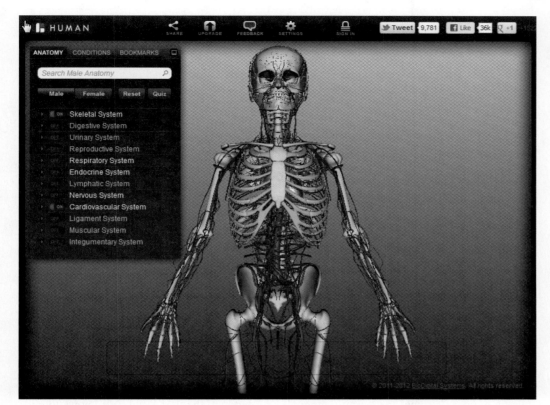

FIGURE 3-13

Sophisticated html5 Application

Source: Image created using the BioDigital Human (www.biodigitalhuman.com).

considerably cheaper to develop than native applications. However, this statement assumes applications of equivalent complexity. A simple native application can be cheaper to develop than a complex thin-client application.

Users obtain thin-client applications via the Web. For example, when you go to *www.picozu.com/editor*, the required html5, CSS3, and JavaScript files are downloaded automatically over the Web. Updates to the application are automatic and seamless. You need not install (or re-install) anything. This difference is an advantage to the user; it makes it more difficult, however, to earn money from your application. Apple, for example, will sell your native application and pay you a royalty. However, unless you require users to buy your thin-client application (which is possible, but rare), you'll have to give it away. To companies like CBI, royalty revenue from their application is not important. To you, it might be.

Which Is Better?

You know the answer to that question. If it were clear-cut, we'd only be discussing one alternative. It's not. The choice depends on your strategy, your particular goals, the requirements for your application, your budget, your schedule, your tolerance for managing technical projects, your need for application revenue, and other factors. In general, thin-client applications are cheaper to develop and maintain, but they may lack the wow factor. You and your organization have to decide for yourselves!

Q4. What Characterizes Quality Mobile User Experiences?

A **user interface (UI)** is the presentation format of an application. It consists of windows, menus, icons, dialog boxes, toolbars, and so on, as well as user content. A **user experience (UX)** is a newer term that refers not only to the UI, but also to the way that the user responds to the application. Effective UX includes enjoyment, desire to use the application again, and a positive emotional experience within that application.

FIGURE 3-14
Characteristics of Quality Mobile UX

- Feature content and support direct interaction
- Use context-sensitive chrome when needed
- Provide animation and lively behavior
- Design to scale and share (display and data)
- Use the cloud

Apple redefined the UX for mobile applications when it introduced the iPhone with touch, gravity sensing portrait/landscape orientation, and other innovative UX behavior. Since then, Microsoft defined its Windows 8 application that builds and (possibly) improves upon Apple's UX. Apple will likely advance UX again. Stay tuned.

Figure 3-14 lists the primary characteristics of a quality mobile user experience.[5] Consider each.

Feature Content

First, quality mobile user interfaces should place the primary emphasis on users' content, giving such content as much of the display as possible. Rather than show menus, toolbars, and heavy window borders, the content should be shown cleanly and in center stage. **Chrome** is a term that refers to the visual overhead in a computer display. It is the windows, the menus, and other apparatus that drive the application. Because mobile screen size is often limited, modern mobile applications eliminate chrome as much as possible. (By the way, do not confuse this use of *chrome* with Google Chrome, the popular browser.)

Figure 3-15 shows the chrome-less mobile Windows Store application. The user doesn't need a toolbar (chrome) for learning more about a product; the user intuitively knows to click the image to see more.

Using content to drive application behavior is called **direct interaction**. For another example, when you see blue, underlined type, you know to tap on it to navigate to that Web site. Similarly, if users want to highlight a word, they know to touch it to see what will happen.

Use Context-Sensitive Chrome

Designing for direct action reduces the need for chrome, but not entirely. In an online store application, once you select the application, say a game, you'll need controls to play it. For such cases, mobile applications do provide chrome, but it is **context-sensitive chrome**, meaning it pops up in the display when appropriate. Ideally, no button or command name is ever shown in a disabled (grayed-out) state. Instead, if it's disabled, the application doesn't show it, thus simplifying the UI and reserving more of the display for the users' content.

Provide Animation and Lively Behavior

Great mobile applications are lively. They capture your attention with motion and sound. If you are not doing something, they are. For example, an icon to play a movie has the movie's preview playing inside it. An unused game displays a sample game under way. When you do act, something happens immediately. The touched word or image changes color, pops up, or does something to give you active feedback that the application is alive and running.

All of this is easy to comprehend for games and entertainment applications. How these ideas pertain to commercial applications is on the leading edge of commercial UX design. Everyone wants activity, but when you access your mobile Vanguard application, do you really want to watch the application shrink if your portfolio value has diminished? Or watch it crash to the bottom of your display if the market is down substantially? Or hear *Money, Money, Money* when the market is up? Probably not. What is appropriate is being determined today; there are a lot of opportunities for techno-savvy, marketing-oriented graphic designers in the business world.

---

[5] See *http://msdn.microsoft.com/en-us/library/windows/apps/hh464920.aspx* for the source of much of this figure, as well as for an extended discussion of Windows 8-style UX.

FIGURE 3-15
Chrome-less Interface

Source: © Microsoft Corporation.

Design to Scale and Share

Mobile applications appear on phones, slates, PCs, and even large displays. Applications must be designed so that they can scale up and down without appearing awkward or taking over the device. Note the slightly different appearances of the application in the displays in Figure 3-16.

Modern operating systems (for native applications) and browsers (for thin-client applications) are designed to support such scaling. IE10, for example, allows applications to provide three sizes and versions of graphics; IE will choose the version that is appropriate for the size of the device on which it is running.

Mobile applications share their device with other mobile applications. They need to be designed to share the display effectively; applications that aggressively take over the screen are unappreciated by users and other application developers.

Mobile applications also need to be designed to share data. For example, Windows 8 introduced a feature called **charms**, which are icons that slide in from the right of the display. One of the default charms is Share; it is used to share data from one mobile application to another. IE10 allows Web pages to share thumbnails, descriptions, and links with other applications. If a user wants to email a page, IE10 will provide the shared thumbnail, description, and link to the email application, as shown in Figure 3-17.

FIGURE 3-16
Example of Application Scaling

Source: Scanrail/Fotolia.

FIGURE 3-17
Example Use of Web Page Data Declared as Shared

Source: Microsoft: http://blogs.msdn.com/b/b8/archive/2012/03/13/web-browsing-in-windows-8-consumer-preview-with-ie10.aspx.

Understand the power of this functionality; in the example, the JetSetter thin-client application in the Web page has declared that it will share the thumbnail picture, the description, and the link as shown underneath the email address in Figure 3-17. Any charm that is invoked can obtain this data. The JetSetter Web page programmer has no idea where that data may go or how it will be displayed. It could be emailed, as shown here, but it could equally go to a graphics application, a travel planning application, a social networking application, an event planning application, and so on.

This example focuses on Windows 8 and IE10, but the concepts pertain equally to iOS, Android, and browsers other than IE as well.

Use the Cloud

You will learn about the cloud in Q7 of this chapter. For now, just realize that quality applications utilize data and computing resources that are remote from the user and are likely not even known by the user.

Roaming occurs when users move their activities, especially long-running transactions (reading a book, for example), across devices. The best mobile applications do this transparently; the user need take no action. *Amazon.com*'s Kindle, for example, will track customers' reading within a book across devices. You can open a book on a Kindle that you had previously been reading on an iPad and the Kindle will take you to the last page you had read on that other device. At some point (not yet), enterprise applications like CRM and ERP (Chapter 7) will support roaming as well. This service is possible because *Amazon.com* stores data about your reading progress out in the cloud somewhere.

Live, active mobile applications are designed to receive the latest application data and automatically show it to the user, perhaps in a graphically exciting *breaking news* type banner. Such data includes industry or employee news, but it could also be SharePoint alerts, updates to orders, changes in credit ratings or banking accounts, and so forth. **Push data** is data that the server sends to or pushes onto the device. **Pull data** is data that the device requests from the server. (Notice that those terms use the server's perspective.) Of the two types, push data is more impressive to users because they need to do nothing to receive data. On the other hand, excessive pushing is annoying.

Q5. What Do Business Professionals Need to Know About Data Communications?

In this question, we will introduce important concepts about computer networks, including the Internet. The subject is quite technical, so we will only discuss essential ideas that you need to know to effectively collaborate with network professionals.

To begin, a computer **network** is a collection of computers that communicate with one another over transmission lines or wireless connections. As shown in Figure 3-18, the three basic types of networks are local area networks, wide area networks, and internets.

A **local area network (LAN)** connects computers that reside in a single geographic location on the premises of the company that operates the LAN. The number of connected computers can range from two to several hundred. The distinguishing characteristic of a LAN is *a single location*. **Wide area networks (WANs)** connect computers at different geographic locations. The computers in two separated company sites must be connected using a WAN. To illustrate, the computers for a College of Business located on a single campus can be connected via a LAN. The computers for a College of Business located on multiple campuses must be connected via a WAN.

The single- versus multiple-site distinction is important. With a LAN, an organization can place communication lines wherever it wants because all lines reside on its premises. The same is not true for a WAN. A company with offices in Chicago and Atlanta cannot run a wire down the freeway to connect computers in the two cities. Instead, the company contracts with a communications vendor that is licensed by the government and that already has lines, or has the authority to run new lines, between the two cities.

An internet is a network of networks. Internets connect LANs, WANs, and other internets. The most famous internet is **"the Internet"** (with an uppercase letter *I*), the collection of networks that you use when you send email or access a Web site. In addition to the Internet, private networks of networks, called *internets*, also exist.

The networks that comprise an internet use a large variety of communication methods and conventions, and data must flow seamlessly across them. To provide seamless flow, an elaborate scheme called a *layered protocol* is used. A **protocol** is a set of rules that two communicating devices follow. There are many different protocols; some are used for LANs, some are used for WANs, some are used for internets and the Internet, and some are used for all of these. We will identify several common LAN protocols in this question, as LANs are the most common networks used by businesses. WANs and their protocols are beyond the scope of this text.

What Are the Components of a LAN?

As stated, a LAN is a group of computers connected together on a single site. Usually the computers are located within a half-mile or so of each other. The key distinction, however, is that all of the computers are located on property controlled by the organization that operates the LAN. This means that the organization can run cables wherever needed to connect the computers.

Type	Characteristic
Local area network (LAN)	Computers connected at a single physical site
Wide area network (WAN)	Computers connected between two or more separated sites
The Internet and internets	Networks of networks

FIGURE 3-18

Three Types of Computer Networks

FIGURE 3-19
**Typical Small Office/
Home Office (SOHO) LAN**

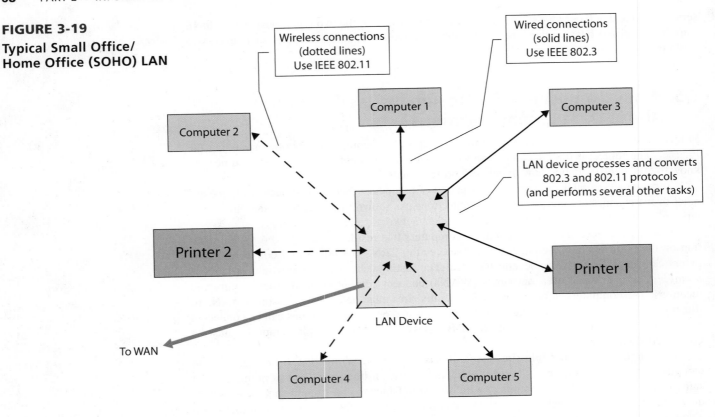

Figure 3-19 shows a LAN that is typical of those in a **small office or a home office (SOHO)**. Typically such LANs have fewer than a dozen or so computers and printers. Many businesses, of course, operate LANs that are much larger than this one, but the principles are the same for a larger LAN.

The computers and printers in Figure 3-19 communicate via a mixture of wired and wireless connections. Computers 1 and 3 and printer 1 use wired connections; computers 2, 4, and 5 as well as printer 2 use wireless connections. The devices and protocols used differ for wired and wireless connectivity. Computers 1 and 3 and printer 1 are wired to a **switch**, which is a special-purpose computer that receives and transmits wired traffic on the LAN. In Figure 3-19, the switch is contained within the box labeled "LAN Device." When either of these two computers communicates with each other or with printer 1, it does so by sending the traffic over wires to the switch, which redirects the traffic to the other computer or printer 1.

The **IEEE 802.3 protocol** is used for wired LAN connections. This protocol standard, also called **Ethernet**, specifies hardware characteristics, such as which wire carries which signals. It also describes how messages are to be packaged and processed for wired transmission over the LAN. The network interface controllers (NICs) in most personal computers today support what is called **10/100/1000 Ethernet**. These products conform to the 802.3 specification and allow for transmission at a rate of 10, 100, or 1,000 Mbps (megabits per second).

In Figure 3-19, three of the computers and one printer are connected to the LAN using wireless technology. The wireless computers and printer have a **wireless NIC (WNIC)** instead of a NIC. Today, nearly all personal computers ship from the factory with an onboard WNIC. (In addition, a NIC or WNIC can be added to most computers that do not have one.)

Wireless LAN connections use the **IEEE 802.11 protocol**. Several versions of 802.11 exist, and as of 2013 the most current one is IEEE 802.11n. The differences among these versions are beyond the scope of this discussion. Just note that the current standard, 802.11n, allows speeds of up to 600 Mbps.

Observe that the LAN in Figure 3-19 uses both the 802.3 and 802.11 protocols. The NICs operate according to the 802.3 protocol and connect directly to the switch, which also operates on the 802.3 standard. The WNICs operate according to the 802.11 protocol and connect to the

Type	Topology	Transmission Line	Transmission Speed	Equipment Used	Protocol Commonly Used	Remarks
Local area network	Local area network	UTP or optical fiber	Common: 10/100/1000 Mbps Possible: 1 Gbps	Switch NIC UTP or optical	IEEE 802.3 (Ethernet)	Switches connect devices, multiple switches on all but small LANs.
	Local area network with wireless	UTP or optical for non-wireless connections	Up to 600 Mbps	Wireless access point Wireless NIC	IEEE 802.11n	Access point transforms wired LAN (802.3) to wireless LAN (802.11).
Connections to the Internet	DSL modem to ISP	DSL telephone	Personal: Upstream to 1 Mbps, downstream to 40 Mbps (max 10 likely in most areas)	DSL modem DSL-capable telephone line	DSL	Can have computer and phone use simultaneously. Always connected.
	Cable modem to ISP	Cable TV lines to optical cable	Upstream to 1 Mbps Downstream 300 Kbps to 10 Mbps	Cable modem Cable TV cable	Cable	Capacity is shared with other sites; performance varies depending on others' use.
	WAN wireless	Wireless connection to WAN	500 Kbps to 1.7 Mbps	Wireless WAN modem	One of several wireless standards	Sophisticated protocol enables several devices to use the same wireless frequency.

FIGURE 3-20
Summary of LAN Networks

wireless access point. The access point must process messages using both the 802.3 and 802.11 standards; it sends and receives wireless traffic using the 802.11 protocol and then communicates with the switch using the 802.3 protocol. Characteristics of LANs are summarized in the top two rows of Figure 3-20.

Bluetooth is another common wireless protocol. It is designed for transmitting data over short distances, replacing cables. Some devices, such as wireless mice and keyboards, use Bluetooth to connect to the computer. Smartphones use Bluetooth to connect to automobile entertainment systems.

How Can You Connect Your LAN to the Internet?

Although you may not have realized it, when you connect your SOHO LAN, phone, iPad, or Kindle to the Internet, you are connecting to a WAN. You must do so because you are connecting to computers that are not physically located on your premises. You cannot start running wires down the street to plug in somewhere.

When you connect to the Internet, you are actually connecting to an **Internet service provider (ISP)**. An ISP has three important functions. First, it provides you with a legitimate Internet address. Second, it serves as your gateway to the Internet. The ISP receives the communications from your computer and passes them on to the Internet, and it receives communications from the Internet and passes them on to you. Finally, ISPs pay for the Internet. They collect money from their customers and pay access fees and other charges on your behalf.

Figure 3-20 shows the three common alternatives for connecting to the Internet. Notice that we are discussing how your computer connects to the Internet via a WAN; we are not discussing the structure of the WAN itself. Search the Web for *leased lines* or *PSDN* if you want to learn more about WAN architectures.

SOHO LANs (like that in Figure 3-19) and individual home and office computers are commonly connected to an ISP in one of three ways: a special telephone line called a DSL line, a cable TV line, or a wireless-phone-like connection.

A **digital subscriber line (DSL)** operates on the same lines as voice telephones, but it operates so that its signals do not interfere with voice telephone service. DSLs use their own protocols for data transmission. A **cable line** is the second type of WAN connection that provides high-speed data transmission using cable television lines. Because up to 500 user sites can share a cable line, performance varies depending on how many other users are sending and receiving data.

A third way that you can connect your computer, iPhone, iPad, Kindle, or other communicating device is via a **WAN wireless** connection. *Amazon.com*'s Kindle, for example, uses a Sprint wireless network to provide wireless data connections. The iPhone uses a LAN-based wireless network if one is available and a WAN wireless network if one is not.

Communication over the Internet

As stated, the Internet is an *internet*, meaning that it is a network of networks. As you might guess, the technology that underlies the Internet is complicated and beyond the scope of this text. However, because of the popularity of the Internet, certain terms have become ubiquitous in twenty-first-century business society. In this question, we will define and explain terms that you need to know to be an informed business professional and consumer of Internet services.

An Internet Example

Figure 3-21 illustrates one use of the Internet. Suppose you are sitting in snowbound Minneapolis and you want to communicate with a hotel in sunny, tropical northern New Zealand. Maybe you are making a reservation using the hotel's Web site, or maybe you are sending an email to a reservations clerk inquiring about facilities or services.

To begin, note that this example is an internet because it is a network of networks. It consists of two LANs (yours and the hotel's) and four WANs. (In truth, the real Internet consists of tens of thousands of WANs and LANs, but to conserve paper we don't show all of them here.)

Your communication to the hotel involves nearly unimaginable complexity. Somehow, your computer communicates with a server in the New Zealand hotel, a computer that it has never "met" before and knows nothing about. Further, your transmission, which is too big to travel in one piece, is broken up into parts and each part passed along from WAN to WAN in such a way that it arrives intact. Then your original message is reassembled, any parts that were lost or damaged (this happens) are resent, and the reconstructed message is delivered to the server for processing. All of this is accomplished by computers and data communications devices that most likely have not interacted before.

FIGURE 3-21

Using the Internet for a Hotel Reservation

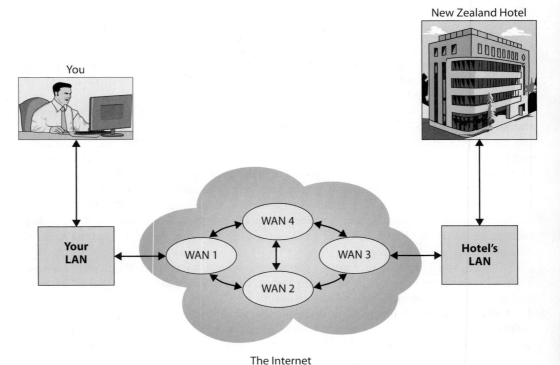

The Internet

What all these devices do know, however, is that they process the same set of protocols. Numerous protocols are used on the internet and they are organized according to the **TCP/IP Protocol architecture**, which is a scheme of five protocol types arranged in layers. We will define the role of several important protocols here.

Hypertext Transport Protocol (http) is the protocol used between browsers and Web servers. When you use a browser like Internet Explorer, Safari, or Chrome, you are using a program that implements the http protocol. At the other end, at the New Zealand Hotel, for example, there is a server that also processes http, as you will learn in Q7. Even though your browser and the server at the hotel have never "met" before, they can communicate with one another because they both follow the rules of http. Your browser sends requests for service encoded in a predefined http *request format*: The server receives that request; processes the request, say, reserves a room for you; and formats a response in a predefined http *response format*.

As you will learn in Chapter 12, a secure version of http is available called **https**. Whenever you see *https* in your browser's address bar, you have a secure transmission and you can safely send sensitive data like credit card numbers. However, when you are on the Internet, unless you are using https, you should assume that all of your communication is open and could be published on the front page of your campus newspaper tomorrow morning.

Hence, when you are using http, email, text messaging, chat, videoconferencing, or anything other than https, know that whatever you are typing or saying could be known by anyone else. Thus, in your classroom, when you send a text message to a fellow student, that message can be intercepted and read by anyone in your class, including your professor. The same is true of people at a coffee shop, at an airport, or anywhere.

Two additional TCP/IP application layer protocols are common. **Smtp, or Simple Mail Transfer Protocol**, is used for email transmissions (along with other protocols as well). **Ftp, or File Transfer Protocol**, is used to move files over the Internet. One very common use for ftp is to maintain Web sites. When a Web site administrator wishes to post a new picture or story on a Web server, the administrator will often use ftp to move the picture or other item to the server. Like http, ftp has a secure version as well, but do not assume you are using it.

With this knowledge, we can clear up one common misconception. You are using the Internet when you use any of these protocols. However, you are using the Web only when you use either http or https. Thus, the **Web** is the Internet-based network of browsers and servers that processes http or https. When you send email, you are using the Internet, but not the Web. It is incorrect to say you are using the Web to send email or text messages.

Before we leave the Internet, you need to know two more terms. A **URL (Uniform Resource Locator)** is an address on the Internet. Commonly, it consists of a protocol (like http:// or ftp://) followed by a **domain name**, which is a worldwide-unique name that is affiliated with a particular Internet address. To obtain a domain name, you can go to GoDaddy (or other similar companies) and, for a small fee, it will register your name on Internet directories. GoDaddy (or other) will first determine if the desired name is unique worldwide. If so, it will then apply to register that name to you. Once the registration is completed, you can affiliate a public Internet address with that domain name. From that point onward, traffic for the new domain name will be routed to your Internet address.

Note two important points: First, several domain names can point to the same Internet address. Second, the affiliation of domain names with Internet addresses is dynamic. The owner of the domain name can change the affiliated addresses at its discretion.

Q6. What Happens on a Typical Web Server?

At this point, you know basic networking terms and have a high-level view of how internets and the Internet work. To complete this chapter's high-level survey of network technology, you need to know a bit about the processing that occurs on a Web server. For this discussion, we will use the example of a Web storefront, which is a server on the Web from which you can buy products.

Suppose you want to buy shoes from Zulily, a private buying site that sells clothing and related goods. To do so, you go to *www.zulily.com* and navigate to the product(s) that you want to buy (see Figure 3-22). When you find something you want, you add it to your shopping cart and keep shopping. At some point, you check out by supplying credit card data.

FIGURE 3-22

Sample of Commerce Server Pages; Product Offer Pages

Source: www.zulily.com.

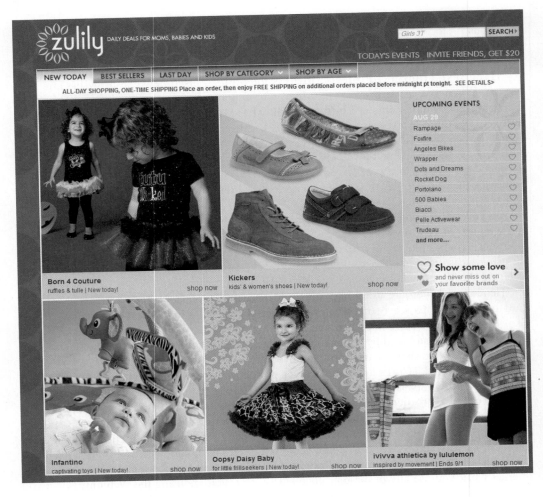

In Q5, we discussed how your traffic crosses over the Internet to arrive at the Zulily server. The next question is: What happens at that server when it arrives? Or, from another perspective, if you want to set up a Web storefront for your company, what facilities do you need?

Three-Tier Architecture

Almost all e-commerce applications use the **three-tier architecture**, which is an arrangement of user computers and servers into three categories, or tiers, as shown in Figure 3-23. The **user tier** consists of computers, phones, and other devices that have browsers that request and process Web pages. The **server tier** consists of computers that run Web servers and process application programs. The **database tier** consists of computers that run a DBMS that processes requests to retrieve and store data. Figure 3-23 shows only one computer at the database tier. Some sites have multicomputer database tiers as well.

When you enter *http://www.zulily.com* in your browser, the browser sends a request that travels over the Internet to a computer in the server tier at the Zulily site. That request is formatted and processed according to the rules of http. (Notice, by the way, that if you just type *www.zulily.com*, your browser will add the *http://* to signify that it is using http.) In response to your request, a server-tier computer sends back a **Web page**, which is a document that is coded in one of the standard page markup languages. The most popular page markup language is the *Hypertext Markup Language (html)*, which is described later in this section.

Web servers are programs that run on a server-tier computer and that manage http traffic by sending and receiving Web pages to and from clients. A **commerce server** is an application program that runs on a server-tier computer. A commerce server receives requests from users via the Web server, takes some action, and returns a response to the users via the Web server. Typical commerce server functions are to obtain product data from a database, manage the items in a

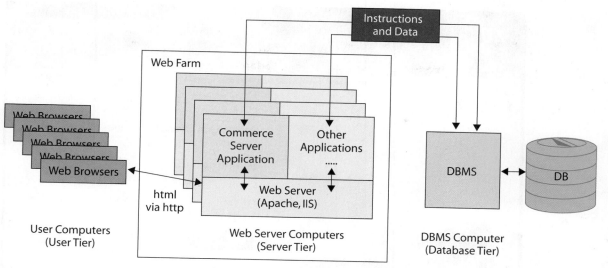

FIGURE 3-23
Three-Tier Architecture

shopping cart, and coordinate the checkout process. In Figure 3-23, the server-tier computers are running a Web server program, a commerce server application, and other applications having an unspecified purpose.

To ensure acceptable performance, commercial Web sites usually are supported by several or even many Web server computers in a facility called a **Web farm**. Work is distributed among the computers in a Web farm so as to minimize customer delays. The coordination among multiple Web server computers is a fantastic dance, but, alas, we do not have space to tell that story here. Just imagine the coordination that must occur as you add items to an online order when, to improve performance, different Web server computers receive and process each addition to your order.

Watch the Three Tiers in Action!

To see a three-tier example in action, go to your favorite Web storefront site, place something in a shopping cart, and consider Figure 3-23 as you do so. When you enter an address into your browser, the browser sends a request for the default page to a server computer at that address. A Web server and possibly a commerce server process your request and send back the default page.

As you click Web pages to find products you want, the commerce server accesses the database to retrieve data about those products. It creates pages according to your selections and sends the results back to your browser via the Web server. Again, different computers on the server tier may process your series of requests and must constantly communicate about your activities. You can follow this process in Figure 3-23.

Suppose the user of the Web page in Figure 3-22 clicks on Kickers and then selects a particular shoe, say the Darkish Gray Dorine Mary Jane shoe. When the user clicks on that shoe, the commerce server requests that shoe's data from the DBMS, which reads it from the database and then returns the data (inlcuding pictures) to the commerce server. That server then formats the Web page with that data into html and sends the html to the user's computer. The resulting page is shown in Figure 3-24.

Hypertext Markup Language (html)

Hypertext Markup Language (html) is the most common language for defining the structure and layout of Web pages. An html **tag** is a notation used to define a data element for display or other purposes. The following html is a typical heading tag:

```
<h2>Price of Item</h2>
```

FIGURE 3-24
Product Page

Source: www.zulily.com.

Notice that tags are enclosed in < > (called *angle brackets*) and that they occur in pairs. The start of this tag is indicated by <h2>, and the end of the tag is indicated by </h2>. The words between the tags are the value of the tag. This html tag means to place the words "Price of Item" on a Web page in the style of a level-two heading. The creator of the Web page will define the style (font size, color, and so forth) for h2 headings and the other tags to be used.

Web pages include **hyperlinks**, which are pointers to other Web pages. A hyperlink contains the URL of the Web page to find when the user clicks the hyperlink. The URL can reference a page on the server that generated the page containing the hyperlink or it can reference a page on another server.

Figure 3-25(a) shows a sample html document. The document has a heading that provides metadata about the page and a body that contains the content. The tag <h1> means to format the indicated text as a level-one heading; <h2> means a level-two heading. The tag <a> defines a hyperlink. This tag has an **attribute**, which is a variable used to provide properties about a tag. Not all tags have attributes, but many do. Each attribute has a standard name. The attribute for a hyperlink is **href**, and its value indicates which Web page is to be displayed when the user clicks the link. Here, the page *www.pearsonhighered.com/kroenke* is to be returned when the user clicks the hyperlink. Figure 3-25(b) shows this page as rendered by Internet Explorer.

Q7. Why Is the Cloud the Future for Most Organizations?

Until 2010 or so, most organizations constructed and maintained their own computing infrastructure. Organizations purchased or leased hardware, installed it on their premises, and used it to support organizational email, Web sites, e-commerce sites, and in-house applications, such

FIGURE 3-25

html Code

```
<!DOCTYPE html PUBLIC "-//W3C//DTD XHTML 1.0 Transitional//EN" "http://www.w3.org/TR/xhtml1/DTD/xhtml1-transitional.dtd">
<html xmlns="http://www.w3.org/1999/xhtml">
<head>
<meta content="en-us" http-equiv="Content-Language" />
<meta content="text/html; charset=utf-8" http-equiv="Content-Type" />
<title>PSI Example HTML</title>
<style type="text/css">
.style1 {
    font-size: xx-large;
    text-align: center;
    font-family: Arial, Helvetica, sans-serif;
}
.style2 {
    color: #FF00FF;
}
.style3 {
    font-size: medium;
    text-align: center;
    font-family: Arial, Helvetica, sans-serif;
}
.style5 {
    font-size: medium;
    text-align: left;
    font-family: Arial, Helvetica, sans-serif;
}
</style>
</head>
<body>
<p class="style1">
    <span class="style2"><strong>Processes, Systems, and Information</strong></span></p>
<p class="style1"> </p>
<p class="style3"><em>Second Edition</em></p>
<p class="style3"> </p>
<p class="style5">Example html Document</p>
<p class="style5"> </p>
<p class="style5"> </p>
<p class="style5">Click <a href="http://www.PearsonHigherEd.com/kroenke">here</a>
for the textbook&#39;s Web site at Pearson Education.</p>
</body>
</html>
```

(a) Sample html Code Snippet

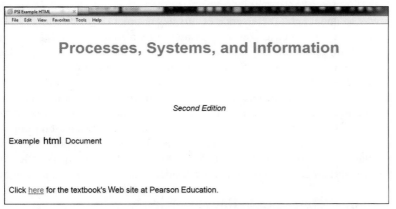

(b) Document Created from html Code in Figure 3-25(a)

as accounting and operations systems (you'll learn about them in the next chapter). After about 2010, however, organizations began to move their computing infrastructure to the cloud, and it is likely that in the future all, or nearly all, computing infrastructure will be leased from the cloud. So, just what is the cloud, and why is it the future?

We define the **cloud** as the *elastic* leasing of *pooled* computer resources over the *Internet*. The term *cloud* is used because most early diagrams of three-tier and other Internet-based systems used a cloud symbol to represent the Internet (see Figure 3-21 for an example), and organizations came to view their infrastructure as being "somewhere in the cloud."

Consider each of the italicized terms in the definition. The term **elastic**, which was first used this way by *Amazon.com*, means that the amount of resources leased can be increased or decreased dynamically, programmatically, in a short span of time and that organizations pay for just the resources that they use. The resources are **pooled** because many different organizations use the same physical hardware; they share that hardware through virtualization. Cloud vendors dynamically allocate virtual machines to physical hardware as customer needs increase or decrease. Finally, the resources are accessed via **Internet protocols and standards**, which are additions to TCP/IP that enable cloud-hosting vendors to provide processing capabilities in flexible yet standardized ways.

FIGURE 3-26

**Apple Data Center
in Maiden, NC**

Source: Google Earth.

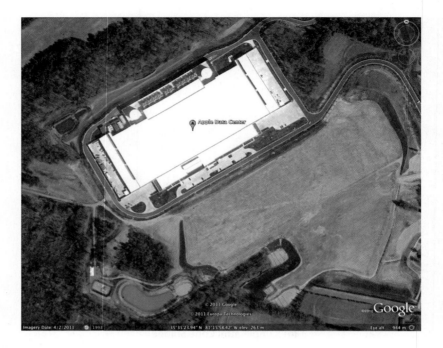

An easy way to understand the essence of this development is to consider electrical power. In the very earliest days of electric power generation, organizations operated their own generators to create power for their company's needs. Over time, as the power grid expanded, it became possible to centralize power generation so that organizations could purchase just the electricity they needed from an electric utility.

Both cloud vendors and electrical utilities benefit from economies of scale. According to this principle, the average cost of production decreases as the size of the operation increases. Major cloud vendors operate enormous Web farms. Figure 3-26 shows the building that contains the computers in the Web farm that Apple constructed in 2011 to support its iCloud offering. This billion-dollar facility contains more than 500,000 square feet.[6] IBM, Google, *Amazon.com*, Microsoft, Oracle, and other large companies each operate several similar farms as well.

Why Is the Cloud Preferred to In-House Hosting?

Figure 3-27 compares and contrasts cloud-based and in-house hosting. As you can see, the positives are heavily tilted toward cloud-based computing. The cloud vendor Rackspace will lease you one medium server for as little as 1.5 cents per hour. You can obtain and access that server today, actually within a few minutes. Tomorrow, if you need thousands of servers, you can readily scale up to obtain them. Furthermore, you know the cost structure; although you might have a surprise with regards to how many customers want to access your Web site, you won't have any surprises as to how much it will cost.

Another positive is that as long as you're dealing with large, reputable organizations, you'll be receiving best-of-breed security and disaster recovery (discussed in Chapter 12). In addition, you need not worry that you're investing in technology that will soon be obsolete; the cloud vendor is taking that risk. All of this is possible because the cloud vendor is gaining economies of scale by selling to an entire industry, not just to you.

The negatives of cloud computing involve loss of control. You're dependent on a vendor; changes in the vendor's management, policy, and prices are beyond your control. Further, you don't know where your data—which may be a large part of your organization's value—is located. Nor do you know how many copies of your data there are or even if they're located in the same country as you are. Finally, you have no visibility into the security and disaster preparedness that is actually in place.

[6] Patrick Thibodeau, "Apple, Google, Facebook Turn N.C. into Data Center Hub," *Computerworld,* last modified June 3, 2011, www.computerworld.com/s/article/9217259/Apple_Google_Facebook_turn_N.C._into_data_center_hub.

Cloud	In-House
Positive:	
Small capital requirements	Control of data location
Speedy development	In-depth visibility of security and disaster preparedness
Superior flexibility and adaptability to growing or fluctuating demand	
Known cost structure	
Possibly best-of-breed security/disaster preparedness	
No obsolescence	
Industry-wide economies of scale, hence cheaper	
Negative:	
Dependency on vendor	Significant capital required
Loss of control over data location	Significant development effort
Little visibility into true security and disaster preparedness capabilities	Annual maintenance costs
	Ongoing support costs
	Staff and train personnel
	Increased management requirements
	Difficult (impossible?) to accommodate fluctuating demand
	Cost uncertainties
	Obsolescence

FIGURE 3-27

Comparison of Cloud and In-House Alternatives

The positives and negatives of in-house hosting are shown in the second column of Figure 3-27. For the most part, they are the opposite of those for cloud-based computing; note, however, the need for personnel and management. With in-house hosting, not only will you have to construct your own data center, you'll also need to acquire and train the personnel to run it and then manage those personnel and your facility.

Why Now?

A skeptic responds to Figure 3-27 by saying "If it's so great, why hasn't cloud-based hosting been used for years?" Why now?

In fact, cloud-based hosting (or a version of it under a different name) has been around since the 1960s. Long before the creation of the personal computer and networks, time-sharing vendors provided slices of computer time on a use-fee basis. However, the technology of that time, continuing up until the first decade of this century, did not favor the construction and use of enormous data centers.

Three factors have made cloud-based hosting advantageous today. First, processors, data communication, and data storage are so cheap as to be nearly free. At the scale of a Web farm of hundreds of thousands of processors, providing a virtual machine for an hour costs essentially nothing, as the 1.5 cent price per hour indicates. Because data communication is so cheap, getting the data to and from that processor is also nearly free.

Second, virtualization technology enables the near instantaneous creation of a new virtual machine. The customer provides (or creates in the cloud) a disk image of the data and programs of the machine it wants to provision. Virtualization software takes it from there.

Finally, new Internet-based protocols and standards have enabled cloud-hosting vendors to provide processing capabilities in flexible yet standardized ways. Using a design philosophy named **service-oriented architecture (SOA)**, applications use standard protocols to publish a menu of services that the application provides, the structure of the data that it expects to receive, the structure of the data that it will produce, and the ways in which services can be requested. The provider of a Web service, such as a cloud-hosting organization, uses these standards to specify the work that it will perform and how it will provide it. Consumers of that service use those standards to request and receive service. Search for the terms *WSDL, OData, XML,* and *JSON* to learn more. The bottom line: SOA design and Web service standards provide a vocabulary and grammar for programs on different computers to interact.

When Does the Cloud Not Make Sense?

Cloud-based hosting makes sense for most organizations. The only organizations for which it may not make sense are those that are required by law or by industry standard practice to have physical control over their data. Such organizations might be forced to create and maintain their own hosting infrastructure. A financial institution, for example, might be legally required to maintain physical control over its data.

Even where physical control is a requirement, it is possible for organizations to obtain some of the benefits of cloud computing in what is termed the **private cloud**, which is in-house hosting, delivered via Web service standards, that can be configured dynamically. Some say that there is no such thing as a private cloud, however, because the infrastructure is owned by the using organization and the economies of scale cannot be shared with others.

In the final analysis, the cloud is the future for most organizations.

How Do Organizations Use the Cloud?

Cloud-based service offerings can be organized into the three categories shown in Figure 3-28. An organization that provides **software as a service (SaaS)** provides not only hardware infrastructure but also an operating system and application programs on top of that hardware. For example, *Salesforce.com* provides programs for customer and sales tracking as a service. Similarly, Microsoft provides Office 365 as a service. Exchange, Lync, and SharePoint applications are provided as a service "in the cloud."

Apple's iCloud is probably the most exciting recent SaaS offering. Using iCloud, Apple will automatically sync all of its customers' iOS devices. Calendar is a good example. When a customer enters an appointment in her iPhone, Apple will automatically push that appointment into the calendars on all of that customer's iOS devices. Further, customers can share calendars with others that will be synchronized as well. Mail, pictures, applications, and other resources are also synched via iCloud.

An organization can move to SaaS simply by signing up and learning how to use it. In Apple's case, there's nothing to learn. To quote the late Steve Jobs, "It just works."

The second category of cloud hosting is **platform as a service (PaaS)**, whereby vendors provide hosted computers, an operating system, and possibly a DBMS. Microsoft Windows Azure, for example, provides servers installed with Windows Server. Customers of Windows Azure then add their own applications on top of the hosted platform. Microsoft SQL Azure provides a host with Windows Server and SQL Server. Oracle On Demand provides a hosted server with Oracle Database. Again, for PaaS, organizations add their own applications to the host.

Cloud Category	Examples
SaaS (software as a service)	Salesforce.com iCloud Office 365
PaaS (platform as a service)	Microsoft Azure Oracle On Demand
IaaS (infrastructure as a service)	Amazon EC2 (Elastic Cloud 2) Amazon S3 (Simple Storage Service)

FIGURE 3-28

Three Fundamental Cloud Types

The most basic cloud offering is **infrastructure as a service (IaaS)**, which is the cloud hosting of a bare server computer or disk drive. The Amazon EC2 provides bare servers, and its Simple Storage Server provides, in essence, an unlimited, reliable disk drive in the cloud. Rackspace provides similar capabilities.

Organizations choose the cloud service they need. Lucas, for example, wants to host Chuck's Bikes' e-commerce server in the cloud. In terms of Figure 3-28, Chuck's Bikes needs to put its Web servers and its database server in the cloud using PaaS. To do so, CBI could use, say, Windows Azure for the Web servers and SQL Azure for the database server. If CBI wanted to, it could also obtain bare servers from an IaaS vendor like *Amazon.com* or Rackspace. Were it to do so, CBI would need to provision an operating system and DBMS on top of the server. Most likely, a small organization like CBI would use PaaS.

Ethics Guide

Showrooming: The Consequences

Showrooming occurs when someone visits a brick-and-mortar store to examine and evaluate products without the intention of them buying at that store. Rather, once the consumer has decided on the most suitable product, he or she purchases that product elsewhere, usually online. Thus, if you visit a Best Buy store, check out the Windows 8 touch computers, ask the sales personnel questions about the various alternatives, and then return home to purchase the one you like best from an online vendor, you are showrooming Best Buy computers.

In most cases, online vendors charge less than brick-and-mortar vendors because they save money on rent, employees, utilities, and other costs of operating a physical retail presence. If they choose, online vendors can pass those savings on to the purchaser, either in the form of lower prices, free shipping, or both.

Online vendors have another advantage. While all brick-and-mortar stores must pay sales tax, unless an online vendor has a physical presence in your state, that vendor need not pay. You, as the purchaser of goods from out of state, are supposed to declare and pay state tax on your purchase, but few people do. Thus, the price charged by a brick-and-mortar store can be the same as the online vendor, but it can be cheaper to buy online if the cost of shipping is less than your state's sales tax (this comparison is subject to recent changes in online taxation).

To facilitate showrooming, Amazon.com developed a mobile native application called *Price Check* that is available for iOS and Android devices. Using mobile devices, consumers can scan the UPC product code, take a picture of a product, or say the name of a product, and Amazon.com will respond with its price as well as prices from many other online vendors.

DISCUSSION QUESTIONS

1. In your opinion, with regard to showrooming, are online vendors behaving unethically? Use both the categorical imperative (page 20) and utilitarianism (page 40) in your answer.
2. In your opinion, is Amazon.com behaving unethically by creating and disseminating the Price Check app? Use both the categorical imperative and utilitarianism in your answer.
3. In your opinion, are consumers behaving unethically when they showroom? Use both the categorical imperative and utilitarianism in your answer.
4. What are the long-term consequences of showrooming? Do they matter?
5. How would you advise senior managers of brick-and-mortar stores to respond to showrooming?
6. Consider a consumer who elects not to pay state tax on online purchases from a vendor who need not pay that tax on his or her behalf:
   a. Is there an ethical responsibility to pay state tax? Again, consider both categorical imperative and utilitarianism perspectives.
   b. Suppose a consumer says, "Look, most of the state tax money just goes to bloated retirement programs anyway. All those old people aren't entitled to my money." Does this posture change your answer to question 6a? Why or why not?
   c. Suppose a consumer says, "I'm just one of millions who are doing this in our state. My piddly $50 really doesn't matter." Does this posture change your answer to question 6a? Why or why not?

d. Suppose a consumer says, "I will do more for society in our state with my $50 than the state government ever will." Does this posture change your answer to question 6a? Why or why not?

e. Suppose a consumer says, "The state makes it so hard to pay this tax. I have to keep track of all my online purchases, and then I don't even know whom to contact. Plus, once they have my name and address and know that I buy online, who knows how they'll hassle me. Amazon.com makes it easy to pay; until the state does the same, they can forget about revenue from me." Does this posture change your answer to question 6a? Why or why not?

7. How would you advise your state legislature to respond to tax avoidance for online purchases?

Active Review

Use this Active Review to verify that you understand the material in the chapter. You can read the entire chapter and then perform the tasks in this review, or you can read the text material for just one question and perform the tasks in this review for that question before moving on to the next one.

Q1. What do business professionals need to know about computer hardware?

List hardware components and explain the purpose of each. Summarize types of hardware and explain the differences between servers and clients. Define *server farm*. Define *bit* and *byte*, and explain why bits are used to represent computer data. Define the units of bytes used to size computer hardware. Explain why you should save your work from time to time while you are using your computer.

Q2. What do business professionals need to know about software?

Define *operating system* and explain the meaning of each cell in Figure 3-5. Describe three types of virtualization. Explain the difference between software ownership and software licenses. Explain the differences among horizontal-market, vertical-market, and one-of-a-kind applications. Describe the three ways that organizations can acquire software. Define *firmware*.

Name three successful open source projects. Describe four reasons programmers contribute to open source projects. Define *open source, closed source, source code,* and *machine code.* In your own words, explain why open source is a legitimate alternative but may or may not be appropriate for a given application.

Q3. What are the differences between native and thin-client applications?

In your own words, summarize the differences between native applications and thin-client applications. In high-level terms, explain the difference between object-oriented languages and scripting languages. Explain each cell of Figure 3-11. State which is better: native or thin-client applications. Justify your answer.

Q4. What characterizes quality mobile user experiences?

Explain the difference between the terms *UI* and *UX.* Describe how each of the following can affect the UX of a mobile application: user content, context-sensitive chrome, animation and lively behavior, scaling and sharing, the cloud. Define *chrome, charms, roaming, push,* and *pull.*

Q5. What do business professionals need to know about data communications?

Define *computer network.* Explain the differences among LANs, WANs, internets, and the Internet. Describe the purpose of a protocol. Explain the key distinction of a LAN. Describe the purpose of each component in Figure 3-19. Define *IEEE 802.3* and *802.11* and explain how they differ. List three ways of connecting a LAN or computer to the Internet. Explain the nature of each. Explain the statement, "The Internet is an internet." Define *TCP/IP* and explain the purpose of http, https, smtp, and ftp. Describe, in general terms, how you would obtain a domain name.

Q6. What happens on a typical Web server?

Explain what a Web storefront is. Define *three-tier architecture* and name and describe each tier. Explain the function of a Web page, a Web server, and a commerce server. Explain the purpose of a Web farm. Explain the function of each tier in Figure 3-23 as the pages in Figures 3-22 and 3-24 are processed.

Q7. Why is the cloud the future for most organizations?

Define *cloud* and explain the three key terms in your definition. Using Figure 3-27 as a guide, compare and contrast cloud-based and in-house hosting. Explain three factors that make cloud computing possible today. Explain the role of service-oriented architecture. When does it not make sense to use a cloud-based infrastructure? Define *SaaS, PaaS,* and *IaaS.* Provide an example of each. For each, describe the requirements for when it would be the most appropriate option.

Key Terms and Concepts

10/100/1000 Ethernet   68
3D printing   60
Additive manufacturing   60
Android   54
Application software   56
ARM   55
Attribute   74
BlackBerry OS   54
Bluetooth   69
Bytes   51
Cable line   69
CAD (computer added design)
    software   60
Central processing unit (CPU)   50
Charms   65
Chrome   64
Client   50
Closed source   58
Cloud   75
Commerce server   72
Context-sensitive chrome   64
Custom-developed software   57
Database tier   72
Desktop virtualization   56
Digital subscriber line (DSL)   69
Direct interaction   64
Domain name   71
Dual-processor   50
Elastic   75
Ethernet   68
Exabyte (EB)   51
File Transfer Protocol (ftp)   71
Gigabyte (GB)   51
Horizontal-market application   56
Host operating system   55
href   74
html (Hypertext Markup
    Language)   73
http (Hypertext Transport
    Protocol)   71

https   71
Hyperlinks   74
IEEE 802.11 protocol   68
IEEE 802.3 protocol   68
Infrastructure as a service (IaaS)   79
Internet   67
Internet protocols and standards   75
Internet service provider (ISP)   69
iOS   54
Kilobyte (K)   51
License   56
Linux   54
Local area network (LAN)   67
Mac OS   53
Machine code   58
Main memory   50
Megabyte (MB)   51
Microsoft Windows   52
Native applications   59
Network   67
Object-oriented   60
Off-the-shelf software   57
Off-the-shelf with alterations
    software   57
One-of-a-kind application   57
Operating system (OS)   52
PC virtualization   55
Personal computer (PC)   50
Petabyte (PB)   51
Platform as a service (PaaS)   78
Pooled   75
Private cloud   78
Protocol   67
Pull data   66
Push data   66
Quad-processor   50
RAM (random access memory)   50
Roaming   66
Server   50

Server farm   50
Server tier   72
Server virtualization   55
Service-oriented architecture (SOA)   78
Showrooming   80
Site license   56
Slates   50
Small office/home office (SOHO)   68
Smartphones   50
smtp (Simple Mail Transfer
    Protocol)   71
Software as a service (SaaS)   78
Source code   58
Storage hardware   50
Switch   68
Symbian   54
Tablets   50
Tag   73
TCP/IP Protocol architecture   71
Terabyte (TB)   51
Thin-client applications   59
Three-tier architecture   72
Unix   54
URL (Uniform Resource
    Locator)   71
User experience (UX)   63
User interface (UI)   63
User tier   72
Vertical-market application   57
Virtual machines (vm)   55
WAN wireless   70
Web   71
Web farm   73
Web page   72
Web server   72
Wide area network (WAN)   67
Windows RT   55
Windows Server   55
Wireless NIC (WNIC)   68

Using Your Knowledge

3-1. Microsoft offers free licenses of certain software products to students at colleges and universities that participate in its DreamSpark program [formerly known as the Microsoft Developer Network (MSDN) Academic Alliance (AA)]. If your college or university participates in this program, you have the opportunity to obtain hundreds of dollars of software for free. Here is a partial list of the software you can obtain:

- Microsoft Access 2013
- OneNote 2013
- Expression Studio 4
- Windows 2012 Server
- Microsoft Project 2013
- Visual Studio Developer
- SQL Server 2012
- Visio 2013

a. Search *www.microsoft.com*, *www.google.com*, or *www.bing.com* and determine the function of each of these software products.

b. Which of these software products are operating systems and which are application programs?

c. Which of these programs are DBMS products (the subject of the next chapter)?

d. Which of these programs should you download and install tonight?

e. Either (1) download and install the programs in your answer to part d, or (2) explain why you would choose not to do so.

f. Does DreamSpark provide an unfair advantage to Microsoft? Why or why not?

3-2. Visit the Open Source Initiative's Web site at *http://opensource.org*. Summarize the mission of this non-profit corporation. Find the definition of open source on this site and summarize that definition in your own words. Explain this corporation's role with regard to open source licenses. Summarize the process for having a license approved by OSI. Describe the advantage of having OSI's approval.

3-3. Suppose that you are Drew at CBI. List five criteria you would use in helping CBI decide whether it should develop a native or a thin-client mobile application. Justify your criteria.

3-4. Suppose you manage a group of seven employees in a small business. Each of your employees wants to be connected to the Internet. Consider two alternatives:

Alternative A: Each employee has his or her own modem and connects individually to the Internet.

Alternative B: The employees' computers are connected using a LAN, and the network uses a single modem to connect.

a. Sketch the equipment and lines required for each alternative.

b. Explain the actions you need to take to create each alternative.

c. Which of these two alternatives do you recommend?

3-5. Suppose that you have a consulting practice implementing LANs for fraternities and sororities on your campus.

a. Consider a fraternity house. Explain how a LAN could be used to connect all of the computers in the house. Would you recommend an Ethernet LAN, an 802.11 LAN, or a combination? Justify your answer.

b. This chapter did not provide enough detail for you to determine how many switches the fraternity house might need. However, in general terms, describe how the fraternity could use a multiple-switch system.

c. Considering the connection to the Internet, would you recommend that the fraternity house use DSL, cable modem, or WAN wireless? Although you can rule out at least one of these alternatives with the knowledge you already have, what additional detail do you need in order to make a specific recommendation?

d. Should you develop a standard package solution for each of your customers? What advantages accrue from a standard solution? What are the disadvantages?

Collaboration Exercise 3

Collaborate with a group of fellow students to answer the following questions. For this exercise, do not meet face to face. Your task will be easier if you coordinate your work with SharePoint, Office 365, Google Docs with Google+, or equivalent collaboration tools. (See Chapter 9 for a discussion of collaboration tools and processes.) Your answers should reflect the thinking of the entire group, not just that of one or two individuals.

In the past few years, Microsoft has been promoting PixelSense, a hardware–software product that enables people to interact with data on the top of a table. PixelSense initiates a new product category, and the best way to understand it is to view one of Microsoft's promotional videos at *www.pixelsense.com*.

PixelSense paints the top of the 30-inch table with invisible, near-infrared light to detect the presence of objects. It can respond to up to 52 different touches at the same time. According to Microsoft, this means that four people sitting around the PixelSense table could use all 10 of their fingers to manipulate up to 12 objects simultaneously.

PixelSense uses wireless and other communications technologies to connect to devices that are placed on it, such as cameras or cell phones. When a camera is placed on PixelSense, pictures "spill" out of it, and users can manipulate those pictures with their hands. Products can be placed on PixelSense, and their product specifications are displayed. Credit cards can be placed on PixelSense, and items to be purchased can be dragged and dropped onto the credit card.

Currently, Microsoft PixelSense is marketed and sold to large-scale commercial organizations in the financial services, healthcare, hospitality, retail, and public service business sectors. Also, smaller organizations and individuals can purchase a PixelSense unit from Samsung (*www.samsunglfd.com/solution/sur40.do*)

One of the first implementers of PixelSense was the iBar lounge at Harrah's Rio All-Suite Hotel and Casino in Las

Vegas, Nevada. The subtitle for the press release announcing iBar's system read, "Harrah's Reinvents Flirting and Offers New Uninhibited Fun and Play to iBar Patrons."[7]

The potential uses for PixelSense are staggering. Maps can display local events, and consumers can purchase tickets to those events by just using their fingers. PixelSense can also be used for new computer games and gambling devices. Children can paint on PixelSense with virtual paintbrushes. Numerous other applications are possible. At the product's announcement, Steve Ballmer, former CEO of Microsoft, said "We see this as a multibillion dollar category, and we envision a time when PixelSense computing technologies will be pervasive, from tabletops and counters to the hallway mirror. PixelSense is the first step in realizing that vision."[8]

As you can see at the PixelSense Web site, this product can be used for many different purposes in many different places, such as restaurants, retail kiosks, and eventually at home. Probably most of the eventual applications for PixelSense have not yet been envisioned. One clear application, however, is in the gambling and gaming industry. Imagine placing your credit card on a PixelSense gambling device and gambling the night away. Every time you lose, a charge is made against your credit card. Soon, before you know it, you've run up $15,000 in debt, which you learn when PixelSense tells you you've reached the maximum credit limit on your card.

Recall the RAND study cited in Chapter 1 that stated there will be increased worldwide demand for workers who can apply new technology and products to solve business problems in innovative ways. PixelSense is an excellent example of a new technology that will be applied innovatively.

1. Consider uses for PixelSense at your university. How might PixelSense be used in architecture, chemistry, law, medicine, business, geography, political science, art, music, or any other discipline in which your team has interest? Describe one potential application for PixelSense for five different disciplines.
2. List specific features and benefits for each of the five applications you selected in question 1.
3. Describe, in general terms, the work that needs to be accomplished to create the applications you identified in question 1.
4. Until June 2012, PixelSense was called Surface. At that time, Microsoft repurposed the name to use on its tablet devices. Surface was changed to PixelSense. What conclusions do you draw from these naming decisions?
5. You will sometimes hear the expression, "Emerging technology is constantly leveling the playing field," meaning that technology eliminates competitive advantages of existing companies and enables opportunities for new companies. How does this statement pertain to PixelSense, Surface, Windows 8, Apple, and Google?

CASE STUDY 3

The Apple of Your i

A quick glance at Apple's stock history in Figure 3-29 will tell you that Apple, Inc., has been an incredibly successful company, but that there might be dark clouds on its horizon. As you can see, its stock price took off in 2003 and didn't look back until its high of $707 in late 2012. Since then, it has fallen back to its price of $459 on February 7, 2013. Where it goes from there, however, is open to question. To assess what might be next, consider Apple's history.

Early Success and Downfall

At the dawn of the personal computer age, in the early 1980s, Apple pioneered well-engineered home computers and innovative interfaces with its Apple II PC for the home and its Macintosh computer for students and knowledge workers. At one point,

Apple owned more than 20 percent of the PC market, competing against many other PC vendors, most of which are no longer relevant (or in business).

However, Apple lost its way. In 1985, Steve Jobs, Apple's chief innovator, lost a fight with the Apple board and was forced out. He founded another PC company, NeXT, which developed and sold a groundbreaking PC product that was too groundbreaking to sell well in that era. Meanwhile, Apple employed a succession of CEOs, starting with John Sculley, who was hired away from Pepsi-Cola where he'd enjoyed considerable success. Sculley's knowledge and experience did not transfer well to the PC business, however, and the company went downhill so fast that CNBC named him the 14th worst American CEO of all time.[9] Two other CEOs followed in Sculley's footsteps.

---

[7] "Harrah's Entertainment Launches Microsoft Surface at Rio iBar, Providing Guests with Innovative and Immersive New Entertainment Experiences," Microsoft Press Release, last updated June 11, 2008, www.microsoft.com/presspass/press/2008/jun08/06-11HETSurfacePR.mspx.
[8] Microsoft Press Release, May 29, 2007.
[9] "Portfolio's Worst American CEOs of All Time," *CNBC.com*, accessed September 4, 2013, www.cnbc.com/id/30502091?slide=8.

FIGURE 3-29

Apple Stock History

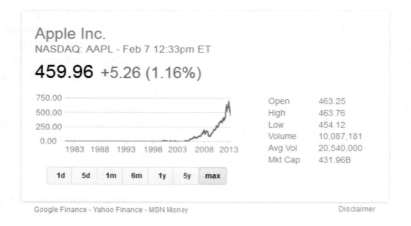

During this period, Apple made numerous mistakes, among them not rewarding innovative engineering, creating too many products for too many market segments, and losing the respect of the retail computer stores. Apple's market PC share plummeted.

Steve Jobs, Second Verse

In 1996, Apple bought Jobs' NeXT Computing and gained technology that became the foundation of Mac OS X, today's Macintosh operating system. The true asset it acquired, however, was Steve Jobs. Even he, however, couldn't create an overnight miracle. It is exceedingly difficult to regain lost market share and even more difficult to regain the respect of the retail channel that had come to view Apple's products with disdain. Even by 2011, Apple's PC market share was in the range of 10 to 12 percent, down from a high of 20 percent in the 1980s.

In response to these problems, Apple broke away from the PC and created new markets with its iPod, iPhone, and iPad. It also countered retailer problems by opening its own stores. In the process, it pioneered the sale of music and applications over the Internet.

iPod, iPhone, and iPad devices are a marvel of creativity and engineering. They exude not only ease of use, but also now/wow/fun coolness. By selling hot music for the iPod, Apple established a connection with a dynamic segment of the market that was willing to spend a lot of money on bright, shiny objects. The ability to turn the iPhone on its side to rotate images probably sold more iPhones than anything else. With the iPad, portable devices became readable, and the market responded by awarding Apple a 44 percent share of the mobile market in 2011.[10]

To encourage the development of iPhone and iPad apps, Apple shares its revenue with application developers. That would be $2.5 billion paid to developers in the first 3 years! Developers responded by creating 445,000 iOS applications in that same period, and an army of developers are at work building thousands more while you read this.

By the way, if you want to build an iOS application, what's the first thing you need to do? Buy a Macintosh. Apple closed its development to any other development method. Adobe Flash? No way. Apple claims that Flash has too many bugs, and perhaps so. Thus, Flash developers are excluded. Microsoft developers are out in the cold, too. The non-Apple development community was furious, and Apple's response was, in essence, "Fine, we'll pay our $2.5 billion to someone else."

The bottom line? Every sales success feeds every other sales success. Hot music fed the iPod. The iPod fed iTunes and created a growing customer base that was ripe for the iPhone. Sales of the iPhone fed the stores, whose success fed the developer community, which fed more applications, which fed the iPhone and set the stage for the iPad, which fed the App Store, which enabled the $30 price on the OS X Lion, which led to more loyal customers and, of course, to more developers.

Apple Today

So much for Apple's history. With the much-lamented loss of Steve Jobs, many analysts wonder if the best days for Apple are behind it. History offers little solace to Apple fans; when Jobs left before, the company foundered. And, meanwhile, Apple is confronting threats from both Google and its Android devices and Microsoft with its Win 8 devices.

[10] Apple presentation at the Apple Worldwide Developers Conference, June 6, 2011.

Questions

3-6. What do you think are the three most important factors in Apple's incredible success? Justify your answer.

3-7. Microsoft took a lead in the development of the technology of early tablets, and it had the world's leading operating system and applications for more than 25 years. Provide five reasons why Microsoft was not able to achieve the same success that Apple has. Most industry analysts would agree that the skills and abilities of Microsoft's 88,000 employees are as good, on average, as Apple's.

3-8. Search the Internet for the latest data on the sales of iOS, Android, and Windows 8 devices. What trends do you see? Is Apple in danger of being surpassed by competition? Why or why not?

3-9. Steve Jobs passed away in the fall of 2011. Until his death, he had been the heart and soul of Apple's innovation. Apple continued on in his absence and did not reach its stock high until nearly a year after his death. But, so far, Apple has not continued its string of amazing products. A question to many investors is whether the company can be successful without him. What is your opinion? What role did he play? How can Apple respond to his loss? Would you be willing to invest in Apple without his leadership? Why or why not?

3-10. Considering your answers to the four questions above, if you had a spare $5,000 in your portfolio and wanted to buy an equity stock with it, would you buy AAPL (Apple)? Why or why not?

arter Jackson is a student at Central Colorado State University and is the coach of an intramural soccer team. Carter recently received a bill on his student account regarding lost soccer equipment, and he's mystified. To his knowledge he's never lost any equipment, so he visits the counter where he checks out equipment.

"What is this?" Carter asks the counter attendant, Jeremy Bates, pointing to his student account billing statement.

"This what?" It's 2:30 in the afternoon, and Jeremy is still waking up.

"This bill... $187.78. What's it for? It's on my university account for last month."

"Don't know. Did you buy something here?" Jeremy's rubbing his eyes.

"No. I have absolutely no idea what this is for. And I'm on a tight budget. I need to get this fixed."

"Well, let me take a look. Give me your ID card."

Jeremy squints his eyes in an attempt to wake up as he scans Jackson's ID card. He clicks a few times to find Jackson's report. "It looks like you were billed $187.78 for soccer equipment that you didn't return."

"What are you talking about? I'm not supposed to return it until the end of the season, which is 3 weeks from now."

"Not for this year. For last year."
Jeremy wishes he were still asleep.

"But I wasn't coach last year. Someone else was." Carter's got a bad feeling about this.

"That's not what it says here. It says here that you're the coach of the Helicopters... by the way, great game on Saturday. I never thought you guys would pull it out, but you did. How's your goalie, by the way?" Jeremy hopes to calm Carter down.

"She's fine... sore, but fine. So, look, I'm the coach of the Helicopters this year, but I wasn't last year."

Q1. What is the purpose of a database?

Q2. What are the contents of a database?

Q3. What are the components of a database application system?

Q4. How do data models facilitate database design?

Q5. How is a data model transformed into a database design?

Q6. Why are NoSQL and Big Data important?

Q7. How can the intramural league improve its database?

"Maybe not. I don't know. All it says here is, Helicopters, Coach, Carter Jackson. Here, look at my screen."

Carter looks over the counter at Jeremy's screen.

"So, where does it show I owe 187 bucks?"

"It doesn't...that comes from another report. But like it shows, you checked out soccer balls and jerseys back in 2010 that were never checked in."

"I did not. I was in New Zealand in 2010!"

"Well, your team did."

"Don't you have another screen, another form, that shows who was coach back then?"

"Not that I know about. To tell you the truth, you're not the first person to complain about this." Jeremy's thinking this is too much...maybe he shouldn't stay up so late on Tuesday nights, especially when he has to work. "Give me your name and somebody will contact you."

"You've already got my name. Right there on your screen." Carter's wondering where they find these guys.

"Oh, yeah."

"But I can't wait. I need to get this fixed *now*. I don't want this debt hanging over me."

"OK, let me see if Dawn is here."

Enter Dawn Jenkins, intramural director. In contrast to Jeremy, Dawn's full of enthusiasm and energy.

"Hi, Jeremy, what seems to be the problem?" she asks.

"I was billed 187, no wait, almost 188 bucks for soccer equipment that wasn't returned last year," Carter interrupts.

"Yeah, you have to return all the equipment...." Dawn starts to give her standard pitch.

"But I wasn't coach last year," Carter interrupts.

"Oh, one of those. OK. I get it." Some of the energy seeps out of her voice. "Here's the problem. Our computer doesn't tell us who was coach last year. But it does remember that the team didn't return its soccer gear. Do you know last year's coach?" she asks hopefully.

"Yeah, Fred Dillingham. He graduated."

"Oh, dear. Well, we need our equipment back."

"Look, Dawn, I never met the guy. I heard he was a great coach, but he's gone. I can't call him up, wherever he is, and ask for your equipment back. Why didn't you bill him before he left?" Carter thinks to himself, "These people are idiots."

"Well, we had a little problem. Mary Anne, who normally does that each year, had her baby and was gone. Nobody knew to run the missing equipment report."

"So, how come I get billed now?"

"Because I figured it out and ran the report last month."

"Dawn, this is a mess."

"What do we do? We need to replace our missing gear."

Chapter Preview

Clearly, the intramural sports league has problems. At least one problem is a *process* problem. The fact that one of the league's employees took maternity leave should not mean that it doesn't send out bills for missing equipment. The league management has confused an *employee*, Mary Anne, with a *role* in a business process. We will address problems like this in Chapters 5 through 8.

For now, we will focus on the problems in its database. Something is not quite right; the database should contain the name of the coaches of past years, at least. But how should the league change it? We will address this issue in Q7 of this chapter.

To begin, realize that businesses of every size organize data records into collections called *databases*. At one extreme, small businesses use databases to keep track of customers; at the other extreme, huge corporations such as Dell and Amazon.com use databases to support complex sales, marketing, and operations activities. In between, we have universities like Central Colorado State that use databases as a crucial part of their operations but lack the trained and experienced staff to manage and support their databases. To obtain

answers to the one-of-a-kind queries they need, employees need to be creative and adaptable in the way they access and use the university databases.

This chapter discusses the why, what, and how of database processing. We begin by describing the purpose of databases and then explain the important components of database systems. We then overview the process of creating a database system and summarize your role as a future user of such systems.

Users have a crucial role in the development of database applications. Specifically, the structure and content of the database depend entirely on how users view their business activity. To build the database, the developers will create a model of that view using a tool called the entity-relationship model. You need to understand how to interpret such models because the development team might ask you to validate the correctness of such a model when building a system for your use. Finally, we describe the various database administration tasks.

This chapter focuses on database technology. Here we consider the basic components of a database and their functions. You will learn about the use of database reporting and data mining in Chapter 11.

Q1. What Is the Purpose of a Database?

The purpose of a database is to keep track of things. When most students learn that, they wonder why we need a special technology for such a simple task. Why not just use a list? If the list is long, put it into a spreadsheet. In fact, many professionals do keep track of things using spreadsheets. If the structure of the list is simple enough, there is no need to use database technology. The list of student grades in Figure 4-1, for example, works perfectly well in a spreadsheet.

Suppose, however, that the professor wants to track more than just grades. Say that the professor wants to record email messages as well. Or perhaps the professor wants to record both email messages and office visits. There is no place in Figure 4-1 to record that additional data. Of course, the professor could set up a separate spreadsheet for email messages and another one for office visits, but that awkard solution would be difficult to use because it does not provide all the data in one place.

Instead, the professor wants a form like that in Figure 4-2. With it, the professor can record student grades, emails, and office visits all in one place. A form like the one in Figure 4-2 is difficult, if not impossible, to produce from a spreadsheet. Such a form is easily produced, however, from a database.

The key distinction between Figures 4-1 and 4-2 is that the data in Figure 4-1 is about a single theme or concept. It is about student grades only. The data in Figure 4-2 has multiple themes; it shows student grades, student emails, and student office visits. We can make a general rule from these examples: Lists of data involving a single theme can be stored in a spreadsheet; lists that involve data with multiple themes require a database. We will say more about this general rule as this chapter proceeds.

FIGURE 4-1

List of Student Grades in a Spreadsheet

	A	B	C	D	E	F	G	H
1	Student Name	Student Number	HW1	HW2	MidTerm	HW3	HW4	Final
2								
3	BAKER, ANDREA	1325	88	100	78			
4	FISCHER, MAYAN	3007	95	100	74			
5	LAU, SWEE	1644	75	90	90			
6	NELSON, STUART	2881	100	90	98			
7	ROGERS, SHELLY	8009	95	100	98			
8	TAM, JEFFREY	3559		100	88			
9	VALDEZ, MARIE	5265	80	90	85			
10	VERBERRA, ADAM	4867	70	90	92			

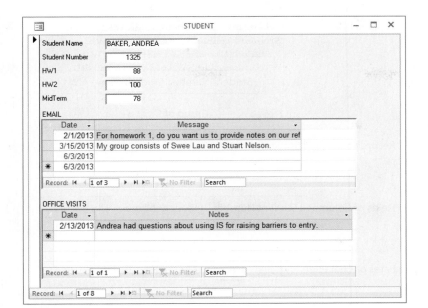

FIGURE 4-2

Student Data in a Form, Data from a Database

Q2. What Are the Contents of a Database?

A **database** is a self-describing collection of integrated records. To understand the terms in this definition, you first need to understand the terms illustrated in Figure 4-3. As you learned in Chapter 3, a **byte** is a character of data. In databases, bytes are grouped into **columns**, such as *Student Number* and *Student Name*. Columns are also called **fields**. Columns or fields, in turn, are grouped into **rows**, which are also called **records**. In Figure 4-3, the collection of data for all columns (*Student Number, Student Name, HW1, HW2,* and *MidTerm*) is called a *row* or a *record*. Finally, a group of similar rows or records is called a **table** or a **file**. From these definitions, you can see that there is a hierarchy of data elements, as shown in Figure 4-4.

It is tempting to continue this grouping process by saying that a database is a group of tables or files. This statement, although true, does not go far enough. As shown in Figure 4-5, a database is a collection of tables *plus* relationships among the rows in those tables, *plus* special data, called metadata, that describes the structure of the database. By the way, the cylindrical symbol labeled "database" in Figure 4-5 represents a computer disk drive. It is used in diagrams like this because databases are normally stored on magnetic disks.

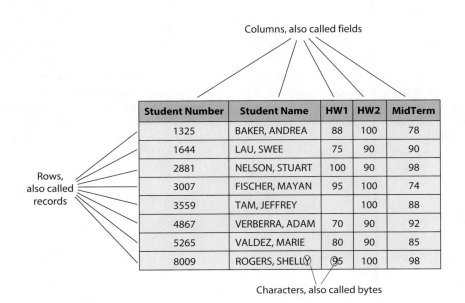

Columns, also called fields

Student Number	Student Name	HW1	HW2	MidTerm
1325	BAKER, ANDREA	88	100	78
1644	LAU, SWEE	75	90	90
2881	NELSON, STUART	100	90	98
3007	FISCHER, MAYAN	95	100	74
3559	TAM, JEFFREY		100	88
4867	VERBERRA, ADAM	70	90	92
5265	VALDEZ, MARIE	80	90	85
8009	ROGERS, SHELLY	95	100	98

Rows, also called records

Characters, also called bytes

FIGURE 4-3

Elements of the Student Table (also called a file)

FIGURE 4-4

Hierarchy of Data Elements

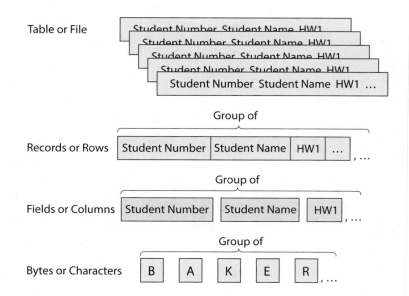

What Are Relationships Among Rows?

Consider the terms on the left-hand side of Figure 4-5. You know what tables are. To understand what is meant by *relationships among rows in tables*, examine Figure 4-6. It shows sample data from the three tables *Email*, *Student*, and *Office_Visit*. Notice the column named *Student Number* in the *Email* table. That column indicates the row in *Student* to which a row of *Email* is connected. In the first row of *Email*, the *Student Number* value is 1325. This indicates that this particular email was received from the student whose *Student Number* is 1325. If you examine the *Student* table, you will see that the row for Andrea Baker has this value. Thus, the first row of the *Email* table is related to Andrea Baker.

Now consider the last row of the *Office_Visit* table at the bottom of the figure. The value of *Student Number* in that row is 4867. This value indicates that the last row in *Office_Visit* belongs to Adam Verberra.

From these examples, you can see that values in one table relate the rows in that table to rows in a second table. Several special terms are used to express these ideas. A **key** (also called a **primary key**) is a column or group of columns that identifies a unique row in a table. *Student Number* is the key of the *Student* table. Given a value of *Student Number*, you can determine one and only one row in *Student*. Only one student has the number 1325, for example.

Every table must have a key. The key of the *Email* table is *EmailNum*, and the key of the *Office_Visit* table is *VisitID*. Sometimes more than one column is needed to form a unique identifier. In a table called *City*, for example, the key would consist of the combination of columns (*City, State*) because a given city name can appear in more than one state.

Student Number is not the key of the *Email* or the *Office_Visit* tables. We know that about *Email* because there are two rows in *Email* that have the *Student Number* value 1325. The value 1325 does not identify a unique row; therefore *Student Number* cannot be the key of *Email*. Nor is *Student Number* a key of *Office_Visit*, although you cannot tell that from the data in Figure 4-6. If you think about it, however, there is nothing to prevent a student from visiting a professor more than once. If that were to happen, there would be two rows in *Office_Visit* with the same value of *Student Number*. It just happens that no student has visited twice in the limited data in Figure 4-6.

FIGURE 4-5

Contents of a Database

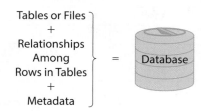

Email Table

EmailNum	Date	Message	Student Number
1	2/1/2013	For homework 1, do you want us to provide notes on our references?	1325
2	3/15/2013	My group consists of Swee Lau and Stuart Nelson.	1325
3	3/15/2013	Could you please assign me to a group?	1644

Student Table

Student Number	Student Name	HW1	HW2	MidTerm
1325	BAKER, ANDREA	88	100	78
1644	LAU, SWEE	75	90	90
2881	NELSON, STUART	100	90	98
3007	FISCHER, MAYAN	95	100	74
3559	TAM, JEFFREY		100	88
4867	VERBERRA, ADAM	70	90	92
5265	VALDEZ, MARIE	80	90	85
8009	ROGERS, SHELLY	95	100	98

Office_Visit Table

VisitID	Date	Notes	Student Number
2	2/13/2013	Andrea had questions about using IS for raising barriers to entry.	1325
3	2/17/2013	Jeffrey is considering an IS major. Wanted to talk about career opportunities.	3559
4	2/17/2013	Will miss class Friday due to job conflict.	4867

FIGURE 4-6
Examples of Relationships

Student Number is, however, a key, but it is a key of a different table, namely *Student*. Hence, the column *Student Number* in the *Email* and *Office_Visit* tables is called a **foreign key**. This term is used because such columns are keys of a different (foreign) table than the one in which they reside.

Before we go on, databases that carry their data in the form of tables and that represent relationships using foreign keys are called **relational databases**. (The term *relational* is used because another, more formal name for a table like those we are discussing is **relation**.) In the past, there were databases that were not relational in format, but such databases have almost disappeared. However, nonrelational databases are making a comeback, as we'll see later in Q6.[1]

Metadata

Recall the definition of database: A database is a self-describing collection of integrated records. The records are integrated because, as you just learned, rows can be tied together by their key/foreign key relationship. But what does *self-describing* mean?

It means that a database contains, within itself, a description of its contents. Think of a library. A library is a self-describing collection of books and other materials. It is self-describing because the library contains a catalog that describes the library's contents. The same idea also pertains to a database. Databases are self-describing because they contain not only data, but also data about the data in the database.

[1] Another type of database, the **object-relational database**, is rarely used in commercial applications. Search the Web if you are interested in learning more about object-relational databases. In this book, we will describe only relational databases.

FIGURE 4-7
Metadata for Email Table

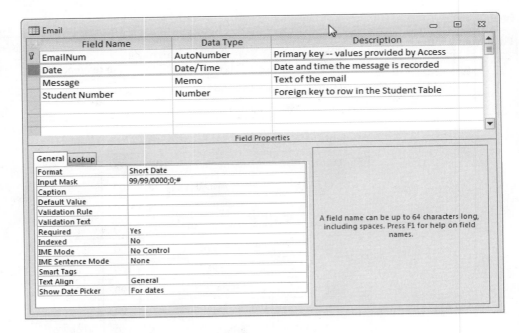

Metadata are data that describe data. Figure 4-7 shows metadata for the *Email* table. The format of metadata depends on the software product that is processing the database. Figure 4-7 shows the metadata as they appear in Microsoft Access. Each row of the top part of this form describes a column of the *Email* table. The columns of these descriptions are *Field Name*, *Data Type*, and *Description*. *Field Name* contains the name of the column, *Data Type* shows the type of data the column may hold, and *Description* contains notes that explain the source or use of the column. As you can see, there is one row of metadata for each of the four columns of the *Email* table: *EmailNum, Date, Message,* and *Student Number*.

The bottom part of this form provides more metadata, which Access calls *Field Properties*, for each column. In Figure 4-7, the focus is on the *Date* column (note the light rectangle drawn around the *Date* row). Because the focus is on *Date* in the top pane, the details in the bottom pane pertain to the *Date* column. The Field Properties describe formats, a default value for Access to supply when a new row is created, and the constraint that a value is required for this column. It is not important for you to remember these details. Instead, just understand that metadata are data about data and that such metadata are always a part of a database.

The presence of metadata makes databases much more useful. Because of metadata, no one needs to guess, remember, or even record what is in the database. To find out what a database contains, we just look at the metadata inside the database.

Q3. What Are the Components of a Database Application System?

Figure 4-8 shows the three major components of a **database application system**: a database, a DBMS, and one or more database applications. We have already described the contents of the database. We will next describe the DBMS and then, finally, discuss database applications, which include computer software.

Of course, as an information system, database application systems also have the other three components: hardware, people and procedures. Because the purpose of this chapter is to discuss database technology, we will omit them from this discussion.

What Is a Database Management System?

A **database management system (DBMS)** is a program used to create, process, and administer a database. As with operating systems, almost no organization develops its own DBMS. Instead, companies license DBMS products from vendors such as IBM, Microsoft, Oracle, and others. Popular DBMS products are **DB2** from IBM, **Access** and **SQL Server** from Microsoft, and

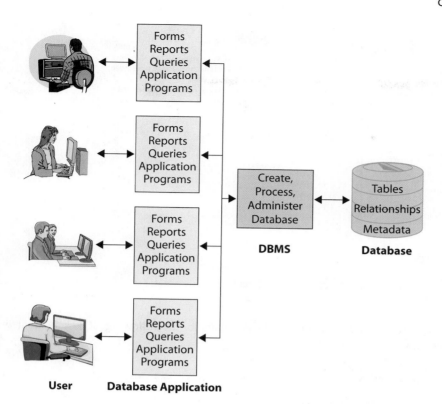

FIGURE 4-8
Components of a Database Application System

Oracle Database from the Oracle Corporation. Another popular DBMS is **MySQL**, an open source DBMS product that is license-free for most applications.[2] Other DBMS products are available, but these five process the bulk of databases today.

Note that a DBMS and a database are two different things. For some reason, the trade press and even some books confuse the two. A DBMS is a software program; a database is a collection of tables of data, relationships, and metadata. The two are very different in nature.

Creating the Database and Its Structures

Database developers use the DBMS to create tables, relationships, and other structures in the database. The form in Figure 4-7 can be used to define a new table or to modify an existing one. To create a new table, the developer just fills the new table's metadata into the form.

To modify an existing table—say, to add a new column—the developer opens the metadata form for that table and adds a new row of metadata. For example, in Figure 4-9 the developer has added a new column called *Response?*. This new column has the data type *Yes/No*, which means that the column can contain only one of two values—*Yes* or *No*. The professor will use this column to indicate whether he has responded to the student's email. A column can be removed by deleting its row in this table, though doing so will also delete its existing data.

Processing the Database

The second function of the DBMS is to process the database. Such processing can be quite complex, but, fundamentally, the DBMS provides four processing operations: *read, insert, modify*, or *delete* data. These operations are requested in different ways. From a form, when the user enters new or changed data, a computer program behind the form calls the DBMS to make the necessary database changes. From a Web application, a program on the client or on the server calls the DBMS to make the change.

Structured Query Language (SQL) (pronounced "see-quell") is an international standard language for processing a database. All five of the DBMS products mentioned earlier

---

[2] MySQL was supported by the MySQL company. In 2008, that company was acquired by Sun Microsystems, which was, in turn, acquired by Oracle later that year. Because MySQL is open source, Oracle does not own the source code, however.

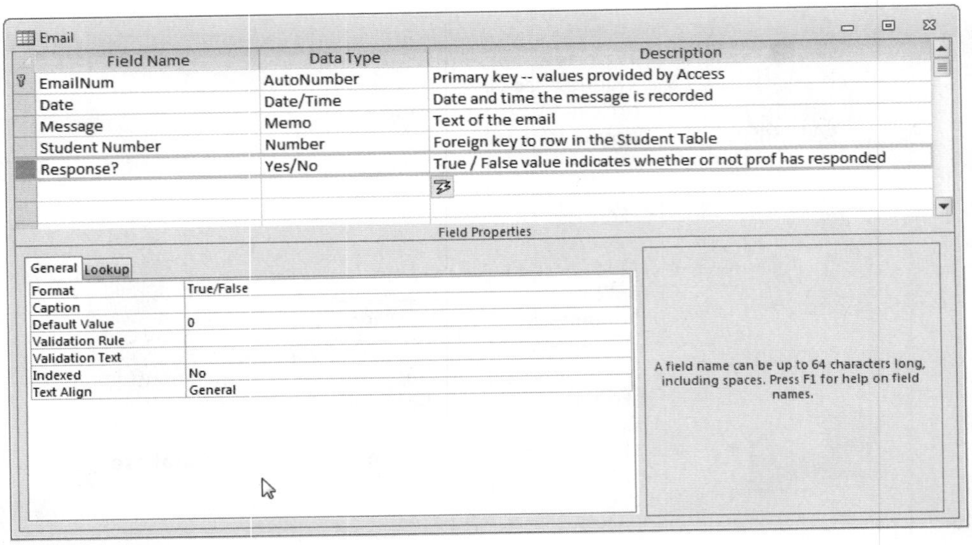

FIGURE 4-9

Adding a New Column to a Table (Microsoft Access)

accept and process SQL statements. As an example, the following SQL statement inserts a new row into the *Student* table:

```
INSERT INTO Student
([Student Number], [Student Name], HW1, HW2, MidTerm)
VALUES
(1000, 'Franklin, Benjamin', 90, 95, 100);
```

As stated, statements like this one are issued "behind the scenes" by programs that process forms. Alternatively, they can be issued directly to the DBMS by an application program.

You do not need to understand or remember SQL language syntax. Instead, just realize that SQL is an international standard for processing a database. SQL can also be used to create databases and database structures. You will learn more about SQL if you take a database management class.

Administering the Database

A third DBMS function is to provide tools to assist in the administration of the database. Database administration involves a wide variety of activities. For example, the DBMS can be used to set up a security system involving user accounts, passwords, permissions, and limits for processing the database. To provide database security, a user must sign on using a valid user account before she can process the database.

Permissions can be limited in very specific ways. In the Student database example, it is possible to limit a particular user to reading only *Student Name* from the *Student* table. A different user could be given permission to read the entire *Student* table, but limited to update only the *HW1, HW2*, and *MidTerm* columns. Other users can be given still other permissions.

In addition to security, DBMS administrative functions include backing up database data, adding structures to improve the performance of database applications, removing data that are no longer wanted or needed, and similar tasks.

For important databases, most organizations dedicate one or more employees to the role of **database administration (DBA)**, which is defined by the major responsibilities listed in Figure 4-10. You will learn more about this topic if you take a database management course.

What Are the Components of a Database Application?

A database, all by itself, is not very useful. The tables in Figure 4-6 have all of the data the professor wants, but the format is unwieldy. The professor wants to see the data in a form like that in Figure 4-2 and also as a formatted report. Pure database data are valuable, but in raw form they are not pertinent or useful. In terms of information, it is difficult to conceive differences that make a difference among rows of data in tables.

A **database application** is a collection of forms, reports, queries, and application programs that use the DBMS to process a database. A database may have one or more applications, and

Category	Database Administration Task	Description
Development	Create and staff DBA function	Size of DBA group depends on size and complexity of database. Groups range from one part-time person to small group.
	Form steering committee	Consists of representatives of all user groups. Forum for community-wide discussions and decisions.
	Specify requirements	Ensure that all appropriate user input is considered.
	Validate data model	Check data model for accuracy and completeness.
	Evaluate application design	Verify that all necessary forms, reports, queries, and applications are developed. Validate design and usability of application components.
Operation	Manage processing rights and responsibilities	Determine processing rights/restrictions on each table and column.
	Manage security	Add and delete users and user groups as necessary; ensure that security system works.
	Track problems and manage resolution	Develop system to record and manage resolution of problems.
	Monitor database performance	Provide expertise/solutions for performance improvements.
	Manage DBMS	Evaluate new features and functions.
Backup and Recovery	Monitor backup procedures	Verify that database backup procedures are followed.
	Conduct training	Ensure that users and operations personnel know and understand recovery procedures.
	Manage recovery	Manage recovery process.
Adaptation	Set up request tracking system	Develop system to record and prioritize requests for change.
	Manage configuration change	Manage impact of database structure changes on applications and users.

FIGURE 4-10
Summary of Database Administration Tasks

each application may have one or more users. As stated, the database application(s), the DBMS, and the database comprise the database application system.

Figure 4-11 shows three applications used at FlexTime, a fitness center. The first one is used to bill and manage FlexTime memberships; the second schedules and bills scheduled classes; and the third tracks and supports personal training sessions. These applications have different purposes, features, and functions, but they all process the same FlexTime customer database.

What Are Forms, Reports, Queries, and Application Programs?

Figure 4-2 shows a typical database application data entry **form**. Data entry forms are used to read, insert, modify, and delete data. **Reports** show data in a structured context. Some reports, like the one in Figure 4-12, also compute values as they present the data. An example is the computation of *Total Points* in Figure 4-12. If forms and reports are well designed, they allow users to readily identify *differences that make a difference*. Thus, they enable users to conceive information.

But there's more. DBMS products provide comprehensive and robust features for querying database data. For example, suppose the professor who uses the Student database remembers that one of the students referred to the topic *barriers to entry* in an office visit, but cannot remember which student or when. If there are hundreds of students and visits recorded in the database, it will take some effort and time for the professor to search through all office visit records to find that event. The DBMS, however, can find any such record quickly. Figure 4-13(a) shows a **query**

FIGURE 4-11

FlexTime's Database Application System

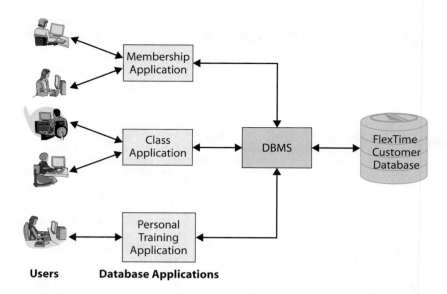

Users   Database Applications

form in which the professor types in the keyword for which she is looking. Figure 4-13(b) shows the results of the query in the *Notes* field of the *Email* table.

Why Are Database Application Programs Needed?

Forms, reports, and queries work well for standard functions. However, most applications have unique requirements that a simple form, report, or query cannot meet. For example, at the university intramural center, what should be done if only a portion of a team's need can be met? If a coach requests 10 soccer balls and only three are available, should a backorder for seven more be generated automatically? Or should some other action be taken?

Application programs process logic that is specific to a given business need. In the Student database, an example application is one that assigns grades at the end of the term. If the professor grades on a curve, the application reads the breakpoints for each grade from a form and then processes each row in the *Student* table, allocating a grade based on the breakpoints and the total number of points earned.

Another important use of application programs is to enable database processing over the Internet. For this use, the application program serves as an intermediary between the Web server and the DBMS and database. The application program responds to events, such as when a user presses a submit button; it also reads, inserts, modifies, and deletes database data.

For example, Figure 4-14 shows four different database application programs running on a Web server computer. Users with browsers connect to the Web server via the Internet. The Web server directs user requests to the appropriate application program. Each program then processes the database via the DBMS.

Multi-User Processing

Figures 4-8, 4-11, and 4-14 show multiple users processing the database. Such multi-user processing is common, but it does pose unique problems that you, as a future manager, should know about. To understand the nature of those problems, consider the following scenario.

FIGURE 4-12

Example Report

Student Report with Emails

Name	Number	HW1	HW2	MidTerm (= 3 HW)	Total Points		Date	Message
BAKER, ANDRE	1325	88	100	78	422			
							3/15/2013	My group consists of Swee Lau and Stuart Nelson.
							2/1/2013	For homework 1, do you want us to provide notes on our references?
LAU, SWEE	1644	75	90	90	435			
							3/15/2012	Could you please assign me to a group?

FIGURE 4-13
Example Database Query

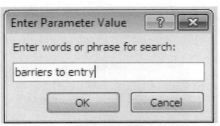

(a) Query Form for Search

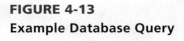

Student Name	▾	Date ▾	Notes	▾
BAKER, ANDREA		2/13/2013	Andrea had questions about using IS for raising barriers to entry.	

(b) Query Result

Suppose two of the users are FlexTime employees using the Class application in Figure 4-11. For convenience, let's call them Andrea and Jeffrey. Assume that Andrea is on the phone with a customer who wants to enroll in a particular spinning class. At the same time, Jeffrey is talking with another customer who wants to enroll in that same class. Andrea reads the database to determine how many vacancies that class has. While doing this, she unknowingly invokes the Class application when she types in her data entry form. The DBMS returns a row showing there is one slot left in that class.

Meanwhile, just after Andrea accesses the database, Jeffrey's customer says she wants to be in that class, and so he also reads the database (via the Class application program) to determine how many slots are available. The DBMS returns the same row to him, indicating that one slot is left.

Andrea's customer now says that he will enroll in the class, and Andrea records this fact in her form. The application rewrites that class row back to the database, indicating that there are no slots left.

Meanwhile, Jeffrey's customer says that she will take the class. Jeffrey records this fact in his form, and the application (which is still using the row it read indicating that a slot is available) rewrites that class row to the database, indicating there are no openings left. Jeffrey's application knows nothing about Andrea's work and hence does not know that her customer has already taken the last slot.

Clearly, there is a problem. Both customers have been assigned the same last slot in the class. When they attend the class, one of them will not have a bike to ride, which will be frustrating to the customers as well as the instructor.

This problem, known as the **lost update problem**, exemplifies one of the special characteristics of multi-user database processing. To prevent this problem, some type of locking must be used to coordinate the activities of users who know nothing about one another. Locking brings its own set of problems, however, and those problems must be addressed as well. We will not delve further into this topic here, however.

FIGURE 4-14

Applications Running on a Web Server

MIS InClass 4

How Much Is a Database Worth?

The Firm, a highly successful health club in Minneapolis (*www. TheFirmMpls.com*) realizes more than 15,000 person-visits a month, an average of 500 visits per day. Neil Miyamoto, one of the two business partners, believes that The Firm's database is its single most important asset. According to Neil:

> **Take away anything else—the building, the equipment, the inventory—anything else, and we'd be back in business 6 months or less. Take away our customer database, however, and we'd have to start all over. It would take us another 8 years to get back to where we are.**
> **Why is the database so crucial? It records everything the company's customers do.**

If The Firm decides to offer an early morning kickboxing class featuring a particular trainer, it can use its database to offer that class to everyone who ever took an early morning class, a kickboxing class, or a class by that trainer. Customers receive targeted solicitations for offerings they care about and, maybe equally important, they don't receive solicitations for those they don't care about. Clearly, The Firm's database has value and, if it wanted to, The Firm could sell that data.

In this exercise, you and a group of your fellow students will be asked to consider the value of a database to organizations other than The Firm.

1. Many small business owners have found it financially advantageous to purchase their own building. As one owner remarked upon his retirement, "We did well with the business, but we made our real money by buying the building." Explain why this might be so.
2. To what extent does the dynamic you identified in your answer to item 1 pertain to databases? Do you think it likely that, in 2050, some small businesspeople will retire and make statements like, "We did well with the business, but we made our real money from the database we generated?" Why or why not? In what ways is real estate different from database data? Are these differences significant to your answer?

Source: Image Source/Alamy.

3. Suppose you had a national database of student data. Assume your database includes the name, email address, university, grade level, and major for each student. Name five companies that would find that data valuable, and explain how they might use it. (For example, Pizza Hut could solicit orders from students during finals week.)
4. Describe a product or service that you could develop that would induce students to provide the data in item 3.
5. Considering your answers to items 1 through 4, identify two organizations in your community that could generate a database that would potentially be more valuable than the organization itself. Consider businesses, but also think about social organizations and government offices.
    For each organization, describe the content of the database and how you could entice customers or clients to provide that data. Also, explain why the data would be valuable and who might use it.
6. Prepare a 1-minute statement of what you have learned from this exercise that you could use in a job interview to illustrate your ability to innovate the use of technology in business.
7. Present your answers to items 1–6 to the rest of the class.

Realize from this example that converting a single-user database to a multi-user database requires more than simply connecting another computer. The logic of the underlying application processing needs to be adjusted as well. Be aware of possible data conflicts when you manage business activities that involve multi-user processing. If you find inaccurate results that seem not to have a cause, you may be experiencing multi-user data conflicts. Contact your IS department for assistance.

Enterprise DBMS Versus Personal DBMS

DBMS products fall into two broad categories. **Enterprise DBMS** products process large organizational and workgroup databases. These products support many, possibly thousands, of users and many different database applications. Such DBMS products support 24/7 operations and can

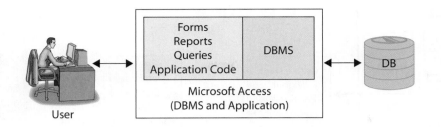

FIGURE 4-15

Microsoft Access as Application Generator and DBMS

manage databases that span dozens of different magnetic disks with hundreds of gigabytes or more of data. IBM's DB2, Microsoft's SQL Server, and Oracle's Oracle Database are examples of enterprise DBMS products.

Personal DBMS products are designed for smaller, simpler database applications. Such products are used for personal or small workgroup applications that involve fewer than 100 users—and normally fewer than 15. In fact, the great bulk of databases in this category have only a single user. The professor's Student database is an example of a database that is processed by a personal DBMS product.

In the past, there were many personal DBMS products—Paradox, dBase, R:base, and FoxPro. Microsoft put these products out of business when it developed Access and included it in the Microsoft Office suite. Today, about the only remaining personal DBMS is Microsoft Access.

To avoid one point of confusion for you in the future, the separation of application programs and the DBMS shown in Figure 4-11 is true only for enterprise DBMS products. Microsoft Access includes features and functions for application processing along with the DBMS itself. For example, Access has a form generator and a report generator. Thus, as shown in Figure 4-15, Access is both a DBMS *and* an application development product.

Q4. How Do Data Models Facilitate Database Design?

In Chapter 12, we will describe the process for developing information systems in more detail. However, business professionals have such a critical role in the development of database applications that we need to anticipate part of that discussion here by introducing two topics—data modeling and database design.

Because the design of the database depends entirely on how users view their business environment, user involvement is critical for database development. Think about the Student database. What data should it contain? Possibilities are: *Students, Classes, Grades, Emails, Office_Visits, Majors, Advisers, Student_Organizations*—the list could go on and on. Further, how much detail should be included in each? Should the database include campus addresses? Home addresses? Billing addresses?

In fact, there are dozens of possibilities, and the database developers do not, and cannot, know what to include. They do know, however, that a database must include all the data necessary for the users to perform their jobs. Ideally, it contains that amount of data and no more. So, during database development, the developers must rely on the users to tell them what to include in the database.

Database structures can be complex, in some cases very complex. So, before building the database, the developers construct a logical representation of database data called a **data model**. This model describes the data and relationships that will be stored in the database; it is akin to a blueprint. Just as building architects create a blueprint before they start building, database developers create a data model before they start designing the database.

Figure 4-16 summarizes the database design process. Interviews with users lead to database requirements, which are summarized in a data model. Once the users have approved (validated) the data model, it is transformed into a database design. That design is then implemented into database structures. We will consider data modeling and database design briefly in the next two sections. Again, your goal should be to learn the process so that you can be an effective user representative for a development effort. Also, Figure 4-16 is just part of the systems development process; other requirements used to develop application programs and features are beyond the scope of this book.

FIGURE 4-16
Database Design Process

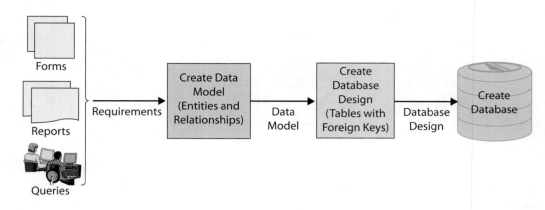

What Is the Entity-Relationship Data Model?

The **entity-relationship (E-R) data model** is a tool for constructing data models. Developers use it to describe the content of a data model by defining the things (*entities*) that will be stored in the database and the *relationships* among those entities. A second, less popular tool for data modeling is the Unified Modeling Language (UML). We will not describe that tool here. However, if you learn how to interpret E-R models, with a bit of study you will be able to understand UML models as well.

Entities

An **entity** is something that the users want to track. Examples of entities are *Order, Customer, Salesperson,* and *Item.* Some entities represent a physical object, such as *Item* or *Salesperson*; others represent a logical construct or transaction, such as *Order* or *Contract.* For reasons beyond this discussion, entity names are always singular. We use *Order,* not *Orders*; *Salesperson,* not *Salespersons.*

Entities have **attributes** that describe characteristics of the entity. Example attributes of *Order* are *OrderNumber, OrderDate, SubTotal, Tax, Total,* and so forth. Example attributes of *Salesperson* are *SalespersonName, Email, Phone,* and so forth. Entities also have an **identifier,** which is an attribute (or group of attributes) whose value is associated with one and only one entity instance. For example, *OrderNumber* is an identifier of *Order* because only one *Order* instance has a given value of *OrderNumber.* For the same reason, *CustomerNumber* is an identifier of *Customer.* If each member of the sales staff has a unique name, then *SalespersonName* is an identifier of *Salesperson.*

Before we continue, consider that last sentence. Is the salesperson's name unique among the sales staff? Both now and in the future? Who decides the answer to such a question? Only the users know whether this is true; the database developers cannot know. This example underlines why it is important for you to be able to interpret data models because only users like you will know for sure.

Figure 4-17 shows examples of entities for the Student database. Each entity is shown in a rectangle. The name of the entity is just above the rectangle, and the identifier is shown in a

FIGURE 4-17
Example Entities

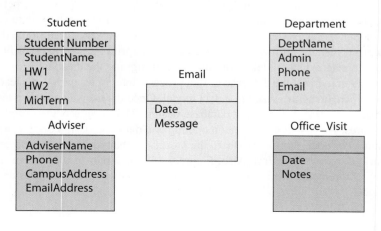

section at the top of the entity. Entity attributes are shown in the remainder of the rectangle. In Figure 4-17, the *Adviser* entity has an identifier called *AdviserName* and the attributes *Phone, CampusAddress,* and *EmailAddress.*

Observe that the entities *Email* and *Office_Visit* do not have an identifier. Unlike *Student* or *Adviser,* the users do not have an attribute that identifies a particular email. *Student Number* will not work because a student could send several emails. We *could* make one up. For example, we could say that the identifier of *Email* is *EmailNumber,* but if we do so we are not modeling how the users view their world. Instead, we are forcing something onto the users. Be aware of this possibility when you review data models about your business. Do not allow the database developers to create something in the data model that is not part of your business world.

Relationships

Entities have **relationships** to each other. An *Order,* for example, has a relationship to a *Customer* entity and also to a *Salesperson* entity. In the Student database, a *Student* has a relationship to an *Adviser,* and an *Adviser* has a relationship to a *Department.*

Figure 4-18 shows sample *Department, Adviser,* and *Student* entity instances and their relationships. For simplicity, this figure shows just the identifier of the entities and not the other attributes. For this sample data, *Accounting* has a relationship to three professors—Jones, Wu, and Lopez—and *Finance* has relationships to two professors—Smith and Greene.

The relationship between *Advisers* and *Students* is more complicated because in this example an adviser is allowed to advise many students and a student is allowed to have many advisers. Perhaps this happens because students can have multiple majors. In any case, note that Professor Jones advises students 100 and 400 and that student 100 is advised by both Professors Jones and Smith.

Diagrams like the one in Figure 4-18 are too cumbersome for use in database design discussions. Instead, database designers use diagrams called **entity-relationship (E-R) diagrams**. Figure 4-19 shows an E-R diagram for the data in Figure 4-18. In this figure, all of the entity instances of one type are represented by a single rectangle. Thus, there are rectangles for the *Department, Adviser,* and *Student* entities. Attributes are shown as before in Figure 4-17.

Additionally, a line is used to represent a relationship between two entities. Notice the line between *Department* and *Adviser,* for example. The forked lines on the right side of that line signify that a department may have more than one adviser. The little lines, which are referred to as **crow's feet**, are shorthand for the multiple lines between *Department* and *Adviser* in Figure 4-18. Relationships like this one are called **1:N**, or **one-to-many relationships**, because one department can have many advisers but an adviser has at most one department.

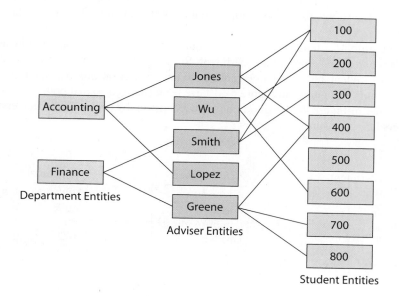

FIGURE 4-18

Example Entity Instances and Relationships

FIGURE 4-19

**Entity Relationships,
Version 1**

Now examine the line between *Adviser* and *Student*. Notice the crow's feet that appear at each end of the line. This notation signifies that an adviser can be related to many students and that a student can be related to many advisers, which is the situation in Figure 4-18. Relationships like this one are called **N:M**, or **many-to-many relationships**, because one adviser can have many students and one student can have many advisers.

Students sometimes find the notation N:M confusing. Just interpret the *N* and *M* to mean that a variable number, greater than one, is allowed on each side of the relationship. Such a relationship is not written *N:N* because that notation would imply that there are the same number of entities on each side of the relationship, which is not necessarily true. *N:M* means that more than one entity is allowed on each side of the relationship and that the number of entities on each side can be different.

Figure 4-20 shows the same entities with different assumptions. Here advisers may advise in more than one department, but a student may have only one adviser, representing a policy that students may not have multiple majors.

Which, if either, of these versions is correct? Only the users know. These alternatives illustrate the kinds of questions you will need to answer when a database designer asks you to check a data model for correctness.

Figures 4-19 and 4-20 are typical examples of an entity-relationship diagram. Unfortunately, there are several different styles of entity-relationship diagrams. This one is called, not surprisingly, a **crow's-foot diagram**. You may learn other versions if you take a database management class. These diagrams were created in PowerPoint, which works fine for simple models. More complex models can be created in Microsoft Visio and other products that were purpose-built for creating E-R models.

The crow's-foot notation shows the maximum number of entities that can be involved in a relationship. Accordingly, they are called the relationship's **maximum cardinality**. Common examples of maximum cardinality are 1:N, N:M, and 1:1 (not shown).

Another important question is, "What is the minimum number of entities required in the relationship?" Must an adviser have a student to advise, and must a student have an adviser? Constraints on minimum requirements are called **minimum cardinalities**.

Figure 4-21 presents a third version of this E-R diagram that shows both maximum and minimum cardinalities. The vertical bar on a line means that at least one entity of that type is required. The small oval means that the entity is optional; the relationship *need not* have an entity of that type.

Thus, in Figure 4-21 a department is not required to have a relationship to any adviser, but an adviser is required to belong to a department. Similarly, an adviser is not required to have a relationship to a student, but a student is required to have a relationship to an adviser. Note, also, that the maximum cardinalities in Figure 4-21 have been changed so that both are 1:N.

Is the model in Figure 4-21 a good one? It depends on the policy of the university. Again, only the users know for sure.

FIGURE 4-20

**Entity Relationships,
Version 2**

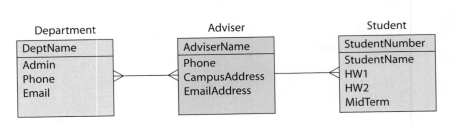

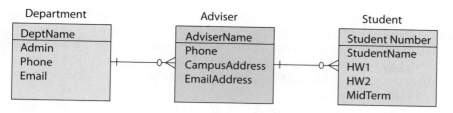

FIGURE 4-21

Entity Relationships, Version 3, Minimum Cardinality Shown

Q5. How Is a Data Model Transformed into a Database Design?

Database design is the process of converting a data model into tables, relationships, and data constraints. The database design team transforms entities into tables and expresses relationships by defining foreign keys. Database design is a complicated subject; as with data modeling, it occupies weeks in a database management class. In this section, however, we will introduce two important database design concepts: normalization and the representation of two kinds of relationships. The first concept is a foundation of database design, and the second will help you understand important design considerations.

Normalization

Normalization is the process of converting a poorly structured table into two or more well-structured tables. A table is such a simple construct that you may wonder how one could possibly be poorly structured. In truth, there are many ways that tables can be malformed—so many, in fact, that researchers have published hundreds of papers on this topic alone.

Consider the *Employee* table in Figure 4-22(a). It lists employee names, hire dates, email addresses, and the name and number of the department in which the employee works. This table seems innocent enough. But consider what happens when the Accounting department changes its name to Accounting and Finance. Because department names are duplicated in this table, every row that has a value of "Accounting" must be changed to "Accounting and Finance."

Data Integrity Problems

Suppose the Accounting name change is correctly made in two rows, but not in the third. The result is shown in Figure 4-22(b). This table has what is called a **data integrity problem**, which is the situation that exists when the database contains inconsistent data. Here two rows indicate

Employee

Name	HireDate	Email	DeptNo	DeptName
Jones	Feb 1, 2010	Jones@ourcompany.com	100	Accounting
Smith	Dec 3, 2012	Smith@ourcompany.com	200	Marketing
Chau	March 7, 2013	Chau@ourcompany.com	100	Accounting
Greene	July 17, 2011	Greene@ourcompany.com	100	Accounting

(a) Table Before Update

Employee

Name	HireDate	Email	DeptNo	DeptName
Jones	Feb 1, 2010	Jones@ourcompany.com	100	Accounting and Finance
Smith	Dec 3, 2012	Smith@ourcompany.com	200	Marketing
Chau	March 7, 2013	Chau@ourcompany.com	100	Accounting and Finance
Greene	July 17, 2011	Greene@ourcompany.com	100	Accounting

(b) Table with Incomplete Update

FIGURE 4-22

Table with Problematic Structure

that the name of Department 100 is "Accounting and Finance," and another row indicates that the name of Department 100 is "Accounting."

This problem is easy to spot in this small table. But consider a table like the *Customer* table in the Amazon.com database or the eBay database. Those databases may have hundreds of millions of rows. Once a table that large develops serious data integrity problems, months of labor will be required to remove them.

Data integrity problems are serious. A table that has data integrity problems will produce incorrect and inconsistent data. Users will lose confidence in their ability to conceive information from that data, and the system will develop a poor reputation. Information systems with poor reputations become serious burdens to the organizations that use them.

Normalizing for Data Integrity

The data integrity problem can occur only if data are duplicated. Because of this, one easy way to eliminate the problem is to eliminate the duplicated data. We can do this by transforming the table in Figure 4-22 into two tables, as shown in Figure 4-23. Here the name of the department is stored just once; therefore no data inconsistencies can occur.

Of course, to produce an employee report that includes the department name, the two tables in Figure 4-23 will need to be joined back together. Because such joining of tables is common, DBMS products have been programmed to perform it efficiently, but it still requires work. From this example, you can see a trade-off in database design: Normalized tables eliminate data duplication, but they can be slower to process. Dealing with such trade-offs is an important consideration in database design.

The general goal of normalization is to construct tables such that every table has a *single* topic or theme. In good writing, every paragraph should have a single theme. This is true of databases as well; every table should have a single theme. The problem with the table in Figure 4-22 is that it has two independent themes: employees and departments. The way to correct the problem is to split the table into two tables, each with its own theme. In this case, we create an *Employee* table and a *Department* table, as shown in Figure 4-23.

As mentioned, there are dozens of ways that tables can be poorly formed. Database practitioners classify tables into various **normal forms**, which are classifications of tables according to the kinds of problems they have. Transforming a table into a normal form to remove duplicated data and other problems is called *normalizing* the table.[3] Thus, when you hear a database designer say, "Those tables are not normalized," she does not mean that the tables have irregular, not-normal data. Instead, she means that the tables have a format that could cause data integrity problems.

FIGURE 4-23
Two Normalized Tables

Employee

Name	HireDate	Email	DeptNo
Jones	Feb 1, 2010	Jones@ourcompany.com	100
Smith	Dec 3, 2012	Smith@ourcompany.com	200
Chau	March 7, 2013	Chau@ourcompany.com	100
Greene	July 17, 2011	Greene@ourcompany.com	100

Department

DeptNo	DeptName
100	Accounting
200	Marketing
300	Information Systems

[3] See David Kroenke and David Auer, *Database Processing*, 13th ed. (Upper Saddle River, NJ: Pearson Education, 2014) for more information.

Summary of Normalization

As a future user of databases, you do not need to know the details of normalization. Instead, understand the general principle that every normalized (well-formed) table has one and only one theme. Further, tables that are not normalized are subject to data integrity problems.

Be aware, too, that normalization is just one criterion for evaluating database designs. Because normalized designs can be slower to process, database designers sometimes choose to accept non-normalized tables. The best design depends on the users' processing requirements.

Representing Relationships

Figure 4-24 shows the steps involved in transforming a data model into a relational database design. First, the database designer creates a table for each entity. The identifier of the entity becomes the key of the table. Each attribute of the entity becomes a column of the table. Next, the resulting tables are normalized so that each table has a single theme. Once that has been done, the next step is to represent relationships among those tables.

For example, consider the E-R diagram in Figure 4-25(a). The *Adviser* entity has a 1:N relationship to the *Student* entity. To create the database design, we construct a table for *Adviser* and a second table for *Student*, as shown in Figure 4-25(b). The key of the *Adviser* table is *AdviserName*, and the key of the *Student* table is *StudentNumber*. Further, the *EmailAddress* attribute of the *Adviser* entity becomes the *EmailAddress* column of the *Adviser* table, and the *StudentName* and *MidTerm* attributes of the *Student* entity become the *StudentName* and *MidTerm* columns of the *Student* table.

The next task is to represent relationships. Because we are using the relational model, we know that we must add a foreign key to one of the two tables. The possibilities are: (1) place the foreign key *StudentNumber* in the *Adviser* table or (2) place the foreign key *AdviserName* in the *Student* table.

The correct choice is to place *AdviserName* in the *Student* table, as shown in Figure 4-25(c). To determine a student's adviser, we just look into the *AdviserName* column of that student's row. To determine the adviser's students, we search the *AdviserName* column in the *Student* table to determine which rows have that adviser's name. If a student changes advisers, we simply change the value in the *AdviserName* column. Changing *Jackson* to *Jones* in the first row, for example, will assign student 100 to Professor Jones.

For this data model, placing *StudentNumber* in *Adviser* would be incorrect. If we were to do that, we could assign only one student to an adviser. There is no place to assign a second student.

This strategy for placing foreign keys will not work for all relationships, however. Consider the data model in Figure 4-26(a); here, advisers and students have a many-to-many relationship. An adviser may have many students, and a student may have multiple advisers (for multiple majors).

The foreign key strategy we used for the 1:N data model will not work here. To see why, examine Figure 4-26(b). If student 100 has more than one adviser, there is no place to record second or subsequent advisers.

To represent an N:M relationship, we need to create a third table, as shown in Figure 4-26(c). The third table has two columns, *AdviserName* and *StudentNumber*. Each row of the table means that the given adviser advises the student with the given number.

What Is the User's Role in the Development of Databases?

As stated, a database is a model of how the users view their business world. This means that the users are the final judges as to what data the database should contain and how the records in that database should be related to one another.

> - Represent each entity with a table
>   - Entity identifier becomes table key
>   - Entity attributes become table columns
> - Normalize tables as necessary
> - Represent relationships
>   - Use foreign keys
>   - Add additional tables for N:M relationships

FIGURE 4-24

Summary of Database Design Process

FIGURE 4-25

Representing a 1:N Relationship

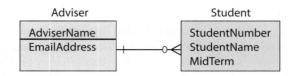

(a) 1:N Relationship Between Adviser and Student Entities

Adviser Table—Key is AdviserName

AdviserName	EmailAddress
Jones	Jones@myuniv.edu
Choi	Choi@myuniv.edu
Jackson	Jackson@myuniv.edu

Student Table—Key is StudentNumber

StudentNumber	StudentName	MidTerm
100	Lisa	90
200	Jennie	85
300	Jason	82
400	Terry	95

(b) Creating a Table for Each Entity

Adviser Table—Key is AdviserName

AdviserName	EmailAddress
Jones	Jones@myuniv.edu
Choi	Choi@myuniv.edu
Jackson	Jackson@myuniv.edu

Student—Key is StudentNumber

StudentNumber	StudentName	MidTerm	AdviserName
100	Lisa	90	Jackson
200	Jennie	85	Jackson
300	Jason	82	Choi
400	Terry	95	Jackson

Foreign Key Column Represents Relationship

(c) Using the *AdviserName* Foreign Key to Represent the 1:N Relationship

The easiest time to change the database structure is during the data modeling stage. Changing a relationship from one-to-many to many-to-many in a data model is simply a matter of changing the 1:N notation to N:M. However, once the database has been constructed, loaded with data, and application forms, reports, queries, and application programs have been created, changing a one-to-many relationship to many-to-many means weeks of work.

You can glean some idea of why this might be true by contrasting Figure 4-25(c) with Figure 4-26(c). Suppose that instead of having just a few rows, each table has thousands of rows; in that case, transforming the database from one format to the other involves considerable work. Even worse, however, is that someone must change application components as well. For example, if students have at most one adviser, then a single text box can be used to enter *AdviserName*. If students can have multiple advisers, then a multiple-row table will need to be used to enter *AdviserName*, and a program will need to be written to store the values of *AdviserName* into the *Adviser_Student_Intersection* table. There are dozens of other consequences, consequences that will translate into wasted labor and wasted expense.

FIGURE 4-26

Representing an N:M Relationship

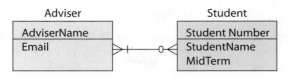

(a) N:M Relationship Between Adviser and Student

Adviser—Key is AdviserName

AdviserName	Email
Jones	Jones@myuniv.edu
Choi	Choi@myuniv.edu
Jackson	Jackson@myuniv.edu

No room to place second or third AdviserName

Student—Key is StudentNumber

StudentNumber	StudentName	MidTerm	AdviserName
100	Lisa	90	Jackson
200	Jennie	85	Jackson
300	Jason	82	Choi
400	Terry	95	Jackson

(b) Incorrect Representation of N:M Relationship

Adviser—Key is AdviserName

AdviserName	Email
Jones	Jones@myuniv.edu
Choi	Choi@myuniv.edu
Jackson	Jackson@myuniv.edu

Student—Key is StudentNumber

StudentNumber	StudentName	MidTerm
100	Lisa	90
200	Jennie	85
300	Jason	82
400	Terry	95

Adviser_Student_Intersection

AdviserName	StudentNumber
Jackson	100
Jackson	200
Choi	300
Jackson	400
Choi	100
Jones	100

Student 100 has three advisers.

(c) Adviser_Student_Intersection Table Represents the N:M Relationship

Thus, *user review of the data model is crucial.* When a database is developed for your use, you must carefully review the data model. If you do not understand any aspect of it, you should ask for clarification until you do. *Entities must contain all of the data you and your employees need to do your jobs, and relationships must accurately reflect your view of the business.* If the data model is wrong, the database will be designed incorrectly, and the applications will be difficult to use, if not worthless. Do not proceed unless the data model is accurate.

As a corollary, when asked to review a data model, take that review seriously. Devote the time necessary to perform a thorough review. Any mistakes you miss will come back to haunt you, and by then the cost of correction may be very high with regard to both time and expense. This brief introduction to data modeling shows why databases can be more difficult to develop than spreadsheets.

Q6. Why Are NoSQL and Big Data Important?

The relational databases that you have learned about in this chapter are the workhorse of information systems both today and for the foreseeable future. However, in the past 5 years something unusual occurred that may portend a major change—or at least a major new dimension to database processing.

Amazon.com determined that relational database technology wouldn't meet its processing needs, and it developed a nonrelational data store called **Dynamo**.[4] Meanwhile, for many of the same reasons, Google developed a nonrelational data store called **Bigtable**.[5] Facebook took concepts from both of these systems and developed a third nonrelational data store called **Cassandra**.[6] In 2008, Facebook turned Cassandra over to the open source community, and now Apache has dubbed it a top-level project (TLP), which is the height of respectability among open source projects.

Such nonrelational DBMS have come to be called **NoSQL DBMS.** This term refers to software systems that support very high transaction rates processing relatively simple, nonrelational data structures replicated on many servers in the cloud. NoSQL is not the best term; *NotRelational DBMS* would have been better, but the die has been cast. You can learn more about the rationale for NoSQL products and some of their intriguing features in Case Study 4, page 121.

Will NoSQL Replace Relational DBMS Products?

Because of the success of these leading companies, is it likely that most companies will follow their examples and convert their existing relational databases to NoSQL databases? Probably not. Such conversion would be enormously expensive and disruptive and, in cases where the relational database meets the organization's needs, would also be unnecessary.

Also, currrent NoSQL DBMS products are very technical and beyond the skill of most business professionals, and even beyond that of some IS professionals. Switching entirely to NoSQL databases would require organizations to make a substantial investment in new employees and in training existing employees to use them. Only those organizations whose data requirements cannot be met in any other way (like Google and Facebook) are likely to justify those expenses.

However, the rise of NoSQL does mean that when selecting a DBMS for organizational IS, there are viable choices other than relational products. For requirements that fit NoSQL's strengths, such products will likely be used for new projects; and for existing systems with performance problems, some relational database conversions may also occur.

How Does Big Data Differ from Relational Data?

Use of NoSQL products led to the definition of a new type of data store. **Big Data** is used to describe data collections that differ from relational databases by their huge *volume*, rapid *velocity*, and great *variety*. Considering volume, Big Data refers to data sets that are at least a petabyte in size, and usually larger. A data set containing all Google searches in the United States on a given day is Big Data in size.

Additionally, Big Data has high velocity, meaning that it is generated rapidly, much more so than relational databases. (If you know physics, you know that *speed* would be a more accurate term, but speed doesn't start with a *v*, and the *vvv* description has become a common way to describe Big Data.) The Google search data for a given day is generated, in, well, just a day. In the past, months or years would have been required to generate so much data.

Finally, Big Data is varied. Like relational databases, Big Data may have structured data, but it also may have nonrelational free-form text, dozens of different formats of Web server and database log files, streams of data about user responses to page content, and possibly graphics, audio, and video files. Such variety is difficult to accommodate in a relational database.

[4] Werner Vogel, "Amazon's Dynamo," All Things Distributed blog, last modified October 2, 2007, www.allthingsdistributed.com/2007/10/amazons_dynamo.html.
[5] Fay Chang, Jeffrey Dean, Sanjay Ghemawat, Wilson C. Hsieh, Deborah A. Wallach, Mike Burrows, Tushar Chandra, Andrew Fikes, and Robert E. Gruber, "Bigtable: A Distributed Storage System for Structured Data," OSDI 2006, Seventh Symposium on Operating System Design and Implementation, Seattle, WA, last modified November 2006, http://labs.google.com/papers/bigtable.html.
[6] Jonathan Ellis, "Cassandra: Open Source Bigtable + Dynamo," accessed June 2011, www.slideshare.net/jbellis/cassandra-open-source-bigtable-dynamo.

In the years ahead, Big Data collections will continue to grow. Considerable information can be gleaned from these growing Big Data stores, but organizations are challenged to find important patterns and relationships in such huge amounts of data. NoSQL DBMS are used for this purpose, along with another open source product named Hadoop. We will discuss it further in Chapter 11.

However, due to the complex user interfaces of NoSQL DBMS and Hadoop, only trained computer scientists can use them. Unlike Access, which a serious business professional can learn to use to query and report data on her own, it is impossible for business professionals to query and report from NoSQL DBMS products. Instead, business users need to employ other products, such as Tableau, as front-ends that integrate in the background with NoSQL DBMS products.

In the future, it is quite likely that NoSQL DBMS will add features and functions that allow business professionals to process Big Data. Is that an important opportunity? Building that product may not be too rewarding if market dynamics force software to be given away. But being on the leading edge of business professionals who learn how to use such products to find important patterns and relationships in data could give you a highly compensated skill and competitive advantage. Keep watching; there may be an important opportunity for you around the corner!

Q7. How Can the Intramural League Improve Its Database?

We conclude this chapter by returning to the intramural league and its database. As you saw in the opening vignette, the league has at least two problems: a process problem that caused the missing equipment report not to have been produced on time and a database problem that allocates equipment to teams but not to coaches, the people who are responsible for returning the equipment. We will address process problems starting in the next chapter. For now, let's consider the database problem.

Figure 4-27 shows the tables in the league database. Each rectangle represents a table, and the items in the rectangles are fields in the table. The key symbol means that ID is the primary key of each table. In fact, the design of these tables uses what are called **surrogate keys**, which are unique identifiers assigned by the DBMS. Every time a new row is created, the DBMS, here Microsoft Access, creates a unique identifier for that row. That identifier has no meaning to the users, but it is guaranteed to be unique. The primary key of all three tables is a surrogate key named *ID*. (These are three different fields; they are just named the same thing in their respective tables.)

There are several ways of solving the league's problem. In the following explanation, we will proceed in a way that avoids messy pitfalls and results in an acceptable result. It will also

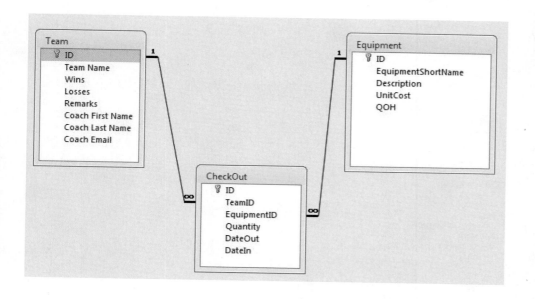

FIGURE 4-27

Tables in the League Database

give you a taste of what database designers do. If you take a database class, you will approach problems like this in a systematic way, based on sound theory. Here we will just work our way through to a solution.

League Database, Revision 1

The problem is that equipment is checked out to teams and teams can have different coaches in different years. So, one way to solve that problem is to add a new field to the *Team* table that indicates the year of the data. Figure 4-28 shows the structure of a new table with a new field called *Season*. It will have values like "2010–2011."

Now, consider the implications of that change. When we add *Season*, we are actually changing the theme of the table. It is no longer about a team; it is about a team's situation (i.e., performance, coach) in a given season. Consequently, we really should change the name of the table from *Team* to something like *Team_Season*. Note this was done in Figure 4-28.

Figure 4-29 shows a report that reflects this change. It makes sense; we are now recording the win/loss record for a particular year as well as the coach for that year. The *Remarks* also pertain to a given team in a given season. By making this change, we have made the table's structure less ambiguous.

However, we've lost something. Where can we store an item of data that belongs to a team but not to a particular season? If the league wants to record, say, the first season a team played, where would that be stored? If we store *FirstSeasonPlayed* in this table, we will create a data integrity problem (you will have a chance to verify this in Using Your Knowledge Exercise 4-3 on page 117). In fact, we have no place to store anything else about the team that does not change from year to year, such as jersey color (if that is fixed).

If this is a problem for the league, it will need to define a new table, called *Team*, and store the data that does not change from year to year in that new table. It would then need to define a new relationship from *Team* to *Team_Season*. (See Using Your Knowledge Exercise 4-4 on page 117.) For now, let's assume that the league has no need for such overall team data and ignore this problem.

However, by solving the problem in this way, we have created a new problem. Notice in the report in Figure 4-29 that by storing a row for each team, each season, we have duplicated the email addresses for those who have coached more than once. For the data shown, if, for

FIGURE 4-28

League Database, Revision1, Team_Season Table

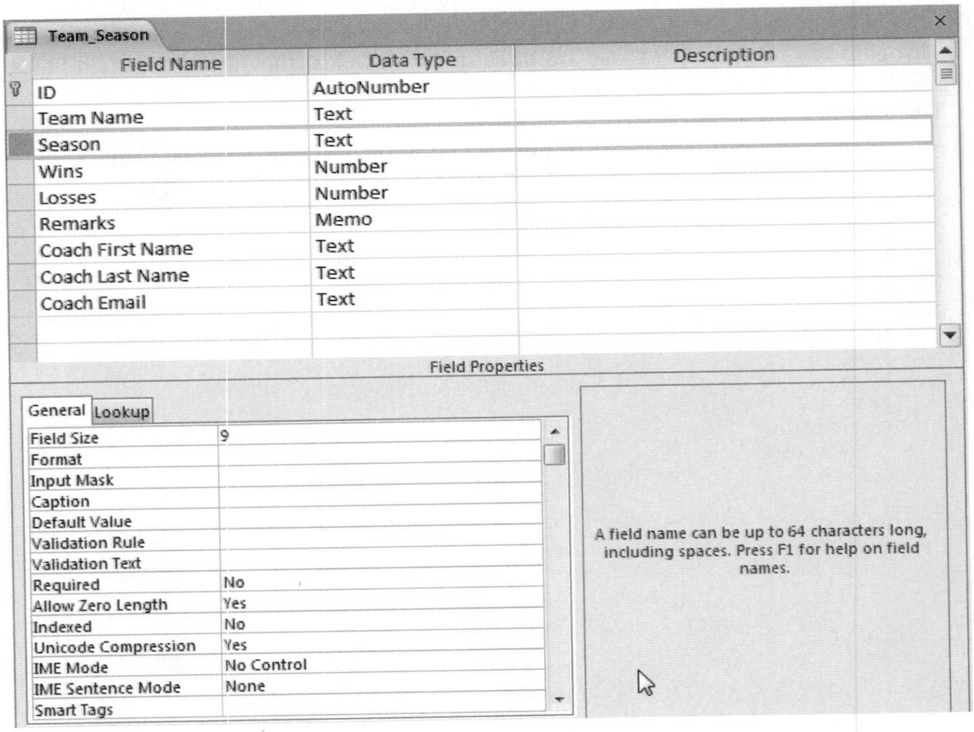

FIGURE 4-29

Report for League DB, Revision 1

Team History Report, Revision 1							
Team Name	Season	Wins	Losses Remarks		Coach First Name	Coach Last Name	Coach Email
Helicopters	2009-2010	7	0	Won the tournament first year.	Fred	Dillingham	FD@ourschool.edu
Helicopters	2010-2011	7	0	Won the tournament last year.	Fred	Dillingham	FD@ourschool.edu
Helicopters	2011-2012	7	0	Won the tournament last year, again.	Carter	Jackson	CJ@ourschool.edu
Huskies	2009-2010	1	5	Nearly won tournament.	Sark	Justin	SJ@ourschool.edu
Huskies	2010-2011	1	5	Lost several games by forefeit.	Sark	Justin	SJ@ourschool.edu
Huskies	2011-2012	1	5	Improving ...	Sark	Justin	SJ@ourschool.edu
Wolverines	2011-2012	5	2	Off to good start.	Daniel	Smith	DS@SmithFamily.com

example, Sark Justin changes his email, three rows will need to be changed. Hence, this new table is vulnerable to data integrity problems; it is not normalized. We need to fix it in the next revision.

League Database, Revision 2

Consider Figure 4-30, which shows an E-R model of the league database after the revision just described. The changed entity is shown in brown, and the new attribute, *Season,* is shown in blue. Neither the *Checkout* nor *Equipment* entities have been changed, so their attributes are omitted for simplicity.

ADDING THE COACH ENTITY Examining the model in Figure 4-30, we can see that *Team_Season* has two themes; one is about the team in a given season, and the second is about a coach and his or her email. Using our normalization criterion, we know that each entity should have a single theme. So, we decide to move the *Coach* attributes from *Team_Season* into a new entity called *Coach*, as shown in Figure 4-31.

OK so far, but what is the relationship between *Coach* and *Team*? If we look at the data in Figure 4-29, it appears that a given coach can coach many teams, in the same or different seasons (note Fred Dillingham, the coach who took off with the gear). It also appears that a team has at most one coach. Thus, the relationship from *Coach* to *Team_Season* seems to be 1:N.

However, it is dangerous to make such conclusions from sample data. We might just have an odd set of data. An experienced database design team knows to interview users (which could be you) to find out. In this case, let's assume that the 1:N relationship is correct.

The decisions yield the E-R diagram in Figure 4-32. Before we continue, notice we've added *Amount Due* to the *Coach* entity. The idea behind this addition is that at the end of the sport's season, an application program will compute the amount due based on the current

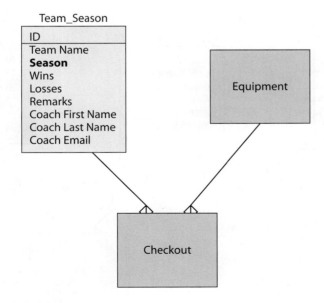

FIGURE 4-30

League E-R Diagram, Revision 1

FIGURE 4-31

League E-R Diagram with Coach Entity

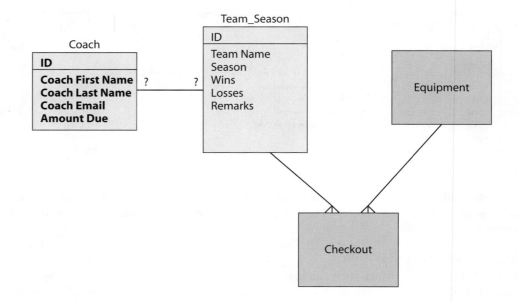

cost of equipment that has not been returned. As equipment is returned, this amount will be decremented appropriately.

REPRESENTING THE RELATIONSHIP IN THE DATABASE DESIGN As described in Q5, we represent a 1:N relationship by adding the key of the parent (the entity on the 1 side) to the child (the entity on the many side). Here we need to add the key of *Coach* to *Team_Season*. Figure 4-33 shows the result; *CoachID* in *Team_Season* is a foreign key that references *ID* in *Coach*.

With this design, every table has a single theme and is normalized. This design is therefore not subject to data integrity problems. Note, however, that it will be necessary to join rows in the table together to produce reports. DBMS products are programmed to do that efficiently, however. The report in Figure 4-34 shows equipment that has been checked out by coaches but has not yet been returned. This report was created by joining data in all four of the tables in Figure 4-33 together.

With these two changes, the intramural league can now allocate equipment checkouts to specific coaches. These changes, in and of themselves, will not solve the league's problem, but it will at least allow the league to know definitively who checked out what equipment. The complete solution to the problem requires a change in process as well.

FIGURE 4-32

League E-R Diagram, Revision 2

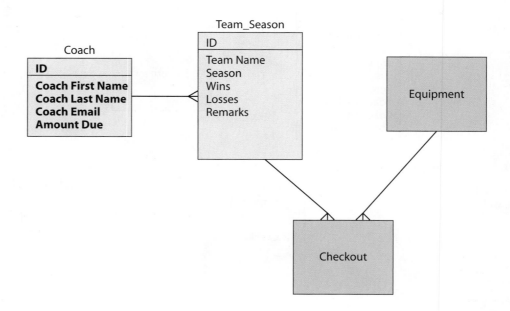

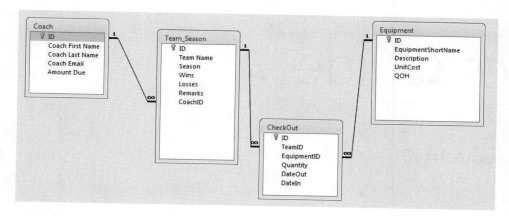

FIGURE 4-33

League Database Design, Revision 2

Coach Equipment Report -- Items Checked Out as of 10/17/2012

Coach First Name	Coach Last Name	Coach Email	Team Name	Season	DateOut	Equipment	Quantity
Fred	Dillingham	FD@ourschool.edu					
			Helicopters	2009-2010			
					11/6/2010	Soccer Jerseys	12
					11/6/2010	Soccer Balls	3
Sark	Justin	SJ@ourschool.edu					
			Huskies	2009-2010			
					10/4/2009	Soccer Balls	3
			Huskies	2011-2012			
					9/6/2012	Soccer Balls	2
					9/6/2012	Soccer Jerseys	12
					9/6/2012	Soccer Balls	1
Daniel	Smith	DS@SmithFamily.com					
			Wolverines	2011-2012			
					9/6/2012	Soccer Balls	3
					9/6/2012	Soccer Jerseys	14
					9/6/2012	Soccer Balls	2
Carter	Jackson	CJ@ourschool.edu					
			Helicopters	2011-2012			
					9/4/2012	Soccer Balls	2
					9/4/2012	Soccer Jerseys	17
					9/4/2012	Soccer Balls	3

FIGURE 4-34

Report Showing Equipment Still Checked Out to Coaches

Querying Inequality?

MaryAnn Baker works as a data analyst in human relations at a large, multinational corporation. As part of its compensation program, her company defines job categories and assigns salary ranges to each category. For example, the category M1 is used for first-line managers and is assigned the salary range of $75,000 to $95,000. Every job description is assigned to one of these categories, depending on the knowledge and skills required to do that job. Thus, the job titles Manager of Customer Support, Manager of Technical Writing, and Manager of Product Quality Assurance are all judged to involve about the same level of expertise and all are assigned to category M1.

One of MaryAnn's tasks is to analyze company salary data and determine how well actual salaries conform to established ranges. When discrepancies are noted, human relations managers meet to determine whether the discrepancy indicates a need to:

- Adjust the category's salary range;
- Move the job title to a different category;
- Define a new category; or
- Train the manager of the employee with the discrepancy on the use of salary ranges in setting employee compensation.

MaryAnn is an expert in creating database queries. Initially she used Microsoft Access to produce reports, but much of the salary data she needs resides in the organization's Oracle database. At first she would ask the IS Department to extract certain data and move it into Access, but over time she learned that it was faster to ask IS to move all employee data from the operational Oracle database into another Oracle database created just for HR data analysis. Although Oracle provides a graphical query interface like that in Access, she found it easier to compose complex queries directly in SQL, so she learned it and within a few months was a SQL expert.

"I never thought I'd be doing this," she said. "But it turns out to be quite fun, like solving a puzzle, and apparently I'm good at it."

One day, after a break, MaryAnn signed into her computer and happened to glance at the results of a query that she'd left running while she was gone. "That's odd," she thought, "all the people with Hispanic surnames have lower salaries than the others." She wasn't looking for that pattern; it just happened to jump out at her as she glanced at the screen.

As she examined the data, she began to wonder if she was seeing a coincidence or if there was a discriminatory pattern within the organization. Unfortunately for MaryAnn's purposes, the organization did not track employee race in its database, so she had no easy way of identifying employees of Hispanic heritage other than reading through the list of surnames. But, as a skilled problem solver, that didn't stop MaryAnn. She realized that many employees having Hispanic origins were born in certain cities in Texas, New Mexico, Arizona, and California. Of course, this wasn't true for all employees; many non-Hispanic employees were born in those cities, too, and many Hispanic employees were born in other cities. This data was still useful, however, because MaryAnn's sample queries revealed that the proportion of employees with Hispanic surnames who were also born in those cities was very high. "OK," she thought, "I'll use those cities as a rough surrogate."

Using birth city as a query criterion, MaryAnn created queries that determined employees who were born in the selected cities earned, on average, 23 percent less than those who were not. "Well, that could be because they work in lower-pay-grade jobs." After giving it a bit of thought, MaryAnn realized that she needed to examine wages and salaries within job categories. "Where," she wondered, "do people born in those cities fall in the ranges of their job categories?" So, she constructed an SQL query to determine where within a job category the compensation for people born in the selected cities fell. "Wow!" she said to herself, "almost 80 percent of the employees born in those cities fall into the bottom half of their salary range."

MaryAnn scheduled an appointment with her manager for the next day.

DISCUSSION QUESTIONS

When answering the following questions, suppose that you are MaryAnn:

1. Given these query results, do you have an ethical responsibility to do something? Consider both the categorical imperative (page 20) and the utilitarian (page 40) perspectives.

2. Given these query results, do you have a personal or social responsibility to do something?

3. What is your response if your manager says, "You don't know anything; it could be that starting salaries are lower in those cities. Forget about it."

4. What is your response if your manager says: "Don't be a troublemaker; pushing this issue will hurt your career."

5. What is your response if your manager says: "Right. We already know that. Get back to the tasks that I've assigned you."

6. Suppose your manager gives you funding to follow up with a more accurate analysis and, indeed, there is a pattern of underpayment to people with Hispanic surnames. What should the organization do? For each choice below, indicate likely outcomes:
   a. Correct the imbalances immediately
   b. Gradually correct the imbalances at future pay raises
   c. Do nothing about the imbalances, but train managers not to discriminate in the future
   d. Do nothing

7. Suppose you hire a part-time person to help with the more accurate analysis, and that person is so outraged at the outcome that he quits and notifies newspapers in all the affected cities of the organization's discrimination.
   a. How should the organization respond?
   b. How should you respond?

8. Consider the adage, "Never ask a question for which you do not want the answer."
   a. Is following that adage ethical? Consider both the categorical imperative and utilitarian perspectives.
   b. Is following that adage socially responsible?
   c. How does that adage relate to you, as MaryAnn?
   d. How does that adage relate to you, as a future business professional?
   e. With regard to employee compensation, how does that adage relate to organizations?

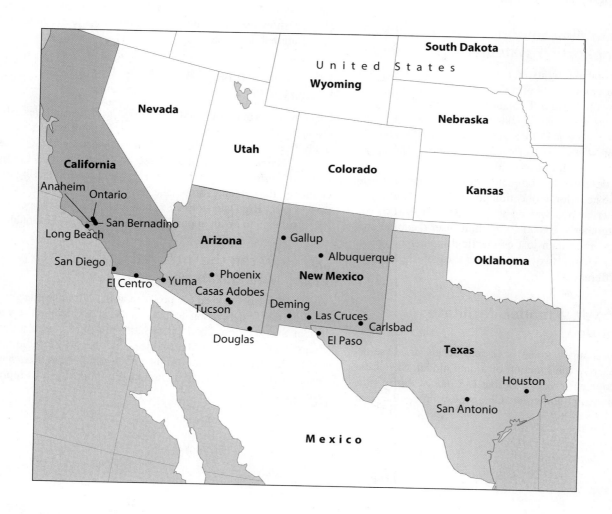

Active Review

Use this Active Review to verify that you understand the material in the chapter. You can read the entire chapter and then perform the tasks in this review, or you can read the text material for just one question and perform the tasks in this review for that question before moving on to the next one.

Q1. What is the purpose of a database?

State the purpose of a database. Explain the circumstances in which a database is preferred to a spreadsheet. Describe the key difference between Figures 4-1 and 4-2.

Q2. What are the contents of a database?

Define the term *database*. Explain the hierarchy of data and name three elements of a database. Define *metadata*. Using the example of *Student* and *Office_Visit* tables, show how relationships among rows are represented in a database. Define the terms *key, foreign key*, and *relational database*.

Q3. What are the components of a database application system?

Explain why a database, by itself, is not very useful to business users. Name the components of a database application system and sketch their relationship. Explain the acronym DBMS and name its functions. List five popular DBMS products. Explain the difference between a DBMS and a database. Summarize the functions of a DBMS. Define *SQL*. Describe the major functions of database administration.

Name and describe the components of a database application. Explain the need for application programs. For multi-user processing, describe one way in which one user's work can interfere with another's. Explain why multi-user database processing involves more than just connecting another computer to the network. Define two broad categories of DBMS and explain their differences.

Q4. How do data models facilitate database design?

Explain why user involvement is critical during database development. Describe the function of a data model. Sketch the database development process. Define *E-R model, entity, relationship, attribute*, and *identifier*. Give an example, other than

one in this text, of an E-R diagram. Define *maximum cardinality* and *minimum cardinality*. Give an example of three maximum cardinalities and two minimum cardinalities. Explain the notation in Figures 4-18 and 4-19.

Describe the users' role in database development. Explain why it is easier and cheaper to change a data model than to change an existing database. Use the examples of Figures 4-25(c) and 4-26(c) in your answer. Describe two criteria for judging a data model. Explain why it is important to devote time to understanding a data model.

Q5. How is a data model transformed into a database design?

Name the three components of a database design. Define *normalization* and explain why it is important. Define *data integrity problem* and describe its consequences. Give an example of a table from this chapter with data integrity problems and show how it can be normalized into two or more tables that do not have such problems. Describe two steps in transforming a data model into a database design. Using an example not in this chapter, show how 1:N and N:M relationships are represented in a relational database.

Q6. Why are NoSQL and Big Data important?

Explain the origins of NoSQL DBMS products and describe the applications for which they're used. Explain why it is unlikely that relational databases will be replaced by NoSQL databases. Name and explain the three key characteristics of Big Data and differentiate them from relational data. Describe the challenge that organizations face in attempting to glean information from Big Data stores. Explain what needs to happen for that challenge to be an opportunity for business professionals.

Q7. How can the intramural league improve its database?

What two factors caused the problem at the intramural league? Explain the first revision to the database. Explain what was lost in this revision. Explain why the revision caused a data integrity problem. Describe the need for the *Coach* table and justify the decision to model the relationship from *Coach* to *Team_Season* as 1:N. Explain how that relationship was represented in the database.

Key Terms and Concepts

Access 94
Attributes 102
Big Data 110
Bigtable 110
Byte 91
Cassandra 110
Columns 91
Crow's feet 103
Crow's-foot diagram 104
Data integrity problem 105
Data model 101
Database 91
Database administration (DBA) 96
Database application 96
Database application system 94
Database management system (DBMS) 94
DB2 94
Dynamo 110
Elastic 122
Enterprise DBMS 100
Entity 102
Entity-relationship (E-R) data model 102
Entity-relationship (E-R) diagrams 103
Fields 91
File 91
Foreign key 93
Form 97
Identifier 102
Key 92
Lost update problem 99
Many-to-many (N:M) relationships 104
Maximum cardinality 104
Metadata 94
Minimum cardinality 104
MySQL 95
Normal forms 106
Normalization 105
NoSQL DBMS 110
Object-relational database 93
One-to-many (1:N) relationships 103
Oracle Database 95
Personal DBMS 101
Primary key 92
Query 97
Records 91
Relation 93
Relational databases 93
Relationships 103
Report 97
Rows 91
SQL Server 94
Structured Query Language (SQL) 95
Surrogate key 111
Table 91

Using Your Knowledge

4-1. Draw an entity-relationship diagram that shows the relationships among a database, database applications, and users.

4-2. Consider the relationship between *Adviser* and *Student* in Figure 4-20. Explain what it means if the maximum cardinality of this relationship is:
a. N:1
b. 1:1
c. 5:1
d. 1:5

4-3. Suppose the intramural league wants to keep track of the first season that a team played in the league. Make that addition to *Team_Season* for the data shown in Figure 4-29. Explain why the table now has duplicated data. Explain potential data integrity problems from that data.

4-4. To solve the problem in Exercise 4-3, create a new entity named *Team.* Extend the E-R diagram in Figure 4-32 to include the *Team* entity. State the cardinality of the relationship between *Team* and *Team_Season.* Show how the database structure in Figure 4-33 will need to be changed to accommodate this new table.

4-5. Identify possible entities in the data entry form in Figure 4-35. What attributes are shown for each? What do you think are the identifiers?

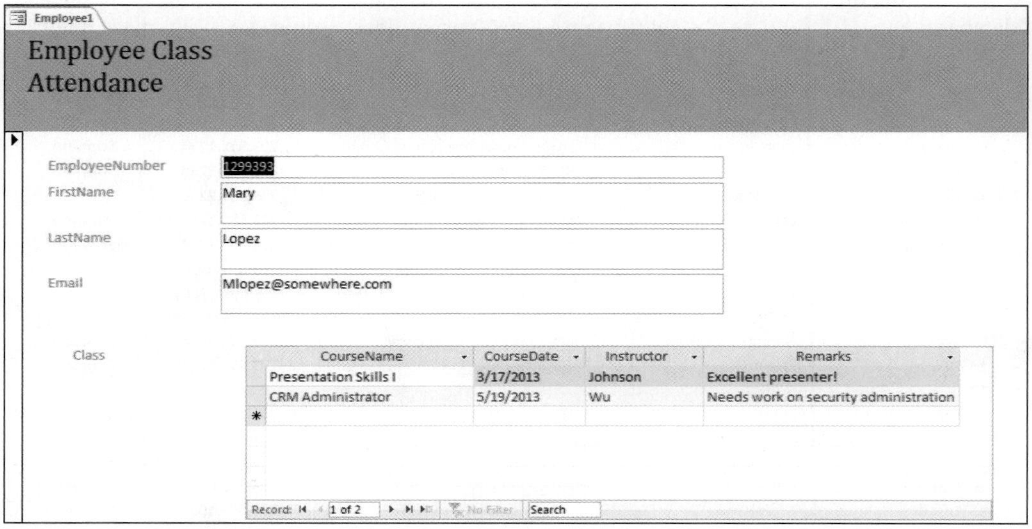

FIGURE 4-35
Sample Data Entry Form

FIGURE 4-36

Partial E-R Diagram for Sales Order

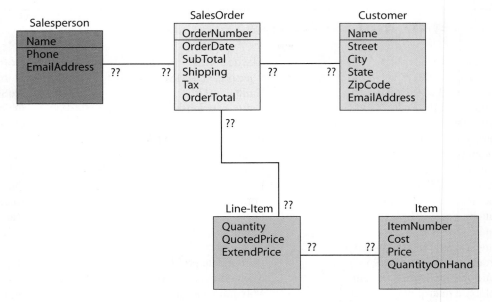

4-6. Using your answer to Exercise 5, draw an E-R diagram for the data entry form in Figure 4-35. Specify cardinalities. State your assumptions.

4-7. The partial E-R diagram in Figure 4-36 is for a sales order. Assume there is only one *Salesperson* per *SalesOrder*.

a. Specify the maximum cardinalities for each relationship. State your assumptions, if necessary.

b. Specify the minimum cardinalities for each relationship. State your assumptions, if necessary.

4-8. Consider the report in Figure 4-12 in the context of information as a *difference that makes a difference*. What differences does the structure of this report show? Describe five ways this report could be changed that would make it easier for humans to conceive information. Name the criteria you used in suggesting these five changes.

Collaboration Exercise 4

Collaborate with a group of fellow students to answer the following questions. For this exercise, do not meet face to face. Your task will be easier if you coordinate your work with SharePoint, Office 365, Google Docs with Google+, or equivalent collaboration tools. (See Chapter 9 for a discussion of collaboration tools and processes.) Your answers should reflect the thinking of the entire group, not just that of one or two individuals.

The purpose of this exercise is to identify the limitations of spreadsheets and the advantages of databases.

Figure 4-37 shows a spreadsheet that is used to track the assignment of sheet music to a choir—it could be a church choir or school or community choir. The type of choir does not matter because the problem is universal. Sheet music is expensive, choir members need to be able to take sheet music away for practice at home, and not all of the music gets back to the inventory. (Sheet music can be purchased or rented, but either way lost music is an expense.

Look closely at this data and you will see some data integrity problems—or at least some possible data integrity

FIGURE 4-37

Sheet Music Spreadsheet

	A	B	C	D	E
1	Last Name	First Name	Email	Phone	Part
2	Ashley	Jane	JA@somewhere.com	703.555.1234	Soprano
3	Davidson	Kaye	KD@somewhere.com	703.555.2236	Soprano
4	Ching	Kam Hoong	KHC@overhere.com	703.555.2236	Soprano
5	Menstell	Lori Lee	LLM@somewhere.com	703.555.1237	Soprano
6	Corning	Sandra	SC2@overhere.com	703.555.1234	Soprano
7		B-minor mass	J.S. Bach	Soprano Copy 7	
8		Requiem	Mozart	Soprano Copy 17	
9		9th Symphony Chorus	Beethoven	Soprano Copy 9	
10	Wei	Guang	GW1@somewhere.com	703.555.9936	Soprano
11	Dixon	Eleanor	ED@thisplace.com	703.555.12379	Soprano
12		B-minor mass	J.S. Bach	Soprano Copy 11	
13	Duong	Linda	LD2@overhere.com	703.555.8736	Soprano
14		B-minor mass	J.S. Bach	Soprano Copy 7	
15		Requiem	J.S. Bach	Soprano Copy 19	
16	Lunden	Haley	HL@somewhere.com	703.555.0836	Soprano
17	Utran	Diem Thi	DTU@somewhere.com	703.555.1089	Soprano

problems. For one, do Sandra Corning and Linda Duong really have the same copy of music checked out? Second, did Mozart and J. S. Bach both write a Requiem, or in row 15 should J. S. Bach actually be Mozart? Also, there is a problem with Eleanor Dixon's phone number; several phone numbers are the same as well, which seems suspicious.

Additionally, this spreadsheet is confusing and hard to use. The column labeled *First Name* includes both people names and the names of choruses. *Email* has both email addresses and composer names, and *Phone* has both phone numbers and copy identifiers. Furthermore, to record a checkout of music the user must first add a new row and then reenter the name of the work, the composer's name, and the copy to be checked out. Finally,

consider what happens when the user wants to find all copies of a particular work: The user will have to examine the rows in each of four spreadsheets for the four voice parts.

In fact, a spreadsheet is ill-suited for this application. A database would be a far better tool, and situations like this are obvious candidates for innovation.

1. Analyze the spreadsheet shown in Figure 4-37 and list all of the problems that occur when trying to track the assignment of sheet music using this spreadsheet.
2. Figure 4-38(a) shows a two-entity data model for the sheet-music-tracking problem.
   a. Select identifiers for the *ChoirMember* and *Work* entities. Justify your selection.

FIGURE 4-38

Three Data Model Alternatives

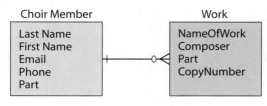

(a) Data Model Alternative 1

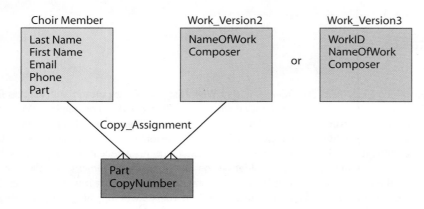

(b) Data Model Alternative 2

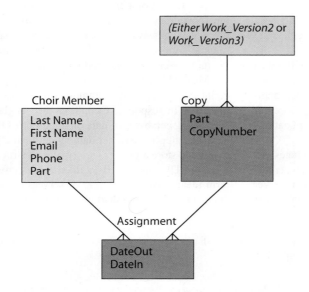

(c) Data Model Alternative 3

b. This design does not eliminate the potential for data integrity problems that occur in the spreadsheet. Explain why not.

c. Design a database for this data model. Specify key and foreign key columns.

3. Figure 4-38(b) shows a second alternative data model for the sheet-music-tracking problem. This alternative shows two variations on the *Work* entity. In the second variation, an attribute named *WorkID* has been added to *Work_Version3*. This attribute is a unique identifier for the work; the DBMS will assign a unique value to *WorkID* when a new row is added to the *Work* table.

a. Select identifiers for *ChoirMember, Work_Version2, Work_Version3,* and *Copy_Assignment*. Justify your selection.

b. Does this design eliminate the potential for data integrity problems that occur in the spreadsheet? Why or why not?

c. Design a database for the data model that uses *Work_Version2*. Specify key and foreign key columns.

d. Design a database for the data model that uses *Work_Version3*. Specify key and foreign key columns.

e. Is the design with *Work_Version2* better than the design for *Work_Version3*? Why or why not?

4. Figure 4-38(c) shows a third alternative data model for the sheet-music-tracking problem. In this data model, use either *Work_Version2* or *Work_Version3*, whichever you think is better.

a. Select identifiers for each entity in your data model. Justify your selection.

b. Summarize the differences between this data model and that in Figure 4-38(b). Which data model is better? Why?

c. Design a database for this data model. Specify key and foreign key columns.

5. Which of the three data models is the best? Justify your answer.

CASE STUDY 4

Fail Away with Dynamo, Bigtable, and Cassandra

During its holiday season, Amazon.com receives nearly 200 order items per second! To support such an enormous workload, it processes customer transactions on tens of thousands of servers. Unfortunately, with that many computers, failure is inevitable. Even if the probability of any one server failing is .0001, the likelihood that not one of them fails is .9999 raised to the 10,000 power, which is about .37. Thus, for these assumptions, the likelihood of at least one failure is 63 percent. For reasons that go beyond the scope of this discussion, the likelihood of failure is actually much greater.

Amazon.com must be able to thrive in the presence of such constant failure. Or, as Amazon.com engineers stated: "Customers should be able to view and add items to their shopping cart even if disks are failing, network routes are flapping, or data centers are being destroyed by tornados."[7]

The only way to deal with such failure is to replicate the data on multiple servers. When a customer stores a Wish List, for example, that Wish List needs to be stored on different, geographically separated servers. Then, when (notice *when*, not *if*) a server with one copy of the Wish List fails, Amazon.com applications obtain it from another server.

Such data replication solves one problem but introduces another. Suppose that the customer's Wish List is stored on servers A, B, and C and server A fails. While server A is down, server B or C can provide a copy of the Wish List, but if the customer changes it, that Wish List can only be rewritten to servers B and C. It cannot be written to A because A is not running. When server A comes back into service, it will have the old copy of the Wish List. The next day, when the customer reopens his or her Wish List, two different versions exist: the most recent one on servers B and C and an older one on server A. The customer wants the most current one. How can Amazon.com ensure that it will be delivered? Keep in mind that 9 million orders are being shipped while this goes on.

None of the current relational DBMS products was designed for problems like this. Consequently, Amazon.com engineers developed Dynamo, a specialized data store for reliably processing massive amounts of data on tens of thousands of servers. Dynamo provides an always-open experience for Amazon.com's retail customers; Amazon.com also sells Dynamo store services to others via its S3 Web Services product offering.

Meanwhile, Google was encountering similar problems that could not be met by commercially available relational DBMS products. In response, Google created Bigtable, a data store for processing petabytes of data on hundreds of thousands of servers.[8] Bigtable supports a richer data model than Dynamo, which means that it can store a greater variety of data structures.

Both Dynamo and Bigtable are designed to be **elastic**; this term means that the number of servers can dynamically increase and decrease without disrupting performance.

---

[7] Giuseppe DeCandia, Deniz Hastorun, Madan Jampani, Gunavardhan Kakulapati, Avinash Lakshman, Alex Pilchin, Swami Sivasubramanian, Peter Vosshall, and Werner Vogels, "Dynamo: Amazon's Highly Available Key-Value Store," *Proceedings of the 21st ACM Symposium on Operating Systems Principles*, Stevenson, WA, October 2007.

[8] Fay Chang, Jeffrey Dean, Sanjay Ghemawat, Wilson C. Hsieh, Deborah A. Wallach, Mike Burrows, Tushar Chandra, Andrew Fikes, and Robert E. Gruber, "Bigtable: A Distributed Storage System for Structured Data," *OSDI 2006: Seventh Symposium on Operating System Design and Implementation*, Seattle, WA, last modified November 2006, http://labs.google.com/papers/bigtable.html.

In 2007, Facebook encountered similar data storage problems: massive amounts of data, the need to be elastically scalable, tens of thousands of servers, and high volumes of traffic. In response to this need, Facebook began development of Cassandra, a data store that provides storage capabilities like Dynamo with a richer data model like Bigtable.[9,10] Initially, Facebook used Cassandra to power its Inbox Search. By 2008, Facebook realized that it had a bigger project on its hands than it wanted and gave the source code to the open source community. As of 2011, Cassandra is used by Facebook, Twitter, Digg, Reddit, Cisco, and many others.

Cassandra, by the way, is a fascinating name for a data store. In Greek mythology, Cassandra was so beautiful that Apollo fell in love with her and gave her the power to see the future. Alas, Apollo's love was unrequited and he cursed her so that no one would ever believe her predictions. The name was apparently a slam at Oracle.

Cassandra is elastic and fault-tolerant; it supports massive amounts of data on thousands of servers and provides durability, meaning that once data is committed to the data store, it won't be lost, even in the presence of failure. One of the most interesting characteristics of Cassandra is that clients (meaning the programs that run Facebook, Twitter, etc.) can select the level of consistency that they need. If a client requests that all servers always be current, Cassandra will ensure that happens, but performance will be slow. At the other end of the trade-off spectrum, clients can require no consistency, whereby performance is maximized. In between, clients can require that a majority of the servers that store a data item be consistent.

Cassandra's performance is vastly superior to relational DBMS products. In one comparison, Cassandra was found to be 2,500 times faster than MySQL for write operations and 23 times faster for read operations[11] on massive amounts of data on hundreds of thousands of possibly failing computers!

Questions

4-9. Clearly, Dynamo, Bigtable, and Cassandra are critical technology to the companies that created them. Why did they allow their employees to publish academic papers about them? Why did they not keep them as proprietary secrets?

4-10. What do you think this movement means to the existing DBMS vendors? How serious is the NoSQL threat? Justify your answer.

4-11. Search the Web to determine what existing vendors such as Oracle and Microsoft are doing with regard to NoSQL databases. Also, search to see what support such vendors are providing for Big Data data stores. Summarize your findings.

4-12. Amazon.com offers cloud services known as *Amazon Web Services (AWS)*. Within the AWS offering is a set of services for accessing Dynamo. Search the Web for the term *AWS Dynamo cases* and find two examples of companies that are using AWS Dynamo. Why did those companies choose AWS Dynamo? Note that the answer to this question has two parts: Why did they use a cloud service? And why did they choose NoSQL rather than a relational database?

4-13. The text describes how organizations need to create information from Big Data data stores but are challenged to do so because NoSQL and Hadoop are difficult to use. Search the Web for easier-to-use query and reporting products for Big Data data stores. Investigate the top two products and determine if they are for you. Summarize your findings.

[9] "Welcome to Apache Cassandra," The Apache Software Foundation, accessed June 2011, http://cassandra.apache.org.

[10] "The Cassandra Distributed Database," Parleys, accessed July 16, 2013, http://www.parleys.com/#st=5&id=1866&sl=20.

[11] "The Cassandra Distributed Database," Slide 21.

supervision removed from the people who execute them. As a result, process objectives may get muddled by layers of management. Managers in large firms must find a way to ensure objectives are well communicated to those executing them.

Process Measures

Process owners must also specify and communicate measures for each objective. **Measures**, also called **metrics**, are quantities assigned to attributes. Measures are also called key performance indicators (**KPIs**) by process improvement experts.

A measure of the Deliver process is the elapsed time in minutes and seconds from leaving the store until arrival at the customer's location. Just as there are many possible objectives for each process, there are many possible ways to measure each objective—it is the manager's job to specify measures or, if necessary, to improve the choice of measures and communicate these measures to process participants.

Specifying measures can be difficult, as it requires a very thorough knowledge of the process. Even then, some objectives are challenging to quantify. Mr. Pizzi at the pizza shop wants to sell to freshmen so that these students become frequent customers over their time at the university. However, it is hard to know which customers are freshmen. As a result, the pizza shop decides to measure the number of deliveries to the dorms as an approximation. Freshmen are not the only dorm residents, but this may be the only measure that is available to the pizza shop.

Although measuring dorm sales is clearly not a perfect measure of freshmen sales, the pizza shop owner realizes that all measures are imperfect to some degree. Einstein once said, "Not everything that can be counted counts, and not everything that counts can be counted." When considering measures, recognize they all have limitations and that the key business challenge is to select the best ones available and know their limits.

The best measures are reasonable, accurate, and consistent, as shown in Figure 5-9. A reasonable measure is one that is valid and compelling. It is reasonable to approximate freshmen pizza orders with dorm orders. Accurate measures are exact and precise. An accurate measure is 26 pizzas; a less accurate one is "more than last week." To accurately assess an objective, it may be appropriate to have multiple measures. For example, to assess selling to freshmen, the pizza shop might also record the number of pizzas delivered to campus during the freshman orientation weekend. A final characteristic of a good measurement is consistency. Managers should develop measures of processes that are reliable, that is, the measure returns the same value if the same situation reoccurs.

Finally, managers should avoid the common trap of falling in love with their favorite measurement. If Mr. Pizzi discovered the freshman orientation weekend measure and it works for several years, he may not be willing to entertain new measurement suggestions even if they are more reasonable, accurate, or consistent. Managers should not marry measures; they need to be able to move on when a better measurement option emerges.

Once managers specify and communicate the stated objectives and measures, the next step is to consider how to improve the process with IS. The results of the improvement will be apparent in the specified measures.

Q4. How Can Information Systems Be Used to Improve Processes?

Today, information systems are playing an increasingly important role in business processes. Because they are so essential, they can often be used to improve the process. An IS can improve a process in a number of ways; here we consider five ways, as shown in Figure 5-10.

Managers must specify and communicate appropriate measures for each objective that are:
• Reasonable—valid and compelling
• Accurate—exact and precise
• Consistent—reliable

FIGURE 5-9

Options for Improving Process Measures

FIGURE 5-10

Options for Improving a Process with an IS

Improve an Activity	
Pizza Shop:	Driving activity improved with GPS
Health Clinic:	Prescription Writing activity improved with Medication Checker
Improve Data Flow Among Activities	
Pizza Shop:	Display Order process data on GPS in Delivery process
Health Clinic:	Prescription data electronically recorded and shared with pharmacy
Improve Control of Activities	
Pizza Shop:	Better control of order details
Health Clinic:	Appointment no-shows reduced
Use Automation	
Pizza Shop:	Send scheduled tweets in Tweet Promotion process
Health Clinic:	Phone answering system in Office Reception process
Improve Procedures	
Pizza Shop:	Payment procedure improved and Payment process performs better
Health Clinic:	Office procedures rewritten to improve Office processes

Improve an Activity

One way to improve a process with IS is to improve one of the activities in the process. At the pizza shop, the Delivery process driving activity can be improved by adding a GPS to each delivery vehicle that displays traffic updates. As a result, the measure of the Delivery objective—delivery time—is improved. Another example is the Sales process. One activity, the Promotion activity, can be improved by using Twitter to identify and attract freshmen.

To broaden our discussion, consider how IS can help improve healthcare service processes at the clinic at Sarah's university. To show how an IS can improve an activity, consider the Write a Prescription process. When a doctor types a prescription for a student on a tablet, software can compare that medicine to other medicines the student has been prescribed. If the new drug conflicts with any previously prescribed drug or interacts with the patient's allergies, a warning message is displayed.

Improve Data Flow Among Activities

Information systems can also improve a process by adding or improving the data flow between activities in the same or different processes. For example, consider the Web site used by the pizza shop for the Order process. The order data from the Order process can be used to improve the Delivery process if the order data flows to GPS displays in the delivery cars in real time. Using this data about upcoming deliveries, drivers can make better plans about when to stop for gas or when to wait for one more pizza to finish cooking before heading out on deliveries.

At the health clinic, improving data flow can improve the process of filling a prescription. When the doctor writes a prescription during an office visit, the prescription data can be sent to the local pharmacy so the prescription is ready when the patient arrives. The data, the prescription, flows from the Write a Prescription process to the Fill a Prescription process at the pharmacy. The data flows automatically rather than being hand-carried by the patient. Not only does the data flow reduce the waiting time in the Fill Prescription process, there are fewer errors about the prescription than when it is handwritten.

Improve Control of Activities

A third way that IS can improve a process is to improve the control of activities in the process. In general, **control** limits behavior. A process is like a river; controls are like dams and sidewalls that limit the behavior of the river. You have controls in your life that help you limit your own behavior, as shown in Figure 5-11. Your alarm clock limits your sleep, the cruise control on your car limits your speed, your phone password limits who can use your phone, your social media privacy controls limit who can see your posts, and your ATM PIN limits who can execute banking transactions.

In the process world, controls help limit wide variations in activities so a process runs more consistently and smoothly. In other words, by limiting the behavior of the activities,

Control	Reduces Variation In
Alarm clock	Wake-up time
Cruise control	Speed of the vehicle
Phone password	Who can use your phone
Social media privacy settings	Who can see your content
ATM PIN	Who can execute banking activities

FIGURE 5-11
Common Controls

control helps the process provide consistent results. Consider how a lack of control can lead to wide variations and even disaster—the absence of control has been blamed for the Enron, WorldComm, and Freddie Mac financial debacles. If you can suggest ways to improve control of a business process, you'll be the life of the process party. For many processes, an information system is the most reliable way to improve control.

Controls at the pizza shop help make every pizza the same size, keep the oven at a consistent temperature, and allow only the manager to void sales on the cash register. An example of an IS control is the new computer for the in-restaurant Order process. Waiters and waitresses now type in orders on the new computer rather than on handwritten slips. One control on this process is that software checks for incomplete orders, and if the order is incomplete it is not sent to the kitchen. For example, if a waiter fails to enter three pizza toppings for a three-topping pizza or a dressing is not specified for a salad, the computer alerts the waiter to enter the missing data. The kitchen is not given the order until it is corrected by the waiter. This control helps reduce variation in delivery time and variations between what the customer ordered and what the customer is served.

At the health clinic, one recurring problem is appointment no-shows. To exercise better control of these problem patients, the clinic now sends voice and text reminders of the appointment to the student's cell phone. In addition, patient healthcare records have been converted to electronic records to improve control of the records and limit who can see them.

Use Automation

A fourth way that IS can improve a process is automation. **Automation** means that a computer does an activity or a part of an activity that was once done by a person. One classic example of this is the ATM that replaced some of the activities of the bank teller; another is e-commerce Web sites that do several activities of salespeople. A more recent automation example is the Google car. Google has developed and tested a driverless car, an automated vehicle designed to improve driving and lower accidents, as shown in Figure 5-12.

FIGURE 5-12

**Automation Example—
Google Driverless Car**

Source: KAREN BLEIER/AFP/Getty Images/
Newscom

FIGURE 5-13

Tweet Customer Process Activities Before and After Automation

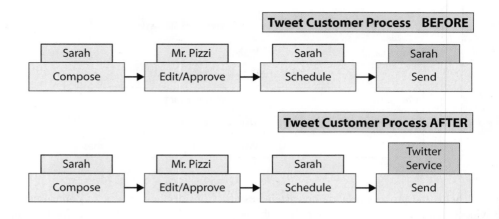

An example of using automation is the Tweet Customers process at the pizza shop, as shown in Figure 5-13. The top diagram shows the Tweet Customer process before automation. Each of these activities is currently done by a person. Sarah composes a list of 5 or 10 tweets and emails the list to Mr. Pizzi. He edits and approves the list and emails these back to Sarah, who then schedules the best time to send them. When each appointed time arrives, Sarah logs into Twitter and sends the tweet. One way to automate an activity is to use a Twitter service to automatically send the tweets at the scheduled times so that Sarah does not need to log in and send them herself; this process is shown in the bottom of Figure 5-13.

At the clinic, an automated phone answering system improved office processes. Before the system was developed, two receptionists were always required in the office to answer calls and admit patients; with an automated answering system, only one receptionist is necessary.

The decision to automate can be challenging. Clearly computers have many advantages—productivity, speed, quality, scale, consistency, and reduction of human injury. They don't go on vacation or leave early for a child's ball game, they are very consistent and easy to control, and they don't have birthdays to remember. But people have their advantages, too—lower development cost, better security, less upfront costs, and much greater flexibility and adaptability. If a comparison of these advantages does not answer the question, "Should a person actor or computer actor do this activity?" then consider the amount of judgment required by the actor. Automated actors are more capable in low-judgment settings where well-known and repeatable activities are performed, like timing the inputs on an assembly line, holding an altitude for an airplane, or checking if every box has been completed on a form. But computers also break down unexpectedly and require maintenance; and while this may only be a nuisance for the pizza shop if it affects the tweeting of discounts, it can be a big deal if it shuts down the ovens. Humans, on the other hand, are uniquely able to deal with high-judgment activities that feature uncertainty or ambiguity like the diagnosis and treatment of illness; risk assessment; and human communication, interaction, and learning.

The decision to automate is even more vexing because the decision is never final. Unrelenting advances in technology will require that businesspeople continually reassess automation decisions. The decision to automate an activity may change as new technologies are developed or made more affordable.

Improve Procedures

Before we can discuss how the procedures of an IS can improve a process, it is important to be clear about how IS and processes are related to each other. In Chapter 2, we first introduced processes, IS, and their relationship. We explained that each process can rely on zero, one, or many IS and that an IS may support one or many processes. In Figure 5-14, we show one IS—your cell phone—supporting two Go To Movie processes.

As shown in Figure 5-14, a procedure anchors an IS to a process. Each application of an IS to a process has a unique procedure. For example, your smartphone supports both Go To Movies processes, but each process has its own procedure. When you execute the Movie With Friends process, you use your phone to view trailers with your friends before you decide. Your procedure

Go To Movie Processes

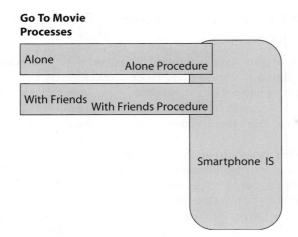

FIGURE 5-14

Two Go To Movies Processes and Smartphone IS

takes you to a movie app, then via some search magic to the trailer of the movie you are considering. When you execute the Movie Alone process, you use your phone only to see showtimes. One phone, two processes, two procedures.

That is nice to know. However, the real advantage of thinking about IS, processes, and procedures is to recognize that the procedure is often the weak link between a process and its IS. As a result, improving a procedure can often lead to process improvement. For example, you might have a great phone but lousy Movie processes because you never learned how to search nearby theaters for showtimes or reviews. Your procedures are holding you back; fix those and your Movie process will get much better.

The pizza shop is in the same pickle. For several years, the university allowed local restaurants to use the student ID card as a charge card. Recently, Mr. Pizzi noticed that only a few pizzas were sold using the student ID card. To improve the Payment process, he asked some of his cashiers what was going on. It turns out they were not sure if they could execute the sale with the student ID card and did not know how to enter the student ID number on the cash register. Mr. Pizzi rewrote the Payment procedure with the help of one of his cashiers, they trained the other cashiers, and soon the Payment process was working better. The Payment process had a poorly understood procedure that was holding it back; once the procedure was improved, the Payment process performed better.

At the clinic, healthcare professionals had to use a new healthcare IT system to comply with the new federal Affordable Care Act. However, when they switched over to the new IS, their office processes suffered. The clinic soon realized that its processes were still fine but that no one knew the procedures for the IS.

Before we move on, recognize the clinic's problem is a common one—anytime an IS or a process changes, a procedure should change. Often, a new IS is purchased or a process is changed but the procedure is left unchanged. Procedures in business need to be constantly refined as technology changes and processes change. As you will find out in your career, keeping procedures current is easier said than done.

These examples show some of the possibilities for improving processes with information systems. The opportunities to use IS to improve processes will continue to grow as the price-performance ratio of computers continues to plummet, new technologies and ideas continue to enter the business world, and young professionals join the workforce who are more comfortable with technology than any previous generation. The most significant information system for improving business processes emerged over the past decade. These are multimillion-dollar ERP systems that are designed to improve a wide range of company processes. These ERP systems are described in Chapter 6.

Although information systems can have a big impact on process performance, there are other ways to achieve process improvement. An entire process management industry has emerged over the past 50 years. This movement acknowledges the role of IS in process improvement but has also developed a wide range of techniques and suggestions to improve processes that do not depend on an IS. We investigate these next.

Q5. How Can Process Management Principles Improve Processes?

Process management experts have developed a number of process principles that can improve processes, as shown in Figure 5-15. Process management experts call these process improvement principles a number of names: systems engineering, workflow/WfMc, Business Process Modeling, Business Process Reengineering, Continuous Improvement, xMatrix, Kaizen, and Six Sigma. From these various approaches we distill the six techniques shown in Figure 5-15.

While we have seen earlier that an IS can improve a process by improving an activity, there are ways to improve a process by improving an activity that do not involve an IS. For example, the Pizza Delivery process can be enhanced by improving the parking activity of the drivers or using better-insulated pizza boxes. One common way to improve an activity is to add resources to it such as adding drivers to the Delivery process.

Another simple improvement is to remove unproductive resources from a process; this is often referred to as cutting slack. For example, if drivers assigned to a particular pizza outlet are not busy, they could be trained to do other jobs so their time is more productive.

A third technique is to improve the feedback generated by the process. At the pizza shop, the Delivery process should generate feedback to Mr. Pizzi on the number of orders delivered by each driver and the number of deliveries that are late. With richer feedback, process managers and participants can identify problems, suggest process improvements, and test potential solutions.

Another technique is to remove a process bottleneck. A **bottleneck** occurs when one activity reduces the performance of the overall process. In the pizza restaurant, a bottleneck occurs when too many customers are being served by one waiter. In a similar way, the elevator is often a bottleneck in the dorm during the move-in process. A process management expert would identify the bottleneck and propose that other employees do waiter activities on busy nights and that the university allow a longer move-in period to reduce spikes in elevator demand.

A business process can also be improved by redesigning it—by changing its structure. To change structure simply means to change the arrangement or roles of the activities of a process. An example of changing a structure can be seen in the Assemble Pizza process. Currently each chef rolls dough, adds toppings, then loads his or her own pizza in the oven and takes it out when it is finished. On hectic nights, a better structure to the process would be to specialize the jobs. That is, one chef rolls dough for all the pizzas, another adds ingredients, and a third moves pizzas in and out. This helps reduce delays, an objective of the Assemble process.

A final way to improve the process may be to outsource an activity—that is, have a supplier, customer, or business partner do one of the activities in the process. Customers seem willing to swipe their own credit cards, change their password, pump their gas, check out their groceries, make their travel arrangements, and check in at an airport. Customers should not be the only ones considered for outsourcing; other businesses should also be considered. For example, the pizza shop can outsource its accounting activities.

Whether it is using process management principles or other methods of improving processes listed in this chapter, most businesspeople can suggest ways to improve processes. The issue is whether it is worth the cost and if the improvements help the process better achieve the

FIGURE 5-15

Options for Improving a Process Using Process Management Principles

Improvement Category	Examples in Pizza Shop
Improve activity	Improve parking activity
Remove unproductive resources	Remove unnecessary drivers
Improve feedback	Give Mr. Pizzi late delivery report
Remove bottleneck	Add waiters
Redesign the structure	Specialize cooks
Outsource activity	Outsource accounting activities

firm's strategy. For example, the pizza shop can always add more drivers or use Twitter to take orders, but managers must decide if these improvements are better than other choices that might be less expensive or time consuming and achieve the strategy better.

While this chapter is a good way to begin your process education, the most common approach to process improvement, particularly in the manufacturing industry, is called Six Sigma. **Six Sigma** seeks to improve process outputs by removing causes of defects and minimizing variability in the process. Each Six Sigma project follows a very structured sequence of steps with quantified financial measures. Six Sigma gets its name from its goal that 99.99966% of process outputs will be free from defects. Without such high quality processes, Six Sigma proponents argue we would be without electricity 10 minutes each week, 810 commercial airliners would crash every month, and 50 newborn babies would be dropped at birth by a doctor every day.[4]

For you to be able to contribute in today's business environment, hone your ability to visualize and assess business processes. That is, once you isolate a particular process, determine its objectives, assess the quality of its measures, and determine if IS or process management principles can improve the process. To this end, this chapter is offered to help you be like Sarah in the chapter vignette—to equip you with a series of questions you can ask to better understand a process and make suggestions for improvement.

Q6. How Do Process Teams Diagram Process Improvement?

Whether it is using our approach, Six Sigma, or another technique, process improvement at medium to large organizations always involves a team. Typically, the team includes the users who are the actors in the process, general managers responsible for the process, IT analysts, and business analysts. Unless the process is very simple like assembling or baking a pizza, diagramming a process is typically necessary in order for team members to understand the process and to identify activities that must be changed. It is necessary for the redesign team to understand how the current process works and what the intended process should look like. Diagrams of the current process are typically called **"as-is" diagrams**, and diagrams of suggested improvements are called **"ought-to-be" diagrams**. Diagrams can take many forms, but as mentioned in Chapter 2, we will use the current gold standard, BPMN.

To better understand how a process improvement team might use BPMN diagramming, consider the ought-to-be Select New Supplier process for the pizza shop. This is the process the pizza franchise company wants to adopt. The company must find and select suppliers for fresh pizza items, cleaning supplies, uniform cleaning, office supplies, and waste removal. The objectives of this managerial process are to find good quality suppliers in a reasonable amount of time. The measures for these objectives are shown in Figure 5-16.

The Select New Supplier process is shown in Figure 5-17. It begins when the franchise communicates a request for proposal (RFP) to potential suppliers (the Request Proposal from Supplier activity). This activity, completed by the warehouse manager, finds potential suppliers, performs a cursory investigation of their products, and contacts the potential supplier's sales office. If the supplier responds positively, the next step is the Receive Proposal from Supplier activity. In this activity, a supplier provides address and contract data and a list of products the supplier expects to sell to the franchise if the supplier is approved. These application data and product data are inserted as new supplier data in a resource labeled Warehouse DB. Once this activity is complete, the warehouse manager evaluates the potential supplier's product list to

Objectives	Measures
Good quality Effectiveness	Difference in scheduled and actual delivery time Number of returned purchases
Reasonable amount of time Efficiency	Time in days to execute this process

FIGURE 5-16

Objectives and Measures of the Select New Supplier Process

---

[4] H. James Harrington and Kenneth C. Lomax, *Performance Improvement Methods* (New York: McGraw-Hill, 2000), p. 57.

FIGURE 5-17
BPMN Diagram of the Select New Supplier Process

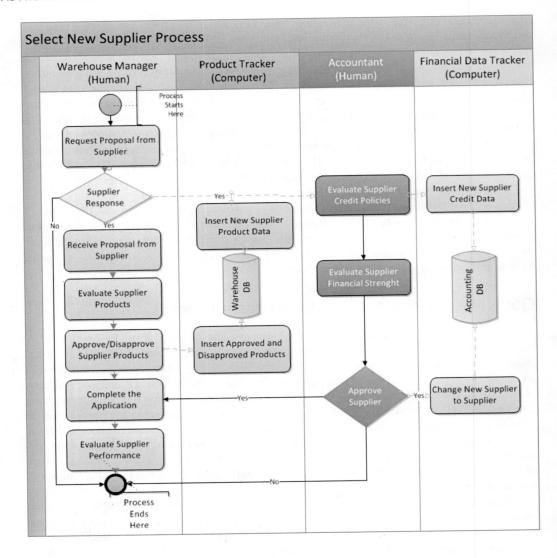

determine items that may be appropriate. While this activity is happening, an accountant is also evaluating the supplier's credit policies in the Evaluate Supplier Credit Policies activity. The data generated about the supplier's credit policies is stored in the Accounting DB. This data will be used later by the accounting department in payment processes. Accounting also collects other data on the supplier in order to reach an approve/disapprove supplier decision. This activity is called Evaluate Supplier Financial Strength. If the accountants approve the potential supplier, a Complete the Application activity is initiated that specifies the potential products to be ordered. Finally, after the first month, the final activity, Evaluate Supplier Performance, is accomplished. The franchise strives to determine quickly if a supplier is working out.

Our goal here is for you to see how process teams use formal tools like BPMN diagramming to depict process improvement. The final chapter of this book is a more complete explanation of the sequence of actions organizations use to improve a process; it is a process of process improvement.

Q7. How Can an IS Hinder a Process?

As we have seen, information systems usually support and improve processes. As we mentioned earlier, one way they do that is by improving the data flow between activities. However, IS are not always the process hero; sometimes they are the goat. If an IS prevents or restricts the flow, this can hinder a process. This situation is called an **information silo**—the data needed for a process activity is unavailable because it is stored in an isolated, separated information system. Let's consider a few silo examples, how silos can be corrected, and why they exist.

Notice that the objectives of the Select New Supplier process are to select suppliers that are good quality in a reasonable amount of time. The final activity in the Select New Supplier process is Evaluate New Supplier Performance. To evaluate the new supplier, an analyst must obtain data on the new supplier's deliveries to the pizza shops. One measure of good quality is the timeliness of delivery—the difference in time between scheduled delivery and actual delivery. Unfortunately, the scheduled delivery times are stored in the franchise information system, but actual delivery times are stored in spreadsheets at the different shops. These spreadsheets are information silos. To make matters worse, the delivery time data is not in a consistent format at the different shops, making it even harder for the data to flow to the franchise.

One other example of information silos may be closer to home: your smartphone. You may have music, email, chat, contact, and other data on your smartphone that is not easily synced with similar programs on your laptop. If you wanted to improve your music listening process or your calendar update process, having two silos can be a hindrance.

One fix to the information silo problem is to duplicate the data—make a copy of the data that is isolated and make it available to the process that needs it. However, when duplicated, the data can quickly become inconsistent when changes are made to only one set of data. The most complete fix to eliminate information silos is to store a single copy of data in a shared database and connect the business processes to that database. A single-copy database solution is a feature of the ERP systems that we will discuss in the next three chapters.

Why Information Silos Exist

Information silos at the pizza franchise are caused in part by the physical separation of the stores from the franchise headquarters. However, this information silo problem occurs even when all the data is under the same roof. For example, at the franchise office, one database stores data on restaurant sales while another database keeps track of the inventory and deliveries. In each database, the data are compiled at the end of the day and shared with the other database. This delay normally does not affect the franchise; however, several times a year sales are quite unusual and this delay leads to running out of items at the restaurants or unneeded deliveries. If the data were all in one system, these problems would be less likely to occur.

If the problems of information silos are so evident, why does this issue ever arise? Organizations store data in separate databases for several reasons. Given a choice, organizational departments prefer to control the data they use; they are, after all, the experts about the data. For example, accountants know more than anyone about how the accounting database should be used, so it is natural for them to want to control how it is set up, what the data will look like, and how the database will be updated. Also, a department may have very different objectives than other departments in the firm. These objectives might be to minimize inventory or serve customers. A department system that supports a key objective, even if it is an information silo, might be a better solution for the department than an enterprise system that doesn't support that objective as well.

There are other reasons for a department to use its own system. Some processes use sensitive data that should not be shared with other processes such as tax data in accounting processes and healthcare claims data in the HR department. Also, a department system can be purchased and implemented more quickly than most enterprise solutions. Finally, departmental IS are much more affordable; enterprise systems can cost as much as 10 to 50 times as much as a single-department application. This is evident at the new pizza shop, where the student union outlet will keep its own data about student Twitter names. The process of tweeting discounts may well work at the other shops, but the cost of restructuring the TPS to record this new data may not be worth the cost.

In the past, a department IS was frequently chosen to support a department process because cross-department IS were rare. Just 20 years ago, the only game in town was the departmental system, as enterprise systems only existed in dreams. Today, the expectation is to minimize information silos and promote data flow among departments, not just in pizza franchises but across global enterprises. This is a theme we continue in the next several chapters.

MIS InClass 5

Improving the Process of Making Paper Airplanes[5]

The purpose of this exercise is to demonstrate process concepts. In this exercise, students will form assembly lines to create paper airplanes. Each assembly line will have the same four activities, each called a Work Center (WC), as shown in Figure 5-18. Raw material is a stack of plain paper, finished goods are the folded airplanes, and WIP is Work In Progress, which is the output of the Work Center prior to the WIP.

One student is assigned to each of the four Work Centers in the assembly line. Student 1 (in WC 1) creates the first fold, as shown at the top of Figure 5-19. Student 2, at WC 2, folds the corners, also shown in Figure 5-19. The location and assembly instructions for Students 3 and 4 are also shown in Figure 5-19. In addition to the four students who fold the planes, seven other students observe, time, and record each assembly line as listed below using the three forms in Figure 5-20:

Source: dotshock/Shutterstock.

> Observer 1: Use Form 1, record WC 1 task times.
> Observer 2: Use Form 1, record WC 2 task times.
> Observer 3: Use Form 1, record WC 3 task times.
> Observer 4: Use Form 1, record WC 4 task times.
> Observer 5: Use Form 2, record cycle time at the end of the line.
> Observer 6: Use Form 3, record colored sheet throughput time.
> Observer 7: Count Work In Progress at the end of each run.

Each assembly line is run to construct 20 airplanes. Prior to beginning the process, each line will run a practice session of four or five planes. Then clear the line, start the clock, and make the 20 airplanes. Each WC continues to work until the 20th plane is finished, which means that more than 20 will be started as there will be WIP when the 20th is finished. About halfway through the run, the instructor will insert a colored piece of paper as raw material. Each student assembler works at his or her own pace. As workers build planes, they should work at a comfortable pace and not speed. This is not a contest for maximum output, but for quality.

After the first run is completed, make a second run of 20 planes with all the same roles. However, each student can work only when there is an airplane in his or her inbox (WIP) and no airplane in his or her outbox (WIP). Again, midway through the run, the instructor will insert a colored sheet of paper.

After the runs:

1. In teams, diagram the Assembly process using BPMN symbols such as roles, swimlanes, activities, and decisions. Name resources assigned to roles.
2. Use the ideas in this chapter to improve this Assembly process. Discuss the objectives of the assembly line. If you were in charge of an assembly line like this one, do you think your objective would be efficiency or effectiveness? Specify the measures used to monitor progress toward your objective(s).
3. Assume the WC folding is done by four machines. In that scenario, the second run uses different software than the first run. Does this new IS improve an activity, data flow, control, automation, or procedure?
4. Is any data in an information silo on the first or second runs?
5. Which measure changed most significantly from the first to the second run? Did you anticipate this? Are other processes with other measures just as subject to change with a similar minor change in information?
6. Were there any controls on the assembly process? Could an IS improve the process by improving control? On which measure(s) will this improvement appear?

FIGURE 5-18
Classroom Assembly Line Setup

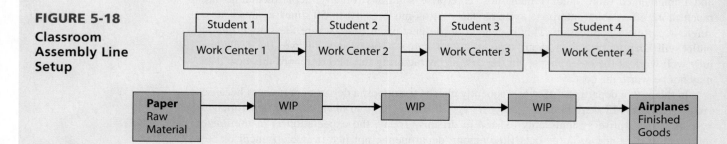

---

[5] Based on "A Classroom Exercise to Illustrate Lean Manufacturing Pull Concepts," by Peter J. Billington, in *Decision Sciences Journal of Innovative Education*, 2(1), 2004, pp. 71–77.

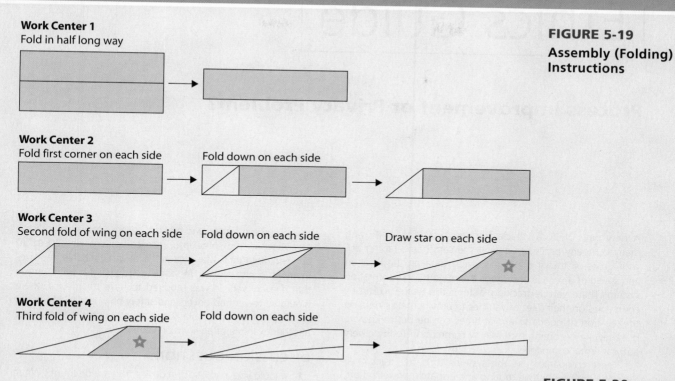

Work Center 1
Fold in half long way

Work Center 2
Fold first corner on each side   Fold down on each side

Work Center 3
Second fold of wing on each side   Fold down on each side   Draw star on each side

Work Center 4
Third fold of wing on each side   Fold down on each side

FIGURE 5-19

Assembly (Folding) Instructions

FIGURE 5-20

Airplane Folding Recording Forms

Work Center _____ (1, 2, 3, or 4)

Unit	Run 1 (seconds)	Run 2 (seconds)
1		
2		
3		
4		
5		
6		
7		
8		
9		
10		
11		
12		
13		
14		
15		
16		
17		
18		
19		
20		
Sum		
Average		

System	Throughput Time for 20 Sheets Run 1	Throughput Time for 20 Sheets Run 2
Start time		
Finish time		
Total time		

Form 2: Airplane manufacturing cycle time for 20 airplanes. Observer 5 uses this form to record start and finish time for entire run of 20 planes.

System	Throughput Time for Colored Sheets Run 1	Throughput Time for Colored Sheets Run 2
Start time		
Finish time		
Total time		

Form 3: Paper airplane manufacturing color sheet throughput time. Observer 6 uses this form to record start and finish time for colored sheet.

Form 1: Airplane manufacturing task time. Observers 1, 2, 3, and 4 use this form to record assembly times for each Work Center.

Ethics Guide

Process Improvement or Privacy Problem?

A new type of IS, a vehicle tracking system, is improving many company processes and at the same time raising privacy issues. A tracking system collects data on the location and speed of a vehicle and sends that data to an information system. These vehicle tracking systems are typically used by companies on their fleet of vehicles to provide better data on the location of goods so arrival times can be better known, but they are becoming increasingly common in food delivery and car rental companies.

These companies use the systems to better track their fleet of vehicles, improve routing and dispatch, prevent theft, and improve vehicle retrieval. Some hotel companies are using the systems to ensure that special guests are appropriately welcomed upon arrival at the hotel.

These systems typically include a wireless device attached to the vehicle and some type of GPS tracking server that receives data from the device, stores it, and creates reports for analysis. Two types of systems are in use. Active systems collect data and transmit the data to the server in real time via cellular networks. Passive systems store the data on board for later download to the server.

Automobile insurance companies are beginning to offer discounts to drivers willing to install a tracking device on their cars. This device can measure distance traveled, acceleration, speed, turning forces, and braking. If these measures indicate a cautious driver, some insurance companies give 20 to 30 percent discounts. Many cautious drivers hail this improvement as a just reward for their good driving. Some argue that if every vehicle was required to have this device, there would be fewer bad drivers and safety on public roads would improve. Others, particularly privacy advocates, see it as yet another example of an invasion of privacy.

DISCUSSION QUESTIONS

1. Would you install such a device to get a discount? What if the discount was 50 or 70 percent?
2. Is it ethical for a parent not to tell his or her 16-year-old driver that he or she installed this device on the car in order to secretly learn from the insurance company how cautiously the teen drives? Consider both the categorical imperative (page 20) and utilitarianism (page 40) in your response.
3. Is it ethical for a company to sell this data to a car manufacturer? The insurance company never specifically asked its customers if it could share this data, and the car company does not want any customer-identifying data, just the driver's age and the measures for each driver.

4. Should the legal system be able to subpoena this data from the insurance company as evidence in a court case? Would your answer change if you were being falsely accused of a hit-and-run accident?

5. Car rental and food delivery companies are required to tell their drivers when these systems are in place. In what ways can these systems lead to abuse, and how could the systems be designed to limit these abuses?

6. Should the pizza franchise require this device for all vehicles used by its drivers? It would not be used for insurance purposes but to determine better delivery routes and to help make its drivers more cautious.

7. For the pizza franchise, this device is an IS that improves a process. The business process is Delivery. What are the objectives of the pizza Delivery process, and what measures are now available?

8. Is this IS improvement an improvement in activity, data flow, control, automation, or procedures?

9. In this scenario, improving a process with IS reduces privacy. Do all IS improvements in processes with employees or customers reduce privacy? Can you think of processes with sensitive employee or customer data in healthcare, finance, or social media where improving the process with IS does not threaten privacy?

Source: © mickey hoo/Fotolia.

Active Review

Use this Active Review to verify that you understand the material in the chapter. You can read the entire chapter and then perform the tasks in this review, or you can read the text material for just one question and perform the tasks in this review for that question before moving on to the next one.

Q1. What are the important characteristics of processes in organizations?

Define *business process* and the key terms that describe business processes: *activity, resource, role,* and *actor*. Name the term that can be fulfilled by either a human or computer. Explain the four characteristics of processes. List the three main categories of process scope, and explain how each one is different from the others. Give examples of processes in each of the categories. Define *efficiency* and *effectiveness*. What things are efficient and effective?

Q2. What are examples of common business processes?

Explain a process in each of the primary activities of the value chain. Specify if that process is operational, managerial, or strategic, and explain why you classified it that way. Explain the support activities. Describe a procurement process and a sales and marketing process. Describe how knowledge of process characteristics can be used.

Q3. How can management improve processes?

What does the term *process improvement* imply? Explain what managers of processes are responsible for. Describe ideal process objectives. Explain measures and discuss why they are difficult to develop. Give examples of reasonable, accurate, and consistent process measures. What should managers avoid about measures?

Q4. How can information systems be used to improve processes?

Explain the five ways IS can be used to improve a particular process. Specify a process and explain how an IS can improve that process. Specify measures and objectives for the process. Give an example of a process where an activity can be improved using an IS. Describe how data flow can improve a process. Explain why control is important for a business process. Describe an example of how IS can improve control in a process. Give an example where automation of an activity improved the process. What makes the decision to automate challenging? Explain the relationship between a process, an IS, and a procedure. Give an example of how a poorly executed procedure limits the performance of a process.

Q5. How can process management principles improve processes?

Explain the ways process management principles can improve a process. Give an example of each and explain the process objective that is improved. State the goal of Six Sigma.

Q6. How do process teams diagram process improvement?

Identify common participants in a process improvement team. Describe the two types of BPMN diagrams. Explain the new supplier process and its roles, resources, and activities.

Q7. How can an IS hinder a process?

Describe how IS configuration in a company can hamper a process and limit its improvement. Describe an information silo. Explain the impact of silos on process objectives. Explain the most common fix to the silo problem. Describe why departments like to control the systems they use. Explain why a department may legitimately seek to keep its data in multiple databases.

Key Terms and Concepts

Using Your Knowledge

5-1. For each of the following processes, suggest how an IS can improve the process. Specify if the improvement is due to improving an activity, improving data flow, improving control, implementing automation, or improving procedures.
  a. the process of selecting a job after college
  b. the process of planning and executing a wedding or a funeral
  c. the process of taking photos and uploading the photos to Facebook
  d. the process the pizza shop uses to buy supplies

5-2. For each process, specify an IS that supports the process and the first three steps of the procedure that links that IS to the process.

5-3. For each of these processes, suggest how they may be improved by non-IS means; that is, by management and by process management principles.

5-4. When you go to a restaurant, that restaurant must execute several operational processes. Apply the concepts in this chapter to several of these processes. These processes might include seating, ordering, cooking, delivering, and paying.

5-5. How can your college use IS to make its processes better? Can you think of ways to use new IS tools like smartphones and social media to make college processes better? Specify the objective and measure that these IS help improve. For two of these processes, describe the procedures. Does your college have information silos? Which departments keep data needed by processes outside the department?

5-6. When you order a meal at McDonald's, that data is stored in an enterprise IS to be used by various processes. Make a list of the McDonald's processes in which your Happy Meal purchase will appear. You may want to review the value chain processes discussed in Q2.

5-7. Make a Facebook cause (*www.facebook.com/causes*). Invite several friends to join. Using paper and pencil or diagramming software, make a BPMN diagram of the three or four key activities in this promotional process. Specify objectives and measures for this process and explain how Facebook (IS) improves the promotional process.

5-8. Assume you are flying to a vacation resort. Create a BPMN diagram of the five to seven key activities in the process of getting your suitcase to your destination. Specify objectives and measures for this process.

Collaboration Exercise 5

Collaborate with a group of fellow students to answer the following questions. For this exercise, do not meet face to face. Your task will be easier if you coordinate your work with SharePoint, Office 365, Google Docs with Google+, or equivalent collaboration tools. (See Chapter 9 for a discussion of collaboration tools and processes.) Your answers should reflect the thinking of the entire group, not just that of one or two individuals.

The county planning office issues building permits, septic system permits, and county road access permits for all county building projects in an eastern state. The planning office issues permits to homeowners and builders for the construction of new homes and buildings and for any remodeling projects that involve electrical, gas, plumbing, and other utilities, as well as the conversion of unoccupied spaces such as garages into living or working space. The office also issues permits for new or upgraded septic systems and permits to provide driveway entrances to county roads.

Figure 5-21 shows the permit process that the county used for many years. Contractors and homeowners found this process to be slow and very frustrating. For one, they did not like its sequential nature. Only after a permit had been approved or rejected by the engineering review process would they find out whether a health or highway review was also needed. Because each of these reviews could take 3 or 4 weeks, applicants requesting permits wanted the review processes to be concurrent rather than serial. Also, both the permit applicants and county personnel were frustrated because they never knew where a particular application was in the permit process. A contractor would call to ask how much longer, and it might take an hour or more just to find which desk the permits were on.

Accordingly, the county changed the permit process to that shown in Figure 5-22. In this second process, the permit office made three copies of the permit and distributed one to each

FIGURE 5-21
Sequential Permit Review Process

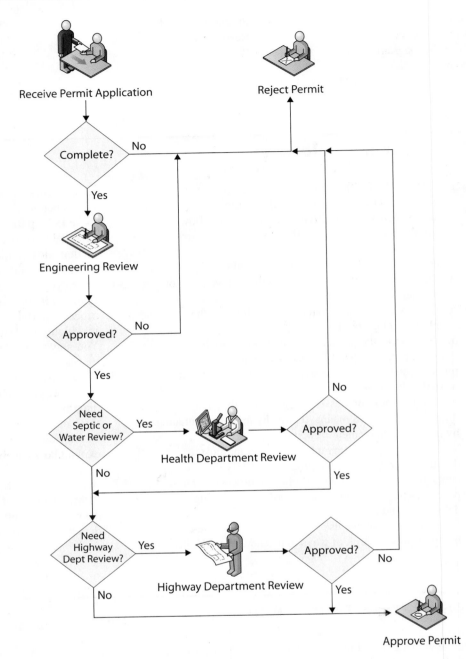

department. The departments reviewed the permits in parallel; a clerk would analyze the results and, if there were no rejections, approve the permit.

Unfortunately, this process had a number of problems, too. For one, some of the permit applications were lengthy; some included as many as 40 to 50 pages of large architectural drawings. The labor and copy expense to the county was considerable.

Second, in some cases, departments reviewed documents unnecessarily. If, for example, the highway department rejected an application, then neither the engineering nor health departments needed to continue their reviews. At first, the county responded to this problem by having the clerk who analyzed results cancel the reviews of other departments when he or she received a rejection. However, that policy was exceedingly unpopular with the permit applicants because

once an application was rejected and the problem corrected, the permit had to go back through the other departments. The permit would go to the end of the line and work its way back into the departments from which it had been pulled. Sometimes this resulted in a delay of 5 or 6 weeks.

Canceling reviews was unpopular with the departments as well because permit-review work had to be repeated. An application might have been nearly completed when it was canceled due to a rejection in another department. When the application came through again, the partial work results from the earlier review were lost.

1. Is this process an operational, managerial, or strategic process?
2. How can the permit process be improved? Identify at least one flaw in each measure.

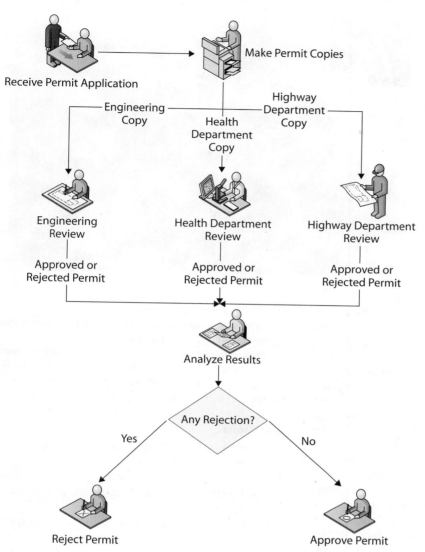

FIGURE 5-22
Parallel Permit Review Process

3. For your proposed IS improvements, specify if they are activity, data flow, control, automation, or procedure improvements.

4. Where are the information silos? Why did these silos develop over the years?

5. Draw the new process using BPMN.

CASE STUDY 5

Google Cars

Zipcars have become a popular method of rental car transportation in a number of cities in the world (Figure 5-23). Essentially, these cars are rented by the hour; customers pick them up at specific parking locations and return them to the same or other parking locations for a specific hourly fee based on each use. Zipcars are a transportation service that allows city dwellers to use cars without owning them in a way similar to cloud storage—the customer gets the service, in this case transportation, without the headaches that come with the hardware. Visit *www.zipcar.com* to better understand the service and see where they are available.

Another interesting transportation approach is being hatched by Google. Recently, state legislatures in Nevada and California approved the operation of driverless cars on public roads. Google, as well as Toyota, has developed driverless cars that have already been safely driven hundreds of thousands of miles. A picture of a Google car was shown earlier in the chapter in Figure 5-12. The cars are able to determine the speed limit based on data stored on Google Maps and acquire data on road objects and other cars with a series of onboard sensors. The specially outfitted Google vehicles avoid other traffic using a system of radar sensors and video cameras and

FIGURE 5-23

Zipcar

Source: © Ulana Switucha / Alamy

use artificial intelligence algorithms to steer. Currently, the cars operate with a safety observer aboard the car to step on a brake or turn the wheel if necessary. To see more current news about the cars, search online for *Google car* or *Google driverless car*.

Google has announced that the goals of this program are to improve driving safety, use fuel more efficiently, and enable more productive commutes for passengers. But there are also side benefits. For example, the cars park themselves after dropping off passengers if they are not needed immediately or pick up another passenger so there is reduced need for parking lots.

While it may be interesting to contemplate owning such a car, Google may be planning something beyond just private ownership for these vehicles. One target may be to equip a town with enough cars to act as public transportation, a pooled transportation system that, like Zipcars, are rented for short intervals.

Currently, the first step of the public transportation process is for the passenger to go meet a bus or vehicle at a common, but often inconvenient, location. With a driverless car, the process changes; the transportation vehicle can come to the passenger. This meeting activity is simple enough to coordinate with a smartphone—a transportation subscriber would only need to say a few words or press a few buttons to summon a vehicle.

Some the potential benefits of driverless cars as public transportation are intriguing. Families could reduce car ownership, including the associated maintenance and upfront costs. Young

children and those too old to safely operate a car could also now be conveniently served. Property values of homes within the area served by the vehicles may also appreciate.

Driverless cars may turn out to be a very interesting event, and one that highlights the theme of this chapter. An IS, a driverless car, can improve the transportation process in significant and unexpected ways by automating the driving activity.

Questions

5-9. For your own transportation process, what are your objectives and measures?

5-10. Make a BPMN of a new transportation process with driverless cars. Specify activities, actors, and the smartphone IS.

5-11. What other processes may be improved with driverless cars?

5-12. Can you think of ways to improve the transportation process further? Try to apply as many concepts from this chapter as possible.

5-13. If you worked at Google, what type of city might you want to pursue for the initial trial and why?

5-14. What are the five components of the driveless car IS, and which lessons from Chapter 2 can be applied to the concept of a Google car?

Chapter 6 Supporting Processes with ERP Systems

"**A**re they out of their minds?" asks Pat Smith, the athletic director at Central Colorado State.

"I'm not sure, Pat, but I will tell you the university is serious about this," replies Heidi, Pat's young, long-suffering assistant.

"University Central Administration wants us to go through them for every purchase?"

"Well, not all the purchases, but the ones above $500, yes. But they say that this new ERP software will save the university more than a half-million dollars in the first year." Heidi is hoping to keep a lid on her volcanic boss.

"Did they say how?"

"Apparently, other places on campus did dumb things. You read about the fraud at the bookstore and the cost overruns with the new computers in the union. The university also mentioned our little adventure with that T-shirt maker. They say we should have known that company used child labor. Oh, and they claim we paid 50 percent more per jersey than the intramural department."

Visibly angry, Pat starts his daily rant, "They have no idea how things work over here! And so the great solution is to go through purchasing for everything. Every order will take a month!"

"Well, they claim this new ERP system will shorten the time. They approve a list of all the suppliers for everyone on campus and negotiate the prices for each item, and we're free to order through the system as we see fit."

"Wait, did I hear you say 'each item'? We order thousands of different things!"

"They did admit this will take a while."

"Did they really say we paid more for our jerseys than intramurals? Do they have any idea how impossible it would be to recruit Division I players and say, 'And you'll look great in this $8 jersey'?"

"But, boss, on the positive side, they said that when other universities went to this system, the suppliers worked harder to stay on everyone's good side because they had more to lose."

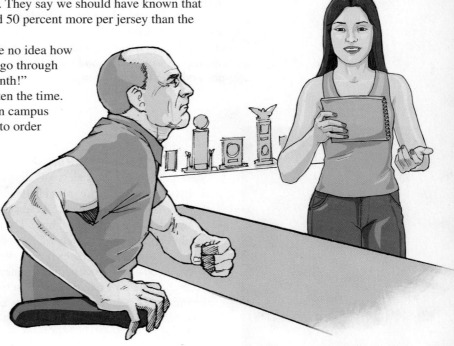

Q1. What problem does an ERP system solve?

Q2. What are the elements of an ERP system?

Q3. What are the benefits of an ERP system?

Q4. What are the challenges of implementing an ERP system?

Q5. What types of organizations use ERP?

Q6. Who are the major ERP vendors?

Q7. What makes SAP different from other ERP products?

Still fuming, Pat asks sarcastically, "So what else good happened at the first meeting?"

"They said start making lists of items you expect to buy this year. Because you blessed me with the duty of being our purchasing agent, I'm invited to configuration meetings every Monday for the rest of my life. And starting in the fall we all have training sessions on the new software to look forward to. Also, we have to tell them something called a *unit of measure* for everything we want to buy. I'm stumped on some of them. Do we buy detergent by the pound or by the gallon, do we buy individual baseballs or dozens of baseballs, stuff like that. They also want to know if one person will approve all purchase requests or if there will be a different person for every department. We also spent about a half-hour trying to figure out how to use the terms *kits* and *bundles*. I guess in an ERP system if you buy things together all the time they are a bundle and I forgot what a kit is, but it seemed important to the ERP people. And we ended on a real positive note—we couldn't decide if we want to officially recognize Cinco de Mayo, Good Friday, or September 11 as holidays."

To lighten the mood, Heidi digs a cheap-looking Superman T-shirt out of her desk drawer. "They gave some of us these great Superman Ts. I know it's a bribe, but I'm good with that. They gave these to people who they think will be super users. They train us on the system, and then we help them do the training for everyone in our department. I think that deserves a pay raise," Heidi says somewhat jokingly.

"Thanks, Heidi. And I thought keeping the boosters' club happy after last year was going to be my biggest headache."

As Heidi leaves, Pat admits to himself that the prospect of saving hundreds of thousands of dollars was too good for the administration to pass up in this time of rising tuition. The school has to save where it can. He is suspicious, though; this new buying process might limit his flexibility to award contracts to suppliers who were consistent givers to the sports program or keep him from buying decent jerseys. Pat thinks the idea of a single way to buy everything on campus won't be a good thing for the athletics department. He knows that no one at the university understands how different an athletics department is from other departments.

Chapter Preview

The athletic director was right. The university has to try to save money, and using an ERP system might help achieve that objective. ERP systems are wonderful tools to help reduce costs and achieve strategic goals, but as the university will find, successfully installing an ERP system is exceptionally challenging. It can take years to implement and cost hundreds of millions of dollars. These systems also require an organization to make difficult changes in the way it does things. The university is heading down a long and bumpy road.

In the previous chapter, we looked at business from a process perspective and examined how to make processes more efficient and effective. Here we discuss the same issue of IS and business process improvement, but from the IS point of view. More specifically, we investigate how one type of IS, a large-scale ERP system like the one implemented at the university, can improve processes across an entire organization and help the processes play well together. To do so, we will examine the components of an ERP system as well as the benefits and challenges of implementing an ERP system, but first we revisit the information silo problem from Chapter 5.

Q1. What Problem Does an ERP System Solve?

To appreciate the popularity of ERP systems today, consider how businesses operated before they were introduced. Businesses were much like Central Colorado State—their departments ran their own processes using their own information systems and databases. Information silos were everywhere. Recall from Chapter 5 that an information silo is isolated data stored in separated information systems. With information silos, the data needed by one process are stored in an information system designed and used in another process. Because information silos exist in isolation from one another, they create islands of automation that can reduce the performance of processes and make process integration difficult.

The silo problem is solved by ERP systems. We will define ERP systems more completely later in this question. For now, ERP systems are very large enterprise IS that bring data together in a big database and help a company improve its processes. We explain this approach in the rest of the chapter. However, before we get there, we briefly consider another approach to the same silo problem. This second solution is a more decentralized approach called enterprise application interface (EAI). ERP and EAI systems are sometimes referred to as *enterprise systems*.

Enterprise Application Integration (EAI)

An **enterprise application integration (EAI)** system tackles the silo problem by providing layers of software that connect information systems together. EAI is software that enables information silos to communicate with each other and to share data. The layers of EAI software are shown in Figure 6-1. For example, when the accounting information system sends data to the human resources information system, the EAI program intercepts the data, converts it to work in the format required by the human resources system, and then sends the converted data on to the human resources system. The reverse action is taken to send data back from the human resources system to the accounting system.

Although there is no centralized EAI database, EAI software keeps files of metadata that describe where all the organization's data are located and how the data must be transformed to work at each location. These details are hidden from users; the EAI system appears to be an integrated database to the user. EAI does the following:

- It connects information silos via a new layer of software.
- It enables existing applications to communicate and share data.
- It provides integrated data.
- It leverages existing systems, leaving departmental information systems as is, but providing an integration layer over the top.
- It enables a gradual move to ERP.

The major benefit of the EAI connect-the-silos approach is that it enables organizations to use existing applications while alleviating many of the problems of information silos.

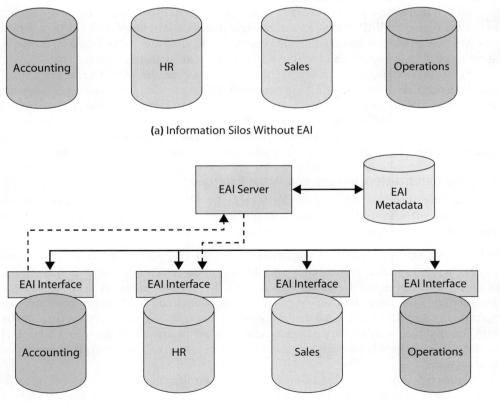

FIGURE 6-1

Enterprise Application Integration (EAI) Architecture

(a) Information Silos Without EAI

(b) Information Silos Connected with EAI

FIGURE 6-2

Two Characteristics of ERP Systems

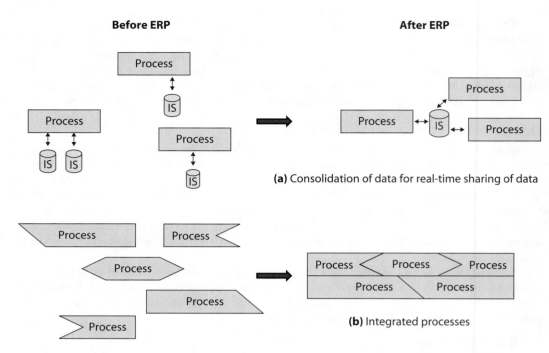

(a) Consolidation of data for real-time sharing of data

(b) Integrated processes

Converting to an EAI system is not nearly as disruptive as converting to an ERP system, it can be less expensive, and it provides many of the benefits of ERP. For some organizations, an ERP system is overkill, or its challenges, which we will soon examine, are too daunting. As a result, an EAI solution is a very smart choice for these organizations.

Enterprise Resource Planning (ERP)

As mentioned, ERP systems also solve the silo problem, but with a centralized approach. Early ERP systems emerged about 20 years ago as advances in network speeds and data storage enabled the development of a large, centralized, well-connected database that could span an entire company.

ERP systems have two key characteristics, as shown in Figure 6-2. First, as shown in the top of the figure, an ERP system creates a single database. By consolidating data, a company can avoid the problem of having multiple versions of the same thing—for example, storing data about a customer in two silos and not knowing which customer data is correct.

By having this single source of truth, this single database, the second key characteristic of ERP systems is made possible. ERP systems provide a set of industry-leading processes that are well integrated with each other as shown in the bottom of Figure 6-2. Process integration has enormous benefit. ERP process integration allows the "left hand of the organization to know what the right hand is doing." For example, data from a new sale is immediately sent to the database and that new data updates the pace of production and the procurement of supplies.

ERP Implementation: Before and After Examples

To better understand the impact of an ERP system, we will examine processes in two organizations before and after an ERP system is implemented. The first organization is the university discussed in the opening vignette; the second is Chuck's Bikes.

EXAMPLE 1: SINGLE PROCESS—UNIVERSITY PURCHASING Compare the university's procurement process before and after implementing an ERP system, as shown in Figure 6-3. In the top half of the figure, each university department works with its own purchasing agent to buy goods and services from three different suppliers. In the bottom half, each department purchasing agent works through a centralized university purchasing agent who in turn buys from the three suppliers. By integrating all the purchasing activity in one central office, the school is better able to standardize its purchasing process, manage it more effectively, and gain bargaining power over suppliers.

Figure 6-3 shows the effect of an ERP system on the university. The effect of an ERP system on a department is shown in the BPMN diagram in Figure 6-4. The top half shows the activities before implementing an ERP system, and the bottom half shows the activities after

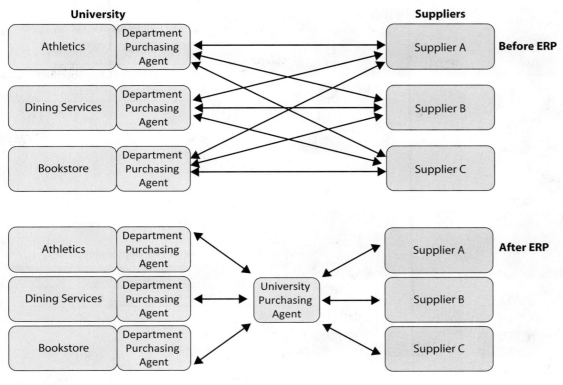

FIGURE 6-3
University Departments Procurement Before and After ERP

implementation. Before implementation, each department's procurement process had three main activities—Create Purchase Order, Receive Goods, and Accounting Activities. The process was initiated by an actor in the Department Purchasing Agent role. Every department at the university had a purchasing agent; in the athletic department, this role was played by Heidi.

Heidi started the process shown at the top left of Figure 6-4 by completing a purchase order (PO). An example PO might be an order for 500 T-shirts for summer camp. The second activity was Receive Goods. Goods were received when the T-shirts arrived on campus at the athletic warehouse where Willy, in the role of Warehouse Manager, signed for the delivery and put them on a shelf. Later, the athletic department accounting office would get a bill from the T-shirt maker and pay it. The purchases by the athletic department were recorded in a department database (not shown for simplicity). Each department on campus maintained its own purchasing database, creating information silos as a result.

The athletic department objectives for this process were to use reliable suppliers who would deliver the goods on time and were reasonably priced. Heidi also had an unstated objective, which was to use suppliers who were also boosters of the athletic department. Measures for these objectives were never specified.

After implementing the ERP system, a new procurement process provided by the ERP vendor is used by every department. This new process is shown in the bottom of Figure 6-4. Now Heidi completes a purchase requisition. A purchase requisition is a PO awaiting approval. The purchase requisition is approved by a University Purchasing Agent as the second activity. The rest of the activities in this process remain the same.

Rather than storing data in department information silos, the new ERP process consolidates all the procurement data for the different departments in a central database. Now when Heidi requests T-shirts, her order goes to a clothing vendor who already supplies the bookstore with thousands of clothing items every year. Because the university buys in bulk from this supplier, the university gets Heidi's T-shirts for less than if she ordered them herself.

With the university purchasing office now orchestrating the process, specific and clear objectives and measures have been developed for the process and shared with all purchasing agents. As mentioned in Chapter 5, in the language of business processes, measures are often

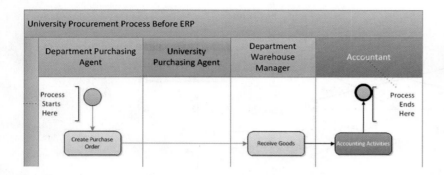

Before ERP Implementation	
Objectives	**Measures**
Use reliable suppliers	Not specified
Use boosters (unstated)	Not specified

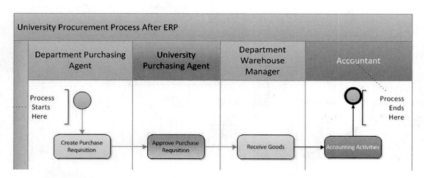

After ERP Implementation	
Objectives	**Measures**
Reduce cost	Cost

FIGURE 6-4

Impact of ERP System on Department

referred to as key performance indicators (KPIs). The university's objective with the new process is efficiency—lowering cost as measured by comparing this month's expenditures to last year's during the same month.

Although it is helpful to understand how an ERP system can improve a single process such as procurement at the university, it is perhaps more important to understand how an ERP system can improve processes for an entire organization. To see these larger-scale impacts, we shift gears to Chuck's Bikes.

EXAMPLE 2: MANY PROCESSES—CHUCK'S BIKES Some of the main processes for CBI before ERP implementation are shown in Figure 6-5. This figure illustrates how many of CBI's processes work together, with the primary activities of the value chain across the top.

Notice the five databases shown as cylinders—Vendor, Raw Material, Manufacturing, Finished Goods, and CRM. CRM is customer relationship management; a CRM database keeps track of data about customers. These five databases are information silos, isolated from each other as they support different processes.

By not having data consolidated in one place, CBI faces difficulty when data need to be shared in real time. For example, if the sales department has the unexpected opportunity to sell 1,000 bicycles, the sales manager must know if the company can produce these bikes in time to meet the delivery date. Unfortunately, the sales manager does not have all the data she needs because the data are stored in isolated databases throughout the firm. She does not know the current data of finished bikes in the Finished Goods database or of bike parts in the Raw Materials database. With data scattered throughout the firm, the potential sale is in jeopardy.

Contrast this situation with the ERP system in Figure 6-6. Here all of CBI's processes are supported by an ERP system, and the data are consolidated into a centralized ERP database. When the sales manager gets the opportunity to sell 1,000 bicycles, the data that the sales manager needs to confirm the order is readily available in the ERP system. From her desk, the sales manager can see how many bikes are finished and ready to sell and how many bikes will be produced in the coming days. Further, the ERP system can show the sales manager that if this

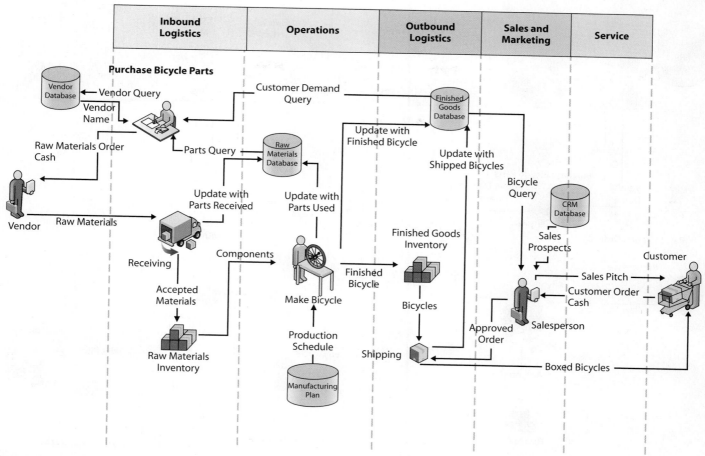

FIGURE 6-5
Pre-ERP Information Systems for Chuck's Bikes

current inventory is not quite enough, the company can double production next week but the cost of the bikes will go up 40 percent.

If the sales manager decides to proceed with the sale and production must double, the ERP system notifies managers in inbound logistics, operations, and outbound logistics with supply and production schedules. By consolidating the data in one place, the impact of the sale can be shared in real time with all affected processes.

As these two examples show, ERP systems consolidate data in one place, which makes it easier to share data. As a result, better process integration is achieved. While the single database and integrated processes are the big magic in ERP systems, the other components of the ERP IS also play a role in the success and failure of ERP systems. We consider these components and ERP processes next.

Q2. What Are the Elements of an ERP System?

To better understand the components of current ERP systems, consider their evolution. Current ERP systems are particularly strong in the areas in which they were first developed, such as manufacturing and supply processes.

Although the term *ERP* is relatively new, businesses have been using IS to support their processes for 50 years, well before the Internet. In the 1960s, a business could use a dedicated phone line, a computer card reader, and punch cards to send inventory orders to a supplier. By the 1970s, businesses began to buy their own mainframe computers, and manufacturing companies began to use software called **material requirements planning (MRP)** to efficiently manage inventory, production, and labor. As computing power became cheaper, **manufacturing resource planning (MRPII)** was developed that added financial tracking capabilities as well as the opportunity to schedule equipment and facilities.

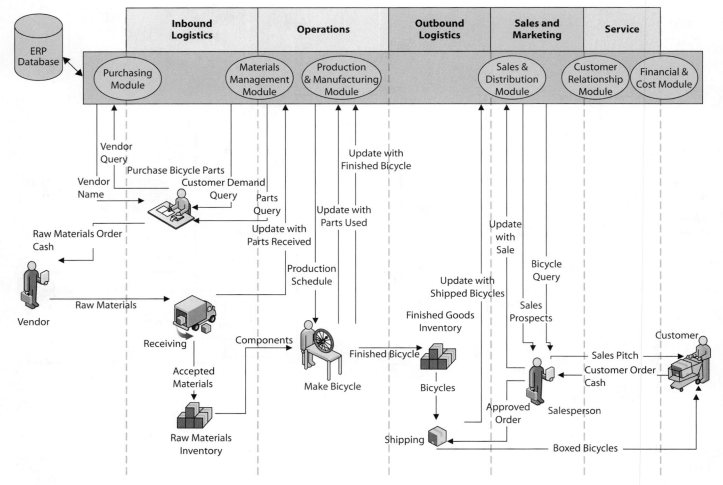

FIGURE 6-6
ERP System for Chuck's Bikes

The business environment continued to evolve with the advent of **just in time (JIT)** delivery. JIT integrates manufacturing and supply—manufacturing occurs just as raw materials arrive. To execute JIT, tight supplier relationships were needed. These relationships depended on unimpeded flows of data between partners. Just as this business need was emerging, Internet technologies globalized supply chains and customer markets in the 1990s.

Businesses began to see newly emerging ERP solutions as a comprehensive way to address their growing supply chain needs, ensure that the looming Y2K problem was solved, and overcome their information silo problem. A short time later, new federal laws such as the **Sarbanes-Oxley Act (SOX)** required companies to exercise greater control over their financial processes, and ERP systems addressed that new requirement. From this brief review, notice that businesses and IS coevolve; one makes progress and has an impact on the other, and vice versa.

As business changes, so must ERP systems. Today, for a product to be considered a true ERP product, it must include applications that integrate processes in the following business functions:[1]

- Supply chain management (SCM; procurement, sales order processing, inventory management, supplier management, and related activities)
- Manufacturing (manufacturing scheduling, capacity planning, quality control, bill of materials, and related activities)
- Customer relationship management (CRM; sales prospecting, customer management, marketing, customer support, call center support)

[1] "ERP101: The ERP Go To Guide," *ERPsoftware360*, accessed September 11, 2013, www.erpsoftware360.com/erp-101.htm.

- Human resources (payroll, time and attendance, HR management, commission calculations, benefits administration, and related activities)
- Accounting (general ledger, accounts receivable, accounts payable, cash management, fixed-asset accounting)

Although ERP solutions can integrate these processes, frequently an organization will purchase and implement just parts of the total ERP package. For example, a defense contractor might rely on just SCM and manufacturing, and a university may only install the human resources and accounting functions. The most common partial implementations are CRM to support promotion, sales, and service processes or SCM to integrate supply chain processes and promote data sharing with supply chain partners.

The Five Components of an ERP IS: Software, Hardware, Data, Procedures, and People

As shown in Figure 6-7, an ERP product provides a set of integrated processes as well as two of the five components of an IS—the software and an empty database. The product that an ERP vendor sells is not the same thing as a living, breathing ERP system used in a company after implementation, which is shown on the right side of Figure 6-7. To implement the ERP system, a company installs the ERP product's software and database on the company's hardware, writes procedures, and trains its people to follow them, as shown in Figure 6-7. Consider each component:

SOFTWARE ERP software typically resides on servers and on client machines in the company. The software can be customized to meet customer requirements without changing program code. This customization is called **configuration**.

This process of configuring the software is similar to the configuration you do when you install an email system. During installation of an email system, you might make 10 to 20 decisions, such as how long old email is retained, what folders are available, and what names are used for address books. In the same way, a company will make more than 8,000 configuration decisions to customize the ERP system to its needs. At the university, for example, to configure the system, many decisions must be made. These include decisions on the number of hours in the standard workweek, the holidays recognized by the university, the hourly wages for different job categories, the wage adjustments for overtime and holiday work, the units of measure for detergent and baseballs, and spending limits for each department.

Of course, there are limits to how much configuration can be done. If a new ERP customer has requirements that cannot be met via configuration, then the customer either needs to adapt its business to what the software can do or write application code to meet its requirements. Writing new code to supplement an ERP system is called **customization**.

For example, the athletics department is allowed to keep some of the money given by boosters for particular items such as greens fees for the golf team. The university could not figure out

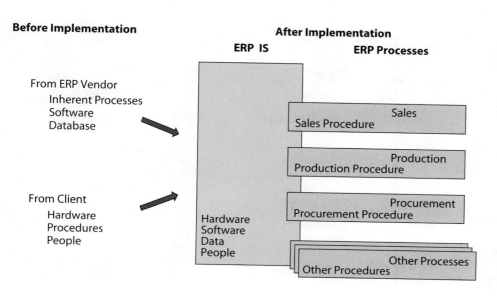

FIGURE 6-7
ERP IS and ERP Processes

how to configure the ERP system to display these funds appropriately. As a result, the university had to either write the code or hire another firm to write the code and add it to the ERP software. Code can be added to any ERP implementation using specific application languages such as Java. The most common use of this application code is to create company-unique reports from ERP data.

DATA An ERP solution includes a gigantic but largely unpopulated database, a database design, and initial configuration data. It does not, of course, contain the company's actual operational data. Operational data are entered during development and use.

ERP systems rely on a DBMS to process and administer the ERP database. Chapter 3 distinguished between the DBMS that creates and maintains the database and the database itself. Figure 6-8 shows this relationship. Common DBMS products used by ERP systems include IBM DB2, Oracle Database, and Microsoft SQL Server. ERP software interacts with the DBMS to update data in the database.

In an ERP database, there are several different types of data. **Transactional data** are data related to events such as a purchase or a student enrollment. For the university, examples of transactional data include purchases at the bookstore, student tuition payments, deliveries, and payroll expenditures. **Master data**, also called reference data, are data used in the organization that don't change with every transaction. Master data includes supplier names and addresses, item names and units of measure, and employee data. ERP systems also designate **organizational data**, data about the university such as the location of its warehouses, the mailing addresses of the buildings, and the names it of its financial accounts.

HARDWARE Each ERP implementation requires a wide variety of hardware, including disk storage, servers, clients, printers, scanners, network devices, and cables. To determine the necessary levels for each of these hardware devices, an organization first estimates the number of users, the processes supported, and the volume of data for the intended system. With these estimates, hardware sizing can be accomplished.

Recently, a new hardware opportunity has emerged that affects ERP systems: cloud computing. Currently, more than 80 percent of ERP products are installed on-premises on company hardware.[2] With the cloud, ERP systems may be rented with a much lower upfront cost, stored on cloud vendor hardware, and paid for by use. Most ERP vendors are offering cloud-based solutions, and this segment of the ERP market is growing three times faster than on-premises ERP. While the cloud is new, the lesson it teaches is an old one. ERP solutions, like all IT solutions, are designed and implemented on hardware that soon becomes dated. Like a forest fire cleans out some of the trees in an old-growth forest, a new technology cleans out an IT sector, creating a new ecology where new ideas and new businesses can take root alongside surviving businesses. New hardware options always create the opportunity for new approaches to emerge and new businesses to get a foothold, but transitioning to the new hardware can be expensive, risky, and challenging. At times, we may miss the old forest.

FIGURE 6-8
ERP Software, DBMS, and Database

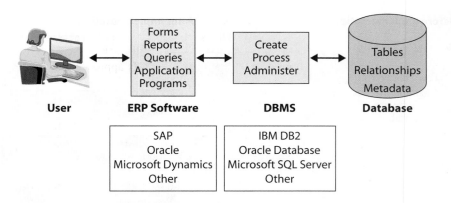

[2] "On-Premise or in the Cloud: How Best-in-Class Deploy their ERP Applications," Aberdeen Group Report, last modified April 2013, http://crawford-software.com/resources/On-Premise-or-in-the-Cloud-ERP-Deployment.pdf.

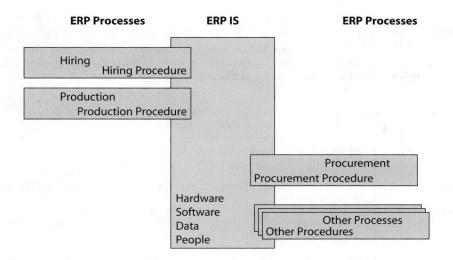

FIGURE 6-9

Example of ERP Processes, IS, and Procedures

PROCEDURES A procedure is a set of instructions for a person to follow when operating an IS. The relationship between ERP systems and processes is shown in Figure 6-9. On the left-hand side of the figure are two processes, Hiring and Production, that are linked to the ERP information system with procedures. Procurement and other processes are shown with their procedures on the right side.

Every ERP installation requires a firm to select ERP processes and then specify how those processes will be executed on the ERP software. These specifications and procedures are unique to the firm. For example, after Central Colorado State selects an Enroll New Student process, it must write a procedure for its employees to use when executing this process. These procedures tell the user which buttons to click and what text to enter into dialogue boxes like usernames and passwords.

Procedures not only specify instructions, they also are an important opportunity for organizations to improve control of a process. In the last chapter, we defined control as limiting behavior; one example was the cruise control of a car and how it limits variation in the car's speed. A well-written procedure for a process can limit the behavior of people executing the process. By limiting behavior, procedures help processes provide consistent results. For example, a good New Student procedure would include specific instructions for what to do with missing data, what to do with students without ID numbers, and how to handle readmitted students.

Crafting the procedure is the first step; training employees to use the procedure is the second step. Training employees how to interact with an ERP system can be a time-consuming and costly operation. To support this need, ERP vendors have developed extensive training classes and training curricula to enable users to learn the ERP system. ERP vendors typically conduct classes on site prior to, during, and after implementation. To reduce expenses, the vendors sometimes train the organization's users to become in-house trainers in training sessions called **train the trainer**. In the opening vignette, Heidi was designated as a potential super user, another term for a user who helps train other users. Even with this approach, the training bill is very large; a firm may budget a third of the total cost of the implementation on training and consulting fees.

PEOPLE The people involved with an ERP system fall into three general categories. *Users* are the employees of the firm implementing the system. **IT analysts**, also called *systems analysts*, are also employees. IT analysts have specialized training or education that enables them to support, maintain, and adapt the system after it has been implemented. Many analysts have a background or education in MIS or IT. A third role is *consultant*. A consultant works for the ERP vendor or a different company, called a *third party*, and helps budget, plan, train, configure, and implement the system. These consultants may work at the implementing firm for a period before, during, and after the implementation.

Although job titles and descriptions vary, a short list of the most common ERP positions is presented in Figure 6-10. Salary estimates are provided, although they vary widely by experience

Title	Job Description	Salary (in U.S. dollars)
Consultant	Employed by firm other than implementing company or ERP vendor, can perform any of the following roles during implementation	70,000–110,000
Systems analyst	Understands technical aspects of ERP; helps plan, configure, and implement ERP system for company use	70,000–90,000
Developer	Writes additional code where necessary for implementing ERP systems	76,000–92,000
Project manager	Defines objectives; organizes, plans, and leads team that implements ERP solution	80,000–120,000
Business analyst	Understands process aspects; helps plan, configure, and implement ERP system for company use	75,000–95,000
Architect	High-level planner of IS at an organization; ensures compatibility of technology and directs technology toward strategic goals	90,000–130,000
Trainer	Trains end users on how ERP system operates, explains their roles, and trains trainers	65,000–78,000

FIGURE 6-10
ERP Job Titles, Descriptions, and Salary Estimates

and location. Like an increasing number of IS jobs, success in these positions is based less on technical skill and more on process understanding and an ability to work with people. According to the Bureau of Labor Statistics, job opportunities in ERP and IS in general are expected to grow by nearly 25 percent from 2012 to 2022.[3]

When using the ERP system, people in an organization play specific roles. For example, one role for Heidi is department purchasing agent. When Heidi logs into the ERP system, she only has access to screens and data based on this role. She does not have access to other ERP data such as personnel salary data or configuration data. These limits are an example of **access control**, specifying limits on who can interact with an IS resource.

Inherent Business Processes

As mentioned earlier, ERP systems are more than an IS. They also specify processes called **inherent processes** or **process blueprints**. For the implementing organization, some of the changes it must make from existing processes to inherent processes are minor and hardly noticed, but some changes can be significant. Organizations implementing an ERP system must either adapt to the predefined inherent processes or design new ones. In the latter case, the design of a new process may necessitate changes to software and database structures, all of which mean great expense!

Now that we've discussed the pieces of the ERP puzzle, let's see how a firm puts these components together to create a functioning ERP system. The steps necessary to put the pieces together is itself a process—a simplified version of this Implementation process is shown in Figure 6-11. First, the top managers of the company revisit their strategy so that the ERP system has clear goals. Next, they conduct a **gap analysis,** a study that highlights the differences between the business requirements that emerge from strategic planning and the capabilities of the ERP system. The Implementation team then develops processes it will use and configures

---

[3] Bureau of Labor Statistics, "Computer and Information Technology Occupations," *United States Department of Labor,* last modified March 29, 2012, www.bls.gov/ooh/computer-and-information-technology/home.htm.

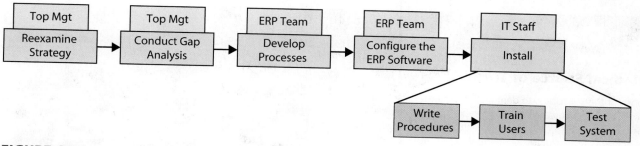

FIGURE 6-11

Implementation Process of an ERP System

the software. In the final steps, the company's IT staff writes procedures, trains the users, and tests the system. This Implementation process can require a year to 18 months for a large firm.

Q3. What Are the Benefits of an ERP System?

An ERP system provides a number of benefits to the organization as a whole. These organizational benefits are listed in Figure 6-12. Notice that the two key characteristics of ERP systems—consolidating data for real-time sharing and inherent processes that integrate well—headline this list of benefits.

One benefit of an ERP system is that real-time data sharing allows managers to see trends as they occur and respond appropriately. For example, the purchasing office at the university can see up-to-the-minute totals for each department's purchases. As a result, if food prices rise significantly, the purchasing office can help dining services re-allocate funds from other dining services accounts or change upcoming orders. Similarly, if an academic department is approaching its enrollment limit on a class, the ERP system can notify the department chair.

A second benefit of an ERP system for the organization is converting its processes to the well-integrated, inherent, best-practice processes of the ERP vendor. For example, at the university, best practices are now a part of the university procurement process. These practices include buying in bulk, negotiating prices prior to purchase, and a centralized procurement requisition approval activity. Prior to implementing the ERP system, the separate university departments purchased individually and not in bulk, they had little opportunity to negotiate price, and if a delivery was late or of poor quality, the department had little training or expertise in making things right.

A third benefit for the organization is that an effective ERP system can lead to better management as more managers have visibility to more data. For example, if the athletic director wants to check on the status of an order before meeting with a coach, that data is only seconds away. Similarly, the university purchasing department can easily total all the purchases from a particular vendor and renegotiate prices.

To help managers spot trends and changes, ERP systems can provide managers with **dashboards**, which are easy to read, concise, up-to-the minute displays of process KPIs. Like a car dashboard displays speed, fuel, and oil readings, a process dashboard will show sales for today, output of a production machine, or a summary of expenditures for the current month.

Benefits of Using an ERP Solution
Data sharing occurs in real time.
Implements integrated processes that are industry best practices.
More managers see more data, leading to better oversight.
The information silo problem is solved.
Better integration with supply chain partners.

FIGURE 6-12

Benefits of Using an ERP Solution

MIS InClass 6

One Medical Source of Truth

The purpose of this exercise is to demonstrate the usefulness of a single database, one source of truth. This exercise re-creates the Prescription Filling process that begins with a doctor writing a script. To begin, your instructor will hand-write a prescription for a medication on the board or projection system.

1. Without the aid of the Internet, write down on your own piece of paper the medication prescribed by your teacher. Then your teacher will read to you or show you the right answer.
2. Do the same exercise again, except now use the Internet on your mobile device and search for similarly spelled medications. For example, if you thought the prescription was for Methylphenidate (which is Ritalin) but you typed in Mathilpendate in a Google search, the Google search will correct it to Methylphenidate.
3. Would your errors be reduced if you had a list of 250 medications?
4. Would errors be eliminated if the doctor selected from a drop-down box?
5. Some hospitals are beginning to use automated pharmacies, a large machine that can dispense common medications like an ATM. What are the benefits and challenges of this technology?
6. Where else in the healthcare field are messages poorly written and interpreted that a consolidated database, a single source of truth, would help?
7. If the federal government establishes a consolidated database of medicine, what impact does this have on hospitals, pharmacies, doctor offices, and other organizations?

Source: VStock LLC/Tanya Constantine/Getty Images, Inc.

8. Which ERP challenges described in this chapter apply to attempting to create a large-scale medical database that can be shared by patients and healthcare and insurance providers?
9. What medical processes will a consolidated database of electronic health records support?

Alternative exercise: Each student folds a paper in half and then in half again. The student then writes a medication on one exposed side of the folded paper, adds a 1 to the end of the prescription, and hands the "prescription" to the next student. This second student rewrites the original prescription on a second section of the paper and labels it with a 2. A third and fourth student follow the same steps only looking at the most recent version. The paper is then handed back to the original owner. Notice the variations in spelling. Then answer questions 3 to 9.

Fourth, as was discussed earlier, another significant benefit of an ERP system is solving the information silo problem. This means that at the university, the different departments no longer create and maintain their own purchasing databases.

Finally, ERP systems make it easier to exchange data with supply chain partners. Sharing data throughout a supply chain can reduce costs and create efficiencies for every business in the chain. For this reason, some customers and suppliers will not want to do business with an organization that does not use an ERP system.

Clearly, the benefits of an ERP system are significant. However, these benefits are hard earned—the many challenges of implementing an ERP system are discussed next.

Q4. What Are the Challenges of Implementing an ERP System?

The process of converting an organization like the one shown in Figure 6-5 to an ERP-supported organization like that in Figure 6-6 is daunting and expensive. Some have called ERP implementation the corporate equivalent of a brain transplant or a nine-month root canal. If not done well, the losses are often very significant. For example, the U.S. Air Force recently pulled the plug on its 10-year ERP implementation having already spent $1 billion. Well-known firms like Kmart[4]

---

[4] C. Ndubisi Madu and K Chu-hua, *ERP and Supply Chain Management* (Chi Publishers Inc.), 2005, p. 20.

Year	Client	Costs	ERP Vendor
2012	U.S. Air Force	$1 billion	Oracle
2011	Montclair State University	$20 million cost overruns	Oracle
2011	Ingram Micro Australia	$22 million reduction in net income	SAP
2010	Dillard's Inc.	$8 million in disputed obligations	JDA
2009	City of San Diego	$11 million over budget	SAP

FIGURE 6-13

ERP Implementation Failures

and Hershey's[5] lost more than $100 million implementing ERP systems. In another debacle, the UK scrapped an ERP system designed to support electronic healthcare records after 10 years and $18 billion.[6] Other well-known recent failures are listed in Figure 6-13.

Here we describe the wide range of implementation challenges that fall into two general categories—decision making and people.

Decision-Making Challenges

Decision-making challenges that are common to ERP implementation are listed in Figure 6-14. One of the most challenging decisions for the client firm comes early: selecting the right ERP vendor. Client firms have unique needs, and ERP vendors have a variety of strengths and weaknesses. Picking the right vendor is an important challenge because it creates a long-term relationship between the firms; this relationship will have an impact on the effectiveness of the ERP system for the length of the contract.

Once the vendor is selected, a second challenge emerges. As mentioned earlier, the organization conducts a gap analysis to identify the differences between the business requirements that emerge from strategic planning and the capabilities of the chosen ERP system. The first difficult decision is deciding what the company would like the ERP system to do. A long list of "likes" will lead to a long list of gaps and a difficult implementation. The top leadership team should ensure that a focused, well-understood, short list of "likes" is adopted. The second decision is what to do about the gaps. The company can write custom code, look for a solution outside of ERP, or live with the gap for now.

A third set of challenging decisions occurs during configuration. As mentioned earlier, firms may need to make as many as 8,000 configuration decisions. To make matters even more challenging, many of the most important decisions require a wide understanding of both the business and the ERP system. Earlier in this chapter, the configuration decisions about wages and holidays were introduced. Figure 6-15 lists a sample of the other kinds of configuration decisions implementation teams must make. For brevity here, we consider just the first three—item identifiers, order size, and bill of material—to give you a glimpse of the overall challenge.

One configuration decision is item identifiers. Does the company want to identify or track every item in an incoming and outgoing shipment, a bundle of items, or just the entire shipment itself? Further, does it want to track material as it is being assembled or only when it is finished?

Implementation Decision Challenges
ERP vendor selection
Gap Analysis—decide on limited number of "like to dos" and what to do with gaps
Configuration—identifiers, order sizes, BOM
Data issues
Cutover pressure

FIGURE 6-14

Implementation Decision Challenges

[5] "Blaming ERP," Andrew Osterland, *CFO Magazine*, 1 January 2000, http://www.cfo.com/article.cfm/2987370.
[6] "10 Biggest ERP Software Failures of 2011," *PCWorld*, last modified December 20, 2011, www.pcworld.com/article/246647/10_biggest_erp_software_failures_of_2011.html.

FIGURE 6-15

A Sample of Configuration Decisions

Configuration Decisions
What do we select as our item identifier?
What will be our order sizes?
Which BOM format should we use?
Who approves customer credit (and how)?
Who approves production capacity (and how)?
Who approves schedule and terms (and how)?
What actions need to be taken if the customer modifies the order?
How does management obtain oversight on sales activity?

Another set of issues is order size—the organization must specify the number of items in a standard order. At one extreme is to order continuously in small amounts to reduce inventory. However, using that approach, transportation and ordering costs become a problem. At the other extreme, order sizes that are larger require warehouse space and tie up substantial capital.

A third detailed decision is the structure of the **bill of material (BOM)**. The BOM is like a recipe; it specifies the raw materials, quantities, and subassemblies needed to create a final product. Most large organizations have a wide variety of BOM structures in place for making their products. Deciding on one BOM standard can be challenging, particularly when the organization makes different types of products in different divisions.

For each of these configuration decisions, the implementation teams must first decide if any of the configuration choices offered by the ERP vendor are suitable. If not, the team must then weigh the advantages and disadvantages of using customized software. Configuring an ERP system is like an 8,000-question multiple-choice test, and on each question, the none-of-the-above answer—customization—is available.

Returning to the list of implementation decision challenges in Figure 6-14, a fourth set of decisions must be made about the data in the ERP system. One issue is the format of the data; for example, the sales department uses a five-digit customer ID, whereas the service department uses a four-digit number. In the past, each department maintained its own data and built processes on that numbering system. Committing to one number format can be a challenge and will make at least one department mad. Other data decisions include how duplications will be avoided and deciding who can enter and edit the data.

A fifth challenging set of decisions occurs during the transition, or cutover, from the current way of doing things to the new ERP system. These cutover decisions are common with any new IS and will be discussed more in Chapter 12; at this point, just recognize that cutover is like deciding which option to use to overcome an addiction. The addict or firm can go cold turkey and cutover all at once, it can do it gradually in a series of steps like rehab, or it can choose another option. The challenge for the addict or the implementation team is making good decisions under the stress of transition.

People Challenges

In addition to the challenge of making good decisions, the actions and attitudes of the people in the client organization can make implementation even more challenging. This challenge is aptly summarized by the saying, "All our problems wear shoes." Although this may overlook the technical ERP challenges, the saying wisely identifies the biggest challenge to successful implementation: people. Common people-related issues are listed in Figure 6-16. These challenges can be classified as top management, team, and individual.

MANAGEMENT MOVES ON PREMATURELY One common problem occurs when top management believes the hard part of the implementation process is the decision to implement. Managers believe that once that decision is made, they can move on. Instead, they need to stay involved and ensure implementation is monitored, resources are committed, good procedures are written, and thorough training is conducted.

Implementation People Challenges
Management
Moves on prematurely
Oversells
Fails to anticipate cultural resistance
Team
Collaboration breaks down
Individual
Users feel pain and get no gain

FIGURE 6-16

Implementation People Challenges

MANAGEMENT OVERSELLS A second top management problem is overselling the vision of what the system will do. Often management can be blinded by the benefits of the promised system and not look carefully at the assumptions behind the promises. This can lead top management to buy more features than it needs or than the organization can implement successfully. Employees who may be more familiar with the assumptions and the necessary change can quickly become jaded when the "grand solution" runs into inevitable implementation problems.

MANAGEMENT FAILS TO ANTICIPATE CULTURAL RESISTANCE An ERP implementation can change the culture of an organization. **Culture** is the day-to-day work habits and practices that workers take for granted. Culture is both difficult to see and difficult to change. When an ERP system is implemented, the way work is done is changed and the culture typically bites back. Changing the culture can lead to employee resistance as the change in work habits may threaten **self-efficacy**, which is a person's belief that he or she can be successful at his or her job. The athletic director in the opening vignette reacted negatively because he felt threatened by the system; he felt that he could not be successful in recruiting or fundraising if his procurement hands were tied by the new system.

COLLABORATION BREAKS DOWN Implementing an ERP system requires extensive and effective collaboration; when collaboration breaks down, implementation suffers. Consultants from the vendor, IT analysts from the client firm, and end users all know things the others don't know; these missing bits of knowledge can only be learned by collaborating. For example, at Central Colorado State, one collaboration team includes Heidi from the athletic department, an ERP expert from outside the university, and a university IT staff member. If Heidi does not tell the group that there are three warehouses that will receive purchased items, the system may be configured based on the assumption that there is only one. If the IT staff member does not tell the team that mobile devices do not work at some locations on campus, a poor procedure will be crafted.

EMPLOYEES SEE LITTLE BENEFIT As mentioned, implementation changes the work people do. However, the people whose work has changed often receive no benefit from the change; they get the pain but no gain. The benefits occur for the organization. For example, Heidi's work doesn't get much easier at the athletics department after the ERP system is implemented, but the organization benefits by the change. As a result, employees may need to be given extra inducement to change to the new system. As one experienced change consultant said, "Nothing succeeds like praise or cash, especially cash." Straight-out pay for change is bribery, but contests with cash prizes among employees or groups can be very effective at inducing change.

There are a lot of challenges when implementing an ERP system. Each one is not pass-fail; each one can take a toll in terms of cost, time, or system performance. We included this long discussion of challenges here to drive home one of the key lessons of this chapter. Implementing an ERP system is a very big deal for any organization. Fortunately, companies are getting better at this, and one reason may be that they have learned to anticipate some of these challenges.

ERP Upgrades

To this point, we have only considered the benefits and challenges of the initial ERP implementation. Today, many firms have survived an initial implementation and are executing a second or third upgrade to their original system. These upgrades frequently involve adding new functions to the system. Often, a company will first implement an ERP on a small scale in one division or function with the intent to expand later.

FIGURE 6-17
ERP Upgrade Challenges

ERP Upgrade Challenges
Surprise and resistance
Justification
Version lock from customization
No long-term upgrade strategy

Aggressive client firms upgrade their ERP systems as frequently as every 2 or 3 years, while 5 to 6 years is more common for less aggressive firms. Often an upgrade is justified on a pending change of service from the ERP vendor or a significant increase in service support fees from the vendor. Companies also upgrade to leverage advances in information technology and to better integrate their processes.

Having survived an initial implementation, most firms have learned how to cope with many of the problems just discussed. However, the challenges described above return for a rematch during the upgrade phase, and although they rarely overcome the firm, they often force delays and cost overruns. Upgrades have unique challenges compared to initial implementation; these are listed in Figure 6-17.

First, discussions about upgrades may need to occur within a year or two after the original implementation. This may come as a disappointing surprise to some in the organization, getting things off to a bad start. This resistance may be particularly strong if people believe the upgrade will be as disruptive as the original implementation.

Second, it may be more challenging to justify upgrades than an original implementation. An original implementation creates unique opportunities, and the contrast of the new ERP system with the old non-ERP system is both stark and encouraging. With an upgrade, these opportunities and the contrast between new and newer are not so vivid.

A third problem with upgrades is sometimes referred to as version lock. To understand **version lock**, recall that during implementation, the client firm may decide to write custom software to enable the system to do things unique to that client. Some organizations choose to customize heavily—they attempt to build into the ERP processes their unique way of doing things. However, when the ERP vendor upgrades their system to a new version, the new ERP software may not be compatible with the customization done by client firms. For firms that do little customization, an upgrade is relatively painless. In contrast, firms that customize extensively have essentially locked themselves into a particular version of ERP software, and upgrading is more difficult.

Finally, upgrades are challenging if the client firm has not developed a long-term strategy for ERP updates. This strategy should specify plans for upgrading different business functions and should allocate sufficient funds and manpower to ensure future upgrades are wisely conceived and executed.

Q5. What Types of Organizations Use ERP?

ERP systems are used by many organizations. Use depends on many factors, two of which are examined next: the organization's industry and the organization's size.

ERP by Industry Type

The first major ERP customers were large manufacturers in the aerospace, automotive, industrial equipment, and other industries. In these industries, ERP use is widespread and typically very effective. Given success in manufacturing, it was natural for ERP vendors to go up the supply chain and sell ERP solutions to those industries that supplied the manufacturers: distributors, raw materials extractors and processors, and the petroleum industry. At the same time, health care was becoming more complex, and hospitals were changing from a service to a profit orientation and began to adopt ERP solutions.

Over time, ERP use spread to companies and organizations in other industries, such as those listed in Figure 6-18. Today, ERP systems are used by governments and utilities, in the retail industry, and in education. However, in industries where ERP use has been less extensive, implementation may not be as smooth.

ERP by Industry
Manufacturing
Distribution
Mining, materials extraction, petroleum
Medical care
Government and public service
Utilities
Retail
Education

FIGURE 6-18
ERP by Industry

ERP by Organization Size

ERP, as stated, was initially adopted by large manufacturing organizations that had complex process problems that needed ERP solutions. Those large organizations also had the resources and skilled personnel needed to accomplish and manage an ERP implementation. Over time, as ERP implementation improved, other smaller organizations were able to implement ERP. Today, 84 percent of organizations with between 100 and 1,000 employees have already implemented ERP.[7] ERP systems are now increasingly common in firms with yearly revenues as low as $5 million.

Value chains and basic business processes are not different in character between small and large organizations. To quote F. Scott Fitzgerald, "The rich are no different from you and me, they just have more money." The steps required to check credit, verify product availability, and approve terms are no different for order processing at Amazon.com than they are at Phil's Muffler Shop. An excellent sales process for a multimillion-dollar company is very helpful to midsize companies. They differ in scale, but not in character.

However, companies of different sizes have one very important difference that has a major impact on ERP: the availability of skilled business and IT analysts. Small organizations employ only one or two IT analysts who not only manage the ERP system but also manage the entire IS department. They are spread very thin and are often in over their heads during an ERP implementation. Smaller, simpler ERP solutions are common among these companies.

Midsize organizations may expand IT from one person to a small staff, but frequently this staff is isolated from senior-level management. Such isolation can create misunderstandings and distrust. Because of the expense, organizational disruption, and length of ERP projects, senior management must be committed to the ERP solution. When IT management is isolated, such commitment is difficult to obtain and may not be strong. This issue is problematic enough that many ERP consultants say the first step for these firms in moving toward ERP is to obtain deep senior-level commitment to the project.

Large organizations have a full IT staff that is headed by the chief information officer (CIO), a business and IT professional who sits on the executive board and is an active participant in organizational strategic planning. ERP implementation will be part of that strategic process and, when begun, will have the full backing of the entire executive group.

International Firms and ERP

One way that the needs of large organizations differ in character from those of small organizations is international presence. Most billion-dollar companies operate in many countries, and the ERP application programs must be available in many languages and currencies.

Once implemented, ERP brings huge benefits to multinational organizations. International ERP solutions are designed to work with multiple currencies, manage international transfers of goods in inventories, and work effectively with international supply chains. Even more

---

[7] Nick Castellina, "A Guide for Successful ERP Strategy in the Midmarket," *Aberdeen Group,* accessed September 11, 2013, http://public.dhe.ibm.com/common/ssi/ecm/en/sml12349usen/SML12349USEN.PDF.

important, ERP solutions provide a worldwide consolidation of financial statements on a timely basis. As a result, they can produce one set of financial reports, better analyze where costs could be saved, and identify where production can be optimized.

While it is advantageous for these international firms to consolidate all their operations within one large ERP implementation, called a **single instance**, some firms maintain **multiple instances**, or an ERP for each country, business unit, or region. For these firms, the advantages of one set of data, a single financial system, and worldwide process standards are outweighed by the cost of consolidating or the disparity among divisions.

Q6. Who Are the Major ERP Vendors?

Although more than 100 companies advertise ERP products, many are designed for one or two business functions: customer relationship management, manufacturing, supply chain, or accounting. At the other end of the functional spectrum are comprehensive ERP systems that support most of the major processes in a business. In this comprehensive ERP industry, three vendors have the lion's share of the market, as shown in Figure 6-19. SAP has the largest market share and longest history, while Oracle and Microsoft have trailed in that order for most of the previous decade. These top three companies are often labeled Tier 1 ERP vendors and comprise about half of the total market share for ERP. A wide variety of vendors compete for the other half of the market.

Over the last several years, SAP's market share has decreased slightly as smaller vendors and cloud offerings have improved. Most of these changes can be attributed to growth in the small-to-medium market and the maturity of ERP systems in large organizations.

ERP Products

MICROSOFT DYNAMICS **Microsoft Dynamics** is composed of four ERP products, all obtained via acquisition: AX, Nav, GP, and SL. AX and Nav have the most capabilities; GP is smaller and easier to use. Although Dynamics has more than 80,000 installations, the future of SL is particularly cloudy; Microsoft outsources the maintenance of the code to provide continuing support to existing customers. Each product is particularly capable in different business functions. Compared with Oracle and SAP products, a Dynamics implementation is typically smaller in scale and functionality and, as a result, a bit less expensive and time consuming to implement. None of these products are well integrated with Microsoft Office, and none of them are integrated at all with Microsoft's development languages. In fact, Microsoft's ERP direction is difficult to determine. It seems to have four horses headed in different directions, and none of them are attached to the primary Microsoft coach.

ORACLE Oracle is an intensely competitive company with a deep base of technology and high-quality technical staff. Oracle developed some of its ERP products in-house and has complemented those products with others obtained through its acquisition of PeopleSoft (high-quality HR products) and Siebel (high-quality CRM products). Beginning with its first DBMS product release, Oracle has never been known to create easy-to-use products. It is known, however, for producing fully-featured products with superior performance. They are also expensive. Oracle CEO Larry Ellison owns 70 percent of NetSuite, a company that offers

FIGURE 6-19
ERP Vendors and Market Share

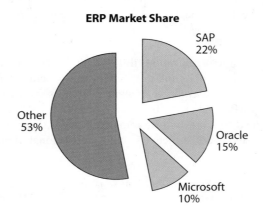

ERP Market Share

SAP 22%

Oracle 15%

Microsoft 10%

Other 53%

a cloud-based solution for integrated financial reporting for large, international organizations. Oracle also recently signed a 9-year agreement with Salesforce.com, indicating Oracle's interest in the cloud-ERP sector.

SAP SAP is the gold standard of ERP products. SAP is used by midsized and large companies and offers the most extensive line of ERP products. It has recently introduced Business ByDesign and Business One as smaller, more lightweight options for small to midsized companies, and it is expanding its cloud offerings with Cloud for Financials and Cloud for Customers. In Q7, we elaborate more on SAP than the other ERP products because we will use it in the next two chapters to explain the procurement and sales processes and how an ERP system improves those processes.

OUTSIDE OF TIER 1 While the titans of Tier 1 duke it out trying to be everything to everybody, smaller firms are establishing a strong niche by offering industry-specific systems, solutions for particular business functions, or pay-as-you-go cloud services. While the functional breadth and opportunity for corporate-wide standardization of processes make Tier 1 vendors appealing to large firms, many midsize to small firms find smaller, more nimble, or cloud-based solutions less disruptive and lower risk. Keep your eye on one of the more popular choices: Salesforce .com, an industry leader in CRM cloud services, mentioned earlier as Oracle's business partner.

We close this chapter with a more thorough look at SAP. While some of you will use the SAP tutorials at the end of Chapters 7 and 8 to practice with SAP software, it is helpful for all of you to better understand some background on the industry leader as well as some of the features of SAP software that are common to all ERP products.

Q7. What Makes SAP Different from Other ERP Products?

SAP is a product of **SAP AG**, a German firm. It is pronounced as three letters, "S-A-P," not as the word *sap*. The letters are an abbreviation for "Systems, Applications, Products," which in German is "*Systeme, Anwendungen, Produkte*." Detractors humorously claim it might also stand for "Stop All Progress" or "Start And Pray," titles that hint at the challenges of using SAP and of its importance to the company.

Founded in 1972 by five former IBM employees, SAP AG has grown to become the third-largest software company in the world, with about 50,000 employees, 100,000 customers, and 10 million users in more than 100 countries. The core business of SAP AG is selling licenses for software solutions and related services. In addition, it offers consulting, training, and other services for its software solutions. The stated goal of SAP software is to help companies make their business processes more efficient and agile. To do this, it relies on a database of more than 25,000 tables.

More than 80 percent of *Fortune* 500 companies use SAP, including Coke, Caterpillar, Exxon Mobile, Procter & Gamble, IBM, Marathon Oil, General Motors, Nike, and General Electric. To install SAP today, those companies might spend $100 million or more. Of this total cost, hardware may account for 20 to 25 percent, software 20 to 25 percent, and "human ware" (training, consulting, and implementation) 50 to 60 percent. Training, consulting, and implementation of SAP products has become a career for many in IT, and it is easy to see why—companies need technical people who understand the business and business processes and can make SAP work for them.

The prices mentioned above vary because getting SAP up and running in a company varies—in some cases the process can take years. One time-consuming process is answering the more than 8,000 configuration decisions mentioned earlier. To speed up the configuration process, SAP produces and sells **industry-specific platforms**. An industry-specific platform is like a suit before it is tailored; it is a preconfiguration platform that is appropriate for a particular industry, such as retail, manufacturing, or health care. All SAP implementations start with an SAP industry-specific platform and are further configured to a particular company with the configuration choices mentioned earlier. A second lengthy and expensive process is training employees of all levels how to use the system.

A common way to view SAP is as a collection of interconnected and interdependent modules, some of which are listed in Figure 6-20. A **module** is a distinct and logical grouping of processes. For example, SD, the Sales and Distribution module, is a collection of processes

FIGURE 6-20
SAP Modules

SAP Modules			
QM	Quality Management	PP	Production Planning
FI	Financial Accounting	CO	Controlling
PM	Plant Maintenance	SD*	Sales and Distribution
HR	Human Resource	MM**	Materials Management
PS	Project Systems	BI	Business Intelligence

*SD includes sales processes, the topic of Chapter 8.
**MM includes procurement processes, the topic of Chapter 7.

supervised by the marketing department. These processes record customer data, sales data, and pricing data. Not every module is implemented in every installation of SAP. Companies that install SAP choose modules for their implementation.

SAP Inputs and Outputs

An example SAP screen is shown in Figure 6-21. When the screen first loads, it is largely empty. On a screen like this, Heidi, following the university's procedure, enters a vendor number in the box numbered 1 and the material in box number 2. After clicking the check icon, marked as 3, SAP populates the screen as shown with data about the company, payment options, and pricing choices for Heidi. The screen shown in Figure 6-21 is called the Create Purchase Order: Overview screen. When SAP is implemented and configured at a particular organization, this screen is made available only to approved purchasing agents in each department. Different roles in the organization give people access to different screens and different data; accountants would have access to their screens, warehouse people their screens, and so on. Although it is difficult to tell from this example, Heidi does not have the option to permanently delete a purchase order once it has been saved. SAP is designed to preclude deleting saved records. This control makes auditing and supervision of the transactions more complete and reduces the risk of fraud. Other controls limit the data the salesperson can enter. For example, items sold must already be in inventory, ZIP codes must match cities, and delivery locations to a warehouse must be specified.

SAP Software

SAP was the first ERP software designed to work at different companies. Prior to SAP, early ERP programs were customized products—companies wrote their own programs to support their own processes. When SAP was launched, its first effort was to consolidate data for

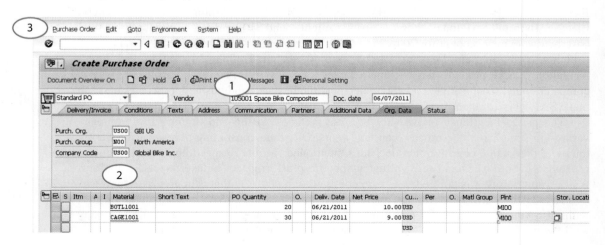

FIGURE 6-21
SAP Procurement Example Screen

Source: Copyright © SAP AG

financial, accounting, inventory, and production-planning processes. Personnel and plant management modules were developed in the 1980s.

One of the more well-known versions of SAP is called **R/3**. The R/3 program (where R means "real time") was the first truly integrated system that was able to support most of an organization's major operational processes. Built in the 1990s, the R/3 platform uses client-server architecture. It experienced runaway growth in the 1990s and was installed in 17,000 organizations. Ironically, this past success creates a problem today. SAP R/3 uses classic, native client, client-server architecture, rather than a browser-based approach that would be easier to use on a wide range of devices, such as smartphones and other thin clients. Because of this large installed base, SAP has lagged the competitions' rapid move to thin-client, cloud-based solutions. Instead, it must focus resources and attention on the needs of its current customers (and the attendant large revenue stream from their maintenance contracts). SAP has the twin challenge of building a stable single platform that makes company processes efficient today while at the same time providing a platform that will adapt to take advantage of new IT developments. SAP overcame its early dependence on mainframe architecture; now it must do so again to overcome its dependence on client-server architecture.

To this end, SAP has rebranded its R/3 software as the **SAP Business Suite**. The SAP Business Suite runs on a program called an *application platform*. The SAP application platform is NetWeaver. NetWeaver is like the operating system in your computer. Recall from Chapter 3 that an operating system helps connect programs, printers, and other devices. Similarly, **NetWeaver** connects SAP to hardware, third-party software, and output devices. NetWeaver also has SOA capabilities that help it integrate SAP with non-SAP applications. These features enable the Business Suite/NetWeaver approach to be more adaptive to new IT developments compared to R/3. **ABAP** is SAP's high-level application language that is used to enhance the functionality of an SAP implementation.

Helping your future company, whether large or small, make wise use of ERP systems will be one of the challenges you will face during your business career. You will be hired initially into a department based on your experience and education, but all businesses want integrated processes. As a result, you will be asked to think about how your department's processes can be improved with the ERP system and how they can be integrated with other processes in the firm.

This will take some of the skills mentioned in Chapter 1: the ability to experiment, collaborate, think about systems, and use abstract reasoning. Employers seek new hires who have mastered some of the aspects of ERP systems. So take time to command the vocabulary in these next several chapters. Learn how the procurement and sales processes work in Chapters 7 and 8 and how an ERP system supports those processes. If you have access to SAP, accomplish the SAP exercises at the end of the next two chapters and, once complete, start over and deliberately make mistakes, try new things, and see how SAP acts. Learn beyond the book; later you'll be glad you did.

Ethics Guide

ERP Estimation

Todd Douglas Jones was the director of IT at Central Colorado State when the ERP system was implemented. He was a big advocate of the ERP system because he had seen such systems work elsewhere and was convinced it would work well at the university.

Todd was charged with the task of determining the costs and benefits for the new system. After some preliminary research on the topic, he decided that cost should primarily be measured in the price of the product and the number of hours of training for the users of the system. Benefits will be determined by the reduction in operating costs.

In order to help the university's president and staff see that the benefits of purchasing and implementing an ERP solution outweighed the costs, Todd shaded the facts in order to make the ERP choice look more promising. Todd did a number of questionable things:

a. He researched 10 schools that had implemented a similar system. He could have used the cost and labor of all 10 schools as estimates for his school. However, in his opinion, three of the schools mismanaged the implementation, and he chose not to include those schools in his estimate, resulting in a lower cost estimate for his university.

b. He estimated that end-user training would be 750 hours, although he expected at least 1,000 hours would be needed. He planned to fund the other 250 hours from his IT training budget for next year.

c. To calculate cost savings, Todd used a different set of 10 schools than he used in item a. He believed that these 10 schools were closer in size to his own school and were more representative of his university, and they made the cost savings look better than the 10 other schools.

Six months after the very successful implementation, Todd was hailed as a visionary. The university is saving thousands of dollars a month. Seven months after the implementation, an auditor discovered the three questionable activities listed above.

You are Todd. Your boss knows what you did. You look into your own motivations and with a clear conscience you tell yourself: I did not tell a lie. I knew that the system would be a tremendous success, and if I did not help the boss come to see that I would have let a great opportunity pass us by. I did what was best for the most people. I did not directly profit from this. If I were the boss, I would want my IT manager to help me reach the right conclusion, too. And look how it turned out—that alone shows I did the right thing.

DISCUSSION QUESTIONS

1. Was Todd ethical in his actions? Use both the categorical imperative (page 20) and utilitarianism (page 40) in your answer.
2. Of the actions taken by Todd, which one was the least ethical?
3. What would you do if you were Todd's boss? How does this change your management of Todd in the future?
4. What is the difference between inappropriate rationalization and justification?
5. How do you know when you are rationalizing inappropriately?
6. Do you agree with Todd's last statement? Does a good result always indicate a good process or a good decision?

Source: Orange Line Media/Shutterstock.

Active Review

Use this Active Review to verify that you understand the material in the chapter. You can read the entire chapter and then perform the tasks in this review, or you can read the text material for just one question and perform the tasks in this review for that question before moving on to the next one.

Q1. What problem does an ERP system solve?

Explain how businesses used IS before ERP systems. Identify the problem solved by an enterprise system. Explain information silos. State the differences between the two enterprise systems: EAI and ERP. Define *EAI* and describe how EAI works. Give several reasons why a firm might want to use an EAI rather than ERP. Describe the two key characteristics of ERP systems.

Q2. What are the elements of an ERP system?

Explain how businesses used computers for inventory purposes before the Internet. Explain the difference between MRP and MRPII. Explain how business and IS have coevolved. Name several of the business functions integrated by ERP. What is the difference between an ERP product and an implemented ERP system at a company? Describe configuration. Explain why a company might create a custom program for its ERP implementation. Describe the relationship between ERP systems and databases. Differentiate among the three types of ERP data. Explain the two ERP hardware issues. Describe how procedures can improve control of a process. Explain several ERP jobs. Describe inherent processes.

Q3. What are the benefits of an ERP system?

Explain why it is not accurate to say that ERP improves existing processes. Describe the advantages of the real-time data benefit of ERP systems. Explain how ERP benefits management. Describe the contents and purpose of a dashboard.

Q4. What are the challenges of implementing an ERP system?

Why is selecting the right ERP vendor an important decision? In a gap analysis, why should a company avoid creating a long list of things it would like the ERP system to do? Give several examples of the types of decisions a firm must make to configure an ERP system. Explain the general options the implementation team has for each decision. Explain the disadvantages of using custom software with ERP. What makes the transition, the cutover, from the old system to the new a challenge? Explain each of the people implementation challenges. Describe culture and why it is important to ERP implementation. What problems are unique to ERP upgrades?

Q5. What types of organizations use ERP?

Explain how the type of firm that uses ERP has changed over time. How can the size of the organization affect ERP success? What ERP needs are unique to large organizations? Describe the unique benefits of ERP systems for international firms.

Q6. Who are the major ERP vendors?

How do the Tier 1 ERP vendors differ? Name the three top vendors and explain how they are unique. Identify the relative market share of each. Explain which ERP vendors serve small and midsized organizations and which serve large organizations.

Q7. What makes SAP different from other ERP products?

Describe SAP AG. Break down the expenses for implementing SAP. Define *module* and give examples of SAP modules. Explain how access to SAP screens can be controlled and how SAP limits or controls data inputs. Describe SAP's NetWeaver. Explain the important characteristics of R/3.

Key Terms and Concepts

Using Your Knowledge

6-1. Give two examples of organizations that you know have information silos. Would either of these organizations choose an EAI solution over an ERP solution? Explain.

6-2. What would happen next fall if the freshman class is unexpectedly 20 percent larger than this year's class? Which campus organizations need to know that data early? Do you think your university has a way to share this data efficiently?

6-3. An ERP can create a digital dashboard of important statistics and measures. What data would you like on your dashboard if you were the athletics director? Are they all measures of process objectives? What data would you like if you were the president of the university? Who else at the university could use a dashboard to do their work more effectively?

6-4. What does this MIS class do differently than other classes? Maybe the assignments are a bit different, maybe the instructor does some things a little differently. What if a university instructional ERP system was invented that featured inherent processes that removed these unique elements? Would that make the school's teaching process more efficient and effective? How could you measure that improvement? Would it be worth it?

6-5. If your school adopts a new ERP-like system to improve class scheduling, procurement, and HR functions, which of the implementation people challenges in Figure 6-16 might be particularly hard in a university setting?

6-6. The athletics director buys sports equipment from a supplier with a well-implemented ERP. What advantages are there for your school to buy from a supplier with an ERP system? You might expect to see an advertising claim from that company like, "We can meet customer orders in 20 percent less time than the industry average." Create a list of two or three measures you would expect to hear from a supplier with an effective ERP system and two or three measures that an ERP system might not improve.

6-7. To have a successful ERP system, a sports equipment supplier will have made a variety of good configuration decisions. Give examples of what you think might be the company's item identifiers and order sizes. Also, who do you think approves customer credit and production capacity increases? What actions need to be taken if a customer modifies an order?

6-8. Assume that a sports equipment supplier chose SAP and is an equipment wholesaler that does not produce the equipment it sells to universities. As a wholesaler, which module in Figure 6-20 might the supplier not purchase from SAP?

6-9. Figure 6-4 shows the procurement process now used at the university and the objectives and measures used by the athletics department. If you worked as the purchasing agent for dining services, buying all the food served in campus dining halls, what would be the objectives and measures of your procurement process?

Collaboration Exercise 6

Collaborate with a group of fellow students to answer the following questions. For this exercise, do not meet face to face. Your task will be easier if you coordinate your work with SharePoint, Office 365, Google Docs with Google+, or equivalent collaboration tools. (See Chapter 9 for a discussion of collaboration tools and processes.) Your answers should reflect the thinking of the entire group, not just that of one or two individuals.

1. Using your local hospital as an example, answer the following questions:
    a. Where might information silos exist if an ERP system is not being used?
    b. Should the hospital pursue more efficient processes or more effective ones? Does it matter if you are a patient?

    c. Using your answer to item b, what measures might be used to assess the benefits of an ERP system at the hospital?
    d. Of the configuration decisions listed in Figure 6-15, which ones apply to the hospital?
    e. Which ERP vendor would you suggest for the hospital? Explain your selection.
    f. Assign each person on your team the task of diagramming a different hospital process using BPMN. Then merge your diagrams and reduce the detail in each of the individual processes so that the overall process diagram has about the same number of activities as the individual processes did before merging.

2. Using your university or college as an example, answer the following questions:
   a. Where might information silos exist if an ERP system is not being used?
   b. Will using an ERP system improve the efficiency or effectiveness of processes? What are the objectives of the process(es) being improved?
   c. Using your answer to item b, what measures might be used to assess the benefits of an ERP system at the university?
   d. Of the configuration decisions listed in Figure 6-15, which ones apply to the university?
   e. Which ERP vendor would you suggest for the university? Explain your selection.

3. The paper airplane exercise in MIS InClass 5 was designed to help you see important aspects of processes and enterprise systems:
   a. What lessons from Chapter 6 can be applied to the process of building paper airplanes?
   b. Rewrite the instructions to make it easier for future classes to learn the lessons you identified in the previous question.
   c. Could this game be used in other business school classes? What learning objectives could this game deliver?

CASE STUDY 6

The Sudden End of the U.S. Air Force[8]

"Why does the country need an independent Air Force?" This question is now being asked by the top brass and the civilian leadership at the Pentagon. Many other government agencies—local, state, and federal—are asking similar types of questions. New enterprise systems available to government agencies are making them question old ways of doing things and old processes. The need for intelligence agencies to overcome their information silos and share data on potential terrorist threats is constantly in the news. The same information silo problem exists with your local police and fire departments and with many other government agencies at all levels. The Air Force issue is a classic case of what happens when a new IS and information silos meet.

The military still needs airplanes, but what it needs more are integrated end-to-end processes that connect soldiers fighting on the ground with airplanes supporting them. Military airplanes provide two important services: They collect data about the war zone, and they drop ordnance on targets. In both cases, these are just activities within larger processes, processes that until now had to be done by different departments using their own isolated databases.

One process is the Collect Battlefield Intelligence (BI) process. Troops currently fighting and managers planning the fighting both need BI. In both cases, the process starts as a Department of the Army request for intelligence. This request is passed to the Department of the Air Force, which then schedules the flight, assigns pilots, specifies locations, and collects data. After the flight, the data is then sent back to the Army. The delivery of ordnance goes through exactly the same interdepartmental process; the only difference is that when the trigger is pulled in the airplane, a bomb goes out rather than data coming in.

These processes have worked this way for about 50 years. Recently, pilotless drones have been developed that do the work that manned airplanes did in the past. These drones have much in common with information systems. The plane, the hardware, is controlled by the software that flies the plane. Data is collected by the drone, and the drone has a database of GPS coordinates and data on the height of every obstacle near it. People operate the drone to drop ordnance and collect BI using well-established procedures.

These flying information systems, these drones, have changed many of the old processes used by the organization in much the same way ERP changes processes. Because they can be much smaller than manned airplanes and much cheaper, drones can be assigned to the Army units doing the fighting. As a result, the process to drop ordnance or gather BI is accomplished much more quickly. Instead of information silos that separated Air Force and Army data, now the drone can quickly respond to the request and the data can be made available in real time to the Army units that need it. If these new processes are completely adopted, there may be no need for an independent Air Force.

Questions

6-10. Using BPMN documentation, diagram the Collect Battlefield Intelligence process before and after the use of drones. Some activities are Request for Intelligence, Schedule Airplane, and Transmit Data. Resources include the Army database and the Air Force database. Roles include Warfighter, Planner, and Airplane Scheduler. Actors can be Airplane and Drone.

6-11. Will the new process have the same objectives as the old process? Are the new objectives focused on effectiveness or efficiency or both? What measures should be used to prove efficiency and effectiveness?

6-12. Beyond the two processes mentioned here, if the Department of Defense implemented an ERP system, which of the benefits in Figure 6-12 could it expect to attain?

6-13. Again, if one ERP system is used in the future, what are the most significant challenges the Department of Defense will encounter?

6-14. Pick another government agency that you understand well. Explain what existing processes would be replaced by an ERP system, what the benefits of an ERP system would be, and the challenges faced.

[8] Based on Greg Jaffe, "Combat Generation: Drone Operators Climb on Winds of Change in the Air Force," *Washington Post,* February 28, 2010.

Chapter 7 Supporting the Procurement Process with SAP

"**T**ell me, Wally, what was the hardest part of your job as a warehouse manager?" asks Jerry Green. The two are huddled around a small table in a warehouse at Chuck's Bikes, Inc. (CBI),[1] a small bicycle company that buys frames, tires, and accessories and then assembles bikes that it sells to retailers. They are discussing Wally's pending retirement.

"It was probably dealing with people. Suppliers would only tell me half the story when my orders were going to be late, and our salespeople seem to think I should be able to read their minds," says Wally.

"And, by the way, this job description doesn't describe what I do," says Wally, pointing to an updated version of his job description.

"Wally, you are one of a kind. We can't replace you, but we can be specific about the skills we need," Jerry replies. Jerry, the head of human resources at CBI, and Wally are tweaking a draft job description to hire Wally's replacement.

"Wally, do you see anything we missed?"

"Nothing is missing, but this description makes my job sound like you need to be a statistics and computer whiz just to apply. I never thought the job was that complicated—just figure out what you need to order, what you have, what is available, and when you need everything. This year's orders are like last year's orders. You keep a little of everything."

Wally continues after a pause. "But maybe we should change the job. I really did not act fast enough when the salespeople told us about those new e-bikes.

Q1. What are the fundamentals of a Procurement process?

Q2. How did the Procurement process at CBI work before SAP?

Q3. What were the problems with the Procurement process before SAP?

Q4. How does CBI implement SAP?

Q5. How does the Procurement process work at CBI after SAP?

Q6. How can SAP improve supply chain processes at CBI?

Q7. How does the use of SAP change CBI?

Q8. What new IS will affect the Procurement process in 2024?

---

[1] At the request of SAP University Alliance, we did not make any changes to the Global Bike, Inc. (GBI) case. Instead, we have created a company that is different, a competitor, for which we can add characters without compromising the GBI SAP materials but that is close enough to enable students to be able to use the GBI SAP simulation, if appropriate.

They had to cancel sales for those bikes because I simply didn't get the little electrical motors here in time. Maybe if we had that SAP program working, it would have helped. But then again that thing is less user friendly than my cat."

"Well, we did add experience with SAP as a requirement to your job description."

"The only person who's not afraid of that system is that guy we just hired—Jake. He seems to know stuff from his college classes about it. For the rest of us, that system is not easy to use. And I didn't realize when we put it in how much it would change my job."

"That's an understatement. I'm still getting used to it. Some days I wish I were the one retiring."

After they work on some details, Jerry thanks Wally for his help and sees him out. Later, Jerry and Wally's boss, Tim, discuss the job description.

"Wally was the best warehouse manager Chuck's Bikes has ever had," Tim says.

"But he's also one reason the new system doesn't run well," adds Jerry. "His skill set matches the job description from 15 years ago, but those skills are outdated now."

"You're right. He hasn't adapted to the SAP system very well. That's one reason I'm glad he took our offer to retire early."

"I don't think it was just the new system. His job was already becoming more complex. Wally was great until we expanded the product line a couple of years ago."

"Wally did mention that he thought this new description overemphasizes math and computer skills."

"I see his point. I think we should balance those with team skills and communication. The new position will require more communication with the other warehouses and departments here."

"I'll add those. But look at this description now. Doesn't it seem odd that someone we both think was terrific at one time couldn't win his own job today?"

"It does seem like a new day."

Chapter Preview

In this chapter, we look into the Procurement process that Wally supervised before and after the implementation of SAP. We are interested in how SAP made that process and other processes at his company better.

In the previous two chapters, we introduced processes and ERP systems. Here and in the next chapter, we show how the general ideas about processes and ERP systems can be applied to two common business processes. We will see how the benefits of ERP—consolidating the data and using inherent processes that integrate well—can improve the Procurement process. In Chapter 8, we examine the Sales process.

We begin by considering how CBI accomplished procurement before implementing SAP. We then examine how SAP improved CBI's Procurement process. Although most of the chapter concerns the Procurement process, toward the end of the chapter we will broaden our discussion to other processes in CBI's supply chain. While the Procurement process can be improved with SAP, the positive impact on the group of procurement-related processes is even more significant.

Q1. What Are the Fundamentals of a Procurement Process?

Before discussing the Procurement process at CBI, a short review of procurement fundamentals will set the stage for understanding this process at CBI. Here we define procurement along with its objectives and activities.

Procurement is the process of obtaining goods and services such as raw materials, machine spare parts, and cafeteria services. Procurement is an operational process executed hundreds or thousands of times a day in a large organization. The three main procurement activities are Order, Receive, and Pay, as shown in Figure 7-1. These three activities are performed by actors in different departments and were briefly introduced in Chapter 6 with the example of procurement at a university.

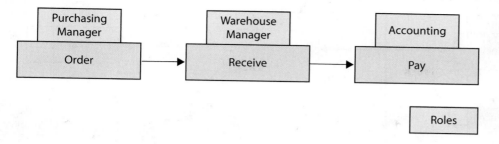

FIGURE 7-1

Main Procurement Process Activities and Roles

Procurement is the most common organizational process. Every organization, from single employee startups to Walmart and from county to federal governments, relies on its Procurement process. For businesses that make products, procurement is a vital process as all the raw material and parts needed for production or assembly must first be procured. However, even firms that provide services depend on procurement. For example, hospitals need thousands of healthcare products, and universities need food, equipment, landscaping services, and mascots. Look around you. Every man-made thing you see passed through at least one procurement process, and that Camry driving down the street has parts that were procured by hundreds of suppliers, each with its own procurement process.

Even college students procure items: You order books and movies online, and you buy clothes and food. Everything you own you procured in some way. And, like procurement at an organization, your process has objectives—you do not want to buy inferior goods, and you do not want to waste time or money.

Many organizations have similar procurement objectives; the most common are saving time and money. According to some estimates, a well-managed procurement process can spend half as much as a poorly managed procurement process to acquire the same goods.[2] The state of Pennsylvania has saved $360 million a year by restructuring its procurement process; other states have saved 10 to 25 percent of their purchasing budgets.[3]

Other procurement effectiveness objectives include finding reliable, high-quality suppliers; maintaining good relationships with existing suppliers; and supporting other processes in the organization such as sales and operations. Procurement processes also seek to be efficient—to be less costly and to generate fewer failures, such as stockouts, errors, and products that need to be returned to suppliers.

In this chapter, we consider the portion of procurement that supports the inbound logistics process in the value chain. In this role, procurement obtains the raw material and semi-finished goods needed for subsequent assembly in the production process of the operations activity in the value chain, as shown in Figure 7-2. Other value chain activities also develop and execute procurement processes to obtain things other than raw materials, such as legal services, machine parts, consulting, computer systems, facilities, and transportation services.

Primary Activity	Description	Process and Chapter
Inbound logistics	Receiving, storing, and disseminating inputs to products	Procurement, Chapter 7
Operations	Transforming inputs into final products	
Outbound logistics	Collecting, storing, and physically distributing products to buyers	
Sales and marketing	Inducing buyers to purchase products and providing the means for them to do so	Sales, Chapter 8
Customer service	Assisting customers' use of products and thus maintaining and enhancing the products' value	

FIGURE 7-2

Procurement Process within the Value Chain of CBI

---

[2] "Supply Management Transformation," Axiom Capital Services, accessed September 27, 2013, http://axicap.com/general_and_administrative_services.html

[3] David Yarkin, "Saving States the Sam's Club Way," *New York Times,* February 28, 2011, p. A23.

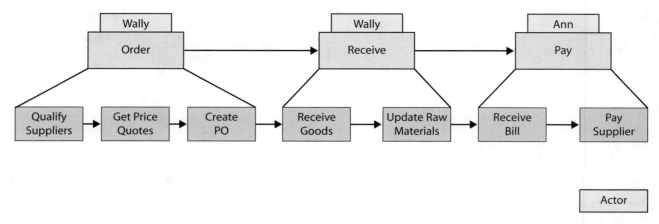

FIGURE 7-3

Main Procurement Process Activities, Subactivities, and Actors at CBI

The activities in the Procurement process at CBI are shown in Figure 7-3. To better understand the activities in Figure 7-3, consider how CBI acquires tires for its bikes. The first activity is to find qualified suppliers who make tires. Once these firms have been identified as potential suppliers, CBI asks each supplier to specify the price it would charge for each type of tire and order quantity. Using this price data, CBI creates a **purchase order (PO)**, a written document requesting delivery of a specified quantity of a product or service in return for payment. At CBI, the Purchase Order specifies a supplier, the tire part number, quantities of tires, and delivery dates. The tires are then received from the supplier in one of CBI's warehouses. Once the tires are received, CBI updates its Raw Materials Inventory database. Soon after, a bill arrives from the supplier and the supplier is paid.

A final key aspect of the procurement process is the resource called inventory. CBI maintains two types of inventory, as shown in Figure 7-4. At the top of Figure 7-4, the Procurement process acquires raw materials, whereas the Production process, shown on the bottom, converts the raw materials into finished goods. **Raw materials inventory** stores components like bicycle tires and other goods procured from suppliers. These raw materials must be on hand

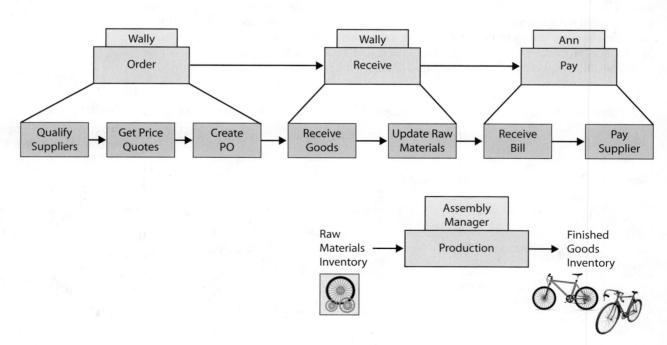

FIGURE 7-4

Main Procurement Process Activities, Subactivities, Production Process, and Inventories

for assembly operations to occur in the Production process. At CBI, raw materials inventory includes bike frames, wheels, and seats. **Finished goods inventory** is the completed products awaiting delivery to customers. At CBI, finished goods inventory is the assembled bikes and accessories.

The fundamentals of procurement are common to most organizations. To better understand the impact of SAP on procurement, we consider its use at CBI. We first examine how procurement worked before SAP was implemented, and then we will determine how SAP changed procurement processes at CBI.

Q2. How Did the Procurement Process at CBI Work Before SAP?

Prior to the implementation of SAP at CBI, Wally was responsible for ordering and receiving raw materials. He issued orders when the raw materials inventory was low, stored parts when they arrived, kept track of where he put them, and planned and managed the people and equipment to accomplish those tasks. His objectives were to avoid running out of raw materials, to use reliable suppliers, and to stay within a budget. The measures for these objectives were number of stockouts, number of late deliveries, and price.

The Procurement process at CBI before SAP is shown in Figure 7-5. As shown, the process has six roles. Two of these, Warehouse Manager and Accountant, are performed by people; the other four are done by computers. As you will see, each of the computer roles uses its own database, creating four information silos.

The first activity in the process shown in Figure 7-5 is Pre-Order Actions. In this step, Wally, in his role as Warehouse Manager, would notice that an item was below its reorder point, look over previous purchases for the item to discover a good supplier, and determine his order quantity. He would often log into the Sales database to see if that item would be needed in the next few days to fulfill recent sales. If he decided to order at the Order decision node, he would start the Create Purchase Order activity and log into his Purchase Order database to obtain supplier data needed to complete the purchase order. Wally would use the purchase order form shown in Figure 7-6. In this example, he ordered 20 water bottles and 30 cages from Space Bike Composites.

The time required for a supplier to deliver an order is called the **lead time**. The lead time ends when the order arrives at the warehouse and the Receive Goods activity occurs. In this

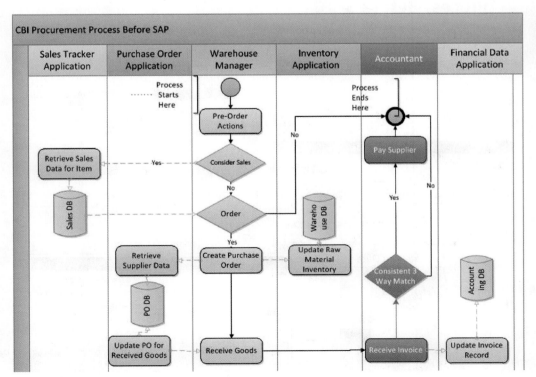

FIGURE 7-5

BPMN Diagram of Procurement Process at CBI Before SAP

FIGURE 7-6

Wally's Purchase Order in Paper Form

CBI			**PURCHASE ORDER**	
			P.O. DATE 10/15/2014	
PURCHASE ORDER:	172		TERMS	
			F.O.B.	
TO:			SHIP VIA	
Space Bike Composites			ADDRESS CORRESPONDENCE TO:	
			Total $470.00	

QTY	UNIT	DESCRIPTION	UNIT PRICE	AMOUNT
20	Single	Water Bottles	10.00	200.00
30	Single	Cages	9.00	270.00

activity, a warehouse worker unpacks the box, counts the items, and updates the raw material inventory quantity in the Warehouse database. At the end of the day, Wally updates the Purchase Order database to reflect all the purchase orders that were received that day.

Several days later, an **invoice**, or itemized bill, is received from the supplier. The data on the invoice—the amount due and the purchase order number for that invoice—are entered into the Accounting database. Before the accountants pay the bill, they make sure that the data on the invoice matches the data in the purchase order and the goods receipt. Figure 7-7 shows a **three-way match** between the invoice, purchase order, and receipt for goods, with color coding for matching data. If the data in this three-way match are consistent, a payment is made and the payment data are posted to the Accounting database.

In the entire Procurement process at CBI, four databases are used—one in sales, two in the warehouse, and one in accounting. Each of these databases was constructed to serve the needs of different departments.

Because each department built its own information system, the inability of these systems to share data increasingly became a concern. These department information silos were not the only problem with CBI's procurement process, as we'll soon see.

Q3. What Were the Problems with the Procurement Process Before SAP?

The problems with the Procurement process before SAP were well known at CBI. They are listed in Figure 7-8.

FIGURE 7-7

Three-Way Match

Matching Data
Supplier Name
PO Number
Ship Items
Ship Quantity
Price

Role	Problems
Warehouse	Warehouse manager does not have data on sales price discounts.
Accounting	Three-way match discrepancies take time to correct. Accounting reports are not real time.
Purchasing	Purchasing agents not centralized; training, experience, and motivation vary. Weak internal controls lead to limited scrutiny of purchases.

FIGURE 7-8

Problems at CBI with Procurement Before SAP

Warehouse Problems

A key problem in the warehouse is that Wally was blind to sales price data. While Wally could see data on the bikes and accessories CBI sold the previous day, this data did not include price discounts; that data only existed in the sales information silo. He did not know if a sudden increase in sales of one bike was due to a deep price discount or whether the product was being bundled with something else that was selling well. The sudden increase might be due to these marketing campaigns, or it might be the first sign of a big spike in popularity for that bicycle. A big spike in e-bike demand was mentioned in the opening vignette. Wally did not have enough sales data to see that the spike in sales of e-bikes was the real deal; he mistakenly thought it was because the new bike was being sold at a very low price to the customer. As a result, Wally did not order enough raw materials to meet the sustained rise in customer orders for these e-bikes.

Accounting Problems

In accounting, Ann supervised the payment activities. Most of Ann's challenges occurred at the end of the Procurement process. One of her activities was to ensure that the three-way match was correct. When discrepancies occurred, the accounting department had to begin a costly and labor-intensive process that required several emails to the warehouse and the supplier to resolve. For example, if the warehouse miscounted or if the supplier shipped the wrong components, Ann would have to access various databases, compare results, and email suppliers to confirm the results of her inquiry.

The other accounting problem was that accounting reports always lagged; they were never up to the minute. Actually, they were never up to the day. This was a result of not sharing real-time accounting data throughout the organization. Instead, accounting reports were produced at the end of the month. It took the accountants several days to **roll up**, or compile and summarize, the accounting transactions into balance sheets and income statements. This was a problem because other firms that competed with CBI had begun to rely on ERP systems to produce real-time accounting reports. With more current data, managers at these other firms could notice problems sooner and respond to customers more quickly.

Purchasing Problems

CBI had no purchasing department, a fact that created numerous problems. First, the purchasing agents, like Wally, were scattered throughout the firm. As a result, they had diverse training, experience, and motivation, which in turn led to a variety of mistakes on the purchase orders. Further, they had little knowledge about what was happening in other parts of the organization. For example, CBI's repair shop had recently found several very good suppliers of bike parts that Wally in the warehouse would have used, too, but he was not aware of them. These suppliers would have granted CBI lower prices if both Wally and the repair shop combined their purchases. The old Procurement process at CBI required each of its purchasing agents to be meticulous record keepers. However, Wally and other purchasing agents sometimes forgot to transcribe data from the handwritten purchase order to the database, used wrong addresses for suppliers, or entered incorrect totals. Doing their primary jobs was their passion; the procurement paperwork was a much lower priority. Further, it was hard to train these dispersed purchasing agents because they were scattered throughout the organization and had great differences in training needs and expectations from their bosses.

A final problem with the old process was that the upper management at CBI was under pressure from the board of directors to exercise more control over financial processes. A lack

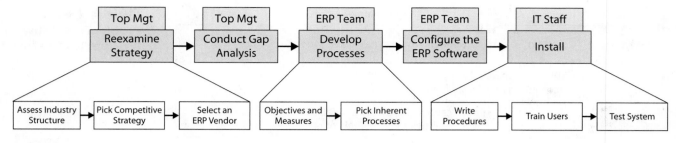

FIGURE 7-9

SAP Implementation Process at CBI

of financial control was at the root of Enron and WorldCom's financial meltdowns, which led to new federal government financial requirements, such as the Sarbanes-Oxley Act. The Sarbanes-Oxley Act of 2002 imposed new regulations on how corporations govern themselves, requiring them to set higher standards for the control of their financial operations. Wally and his procurement colleagues could make costly mistakes, favor suppliers for the wrong reasons, or succumb to the temptation to procure items based on their own interests and not the firm's. By bringing all the purchasing to one office in the company, CBI could exercise much better oversight.

This improved oversight is an example of **internal control**. Internal controls systematically limit the actions and behaviors of employees, processes, and systems within the organization to safeguard assets and achieve objectives. These internal controls are an example of the control of activities first mentioned in Chapter 5. At CBI and elsewhere, ERP systems often dramatically improve internal controls.

To conclude, CBI, like many other companies, had evolved to the point where the problems of isolated processes and information silos could no longer be tolerated. CBI wanted a comprehensive and lasting solution to these problems and decided an ERP system was the most appropriate choice.

Q4. How Does CBI Implement SAP?

The steps required for CBI to install an ERP system are called the Implementation process, briefly discussed in Chapter 6. While this process may have hundreds of activities, the most general are listed in Figure 7-9. The process begins with CBI examining and refocusing its strategy.

CBI began its Implementation process by using Porter's five forces model to determine the structure of its industry, as shown in Figure 7-10. CBI determined that the bike wholesale industry has strong rivalry and that customers have low switching costs. Because of low switching costs, a bike retailer could easily switch from one bike wholesaler to another.

To survive and flourish in such an industry, CBI decided to pursue a competitive strategy that focused on high-end bikes and a differentiation strategy of responsiveness to retailers. This competitive strategy is shown in the bottom-right quadrant of Figure 7-11. The high-end bike industry segment includes very lightweight racing bikes and touring bikes with composite

FIGURE 7-10

Determine Industry Structure with Five Forces Model

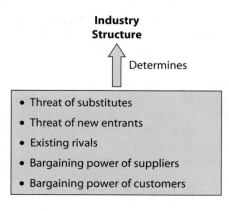

	Cost	Differentiation
Industry-wide	Lowest cost across the industry	Better product/service across the industry
Focus	Lowest cost within an industry segment	Better product/service within an industry segment

(a) Competitive strategies

		Responsiveness
High-End Bikes		**Competitive Strategy** High-end bikes Responsiveness to retailers

(b) Competitive strategy chosen by CBI of high-end bikes; customer responsiveness differentiation

FIGURE 7-11
Four Competitive Strategy Options and CBI's Competitive Strategy

frames and sophisticated gear-shifting systems. Responsiveness means that orders from retailers are fulfilled rapidly; a retailer could order a wide range of products, and new hot-selling items would be available.

Next, CBI picked an ERP vendor. CBI top managers realized that as a large international firm, only SAP, Oracle, and Microsoft could support the wide variety of processes they wanted to integrate. After further investigation, they realized that most of their suppliers and customers used SAP and decided that SAP would be the best choice if they wanted to seamlessly fit into the supply chain of their business partners. Once SAP was selected, they spent several months on a gap analysis identifying where their process expectations and SAP capabilities differed. The most significant gap occurred in some promotions that CBI wanted to use with its newest customers. One example is that CBI wanted to give a price discount to new bike retailers who sold more than $250,000 worth of CBI products in the first 6 months.

Once the gap analysis was complete, CBI management crafted objectives and measures for each of CBI's processes. Wally participated on the team that created the objectives and measures for the Procurement process. This team decided on the two objectives shown in Figure 7-12.

Wally's team decided on one efficiency objective: reducing administrative time. It decided to measure this objective by tracking the average time spent to complete each of the most

Objective	Measure
Efficiency Reduce Administrative Time	Average time of Create Purchase Order activity Average time of Receive Goods activity Average time of Pay Supplier activity
Effectiveness More Responsive to Customers	Average lead time to supply customer orders Number of products to sell Stockouts of new, hot-selling products

FIGURE 7-12
Objectives and Measures for the New Procurement Process

FIGURE 7-13

**Goods Receipt
Procedure at CBI**

Source: Copyright © SAP AG

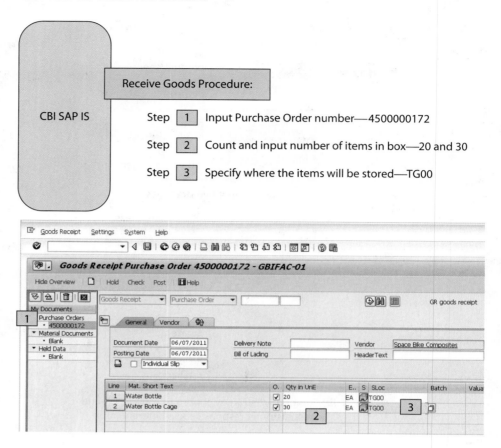

time-consuming activities: complete a PO, receive goods, and pay a supplier. On the effectiveness side, the team also decided on one objective: responsiveness to customers. To measure the responsiveness of procurement, the team picked average customer lead time; number of products to sell; and stockouts of new, hot-selling products such as the e-bike. The ultimate goal of the effectiveness objective was to have bikes ready to sell so CBI could quickly respond to shifting customer demand.

CBI then selected processes from the set of inherent processes that SAP had developed for companies in the material assembly industry and configured the software as described in Chapter 6. Then CBI wrote procedures for its employees on how to use SAP to execute these processes. For example, the procedure for one activity, Receive Goods, is shown in Figure 7-13. In this activity, Wally logs into SAP and inputs three data elements: the purchase order number, the item counts, and the location where these items will be stored in the warehouse. We will explain more about this activity in the next section. At this point, we want you to see that for each activity, CBI must write a procedure for its employees to use. In this example, the procedure has three simple steps. In Appendix 7A, you will accomplish many of the procedures for the activities in the procurement process at CBI.

To complete the implementation process, CBI trained users and tested the system.

Q5. How Does the Procurement Process Work at CBI After SAP?

Let's fast-forward 2 years. CBI has now successfully completed the implementation process outlined above, and Wally, as first introduced in the opening vignette to this chapter, is approaching retirement. The SAP inherent Procurement process has replaced CBI's previous Procurement process. Although the new process has the same major activities—Order, Receive, and Pay—the Order activity has changed significantly.

Figure 7-14 shows a BPMN diagram of the new SAP-based Procurement process. The Order activity in the new Procurement process begins with the Create Purchase Requisition activity. A **purchase requisition (PR)** is an internal company document that issues a request for a purchase. This activity is automated at CBI; a computer is the actor, not a human. For example, a PR is automatically

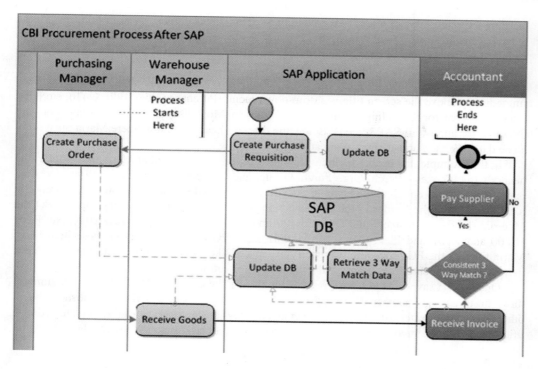

FIGURE 7-14

Procurement Process at CBI After SAP

generated when the amount of raw material inventory goes below the reorder point. In the example that follows, the PR is for 20 water bottles and 30 water bottle cages. After the Create Purchase Requisition activity, the next activity is Create Purchase Order, which is done by the Purchasing Manager.

Purchasing

In the new purchasing department, if Maria, the purchasing manager, approves the purchase, she converts the PR into a purchase order (PO). Whereas the automatically-generated PR is a CBI document, the PO is a document that CBI shares with its suppliers and, if accepted, is a legally binding contract. In this example, when the PO is completed and accepted, the supplier, Space Bike Composites, has agreed to deliver the goods.

To execute this activity, Maria follows the Create Purchase Order procedure: She logs into SAP and navigates to one of her screens, the Create Purchase Order screen, which is shown in Figure 7-15. We will return to Maria in a moment, but first a few words about the SAP screens you will see here and in the next chapter. Tens of thousands of such screens exist in SAP, so

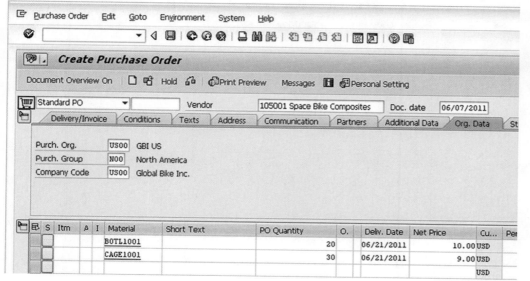

FIGURE 7-15

Create Purchase Order Subactivity Screen in SAP of Water Bottles and Cages from Space Bike Composites

Source: Copyright © SAP AG

learning the particulars of a few of them is not of great value. Rather, we want you to learn the recurring features of an SAP screen, the data typed in by employees, and how the Procurement activity flows from one screen to the next. These skills will be useful for you no matter which ERP screens or processes you use.

Every screen has a title. Here the Create Purchase Order title is shown on the top left. Immediately above the screen title is a drop-down menu (Purchase Order, Edit, GoTo, etc.) and a series of icons for navigating, saving, and getting help. Most of these menu items and icons are the same for almost all SAP screens. Below the title is a header section where Maria must input some data. We pick up her story again at this point.

In this example, the header includes three identifying data items that Maria must input. The header's three boxes—Purch. Org., Purch. Group, and Company Code—are used to identify a particular CBI warehouse.[4] Other inputs would identify CBI's other divisions and warehouse locations. Below the header is the items section that allows Maria to specify for this PO the Material (bottles and cages), PO Quantity (20 and 30), Delivery Date (06/21/2011), Net Price (10.00 and 9.00), and Plant (MI00 for Miami). Each PO can have many of these item lines. Maria finishes the PO procedure by specifying Space Bike Composites (105001) as the vendor in the box in the center of the screen above the header section.

Once Maria saves this PO, SAP records the data in the database. At that point, Maria might move on to entering another PO or log out. After each PO is saved, SAP accomplishes several other tasks. SAP creates a unique PO number and displays this number on Maria's screen. SAP notifies Space Bike Composites via email, a Web service, or an electronic message of the PO details.

Warehouse

Once the PO is saved and transmitted to Space Bike Composites, the next activity at CBI is Receive Goods when the shipment arrives. The Receive Goods activity is shown in the Warehouse Manager swimlane in Figure 7-14; Wally plays the Warehouse Manager role. Let's move the clock forward 7 days from when the PO was sent. The bottles and cages have arrived in a box delivered to Wally's warehouse. On the outside of the box, Space Bike Composites has printed the PO number and the contents of the box. Wally notes the PO number, opens the box, and counts and inspects the contents. He then goes to his computer and executes the Receive Goods procedure. First, he logs into SAP and the Goods Receipt screen. This screen is shown in Figure 7-16, and it is the same screen shown earlier in Figure 7-13.

The title of this screen, near the top, is Goods Receipt Purchase Order. The header includes a Document Date of 06/07/2011, the Vendor (Space Bike Composites), and the purchase order Wally types in. He counts the quantity of bottles and cages in the box and discovers that

FIGURE 7-16
Goods Receipt Subactivity Screen in SAP

Source: Copyright © SAP AG

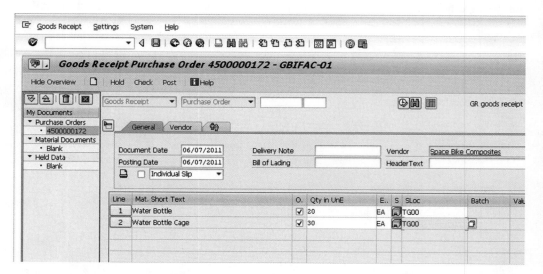

[4] Note that the figures refer to Global Bike Inc. (GBI), not CBI. CBI is used in this textbook; GBI is the dataset provided by SAP to all University Alliance members.

20 bottles and 30 cages were shipped. He moves to the item section and enters 20 and 30 for the quantities that arrived. For larger orders, several shipments may be required. Here, one PO has one goods receipt. His last input is TG00 as the storage location for these bottles and cages. He clicks Save and exits SAP.

Once Wally saves the goods receipt, SAP creates a document number for this particular goods receipt. In addition, it updates records in the Raw Material Inventory table in the database to reflect the addition of these new bottles and cages. Because CBI now owns the goods, SAP posts a debit to the raw materials inventory account. Finally, an entry is made in the PO record to show that a goods receipt occurred that corresponds to that PO.

Accounting

The next activity, Receive Invoice, occurs when Space Bike Composites sends CBI an invoice for the material. Ann, playing the role of Accountant as shown in Figure 7-14, receives the invoice the day after the material arrives. To record the arrival of the invoice, she executes the Enter Incoming Invoice procedure. She navigates to the Enter Incoming Invoice screen, shown in Figure 7-17. In the header section, she enters the date of the invoice (06/07/2011), the Amount ($470.00), and the Purchase Order number (4500000172). After she enters this data, the system finds other data about the PO and displays it on the screen. This data includes the vendor name and address and the two items that were ordered, each on its own row in the items section. When Ann saves this data, SAP records the invoice, displays a new document number for the invoice, and updates the accounting data records to reflect the arrival of the invoice.

The final activity, Pay Supplier, posts an outgoing payment to Space Bike Composites. This is the electronic equivalent of writing a check. Before she posts the payment, the process requires that Ann performs a three-way check. She compares the data on the PO, the goods receipt, and the invoice to make sure that all three agree on supplier name, PO number, items, quantities, and price. Ann opens the final SAP screen, Post Outgoing Payment, shown in Figure 7-18. Here she specifies the date of the payment (06/07/2011), the bank Account (100000), and the Amount (470.00). She also must specify an existing vendor in the Account box at the bottom of the screen (the vendor number for Space Bike Composites is 105001). She clicks the Process Open Items icon in the upper-left side of the screen and then saves the transaction. A document number is again created, and an accounting update is made to reflect the outgoing payment.

As you can see, each actor—Maria, Wally, and Ann—interacts with SAP using different screens, and CBI has created procedures for each activity.

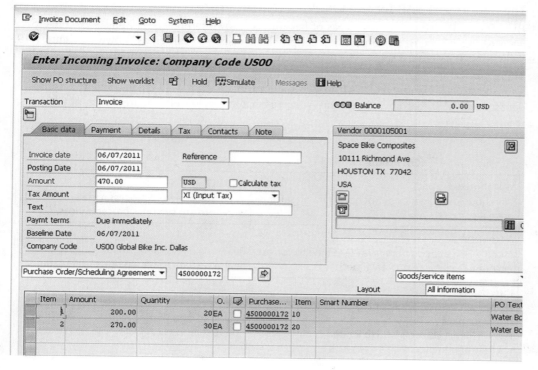

FIGURE 7-17
Receive Bill Subactivity Screen in SAP

Source: Copyright © SAP AG

FIGURE 7-18

Pay Supplier Subactivity Screen in SAP

Source: Copyright © SAP AG

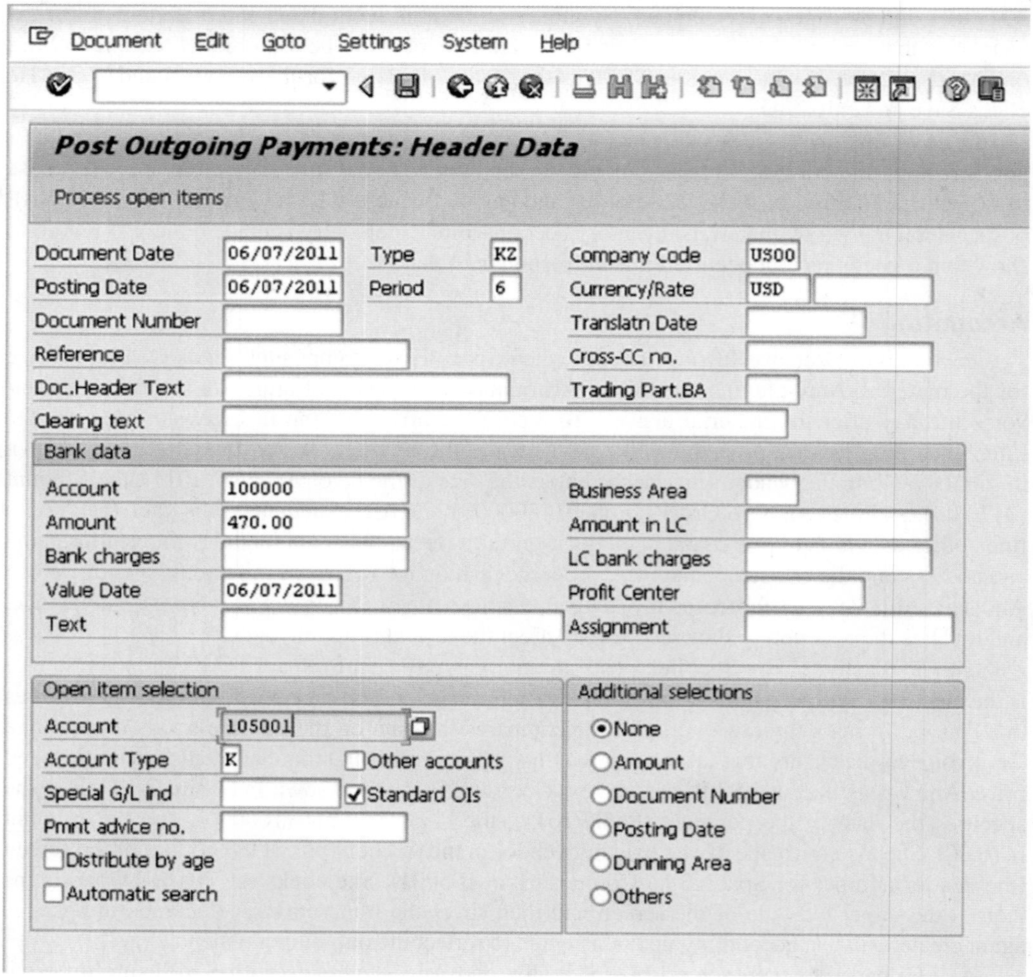

The Benefits of SAP for the CBI Procurement Process

By using SAP, CBI enjoys two types of benefits, as shown in Figure 7-19 and 7-20. First, SAP addresses each of CBI's five procurement problems discussed earlier, as shown in Figure 7-19. Second, SAP helps CBI achieve its two procurement objectives, also mentioned earlier, as shown in Figure 7-20.

The two key features of SAP first introduced in Chapter 6—a database that consolidates data for real-time sharing and inherent processes that integrate well—address each of CBI's five

FIGURE 7-19

CBI Problems and SAP Benefits

CBI Problems	SAP Benefits
Warehouse Warehouse manager does not have data on sales price discounts.	Integrated inherent process allows warehouse to see sales process prices.
Accounting Three-way match discrepancies take time to correct. Accounting data are not real time.	Real-time data sharing limits errors. Real-time data sharing reduces roll-up time.
Purchasing Agents not centralized; training, experience, motivation vary. Weak internal controls lead to limited scrutiny of purchases.	Integrated purchasing activity of ERP system. Real-time data sharing increases use of financial reports.

CBI Objectives	SAP Benefits
Efficiency Reduce administrative time	Data entered once then later shared.
Effectiveness More responsive to customers	Forecast data shared with supply chain partners reduces times.

FIGURE 7-20

CBI Procurement Process Objectives and SAP Benefits

procurement problems. Consolidated, real-time data leads to fewer three-way match errors as input mistakes are reduced. The data are entered into only one database, and controls on inputs reduce input mistakes. For example, before SAP, Wally had to enter supplier data in both the PO database and the Inventory database. If he mistyped data in either system, that error would not be caught. Also, with real-time data, Ann in accounting has up-to-the minute accounting data and does not have to wait until the end of the month to roll up the financial reports. Scrutiny of purchases is improved as real-time financial data is more informative to managers, who now request more financial reports and use them more frequently.

Also shown on Figure 7-19 is the impact of inherent processes that integrate on CBI's other two problems. Wally can see sales price discounts because the sales process and procurement process are integrated. The lack of a centralized office is also overcome as SAP's inherent procurement process integrates all the procurement in CBI into one office, enabling more consistent training and motivation of purchasing agents.

As stated, CBI implemented SAP not only to overcome problems but also to pursue its particular strategy. This strategy and the Procurement process objectives that support it were listed earlier in Figure 7-12 and shown in Figure 7-20 with SAP's benefits.

With real-time data sharing, administrative time spent on procurement can be reduced. The Create PO, Receive Goods, and Pay Supplier activities are more efficient when data is entered once, then shared in later steps.

Consolidating data also helps CBI's Procurement process be more responsive to customer demands. CBI uses SAP to share sales and sales forecast data with its suppliers. As a result of having more data, forecasts by each supplier in the chain can be more accurate. The improved supply chain helps CBI reduce order lead times to its customers, increase product variety, and suffer fewer stockouts. Ideally, with this more responsive Procurement process, the e-bike fiasco will not recur.

Q6. How Can SAP Improve Supply Chain Processes at CBI?

To this point, for simplicity we have focused on one process: Procurement. However, no organization would implement an ERP system for just one process. The real payoff is evident only when a set of processes is examined. So we shift our focus from the single Procurement process and examine how SAP improves a collection of processes. We consider how SAP improves the set of processes related to procurement called Supply Chain processes.

Supply Chain Processes

Several processes in CBI's supply chain are listed in Figure 7-21. The **Supplier Relationship Management (SRM) process** automates, simplifies, and accelerates a variety of supply chain processes. Broader than the single Procurement process, SRM is a management process that helps companies reduce procurement costs, build collaborative supplier relationships, better manage supplier options, and improve time to market. The **Returns Management process** manages returns of faulty products for businesses. At CBI, if a bike is returned to a customer such as Philly Bikes, Philly might provide a new bike, tag the returned bike, and annotate the customer complaint. The returned bike is shipped back to CBI to determine where the fault occurred. Efficiently getting the defect to the right supplier and charging the right cost to each company in the supply chain are the goals of the Returns Management process. The **Supplier Evaluation process** determines the criteria for supplier selection and adds and removes suppliers from the list of approved suppliers.

FIGURE 7-21

Sample of Supply Chain Processes

Process Scope	Supply Chain Processes
Operational	Procurement
Managerial	Supplier Relationship Management (SRM) Returns Management
Strategic	Supplier Evaluation

The administration of supply chain processes is called **supply chain management (SCM)**. More specifically, SCM is the design, planning, execution, and integration of all supply chain processes.[5] SCM uses a collection of tools, techniques, and management activities to help businesses develop integrated supply chains that support organizational strategy. SAP offers SCM capabilities and can help CBI improve this set of processes. The improvement in a collection of processes can be attributed to sharing data between processes in real time and improving integration.

Improving Supply Chain Processes by Sharing Data

Supply chain processes are improved when processes share data. Figure 7-22 shows two examples where processes are improved by sharing data. For example, data from the Returns Management process about defective bicycle parts should be shared with the Supplier Evaluation process to ensure that suppliers with high defect rates are removed from the list of approved suppliers.

Not only can data sharing help improve the supply processes at CBI, data sharing with CBI suppliers also can improve CBI's processes, as shown in the bottom of Figure 7-22. Before CBI and its suppliers shared data, CBI's raw material inventories were quite large. For example, CBI maintained a large quantity of tires and other raw materials to feed its production lines. In those days, procuring raw materials could take weeks, so running out of a raw material could shut down production for days. One reason that procurement was a slow process was that CBI's suppliers only produced raw materials when orders arrived. Today, CBI shares its sales data with its suppliers in real time. As a result, suppliers can anticipate CBI's orders and make raw materials in anticipation of orders, reducing lead time. By sharing more data and sharing this data rapidly, raw material inventory at CBI could shrink as suppliers become better informed

FIGURE 7-22

Examples of Data Sharing Among Supply Chain Processes

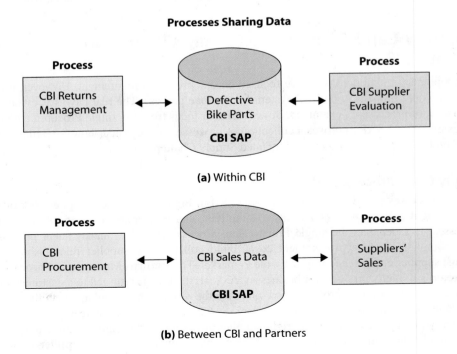

Processes Sharing Data

(a) Within CBI

(b) Between CBI and Partners

---

[5] Association for Operations Management, *APICS Dictionary*, 13th ed. (Chicago: 2011).

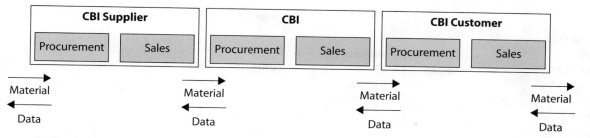

FIGURE 7-23

Procurement Processes, Material, and Data Flow in a Supply Chain

about changes in CBI's sales, allowing them to be more responsive to CBI's orders. Inventories shrink and customer responsiveness improves as more and more data are shared.

This link between CBI procurement and its supplier's sales process can be extended to all firms in a supply chain. Figure 7-23 shows a series of suppliers and the sales process of each supplier integrated with the procurement process of each customer. Also notice in this chain that as material moves from left to right, from suppliers to customers, data is shared from right to left. For example, the sales data to CBI's customers that are collected in the CBI ERP system are shared with CBI's suppliers, who share their sales data with their suppliers. In this way, the ERP system at CBI talks to the ERP systems of its suppliers. Overall, the more data moves, the more efficient the process becomes as less inventory is needed.

Sharing data not only reduces raw material inventory at CBI, it helps reduce the bullwhip effect in the supply chain. The **bullwhip effect** occurs when companies order more supplies than are needed due to a sudden change in demand. For example, if a spike in sales occurred in the old days, CBI would increase its orders to its suppliers. However, in the old days it might be several days after the initial spike for the order to arrive at the supplier. By this time, if sales keep up, CBI could be facing a critical shortage and its order would increase. This type of delay in ordering would also occur for CBI's supplier, the frame manufacturer. While the middle man, the frame maker, was waiting for parts from its supplier, CBI might increase its demand still more as it sees even stronger retailer demand and grow increasingly impatient. If the frame manufacturer was pressed by CBI and others it sells to, the frame manufacturer may raise its order to its suppliers, too. By the time upstream suppliers crank up supply for parts for the new bike frame, demand from customers may recede, leaving the frame manufacturer or CBI holding extra inventory that cannot be sold. This effect can be diminished by real-time sharing of sales order data among collaborating firms in the supply chain.

Improving Supply Chain Processes with Integration

The second characteristic of ERP, process integration, can improve the set of supply chain processes at CBI. Up to this point, we have not been specific about the notion of process integration. Integration, to be more precise, occurs when processes are mutually supportive; that is, when one process is done well, the objectives of another process are also achieved. You integrate your dating and studying processes when you study with your significant other. You integrate your shopping and your banking by doing both on one trip. Examples of integration among CBI supply processes are shown in Figure 7-24.

One example of process integration occurs at CBI between the Returns Management process and the Production process. One of the objectives of production is to reduce defective bikes. The Returns Management process collects data on defective returns from retailers of CBI bikes and accessories. The final step of the Returns Management process is to analyze how to improve the Production process to create fewer defects and thus fewer returns. When the Returns Management process is done well, an objective of the Production process is supported.

The benefits of SAP process integration can also be seen in CBI's supply chain. If retailer demand shifts suddenly, CBI and its suppliers can quickly shift production lines to meet the new demand. CBI and its suppliers rely on the SW Trucking Company to deliver raw materials. In the old days without process integration, SW Trucking had no excess capacity to support the extra shipping needed to move the bike parts from suppliers to CBI to retailers. SW Trucking was a bottleneck. A **bottleneck** occurs when a limited resource greatly reduces the output of an

FIGURE 7-24

Examples of Process Integration Among Supply Chain Processes

Integrating Processes

Process   →Improves→   **Process**

| CBI Returns Management | | CBI Production |

(a) Within CBI

Process   →Improves→   **Process**

| SWT Shipping | | CBI Production |

Process   →Improves→   **Process**

| SWT Shipping | | CBI Procurement |

(b) Between CBI and Partners

integrated series of activities or processes. SW Trucking decided to improve its Shipping process by keeping excess capacity available. As a result, the Production process at CBI was improved because one of its objectives was being responsive to customer demand. Not only did this improve production at CBI, it also improved procurement because the additional shipping capacity meant that CBI's Procurement process could better achieve its objective of being more responsive to customers.

Improving CBI Processes Beyond the Supply Chain

We have progressed from seeing how SAP can improve one procurement process to seeing how SAP can improve a set of processes in supply chain management. Many firms first use SAP to improve just one function of the business, such as the supply chain. Of course, there is one more level: multiple functions throughout a firm. Some firms like CBI use SAP to improve processes throughout the enterprise, as shown in Figure 7-25. The most common enterprise-wide approach is to use SAP in Accounting, Procurement, Production, and Sales.

By sharing data and integrating processes in the supply chain, and in sales as we will see in Chapter 8, CBI became a more successful company. While this significant accomplishment clearly benefits CBI, these changes affect CBI and its workers in a number of ways, some of which are unexpected. We consider the changes to CBI next.

FIGURE 7-25

Major Categories of Business Process in Enterprise-wide Systems

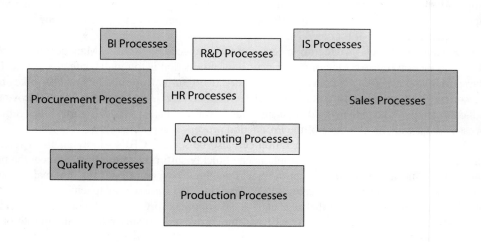

MIS InClass 7

The Bicycle Supply Game[6]

The purpose of this exercise is to better understand how supply chains are affected by information systems. In this game, the class will form supply chains and attempt to be the most efficient supplier.

The four links in each chain are retailer, distributor, wholesaler, and frame maker. The game is played for a period of 50 weeks. Each week each of the four teams in the supply chain orders bikes from its supplier and each team fulfills the orders from its customer. Pennies represent bicycles as the sole item in the supply chain, drinking cups are used to transport pennies between stations, and Post-it notes are used to make orders.

The goal is for each supplier in the chain to have the most efficient procurement process; that is, minimizing inventory and back orders.

Set up as many identical supply chains as needed, as shown in Figure 7-26. Notice that the supply chains are constructed with delays between the ordering of bicycles and their arrival. Each supplier is a team of one to three students. Each supplier records its orders, inventory, and backlog on a form like the one shown in Figure 7-27.

The retailers perform the same actions as the other groups, except their orders come from a stack of 3 × 5 cards that contain prerecorded orders that specify customer demand for the 50 weeks. Students are not to look at incoming orders, prerecorded

Source: Peter Burian/Stock Connection Blue/Alamy.

orders, or supplies until that activity, and then they may look at only that week's order and supply.

Each week follows the same process with these five activities:

1. Receive inventory and advance the shipping delay.
2. Receive incoming orders and advance the order delay.
3. Fill the order.
4. Record inventory or backlog.
5. Place and record orders.

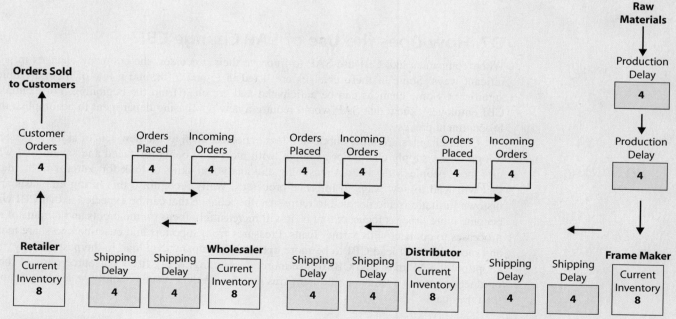

FIGURE 7-26

Supply Chain Game Setup

---

[6] See the "MIT Beer Game" in Chapter 3 of Peter Senge's *The Fifth Discipline: The Art and Practice of the Learning Organization,* rev. ed. (New York: Random House, 2006). Also see Wikipedia, "Beer Distribution Game," http://en.wikipedia.org/wiki/MIT_Beer_Game.

FIGURE 7-27
Supply Chain Game Record Form

Game Record

Position:_____   Team Member Names:_____

Week	Inventory	Backlog	Total Cost for Week
1.	4	0	$ 2.00
2.			
3.			
4.			
5.			

When the game is played, follow these activities as the instructor directs so that every team has accomplished each activity before any team moves on to the next. The game begins with a balanced condition in the supply chain; that is, every existing order is for four pennies, every delivery cup is filled with four pennies, and every supplier begins with eight pennies in inventory.

At the end of the game, each supplier calculates its overall costs.

Cost = .50 (inventory) + 1.00 (backlog)

A backlog occurs when an order is made that cannot be fulfilled. This backlog accumulates from week to week until it is paid off completely. The supplier with the lowest value is the winner.

At the end of the game, discuss the following:

1. Describe the order pattern from the customers to the retailer every week.
2. Why did the ordering pattern between the suppliers in the supply chain evolve the way it did?
3. What are the objectives and measures for each team's procurement process?
4. Where is the IS? What would more data allow? What data are most needed?
5. If you spent money on an IS to improve your procurement process, would it improve an activity, data flow, control, automation, or procedure?
6. Create a BPMN diagram of your team's weekly procurement process.

Q7. How Does the Use of SAP Change CBI?

When companies like CBI use SAP to improve their processes, the company changes in significant ways. Some of these changes are listed in Figure 7-28, and a few of them are quite significant. Some changes can be anticipated and are clear from the beginning. For example, CBI employees knew that SAP would require a new purchasing department to accomplish the Procurement process.

Other changes are more subtle and less expected, such as the new sets of skills necessary to optimize a supply chain. For example, with more data being produced and saved, CBI will hire more people with abstract reasoning and analytical skills to look for patterns in the data that will lead to new ways to improve processes. Wally recognized this hiring emphasis and his own limitations and decided to retire. Another change that can be expected is that CBI will become more process focused; that is, it will increasingly focus on the inputs and outputs of its processes to connect with partner firms. Pressures from suppliers and customers to share more and more data will lead CBI to be more open with company data than in the past. Finally, the adoption of SAP may lead CBI to use more outsourcing. Many firms outsource parts of their production to take advantage of other firms that can produce a subassembly or service cheaper than they can.

FIGURE 7-28
Impacts of SAP on Organizations

New skills needed
Process focus
More data sharing
Outsourcing

In the CBI warehouse, Wally has seen these organizational and technological changes in the past few years. One result is that CBI is doing less production of bicycles and is instead purchasing more finished bicycles. CBI believes this will help it reduce costs by shifting production to suppliers who can do the work at a lower cost. CBI is also lowering costs by using more full-truck shipments rather than partial loads. Because of these large shipments, storage of the finished goods is optimized across CBI's worldwide system and is not done locally. The inventory system dictates where each item is stored in the warehouse; in fact, at Wally's warehouse, the SAP system now dictates an item's location to the robot forklifts. Another recent change is that much more data are produced by the new system and shared with CBI customers and suppliers than was ever done in the past. This willingness to share inventory and pricing data gives CBI customers the opportunity to compare prices.

Finally, one more change is significant for Wally and the other warehouse managers at other locations. Before SAP, they were the ones who decided what was purchased. They would notice low raw material levels and then use their experience to decide if, when, and how many parts or bikes were ordered. Now, the system automatically tracks raw material inventory and generates purchase requisitions when reorder levels are reached.

Wally's Job Change

These changes have taken a toll on Wally. Before the installation of SAP, Wally's job was to manage the inventory levels in the warehouse. And he was good at it. Using Excel spreadsheets, some freeware programs he found on the Internet, and his fax machine, Wally did the job well. When the new company-wide SAP system was announced, he could see that it was a good idea and he supported its implementation as it looked like it was the only way for the firm to stay in business. Although helping to implement the system in the warehouse was a time-consuming challenge, Wally looked forward to seeing the project through.

He took on the responsibility of scheduling training classes for everyone at the warehouse. However, he encountered his first disappointment when he noticed that the budget for these classes was much less than initially planned, apparently a victim of cost overruns during implementation.

As the system went online, he helped sell the system to frustrated and disgruntled workers. Some of his people were not able to see the big picture and resisted the changes necessary to efficiently and effectively use the new system. He could understand their frustration with this new technology. Data that was easy to find now seemed needlessly hidden, reports were different and not as informative as before, and the error messages were very confusing. Wally faithfully helped triage the complaints for upper management and for the IT staff, who appreciated his support and ability to keep things working during a difficult implementation. As time went on, other problems left him wondering about his future. Most of the jobs in the warehouse were redesigned. A few people had to be let go, and others found work elsewhere in the company. The substitution of robots for forklift drivers was the most obvious job change. But other changes were also noticeable. Much more time was spent entering data into the system, checking and producing reports, or responding to questions from the system or from offices within the company he didn't even know existed. His particular job changed quite a lot. He was no longer the purchasing agent; instead, he monitored the purchase requisitions the system kicked out every day.

Recently, he came to realize that he missed being more involved. He wanted to use his wits and experience rather than watch numbers on a screen. He decided to take an early retirement and go find his old job.

Wally's experiences are not uncommon. They are included here to present some of the human challenges when ERP systems are implemented. ERP implementations change the type of work many people do. Change, a constant in IT and in business, can be hard on the people experiencing it. And although change is hard on people, it is necessary for businesses to stay competitive. Jack Welch, the CEO of General Electric, once said that if change is happening on the outside of a company faster than on the inside, the end of that company is in sight.

FIGURE 7-29

New IS that Will Impact Supply Chain Processes by 2024

Augmented reality
RFID
Sensors
Robotics
3D printing

Q8. What New IS Will Affect the Procurement Process in 2024?

Before we wrap up this chapter, you should understand that SAP is just one IS that has an impact on procurement processes. Other IS, just now emerging, will have a significant impact on procurement over the next 10 years. The impact of these technologies will vary by company and industry, but these IS technologies, listed in Figure 7-29, will drive the next generation of Procurement process improvements.

With **augmented reality (AR)**, computer data or graphics are overlaid onto the physical environment. An example of augmented reality is shown in Figure 7-30. Another example of AR is Google Glass, which superimposes computer data on eyeglasses to augment what the user sees when looking through the glasses. Using these glasses, warehouse workers at CBI can look at the warehouse and see overlaid on top data about the location of a product they are looking for, the arrival date of the next shipment of a particular item, or the weight of a container. By augmenting reality with procurement data, CBI can save time looking for items and make other procurement and production activities more efficient.

Radio-frequency identification (RFID) technology, as shown in Figure 7-31, can be used to identify and track items in the supply chain. As small and as cheap as a grain of rice, RFID chips broadcast data to receivers that can display and record the data. In the supply chain domain, suppliers put RFID chips on the outside of boxes and shipping pallets so that when those boxes get to their destination, the receiving company can know the contents of the box without opening it. This makes tracking inventory faster and cheaper for all collaborating companies in a supply chain. CBI and its supplier partners can also outfit their trucks with sensors and tracking devices to make the Transportation activity of the Procurement process more efficient. Transportation is one of the highest-cost activities in the Procurement process, and equipping every truck with two-way data exchange can lower costs by optimizing routes to avoid traffic jams, using onboard sensors to better plan vehicle maintenance, and alerting warehouse personnel when delivery trucks are approaching a warehouse.

At CBI and other warehouses, pallets of raw material inventory are moved from inbound delivery trucks to storage locations and then to outbound trucks using robotic forklifts. These

FIGURE 7-30

Augmented Reality

Source: Kazuhiro Nogi/Getty Images, Inc. AFP.

FIGURE 7-31
RFID Chip

Source: Noah Addis/Star-Ledger/Corbis

forklifts rely on RFID chips on pallets to locate the pallet in the warehouse and to know where to deliver the pallet. Although the initial costs are significant, robots can reduce inventory costs markedly for CBI and other firms.

Three-dimensional (3D) printing technologies will also affect CBI's Procurement process. With **3D printing**, also called *additive manufacturing*, objects are manufactured through the deposition of successive layers of material, as shown in Figure 7-32. Just as two-dimensional printers deposit ink in two dimensions, 3D printers deposit material in three dimensions, layering material in the third dimension as it dries. Rather than rely on suppliers for all its raw materials, CBI may choose to "print" some raw materials in-house.

These IS are affecting procurement now, and other, new IS technologies are on the way. As companies continue to pursue their strategies, new technologies will be absorbed into the companies' processes. SAP will choose to adapt its applications to some of these new technologies, but for the rest, organizations will need to develop their own patches of the new technology into SAP. The bottom line: SAP and other new IS can significantly improve the Procurement process, but they will need to work together.

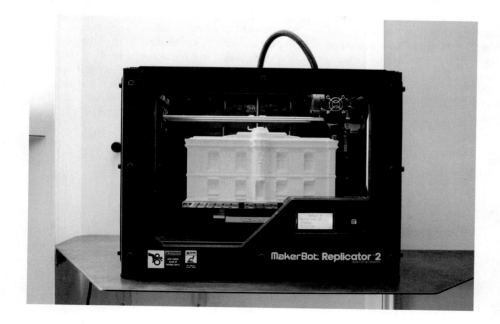

FIGURE 7-32
3D Printing

Source: © James Leynse/Corbis

Ethics Guide

Estimation Ethics

A **buy-in** occurs when a company agrees to produce a system or product for less money than it knows the project will require. An example at CBI would be if a consultant proposed $15,000 to provide some software code when good estimating techniques indicate it would take $35,000. If the contract for the system or product is written for "time and materials," CBI will ultimately pay the $35,000 for the finished system. Or the project will fail once the true cost is known. If the contract for the code is written for a fixed cost, then the consultant will absorb the extra costs. The consultant would use the latter strategy if the contract opens up other business opportunities that are worth the $20,000 loss.

Buy-ins always involve deceit. Most would agree that buying-in on a time-and-materials project, planning to stick the customer with the full cost later, is wrong. Opinions on buying-in on a fixed-priced contract vary. You know you'll take a loss, but why? To build intellectual capital for sale elsewhere? For a favor down the road? Or for some other unethical reason?

What about in-house projects? Do the ethics change if an in-house coding team is doing the work? If team members know there is only $15,000 in the budget, should they start the project if they believe that its true cost is $35,000? If they do start, at some point senior management will either have to admit a mistake and cancel the project with a loss or find the additional $20,000. Project sponsors can state all sorts of reasons for such buy-ins. For example, "I know the company needs this system. If management doesn't realize it and fund it appropriately, then we'll just force its hand."

These issues become even stickier if team members disagree about how much the project will cost. Suppose one faction of the team believes the project will cost $20,000, another faction estimates $30,000, and a third thinks $40,000. Can the project sponsors justify taking the average? Or should they describe the range of estimates?

Other buy-ins are more subtle. Suppose you are a project manager of an exciting new project that is possibly a career-maker for you. You are incredibly busy, working 6 days a week and long hours each day. Your team has developed an estimate of $50,000 for the project. A little voice in the back of your mind says that maybe not all costs for every aspect of the project are included in that estimate. You mean to follow up on that thought, but more pressing matters in your schedule take precedence. Soon you find yourself in front of management, presenting the $50,000 estimate. You probably should have found the time to investigate the estimate, but you didn't. Is there an ethical issue here?

Or suppose you approach a more senior manager with your dilemma. "I think there may be other costs, but I know that $50,000 is all we've got. What should I do?" Suppose the senior manager says something like, "Well, let's go forward. You don't know of anything else, and we can always find more budget elsewhere if we have to." How do you respond?

You can buy-in on schedule as well as cost. If the marketing department says, "We have to have the new product for the trade show," do you agree, even if you know it's highly unlikely you will make the deadline? What if marketing says, "If we don't have it by then, we should just cancel the project." Suppose it's not impossible to make that schedule; it's just highly unlikely. How do you respond?

DISCUSSION QUESTIONS

1. Assess the ethics of buying-in on a cost-and-materials project from both the perspective of the categorical imperative (page 20) and utilitarianism (page 40).
2. Are there circumstances in which buying-in on a cost-and-materials contract could be illegal? If so, state them.
3. Suppose you learn through the grapevine that your opponents in a competitive bid are buying-in on a time-and-materials contract. Does this change your answer to question 1?
4. Suppose you are a project manager who is preparing a request for a proposal on a cost-and-materials systems development project. What can you do to prevent buy-ins?
5. Under what circumstances do you think buying-in on a fixed-price contract is ethical? Use either the categorical imperative or utilitarianism perspectives or both. What are the dangers of this strategy?
6. Explain why in-house development projects are always time-and-materials projects.
7. Given your answer to question 6, assess the ethics of buying-in on an in-house project from the perspective of the categorical imperative and utilitarianism. Are there circumstances that will change your ethical assessment? If so, state what they are and why.
8. Suppose you ask a senior manager for advice as described in the guide. Does the manager's response absolve you of ethical responsibility? Suppose you ask the manager and then do not follow her guidance. What problems could result?
9. Explain how you can buy-in on schedule as well as costs.
10. For an in-house project, what is an ethical response to the marketing manager who says that the project should be canceled if it will not be ready for the trade show? In your answer, suppose that you disagree with this opinion—suppose you know the system has value regardless of whether it is done by the trade show.

Source: Studio_G/Shutterstock and Mmaxer/Shutterstock

Active Review

Use this Active Review to verify that you understand the material in the chapter. You can read the entire chapter and then perform the tasks in this review, or you can read the text material for just one question and perform the tasks in this review for that question before moving on to the next one.

Q1. What are the fundamentals of a Procurement process?

Define *procurement* and explain its three main activities. Explain possible objectives for a procurement process. Name the value chain activity in which the Procurement process, as addressed in this chapter, operates. Explain the common subactivities in the Procurement process. Explain how raw material and finished goods inventories differ.

Q2. How did the Procurement process at CBI work before SAP?

Explain the Procurement process at CBI before SAP. Describe the Pre-Order Actions activity, particularly with regard to the Sales database. Describe which data are stored in the four different databases. Explain what an invoice is, who sends it, and what happens when it arrives. Describe which data must match for a three-way match.

Q3. What were the problems with the Procurement process before SAP?

Explain the problems at CBI in the warehouse, in accounting, and in purchasing prior to the implementation of SAP. Explain how not having price data affects the Procurement process. Describe why a company might want to restrict purchasing to just one department and not scatter it throughout the organization. Explain what the Sarbanes-Oxley Act requires and how ERP systems address that requirement.

Q4. How does CBI implement SAP?

Describe the activities in CBI's ERP Implementation process. Explain the competitive strategy chosen by CBI. Describe why CBI selected SAP as its ERP vendor. Describe a gap analysis. Explain the objectives and measures selected by CBI for the Procurement process.

Q5. How does the Procurement process work at CBI after SAP?

Describe the Procurement process after the implementation of SAP. Explain the difference between a purchase requisition and a purchase order. Explain the three roles in the new Procurement process and the name of the CBI employee who plays each role. Describe the main sections of an SAP screen. Explain the actions that automatically occur after a purchase order is saved and after a goods receipt is saved. Describe how the new Procurement process with SAP overcomes CBI procurement problems and achieves procurement objectives.

Q6. How can SAP improve supply chain processes at CBI?

Describe the processes of Supplier Relationship Management, Returns Management, and Supplier Evaluation. Define *supply chain management (SCM)* and explain the benefits of effective SCM. Explain how data sharing and process integration can improve the family of supply chain processes. Explain the bullwhip effect and bottlenecks and explain how they occur. Also describe how ERP systems can alleviate these situations. What other domains of a business outside of supply and sales are common to enterprise-wide ERP implementations?

Q7. How does the use of SAP change CBI?

Explain some of the new skills needed at CBI after SAP is implemented. Describe why CBI is becoming more process-focused after implementing SAP. How does the adoption of SAP lead CBI to share more data with suppliers and customers? Explain the advantages of outsourcing. Explain some of the changes at CBI due to SAP. Explain how Wally accomplished his Procurement process before SAP. Describe some of the actions Wally took to support a smooth transition to SAP. Describe how Wally's job changed.

Q8. What new IS will affect the Procurement process in 2024?

Explain AR and how it might be used to support the procurement process. What is RFID technology, and how can it affect procurement? What is another name for 3D printing, and how can 3D printing improve procurement?

Key Terms and Concepts

3D printing   203
Augmented reality (AR)   202
Bottleneck   197
Bullwhip effect   197
Buy-in   204
Finished goods inventory   185
Internal control   188
Invoice   186

Lead time   185
Procurement   182
Purchase order (PO)   184
Purchase requisition (PR)   190
Radio-frequency identification
    (RFID)   202
Raw materials inventory   184
Returns Management process   195

Roll up   187
Supplier Evaluation process   195
Supplier Relationship Management
    (SRM) process   195
Supply chain management
    (SCM)   196
Three-way match   186

Using Your Knowledge

7-1. Two supply chain processes introduced in this chapter are Returns Management and Supplier Evaluation.
   a. Create a BPMN diagram of each of these processes.
   b. Specify efficiency and effectiveness objectives for each process and identify measures appropriate for CBI.
   c. What new information system technologies could be used by CBI to improve these processes, as specified by your measures in part b? Can AR, RFID, or 3D printing be used to improve these processes?

7-2. Which of the four nonroutine cognitive skills identified in Chapter 1 (i.e., abstract reasoning, systems thinking, collaboration, and experimentation) did you use to answer the previous question?

7-3. Which of the four skills in Exercise 7-2 would be most important for Wally's replacement?

7-4. The Procurement process in this chapter is an inbound logistics operational process. Name two other operational processes at CBI. Describe two inbound logistics managerial processes and two strategic processes.

7-5. If a warehouse worker opens a box and the contents are broken, those items will be returned to the supplier. Add this activity to the BPMN diagram of the Procurement process (Figure 7-14).

7-6. For the Procurement process after SAP implementation, what are the triggers for each activity to start? For example, what event or action (trigger) initiates the Create PO activity?

7-7. What kinds of errors can Wally, Maria, and Ann make that are not captured by SAP? One example is that Wally might count 20 bottles and 30 cages but mistakenly enter 20 cages and 30 bottles. Describe a particularly harmful mistake that each can make and how the process could be changed to prevent that error.

7-8. How does a pizza shop's Procurement process differ from CBI's? What do you believe is the corporate strategy of your favorite pizza franchise? What are the objectives and measures of its Procurement process to support this strategy?

7-9. 3D printing has many benefits for businesses. Suggest three products that CBI might print instead of procure with traditional means and three that your university might print. Which procurement objectives does 3D printing support?

7-10. Augmented reality will help employees find items in a warehouse, but this IS may also support many other processes. Name two and describe how AR will improve them. Use Google Glass as one example of using AR, and use another example of AR for your other process.

Collaboration Exercise 7

Collaborate with a group of fellow students to answer the following questions. For this exercise, do not meet face to face. Your task will be easier if you coordinate your work with SharePoint, Office 365, Google Docs with Google+, or equivalent collaboration tools. (See Chapter 9 for a discussion of collaboration tools and processes.) Your answers should reflect the thinking of the entire group, not just that of one or two individuals.

In Chapter 6, a university implemented an SAP system. One of the changes is that most purchases must now be

approved by a new university purchasing office. The athletics director is concerned that centralizing the purchasing at the university will impose difficulties on the athletics department.

1. Figure 7-8 lists problems with the Procurement process at CBI. Which of these would apply to the university? Which would not? What are some procurement problems that might be unique to an athletics department?
2. Figure 7-12 lists objectives and measures that the managers at CBI determined for the Procurement process. What objectives and measures would you suggest

for the university? What objectives and measures would you expect the athletics director to suggest (do not use the objectives and measures from Chapter 6)?

3. Figure 7-28 lists the impacts of SAP on an organization. Which of these impacts would affect the athletics department?

4. Chapter 1 explained four nonroutine cognitive skills: abstract reasoning, systems thinking, collaboration, and experimentation. Explain how implementing the new Procurement process at CBI will require each of these skills from the members of the SAP implementation team.

ACTIVE CASE 7: SAP PROCUREMENT TUTORIAL

A tutorial for a Procurement process using SAP is located in the appendix to this chapter. That tutorial leads the student through a Procurement process that orders, receives, and pays for 20 bicycle water bottles and 30 water bottle cages. Once the tutorial is complete, students should answer the following questions.

Questions

7-11. Describe your first impressions of SAP.

7-12. What types of skills are necessary to use this system?

7-13. Create a screen capture of an SAP screen. Underneath the image, provide an answer to each of the following questions:
   a. In which of the activities does this screen occur?
   b. What is the name of this screen?
   c. What is the name of the screen that precedes it? What screen comes after it?
   d. Which actor accomplishes this activity?
   e. Describe an error that this actor may do on this screen that SAP will prevent.

7-14. Make an informal diagram of the four main actors: Supplier (Composite Bikes), Purchasing (Maria), Warehouse (Wally), and Accounting (Ann). Draw

arrows that show the data that flows among the actors during this process. Number the arrows and include on each arrow what data are included in the message.

7-15. Using the same four main actors as in question 7-14, this time show with the arrows how the material (the water bottles and cages) moves.

7-16. One concern of a business is fraud. One fraud technique is to create suppliers who are not suppliers but are co-conspirators. The conspirator inside the business accepts invoices for nonexistent deliveries. For this fraud scheme to work, who at CBI has to take part? How can SAP processes decrease the chance of this type of fraud?

7-17. Select any of the main activities or subactivities in the Procurement process.
   a. What event triggers this activity?
   b. What activity follows this activity?
   c. For one data entry item for this activity, describe what would happen in the rest of the process if that entry was erroneous.
   d. For one data entry item for this activity, describe what limits (controls) you would put in place on the data to prevent the type of error described in item c.

APPENDIX 7—SAP PROCUREMENT TUTORIAL

This tutorial follows the Procurement process shown in Figure 7A-1. The top of Figure 7A-1 appears in Chapter 7 as Figure 7-3. This top figure shows the three main Procurement activities—Order, Receive, and Pay—and their subactivities (Qualify Suppliers, etc.). At the bottom of Figure 7A-1, we have added the six SAP screens that are completed during the Procurement process. This tutorial directs you through the procedures for completing each screen. These six screens were chosen to keep this tutorial simple. To further simplify the process, we begin with screen 3, Create Purchase Order. As shown in Figure 7A-1, you will play the roles of Wally and Ann.

FIGURE 7A-1
Procurement Process and SAP Screens

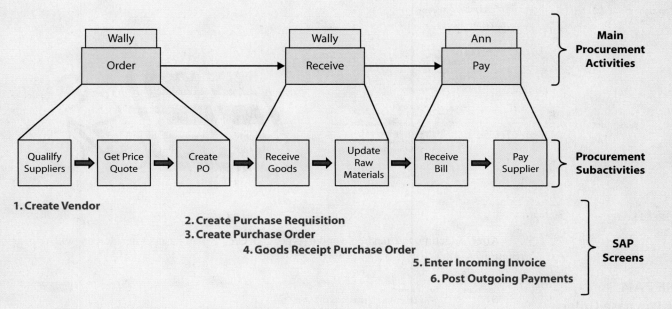

Main Procurement Activities

Procurement Subactivities

1. **Create Vendor**
2. **Create Purchase Requisition**
3. **Create Purchase Order**
4. **Goods Receipt Purchase Order**
5. **Enter Incoming Invoice**
6. **Post Outgoing Payments**

SAP Screens

Navigate to the SAP Welcome screen (Figure 7A-2).

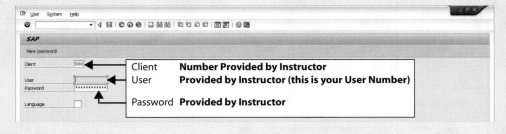

FIGURE 7A-2
Welcome Screen

Source: Copyright © SAP AG.

Client   **Number Provided by Instructor**
User   **Provided by Instructor (this is your User Number)**
Password   **Provided by Instructor**

First Exercise

In this first exercise, we will purchase 20 water bottles and 30 water bottle cages from an existing vendor called Space Bike Composites. The bottles cost $10.00 and the cages $9.00. While our company in this tutorial is Global Bike Inc., our actors—Wally and Ann—and our Procurement process are from Chuck's Bikes.[1] The three digits at the end of your User ID will be used throughout this tutorial. For example, if your User ID is GBI-123, then 123 is your User Number. In this tutorial, 001 is used as the User Number.

[1] All tutorials in this text use SAP GBI Intro to ERP (SCC).

1. Create Vendor

Skipped—does not apply to this first exercise; it is introduced later.

2. Create Purchase Requisition

Skipped—does not apply to this first exercise; it is introduced later.

3. Create Purchase Order

A purchase order, when received and accepted by a vendor, creates a legally binding contract between two parties. As a warehouse manager like Wally, the first screen to complete is the Create Purchase Order Screen. From the SAP Easy Access screen (Figure 7A-3), navigate to the Create Purchase Order screen by selecting:

Logistics > Materials Management > Purchasing > Purchase Order > Create > Vendor/Supplying Plant Known

FIGURE 7A-3

SAP Easy Access Screen

Source: Copyright © SAP AG.

After selecting the desired vendor type, the Create Purchase Order screen will appear (Figure 7A-4).

FIGURE 7A-4

Create Purchase Order Screen

Source: Copyright © SAP AG.

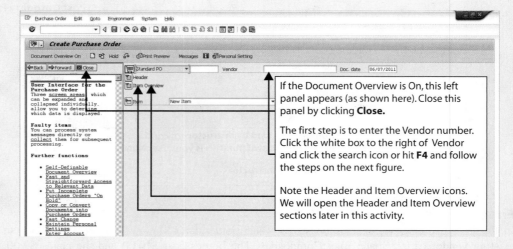

The next screen is the Vendor Search screen (Figure 7A-5). We need to find the vendor number for Space Bike Composites to complete the Purchase Order. While Wally might have this number memorized, we want to search in order to demonstrate how searching is done within SAP. Please note that where 001 appears in Figure 7A-5, you will type in your User Number.

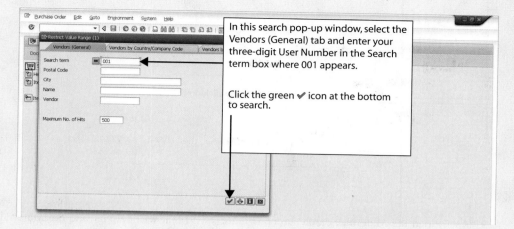

FIGURE 7A-5
Vendor Search Screen

Source: Copyright © SAP AG.

The Vendor List screen (Figure 7A-6) now loads.

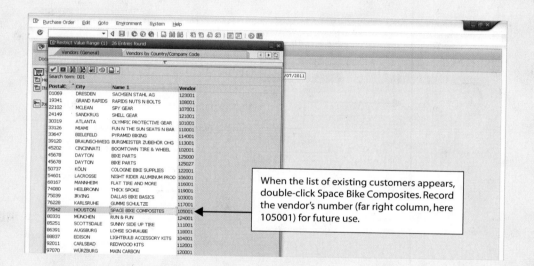

FIGURE 7A-6
Vendor List Screen

Source: Copyright © SAP AG.

After double-clicking on Space Bike Composites, the system returns to the Create Purchase Order screen. On this screen (Figure 7A-7), you will enter three inputs for Purch. Org. (Purchasing Organization), Purch. Group (Purchasing Group), and Company Code. The last two digits of each of the inputs are zeros, not the letter "O." These three inputs specify which office at Global Bikes is making the order.

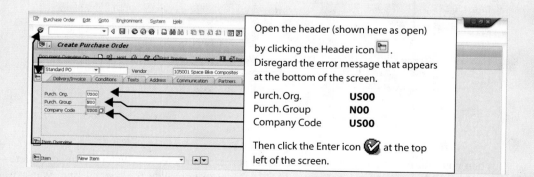

FIGURE 7A-7
Create Purchase Order with Vendor Screen

Source: Copyright © SAP AG.

After clicking Enter, the system loads more data on the screen. Next, we will enter data about the Material (the water bottles and cages) we are purchasing (Figures 7A-8 through 7A-11).

FIGURE 7A-8

Create Purchase Order with Item Overview On Screen

Source: Copyright © SAP AG.

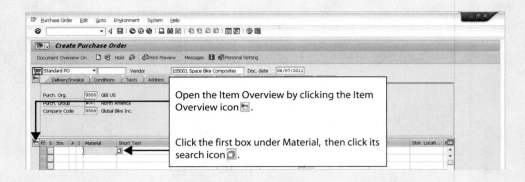

This will load the Material Search screen (Figure 7A-9) that will help us find the Material numbers we need for the Purchase Order.

FIGURE 7A-9

Material Search Screen

Source: Copyright © SAP AG.

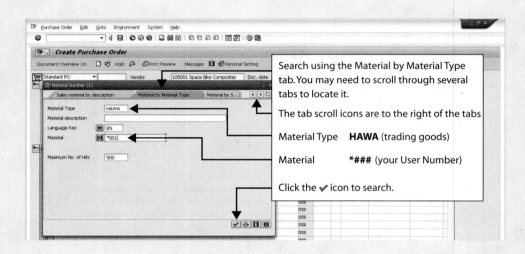

HAWA is the code used by SAP to identify trading goods. The next screen (Figure 7A-10) will show the trading goods you can order.

FIGURE 7A-10

Material List Screen

Source: Copyright © SAP AG.

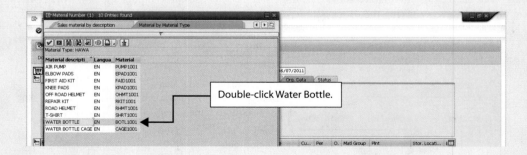

When you return to the Create Purchase Order screen after selecting Water Bottle, complete the following inputs (as shown in Figure 7A-11). Then to complete the second line, you can search for *Water Bottle Cages* or simply type in *Cage1###* (where ### is your User Number). On the following screen (Figure 7A-11), you will enter a date (for the delivery date). To enter date data, use the convenient Search button located to the right of the date input box. Also note, the plant (Plnt on the screen) is MI00, not M100.

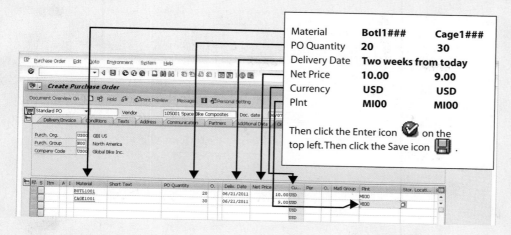

FIGURE 7A-11

Create Purchase Order with Material Screen

Source: Copyright © SAP AG.

A pop-up box appears (Figure 7A-12). Click the Save button.

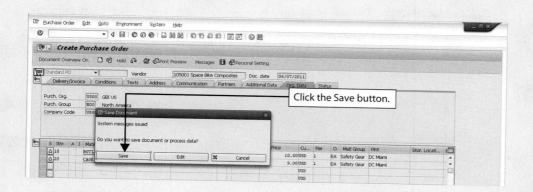

FIGURE 7A-12

Create Purchase Order Save Screen

Source: Copyright © SAP AG.

The SAP database now updates. When complete, the Purchase Order screen reappears; the bottom of the screen is shown in Figure 7A-13.

FIGURE 7A-13

Purchase Order Number Screen

Source: Copyright © SAP AG.

Return to the SAP Easy Access menu by clicking the yellow circle Exit icon near the top of the screen. This icon is located on the same ribbon as the Enter and Save icons.

4. Goods Receipt Purchase Order

The next screen to complete is the Goods Receipt Purchase Order screen. Wally will complete this screen when the water bottles and cages arrive at the warehouse. From the SAP Easy Access screen, navigate to the Goods Receipt Purchase Order screen by selecting:

Logistics > Materials Management > Inventory Management > Goods Movement > Goods Receipt > For Purchase Order > GR for Purchase Order (MIGO)

A goods receipt is recognition that the goods ordered in the PO have arrived. Once the goods receipt has been created, inventory for these items is increased and accounts payable is increased (Figure 7A-14).

FIGURE 7A-14
Goods Receipt Screen

Source: Copyright © SAP AG.

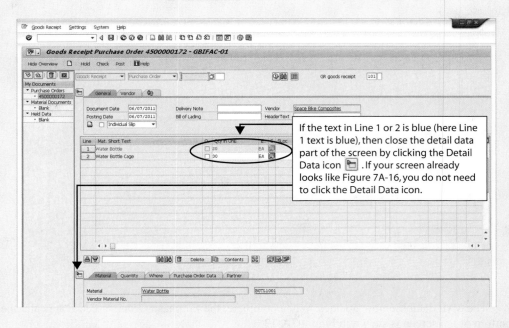

The system loads data from the PO, as shown in Figure 7A-15.

FIGURE 7A-15
Goods Receipt with Detail On Screen

Source: Copyright © SAP AG.

By closing the detail data part of the screen, your screen will look like Figure 7A-16. The reason the Water Bottle line was grayed out in 7A-15 is that the Detail Data section was open at the bottom of the screen. Notice in 7A-16 that the Detail Data section is closed.

FIGURE 7A-16
Goods Receipt with Detail Off Screen

Source: Copyright © SAP AG.

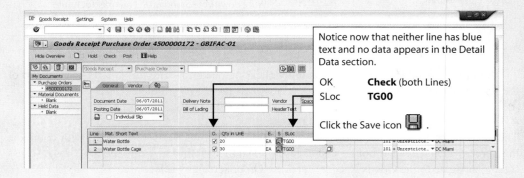

By checking OK, you are verifying that 20 water bottles and 30 cages were delivered as shown in Figure 7A-16. If not, you would not check OK and would instead enter the quantity that did arrive. Figure 7A-16 shows this column header as O. instead of O.K., which can be shown by adjusting the column width. When the Goods Receipt screen is complete and saved, a Material document is created (Figure 7A-17).

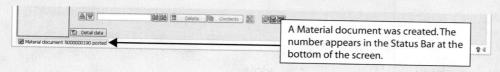

A Material document was created. The number appears in the Status Bar at the bottom of the screen.

FIGURE 7A-17
Goods Receipt Material Document Screen

Source: Copyright © SAP AG.

Return to the SAP Easy Access menu by clicking the Exit icon.

5. Enter Incoming Invoice

An accountant, like Ann, would complete the final two screens in this tutorial: Enter Incoming Invoice and Post Outgoing Payments. From the SAP Easy Access screen, navigate to the Enter Incoming Invoice screen by selecting:

> *Logistics > Materials Management > Logistics Invoice Verification > Document Entry > Enter Invoice*

Shortly after the goods arrived, the vendor has sent us a bill for $470 for the bottles and cages, and here we record this bill in our system (Figure 7A-18). Note, in Figure 7A-18 that the Tax Amount is entered via a drop-down box, which is the rightmost input box for Tax Amount.

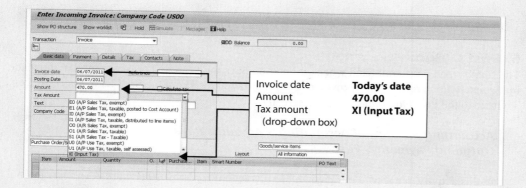

Invoice date   **Today's date**
Amount   **470.00**
Tax amount   **XI (Input Tax)**
   (drop-down box)

FIGURE 7A-18
Enter Incoming Invoice Screen

Source: Copyright © SAP AG.

We also enter our PO number, which was generated earlier in this process at the end of screen 3 (Figure 7A-13). This is shown below in Figure 7A-19.

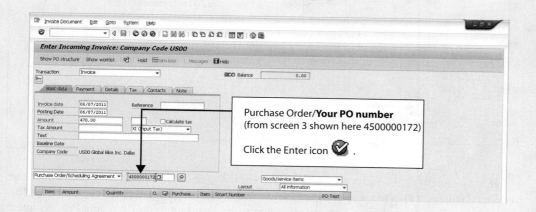

Purchase Order/**Your PO number**
(from screen 3 shown here 4500000172)

Click the Enter icon.

FIGURE 7A-19
Enter Incoming Invoice with PO Number Screen

Source: Copyright © SAP AG.

The system loads vendor data and displays the updated Enter Incoming Invoice screen (Figure 7A-20).

FIGURE 7A-20

**Enter Incoming Invoice
Final Screen**

Source: Copyright © SAP AG.

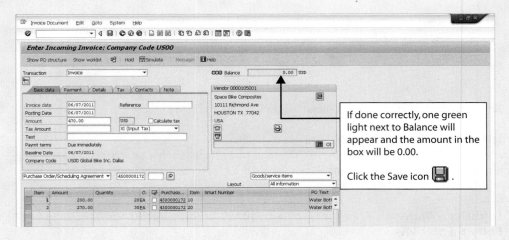

If there are no errors, a document number is produced on the bottom of the next screen (Figure 7A-21).

FIGURE 7A-21

**Enter Incoming Invoice
Document Number Screen**

Source: Copyright © SAP AG.

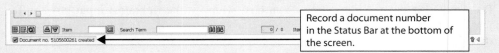

Return to the SAP Easy Access menu by clicking the Exit icon.

6. Post Outgoing Payments

The final screen gets completed when you or Ann pays the vendor. This payment may be made immediately upon receipt of the invoice or shortly thereafter. From the SAP Easy Access screen, navigate to the Post Outgoing Payments screen by selecting:

> *Accounting > Financial Accounting > Accounts Payable > Document Entry >
> Outgoing Payment > Post*

In this activity, we record our payment to the vendor for $470.00 (Figure 7A-22). A journal entry is made to decrease accounts payable.

FIGURE 7A-22

**Post Outgoing Payments
Screen**

Source: Copyright © SAP AG.

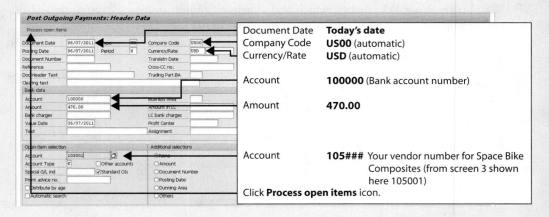

If you have to search for your vendor number in the bottom Account text box, select the Vendors (General) tab in the search pop-up window and use your three-digit User Number as the search term. Once you click on Process open items, the Post Outgoing Payments Process open items screen appears (Figure 7A-23).

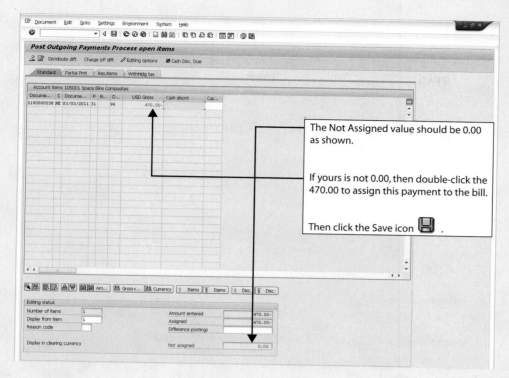

The SAP database is again updated and the Post Payment Document Number screen (Figure 7A-24) appears.

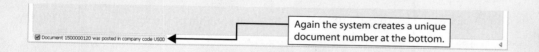

Record the document number that once again appears on the Status bar. Return to the SAP Easy Access screen by clicking the Exit icon. This will generate a pop-up window that is misleading. There is no data to be lost at this point, so click Yes.

You have finished the first exercise.

You Try It 1

Purchase the following three materials from a different vendor—Rapids Nuts N Bolts:

5	Air Pumps	$14.00 each
10	Elbow Pads	$37.50 each
15	First Aid Kits	$20.00 each

Request delivery in 2 weeks. Use Miami for the plant. The total amount is $745.00.

3. Create Purchase Order

Logistics > Materials Management > Purchasing > Purchase Order > Create > Vendor/Supplying Plant Known

Data needed:

Vendor	**108###** (Your Rapids Nuts N Bolts vendor number based on your User Number)
Purch. Org.	**US00**
Purch. Group	**N00**
Company Code	**US00**
Material	**PUMP1###, EPAD1###, FAID1###** (These are Trading Goods)
Quantity	**5, 10, 15**
Delivery Date	**Two weeks from today**
Net Price	**14.00, 37.50, 20.00**
Currency	**USD**
Plnt	**MI00**

Please note: Not every screen is shown here. Refer to the first exercise to see each screen. The completed Create Purchase Order screen as it appears at the *end* of screen 3 is shown in Figure 7A-25.

FIGURE 7A-25
Completed Create Purchase Order

Source: Copyright © SAP AG.

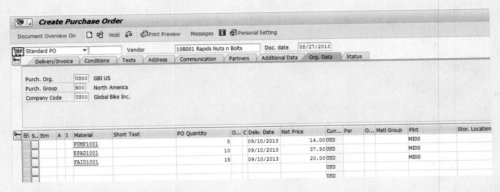

Click the Save icon. Record the PO number at the bottom of the screen. Return to the SAP Easy Access menu by clicking the Exit icon.

4. Goods Receipt Purchase Order

Logistics > Materials Management > Inventory Management > Goods Movement > Goods Receipt > For Purchase Order > GR for Purchase Order (MIGO)

Data needed:

Gr Goods Receipt	**101**
Purchase Order	**From previous screen** (4500000019 shown here)
OK	**Three check marks**
SLoc	**TG00** (Trading Goods)

The completed Goods Receipt Purchase Order screen is shown in Figure 7A-26.

FIGURE 7A-26
Goods Receipt Final Screen

Source: Copyright © SAP AG.

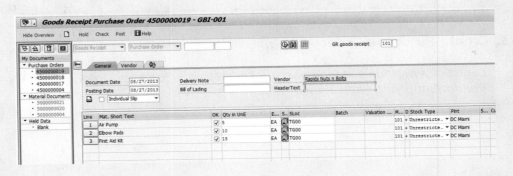

Click the Save icon. Return to the SAP Easy Access menu by clicking the Exit icon.

5. Enter Incoming Invoice

Logistics > Materials Management > Logistics Invoice Verification > Document Entry > Enter Invoice

Data needed:

Invoice Date	**Today's date**
Amount	**745.00**
Tax Amount	**XI (Input Tax)**
Purchase Order	**Your PO number** (4500000019 shown here)

Once these four items have been entered and the Enter icon has been clicked, the Enter Incoming Invoice screen will appear, as shown in Figure 7A-27. If done correctly, the Balance box in the upper right-hand corner should indicate 0.00.

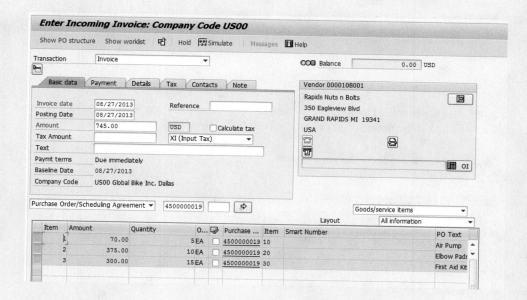

FIGURE 7A-27

Enter Incoming Invoice Final Screen

Source: Copyright © SAP AG.

Click the Save icon. Return to the SAP Easy Access menu by clicking the Exit icon.

6. Post Outgoing Payments

Accounting > Financial Accounting > Accounts Payable > Document Entry > Outgoing Payment > Post

Data needed:

Document Date	**Today's date**
Company Code	**US00** (automatic)
Currency/Rate	**USD** (automatic)
Account	**100000** (Bank account number)
Amount	**745.00**
Account	**108###** (Rapids Nuts N Bolts vendor number based on your User Number)

Before clicking Process Open Items, the Post Outgoing Payments screen appears as shown in Figure 7A-28:

FIGURE 7A-28

Post Outgoing Payments Header Screen

Source: Copyright © SAP AG.

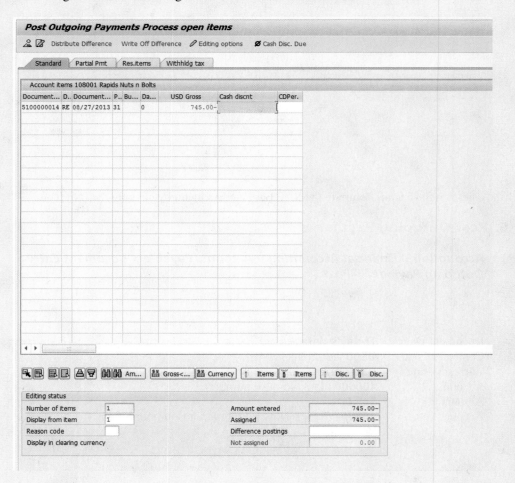

After clicking Process Open Items, the screen appears as shown in Figure 7A-29. If correct, the Not Assigned at the bottom-right corner will be 0.00. Then click the Save icon.

FIGURE 7A-29

Post Outgoing Payments Final Screen

Source: Copyright © SAP AG.

You are now finished with You Try It 1. Return to the SAP Easy Access menu by clicking the Exit icon.

You Try It 2

In screen 1 of You Try It 2, you will create a new vendor called Bike Parts. Then, in screen 2, Creating a Purchase Requisition, you will request a price quote for 10 repair kits. In screen 3, you will once again create a PO; however, this time the PO is based on the purchase requisition you created in screen 2.

1. Create Vendor

Logistics > Materials Management > Purchasing > Master Data > Vendor > Central > Create

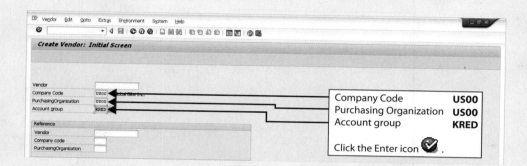

FIGURE 7A-30

Create Vendor Initial Screen

Source: Copyright © SAP AG.

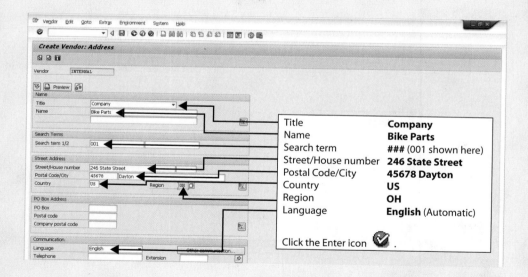

FIGURE 7A-31

Create Vendor Address Screen

Source: Copyright © SAP AG.

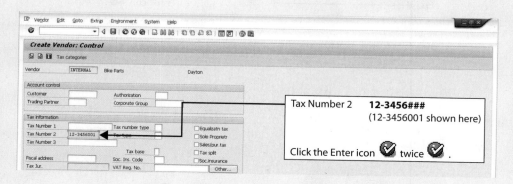

FIGURE 7A-32

Create Vendor Tax Screen

Source: Copyright © SAP AG.

FIGURE 7A-33

Create Vendor Accounting Screen

Source: Copyright © SAP AG.

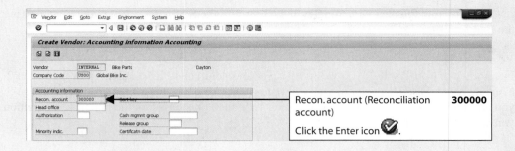

Recon. account (Reconciliation account)   **300000**

Click the Enter icon ✅.

FIGURE 7A-34

Create Vendor Payment Screen

Source: Copyright © SAP AG.

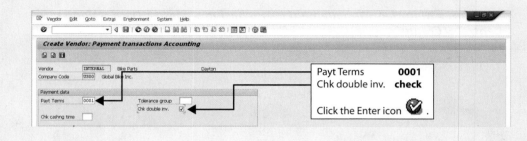

Payt Terms   **0001**
Chk double inv.   **check**

Click the Enter icon ✅.

FIGURE 7A-35

Create Vendor Correspondence Screen

Source: Copyright © SAP AG.

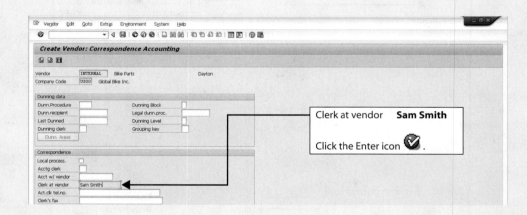

Clerk at vendor   **Sam Smith**

Click the Enter icon ✅.

FIGURE 7A-36

Create Vendor Purchasing Screen

Source: Copyright © SAP AG.

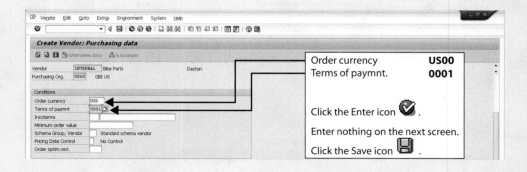

Order currency   **US00**
Terms of paymnt.   **0001**

Click the Enter icon ✅.

Enter nothing on the next screen.

Click the Save icon 💾.

FIGURE 7A-37

Create Vendor Number Screen

Source: Copyright © SAP AG.

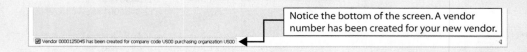

Notice the bottom of the screen. A vendor number has been created for your new vendor.

2. Create Purchase Requisition

Logistics > Materials Management > Purchasing > Purchase Requisition > Create

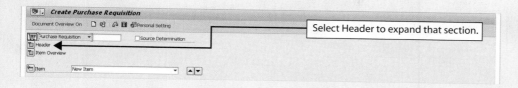

FIGURE 7A-38

Purchase Requisition Screen

Source: Copyright © SAP AG.

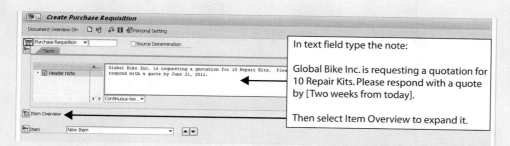

FIGURE 7A-39

Purchase Requisition Text Screen

Source: Copyright © SAP AG.

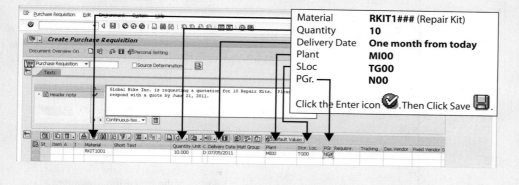

FIGURE 7A-40

Purchase Requisition Item Screen

Source: Copyright © SAP AG.

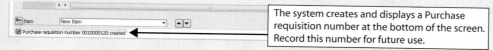

FIGURE 7A-41

Purchase Requisition Number Screen

Source: Copyright © SAP AG.

3. Create Purchase Order (now from Requisition)

Logistics > Materials Management > Purchasing > Purchase Order > Create > Vendor/Supplying Plant Known

Screen 3 was completed in the first exercise and in You Try It 1. This time you are creating the PO from the purchase requisition you created in screen 2.

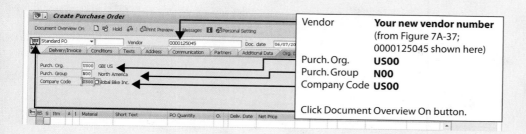

FIGURE 7A-42

Purchase Order Screen

Source: Copyright © SAP AG.

FIGURE 7A-43

Purchase Order from Purchase Requisition Screen

Source: Copyright © SAP AG.

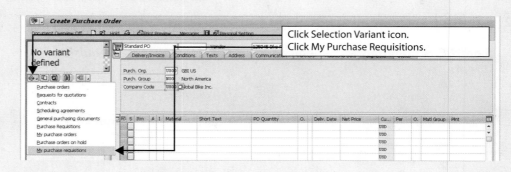

FIGURE 7A-44

Purchase Order from Purchase Requisition Selection Screen

Source: Copyright © SAP AG.

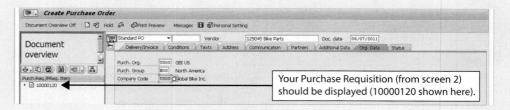

FIGURE 7A-45

Purchase Order Adopt from Purchase Requisition Screen

Source: Copyright © SAP AG.

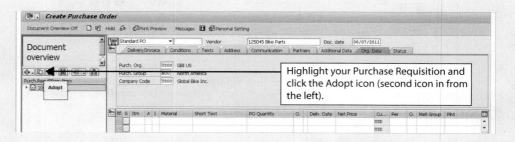

FIGURE 7A-46

Purchase Order Price Screen

Source: Copyright © SAP AG.

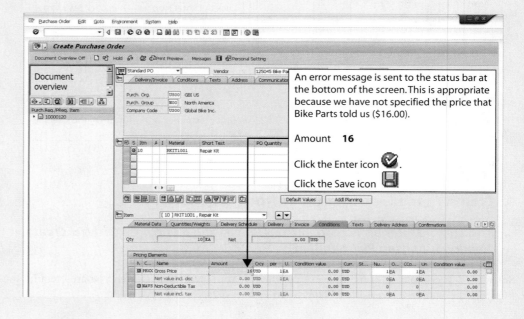

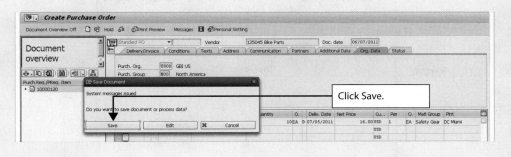

FIGURE 7A-47

Purchase Order Save Screen

Source: Copyright © SAP AG.

FIGURE 7A-48

Purchase Order Number Screen

Source: Copyright © SAP AG.

You have finished You Try It 2.

"**O**ur best client! And we lost the sale!" Sue, CBI's top salesperson, is having one of *those* days.

"Nothing you could have done, Sue. You can't sell bikes that we don't have."

"But Doug, why, why, why does this keep happening? Don't they know we're losing sales left and right? And now Heartland, our biggest customer!"

"I guess this won't happen with the new SAP system. It will give us up-to-the-minute inventory figures."

"I hope CBI is still in business by the time we get the system."

Sue later hears the full story from Ann in accounting. "Ann, when I looked at my screen, I saw that we had 55 of the new e-bikes they wanted, and I only needed 50 for the sale."

"Yeah, it did show that. But what it didn't show is that Doug had sold 10 of them earlier that day."

"So, when I thought we had 55, which is what the computer showed, we actually had 45?"

"Right."

"But, Ann, Doug sold those bikes to that little outfit in Kansas City. Those guys make three orders a year. Heartland makes 300. Why are we selling to the Smurfs? Couldn't we cancel their order instead of Heartland's?"

"That makes sense, but we've never done that."

"Even worse, Ann, and it kills me to say it, Heartland didn't want the bikes

Q1. What are the fundamentals of a Sales process?

Q2. How did the Sales process at CBI work before SAP?

Q3. What were the problems with the Sales process before SAP?

Q4. How does CBI implement SAP?

Q5. How does the Sales process work at CBI after SAP?

Q6. How can SAP improve customer-facing processes at CBI?

Q7. How does e-commerce improve processes in an industry?

Q8. What new IS will affect the Sales process in 2024?

until next month. Couldn't we order the frames and parts and put them together in the next 2 weeks or so? We've done that before to save sales."

"Wouldn't work. Space Bike Composites is our only supplier of that frame, and they were completely sold out."

"Why wasn't the sales department told?"

"We thought another supplier was going to come through with the frame, but that was a dead end."

Sue is now really frustrated. "We've got to find a way to keep the sales reps in the loop. We're going to lose Heartland if I have to cancel more orders."

"I agree, but how? There are hundreds of items we sell and hundreds of suppliers, and the suppliers have suppliers. Would sales reps read hundreds of emails about possible problems?"

"Fine. That doesn't do anything about Heartland, though…or my commission check."

In this chapter, we examine sales. More specifically, the Sales process at a bicycle company called Chuck's Bikes Inc. before and after the implementation of SAP. To accomplish this, we will examine the same questions we used in Chapter 7 when we discussed the Procurement process. It is not a coincidence that our approach here is the same as in Chapter 7. One of the most valuable aspects of a process perspective is that its lessons are reusable—once its lessons are learned, many of those lessons can be applied to other business processes.

We begin by examining the Sales process at CBI before SAP and learning how SAP ultimately improved it. We conclude the chapter by considering other processes that involve customers and how SAP and IS can be used to improve them. As with the procurement discussion, it is easy to get lost in the details. Keep in mind that sales is all about building relationships with customers. As you will see, SAP can help with that.

Chapter Preview

Q1. What Are the Fundamentals of a Sales Process?

Sue made, and lost, a large sale to CBI's best customer. CBI is a bicycle company that buys frames, tires, and accessories and assembles bikes that are then sold to retailers. Before we rush to find fault at CBI, let's make sure we understand the activities involved in a typical sales process. The business definition of a **sale** is an exchange of goods or services for money. More precisely, a sale is revenue from delivery of merchandise or a service where payment may be made in cash or other compensation. The Sales process is an operational process with three main activities—Sell, Ship, and Payment—as shown in Figure 8-1.

The sales activities—Sell, Ship, and Payment—are accomplished by actors playing the roles of Sales Agent, Warehouse Manager, and Accountant. The Sales process is located within the value chain in the sales and marketing primary activity shown in Figure 8-2.

For a business, sales is one of the most important processes. Without sales, no one gets paid and buildings go dark. Although sales is a complex and difficult process, it is also governed by one simple overriding principle: Satisfy the customer. Peter Drucker, one of the fathers of modern management theory, once said that there are no results that matter inside the company; the only result that matters is a satisfied customer.[1]

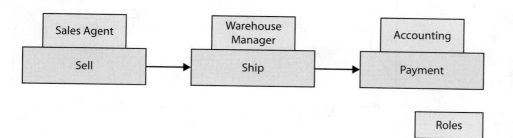

FIGURE 8-1

Main Sales Process Activities and Roles

[1] Peter Drucker, "Infoliteracy," *Forbes*, August 29, 1994, S104.

FIGURE 8-2

Sales Process Within the Value Chain of CBI

Primary Activity	Description	Process & Chapter
Inbound logistics	Receiving, storing, and disseminating inputs to products	Procurement, Chapter 7
Operations	Transforming inputs into final products	
Outbound logistics	Collecting, storing, and physically distributing products to buyers	
Sales and marketing	Inducing buyers to purchase products and providing the means for them to do so	Sales, Chapter 8
Customer service	Assisting customers' use of products thus maintaining and enhancing the products' value	

The online sale of flowers provides a good overview of the Sales process. Online florists use effective sales processes to build long-term, mutually beneficial relationships with customers. For example, when you send flowers to your mother for her birthday and include a birthday greeting, the flower company keeps track of this transaction and will send you a reminder email a few days before her next birthday. If you regularly send flowers to a particular person and then lapse, the company may again send a reminder: "It's been 2 months since you last sent Debbie flowers." The florist may also suggest a particular arrangement or offer you a discounted price to retain you as a frequent customer.

The florist would like to retain good customers, as acquiring new customers can cost 5 to 10 times as much as retaining existing ones. To retain customers, the florist needs to know things about its customers, like buying preferences, important dates, and how to address its customers—does Daniel Smith prefer to be called Mr. Smith, Dr. Smith, Dan, Danny, or Daniel? The more the company knows about its customers and their needs, the greater the likelihood it will keep that customer satisfied.

While understanding customers is key to making a sale, the sales process is key to delivering on the sale. To begin our discussion of the Sales process, consider the Sales process at CBI in the chapter-opening scenario. Figure 8-3 shows the main sales activities and subactivities. The first subactivity is to create a sales order that specifies that Heartland wants 50 bikes in 1 month. Later, on the planned shipping date, Wally, the warehouse manager, ensures that the bicycles are picked, packed in a box, and shipped to Heartland. Soon after, Ann sends Heartland an invoice, and when its payment arrives, she posts the payment to the CBI bank account.

We make two simplifications to the Sales process in this chapter. First, we address sales from one business to another rather than from a business to its consumers. These **business-to-business (B2B)** sales are much more common than **business-to-consumer (B2C)** sales like the florist example given earlier. This is because each B2C sale typically requires many B2B sales to acquire and assemble the product before it can be sold to a customer. A second simplification is that this chapter primarily addresses the sale of products, not services.

The basic fundamentals of the sales process we have discussed in this question are common to most firms. To better understand the impact of SAP on sales, we consider its use at CBI. We first investigate how sales worked before SAP was implemented.

FIGURE 8-3

Main Sales Process Activities, Subactivites, and Actors at CBI

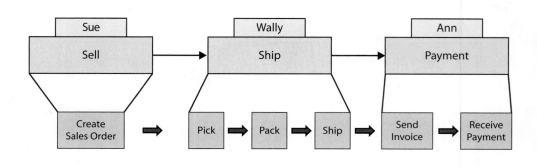

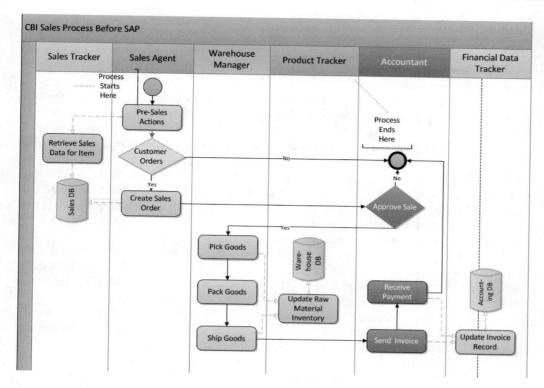

FIGURE 8-4

BPMN Diagram of Sales Process at CBI Before SAP

Q2. How Did the Sales Process at CBI Work Before SAP?

Before we can appreciate the benefits of using SAP, we will start with the lost sale described earlier. To understand why Sue's sale was canceled, consider the Sales process for CBI. The significant activities in this process are shown in Figure 8-4. This process has six roles, three performed by human actors—Sue, Wally, and Ann—and three by computer. Each computer actor is served by its own database, creating three information silos.

The first activity in Figure 8-4 is Pre-Sales Actions. In this activity, Sue and other sales reps contact customers, give price quotes, verify that products are available, check on special terms, and confirm delivery options. If the customer decides to order, the next activity is Create Sales Order. An example of a sales order (SO) is shown in Figure 8-5. On the example shown, Sue is selling Heartland Bike 50 Stream bikes at $300 each for a total price of $15,000.

As shown in Figure 8-4, once complete, the SO is sent to accounting for approval. To approve the SO, Ann in accounting gets price data from the Sales database, customer data from the Accounting database, and inventory data from the Warehouse database. She can also see what was sold and approved earlier in the day. These data flows to Ann are not shown in

FIGURE 8-5

Sue's Sales Order in Paper Form

Sales Order

CBI

June 24, 2014

To: Heartland Bike

Salesperson	Job	F.O.B Point	Delivery Date	Due Date
Sue Clark		Midpoint	7/11/14	

Qty	Item #	Description	Unit Price	Line Total
50.00	TXTR1001	Stream N3	$ 300.00	$ 15,000.00

Figure 8-4 for sake of simplicity. For existing customers, Ann uses data in the Accounting database to determine the history of payments by the customer—Heartland, in this case—before approving the sale. If this sale is for a new customer, there would be no customer data in the Accounting database, and Ann would add the new customer to that database and determine the risk of selling to this customer.

During this activity, Ann also accesses data in the Warehouse database to make sure there is sufficient inventory to sell. If there is not enough inventory, the sale is usually disapproved. However, as in the case of Sue's sale to Heartland, if the delivery for the sale can be delayed, Ann will call the warehouse to ask if future deliveries are expected that will replenish the inventory in time.

If approved by accounting, the SO is passed onto the warehouse where Wally and his staff will collect (or "pick"), pack, and ship the bicycles on the correct day, as shown in Figure 8-4. Once the bikes are shipped by the warehouse, Wally sends a notice to accounting that the goods have shipped so that accounting can send Heartland the invoice. The final activity, Receive Payment, occurs when Heartland sends a payment to CBI for the sale.

This process rejected Sue's sale for two reasons. When Sue made the sale, her sales database indicated the inventory at the beginning of the day—55 Stream bikes. However, 10 of those bikes were sold to a little retailer in Kansas City before Sue's sale to Heartland. When the SO of 50 bikes arrived at accounting, there were only 45 Streams available to sell. As mentioned in the opening vignette, Ann in accounting will coordinate to get an additional shipment of bike frames if the delivery of the sale provides enough time. However, in this case, Ann discovers that the supplier had sold out of the frame.

As you can see, the Sales process at CBI, like the Sales process at most organizations, involves several different people in several different departments. For the process to work well, these people need to be able to share data and integrate their activities. CBI struggled on both accounts, as we discuss next.

Q3. What Were the Problems with the Sales Process Before SAP?

The pre-SAP Sales process at CBI was plagued with problems, which are summarized in Figure 8-6. These are the problems that Sue has had to deal with over the years with this old system.

Sales Problems

Salespeople need to have the authority and data available to offer **real-time price discounts** to close some sales. For example, with the current process, if a customer is considering doubling the size of an order but needs a price discount to close the deal, Sue would have to request a price discount from the sales manager and contact the customer later. To be effective in today's competitive environment, salespeople need to be able to offer real-time price discounting—offering discounts during a sales call.

A second problem in sales at CBI is that Sue did not have accurate data on bikes available for sale. At CBI, inventory data are sent to the salespeople during the overnight hours. When CBI opens in the morning, the salespeople know which bikes and accessories are available in the warehouse that day. At times, as in the opening scenario, this can lead to the sale of too many bicycles, as salespeople only know how many bikes and accessories were available at the

FIGURE 8-6

Problems at CBI with Sales Before SAP

Role	Problems
Sales	No opportunity for real-time price discounting. Inaccurate data on products available for sale.
Warehouse	No communication to Sales on significant changes to future inventory.
Accounting	Time spent on invoice and other errors. New customer delays.

beginning of the day. As a result, salespeople promise bikes and delivery dates to customers that cannot be met. This overselling is particularly common when new or popular items like the e-bike are selling fast.

Warehouse Problems

The most significant problem for Wally is that he cannot easily communicate inventory forecasts to the sales force. For example, he knew that the e-bike frame supplier had sold CBI the last of its inventory, but he had no way to communicate this. He knows this would be useful for salespeople, but the current system does not offer any way to communicate big changes in future inventory.

Accounting Problems

Things are not much better in accounting. Ann supervises a staff of very careful accountants who make the occasional data entry and arithmetic errors. Some problems are unique to the Accounting role. Her office occasionally receives payments from customers with incorrect or missing invoices. The staff may also credit the wrong account or make other update errors. These infrequent errors can take hours to sort out and damage customer relations.

Delays also occur in checking the credit of new customers. When a salesperson makes a sale to a new customer, he or she inputs the customer data and tells the accounting department that a credit check is needed. When accounting receives a sales request for a new customer, an accountant must enter the new customer data into the Accounting database before the new customer approval process can begin. In this old system, the customer data must be entered by two different departments, delaying the process and introducing the opportunity for more input errors.

These problems cost CBI sales and customers over the years. As industry competition increased, CBI had to change or it would go out of business. CBI believed that SAP would help correct these Sales process deficiencies.

Q4. How Does CBI Implement SAP?

Many of the problems with the current Sales process can be overcome with an effective ERP system like SAP. However, as mentioned in Chapter 7, ERP systems are implemented not only to overcome problems but also to achieve strategy. To implement SAP successfully, top management reexamined CBI's strategy and committed to a competitive strategy that focused on a particular industry segment—high-end bikes—and a differentiation on responsiveness to retailers. CBI then selected the SAP Sales process most appropriate for this strategy. Sales managers decided on one efficiency objective and two effectiveness objectives, which are shown in Figure 8-7.

CBI believed that one way to be more efficient in sales is to encourage the sales force to make larger individual sales. Every sale takes time and delivery costs, so less frequent but larger sales increase efficiency. As a result, CBI decided an efficiency objective should be larger sales, as measured by the average sale amount.

The first effectiveness objective—faster customer response—will be measured by customer lead time, or instead of an additional—the time from creation of a sales order to the arrival of

Objective	Measure
Efficiency Increase customer order size	Average sale amount.
Effectiveness Faster customer response	Elapsed time from order to arrival. Percentage of sales of first-year products.
Reduce canceled sales to top customers	Revenue of canceled sales to top 20 customers.

FIGURE 8-7

Objectives and Measures for the New Sales Process

ordered products. A second measure will be the percentage of sales of first-year products. CBI offers new bikes and accessories based on customer input. If these new products are being purchased by retailers, this is a sign that CBI is responding well to customer requests. A second effectiveness objective is to reduce lost revenue from canceled sales to their best customers. CBI wants to maintain the right to cancel lower-revenue sales when they conflict with higher-revenue sales.

Based on these three objectives, CBI selected a sales process from SAP's inherent processes that would best support these objectives. They then organized teams of ERP analysts to configure the system and develop procedures appropriate for CBI employees to use and trained their employees to complete the implementation process.

Q5. How Does the Sales Process Work at CBI After SAP?

Now consider the situation 2 years later. CBI has implemented the SAP system, and employees know how to use it. Figure 8-8 shows the SAP inherent Sales process implemented at CBI.

Sales

The new Sales process features the same three actors as the previous Sales process—Sue, Wally, and Ann. However, the three computer actors are reduced to the single SAP system that tracks all the sales data. For comparative purposes, we will trace the same Sales process as before. This is the sale of 50 Stream bikes to Heartland when only 45 are available.

The Pre-Sales Actions activity is the same with three exceptions. The inventory and price data are now current. Sue can see that 55 bikes are available and that 10 of the 55 have been sold. She can see that the 10 bikes have not been shipped and that her customer will have priority.

FIGURE 8-8

Sales Process at CBI After SAP

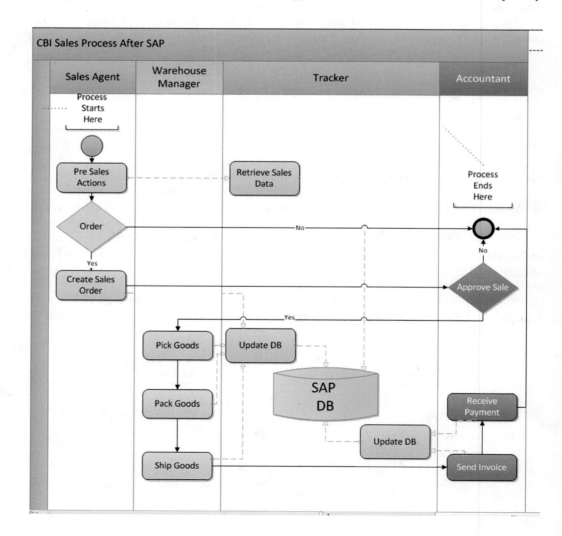

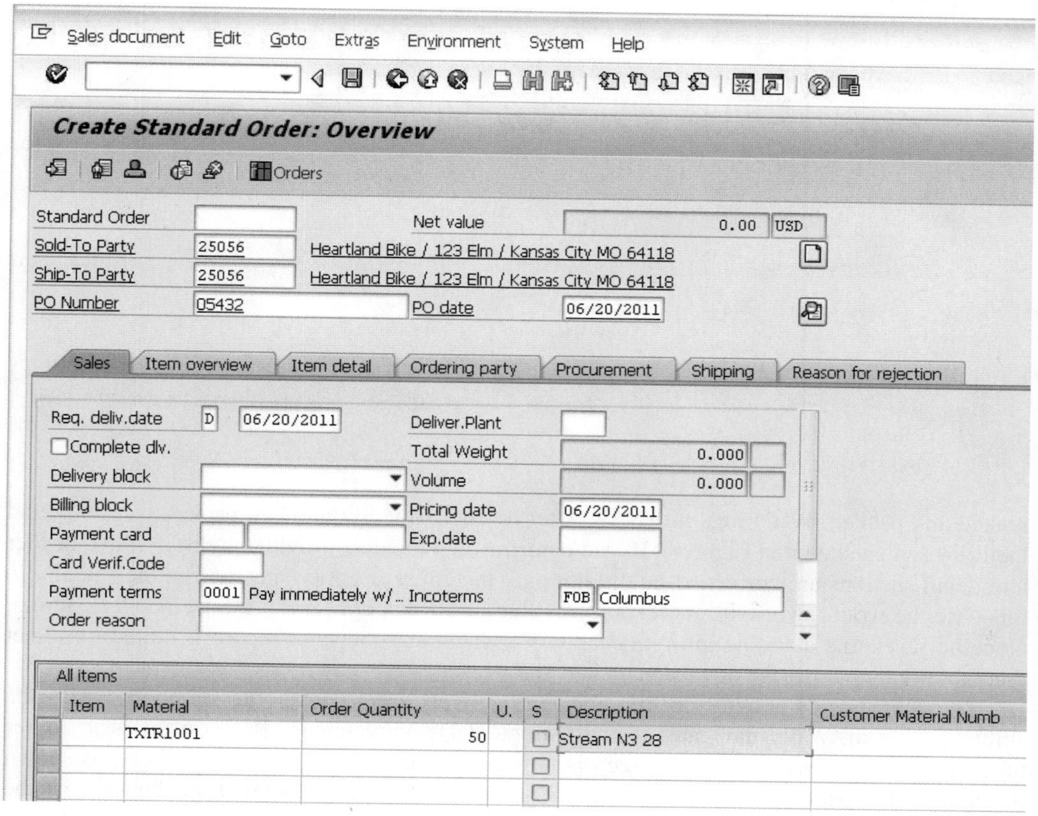

FIGURE 8-9

Create Sales Order Subactivity Screen in SAP of 50 Stream Bikes to Heartland

Source: Copyright © SAP AG.

In addition, Sue has access to real-time price discounts to enable her to offer Heartland additional pricing options. Finally, Sue can see long-term inventory availability; in this case, she can see that Wally has indicated no future inventory of Streams.

As we pick up Sue's story, she has just made the sale and is sitting down in her office to input the sales data into SAP in the Create Sales Order activity. She initiates the Create Sales Order procedure by logging into SAP. Her Sales Order screen looks like Figure 8-9.

The Sales Order screen has many of the same features as the Procurement process screens in Chapter 7. The title, at the top left in this case, is Create Standard Order: Overview. In the header section, Sue enters Heartland's customer number (25056), the date of the transaction (PO date of 06/20/2011), and the transaction number (PO Number 05432). The PO date for Heartland is the sales date for CBI—the date the sale was made. Once Sue enters these three data elements, SAP retrieves the customer's name and address. In the detail section at the bottom of the screen, Sue inputs the material number for Stream bikes (TXTR1001) and the number ordered (50). Sue then saves the data and enters another sale or exits the system.

Once Sue saves the SO, SAP creates a SO number and updates the inventory table in the database to reflect the sale of 50 Streams. In addition, a new SO record is created that will subsequently be updated when the warehouse picks, packs, and ships the bikes.

In addition to updating data, several other actions are triggered. First, a message is sent to the accounting department to approve or disapprove the sale. A second action updates the assembly schedule for CBI. SAP recognizes that the warehouse only has 45 Stream bikes and attempts to acquire from suppliers the additional bike frames and parts to assemble. When automated responses in the supply chain indicate no opportunity to acquire these frames, Ann in accounting receives a message. She sees Sue's pending sale to a preferred customer, the 45 bikes in inventory, and the 10 bikes sold earlier that day to another customer. Because Heartland is a preferred customer, Ann is able to cancel the sale of 10 bikes and move 5 of these bikes to Heartland.

Warehouse

Once this sale is approved, SAP sends a message to Wally in the warehouse to ship the bikes on the scheduled date. On the appointed day, Wally removes the bikes from finished goods inventory, packs them into a crate, and places the crate in the truck loading bay. Once the bikes are

FIGURE 8-10

Picking Subactivity Screen in SAP

Source: Copyright © SAP AG.

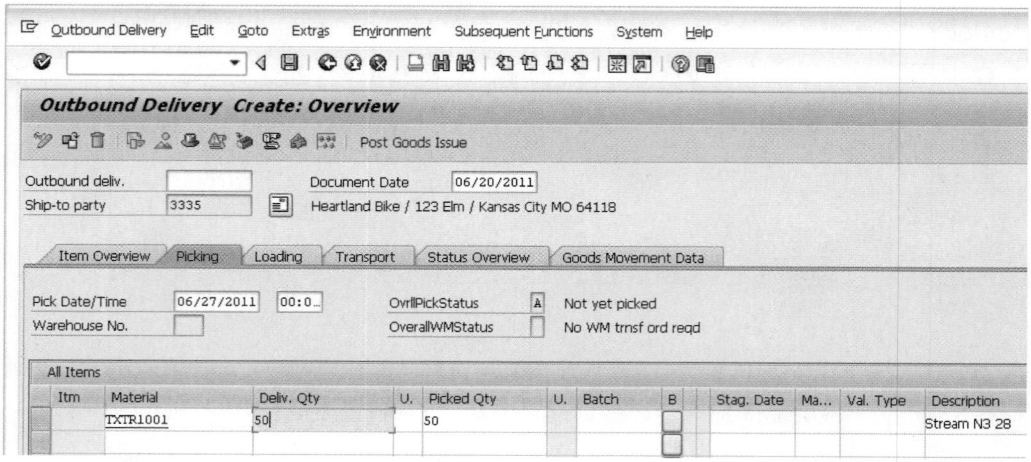

picked and packed, Wally logs into SAP. After he enters the SO number, he sees the Outbound Delivery screen shown in Figure 8-10. He confirms that the data provided by SAP in the header and detail sections are correct. If he did not pick the entire quantity specified in the sale, 50 in this case, he would overwrite the defaulted value of 50 that appears in the Deliv. Qty column. Once he saves this data, the inventory table is updated and the sales record is edited to reflect that the Stream bikes have now been picked and packed.

The Ship Goods activity occurs when the delivery truck leaves the warehouse with the shipment. Again, Wally navigates to the Outbound Delivery screen. Because this sales order has been picked and packed, the screen is now labeled Change Outbound Delivery, as shown in Figure 8-11. Wally executes the procedure by selecting the Post Goods Issue button near the middle of the screen. **Posting** means that legal ownership of the material has changed. The bikes are no longer owned by CBI; they are now the property of Heartland. Posting in this example occurs when the bikes are shipped.

Accounting

After Wally has posted the goods issue and the bicycles have changed ownership, Ann in accounting receives a message that she can bill Heartland for the 50 Streams. She logs into SAP and begins the Send Invoice procedure with the Maintain Billing Due List screen that is shown in Figure 8-12. She enters Heartland's number in the Sold-To Party field (25056) and selects the DisplayBillList icon near the top of the screen. On the following screen (not shown), Ann selects from a list of sales orders to Heartland, adds the sales order for the 50 Stream bikes, and clicks the Save icon.

This action triggers SAP to send a bill, called an invoice, to Heartland Bike for the 50 bikes. A week later, Ann in accounting receives a check in the mail for the 50 Streams.

To accomplish the Receive Payment activity in Figure 8-8, Sue navigates to the Post Incoming Payments screen shown in Figure 8-13. Here she specifies that Heartland, with Account number 25056, has paid $15,000 and that the money has been placed in Account number 100000. Once Ann saves the documents, SAP updates the sales record and makes the appropriate accounting entries.

FIGURE 8-11

Posting Subactivity Screen in SAP

Source: Copyright © SAP AG.

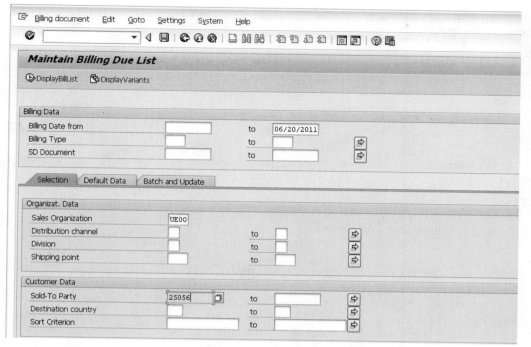

FIGURE 8-12

Send Invoice Subactivity Maintain Billing Due List Screen in SAP

Source: Copyright © SAP AG.

The Benefits of SAP for the CBI Sales Process

By implementing SAP, CBI enjoys two types of benefits. First, SAP addresses each of CBI's Sales process problems discussed earlier, as shown Figure 8-14. Second, SAP helps CBI achieve its sales objectives, also mentioned earlier, as shown in Figure 8-15.

FIGURE 8-13

Receive Payment Subactivity Post Incoming Payments Screen in SAP

Source: Copyright © SAP AG.

Document   Edit   Goto   Settings   System   Help

Post Incoming Payments: Header Data

Process open items

Document Date	06/20/2011	Type	DZ	Company Code	☑
Posting Date	06/20/2011	Period		Currency/Rate	☑
Document Number				Translatn Date	
Reference				Cross-CC no.	
Doc.Header Text				Trading Part.BA	
Clearing text					

Bank data

Account	100000		Business Area	
Amount	15000		Amount in LC	
Bank charges			LC bank charges	
Value Date			Profit Center	
Text			Assignment	

Open item selection

Account	25056	Additional selections
Account Type	D	☐ Other accounts	⦿ None
Special G/L ind		☑ Standard OIs	○ Amount
Pmnt advice no.			○ Document Number
			○ Posting Date

Problems	SAP Benefits
Sales No opportunity for real-time price discounting. Inaccurate data on products available for sale.	Real-time price discounting activity a part of SAP inherent process. Real-time data sharing.
Warehouse Limited communication to Sales on inventory changes.	Inventory forecasts available to sales due to integration of SAP processes.
Accounting Time spent on invoice and other errors. New customer delays.	SAP Inherent processes enforce input controls that reduce errors. Real-time data sharing.

FIGURE 8-14

CBI Sales Process Problems and SAP Benefits

By sharing data through SAP, the warehouse and sales office no longer maintain information silos. As a result, sales has accurate, current data on what's in the warehouse inventory. Further, with data sharing, the checking of credit for new customers is faster because the accounting department does not retype this data into its own database. Instead, new customer data gets entered once by the salesperson and the process of checking credit kicks off immediately.

Also shown in Figure 8-14 is the impact of SAP's inherent integrative processes on CBI's three other problems. First, the SAP inherent Sales process includes a real-time price discounting feature. Second, due to the integration of sales, procurement, and production processes, salespeople can check future inventory availability and make informed commitments to customers about upcoming sales. Finally, there are fewer errors in accounting as the data is entered only once, and SAP imposes controls on the data as it is typed into the database.

Although these are very helpful improvements, CBI implemented SAP to help it achieve a specific strategy, as shown in Figure 8-15. The implementation of SAP helps CBI achieve its efficiency objective. With real-time data on inventory and price discounting options, larger orders can be expected. One of the effectiveness objectives is faster customer response. With SAP, the warehouse can ship orders as soon as the sale is made. Also, the sale of first-year products, the second customer response measure, has increased with SAP. With SAP, sales reps have more accurate data on current and future inventory levels of the new products throughout the supply chain. Prior to SAP, these new products would not appear as inventory in the Warehouse database for potential sale until the day they arrived. Now, sales reps can see when these new products will be available and have accurate data on pending sales of these new items.

The second effectiveness objective of reducing canceled sales to the best customers is also achieved. The SAP inherent process allows the accounting department to give priority to its better customers when products are limited.

Having considered the benefits of SAP on the Sales process, we now broaden our consideration of the impact of SAP to a set of customer-facing processes.

FIGURE 8-15

CBI Sales Process Objectives and SAP Benefits

Objectives	SAP Benefits
Efficiency Increase customer order size	Real-time inventory data and price discounting.
Effectiveness Faster customer response Reduce canceled sales to top customers	With real-time sales data, warehouse can ship orders immediately. Top customers have higher priority.

MIS InClass 8

Building a Model

The purpose of this exercise is to participate in a process that satisfies an external customer. In this exercise, student teams will build replicas of a model that is hidden from their sight.

Before class, the instructor, the external customer, constructed a model that is now hidden from view. The goal of the student team is to build a model identical to that one. The model is concealed in the hallway immediately outside the classroom. The class is divided into teams, and each person on the team is assigned one of four roles. Each team is composed of between four and six students with the following roles:

- **Looker:** The looker looks at the instructor's model and remains in the hallway. The looker cannot write anything down. The looker explains to the messenger how to assemble the model.

- **Messenger:** The messenger listens to the looker's description. The messenger relays these verbal instructions to the builders in the room. The messenger cannot look at either the instructor's model or the team's model as it is being assembled.

- **Feedbacker:** The feedbacker can look at the instructor's model and the team's model. The feedbacker can say only "yes" or "no" to questions asked by any other team member.

- **Builders:** The rest of the team is made up of builders. Builders construct the replica of the instructor's model. They acquire the pieces from a supplier who supplies all the teams.

The game begins with the lookers in the hallway each giving their messenger an initial set of instructions. Play the game until the last team has built the replica.

After the game, discuss the following:

1. Do the roles in the game correspond to business roles?
2. Describe your team's building process and its objectives. Construct a BPMN diagram of your team's building process. Use the looker–messenger exchange as the first activity and assembling pieces as the last activity.

Source: Andresr/Shutterstock.

3. How did your process evolve from the first iteration of the process to the last? How did you learn to use the feedbacker? If the feedbacker is considered a simple IS, how does this IS lead to process improvement?
4. Vocabulary is necessary for effective communication. Did the looker, messenger, and builders use the same vocabulary to describe the building pieces?
5. How well is data shared in the building process?
6. There is no (computer) IS in this game. If your team had some money to spend on an IS, what would you buy? In Chapter 5, we discussed five ways an IS can improve a process. For the IS you purchase, which of these five best describes how your IS will improve your process?
7. After spending money on an IS, which player's job would change? What is the relationship between a new IS and job change in general?
8. With the process used at the end of the game, how much time would it take to construct the next model?

Q6. How Can SAP Improve Customer-Facing Processes at CBI?

The Sales process is just one of many customer-facing processes that SAP can support. These processes are listed in Figure 8-16. The Promotion process is designed to increase sales, stimulate demand, or improve product availability over a predetermined limited time. The Sales process,

Process Scope	Customer-Facing Processes
Operational	Promotion Sales Service
Managerial	Promotional Discounting Service Trends
Strategic	New Product Launch Promotion Evaluation

FIGURE 8-16

Sample of Customer-Facing Processes

FIGURE 8-17

CRM and SCM Processes

CRM Processes—Chapter 8	SCM Processes—Chapter 7
Front Office—Customer Facing	**Back Office—Supply Chain**
Sales	Procurement
Service	Demand Management
Promotion	Returns Management
Other Processes	Other Processes

defined earlier, is the exchange of goods or services for money. The Service process, first defined in Chapter 5, provides after-sales support to enhance or maintain the value of a product.

The administration of customer-facing processes and managing all the interactions with customers is called **customer relationship management (CRM).** The relationship of the Sales process to other customer-facing processes and CRM is the same as the Procurement process, other supply chain processes, and supply chain management (SCM), as shown in Figure 8-17. Just as supply chain processes were improved with data sharing and integration, so too are customer-facing processes.

Improving Customer-Facing Processes by Sharing Data

Customer-facing processes improve when processes share data. To see how this works, consider your process of returning merchandise to a retailer. It is easier for you to return your merchandise if you have a receipt. If this receipt was emailed to you, it may be easier to find than a printed receipt. By using electronic receipts, your retailer's Sales process has made your Returns process easier. Rather than issue paper receipts, which are more costly and more frequently lost, many retailers are sharing receipt data with customers electronically by sending an email or a message to a customer's smartphone. Not only does this reduce sales costs, an objective of the retailer's Sales process, it also improves the customer's Returns process because customers can find their receipts more frequently.

Examples of improving processes by sharing data at CBI are shown in Figure 8-18. Both sales and service are improved when they share customer data. By having access to customer sales data, CBI service is improved. For example, when a customer calls for service about a problem with a particular shipment, the service agent at CBI knows the sales data for that shipment and all shipments to that customer. By having the sales data, the agent is better informed about the customer's situation. Likewise, the Sales process is improved with customer service

FIGURE 8-18

Examples of Data Sharing Among Customer-Facing Processes

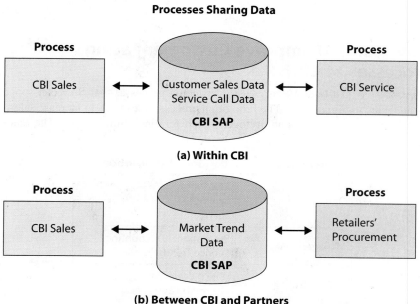

call data. A sales representative can review service data from a customer before initiating a sales call. That way the sales representative can offer the customer products that were not the subject of a service call.

By sharing data, the Sales process of CBI and the Procurement processes of its customer retailers can be improved. For example, CBI sells to many small outlets. These small retailers do not have the resources to collect data on market trends, but CBI does. CBI can share its market trend data with retailers, who can then make better procurement decisions about what bikes to buy from CBI. Both firms win when CBI's Sales process and the small retailer's Procurement process share this market trend data because they both sell more bikes.

Improving Customer-Facing Processes with Integration

The second way to improve the collection of customer-facing processes is to increase their integration, or their synergy. Process synergy occurs when processes are mutually supportive—when one process is done well, then the objectives of another process are supported. Synergy between sales and procurement is evident in your personal life. Amazon.com recognizes the synergy between its Sales process and your personal Procurement process. When people want to buy something, they want to do it quickly. Therefore, it can be said that people have a Procurement process objective of not wasting time. Amazon.com has found that online sales revenue increases 1 percent for every one-tenth of a second decrease in load time.[2] As a result, it makes download time an objective of its Sales process, and this mutually supports your personal Procurement process.

Examples of increasing synergy at CBI are shown in Figure 8-19. At CBI, the Production process can support the objectives of the Sales process. If the Production process times are consistent, the assembly of bikes is on time and the delivery of a sale is rarely late. As a result, customers are satisfied and opportunities for future sales are improved. The objective of the Sales process, repeat customers, is supported by the Production process.

A second example of process synergy is the support of the Sales process by the Billing process. When an accountant at CBI is contacted by a customer or the accountant contacts a customer to clarify a bill, the Billing process requires the accountant to share current pricing of products with the customer. More specifically, the accountant shares prices on products if the new price is better than the price on the bill, which, in turn, leads to future sales.

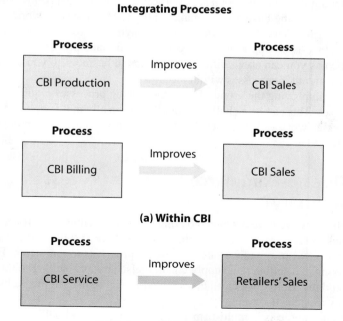

Integrating Processes

FIGURE 8-19

Examples of Process Integration Among Customer-Facing Processes

Process

CBI Production

Improves

Process

CBI Sales

Process

CBI Billing

Improves

Process

CBI Sales

(a) Within CBI

Process

CBI Service

Improves

Process

Retailers' Sales

(b) Between CBI and Partners

---

[2] Jolie O'Dell, "Why Web Sites Are Slow and Why Speed Really Matters," *Mashable*, last modified April 5, 2011, http://mashable.com/2011/04/06/site-speed/.

FIGURE 8-20
Challenges of Improving a Group of Processes

> People are distracted from their most important process.
> Processes change constantly.
> People must know objectives of many processes.

To improve process synergy with retailers, CBI can use its Service process to support the Sales processes of its customer retailers. For example, when a defective bike is returned to CBI from one of its retailers, the CBI Service process uses overnight shipping to give the retailer a new bike within 24 hours. As a result, the retailer's Sales process is improved because each of CBI's retailers can promise customers 24-hour replacements.

In both this chapter and the previous one, we have seen that with SAP, CBI can share data and integrate processes with its suppliers and customers. While we have been quick to sing the virtues of this closer arrangement, there is also a curse. ERP systems are a difficult and expensive necessity to keep up with the competition. In today's tech-savvy environment, customers have high technical expectations of sellers. Retailers like Heartland only want to purchase from bike wholesalers who have a state-of-the-art ERP system supporting their sales and service. For CBI and other wholesalers, this expectation curse increases pressure to spend and spend and spend to keep ERP systems current.

Challenges

Although it is clear that SAP can help improve the collection of customer-facing processes, improving CRM processes or any set of processes also presents challenges, as shown in Figure 8-20.

First, focusing on a single process is easier than trying to achieve the goals of many processes at one time. Trying to improve all the CRM processes can be seen as a distraction by sales representatives who believe the sales process deserves all their focus. These representatives may see their job as building relationships with customers. They may view time spent with technology or time spent on sales-related processes as time they could use to improve these vital relationships.

A second challenge is that all of the processes are in a state of change. Processes change, as we have mentioned in earlier chapters, due to changes in technology, strategy, people, and products. Keeping all these processes working well together while they all change is difficult.

Finally, achieving the objectives of a set of processes can only happen when businesspeople understand other parts of the business. To make all the CRM processes work well, salespeople need to know their firm's Service processes and how payments are processed in accounting. By the way, this challenge is an opportunity for you. To help make processes work at your future firm, learn as much as you can about different functions in business so you can make your processes work well with other processes within the firm.

To summarize, improving the group of customer-facing processes requires sharing data and integrating processes. This can be a challenge, but SAP is an ally in this fight, and there are other IS that help processes work well together. Next, we consider IS that help processes in multiple firms work well together.

Q7. How Does E-Commerce Improve Processes in an Industry?

In the past two chapters, we have discussed buying and selling between CBI and its partners and how SAP can make processes better for both. However, ERP systems are not the only way to improve processes between organizations. Another approach is e-commerce. E-commerce not only supports buying and selling in a supply chain, it also supports selling to the final customer, people like you and me. Before we close this chapter, it will be helpful to you in the future if we consider some key aspects of e-commerce.

Formally, **e-commerce** is a multi-firm process of buying and selling goods and services using Internet technologies. While popular B2C e-commerce is accomplished via the Web at places like Amazon.com and Apple, much of B2B e-commerce uses private networks and company- or industry-specific software.

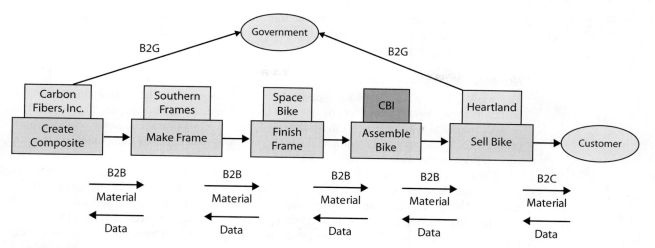

FIGURE 8-21

E-Commerce in Bike Supply Chain

CBI participates in B2B e-commerce as shown in Figure 8-21. Starting on the left end of Figure 8-21, composites, which are raw materials for bike frames, are created by Carbon Fibers, Inc. The composites are sold to a frame manufacturer, Southern Frames, who makes the bicycle frames. The frames are sold to a frame wholesaler, Space Bike Composites in this scenario, where the frames are finished. CBI assembles the bikes and sells the finished product to retailers such as Heartland who, in turn, sell to a final customer.

As defined earlier, e-commerce consists of both a multi-firm buying and selling process and the internet-based IS that supports it. ERP systems can support e-commerce, as do IS that support fund transfers, inventory management, and transaction processing systems. These systems are often referred to as **interorganizational IS,** which are IS used by more than one firm.

Figure 8-22 lists categories of companies that participate in e-commerce. The U.S. Census Bureau, which publishes statistics on e-commerce activity, defines **merchant companies** as those that own the goods they sell. They buy goods and resell them. It defines **nonmerchant companies** as those that arrange for the purchase and sale of goods without ever owning or taking title to those goods. With regard to services, merchant companies sell services that they provide; nonmerchant companies sell services provided by others. Of course, a company can be both a merchant and nonmerchant company.

E-Commerce Merchant Companies

The three main types of merchant companies are those that sell directly to consumers, those that sell to companies, and those that sell to government. Each uses slightly different IS in the course of doing business. B2C e-commerce concerns sales between a supplier and a retail customer (the consumer). IS that support the Sales process of B2C companies are typically **Web storefronts** that customers use to enter and manage their orders. Amazon.com, REI.com, and LLBean.com are examples of companies that use Web storefronts.

B2B e-commerce refers to sales between companies. As Figure 8-21 shows, raw materials suppliers and other firms use interorganizational IS like ERP systems to integrate B2B supply

Merchant Companies	Nonmerchant Companies
Business-to-consumer (B2C)	Auctions
Business-to-business (B2B)	Clearinghouses
Business-to-government (B2G)	Exchanges

FIGURE 8-22

E-Commerce Merchant and Nonmerchant List

chains. **B2G,** or **business-to-government** merchants, sell to governmental organizations. In Figure 8-21, the composite raw material supplier and the bike retailer might sell their products to government agencies.

Nonmerchant E-Commerce

The most common nonmerchant e-commerce companies are auctions and clearinghouses. **Auctions** match buyers and sellers by using an IS version of a standard auction. This application enables the auction company to offer goods for sale and to support a competitive bidding process. The best-known auction company is eBay, but many other auction companies exist; many serve particular industries.

Clearinghouses provide goods and services at a stated price and arrange for the delivery of the goods, but they never take title. One division of Amazon.com, for example, operates as a nonmerchant clearinghouse, allowing individuals and used bookstores to sell used books on the Amazon.com Web site. As a clearinghouse, Amazon.com uses its Web site as an IS to match the seller and the buyer and then takes payment from the buyer and transfers the payment to the seller, minus a commission.

Another type of clearinghouse is an **electronic exchange** that matches buyers and sellers, similar to that of a stock exchange. Sellers offer goods at a given price through the electronic exchange, and buyers make offers to purchase over the same exchange. Price matches result in transactions from which the exchange takes a commission. Priceline.com is an example of an exchange used by consumers.

How Does E-Commerce Improve Market Efficiency?

E-commerce, both the processes and interorganizational IS that support them, improves market efficiency in a number of different ways, as shown in Figure 8-23. For one, e-commerce leads to **disintermediation**, which is the elimination of middle layers of distributors and suppliers. You can buy a bicycle from a typical "brick-and-mortar" retailer like Heartland, or you can use CBI's Web site and purchase the bike directly from CBI. If you take the latter route, you eliminate the retailer. The product is shipped directly from CBI's finished goods inventory to you. You eliminate the retailer's inventory-carrying costs, and you eliminate shipping overhead and handling activity. Because the retailer and associated inventories have become unnecessary waste, disintermediation increases market efficiency.

E-commerce also improves the flow of price data. As a consumer, you can go to any number of Web sites that offer product price comparisons. You can search for the bike you want and sort the results by price and vendor reputation. You can find vendors that avoid your state sales tax or that omit or reduce shipping charges. The improved distribution of data about price and terms enables you to pay the lowest possible cost and serves ultimately to remove inefficient vendors. The market as a whole becomes more efficient.

A third way e-commerce improves market efficiency is sharing customer marketing data. Two examples of improved consumer data sharing come from Google: AdWords and Analytics.

Google pioneered Web 2.0 advertising with its AdWords software. AdWords is Google's popular pay-per-click advertising product. With AdWords, companies pay a predetermined price for particular search words. For example, Oracle might agree to pay $2 for the words *software* and *business*. When a customer uses Google to search for those terms, Google will display a link to Oracle's Web site. If the user clicks that link (and *only* if the user clicks that link), Google charges Oracle $2. Oracle pays nothing if the user does not click.

Customer data sharing is also improved with free Google Analytics software that enables the Web site owner to collect Web traffic data. This data includes where the customer came from (from a search engine, another site, and so on), where the customer visited in the site, and the conversion rate, which is the ratio of the number of customers who eventually purchased divided by the number who visited. Analysts can examine this type of data and make changes to the site with the objective

FIGURE 8-23
Three Ways E-Commerce Improves Market Efficiency

1. Disintermediation—e-commerce removes inefficient middle layers
2. Data Flow—e-commerce allows more data to be available to buyers and sellers
3. Software—e-commerce software improves sharing of customer marketing data

of increasing sales. Installed on more than a half million of the most popular Web sites, Google Analytics improves market efficiencies by improving the collection and sharing of customer data.

Q8. What New IS Will Affect the Sales Process in 2024?

SAP and e-commerce will continue to have a significant impact on Sales processes for years to come. However, other IS that are just now emerging may also help improve the Sales process. These IS include wearable technology, smartphones, social CRM, and cloud CRM.

WEARABLE TECH When customers began to carry mobile phones, many companies changed their Sales processes to take advantage of the new platform. The next step in hardware evolution is for customers to wear devices, and that step will also affect the sales process. While Google Glass was one of the first wearable devices, Disney is demonstrating how another type of wearable device can be put to use. Disney World is giving electronic bracelets called MagicBands, like the bracelet shown in Figure 8-24, to some of its park visitors to support its customer-facing processes. The bracelet allows customers to charge food and drinks, view ride wait times, and enter their locked hotel rooms without a key. This is no Mickey Mouse operation; Disney intends to invest $800 million dollars in the MagicBands concept.[3] In addition to the services just mentioned, at the option of parents, a child's name can be encoded on the child's band so that as Cinderella parades by she can greet the child by name. While most of the examples in this chapter were sales of products, this Disney example suggests that the use of wearable technology to support the sale of services in entertainment, health care, and public safety may only be beginning.

SMARTPHONE PAYMENT Customers are increasingly using their smartphones to make purchases. For example, customers at Starbucks can use their phone to buy coffee and other products. To do so, customers first purchase a QR code online for their phone from Starbucks. Then, when they visit a Starbucks, they display the QR code on their phone and allow the cashier to scan it. Coffee is not the only thing people are buying with smartphones. In Shanghai, China, customers use their phones to shop for groceries at subway stations. On posters in the subway, a grocery chain displays images of products along with a QR code for each item, as shown in Figure 8-25. Shoppers scan the QR code on their smartphones to register a purchase, and the groceries are delivered to their home of record later that day.

SOCIAL CRM As mentioned previously, one way customer processes are improved is by sharing data. **Social CRM** is an information system that helps a company collect customer data from social media and share it among its customer-facing processes.

In today's social media environment, the vendor–customer relationship is complex and is not controlled by the vendor. Businesses offer many different customer touch points, and customers craft their own relationship with the business by their use of those touch points.

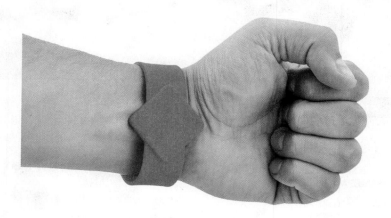

FIGURE 8-24
Electronic Bracelet

Source: vetkit/fotolia

---

[3] Brooks Barnes, "The Digital Kingdom," *New York Times*, January 7, 2013, B1.

FIGURE 8-25

Shopping for Groceries Using QR Codes

Source: © Imaginechina/Corbis.

Social CRM data is collected through interactions on Facebook, Twitter, wikis, blogs, discussion lists, frequently asked questions, sites for user reviews, and other social media. Social CRM systems collect and distribute this data to a variety of customer processes.

CLOUD-BASED CRM: SALESFORCE.COM Salesforce.com is the preeminent cloud-based CRM vendor. Rather than purchasing CRM software and installing it onsite, companies utilize a pay-as-you-go plan to use the online software and run it offsite at Salesforce.com. With more than 80,000 customer firms, Salesforce.com is growing rapidly, particularly with small to medium-sized firms. The Salesforce.com homepage is shown in Figure 8-26.

FIGURE 8-26

Salesforce.com Homepage

Source: www.salesforce.com/ Accessed July 5, 2013.

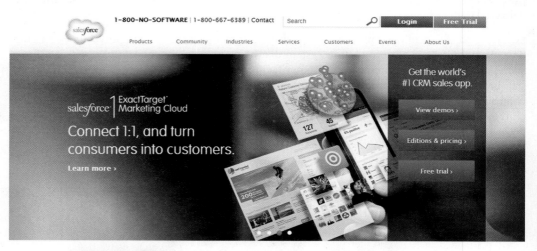

Salesforce.com helps a company integrate its customer processes in several ways. First, by keeping data in the cloud with Salesforce.com, a small company's data is stored in a format that is compatible with a wide variety of software. Because of the universal format, it is easier for the company to share this data among its various customer processes. Second, the software is scalable. A company can conduct a small-scale trial of the CRM software at one office to test the integration of its customer processes before rolling it out to the whole company. Finally, startup costs are zero; firms pay as they use the service without a big up-front contract. A company can therefore conduct its integration trial at one location without significant investment.

Process Integration and You in 2024

While technology will help businesses integrate sales processes, so too will you. One of the goals of this textbook is to help you become comfortable with processes and begin to see how they can work together. We first explained processes and then discussed how a set of processes work together in a supply chain and in the customer-facing processes within one firm. We also applied integration concepts to processes between firms. Our goal all along was to get to the following conclusion: *Processes must work well together.*

In every job you will have, in every company large and small, you will play a role in many processes. If you are an accountant, your accounting classes will prepare you well to do those roles; if you are in sales like Sue, your marketing courses will get you ready for your role as a salesperson. But in every job and in every role you play, you will be more effective if you keep in mind the big picture that processes must work well together.

In Chapter 1, we suggested that four skills will be valuable to you in your career: abstract reasoning, systems thinking, collaboration, and experimentation. Recall from that chapter that a systems thinker is one who understands how the inputs and outputs of processes relate. Here we can express that in a more specific way. A systems thinker is a process thinker. A good systems thinker considers how the change in one process output affects other processes.

Where there are business processes, there is likely to be an ERP system. Whether you are an accounting, supply chain, marketing, or finance student, chances are that you will work with SAP or another ERP system on your very first job after college. As an accountant, you will post payments and configure SAP to allow different payment schedules and to create automatic price discounts. As a salesperson, you may record every customer interaction in your CRM module, post and edit sales, and invent new reports that will help your company identify new trends and opportunities. These activities will affect other processes outside your office. You and your employer will be pleased if, by the time you start, you have mastered some aspects of SAP so you can anticipate these impacts. So take this time to master the vocabulary in these chapters. Learn how to navigate to different screens and to move around within the screens. Think about processes and how ERP systems change and improve processes. If you can, do the tutorials in the appendix, make mistakes, start over—learn beyond the book.

Ethics Guide

Are My Ethics for Sale?

Suppose you are a salesperson at CBI. CBI's sales forecasting system predicts that your quarterly sales will be substantially under quota. You call your best customers to increase sales, but no one is willing to buy more.

Your boss says that it has been a bad quarter for all of the salespeople. It's so bad, in fact, that the vice president of sales has authorized a 20 percent discount on new orders. The only stipulation is that customers must take delivery prior to the end of the quarter so that accounting can book the order. "Start dialing for dollars," she says, "and get what you can. Be creative."

Using CBI's CRM system, you identify your top customers and present the discount offer to them. The first customer balks at increasing her inventory: "I just don't think we can sell that much."

"Well," you respond, "how about if we agree to take back any inventory you don't sell next quarter?" (By doing this, you increase your current sales and commission, and you also help your company make its quarterly sales projections. The additional product is likely to be returned next quarter, but you think, "Hey, that's then, and this is now.")

"OK," she says, "but I want you to stipulate the return option on the purchase order."

You know that you cannot write that on the purchase order because accounting won't book all of the order if you do. So you tell her that you'll send her an email with that stipulation. She increases her order, and accounting books the full amount.

With another customer, you try a second strategy. Instead of offering the discount, you offer the product at full price, but agree to pay a 20 percent credit in the next quarter. That way you can book the full price now. You pitch this offer as follows: "Our marketing department analyzed past sales using our fancy new computer system, and we know that increasing advertising will cause additional sales. So, if you order more product now, next quarter we'll give you 20 percent of the order back to pay for advertising."

In truth, you doubt the customer will spend the money on advertising. Instead, they'll just take the credit and sit on a bigger inventory. That will kill your sales to it next quarter, but you'll solve that problem then.

Even with these additional orders, you're still under quota. In desperation, you decide to sell product to a fictitious company that you say is owned by your brother-in-law. You set up a new account, and when accounting calls your brother-in-law for a credit check, he cooperates with your scheme. You then sell $40,000 of product to the fictitious company and ship the product to your brother-in-law's garage. Accounting books the revenue in the quarter, and you have finally made quota. A week into the next quarter, your brother-in-law returns the merchandise.

Meanwhile, unknown to you, CBI's SAP system is scheduling bike assemblies. The assembly schedule reflects the sales from your activities (and those of the other salespeople) and finds a sharp increase in product demand. Accordingly, it generates a schedule that calls for substantial assembly increases and schedules workers for the assemblies. The production system, in turn, schedules the material requirements with the inventory application, which increases raw materials purchases to meet the increased production schedule.

DISCUSSION QUESTIONS

1. Considering the email you write that agrees to take the product back:
   a. Is your action ethical according to the categorical imperative (page 20) perspective?
   b. Is your action ethical according to the utilitarianism perspective (page 40)?
   c. If that email comes to light later, what do you think your boss will say?
2. Regarding your offer of the "advertising" discount:
   a. Is your action ethical according to the categorical imperative perspective?
   b. Is your action ethical according to the utilitarianism perspective?
   c. What effect does that discount have on your company's balance sheet?
3. Regarding your shipping to the fictitious company:
   a. Is your action ethical according to the categorical imperative perspective?
   b. Is your action ethical according to the utilitarianism perspective?
   c. Is your action legal?
4. Describe the effect of your activities on next quarter's inventories.
5. Setting aside ethical and legal issues, would you say the ERP system is more a help or a hindrance in this example?

Source: privilege/Shutterstock.

Active Review

Use this Active Review to verify that you understand the material in the chapter. You can read the entire chapter and then perform the tasks in this review, or you can read the text material for just one question and perform the tasks in this review for that question before moving on to the next one.

Q1. What are the fundamentals of a Sales process?

Define *sale* and explain the activities and subactivities in the Sales process. Explain the overriding principle of sales. Locate the Sales process within the value chain.

Q2. How did the Sales process at CBI work before SAP?

Explain the major activities in the Sales process at CBI before SAP and identify the actor who accomplishes each activity and what data are used. Explain how the Sales process is different at CBI for new customers. Identify the two reasons that Sue's sale was disapproved.

Q3. What were the problems with the Sales process before SAP?

Explain the problems in the Sales process at CBI for sales, the warehouse, and accounting.

Q4. How does CBI implement SAP?

State CBI's competitive strategy. Describe the efficiency objective and how it will be measured. Identify the two effectiveness objectives and the measures used to assess each one.

Q5. How does the Sales process work at CBI after SAP?

How is the Pre-Sales Action activity different after SAP is implemented? Explain the major activities in the Sales process after SAP. Specify what data each actor supplies for each activity and what SAP does once each actor saves the data on his or her screen. Describe how the new Sales process with SAP overcomes CBI sales problems and achieves sales objectives.

Q6. How can SAP improve customer-facing processes at CBI?

Describe CRM. Explain how data sharing and process integration can improve the set of customer-facing processes. Why is trying to improve a family of processes like the customer-facing processes a challenge?

Q7. How does e-commerce improve processes in an industry?

Define *e-commerce*. Describe an interorganizational IS. How do merchant and nonmerchant companies differ? Explain the three types of nonmerchant companies. Describe how e-commerce can improve market efficiency. Explain how Google AdWords and Analytics support e-commerce.

Q8. What new IS will affect the Sales process in 2024?

Explain the advantages of wearable technology. Describe how QR codes and smartphones can be used in the Sales process. Explain social CRM and how it can be used to improve a company's sales. Describe the advantages of using Salesforce. com or another cloud-based CRM vendor. Explain how process integration impacts your business future.

Key Terms and Concepts

Using Your Knowledge

8-1. This chapter introduced the Service process and the Promotion process:
  a. Diagram each process with a BPMN.
  b. For each process, specify efficiency and effectiveness objectives and measures appropriate for CBI.
  c. What new IS technologies could CBI use to improve these processes, as specified by your measures in item b?

8-2. Which of the four nonroutine cognitive skills discussed in Chapter 1 (abstract reasoning, systems thinking, collaboration, or experimentation) did you use to accomplish question 8-1?

8-3. Even after SAP is implemented, input errors can still be made. What kinds of errors can Wally, Sue, and Ann still make? Describe a particularly harmful mistake that each can make and how the process could be changed to prevent that error.

8-4. Think of a company from which you buy a product or service. Specify when and where you share data with that company. Do you believe the company does a good job collecting data from these encounters?

8-5. Think of another company from which you have purchased a product and been disappointed. Identify the customer-facing process that may be at fault. Specify how that process could be improved.

8-6. Using the example of a fast food restaurant or coffee shop, identify three processes that must integrate well for the outlet to run smoothly. Specify what data the processes must share or which processes can support the objectives of other processes. Give an example of how the processes not integrating well would be apparent to you as a customer.

8-7. This chapter focused on product sales, but service sales processes are also useful to investigate. Consider the outpatient surgery process at a local hospital.
  a. Diagram the outpatient surgery process using BPMN.
  b. What other processes at the hospital would a patient be a part of when he or she receives outpatient surgery services?
  c. What data should be exchanged among the processes, and how can process synergy with these processes be achieved?

Collaboration Exercise 8

Collaborate with a group of fellow students to answer the following questions. For this exercise, do not meet face to face. Your task will be easier if you coordinate your work with SharePoint, Office 365, Google Docs with Google+, or equivalent collaboration tools. (See Chapter 9 for a discussion of collaboration tools and processes.) Your answers should reflect the thinking of the entire group, and not just that of one or two individuals.

Groupon offers a "Daily Deal" through its Web site, www.groupon.com. Groupon originated in Chicago in 2008 and quickly spread to other cities in North America and then around the world. Groupon offers a Daily Deal in each of its geographic areas each day. If a specified minimum number of customers accept the deal, the deal becomes available to everyone who signed up. The coupon for each deal is made available to participating customers the day following its announcement. If the minimum number of customers is not met, the deal is canceled for all.

For example, a popular health spa may offer through Groupon a $50 savings on a $125 weekend pass. If the minimum number of customers was set at 500 and, for purposes of this example, 800 accept the offer, then the 800 are notified that "The deal is on." Groupon charges each customer's credit card for $75. Groupon stores customers' credit card data so that customers can accept and participate in deals with minimal fuss. By charging the credit cards for each customer, Groupon receives cash up front. The next day, each of the 800 customers who purchased the Groupon can log into Groupon, navigate to his or her list of Groupons, and print the $125 voucher. Customers take the voucher to the spa and redeem it on arrival.

Participating firms, such as the spa, do not pay Groupon up front. Groupon takes a percentage of the $75 for each customer and pays the spa the rest. Visit Groupon at www.groupon.com to read more about its customer-facing processes.

As a team, complete the following:
1. Create a process diagram in BPMN to show Groupon's Sales process.
2. Create a process diagram in BPMN for the spa that shows activities from contacting Groupon for the first time through the end of the spa's promotion.
3. What are the objectives of the processes in Questions 1 and 2? Label each as either an effective or efficient objective.
4. What measures should both firms use to assess accomplishment of the objectives identified in step 3?
5. Describe how Groupon's IS supports this process.
6. Groupon's Procurement process integrates with the spa's Sales process. How is this integration accomplished?
7. Groupon's Sales process integrates with a customer's Procurement process. How is this integration accomplished?
8. What other IS (social media, smartphones, and so on) could Groupon use to improve its Promotion or Sales process?

ACTIVE CASE 8: SAP SALES TUTORIAL

A tutorial for the Sales process using SAP is included in the appendix to this chapter, Appendix 8. The tutorial leads the student through a Sales process that sells five bicycles to a customer called Philly Bikes. Once the tutorial is complete, students should answer the following questions.

Questions

8-8. If you completed the case study/tutorial in Chapter 7, how is the Sales process in SAP similar to the Procurement process in SAP? In what important ways are they different?

8-9. Create a screen capture of an SAP screen. Underneath the image, provide an answer to each of the following questions:
   a. In which of the activities does this screen occur?
   b. What is the name of the screen?
   c. What is the name of the screen that precedes it? What screen comes after it?
   d. What actor accomplishes this activity?
   e. Describe an error that this actor could make on this screen that SAP will prevent.

8-10. Make an informal diagram of the four main actors: the Customer (Philly Bikes), Sales (Sue), the Warehouse (Wally), and Accounting (Ann). Draw arrows that show the data that flows between each of the actors

during this process. Number the arrows and include on each arrow what data are included in the message.

8-11. Using the same four main actors, this time show with the arrows how the material (the bikes) moves.

8-12. One concern of a business is fraud. One fraud technique is to create customers who are not customers but who are co-conspirators. The conspirator inside the business credits the account of the co-conspirator for payments that were never actually received. For this fraud scheme to work, who at CBI has to take part? How can SAP processes decrease the chance of this type of fraud?

8-13. Select any of the main activities or subactivities in the Sales process and:
   a. Specify what event triggers this activity to occur.
   b. Identify what activity follows this activity.
   c. For one data entry item, describe what would happen in the rest of the process if that entry was erroneous.
   d. For one data entry item, describe what limits (controls) you would put in place on the data to prevent the type of error described in item c.

8-14. Having completed one or both tutorials, make two suggestions about how:
   a. SAP could make its software easier to use.
   b. the tutorial(s) could be improved to help new students learn about processes and SAP.

APPENDIX 8—SAP SALES TUTORIAL

This tutorial follows the Sales process shown in Figure 8A-1. The top of this diagram appears in Chapter 8 as Figure 8-3. This top figure shows the three main Sales activities—Sell, Ship, and Payment—and their subactivities (Create Sales Order, etc.). At the bottom of Figure 8A-1, we have added the eight SAP screens that are completed during the Sales process. This tutorial directs you through the procedures for completing each screen. These eight screens were chosen to keep this tutorial simple. To further simplify the process, we begin with screen 3, Create Standard Order.

FIGURE 8A-1

Sales Process and SAP Screens

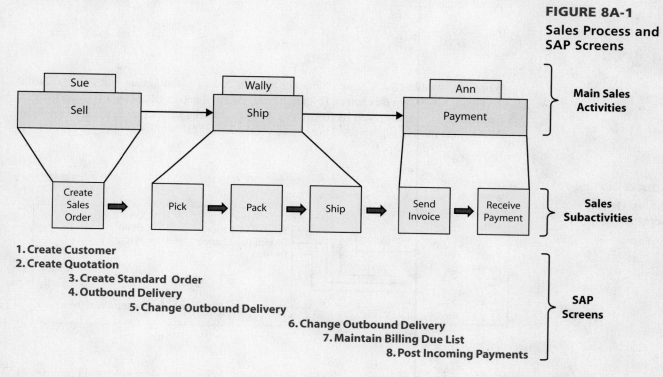

1. Create Customer
2. Create Quotation
3. Create Standard Order
4. Outbound Delivery
5. Change Outbound Delivery
6. Change Outbound Delivery
7. Maintain Billing Due List
8. Post Incoming Payments

First Exercise

In this first exercise, we will sell five black Deluxe Touring bicycles to Philly Bikes. While our company in this tutorial is Global Bike, Inc., our actors—Sue, Wally, and Ann—and our Sales process are from Chuck's Bikes. Log in using data provided by your instructor (see Figure 7A-2).

1. Create Customer

Skipped—does not apply to this first exercise. It is introduced later.

2. Create Quotation

Skipped—does not apply to this first exercise. It is introduced later.

3. Create Standard Order

This first activity, creating a sales order, is accomplished by a salesperson. At CBI, this is Sue. From the SAP Easy Access screen (Figure 8A-2), navigate to the Sales Order screen by selecting:

Logistics > Sales and Distribution > Sales > Order > Create

FIGURE 8A-2
SAP Easy Access Screen

Source: Copyright © SAP AG.

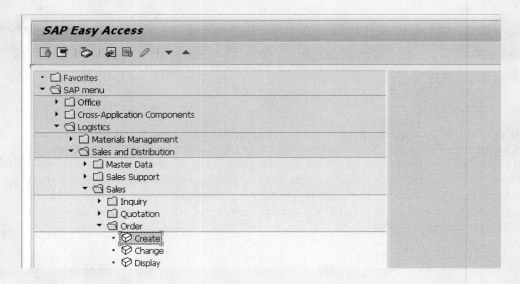

When you double-click Create, the next screen to appear is the Create Sales Order: Initial screen (Figure 8A-3). On this screen (Figure 8A-3), you will enter OR (Standard Order), UE00 (US East), WH (Wholesale), and BI (Bicycles). As in the tutorial in Chapter 7, the last two digits in Sales Organization in Figure 8A-3 are zeros, not the letter "O."

FIGURE 8A-3
Create Sales Order: Initial Screen

Source: Copyright © SAP AG.

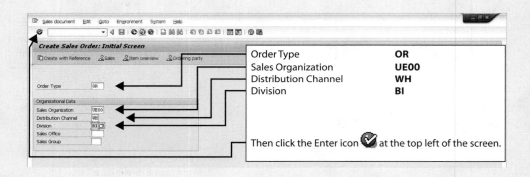

The next screen to appear is the Create Standard Order: Overview screen (Figure 8A-4). This is the same screen Sue completed in Figure 8-9.

FIGURE 8A-4
Create Standard Order: Overview Screen

Source: Copyright © SAP AG.

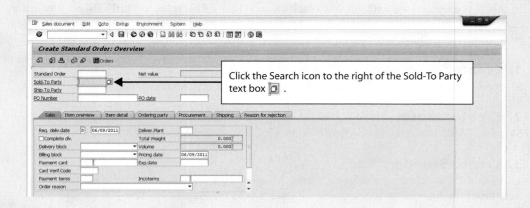

This will produce the pop-up search window shown in Figure 8A-5.

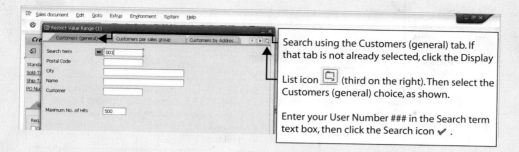

FIGURE 8A-5

Customer Search Screen

Source: Copyright © SAP AG.

Search using the Customers (general) tab. If that tab is not already selected, click the Display List icon (third on the right). Then select the Customers (general) choice, as shown.

Enter your User Number ### in the Search term text box, then click the Search icon ✔.

A list of potential customers is shown (Figure 8A-6).

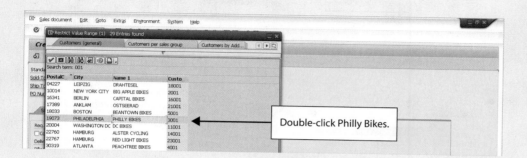

FIGURE 8A-6

Customer List Screen

Source: Copyright © SAP AG.

Double-click Philly Bikes.

After you select Philly Bikes, you are returned to the Create Standard Order: Overview screen (Figure 8A-7). Notice that the Philly Bikes ID number appears in the Sold-To Party box. The PO number (65430 in this exercise) was specified by Philly Bikes and included in the sales order to provide the link between their purchase order and our sales order.

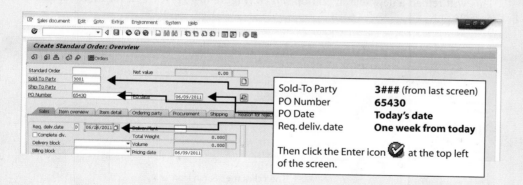

FIGURE 8A-7

Create Standard Order: Overview Screen, with Philly Bikes ID Number and PO Number

Source: Copyright © SAP AG.

Sold-To Party   3### (from last screen)
PO Number   65430
PO Date   Today's date
Req. deliv. date   One week from today

Then click the Enter icon at the top left of the screen.

Click the Enter icon, and a warning pop-up window will be displayed (Figure 8A-8).

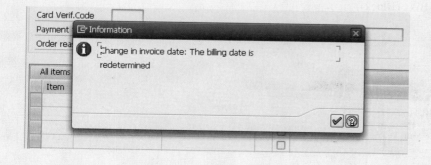

FIGURE 8A-8

Pop-up Warning Screen, Change in Invoice Date

Source: Copyright © SAP AG.

Change in invoice date: The billing date is redetermined

Click the Enter icon to continue. The system retrieves data about the Philly Bikes customer and displays an updated Create Standard Order: Overview screen (Figure 8A-9).

FIGURE 8A-9

Create Standard Order: Overview Screen, with Philly Bikes Customer Info

Source: Copyright © SAP AG.

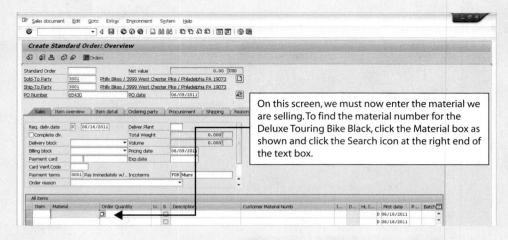

This will load the material search pop-up screen (Figure 8A-10).

FIGURE 8A-10

Material by Description Search Screen

Source: Copyright © SAP AG.

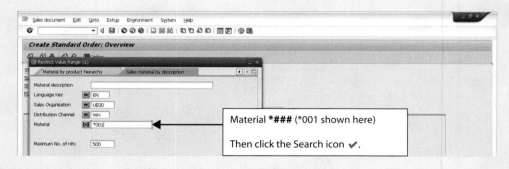

This will reload a new search pop-up screen (Figure 8A-11). Search for Material as shown in Figure 8A-11.

FIGURE 8A-11

Sales Material by Description Search Screen

Source: Copyright © SAP AG.

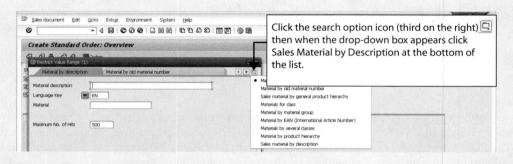

This will show you the sales material you can sell (Figure 8A-12). Find and select Deluxe Touring Bike (Black).

FIGURE 8A-12

Material List Screen

Source: Copyright © SAP AG.

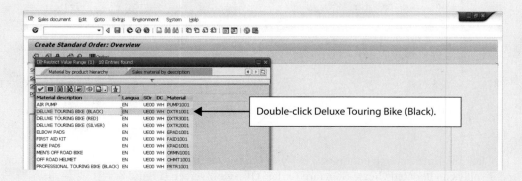

This returns you to the Create Standard Order: Overview screen. The material number for the Deluxe Touring Bike (Black) is now displayed in the Material column (Figure 8A-13).

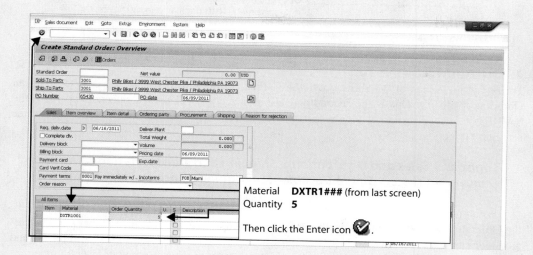

FIGURE 8A-13

Create Standard Order: Overview Screen, with Material Number Displayed

Source: Copyright © SAP AG.

The system will check availability and retrieve Item Number, Total Weight, Net Value, and other data to complete your sales order, as shown in Figure 8A-14.

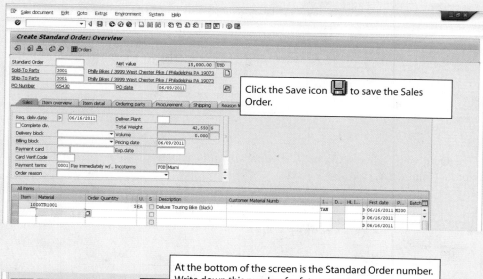

FIGURE 8A-14

Create Standard Order: Overview Screen, with Item Description Added

Source: Copyright © SAP AG.

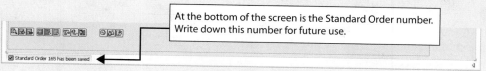

FIGURE 8A-15

Standard Order Number Screen

Source: Copyright © SAP AG.

The sales order is now complete. To return to the SAP Easy Access Screen, click on the exit icon as shown in Figure 8A-16.

FIGURE 8A-16

Toolbar Screen

Source: Copyright © SAP AG.

The Easy Access Screen can be returned to its original structure by clicking on the SAP Menu icon (Figure 8A-17).

FIGURE 8A-17

Easy Access Screen

Source: Copyright © SAP AG.

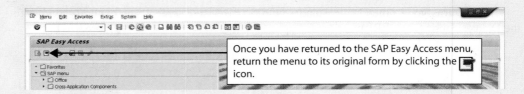

4. Outbound Delivery

To initiate the series of warehouse activities—Pick, Pack, and Ship—we must first create an Outbound Delivery. This is the second and last step accomplished by a salesperson. From the SAP Easy Access screen, navigate to the Create Outbound Delivery with Order Reference screen by selecting:

> *Logistics > Sales and Distribution > Shipping and Transportation > Outbound Delivery > Create > Single Document > With Reference to Sales Order*

When the Create Outbound Delivery with Order Reference screen appears (Figure 8A-18), the Order number should automatically load, and it should correspond to the number you just created in the Sales Order activity. Note that our Shipping point is our Miami plant, and the second digit is the letter "I," not the number 1. Also, the sales order number is not your User Number.

FIGURE 8A-18

Create Outbound Delivery with Order Reference Screen

Source: Copyright © SAP AG.

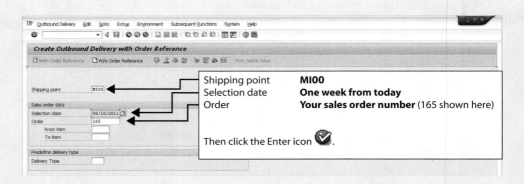

The Outbound Delivery Create: Overview screen is displayed containing the data from the sales order (Figure 8A-19).

FIGURE 8A-19

Outbound Delivery Create: Overview Screen

Source: Copyright © SAP AG.

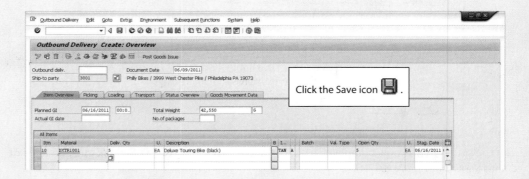

By saving the document, the SAP system ensures that the material is available and can meet the specified delivery date. The SAP system assigns a unique number to this delivery document and displays it at the lower-left corner of the Status bar (Figure 8A-20).

FIGURE 8A-20

Outbound Delivery Document Number

Source: Copyright © SAP AG.

Return to the SAP Easy Access screen by clicking the Exit icon.

5. Change Outbound Delivery

Logistics > Sales and Distribution > Shipping and Transportation > Outbound Delivery > Change > Single Document

When a sales order is picked, the material is moved from its storage location to the packing area. This picking activity, as well as the next two activities, packing and shipping, are accomplished by the warehouse manager. At CBI, this is Wally. To do this, we must change the delivery document. The first screen in this activity is the Change Outbound Delivery screen (Figure 8A-21).

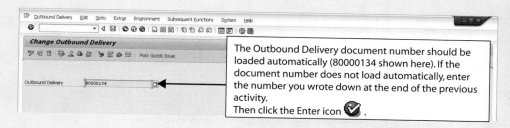

FIGURE 8A-21

Change Outbound Delivery Screen

Source: Copyright © SAP AG.

The Outbound Delivery Change: Overview screen will appear (it is very similar to the Outbound Delivery Create: Overview screen in the previous activity). Notice in the item detail section that the Item Overview tab has been selected (Figure 8A-22).

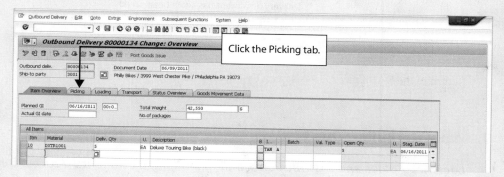

FIGURE 8A-22

Outbound Delivery Change: Overview Screen, Item Overview Tab

Source: Copyright © SAP AG.

Add the SLoc (Storage Location) and Picked Qty (Picked Quantity) as shown in Figure 8A-23. On this screen, SLoc may appear as a very narrow column with its visible heading shortened as "S..."

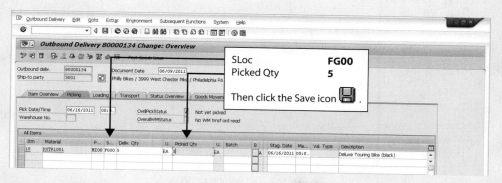

FIGURE 8A-23

Outbound Delivery Change: Overview Screen, Picking Tab

Source: Copyright © SAP AG.

Again, a message in the Status bar appears that confirms that the outbound delivery document is saved. It should be the same document number you created in screen 4. Return to the SAP Easy Access screen by clicking the Exit icon.

6. Change Outbound Delivery

Logistics > Sales and Distribution > Shipping and Transportation > Outbound Delivery > Change > Single Document

After the picking activity, Wally accomplishes the packing activity. No SAP screens are required for packing. Posting, also called shipping, occurs next. When posting occurs, possession of the material transfers from Global Bike to Philly Bikes, and inventory at Global Bike is reduced. Legal ownership of the material also changes hands. The first screen that appears in this activity, Change Outbound Delivery (Figure 8A-24), is the same as the first and last screen in the previous activity (Figure 8A-21).

FIGURE 8A-24

Change Outbound Delivery Screen

Source: Copyright © SAP AG.

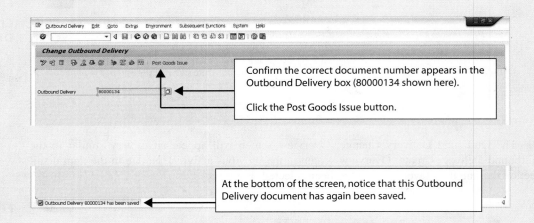

Confirm the correct document number appears in the Outbound Delivery box (80000134 shown here).

Click the Post Goods Issue button.

FIGURE 8A-25

Change Outbound Delivery Screen, Saved Confirmation

Source: Copyright © SAP AG.

At the bottom of the screen, notice that this Outbound Delivery document has again been saved.

Return to the SAP Easy Access screen by clicking the Exit icon.

7. Maintain Billing Due List

Logistics > Sales and Distribution > Billing > Billing Document > Process Billing Due List

This activity creates an invoice for the bikes that have been shipped. This invoice is sent to the customer. Sending the invoice and receiving payment are activities accomplished by an accountant. At CBI, this is accomplished by Ann. The first screen is the Maintain Billing Due List screen (Figure 8A-26).

FIGURE 8A-26

Maintain Billing Due List Screen

Source: Copyright © SAP AG.

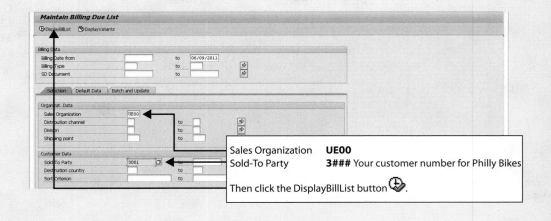

Sales Organization   **UE00**
Sold-To Party   **3###** Your customer number for Philly Bikes

Then click the DisplayBillList button.

The bill list will be displayed with the new bill highlighted, as shown in Figure 8A-27. Click the Collective Billing Document button.

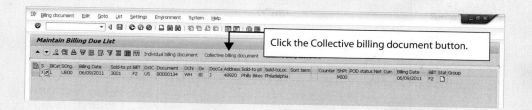

FIGURE 8A-27

Maintain Billing Due List Screen, Bill List Displayed with New Bill Highlighted

Source: Copyright © SAP AG.

After you click the Collective Billing Document icon, the background color of this row will disappear, as shown in Figure 8A-28. An invoice has now been created.

FIGURE 8A-28

Maintain Billing Due List Screen, Bill List Displayed without Background Color

Source: Copyright © SAP AG.

The Maintain Billing Due List screen is now complete. Because this data is automatically saved, you do not need to click Enter or Save. Return to the SAP Easy Access screen by clicking the Exit icon twice.

8. Post Incoming Payments

Accounting > Financial Accounting > Accountants Receivable > Document Entry > Incoming Payments

In the previous activity we sent Philly Bikes a bill. It has now sent us a $15,000 payment. In this activity we record receipt of that payment. The first screen is the Post Incoming Payments: Header Data screen (Figure 8A-29).

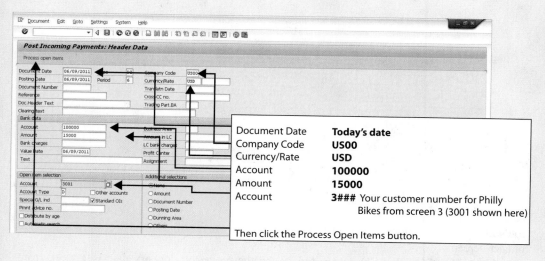

FIGURE 8A-29

Post Incoming Payments: Header Data Screen

Source: Copyright © SAP AG.

Document Date	Today's date
Company Code	US00
Currency/Rate	USD
Account	100000
Amount	15000
Account	3### Your customer number for Philly Bikes from screen 3 (3001 shown here)

Then click the Process Open Items button.

The Post Incoming Payments Process Open Items Screen will appear, as shown in Figure 8A-30.

FIGURE 8A-30

Post Incoming Payments Process Open Items Screen, Standard Tab

Source: Copyright © SAP AG.

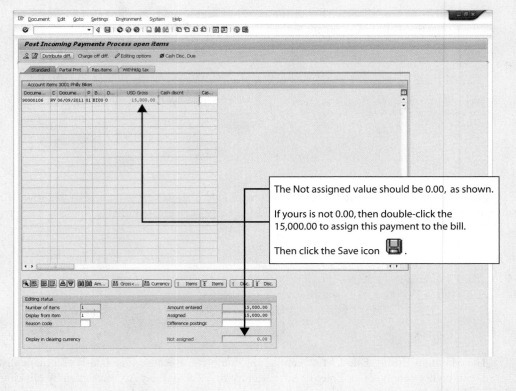

The Not assigned value should be 0.00, as shown.

If yours is not 0.00, then double-click the 15,000.00 to assign this payment to the bill.

Then click the Save icon.

FIGURE 8A-31

Payment Document Screen

Source: Copyright © SAP AG.

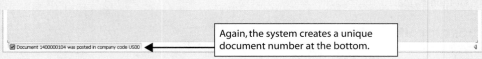

Again, the system creates a unique document number at the bottom.

Return to the SAP Easy Access screen by clicking the Exit icon. This will generate a pop-up window that is misleading (Figure 8A-32). There is no data to be lost at this point, so click Yes. You are finished with the first exercise.

FIGURE 8A-32

Data Lost Pop-up Warning Screen

Source: Copyright © SAP AG.

You Try It 1

You will sell 10 Professional Touring Black Bikes to Philly Bikes. All the data necessary is included for each screen.

This is PO 65431, the PO date is today, and the requested delivery date is 1 week from today. Ship the order a week from today. Use Miami as the shipping point. The total price is $32,000.

Please note: Not every screen is shown here. Refer to the first exercise to see each screen.

3. Create Standard Order

Logistics > Sales and Distribution > Sales > Order > Create

Input the following data in the Create Sales Order: Initial Screen.

Order Type	**OR**
Sales Organization	**UE00**
Distribution Channel	**WH**
Division	**BI**

When these four inputs have been made, your screen will look like Figure 8A-33.

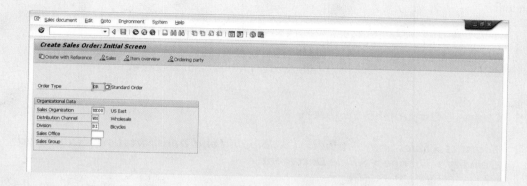

FIGURE 8A-33

Create Sales Order Screen

Source: Copyright © SAP AG.

Enter the next four items on the Create Standard Order: Overview screen.

Sold-To Party	**3###** (3001 shown here)
PO Number	**65431**
PO date	**Today's date**
Req. delv.date	**One week from today**

After entering these four data items, click the Enter icon and then click the check icon on the pop-up warning message. The Create Standard Order: Overview screen appears, as shown in Figure 8A-34.

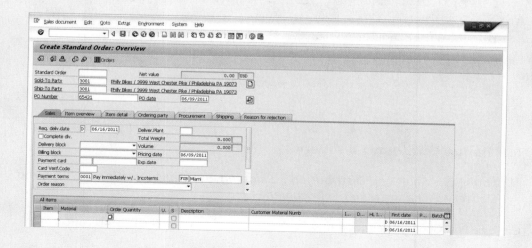

FIGURE 8A-34

Create Standard Order Screen

Source: Copyright © SAP AG.

Enter the material data:

Material   **PRTR1###**
Order Quantity   **10**

After entering these two data items, click the Enter icon and then the Save icon.

4. Outbound Delivery

Logistics > Sales and Distribution > Shipping and Transportation > Outbound Delivery > Create > Single Document > With Reference to Sales Order

Enter the following data, then save the document and record the Outbound Delivery document number.

Shipping point   **MI00**
Selection date   **One week from today**
Order   **Your sales order number** (automatic, from screen 3)

5. Change Outbound Delivery

Logistics > Sales and Distribution > Shipping and Transportation > Outbound Delivery > Change > Single Document

Input the following data in the Outbound Delivery Change: Overview screen. Remember to click on the Picking tab first.

SLoc   **FG00**
Picked Qty   **10**

After you have made these two inputs, your screen will look like Figure 8A-35. Save the document.

FIGURE 8A-35
Outbound Delivery Change Screen

Source: Copyright © SAP AG.

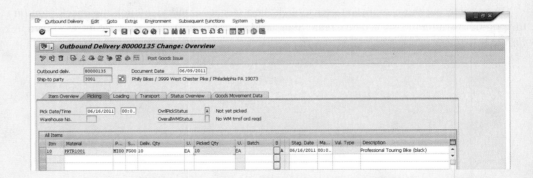

6. Change Outbound Delivery

Logistics > Sales and Distribution > Shipping and Transportation > Outbound Delivery > Change > Single Document

Click the Post Goods Issue button after confirming that the document number is correct.

7. Maintain Billing Due List

Logistics > Sales and Distribution > Billing > Billing Document >
Process Billing Due List

Input the following data in the Maintain Billing Due List:

Sales Organization   **UE00**
Sold-To Party   **3###** Your customer number for Philly Bikes

After clicking the DisplayBillList button and the Collective Billing Document button, the
Maintain Billing Due List screen appears, as shown in Figure 8A-36.

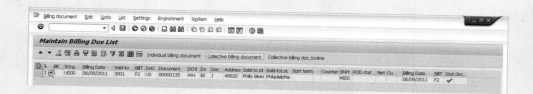

FIGURE 8A-36
**Maintain Billing
Due List Screen**

Source: Copyright © SAP AG.

8. Post Incoming Payments

Accounting > Financial Accounting > Accountants Receivable >
Document Entry > Incoming Payments

Enter the following data in the Post Incoming Payments: Header Data screen. Your screen
should look like Figure 8A-37.

Document Date   **Today's date**
Company Code   **US00**
Currency/Rate   **USD**
Account   **100000**
Amount   **32000**
Account   **3###** (3001 shown here)

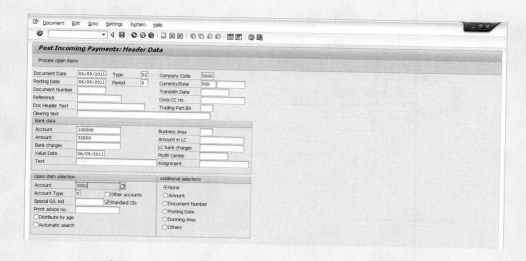

FIGURE 8A-37
**Post Incoming
Payments Screen**

Source: Copyright © SAP AG.

After clicking the Process Open Items button, the Post Incoming Payments Process Open Items
screen will appear, as shown in Figure 8A-38.

FIGURE 8A-38

Post Incoming Payments Process Open Items Screen

Source: Copyright © SAP AG.

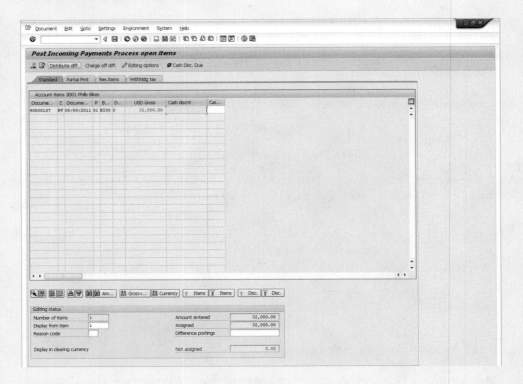

You Try It 2

Sell three Deluxe Touring Black Bikes to a new customer—Cycle Works—and give it a price quote. The Cycle Works data can be found on the following New Customer screens (Figures 8A-39 through 8A-45).

1. Create Customer

Logistics > Sales and Distribution > Master Data > Business Partner > Customer > Create > Complete

FIGURE 8A-39

Customer Create: Initial Screen

Source: Copyright © SAP AG.

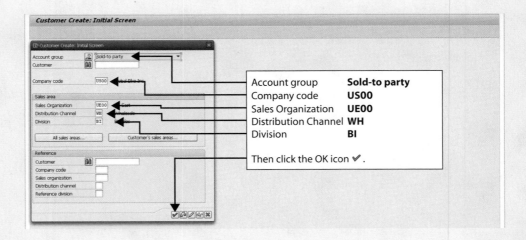

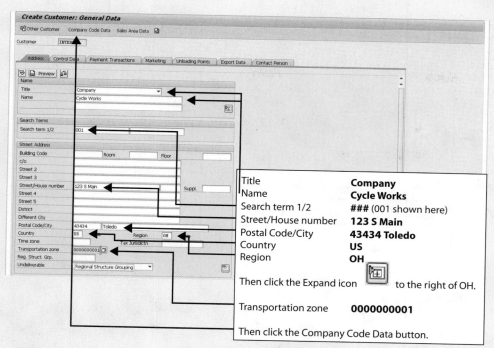

FIGURE 8A-40

Create Customer: General Data Screen

Source: Copyright © SAP AG.

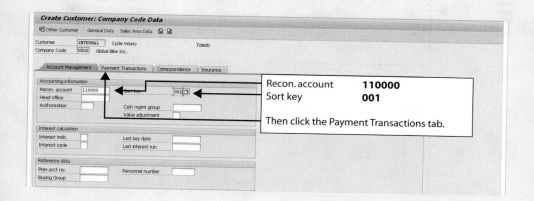

FIGURE 8A-41

Create Customer: Company Code Data Screen, Account Management Tab

Source: Copyright © SAP AG.

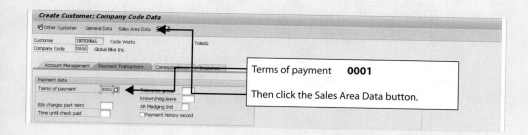

FIGURE 8A-42

Create Customer: Company Code Data Screen, Payment Transactions Tab

Source: Copyright © SAP AG.

FIGURE 8A-43

Create Customer: Sales Area Data Screen, Sales Tab

Source: Copyright © SAP AG.

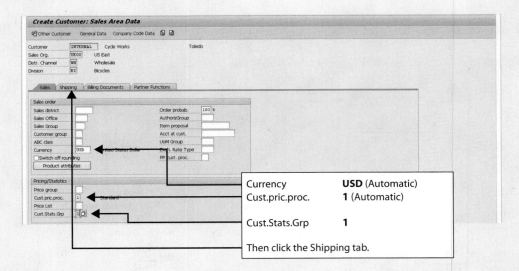

FIGURE 8A-44

Create Customer: Sales Area Data Screen, Shipping Tab

Source: Copyright © SAP AG.

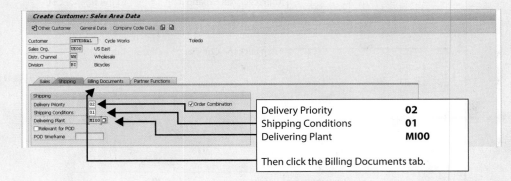

FIGURE 8A-45

Create Customer: Sales Area Data Screen, Billing Documents Tab

Source: Copyright © SAP AG.

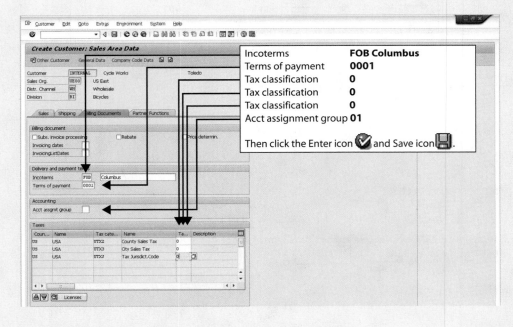

A new customer is created (Figure 8A-46).

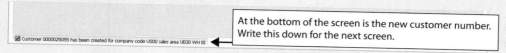

At the bottom of the screen is the new customer number. Write this down for the next screen.

☑ Customer 0000025055 has been created for company code US00 sales area UE00 WH BI

FIGURE 8A-46

Create Customer Number Screen

Source: Copyright © SAP AG.

2. Price Quotation

Logistics > Sales and Distribution > Sales > Quotation > Create

Cycle Works, our new customer, has asked for a price quote on Deluxe Black Bikes (Figures 8A-47 and 8A-48). You will sell these bikes to Cycle Works in screen 3.

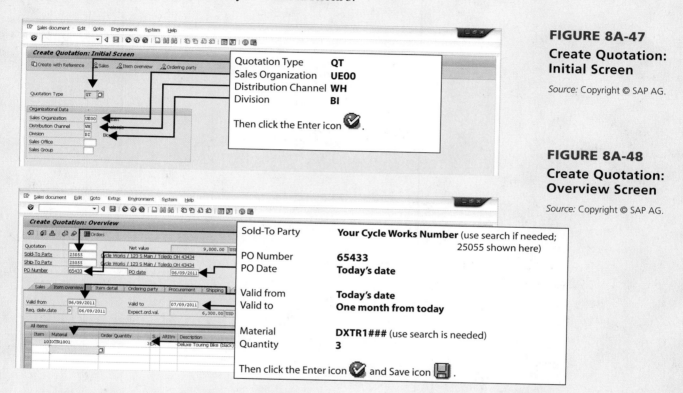

FIGURE 8A-47

Create Quotation: Initial Screen

Source: Copyright © SAP AG.

FIGURE 8A-48

Create Quotation: Overview Screen

Source: Copyright © SAP AG.

Record the Quotation number at the bottom of the screen.

3. Create Standard Order

In this activity, create a sales order to sell the three Deluxe Touring Black Bikes to Cycle Works. To do this, navigate to the Create Sales Order screen as shown in Figure 8A-2; then after you have entered the four data fields as shown in Figure 8A-49, click on "Create with Reference"—see Figure 8A-49. Enter your Quot. number from screen 2: Price Quotation. The PO is 65433, the PO date is today, and Req. Deliv. Date is a week from today. Follow this order through to screen 8. Then in screen 8, record a payment from Cycle Works for $9,000. All the other data is the same as in the first exercise.

FIGURE 8A-49

Create with Reference Sales Order Screen

Source: Copyright © SAP AG.

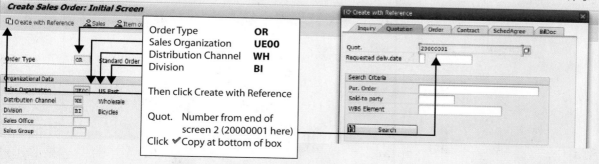

PART 4
DYNAMIC PROCESSES AND INFORMATION SYSTEMS

In Chapters 5 through 8 of Part 3, we discussed structured, operational processes and the information systems that support them. The three chapters in this part continue the discussion of processes and information systems, but for less structured, more dynamic processes. These chapters discuss information systems in three areas—collaboration, social media, and business intelligence—and the dynamic business processes by the same name. These dynamic processes are not like the Procurement and Sales processes that you studied in Chapters 7 and 8; dynamic processes are neither predefined nor fixed. That does not mean, however, that they are unstructured. Dynamic processes have a structure, but their structure is often created on the fly, the activities are fluid and frequently changed and intermingled with other processes, and they often include a lot of backtracking and repetition. You execute a dynamic process when you and your friends collaborate about where to go out to eat—topics are made up on the fly and change rapidly, and you backtrack and start over when someone vetoes a choice or a time.

Dynamic processes such as collaboration, social media, and business intelligence are not typically an end unto themselves. Instead, they are executed to support other business processes. You and your friends collaborate about where to go out to eat; the goal is going, not just collaborating. In these chapters, we will examine how the three dynamic processes support business processes such as project management, promotion, and decision making.

Although specifying objectives and measures is as important to dynamic processes as it is to structured operational processes, dynamic processes typically have fewer well-accepted objectives and measures. Objectives are not as well accepted because they also tend to be dynamic, changing as actors, outputs, and situations change. Further, while dynamic processes have activities in which particular objectives are achieved, the means by which those objectives are achieved vary widely. A final difference with structured processes is that dynamic processes are typically not diagrammed using techniques such as BPMN. As you will see, when we do use such techniques, the activities become very high level and generic, such as "analyze data."

To help you organize your thinking about the three dynamic processes and the business processes they support, each of the three chapters follows a similar outline. First, we address the process—collaboration, social media, or business intelligence—and then we explain the information systems that support the activities of the process. We conclude by examining how IS support these activities in actual business processes. A summary of the chapter topics is shown in Figure 9-1.

Before we begin, keep in mind that the title of each chapter—collaboration, social media, and BI—can apply to both the processes and the IS that support them. In this text, we make them distinct to better understand them. However, realize that people often confuse a process with the IS that supports it, so don't be surprised when they don't distinguish between the two.

Dynamic Process	Objectives	Key Activities	Example IS	Business Processes Containing Activities
Collaboration Chapter 9	Successful output Growth in team capability Meaningful and satisfying experience	Communication Iteration	SharePoint Google Drive E-mail	Project Management Workflow
Social Media Chapter 10	For people—belonging For businesses—support strategy For app providers—market share	Create content Share content	Facebook Twitter LinkedIn	Promotion Customer Service
Business Intelligence Chapter 11	Inform to assess Inform to predict	Acquire Analyze Publish	Excel SAP Business Objects Tableau	Decision Making Next Best Offer Counterterrorism

FIGURE 9-1
Three Dynamic Processes of Part 4

Chapter 9 Collaboration and IS

At Chuck's Bikes, a meeting is about to begin. The meeting involves several sales reps including Sue, soon-to-retire Wally who runs procurement, and several others.

"Wally, why don't we have those racing bikes I need for the race promotion next week?"

Wally, looking at his procurement screen, replies "What promotion?"

"Wally, you didn't get the word? We decided this 10 days ago! I emailed you 2 days ago. Didn't you get my email?"

"Sue, who is 'we'? I don't remember a request for a special order."

"I have the spreadsheet in my hand, Wally, from that meeting 10 days ago. It shows the new amounts were approved."

"OK, that makes sense. I was at another meeting filling in for Tim and couldn't make that meeting. What else did I miss?"

"Wally, how do I know what you missed? There were meeting notes. Did you look at those? This promotion got approved. I have the document in my hand."

"Sue, don't take this wrong, but how do I know that document is the approved version? Remember last month a sales rep called and asked me to manually add 50 Olympic air pumps that he thought were approved but really weren't. We never sold any of those, so Tim insisted that all new emergency orders and promotions go through his office. I've been told that I can't accept documents he hasn't approved. I know you had your meeting 2 weeks ago and that the promotion was approved by those people, but has Tim approved it, too?"

"So now I have to get Tim to sign it, then I make it a PDF or something, then I email it to you…is that right?"

"Sue, that's close. If you email it to Tim, he can approve it and forward it to me. Then I will forward it back to you so you know I acted on it."

Q1. **What is collaboration, and why is it important to business?**

Q2. **What are the objectives of the collaboration process?**

Q3. **What are the key components of a collaboration IS?**

Q4. **How can collaboration IS support the communicating activity?**

Q5. **How can collaboration IS support the iterating activity?**

Q6. **How can collaboration IS support business processes?**

Q7. **Which collaboration IS is right for your team?**

Q8. **2024?**

After a sad-sounding pause, Wally continued, "I know it won't help much, but even if you found Tim today and somehow got him the document, your bikes won't make it here in time for us to put them together anyway."

"Great. Because neither Tim nor you were at the meeting, I'm not going to get the bikes in time."

"I'm sorry, Sue, you're the best. Do you have any ideas about how to keep this from happening again?"

"I guess we could have attached the new agreement to an email and sent it to everyone."

"That would be a start, but you wouldn't know that I acted on it."

"What if I marked the important emails with REPLY NEEDED in the subject line?"

"Sure, let's try that!"

Chapter Preview

CBI has a problem: Sue and the other sales reps could have made a killing selling racing bikes, but the word never got to Wally in the warehouse. Obviously, the company needs to prevent this from happening again, but rather than fixing just this racing bike snafu, CBI needs to improve collaboration in general. With better collaboration, it can answer questions like: How and when should we meet? How can we keep track of what has been decided? How will we share documents with one another? How will we make sure that others on the team have read a document and respond? What software should we use?

These are common questions for all collaborating teams. To address these questions, this chapter has three major sections. First, we discuss the dynamic collaboration process and the information systems used in collaboration. Next, we discuss how collaboration information systems support specific collaboration activities, and then we discuss how collaboration IS support collaboration activities in actual business processes.

You are already familiar with some collaboration IS—texting, Skype, and FaceTime. The point of this chapter is for you to understand how those and other tools are used to support collaboration activities in actual business processes. This understanding is practical and useful, and you can apply it as soon as tonight. Many of your classes require collaboration of some sort, and you will improve the quality of your work if you apply this knowledge to your collaboration.

Q1. What Is Collaboration, and Why Is It Important to Business?

Business is collaboration—it's a social activity, a team sport. Collaborating teams accomplish work that creates value for customers; it is the glue that holds an organization together.[1] Absent the glue, the business struggles. If CBI can't learn to collaborate between the sales and procurement offices, it will miss many opportunities, not just the racing bikes.

While collaboration has always been important, it is becoming increasingly essential as strategies, processes, products, and services become more complex. The more complicated the work, the more collaboration is needed to take action. For example, look at how systems that bring data to your dorm room have changed over time. The business of delivering high-speed Internet is much more complicated than delivering telephone services a few years ago. When you encounter problems with your Internet service, the person that troubleshoots your problem will need to collaborate much more often than the phone tech of yesteryear.

While collaboration is now more common, its payoffs can be quite uncommon. In the airline industry just 20 years ago, the captain on the flight deck was the king (most captains were male), the copilot and flight engineer were expected to kept quiet or risk losing their jobs, and flight attendants kept their distance. Collaboration meant getting coffee for the captain. Today,

[1] Hackman, J. Richard, and A. C. Edmondson. "Groups as Agents of Change." In *Handbook of Organizational Development*, edited by T. Cummings. Thousand Oaks, CA: Sage Publications, 2007 p. 217.

the flight deck is much more collaborative, not just about the flight, but about passenger concerns, too. According to Captain Sullenberger, who safely landed his crippled Airbus in the Hudson River, this better collaboration has led to a remarkable decrease in airline accidents over the past 20 years. Adopting many of the same collaborating ideas, healthcare teams of doctors, nurses, and other professionals are becoming much more collaborative about patient diagnoses and treatments. The result has been a noticeable decline in treatment errors. However, you don't have to fly or volunteer for surgery to see effective teams. As mentioned in Chapter 1, effective collaboration is an increasingly common business skill.

As collaboration has grown over the years, so too has the technology that supports collaborative work. In your grandparents' day, communication was done using letter, phone, and office visits. Those technologies were augmented in the 1980s and 1990s with fax and email and more recently by texting, conference calls, and videoconferencing. Today, products such as Google Drive and Office 365 provide a wide array of tools to support collaborative work. By the time you land your first job, there will surely be other new technologies to use.

To get started, we need to first distinguish between the terms *cooperation* and *collaboration*. **Cooperation** is a process where a group of people work together, all doing essentially the same type of work, to accomplish a job. A group of four painters, each painting a different wall in the same room, are working cooperatively. Similarly, a group of checkers at the grocery store or clerks at the post office are working cooperatively to service customers. A cooperative team can accomplish a given task faster than an individual working alone, but the cooperative result is usually not better in quality than the result of someone working alone.

The Two Key Activities of Collaboration

In this text, we define **collaboration** as a dynamic process: a group of people working together to achieve common objectives *via communication and iteration*. One person will produce something, say the draft of a document, and communicate that draft to a second person, who will review that draft and communicate feedback. Given the feedback, the original author or someone else will then revise the first draft to produce a second. The work proceeds in a series of stages, or *iterations*, in which something is produced, members create feedback, and then another version is produced. Using iteration and communication, the group's result can be better than what any single individual can produce alone. This is possible because different group members provide different perspectives. "Oh, I never thought of it that way," is a typical signal of collaboration success.

Many, perhaps most, student groups rely on cooperation rather than collaboration. Given an assignment, a group of five students will break it up into five pieces, work to accomplish their pieces independently, and then merge their independent work for grading by the professor. Such a process will enable the project to be completed more quickly, with less work by any single individual, but it will not be better than the result obtained if the students were to work alone.

In contrast, when students work collaboratively, they set forth an initial idea or work product, communicate feedback to one another on those ideas or products, and then revise in accordance with feedback. Such a process can produce a result far superior to that produced by any student working alone.

Importance of Effective Critical Feedback

One key aspect of team communication is feedback—for collaboration to be successful, members must provide and receive *critical* feedback. A group in which everyone is too polite to say anything critical cannot collaborate. As Darwin John, the world's first chief information officer (CIO), once said, "If two of you have the exact same idea, then we have no need for one of you." On the other hand, a group that is so critical and negative that members come to distrust, even hate, one another cannot effectively collaborate, either. For most groups, success is achieved between these extremes.

To underline this point, consider the research of Ditkoff, Allen, Moore, and Pollard. They surveyed 108 business professionals to determine the qualities, attitudes, and skills that make a good collaborator.[2] Figure 9-2 lists the most and least important characteristics reported in

[2] Mitch Ditkoff, Tim Moore, Carolyn Allen, and Dave Pollard, "The Ideal Collaborative Team," Idea Champions, accessed July 5, 2013, http://www.ideachampions.com/downloads/collaborationresults.pdf.

FIGURE 9-2

Importance of Collaboration Characteristics

Twelve Most Important Characteristics for an Effective Collaborator

1. Is enthusiastic about the subject of our collaboration.

2. Is open-minded and curious.

3. Speaks his or her mind even if it's an unpopular viewpoint.

4. Gets back to me and others in a timely way.

5. Is willing to enter into difficult conversations.

6. Is a perceptive listener.

7. Is skillful at giving/receiving negative feedback.

8. Is willing to put forward unpopular ideas.

9. Is self-managing and requires "low maintenance."

10. Is known for following through on commitments.

11. Is willing to dig into the topic with zeal.

12. Thinks differently than I do/brings different perspectives.

Nine Least Important Characteristics for an Effective Collaborator

31. Is well organized.

32. Is someone I immediately liked. The chemistry is good.

33. Has already earned my trust.

34. Has experience as a collaborator.

35. Is a skilled and persuasive presenter.

36. Is gregarious and dynamic.

37. Is someone I knew beforehand.

38. Has an established reputation in field of our collaboration.

39. Is an experienced businessperson.

---

the survey. Most students are surprised to learn that five of the top 12 characteristics involve disagreement (highlighted in blue in Figure 9-2). Most students believe that "we should all get along" and more or less have the same ideas and opinions about team matters. Although it is important for the team to be social enough to work together, this research indicates that it is also important for team members to have different ideas and opinions and to express them to each other.

When we think about collaboration as an iterative process in which team members give and receive feedback, these results are not surprising. During collaboration, team members learn from each other, and it is difficult to learn if no one is willing to express different, or even unpopular, ideas. The respondents also seem to be saying, "You can be negative, as long as you care about what we're doing." These collaboration skills do not come naturally to people who have been taught to "play well with others," but that may be why they were so highly ranked in the survey.

The characteristics rated *not relevant* are also revealing. Experience as a collaborator or in business does not seem to matter. Being popular also is not important. A big surprise, however, is that being well organized was rated 31st out of 39 characteristics. Perhaps collaboration itself is not a very well-organized process?

Guidelines for Giving and Receiving Critical Feedback

Giving and receiving critical feedback is the single most important collaboration skill. So, before we discuss the role that information systems can play in collaboration, study the guidelines for giving and receiving critical feedback shown in Figure 9-3.

Many students have found that when they first form a collaborative group, it's useful to begin with a discussion of critical feedback guidelines like those in Figure 9-3. Begin with this list, and then, using feedback and iteration, develop your own list. Of course, if a group member does not follow the agreed-upon guidelines, someone will have to provide critical feedback to that effect as well.

Warning!

If you are like most undergraduate business students, especially freshmen or sophomores, your life experience is keeping you from appreciating the value of collaboration. So far, almost everyone you know has the same experiences as you and thinks like you. Your friends and associates have the same educational background, scored more or less the same on standardized tests, and have the same orientation toward success. Most of the time, your teams have included others who are similar in age, experience, and education. So, why should you collaborate instead of just cooperating? You may feel that everyone in your group thinks the same way anyway. In your effort to get the project done, your group asks, "What does the professor want and what's the easiest, fastest way to get it to her?" instead of "How can we complete this project with the highest quality possible?"

Consider this thought experiment. Your company is planning to build a new facility that is critical for the success of a new product line and will create 300 new jobs. The county government won't issue a building permit because the site is prone to landslides. Your engineers believe your design overcomes that hazard, but your CFO is concerned about possible litigation in the event there is a problem. Your corporate counsel is investigating the best way to overcome the county's objections while limiting liability. Meanwhile, a local environmental group is protesting your site because it believes it is too close to an eagle's nest. Your public relations director is meeting with this local group every week.

Do you proceed with the project?

To decide, you create a working team of the chief engineer, the chief financial officer (CFO), your legal counsel, and the PR director. These people vary widely in age, education and expertise, life experience, and values. In fact, the only thing they have in common is that they are paid by your company. Now compare this group to your student group. Although the business

Guideline	Example
Be specific.	"I was confused until I got to Section 2" rather than "The whole thing is a disorganized mess."
Offer suggestions.	"Consider moving Section 2 to the beginning of the document."
Avoid personal comments.	Never: "Only an idiot would miss that point … or write that document."
Strive for balance.	"I thought Section 2 was particularly good. What do you think about moving it to the start of the document?"
Question your emotions.	"Why do I feel so angry about the comment he just made? What's going on? Is my anger helping me?"
Do not dominate.	If there are five members of the group, unless you have special expertise, you are entitled to just 20 percent of the words/time.
Demonstrate a commitment to the group.	"I know this is painful, but if we can make these changes our result will be so much better." or "Ouch. I really didn't want to have to redo that section, but if you all think it's important, I'll do it."

FIGURE 9-3

Guidelines for Giving and Receiving Critical Feedback

group will participate collaboratively in ways that are far different from your experience as a student, the groups may be more alike than you think. Although you may initially believe that other students think like you, that may be an illusion based on not knowing them well. Each student will bring a unique perspective to the group, which will become more evident as you get to know the group members.

While underappreciated by most young people, collaboration is both common and essential to every organization. To help you get ready to be productive in that environment, we start by considering the types of objectives collaborating teams pursue.

Q2. What Are the Objectives of the Collaboration Process?

Like most business processes, the key to understanding collaboration is to understand its objectives. As mentioned in Chapter 2, dynamic processes typically emphasize effectiveness more than efficiency. Here we outline three effectiveness objectives while recognizing that collaboration also has an underlying efficiency objective: to meet time and cost limits.

J. Richard Hackman studied teamwork for many years, and his book *Leading Teams* contains many useful concepts and tips for future managers.[3] According to Hackman, there are three general objectives for collaboration, as shown in Figure 9-4.

Product Objective: Successful Output

The output of collaboration is the deliverable—a homework assignment for a student team, a budget plan or new product for a business team. Most students are primarily concerned with this first objective, making a successful deliverable. Whatever the intended output is, the first objective is "Did we do it?"

Team Objective: Growth in Team Capability

The other two objectives are process, not output, objectives—they address how well the team worked together, not the product they delivered. These can be surprising to many students, probably because most student teams are short-lived. But, in business, where teams often last months or years, it makes sense to ask, "Did the team get better?" If you're a football fan, you've undoubtedly heard your college's coach say, "We really improved as the season progressed." Football teams last only a season. If the team is permanent, say a team of customer support personnel, the benefits of team growth are even greater. Over time, as the team gets better, it becomes more efficient; thus, over time the team provides more service for a given cost or the same service for less cost.

How does a team get better? For one, it develops better work processes. Activities are combined or eliminated. Communication is improved so that "the left hand knows what the right hand is doing," or needs, or can provide. Teams also get better as individuals improve at their tasks. Part of that improvement is the learning curve; as someone does something over and

FIGURE 9-4
Collaboration Process Objectives

| **Effectiveness** |
| Product objective—Successful output |
| Team objective—Growth in team capability |
| Individual objective—Meaningful and satisfying experience |
| **Efficiency** |
| Time and cost |

[3] J. Richard Hackman, *Leading Teams: Setting the Stage for Great Performances* (Boston: Harvard Business Press, 2002).

over, he or she gets better at it. But team members also teach task skills, give knowledge to one another, and provide perspectives that other team members need.

Individual Objective: Meaningful and Satisfying Experience

The third objective of Hackman's definition of team success is that team members have a meaningful and satisfying experience. Of course, the nature of team goals is a major factor in making work meaningful. But few of us have the opportunity to develop a life-saving cancer vaccine or safely land a stricken airliner in the Hudson River. For most of us, it's a matter of making the product, creating the shipment, accounting for the payment, or finding the prospects, and so on.

So, in that world, what makes work meaningful? Hackman cites numerous studies in his book, and one common thread is that the work is perceived as meaningful by the team. Keeping prices up to date in the product database may not be the most exciting work, but if that task is perceived by the team as important, it will become meaningful.

Furthermore, if an individual's work is not only perceived as important, but the person doing that work is also given credit for it, then the experience will be perceived as meaningful. So, recognition for work well done is vitally important for a meaningful work experience.

Another aspect of team satisfaction is camaraderie. Business professionals, just like students, are energized when they have the feeling that they are part of a group; each person is doing his or her own job and combining efforts to achieve something worthwhile that is better than any could have done alone.

As mentioned earlier in the text, dynamic processes tend to have less well-accepted objectives than structured processes. If you asked team members, "What is the objective of the team—a successful outcome, growth of capability, or a satisfying experience?" you will likely hear a different answer from every team member. Not only do objectives vary by team member, they also vary over the course of the life of the team; at different points in time, different objectives have higher priority. So a word to the wise—don't expect everyone on the team to be on the same page or to have the same objectives.

Now that we have explained the collaboration process and its objectives, we turn to the main focus of this chapter—the role of collaboration information systems in supporting business processes. Figure 9-5 depicts the relationship between collaboration IS, collaboration process activities, and business processes. Starting on the left, the five components of a collaboration IS are discussed next in Q3. Then the two collaboration activities—communicating and iterating—are described in Q4 and Q5. Finally, in Q6 we will describe how collaboration IS support the collaboration activities contained in business processes. Reading left to right, collaboration IS support collaboration activities that are contained in business processes. For simplicity, we display business processes as a rectangle, a display more suited for structured processes; in reality, these dynamic processes defy conventional diagramming.

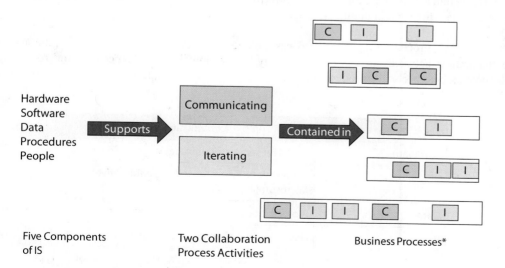

FIGURE 9-5

Collaboration IS Components and Business Processes

* White space represents other activities in the business process

Q3. What Are the Key Components of a Collaboration IS?

Some collaboration systems used in business are familiar to you from use in your personal life—Skype, Google+ Hangouts, and FaceTime. To better understand these systems and other systems used in businesses, let's consider their five components.

As you would expect, a **collaboration information system** is an information system that supports collaboration. Given our discussion in Q1, this means that the system needs to support iteration and communication among team members. As information systems, collaboration systems have the five components of every information system: hardware, software, data, procedures, and people. The distinguishing attributes of a collaboration IS are listed in Figure 9-6. Our goal here is to help you understand how collaboration systems are different from other IS like ERP or social media systems so you can employ them wisely.

The Five Components of a Collaboration IS

HARDWARE Concerning hardware, most collaboration systems are hosted on organizational servers or in the cloud, which you read about in Chapter 3. We will ignore that component in the discussion in this chapter. Just know that the tools you're using and the data you're sharing are supported by computer hardware somewhere. While servers are in the cloud, users interact with the collaboration system with client devices. These devices can be mobile platforms, laptops, or even traditional phones.

SOFTWARE Collaboration software programs are applications like email or text messaging that support collaborative activities. Throughout this chapter we will discuss a variety of collaboration software such as email, Google+, Google Drive, Microsoft SharePoint, and others. Figure 9-7 lists the most popular business collaboration software. This list is long because there is a wide range of combinations of people, work products, meeting schedules, and business contexts. For example, a two-member team editing a video for an online tutorial will need a different set of collaboration software programs than a 100-member team iterating plans for an ERP upgrade. The key for you as a student is to practice with many of these apps so you can learn their strengths and weaknesses and use them effectively when the time comes.

DATA Collaboration involves two types of data. **Project data** is data that is part of the collaboration's work product. For example, for a team that is designing a new product, design documents are examples of project data. A document that describes a recommended solution is project data for a problem-solving project. **Project metadata** is data that is used to manage the project. Schedules, tasks, budgets, and other managerial data are examples of project metadata. Another example of project metadata is the version number of a document. If Alice, Bruce, and Charlie iterate a document, each version of the document is stored; with the document, one piece of metadata—the version number—is also stored.

PROCEDURES Procedures specify standards, policies, and techniques for conducting the team's collaboration activities using the technology. An example is the procedure for reviewing documents or other work products online. To reduce confusion and increase control, the team

FIGURE 9-6

Five Components of Collaboration IS

Five Components of IS	Collaboration IS
Hardware	Cloud for servers; various devices for clients
Software	Wide variety: email, Google+, Google Drive, Microsoft SharePoint
Data	Project data and project metadata
Procedures	Necessary but often implicit or assumed
People	People vary on time and place for collaboration People vary on ability to use IS and in motivation

Collaboration Software
Email
Google+ Hangouts
FaceTime
GotoMeeting
SurveyMonkey
Mind Meister
Prezi
Yammer
SharePoint
Wikis
Google Drive and Docs

FIGURE 9-7

Examples of Collaboration Information Systems

might establish a procedure that specifies who will review documents and in what sequence. Rules about who can do what to which data are also codified in procedures. Procedures for collaboration systems are often implicit. No one follows a procedure to read email, nor should they; it's simple. However, teams need to figure out the procedure to share documents, store meeting notes, update the team task list, and perform other activities. Teams are often careless about procedures—team members often assume others will use the same procedure they do. As a result, unless you raise the issue, you can expect that procedures will be followed differently by different people.

PEOPLE The final component of a collaboration system is, of course, people. We discussed the importance of the ability to give and receive critical communication in Q1. But people affect the collaboration IS in a couple of other ways, too. Will the participants collaborate for multiple projects? If so, a more complex system might be selected than if this is a one-time project for these participants. Also, will collaboration occur during face-to-face meetings or over a period of time when the participants will not be together? Another issue is whether the participants are co-located or are in different geographic locations. Finally, team members vary in their ability and motivation to use collaboration software. Some people know many of the procedures necessary to use the software, but most people have only mastered the simplest procedures.

Key Attributes of Collaboration IS

Collaboration IS have a number of important features that distinguish them from other IS. One fundamental feature is that there is a wide variety of *software* from which to choose. This variety is driven by the wide assortment of *people*, work products, team schedules, and business settings. As a result, the key to successful use of collaboration IS is choosing the right software based on the objectives and the people. *Procedures* are often used carelessly, and people differ on ability and motivation to use collaborative tools.

The components of a collaboration IS are important to understand, but it is more important to see how they collectively support the collaboration activities of teams. Next, we explore how they support the communication activity; then, in the following question, we see how they support iteration.

Q4. How Can Collaboration IS Support the Communicating Activity?

Information systems support the communicating activity. As we will see, there are three general types of communication, and different collaboration IS are well suited to support each. These three types are based on how and where people on the team communicate, as shown in Figure 9-8.

Synchronous communication occurs when all team members meet at the same time, such as with conference calls or face-to-face (F2F) meetings. **Asynchronous communication** occurs when team members do not meet at the same time. Employees who work different shifts at the same location or team members who work in different time zones around the world must meet asynchronously.

FIGURE 9-8
Three Types of Communication and Collaboration IS

	Synchronous		Asynchronous
Shared calendars Invitation and attendance			
Single location	Multiple locations		Single or multiple locations
Office applications such as Word and PowerPoint	Conference calls Webinars Multiparty text chat Microsoft Web Apps Videoconferencing		Email Discussion forums Team surveys Microsoft SkyDrive Google Drive Microsoft SharePoint

Virtual meetings

Most student teams attempt to meet F2F, at least at first. Arranging such meetings is always difficult, however, because student schedules and responsibilities differ. If you are going to arrange such meetings, consider creating an online group calendar in which team members post their availability week by week. Also, use the meeting facilities in Microsoft Outlook to issue invitations and gather RSVPs. If you don't have Outlook, use an Internet site such as Evite (*www.evite.com*) for this purpose.

For most F2F meetings, you need little; the standard Office applications or their freeware lookalikes, such as Open Office, will suffice. However, recent research indicates that F2F meetings can benefit from shared, online workspaces, such as the whiteboard shown in Figure 9-9.[4] Using a whiteboard, team members can type, write, and draw simultaneously, which enables more ideas to be proposed in a given period of time than when team members must wait in sequence to express ideas verbally. If you have access to such a whiteboard, try it in your F2F meetings to see if it works for your team.

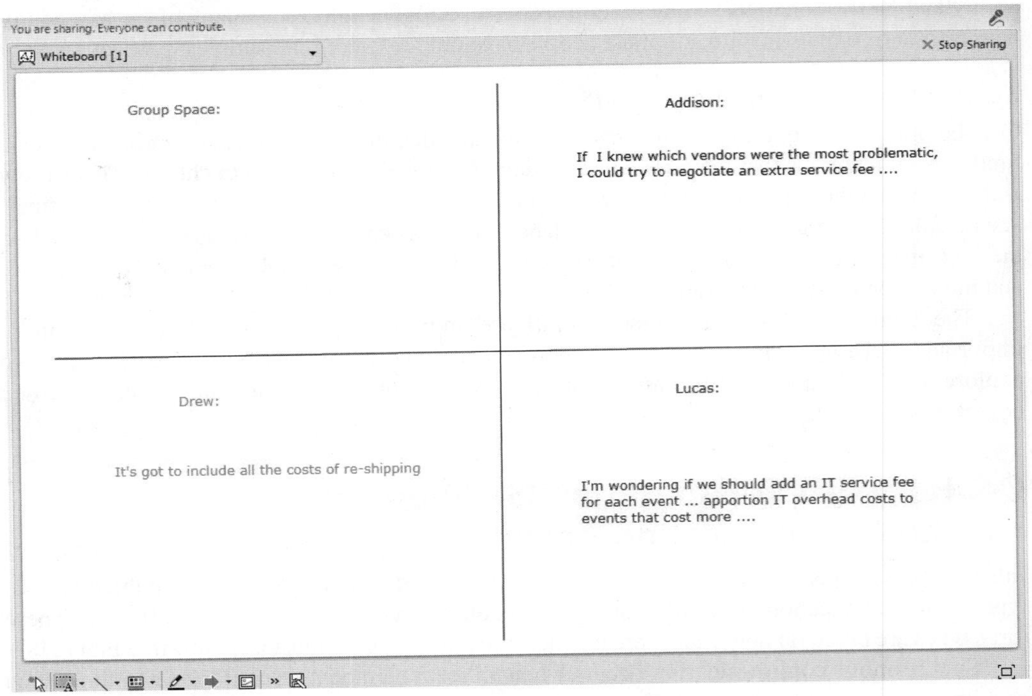

FIGURE 9-9
Whiteboard Example

[4] Wouter van Diggelen, *Changing Face-to-Face Communication: Collaborative Tools to Support Small-group Discussions in the Classroom* (Groningen: University of Groningen, 2011).

However, *given today's communication technology, students can forgo the hassle of sched-uling a F2F meeting in most circumstances* by using a virtual meeting instead. **Virtual meetings** are meetings in which participants do not meet in the same place and possibly not at the same time. F2F meetings are often too difficult to arrange and seldom worth the trouble when a virtual meeting will produce the same results with fewer scheduling problems.

If your virtual meeting is synchronous (all meet at the same time), you can use conference calls, multiparty text chat, screen sharing, webinars, or videoconferencing. Some students find it weird to use text chat for school projects, but why not? You can attend meetings wherever you are without using your voice. Google Text supports multiparty text chat, as does Microsoft Lync. Google or Bing *multiparty text chat* to find other, similar products.

Screen-sharing applications enable virtual meeting members to view the same whiteboard, application, or other display. Figure 9-9 shows an example whiteboard for a business meeting. This whiteboard allows multiple people to contribute simultaneously. To organize the simulta-neous conversation, the whiteboard real estate is divided among the members of the group as shown. Some groups save their whiteboards as minutes of the meeting.

A **webinar** is a virtual meeting in which attendees view one of the attendees' computer screens for a more formal and organized presentation. WebEx (*www.webex.com*) is a popular commercial webinar application used in virtual sales presentations.

If everyone on your team has a camera on his or her computer, you can also do **video-conferencing**, like that shown in Figure 9-10. **Microsoft Lync** is one such product. Google+ works, too, and you can find others on the Internet. Videoconferencing is more intrusive than text chat; you have to comb your hair, but it does have a more personal touch.

In some classes and situations, synchronous meetings, even virtual ones, are impossible to arrange. You just cannot get everyone together at the same time. In this circumstance, when the team must meet asynchronously, most students try to communicate via email. The problem with email is that there is too much freedom. Not everyone will participate because it is easy to hide from email. (Did Wally, in the opening scenario, really not get Sue's email?) Discussion threads become disorganized and disconnected. After the fact, it is difficult to find particular emails, comments, or attachments.

Discussion forums are an alternative. Here one group member posts an entry, perhaps an idea, a comment, or a question, and other group members respond. Figure 9-11 shows an ex-ample. Such forums are better than email because it is harder for the discussion to get off track. Still, however, it remains easy for some team members not to participate.

FIGURE 9-10
Videoconferencing Example

Source: Tom Merton/Getty Images

FIGURE 9-11
Discussion Forum
Example

Team surveys are another form of communication technology. With these, one team member creates a list of questions and other team members respond. Surveys are an effective way to obtain team opinions; they are generally easy to complete, so most team members will participate. Also, it is easy to determine who has not yet responded. Figure 9-12 shows the results of one team survey. SurveyMonkey (*www.surveymonkey.com*) is one common survey application program. You can find others on the Internet.

FIGURE 9-12
Survey Report Example

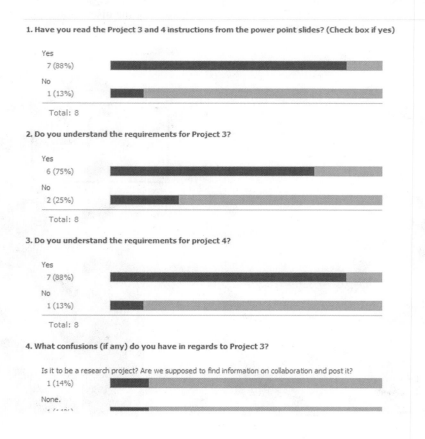

Video and audio recordings are also useful for asynchronous communication. Key presentations or discussions can be recorded and played back for team members at their convenience. Such recordings are also useful for training new employees.

A wiki is also a communication technology that a team can use. A work document or supporting documents can be stored in a wiki for team members to edit and iterate much like Wikipedia pages are stored and edited on the Web.

Finally, collaboration can also use texting systems. Unlike Twitter and other public texting systems, organizations can license products like Chatter and Yammer for internal communication so team members can collaborate privately.

To recap, there are three different types of communication on a team, and each has collaboration IS well suited for it. Teams not only differ on their type of communication but also on how they iterate their work product, our next topic. Just as a collaboration IS should be chosen based on which of the three types of communication it supports, it should also be chosen for how it supports iteration.

Q5. How Can Collaboration IS Support the Iterating Activity?

As mentioned earlier, collaborative teams typically produce a work product—a diagram, a new process, a budget, a healthcare record of a patient, or even a healthy patient. When the team iterates, it produces a new version of the work product. But not only does the work product iterate, so too do the supporting documents, illustrations, spreadsheets, PowerPoint presentations, video, and other data. Figure 9-13 lists three options of content iteration management: no iteration control, iteration management, and iteration control. Next, we consider each and the IS that support each option.

No Iteration Control

The most primitive way to iterate content is via email attachments. However, email attachments have numerous problems. For one, there is always the danger that someone does not receive an email, does not notice it in his or her inbox, or does not bother to save the attachments. Then, too, if three users obtain the same document as an email attachment, each changes it, and each sends back the changed document via email, different, incompatible versions of that document will be floating around. So, although email is simple, easy, and readily available, it will not suffice for collaborations in which there are many document versions or for which there is a desire for content control.

Another way to iterate content is to place it on a shared **file server**, which is simply a computer that stores files just like the disk in your local computer. If your team has access to a file server, you can put documents on the server and others can download them, make changes, and upload them back onto the server using ftp (discussed in Chapter 3). Storing documents on servers is better than using email attachments because documents have a single storage location. They are not scattered in different team members' email boxes. Team members have a known location for finding documents.

However, without any additional control it is possible for team members to interfere with one another's work. For example, suppose team members A and B download a document and edit it, but without knowing about the other's edits. Person A stores his version back on the server and then person B stores her version back on the server. In this scenario, person A's changes will be lost.

Alternatives for Iterating Content		
No Iteration Control	Iteration Management	Iteration Control
Email with attachments Shared files on a server	Google Drive Microsoft SkyDrive	Microsoft SharePoint

FIGURE 9-13

Collaboration Tools for Iterating Content

Increasing degree of content control

Furthermore, without any iteration control it will be impossible to know who changed the document and when. Neither person A nor person B will know whose version of the document is on the server. To avoid such problems, some form of iteration management is recommended.

Iteration Management

Systems that provide **iteration management** track changes to documents and provide features and functions to accommodate concurrent work. The means by which this is done depends on the particular system used. In this section, we consider two systems that you should consider for your team's work: Google Drive and Microsoft SkyDrive.

GOOGLE DRIVE Google Drive is a free thin-client application for sharing documents, presentations, spreadsheets, drawings, and other data. Google Drive is rapidly evolving; by the time you read this, Google may have added additional file types or changed the system from what is described here. Google recently changed the name of this service from Google Docs to Google Drive, so search the name *Google Drive* to obtain the latest data.

To create a Google document, log into your Gmail account, select Drive from the top ribbon menu, and click on Create, or go to *http://drive.google.com* (note there is no www in this address). From that point on, you can create, upload, process, save, and share documents, spreadsheets, presentations, and other content. You can also save most of those documents to PDF and Microsoft Office formats, such as Word, Excel, and PowerPoint.

With Google Drive, you can make documents available to others by entering their email addresses or Gmail accounts. Those users are notified in an email that the document exists and are given a link by which they can access it.

Documents are stored on a Google server. Users can access the documents from Google and simultaneously see and edit documents. In the background, Google merges the users' activities into a single document. You are notified that another user is editing a document at the same time you are. Google tracks document revisions, with brief summaries of changes made. Figure 9-14 shows a sample revision for a document that has been shared among three users.

MICROSOFT SKYDRIVE Microsoft **SkyDrive** is Microsoft's answer to Google Drive. It provides the ability to store and share Office documents and other files and offers free storage. Additionally, SkyDrive includes license-free Web application versions of Word, Excel, PowerPoint, and OneNote that are called **Office Web Apps**. These applications run in the browser and are quite easy to use. Figure 9-15 shows an instance of the Word Web App. These programs have less functionality than desktop Office programs, but they are free and readily accessed on the Web.

In addition to Office Web Apps, the desktop Office 2013 applications are tightly integrated with SkyDrive. You can open and save documents directly from and to SkyDrive from inside Microsoft Office products.

To set up a SkyDrive, you need a Microsoft account, which used to be called a Windows Live ID. If you have either a Hotmail or MSN email account, that account is your Microsoft account. If you do not have a Hotmail or MSN email account, you can create a Microsoft account with some other email account, or you can create a new Hotmail account, which is free.

Once you have a Microsoft account, go to www.skydrive.com and sign in. You will be given 25 GB of storage. You can create file folders and files and use either Office or Office Web Apps as well.

FIGURE 9-14

Example of Iterating a Document on Google Drive

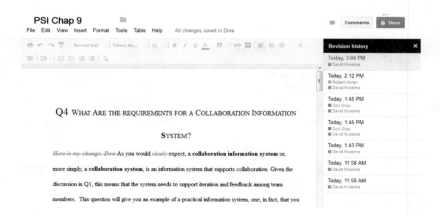

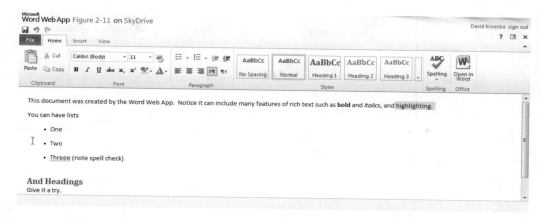

FIGURE 9-15

Example Use of Word Web App

Similar to Google accounts, you can share folders with others by entering their Microsoft account or their email account. Users who have a Microsoft account can view and edit documents; users who do not have a Microsoft account can only view documents.

Only one user at a time can open SkyDrive documents for editing. If you attempt to open a document that someone else is editing, you'll receive an error message. As you can open the document in read-only mode, you can have your changes merged with the document when it is available or you can simply be notified when the document is available.

Both Google Drive and Microsoft SkyDrive are free and very easy to use. They are both far superior to exchanging documents via email or via a file server. If you are not using one of these two products, you should be. Go to *http://drive.google.com* or *www.skydrive.com* and check them out. You will find easy-to-understand demos if you need additional instruction.

Iteration Control

Iteration management systems improve the tracking of iterated content and potentially eliminate problems caused by concurrent document access. They do not, however, provide **iteration control**, the technique that occurs when the collaboration tool limits, and sometimes even directs, user activity. Iteration control provides one or more of the following options:

- User activity limited by permissions
- Document checkout
- Version histories

PERMISSION-LIMITED ACTIVITY With most iteration control tools, each team member is given an account with a set of permissions. Then shared documents are placed into shared directories, sometimes called **libraries.** For example, on a shared site with four libraries, a particular user might be given read-only permission for library 1; read and edit permission for library 2; read, edit, and delete permission for library 3; and no permission even to see library 4. Wikipedia and other wikis also use permission limits; if a contributor has a history of disruptive edits to Wikipedia, that contributor can be restricted from editing pages in the future.

DOCUMENT CHECKOUT With iteration control applications, document directories can be set up so that users are required to check out documents before they can modify them. When a document is checked out, no other user can obtain it for the purpose of editing it. Once the document has been checked in, other users can obtain it for editing.

Figure 9-16 shows a screen for a user of Microsoft SharePoint. The user, Allison Brown (shown in the upper right-hand corner of the screen), is checking out a document named Project One Assignment. Once she has it checked out, she can edit it and return it to this library. While she has the document checked out, no other user will be able to edit it, and her changes will not be visible to others.

VERSION HISTORY Because collaboration involves feedback and iteration, it is inevitable that dozens, or even hundreds, of documents will be created. Imagine, for example, the number of versions of a design document for the Boeing 787. In some cases, collaboration team members attempt to keep track of versions by appending suffixes to file names. The result for a student project is a file name like *Project1_lt_kl_092911_most_ recent_draft.docx* or something similar. Not only are such names ugly and awkward, no team member can tell whether this is the most current version.

FIGURE 9-16
Document Checkout

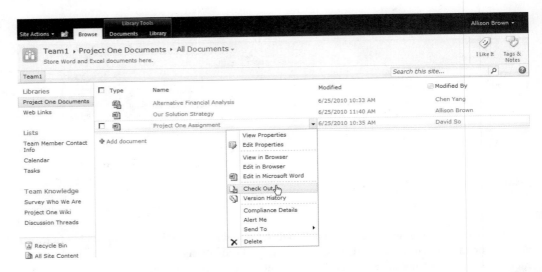

Collaboration tools that provide iteration control have the data to readily provide histories on behalf of the users. When a document is changed (or checked in), the collaboration tool records the name of the author and the date and time the document is stored. Users also have the option of recording notes about their version.

While most of this question examined the three types of iteration control of text documents, the iteration needs of other work products are also supported. Whatever the product, teams should select collaboration software based on the type of iteration control they need as well as the type of communication they will use, as discussed in the previous question.

Q6. How Can Collaboration IS Support Business Processes?

Having described the two activities in the generic collaboration process and how collaboration IS support these activities, we now consider how collaboration IS support actual business processes. There are a great number of business processes that rely on collaboration activities, as shown in Figure 9-17. In fact, virtually all important business processes depend on some collaboration. To demonstrate the usefulness of collaboration IS, we investigate two processes: Project Management and Workflow.

The Project Management Process

One common business process that contains collaboration activities is project management. **Project management** is the process of applying principles and techniques for planning, organizing, and monitoring temporary endeavors. It is a rich and complicated subject, with many theories and methods and techniques. To illustrate how they are supported by collaboration IS, here we will just touch on the basics of project management.

FIGURE 9-17

Business Processes Supported by Collaboration IS

Business Processes Supported by Collaboration IS
Problem solving
Decision making
New product/location selection
Strategic planning
Sales
Brainstorming
Training
Promotion
Health care
Financial services
Project management
Workflow

Projects are formed to create or produce something; as a result, they have a defined beginning and end. The desired outcome might be a marketing plan, the design of a new factory or a new product, or an annual audit. Project teams may include two or three individuals or as many as a few hundred. Project management activities vary widely, but most include setting milestones, keeping track of progress, and allocating funds.

Project team members communicate incessantly about the tasks they have completed, the next milestones, and problems they are encountering that may create havoc with the schedule. The type of communication they use is a mixture of F2F and virtual meetings, and they also use both synchronous and asynchronous communication. They produce and iterate a variety of work products such as their chart of milestones and flowchart of pending activities as well as budgetary documents. These products typically use iteration management controls, but other teamwork products such as meeting agendas and email correspondence may iterate without much control.

Project teams use a variety of collaboration information systems discussed in this chapter for their communication and iteration activities. Larger projects will often also use special project management software such as Microsoft Project and Oracle Primavera. This type of software is particularly helpful in organizing the flow of team activities and managing lists of tasks. A flowchart example using Microsoft Project showing team milestones is shown in Figure 9-18. Project management software also supports communication among team members. Email and text can be sent from within the software, and permissions to view or edit flowcharts and task list are tightly controlled and previous versions automatically archived.

The Workflow Process

The **Workflow** process is a sequence of activities by which original content is created and subsequently acted upon by others within the organization. A workflow could help CBI in the opening vignette—Sue would begin the workflow by creating a message that then would be approved by her sales manager before being sent to the procurement office for its response. The workflow is complete only after the salesperson reads the procurement reply. Another workflow is created when Jerry in the human resources department accumulates résumés of candidates for a position and circulates them to several individuals within the company to pick candidates for follow-up interviews. A final example is a process used by a company to ensure its employees have been briefed on new security procedures. In this company, every year employees are required to hear a security update from their supervisor. The director of IT in charge of this workflow must notify

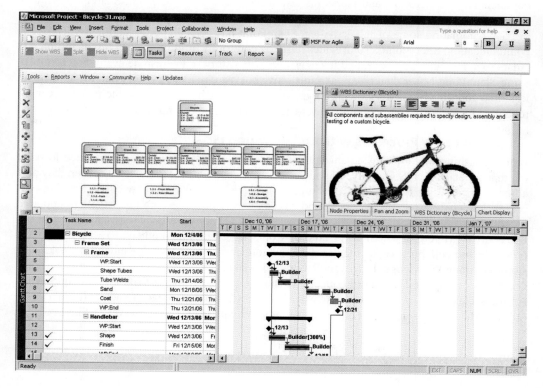

FIGURE 9-18

Microsoft Project Milestones Example

all 411 supervisors in the organization of the update and record when training occurs. In each of these examples, a workflow is executed—initial content is first created, then the content is acted on by a number of people in the organization. Unlike simple collaboration described earlier, a workflow often includes actors outside a team.

In each workflow, communication is essential. Sue, Jerry, and the IT director need to communicate with others in the organization. Further, their original content must be iterated and acted upon; these actions must be controlled and recorded, so iteration control is often used.

Collaboration software has long supported this process. Jerry could write an email with candidate review instructions, attach the résumés, and send it to the individuals that select the candidates for follow-up interviews. Or he could put the résumés on a shared drive along with the instructions or create a Google Doc and share it. But imagine how poorly email or a shared drive would support the security training process. A better collaboration IS choice for workflow is often SharePoint.

SharePoint offers a better way to communicate and exercise iteration control over work documents. SharePoint supports a workflow by automating many of the activities. It helps automate activities involving documents, lists, and other types of content in a workflow. SharePoint ships with several built-in workflows; we will illustrate one of them here. In addition, business analysts can create custom workflows using a graphical interface in SharePoint Designer.[5]

To illustrate a simple workflow, suppose that Jerry wants just two people to review all résumés of job applicants that are submitted to a particular SharePoint **document library**, which is a named collection of documents in SharePoint. Whenever a document is added to the document library, it should be reviewed first by Joseph Schumpeter and then by Adam Smith. Such an arrangement is called a **sequential workflow** because the review activities occur in sequence. In a **parallel workflow,** the reviews would occur simultaneously. Numerous other types of workflows are possible, but we will not consider them here.

Figure 9-19 illustrates this workflow. When a document creator submits a document to a particular SharePoint library (labeled *Data Repository* in Figure 9-19), SharePoint starts a workflow. It sends an email announcing the start of the workflow to Jerry as well as an email to Joseph Schumpeter telling him that he has been requested to review the document.

Schumpeter reviews the document (he will need to obtain it from the data repository, but this arrow has been omitted from Figure 9-19 for clarity). After he has made his review, he will store his comments on the task and mark it as completed. At that point, SharePoint sends an email to the next reviewer, Adam Smith. After Smith has completed his review, he stores his comments in the Tasks list and marks his task as completed. At this point, SharePoint sends a Workflow Completed email to Jerry.

By automating some of the activities, SharePoint has helped coordinate the asynchronous communication. SharePoint also provides iteration control by limiting the activity of Joseph and Adam to a particular sequence, and it keeps a version history of the resume evaluation form. By using SharePoint rather than email, administrative costs are reduced as Jerry and his staff spend less time coordinating and following up on the status of each resume. And the process is more reliable—for each applicant, both reviewers get the same time and reminders.

Supporting New Processes with Collaboration IS

Before finishing this topic of organizational processes and collaboration IS, we need to point out that collaboration IS not only support the existing business processes listed earlier, they also allow new processes to emerge. Collaboration IS have helped enable new online training processes, knowledge storage processes, and find-an-expert processes. Online training supported by collaboration systems are rapidly growing. Larger versions are known as massive open online courses (MOOCs), which are offered by Coursera, Udacity, and others. Knowledge storage processes use collaboration IS such as wikis to store company knowledge much like Wikipedia stores common knowledge. Finally, collaboration systems can enable a new find-an-expert process. This process is designed to collect and share expertise within a firm. For example, when software engineers join a company like Microsoft, they input their areas of knowledge in a series of "Ask Me About" screens, where they can indicate expertise on SQL Server or SharePoint or

[5] For more information about workflows and the Windows Workflow Foundation, see Mark J. Collins, *Office 2010 Workflow* (New York: Apress, 2010).

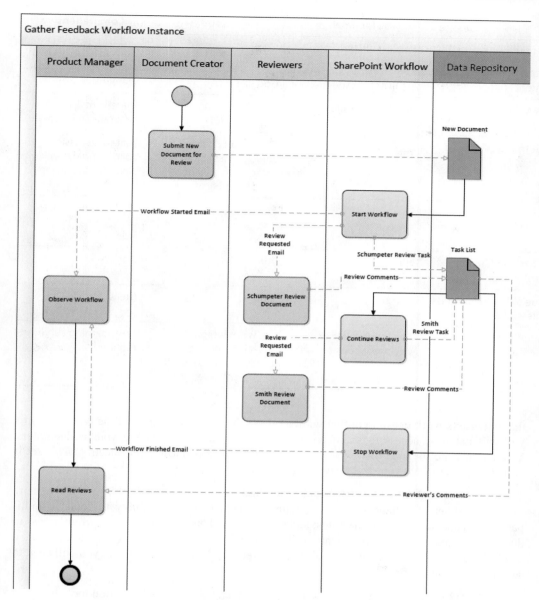

FIGURE 9-19

Gather Feedback Workflow

fluency in Greek. Later, when someone at Microsoft needs to find a Greek-speaking SharePoint expert to help on a project for a company in Greece, the collaboration system helps with the process of finding the right people.

Q7. Which Collaboration IS Is Right for Your Team?

Earlier we mentioned that half the battle is picking the right collaboration IS for the team. In this question, we will define and set up your evaluation of three sets of collaboration tools. Most business courses involve a team project; why not use what you've learned in this chapter to pick a collaboration IS that will make teamwork easier and help you achieve a better product?

Three Sets of Collaboration Tools

Figure 9-20 summarizes three different sets of collaboration tools that you might use.

THE MINIMAL COLLABORATION TOOL SET The first, the Minimal set, has the minimum possible set of tools and is shown in the second column of Figure 9-20. With this set, you should be able to collaborate with your team, though you will get little support from the software. In particular, you will need to manage concurrent access by setting up procedures and agreements to ensure

FIGURE 9-20
Collaboration Tool Sets

	Minimal	Good	Comprehensive
Communication	Email; multi party text chat	Skype	Microsoft Lync
Content Sharing	Email or file server	Google Drive	SharePoint
Task Management	Word or Excel files	Google Calendar	SharePoint lists integrated with email
Nice-to-Have Features		Discussion boards, surveys, wikis, blogs, share pictures/videos from third-party tools	Built-in discussion boards, surveys, wikis, blogs, picture/video sharing
Cost	Free	Free	$10/month per user Or Free
Ease of Use (time to learn)	None	1 hour	3 hours
Value to Future Business Professional	None	Limited	Great
Limitations	All text, no voice or video; no tool integration	Tools not integrated, must learn to use several products; cannot share documents live	Cost, learning curve required

that one user's work doesn't conflict with another's. Your collaboration will be with text only; you will not have access to audio or video, so you cannot hear or see your collaborators. You also will not be able to view documents or whiteboards during your meeting. This set is probably close to what you're already doing.

THE GOOD COLLABORATION TOOL SET The third column of Figure 9-20 shows a more sophisticated set of collaboration tools. With it, you will have the ability to conduct multi-party audio and video virtual meetings; and you will also have support for concurrent access to document, spreadsheet, and presentation files. You will not be able to support surveys, wikis, and blogs and share pictures and videos with this set. If you want any of them, you will need to search the Internet to find suitable tools.

THE COMPREHENSIVE COLLABORATION TOOL SET The third set of collaboration tools is shown in the last column of Figure 9-20. This IS is provided by Microsoft's product Office 365. Office 365 is provided as a service over the Internet. Lync is a communications application that provides IM, audio and video conferencing, and shared whitespaces as well as shared desktops and shared applications. This set is the best of these three because it has a full set of features, including iteration management and control and online meetings with sharing as just described. Furthermore, this set is integrated: SharePoint alerts can send emails via the Microsoft email server Exchange when tasks or other lists and libraries change. You can click on users' names in emails or in SharePoint, and Office 365 will automatically start a Lync text, audio, or video conversation with that user if he or she is currently available. All text messages that you send via Lync are automatically recorded and stored in your email folder.

Choosing the Set for Your Team

Which set should you choose for your team? Unless your university has already standardized on Office 365, you will have to pay for it. You can obtain a 30-day free trial, and if your team can finish its work in that amount of time, you might choose to do so. Otherwise, your team will need to pay a minimum of $10 per month per user. So, if cost is the only factor, you can rule out Office 365.[6]

[6] To sign up for Office 365, go to http://office.microsoft.com/en-us/.

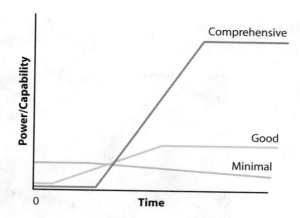

FIGURE 9-21
Power Curve

Even if you can afford the most comprehensive set of tools, you may not want to use it. As noted in the Ease of Use row of Figure 9-20, most team members will need to invest around 3 hours to understand the basic Office 365 features. Less time, on the order of an hour, will be required to learn the Good toolset, and you most likely already know how to use the Minimal set.

When evaluating learning time, consider Figure 9-21. This diagram is a product **power curve**, which is a graph that shows the relationship of the power (the utility that one gains from a software product) as a function of the time using that product. A flat line means you are investing time without any increase in power. The ideal power curve starts at some value at time zero and has no flat spots.

The Minimal product set gives you some power at time zero because you already know how to use it. However, as you use it over time, your project will gain complexity and the problems of controlling concurrent access will actually cause power to decrease. The Good set has a short flat spot as you get to know it. However, your power then increases over time until you reach the most capability your team can do with it. The Comprehensive set has a longer flat spot in the beginning because it will take longer to learn. However, because it has such a rich collaboration feature set, you will be able to gain considerable collaborative power, and the maximum capability is much greater than the Good set.

Finally, consider the Value row in Figure 9-20. The Minimal set has no value to you as a future professional and contributes nothing to your professional competitive advantage. The Good set has some limited value; there are organizations that use Google Drive and Skype. However, the Comprehensive toolset has the potential to give you a considerable competitive advantage, particularly because SharePoint skills are highly valued in industry. You can use knowledge of Office 365 to demonstrate the currency of your knowledge in job interviews.

So, which is the right set for your team? It's up to you. See Exercise 9-2 on page 297.

Don't Forget Procedures and People!

One last and very important point: Most of this chapter focuses on collaboration software. Regarding the other four components of a collaboration IS—you need not worry about hardware, at least not for the Good or Comprehensive sets, because those tools are hosted on hardware in the cloud. The data component is up to you; it will be your content as well as your metadata for project management and for demonstrating that your team practiced iteration and feedback.

As you evaluate alternatives, however, you need to think seriously about the procedure and people components. How are team members going to use these tools? Your team needs to have agreement on tools usage, even if you do not formally document procedures. As noted, such procedures are especially necessary for controlling concurrent access in the Minimal system. You need to have agreement not only on how to use these tools but also on what happens when teammates don't use these tools. What will you do, for example, if teammates persist in emailing documents instead of using Google Drive or SharePoint?

MIS InClass 9

Virtual Practice!

In this contest, you and a group of your classmates will compete against other teams in a short collaborative project. Every member of your team will need access to a networked computer with a browser in order to participate.

The ground rules of this contest are as follows:

a. This contest tests, in part, your ability to meet virtually. Consequently, in Phase 2 you are not allowed to meet and communicate face-to-face with your team members.
b. You will be assigned the use of either Google Drive or Microsoft SkyDrive. You must use your assigned product, along with email or texting, for all of your work.
c. Your work will be judged in terms of the speed with which you can create results as well as on the quality of your team's work product.

The contest is divided into two phases as described below.

Source: Goodshoot/ThinkStock/Getty Images.

5. Review Phase 2 with your teammates to be certain that everyone understands what is required.
6. After this point, no face-to-face communication is allowed.

Phase 1

1. Your team has been assigned the use of either Google Drive or Microsoft SkyDrive. Each of your team members needs to obtain an account that will enable him or her to edit documents using the collaborative tool you have been assigned. Meet with your team members and determine what each person needs to do to make that happen. Agree on the methods by which your team will work. Assign one person as the team leader.
2. Each team member should:
   a. Obtain an account from either Google or Microsoft.
   b. Share the name of your account with your teammates.
   c. Create a document that contains your name, contact data for this exercise, your hometown, and your hobbies. Store this document on Google Drive or SkyDrive, depending on which you are assigned.
   d. Share the stored document with your teammates.
3. Consolidate all of your documents into a single document. Your team leader can determine how best to do that and communicate the technique to be used to the rest of the team.
4. When you have completed this activity, your team leader should send a link to your consolidated document to your instructor so that he or she can verify that you have accomplished this activity. Your instructor will need read-only access to your document. Your team will score points based upon how quickly it has accomplished this activity.

Phase 2

Suppose you made a serious mistake when scheduling your classes, and you discover that you are not enrolled in a class that you must take this term in order to graduate. Unfortunately, all sections of that class are full. In this phase, your team will work collaboratively to determine the best strategy that your team can conceive for getting into this needed, but closed, class.

1. Working as an individual:
   a. Create a document that describes your best idea for getting into the class.
   b. Use Google Drive or Microsoft SkyDrive to share your documents with your team.
2. Have one team member combine all of the team members' documents into a single document.
3. Working as an individual:
   a. Review the consolidated document and edit it as you think appropriate.
   b. Add new ideas, raise issues about existing ideas, or resolve problems.
   c. Leave evidence in the document that you have contributed.
   d. When you are satisfied with your team's answer, leave a statement to that effect, with your name, in the document.
4. When all team members have indicated that they are satisfied with the answer, the team leader should send a link to the document to your instructor. Your team will score points based on the speed and quality of your work.
5. Present your document to the rest of the class.

Q8. 2024?

So, how will we collaborate in 2024? Where will the current trends in collaboration systems take us? One thing is clear—businesses are creating products and services that are more and more complicated and will require greater collaboration than ever. We believe the most important developments in the next decade will be the impact of collaboration on F2F meetings, the rise of more mobile collaboration platforms, the blending of collaboration and social media, and the growing use of collaboration in government and health care.

Clearly, free data communications and data storage will make collaboration systems cheaper and easier to use. One consequence is that by 2024, F2F meetings will be rare. F2F meetings require everyone to be in the same place at the same time, and both of those *sames* can be problematic. When employees work in different locations, bringing them together is expensive in travel cost and time. Employees standing in line in airport security or waiting in their cars in traffic are hardly productive. And bringing everyone together is unfriendly to the environment.

Even when employees work at the same location, they may have schedule conflicts or they may not work at that location at the same time. And unless employees are providing an in-person service, such as physical training or surgery or construction, why do they need to work in the same location?

A mining company in Washington State provided an international example in 2011. The company is located in the United States, close to the Canadian border, but owns several mines in Canada. For its annual audit, the company needed the services of a Canadian-chartered accounting firm from Vancouver, British Columbia. During the audit period, the border crossing was crowded, and the auditors were billing dozens of hours of expensive time while sitting unproductively in their cars at the crossing. To reduce the audit expense, the company eliminated most of this travel by storing audit data in SharePoint libraries.

But, by 2024, why be unproductive in your car? By then you should be able to use the full capabilities of Office 365 or whatever collaboration tools replace it on any mobile device. So, as long as you're not driving, you'll use your device in your car or your golf cart or your boat to get work done.

Further, as the example provided shows, by 2024 collaboration systems will greatly ease international business. If teams meet virtually most of the time and if it doesn't matter where team members are located, then projects can involve the best, or perhaps the most affordable, workers worldwide. Further, work can follow the sun. Workers in the United States can submit documents for feedback by team members in Asia. The Asian workers can contribute their feedback during their normal workday and pass the documents along to European team members for review during *their* normal workday. All the reviewed work will be available to the U.S. workers when their next day begins.

We can also expect that use of mobile collaboration will increase. New collaboration software for tablets and smartphones will take advantage of better networks and increased sophistication by end users. Mobile collaboration tools will help sales reps on the road with clients, home healthcare providers with patients, and maintenance workers with remote machine problems.

We also expect continued blurring of the distinction between collaboration and social media. When you contribute to a firm's social media application, you are collaborating with employees at that firm. Both you and the firm prosper in some fashion. It seems inevitable that both collaboration and social media use will grow and overlap.

Finally, this chapter has focused primarily on business collaboration. However, the need for effective collaboration will also grow as teamwork expands in health care and government. Collaboration by healthcare providers is expanding rapidly, and as collaboration systems improve, processes from telemedicine to patient billing will become more effective. Collaboration between citizens and government employees will also increase in the coming decade. For example, collaboration during natural disasters such as floods and fires will increase as citizens share firsthand knowledge of current conditions with government responders.

Ethics Guide

Virtual Ethics?

The term *virtual* means something that appears to exist but does not exist in fact. A virtual private network (VPN) is a computer network that appears to be private but in fact operates on a public network. The term *virtual meeting* describes a meeting in which everyone is present, but via an information system and not face to face.

However, and it is a big however, "Is everyone present?" Is the person who signed on as Adam truly Adam? Or is it someone else? Or is it Adam with a staff of seven people, all of whom are anonymous to the rest of the group? Consider a team composed of Allison, Abby, and Amy. What if none of them was really involved? What if, in fact, those contributions were really made by Betty, Betsy, and Beatrice, but none of them knew the others were spoofing (pretending to be someone they are not)?

Suppose you run a consulting company and you want to send less experienced consultants out on jobs. During an initial meeting (held electronically, using text chat) with a potential client, you tell the client that he is meeting with Carl, a new and inexperienced employee. But the meeting actually includes Carl and Cathy, your most experienced and senior consultant. During the meeting, all of the remarks attributed to Carl were actually made by Cathy. The client is most impressed with what it thinks are Carl's perceptive comments about its situation and agrees to hire Carl, even though he is inexperienced. You keep using Cathy this way, spoofing several of your young associates to get jobs for them. You justify this by saying, "Well, if they get into trouble, we'll send Cathy out to fix the problem."

Or suppose you have an archrival, Danny. You and Danny compete for a future promotion, and you just cannot stand the idea of him moving ahead of you. So you set up a sequence of virtual meetings, but you never invite Danny. Then, just before a crucial meeting, one that involves senior members of your organization, you invite Danny to be your silent helper. You tell him you do not have the authority to invite him, but you want him to have a chance to express his thoughts. So you attend the meeting and you incorporate Danny's thinking into your chat comments. People think you are the sole author of those ideas and are impressed. Danny's work is never attributed to him.

Consider another possibility. Suppose Earl is an independent consultant who has been hired to write a blog. Earl, who is very busy, hires Erin to write the blog for him. Earl bills his time for $110 an hour and pays Erin $45, keeping the difference. And he has free time for more paid work. Earl reviews her work, but he does none of it himself. The client never knows that it's Erin, not Earl, who writes the blog.

Or let's bring it closer to home. Suppose you take online tests as part of your class. What keeps you from taking the test with your brother, who happens to work for Google as a product manager for Google Drive? Suppose you take the test by yourself, but you believe others are taking their tests with silent helpers. Given that belief, are you justified in finding your own helper? What do you think? Are your ethics virtual?

DISCUSSION QUESTIONS

1. Is it *illegal* to spoof someone? Does it matter whether you have that person's permission to spoof them?
2. Is it *ethical* to spoof someone? Does it matter whether you have that person's permission? Consider both the categorical imperative (page 20) and utilitarianism (page 40) in your response to this question and the remaining questions.
3. Under what circumstances do you believe it is ethical to spoof someone?
4. Consider the virtual meeting of Allison, Abby, and Amy (but Amy is actually not at the meeting; Beatrice is pretending to be Amy because Amy is taking her kid to a doctor's appointment). What are the consequences to the organization of such a meeting? What happens when Abby meets Amy in the hallway and Abby asks, "What did you think of our meeting?" Who has the knowledge of the meeting? Who knows that they have that knowledge?
5. Considering Cathy's spoofing of young associates. What is different between text chat and a speaker phone? Haven't we always had these problems, except Cathy was passing notes and making comments while the phone was muted? What behavior should you follow when talking with someone who is on a speaker phone? How does the videoconferencing capability of products like Lync change this situation?
6. Is it ethical to take credit for Danny's thinking? Suppose you are later heavily criticized for the quality of Danny's ideas that you appropriated. Do you disclaim them? How?
7. Is it cheating to have a helper on an online test? Are you justified if everyone else is doing it? What control is possible for online tests? Should such tests be used at all?

Active Review

Use this Active Review to verify that you understand the material in the chapter. You can read the entire chapter and then perform the tasks in this review, or you can read the text material for just one question and perform the tasks in this review for that question before moving on to the next one.

Q1. What is collaboration, and why is it important to business?

Explain why collaboration is increasingly important in business. Distinguish between cooperative and collaborative teams and give an example of each. Explain the importance of communication and iteration. What aspect of team communication is essential to collaboration? List critical collaboration skills. Explain why undergraduate business students undervalue collaboration.

Q2. What are the objectives of the collaboration process?

Describe how the objectives of a dynamic process differ from a structured process. Explain the three effectiveness objectives and the efficiency objective of the typical collaboration process. Describe how collaboration IS support collaboration activities and business processes.

Q3. What are the key components of a collaboration IS?

Describe the client and server hardware in a collaboration IS. Explain the variety of collaboration software. Describe the two types of collaboration IS data and give an example of each. Explain why collaboration IS procedures are often unstated. Describe the important attributes of the people using collaboration IS.

Q4. How can collaboration IS support the communicating activity?

Describe the three types of communication and give an example. Explain the types of collaboration technology designed to support the communication of teams.

Q5. How can collaboration IS support the iterating activity?

Explain the three options for iterating content. For each option, describe a collaboration technology that can support the iteration activity of teams. Explain iteration control and describe three options of iteration control.

Q6. How can collaboration IS support business processes?

Describe the Project Management process and specify its common activities. What collaboration IS are available to support the Project Management process? Describe the Workflow process and explain what makes the iteration of a Workflow process different from the iteration of the typical collaborative team.

Q7. Which collaboration IS is right for your team?

Describe the three collaboration tool sets. Explain the differences among them. Summarize the criteria for choosing the right set for your team. Explain the meaning of the power curve and discuss the power curve for each of the three alternatives. Describe different ways that people can limit collaboration.

Q8. 2024?

Which type of team communication will be less frequent in the future? Describe the impact of mobile technology and social media on collaboration. Explain non-business domains where collaboration will increase.

Key Terms and Concepts

Using Your Knowledge

9-1. Reread about 2024 in Q8. Do you agree with the conclusions? Why or why not? If F2F meetings become rare, what impacts do you see on the travel industry?

9-2. Choose one of the three alternatives described in Q7 for use by your collaborative team. To do so, answer the following questions (if possible, answer these questions with your team):

a. List your team's collaboration requirements. Break them into mandatory and nice-to-have categories.

b. Create a list of criteria for selecting collaboration tools and creating a collaboration IS. Start with the items in the first column of Figure 9-20, but add, modify, or delete items depending on your answer to question 9-2a.

c. Score the three alternatives in Q7 against your requirements and your criteria. If you wish, change any of the elements of those three alternatives to create a fourth alternative. Score it as well.

d. Based on your answer to question 9-2c, select a collaboration tool set. Explain your selection.

e. Given your answer to question 9-2d, how will you construct your collaboration IS? Specifically, what procedures will you need to develop and how will your team members obtain training? Will you need to have any special jobs or roles for your team members? If so, describe them.

9-3. Reflect on your experience working on teams in previous classes as well as on collaborative teams in other settings, such as a campus committee. To what extent was your team collaborative? Did it involve communication and iteration? If so, how? Was critical feedback provided? How did you use collaborative information systems, if at all? If you did not use collaborative information systems, describe how you think such systems might have improved your work methods and results. If you did use collaborative information systems, explain how you could improve on that use, given the knowledge you have gained from this chapter.

9-4. Think back over your past week. When did you use either of the collaboration activities of communication and iteration outside of an academic setting? What process was your team engaged in? What were your team's objectives? Would any of the IS tools discussed in this chapter have made your process more effective?

9-5. This exercise requires you to experiment with Google Drive. You will need two Google accounts to complete this exercise. If you have two different email addresses, then set up two Google accounts using those addresses. Otherwise, use your school email address and set up a Google Gmail account. A Gmail account will automatically give you a Google account.

a. Using Microsoft Word, write a memo to yourself. In the memo, explain the nature of the communication collaboration driver. Go to *http://drive.google.com* and sign in with one of your Google accounts. Upload your memo using Google Drive. Save your uploaded document and share your document with the email in your second Google account. Sign out of your first Google account.
(If you have access to two computers situated close to each other, use both of them for this exercise. You will see more of the Google Drive functionality by using two computers. If you have two computers, do not sign out of your Google account. Perform step b and all actions for the second account on that second computer. If you are using two computers, ignore the instructions in the following steps to sign out of the Google accounts.)

b. Open a new window in your browser. Access *http://drive.google.com* from that second window and sign in using your second Google account. Open the document that you shared in step a.

c. Change the memo by adding a brief description of the content-management driver. Save the document from your second account. If you are using just one computer, sign out from your second account.

    d. Sign in on your first account. Open the most recent version of the memo and add a description of the role of version histories. Save the document. (If you are using two computers, notice how Google warns you that another user is editing the document at the same time. Click Refresh to see what happens.) If you are using just one computer, sign out from your first account.

    e. Sign in on your second account. Reopen the shared document. From the File menu, save the document as a Word document. Describe how Google processed the changes to your document.

9-6. This exercise requires you to experiment with Microsoft SkyDrive. You will need two Microsoft accounts to complete this exercise. The easiest way to do it is to work with a classmate. If that is not possible, set up two Microsoft accounts using two different Hotmail addresses.

    a. Go to *www.skydrive.com* and sign in with one of your accounts. Create a memo about collaboration tools using the Word Web App. Save your memo. Share your document with the email in your second Microsoft account. Sign out of your first account. (If you have access to two computers situated close to each other, use both of them for this exercise.

If you have two computers, do not sign out of your Microsoft account. Perform step b and all actions for the second account on that second computer. If you are using two computers, ignore the instructions in the following steps to sign out of the Microsoft accounts.)

    b. Open a new window in your browser. Access *www.skydrive.com* from that second window and sign in using your second Microsoft account. Open the document that you shared in step a.

    c. Change the memo by adding a brief description of content management. Do not save the document yet. If you are using just one computer, sign out from your second account.

    d. Sign in on your first account. Attempt to open the memo and note what occurs. Sign out of your first account and sign back in with your second account. Save the document. Now, sign out of your second account and sign back in with the first account. Now attempt to open the memo.
(If you are using two computers, perform these same actions on the two different computers.)

    e. Sign in on your second account. Reopen the shared document. From the File menu, save the document as a Word document. Describe how Microsoft SkyDrive processed the changes to your document.

Collaboration Exercise 9

The purpose of this exercise is for you and a team of your fellow students to improve your collaboration skills. It has two activities. During the first, you are asked to reflect on ways you can improve your collaboration skills. During the second, your team will build a collaboration IS, including choosing a communication method, building a content sharing method, and building a task management method. Then you will use your new collaboration IS to answer a series of questions about collaboration. Use Google Drive, Microsoft SkyDrive, SharePoint, Office 365, or some other collaboration system to conduct your meetings.

Activity 1: Set Goals for Improving Collaboration Skills

  1. With your team, discuss the collaboration skills presented in Figure 9-2. Create your own ranking of what you believe to be the most important collaboration skills. Justify any differences between your team's conclusion and the results of the survey in Figure 9-2.

  2. As a team, choose the two highest skills in your list in Figure 9-2 that your team believes it needs to improve. Explain your choice. Use feedback and iteration as much as possible.

  3. For the two skills you chose in item 2, identify specific ways in which you can improve. State goals both for individuals and for your team.

Activity 2: Building a Collaboration IS

In this exercise, you will first build a collaboration IS and then use that IS to answer four questions in a collaborative fashion. You might want to read the four questions (in item 4 below) before you build your IS.

    Until you answer question 1, you'll have to make do with email or face-to-face meetings. Once you've answered that question, use your communication method to answer question 2. Once you've answered question 2, use your communication and your content sharing method to answer question 3. Then use the full IS to answer question 4.

  1. Choose a communication method:

    a. Meet with your team and decide how you want to meet. Use Figure 9-8 as a guide.

    b. From the discussion in item a, list the requirements for your communication system.

    c. Select and implement a communication tool. It could be Skype, Google+ Hangouts, Microsoft Lync, or some other communication tool.

    d. Write procedures for the team to use when utilizing your new communication tool.

  2. Build a content sharing method:

    a. Meet with your team and decide the types of content that you will be creating.

    b. Decide, as a team, whether you want to process your content using desktop applications or cloud-based applications. Choose the applications you want to use.

c. Decide, as a team, the server you will use to share your content. You can use Google Grid, Microsoft SkyDrive, Microsoft SharePoint, or some other server.

d. Implement your content sharing server.

e. Write procedures for the team to use when sharing content.

3. Build a task management method:

a. Meet with your team and decide how you want to manage tasks. Determine the task data that you want to store on your task list.

b. Decide as a team the tool and server you will use for sharing your tasks. You can use Google Docs, Microsoft SkyDrive, Microsoft SharePoint, or some other facility.

c. Implement the tool and server in item b.

d. Write procedures for the team to use when managing tasks.

4. Using your new collaboration information system, answer the following questions:

a. What is collaboration? Reread Q1 in this chapter, but do not confine yourselves to that discussion. Consider your own experience working in collaborative teams, and search the Web to identify other ideas about collaboration. Dave Pollard, one of the authors of the survey that Figure 9-2 is based on, is a font of ideas on collaboration.

b. What characteristics make for an effective team member? Review the survey of effective collaboration skills in Figure 9-2 and the guidelines for giving and receiving critical feedback in Figure 9-3 and discuss them as a group. Do you agree with them? What skills or feedback techniques would you add to these lists? What conclusions can you, as a team, take from this survey? Would you change the rankings in Figure 9-2?

c. What would you do with an ineffective team member? First, define an ineffective team member. Specify five or so characteristics of an ineffective team member. If your group has such a member, what action do you, as a group, believe should be taken?

d. How do you know if you are collaborating well? When working with a group, how do you know whether you are working well or poorly? Specify five or so characteristics that indicate collaborative success. How can you measure those characteristics?

e. Briefly describe the components of your new collaboration IS.

f. Describe what your team likes and doesn't like about using your new collaboration system.

CASE STUDY 9

Eating Our Own Dog Food

Dogfooding is the process of using a product or idea that you develop or promote. The term arose in the 1980s in the software industry when someone observed that the company wasn't using the product it developed. Or "they weren't eating their own dog food." Wikipedia attributes the term to Brian Valentine, test manager for Microsoft LAN Manager in 1988, but I recall using the term before that date. Whatever its origin, if, of their own accord, employees choose to dogfood their own product or idea, many believe that product or idea is likely to succeed.

You may be asking, "So what?" Well, this text was developed by a collaborative team, using Office 365 and many of the techniques described in this chapter. We dogfooded the ideas and products in this chapter.

Figure 9-22 shows a diagram of the process that transforms a draft chapter in Word, PowerPoint, and PNG image format into PDF pages. For now, just realize that each column represents the activities taken by a role, which in this case is a particular person. The process starts with the thin-lined circle in the top left and ends with the thick-lined circle near the bottom right. The dashed lines represent the flow of data from one activity to another.

As shown in this diagram, the author works closely with the developmental editor, who ensures that the text is complete and complies with the market requirements, as specified by the acquisitions editor. We need not delve into this process in detail here; just observe that many different versions of chapter text and chapter art are created as people playing the various roles edit and approve and adjust edits.

Face-to-face meetings are impossible because the people fulfilling the roles in Figure 9-22 live in different geographic locations. In the past, the developmental process was conducted using the phone, email, and an FTP server. As you can imagine, considerable confusion can ensue with the hundreds of documents, art exhibits, and multiple reviewed copies of each. Furthermore, task requests that are delivered via email are easily lost. Dropped tasks and incorrect versions of documents and art are not common, but they do occur.

For this text, the development team decided to eat its own dog food and use Office 365 for the production of this text. During this process, the authors, the developmental editor Laura Town, and the production editor Jane Bonnell met frequently on Lync. Figure 9-23 shows a typical Lync meeting. Notice that the three actors in this process are sharing a common whiteboard. Each can write or draw on that whiteboard. At the end of the meeting, the whiteboards were saved and placed on the team's SharePoint site to be used as minutes of the meeting.

Figure 9-24 shows the team's SharePoint site. The Quick Launch (left-side vertical menu) has links to important content on

FIGURE 9-22
Chapter PDF Development Process

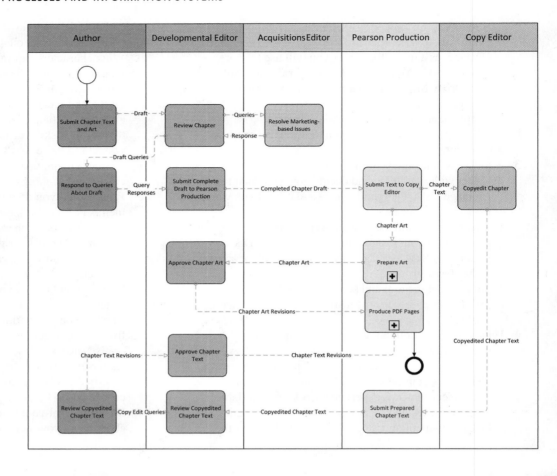

FIGURE 9-23
Lync Weekly Meeting

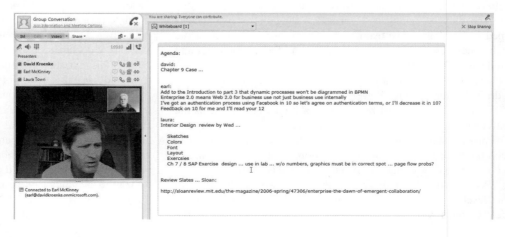

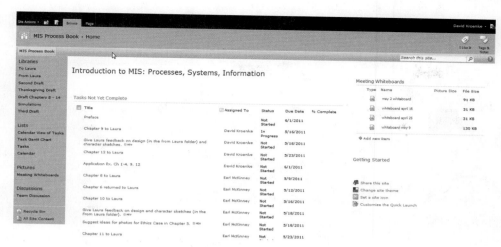

FIGURE 9-24

SharePoint Team Home Page

the site. The center portion has tasks that have a value other than "Completed" for Status. The right-hand section has a list of links to online articles of particular importance to the production of this edition.

The team set up alerts so that when new tasks were created in the Tasks list, SharePoint would send an email to the person who had been assigned that task. Figure 9-25 shows an email that was sent to David when Laura added a task to the Tasks list.

All documents and figures were stored and managed in SharePoint libraries. Figure 9-26 shows the library that contains the figures for this chapter. With so many figures and so much reviewing and editing, it is easy to confuse figures and versions. By storing them in SharePoint, the team took advantage of library version tracking. Figure 9-27 shows a portion of the version history of the text of this chapter.

When it is completed, Laura will need to review the final chapter version, so a task should be created asking her to do so. That new task will spawn an email to her like the email in Figure 9-25. I will create that task just as soon as I finish this sentence! That's dogfooding!

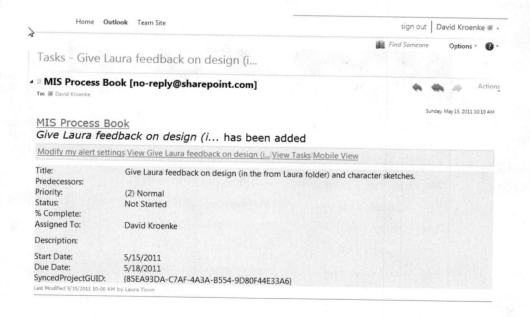

FIGURE 9-25

Task Alert Email

FIGURE 9-26
Figure Library

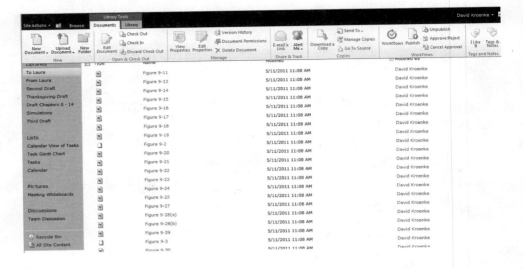

Questions

9-7. In your own words, define *dogfooding*. Do you think dogfooding is likely to predict product success? Why or why not? When would dogfooding not predict product success?

9-8. Is dogfooding a structured or dynamic process? List possible objectives of dogfooding processes.

9-9. Explain how this team uses the shared whiteboard to generate minutes. What are the advantages of this technique?

9-10. Explain how this team uses alerts. Summarize the advantages to this team of using alerts.

9-11. Summarize the advantages to this team of using Lync.

9-12. Summarize the advantages to this team of using SharePoint.

9-13. Explain how you think Office 365 contributes to the efficiency of the development team. How might it contribute to the quality of this text?

9-14. Which aspects of Office 365 described here could have value to you when accomplishing student team projects? Explain why they add value compared to what you are currently doing.

FIGURE 9-27
Version History

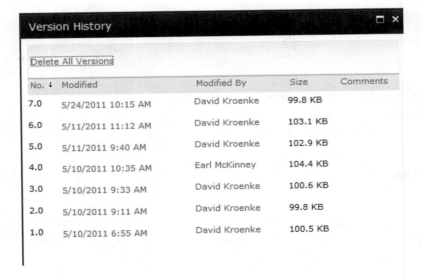

"Central doesn't know what it is doing anymore. Pat Smith has made the athletic department a complete circus. What used to count as loyalty is now rewarded by getting fired. While the football team takes all the money, other sports are left to fend for themselves. The golf team was once a fine tradition when I was there, but last month its longtime coach Sam Murray was dumped even though he ran that program on a shoestring. We need to find a grown-up to run our sports programs. I say we should fire the head clown!"

"**B**oss, you're not going to like this," said Heidi to the athletic director as he walked into the office.

"Heidi, how about starting the day with "Hello, or nice win last night, or…"

"OK, Nice win…but you're still not going to like this."

"Thanks. OK, I'll bite. What will I not like?"

"Do you remember the Facebook page we started for alumni and former athletes to connect and reminisce? I think you said at the time 'bask in the glow of Central Colorado State.'"

"Yeah, I thought you talked me into that, and I thought it was working."

"Well, OK, maybe I did think it was a good idea. Maybe it is still a good idea. It does seem to be generating some

Q1. **What is social media, and why is it important to business?**

Q2. **What are the objectives of the social media process?**

Q3. **What are the key components of a social media IS?**

Q4. **How do social media IS support social media activities?**

Q5. **How can social media IS support business processes?**

Q6. **How can social media IS support the process of building social capital?**

Q7. **How do businesses manage the risks of social media?**

Q8. **2024?**

discussion, and there is a lot of traffic. By last count we had 250 Likes, which was double our goal."

"So, again, what will I not like?"

"Well, one troll yesterday was pretty nasty about you firing the golf coach and claims this office doesn't care about alumni input. And he sort of calls you a clown."

"Can't we just delete that post?"

"Sure, but I think others may have seen it. Forty percent of our page visits are after 9 p.m., and this one loaded about 9."

Pat Smith then read the post. After fuming and ranting for a couple of minutes, he asked, "So if we don't delete it, do we respond? How do I respond?"

"Good question. If we delete it we'll lose some credibility, but if we respond to it we're justifying it. Remember how we came down hard last year on that swimmer who tweeted about the Durango athletes? We got lit up on Twitter for making him apologize."

"All I remember is that that guy was an idiot and some people thought I botched our response."

"Boss, there is something else we could do. We could hide this post from everyone while making it look like it's still there to the original guy. Maybe we need a policy. Something for employees and something that covers user posts on our sites so we don't have to figure this out every time."

"That might be good, but think how much time that will take to enforce. Doing Facebook and Twitter is sucking up time every week. Whoever told me that these sites were free never had to pay anyone for their time!"

Chapter Preview

The Web is changing. Applications like Twitter, Facebook, Wikipedia, and YouTube change what we do and what we can see on the Web. Not long ago, the Web was a one-way street, and we could only read on the Web. But a remarkable change occurred. The Web became a two-way street, bustling with tweets, wall posts, photos, images, videos, votes, reviews, blogs, and other content. While this has made the Web much more interesting for us, businesses also became interested in this new way of doing things. But businesses discovered that the new Web comes with its own surprises.

There is an old saying in the new field of IT—technique follows technology. It means that when a new technology appears on the scene, it takes a while for people to figure out the right technique for its use. New technology is always mesmerizing, and so it is with these new social media technologies. The technology is here—cheap storage and the bandwidth to store and retrieve every embarrassing post or photo—but the technique to apply it to business is still a work in progress.

To us, the right technique is to apply enduring principles. In this chapter, we focus on the principles you have seen throughout the book: the five components of an IS, process activities, and how an IS supports business processes.

Just as we did in earlier chapters where we demonstrated the impact of SAP on processes such as procurement and sales, here we suggest ways to use social media information systems to make business processes better. Our approach is similar to Chapter 9—we first examine the components of a social media IS, then the activities of social media, and finally how social media IS support social media activities in actual business processes. But we begin with the topic of social media—and its importance to business.

Q1. What Is Social Media, and Why Is It Important to Business?

With the arrival of Facebook and Twitter at the end of the last decade, the term *social media* was coined. **Social media** are Web apps that support the creation and sharing of user-generated content. User-generated content is publically available content created by end users. A **social media information system** supports the two activities in the social media process: creating and sharing user-generated content.

94% of all businesses with a marketing department use social media.

60% of marketers are devoting 6 hours or more per week to social media.

43% of people ages 20–29 spend more than 10 hours a week on social media sites.

85% of all businesses that use social media report an increase in their market exposure.

58% of businesses that have used social media for more than 3 years reported an increase in sales.

56% of customers say that they are more likely to recommend a business after becoming a Facebook fan.

90% of people trust peer recommendation via social media.

FIGURE 10-1

Social Media Industry Trends

Source: http://socialmediatoday.com/alexhisaka/1203526/how-use-facebook-business.

The social media process begins when a user creates content by posting on Facebook, tweeting, reviewing a product, updating a LinkedIn résumé, or participating in another creative act. This content is then collected and shared with other users by a social media application provider such as Facebook or YouTube.

While this two-step process is quite simple, people still buzz about it and proclaim "This changes everything!" With social media, the reality has lived up to the hype: social media is fundamentally changing the way people #communicate. It's hard to ignore one billion Facebook users; 200 million resumes on LinkedIn; and 250 million tweets, 4 billion YouTube videos, and 500 million photos posted *every day*.

As the technology grows, the opportunities for organizations to use these technologies to improve their processes grow as well. For example, American Express is tweeting product discounts to valued customers to improve their customer service process, and the FBI used social media to help find the Boston Marathon bombers. And although social media comes with some quirky risks, as in the opening vignette, most businesses are wisely jumping on board, as highlighted in Figure 10-1. *Forbes'* pithy advice is spot on: "Social media is a must for any business."[1]

To engage their customers on social media, businesses depend on social media application providers. The most popular providers are listed in Figure 10-2. While the list contains the usual suspects, notice the wide variety of apps and the popularity of non-English-speaking apps. Also notice the number of new apps that enable users to create and share images such as Tumblr, Pinterest, and Instagram.

While you may have personal experience using many of the apps in Figure 10-2, in this chapter we focus on the business use of social media. When you take your first job after graduation, you may be asked how your new firm might use social media to support their processes. To be ready, practice with the different social media apps while you are in school and use this chapter to learn how businesses can leverage social media to their advantage.

Q2. What Are the Objectives of the Social Media Process?

For any business to use social media successfully, its managers need to understand the objectives of the social media process. However, like other dynamic processes, the social media process has few well-accepted objectives. For example, people use social media to communicate, share, support, and entertain while the objectives of a business may be to boost sales or respond to customer complaints.

To make things a bit more challenging, social media has a unique wrinkle; unlike all the other processes in this book, the social media process is not controlled by the business. Businesses must share control of the social media process with other participants—the app

---

[1] Jessica Bosari, "The Developing Role of Social Media in the Modern Business World," *Forbes,* last modified August 8, 2012, www.forbes.com/sites/moneywisewomen/2012/08/08/the-developing-role-of-social-media-in-the-modern-business-world/.

App Provider	Description	Users as of July 2013
Facebook	General. Photos, videos, blogs, apps	1,000,000,000
Twitter	General. Microblogging, RSS, updates	500,000,000
Qzone	General. Mainland China users	480,000,000
Google+	General	400,000,000
Sina Weibo	Chinese microblog site	300,000,000
Habbo	General. Chat room and user profiles	268,000,000
Renren	China. Was known as Xiaonei until 2009.	200,000,000
LinkedIn	Business and professional	200,000,000
Pinterest	Pinboard photo sharing	200,000,000
Instagram	Photo and video sharing	175,000,000
Tumblr	Multimedia microblog	175,000,000
Vkontakte	General. Popular in Russia and former Soviet republics	123,612,100
Bebo	General	117,000,000
Tagged	General	100,000,000
Orkut	General. Google owned, popular in India and Brazil	100,000,000
Netlog	General. Popular in Europe, Turkey, Mideast	95,000,000

FIGURE 10-2
Popular Social Media App Providers

providers like Facebook and Twitter, and the users. Because businesses don't control it, they do not get to change it or determine its objectives. This lack of exclusive control can be unsettling for control freaks; for others it makes the game much more interesting.

Businesses, app providers, and users share the social media process, and they all have their own objectives. These objectives are shown in Figure 10-3 and include both effectiveness objectives and efficiency objectives. While at times these objectives can align, at times they are in conflict.

Effectiveness Objectives

First, we will examine the effectiveness objectives for each of the three participants—the users, businesses, and app providers. These effectiveness objectives reflect the needs or goals of each participant.

> **Effectiveness**
> Users—Belonging, Communication
> Businesses—Support strategy
> App Providers—Market share, Revenue
>
> **Efficiency**
> Time and cost

FIGURE 10-3

Social Media Participants and Social Media Process Objectives

USERS Joining communities is a deep-seated emotional need for users, and this need is reflected in the first objective: belonging. Belonging to communities greater than oneself fosters a positive self-esteem. In the past, communities were based on family relationships or geographic location—everyone in the village formed a community. While belonging is an old objective, what's new with social media communities is the breathtaking variety of opportunities to belong to communities and the ease of joining them. In addition to belonging, users also appreciate the opportunity to express themselves and communicate. Humans are a particularly communicative animal, and social media feeds that need.

BUSINESSES The primary objective for a business is to use social media to support strategy. For example, a business that differentiates on service uses social media to improve service; a low-cost leader uses social media to reduce expenses and improve efficiencies. These general strategies provide more specific objectives such as gain feedback from customers, build trust and brand identity, generate loyalty and authority, learn about potential hires, develop sales leads, and evaluate new products. We will examine several business objectives later in Q5 when we examine how social media supports business processes.

APP PROVIDERS Most app providers seek either market share or revenue. Early on, most providers focus on growing the market share of their new app, but as the app reaches puberty, the objective shifts to revenue and the nagging question, "How are we going to make money with this thing?" Many app providers fail to make the transition from market share to revenue.

Efficiency Objectives

Users, businesses, and app providers usually share a common efficiency objective: operate within time and cost constraints. While the objective is the same, it leads to different goals. Users want free apps that take little time to master. Businesses seek to limit their labor costs, and app providers use this objective to constrain their development costs.

Now that we have explained social media and its varied objectives, we turn to the main focus of this chapter: how social media information systems support business processes. Figure 10-4

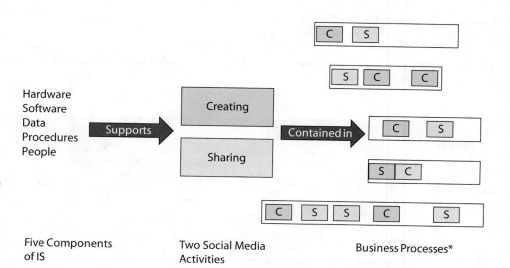

FIGURE 10-4

Social Media IS Components and Business Processes

Hardware
Software
Data
Procedures
People

Supports → Creating / Sharing → Contained in

Five Components of IS

Two Social Media Activities

Business Processes*

*White space represents other activities in the business process

depicts the relationship between social media IS, social media activities, and business processes. Starting on the left, the five components of a social media IS are discussed next in Q3. Then the two social media activities—creating and sharing—are described in Q4 and Q5. Finally, in Q6 we describe how social media IS support the social media activities contained in business processes. As in Chapter 9, we display in Figure 10-4 those business processes as a rectangle, as a structured process would look; in reality, these dynamic processes defy conventional diagramming.

Q3. What Are the Key Components of a Social Media IS?

In common use, the term *social media* can refer to apps, the use of the apps, or the industry. This ambiguity of terms, discussed in the Introduction to Part 4, is fairly common. When you use the term *social media*, try to be clear about whether you are referring to a process, an IS, or just software.

As mentioned earlier, a social media IS supports the creation and sharing of user-generated content. This definition means that the Twitter or Tumblr apps on your iPad are not social media IS by themselves, they are just the technology: the hardware and software. As businesspeople, we think the other components of an IS are also important—the data, procedures, and people.

After we have presented the five components of a social media IS, we will summarize the highlights before discussing how they are used in social media activities.

The Five Components of a Social Media IS

The key elements of the five components are shown in Figure 10-5. Let's consider each.

HARDWARE The hardware employed by users and app providers is different. Users interact with social media on mobile devices, laptops, and desktop systems. On the server end, most social media application providers use elastic servers in the cloud.

One important consideration of hardware is the size of the screen. As users move from PCs to mobile devices, particularly small-screen smartphones, there is much less space for advertising. Businesses love the opportunity to advertise to customers on the move, so ad revenue is a key source of funding for many social media application providers. The emergence of mobile social media on a small screen may affect ad revenue significantly.

SOFTWARE For users, social media apps are free, fun to use, and frequently changed. Most of the features on social media apps are offered to the user at no cost, although advanced features may have a fee. The software is also updated frequently, sometimes with little notification to users. App providers expect users to experiment with the updated app to figure it out. For a business using social media, the attributes of free, fun, and frequently changed also hold true. However, unlike other software the business uses, it has little input on the features of the software. In some cases, like Facebook applications, businesses create their own applications and interface those applications with the social media site. App providers develop and operate their own custom, proprietary social media apps.

As you will learn in Case Study 10, many social media application providers use a NoSQL database management system to process their data, although traditional relational DBMS products are used as well.

FIGURE 10-5

Five Components of a Social Media IS

Five Components of IS	Social Media IS
Hardware	Cloud for servers; various devices, increasingly mobile for clients
Software	Free, fun, frequently changed, wide variety, businesses have little input
Data	Content and connection data are both valuable
Procedures	Informal for users, governed by social media policy for businesses
People	Freedom for users, users seek belonging and communication opportunities, business users should follow established social media policies

DATA Social media data falls into two categories: content and connections. **Content data** is user-generated content and the responses to that content contributed by other users. You provide the content data for your Facebook site, and your friends provide response content when they write on your wall, make comments, tag you, or otherwise publish on your site. Content data also includes metadata such as the location of a photo, its date and time, and copyright data.

Connection data is data about relationships. On Facebook, for example, the relationships to your friends are connection data. The fact that you've liked particular organizations is also connection data. Connection data differentiates social media IS from other Web apps. Both Web sites and social media sites present user and responder content, but only social media applications store and process connection data. Connection data is a clunky term; most social media sites use a related term, **social graph,** which is a mapping that depicts the relationships among connected people.

One unique feature of social media data is tags. A **tag** is a keyword or term given to a piece of data by its creator. A tag or hashtag makes it easier to search for that term or keyword. A **hashtag** is a user-created tag that adds the prefix # to a word. Hashtags are one type of tag, but names of people and Likes in Facebook photos, keywords in YouTube videos, and hyperlinks in wikis are also tags. Tags are important tools for search engines and also because they can be organized into structures, such as bookmark categories at sites like Delicious (*www.delicious.com*). These structures organize tags as any classification would, but unlike classifications, they are not preplanned; they emerge. A term for this emergent classification is **folksonomy**—a content structure that has emerged from the processing of many user tags.

PROCEDURES When you upload a photo to Facebook, retweet, or pin a photo on Pinterest, you are executing a procedure. Social media procedures are typically simple, informal, evolving, and socially oriented. You do what your friends do. When friends learn how to do something new and interesting, you copy them. Software is designed to be easy to learn and use, so the procedures are simple to follow.

While informality makes using social media easy, it also can lead to unintended consequences for the user. The most troubling examples concern user privacy. Many people have learned not to post pictures of themselves in front of their house numbers on the same publicly accessible site on which they're describing their new high-definition television. Many others, alas, have not.

For businesses using social media, procedures cannot be so informal and simple. Before initiating a social media presence, organizations must develop procedures for users to create content, manage user responses, and extract value from content. For an example of the latter, setting up a social media IS to gather data on product problems is a wasted expense unless procedures exist to extract knowledge from that social media data. Organizations also need to develop procedures to manage objectionable content as described in the opening vignette and in Q6.

PEOPLE Users of social media do what they want to do depending on their objectives and their personalities. They behave in certain ways and observe the consequences. This may or may not lead them to change their behavior.

For businesses using social media, this freedom of behavior for users is both exciting and unnerving. Businesses depend on users to experiment with social media—to be willing to click here and there and write their first product reviews. However, this experimentation can also be hard to limit after the cat gets out of the bag.

While businesses exert little control over users, they can control their employees who represent the company on social media sites. The employees who speak for an organization should be trained on both social media IS user procedures as well as on the organization's social media policy. Selecting these employees raises some interesting questions: What makes for a good tweeter? What makes for an effective wall writer? What type of person should be hired for such jobs? What education should he or she have? How does one evaluate candidates for such positions, and what measures can be used? All of these questions are being asked and answered today. Clearly it's a hot field, and social media jobs are not likely to disappear anytime soon.

Key Attributes of a Social Media IS

Social media IS have a number of important distinguishing features. First, the client *hardware* for social media will increasingly be mobile devices. Second, social media apps are designed for personal use, not business use. As a result, organizations have little input on the *hardware* or *software* features, nor do they control much of the *data*; businesses are guests at the party. Third, the relationship data among the participants is key: if you post an image of the company's product on your wall or tweet about good service, the key for an organization is your relationships, your connection data—how many of your friends are reached. Finally, the social media phenomenon is based on the need for *people* to belong and communicate. This is the engine driving this train, and if an organization is successful with social media, it is because it piggybacks on this force.

While it is helpful to understand the components of a social media IS, it is also important to see how these components work together to support social media activities. Next, we explore how these components support the creation and sharing activities.

Q4. How Do Social Media IS Support Social Media Activities?

Social media information systems support the two social media activities: creating and sharing. Here we focus exclusively on the aspects of creating and sharing that affect business use. These dimensions are listed in Figure 10-6.

Creating

The first issue regarding content creation is that while users create content without any incentive from a business, they often create more when they are rewarded. Rewards vary from icons and status symbols to privileged placement, gifts, or entries in sweepstakes. Businesses need to understand reward system opportunities if they want to encourage users to create and disseminate content about the business.

Users create a wide variety of content that may be of interest to a business; they create tweets, posts, Likes, reviews, resumes, photos, images, and geolocation data. They can also create **mashup** content—content that combines data from two or more web services, as shown in Figure 10-7. For a business, this variety means that users are talking about their products or services on a wide variety of social media apps. To hear what their customers are saying, businesses must also listen on a wide variety of social media apps.

While most content is routine, occasionally it erupts and goes **viral**—becoming extremely popular in a short time. For example, in 2010, Old Spice ran a highly successful viral campaign using YouTube videos that were watched 23 million times in a 35-hour window. Viral content could be very good news for a business if the content shows the business in a positive light. However, viral content can also be risky—Starbucks wanted to give free iced coffee to friends and family members of its employees, but when the announcement went viral, it had to pull the plug on the offer. Bottom line—the impact of a viral event on a business is difficult to predict.

Finally, businesses should strive to make content creation convenient. When a customer buys a bicycle online from CBI, the CBI Web site should provide a simple process for the user to copy a photo of the new bike to post it on Facebook, Instagram, or Pinterest or a link to a page with a photo for Twitter. Businesses should support their customers' willingness to create content about them.

FIGURE 10-6

Business Aspects of Creating and Sharing

Creation
User-created content
Learn to reward customers.
Listen on a variety of platforms used by customers.
Be alert for unpredictable viral content.
Make content creation convenient for customers.
Business-created content
Focus on customers' needs more than the features of the product.
Use a variety of accounts to have a variety of voices on key apps.
Sharing
Learn how your customers search.
Use apps that measure the impact of your content, your buzz.
Look for opportunity in new interactive content.

FIGURE 10-7
My Maps Mashup
Source: © 2011 Google.

Having discussed customer-created content, let's turn to business-created content on social media. When businesses create content, their goal should be a closer connection with their customers. As a result, their content should be less about their products and services and more often about their customers. One social media guideline is for a business to discuss its own products and services with fewer than 10 percent of its content. Instead, businesses should post content about how their product plays a positive role in society, the social causes or volunteer activities of the business, interesting information for customers to use to solve their problems, attractive or humorous images, heart-warming stories about their customers, or thoughtful responses to their questions.

To better connect with customers, a business might consider having a variety of accounts on the same platform. For example, a college may use several Twitter accounts, one for school officials to post content in a formal and structured style and another for designated students to connect with prospective students in a less formal way. For example, these designated students may be tour guides who meet prospective students during campus tours and encourage them to stay in touch via social media. In the end, the goal for the college is for the prospective student to connect to several people on the campus.

Sharing

For businesses, the trick to understanding sharing is to learn how their customers search. A big segment of social media content is shared results from a search. Searching is essential to social media apps because all successful apps have an enormous database of content to share. One reason these apps became successful was that users could quickly learn how to search to find their friends' photos and their favorite talking cat videos. Twitter's easy-to-use search function allows users to find particular tweets in the torrent of the twitterverse. For a business to be successful in social media, it must learn how searching is done—it needs to learn how its customers search for tweets, how its customers use hashtags and expressions, and how its customers find content by geographic location. If a business understands search, it can improve the likelihood that the content it creates will be found by the customers it seeks. Search is a powerful user procedure and a must for businesses to master.

When businesses create content, they are particularly interested in impact—the buzz it creates when it is shared. Impact grows if their tweets are retweeted, if their Likes lead to other Likes, or if their help-wanted ads in LinkedIn are widely shared. A number of third-party apps help businesses measure the impact of their social media content. Figure 10-8 shows the impact measures of one widely used third party app, Klout. In the figure, you can see the impact of Mark Benioff's content on other people, who influences Mark, and his overall Klout score.

FIGURE 10-8
Klout, App that Measures Social Media Impact

Source: Klout.com, accessed 5/30/2013.

Finally, businesses should be aware of new forms of content that can be shared on social media. Recently, Microsoft made it possible for users to create a document, spreadsheet, or presentation and share that content with others on social platforms. For example, a user can make a spreadsheet and embed it on his blog where visitors can see it and interact with it. A visitor can change the values in spreadsheet's cells and see how those changes ripple through the spreadsheet while still on the blog. Other software companies are also making it easy for their users to create content and share it in interactive form. Figure 10-9 shows how this is done with a

FIGURE 10-9
Html Code to Embed a YouTube Video on Another Platform

Source: http://www.youtube.com/watch?v=zncqb-n3zMo, accessed 8/20/2013.

Business Processes Supported by Social Media IS
Promotion
Customer service
Crowdsourcing
Knowledge management
Innovation
Product development
Financing
Project management
Sales

FIGURE 10-10

Business Processes Supported by Social Media IS

YouTube video. To embed this video on a blog or on Tumblr, a user simply copies the html code in the red box. Businesses should look for opportunities to take advantage of these new forms of interactive sharing.

In Q4 we wanted to call your attention to the business aspects of social media activities. We continue this business focus by considering in Q5 how social media IS support business processes.

Q5. How Can Social Media IS Support Business Processes?

A number of essential business processes rely on social media, including collaboration, project management, promotion, product design, knowledge management, medical care, sales lead management, and others, as shown in Figure 10-10. Here we present a sample of the processes supported by social media IS in order to show the many ways businesses are using social media.

The Promotion Process

Perhaps the most common way that social media helps business is by supporting the promotion process. **Promotion** is the process of sharing data about a product or service with the objective to improve awareness and sales. Traditionally, businesses executed promotion via well-crafted messages from the business to the customer; however, with social media, promotion now includes informal messages and messages among customers.

Social media promotions involving consumers have two important characteristics. One is the network effect: If a network of consumers is buzzing about a product, the network itself draws an even bigger crowd because nothing draws a crowd like a crowd. The second important aspect of consumer promotion is trust. Consumers trust their friends much more than they do businesses. One study suggests that individuals trust their friends 90 percent of the time while they trust a marketing promotion 14 percent of the time.[2] Interestingly, the level of trust in marketing promotions has dropped rapidly from a high of 52 percent in 1997. That was the year the forerunner of social media got started, **Web 2.0**.

Figure 10-11 lists the objectives and measures of the general promotion process. Notice in the examples that follow the variety of products promoted and how the results of the promotions were measured.

Social Media Promotion Process Objectives and Measures
Objectives: Increase awareness, increase brand
Measures: Counts of Likes, retweets, downloads, conversion rates

FIGURE 10-11

Example Promotion Process Objectives and Measures

[2] Erik Qualman, *Socialnomics: How Social Media Transforms the Way We Live and Do Business* (Hoboken, NJ: Wiley, 2009).

- Stride Gum funded a YouTube video of Matt Harding dancing around the world in 42 different countries. At the end of this upbeat video, a Stride Gum announcement appears identifying Stride Gum as the video's sponsor. The Dancing Matt video was viewed 33 million times in its first 2 years. The promotion is credited with increasing sales by 8 percent and moving Stride Gum to fifth in the sugarless gum industry.
- Volkswagen posted its Passat Super Bowl commercial of 2012 on YouTube after the Super Bowl and was rewarded with more than 58 million views. Other Super Bowl advertisers put their ads on YouTube before or after the game and used shorter versions of those commercials during the game to reduce their on-game advertising costs.
- Promedica Hospital of Ohio used Facebook, Twitter, and other social media outlets to tell the story of a child's traumatic birth and the medical care the hospital provided in his first year. While thousands of dollars of contributions were raised for the baby's health care, the hospital also benefited from the internal promotion by the positive impact it had on employees who enjoyed seeing a vivid example of the value of their work.
- Lands' End Canvas created a promotion on Pinterest called "Lands' End Canvas Pin It to Win It." Fans who pinned items from Lands' End Web site to Lands' End Canvas pinboards were given a chance to win one of those products.
- Social media can also be used to promote social causes. The site Change.org allows visitors to promote causes and petitions and collect "signatures." Businesses can use social media to promote social issues; when this results in profit for the business, this process is called **cause marketing**.

The Customer Service Process

A second common process supported by social media is the customer service process. **Customer service** is the series of activities before, during, or after a sale with the goal of increasing customer satisfaction. Social media provides many new options for businesses to improve customer service. Figure 10-12 shows the variety of objectives for the customer service process as well as some of its measures. Notice in the examples that follow the variety of organizations and types of services that social media can support.

- A key service that Amazon provides its customers is a set of product reviews. In order to provide reviews for new products, Amazon asks its most trusted reviewers to create a review before the product is made available for public purchase. These trusted reviewers, called Vine Voices, are selected based on the quality and usefulness of their existing reviews as determined by other Amazon customers.
- Local and state government agencies use social media to coordinate garbage pickup, to share updates on wildfire and flood locations, and to post school closure data.
- Hospitals help families share medical updates of patients with family and invited friends. One example is a social media platform called CarePages; another is CaringBridge. Both allow families to create free private pages on which they post patient updates and read encouraging posts from friends.
- After an Icelandic volcano erupted in 2010 that canceled many flights, KLM, the Dutch airline, used social media to respond to its thousands of stranded passengers. KLM used social media to quickly reply to customer questions and redirect them to other means of travel.
- Xbox not only has 22 million fans on Facebook, but its "Elite Tweet Fleet" service earned it recognition as one of the most responsive brands on Twitter. Using Twitter, it responds to rapid-fire, live gamer issues, and its Facebook team has one of the fastest average first

FIGURE 10-12

Example Customer Service Process Objectives and Measures

Social Media Customer Service Objectives and Measures
Objectives: Increase communication to and from customers
Measures: Counts of email, tweets, followers, page loads, subscribers

response times in any industry. Not only does this service help to build strong relationships with its customers, it also reduces the number of live service calls, a much more expensive customer service method.

● While the previous examples involve B2C players, social media can also help improve B2B customer service. Cisco posts product demo videos, presentations from events, and question-and-answer forums for its customers. Its YouTube channel has more than 33,000 subscribers and 5 million video views.

Supporting New Processes with Social Media IS

In the examples in the previous two sections, we examined how social media IS could improve existing processes. However, social media can also support the emergence of new processes within the organization. Businesses have used social media to create a number of new processes. Here we will highlight two: crowdsourcing and social media listening.

One popular new process is crowdsouring. **Crowdsourcing** is outsourcing a task to a large number of users. One example is Netflix, which created a competition to build a better algorithm for recommending the next movie for a customer. Another example was how the FBI used crowdsoucing to solicit inputs to find the Boston Marathon bombers. Traditionally, the outsourced task has been product design or redesign, but now crowdsourcing is used in a variety of ways, as shown in Figure 10-13 and the examples below.

● Quirky.com uses crowdsourcing to identify products to design, manufacture, and sell. Inventors contribute ideas for products to the site, and site visitors vote. High-scoring products are then made and sold, and the profit is split with the inventor.

● The Vancouver Police Department used social media to enable people to contribute pictures from the riot after the 2011 Stanley Cup, and the pictures contributed to the arrests of more than 100 rioters.[3]

● Kickstarter.com provides tools for entrepreneurs to raise funds for new projects, disaster relief, and software development.

● Foldit asks site visitors to fold proteins in novel ways that are later analyzed by scientists to determine if these folded protein structures may help address diseases.

● You can raise funds for a new car using the Dodge Dart Registry. Select the options for your new ride on the Dart Web site, and share a link to the site with family and friends and ask them to sponsor a part of the car.

Social Media Crowdsourcing Objectives and Measures
Objectives: Improve quality of customer inputs; increase participation by customers
Measures: Count of the number of participants; count of the number of ideas adopted by crowdsourcing

Social Media Listening Objectives and Measures
Objectives: Improve service, promotion, and other processes
Measures: Count of the number of participants and the number of apps listened to; number of managers reading listening reports

FIGURE 10-13
Example Crowdsourcing and Listening Process Objectives and Measures

[3] Brenda Bouw, "Faces in the Mob Seek Forgiveness After Vancouver's Stanley Cup Riots," *The Globe and Mail,* last modified September 7, 2012, www.theglobeandmail.com/news/national/british-columbia/faces-in-the-mob-seek-forgiveness-after-vancouvers-stanley-cup-riots/article2067208/.

A second new process is social media **listening**. Social media listening is collecting and responding to customer-generated content that is either positive or negative. While companies have long solicited feedback from customers, social media enables companies to obtain feedback without solicitation, to listen in more varied channels, and to do so without being noticed. The objectives of listening, as shown in Figure 10-13, are to improve customer service, promotions, or other business processes. Listening retains customers, as FedEx has learned; satisfying a disgruntled customer triples the likelihood that customer is retained.

Consider the benefits of the listening process in the following examples.

- A customer on a Virgin Atlantic cross-country flight tweeted that he was offended by a fellow traveler's odor. Within minutes, Virgin Atlantic customer service had read the tweet, determined which flight most likely generated it, and notified the flight attendant. The flight attendant then strolled the aisle asking casually if anyone would like to move seats to another location in the plane.
- Hospitals like the Mayo Clinic use Facebook, Twitter, YouTube, and Pinterest to create opportunities for their patients to communicate with each other about common illnesses, treatments, and medicines. By creating these platforms, the hospitals build brand recognition and also have the opportunity to listen to patients candidly discussing their treatments, reactions, and frustrations.
- IBM employees listen on social media for posts and comments that refer to **requests for proposals (RFPs)**. An RFP is a document that an organization posts to solicit bids from potential vendors. IBM has a long history of responding to RFPs posted on traditional sources such as Web sites and government announcements; what is new is that it is listening to social media chatter that refers to RFPs. The post may be something like "I'm about to issue an RFP. Does anyone have a sample RFP that I can use?" or "I'm looking to replace my old database."
- Seton Hall built a Facebook page for an incoming class in order to listen to students chatting about orientation, placement testing, and other upcoming school events. Not only were students who used these services more likely to make an early commitment to the school, Seton Hall was able to listen and discover how to make these early events more appealing for future students.[4]
- An arriving hotel guest was standing in a long line at a Las Vegas hotel and tweeted "No Vegas hotel could be worth this long wait. Over an hour to check in at the Aria. #fail." No one at the Aria was listening, but a competitor was and tweeted back "Sorry about your bad experience, Dave. Hope the rest of your stay in Vegas goes well." Next time, Dave stayed at the competitor's hotel.

You can take advantage of social media listening too. Most business professionals have learned how to listen and learn on social media platforms like Twitter, YouTube, and Wikipedia. Before you graduate, learn to follow, find, and discover content useful for your career using social media platforms.

Tips for Conducting Social Media Promotions

As we close this section on how social media can improve business processes, we wanted to offer a few practical words of advice when using social media for promotion. While still in school, these tips may help you promote your service, club, or volunteer activities that use social media.

Creating a successful promotional campaign on social media can be a challenge. Early studies of successful campaigns suggest that there are five keys to success, as shown in Figure 10-14. First, find and connect to leaders in the community. Follow them on Twitter, Like them, connect with them on LinkedIn, and a number of them will connect to you in return. As a result, when you tweet or post, your message has a greater chance to reach more of your targeted audience. Second, stay involved. Create a plan about how the promotion will be updated, and stay active with the promotion by including new content daily. Third, motivate your early consumers to contribute to the promotion. These early supporters might be willing to make a positive post,

---

[4] Sandy Carter, "Four Steps to Create a Social Listening Strategy," *Social Media Examiner,* last modified December 29, 2011, www.socialmediaexaminer.com/4-steps-to-create-a-social-listening-strategy/.

Social Media Promotion Keys to Success
Connect to leaders in the community
Stay involved—have a plan to update the promotion daily
Motivate early consumers to contribute
Develop a reward mechanism for prosumers
Don't underestimate time required

FIGURE 10-14
Social Media Promotion Keys to Success

write a good review, or retweet your Twitter messages. Rely on their natural desire to belong and to communicate. Fourth, develop a reward mechanism to give status to contributors. You might award icons to screen names that are frequent posters or give them access to people or services at your upcoming event. Reward systems help convert customers into **prosumers**—those who promote for you. Finally, do not underestimate the time required. Promotions can be very time consuming. Often people say that social media is "free," and while the incremental cost in hardware, software, and data for promotions may be near zero, it can take a surprising amount of time and money for people to learn and execute the procedures.

Q6. How Can Social Media IS Support the Process of Building Social Capital?

In the previous question, we considered how social media IS can support business processes. Here we consider one more process—the process of building social capital. Karl Marx defined **capital** as the investment of resources for future profit. Business literature defines three types

MIS InClass 10

Using Twitter to Support the Class Discussion Process

Prior to class, your instructor will decide on a unique hashtag to use for this exercise. During class, use your Twitter account and create tweets that include this hashtag. Make sure your privacy setting is not turned on. Tweets can include observations about class ideas or questions about the day's topic. At the end of the class, you will discuss the tweets.

If you do not have a Twitter account, obtain one at the beginning of class.

As an alternative, rather than send tweets to the public twittersphere, you can use Twitter's direct message feature to send private tweets to a class Twitter account. To use this approach, your instructor must first create the class Twitter account. Prior to sending a direct message to that account, each student must be followed by the class account. The teacher can log in and display the direct messages at the end of class.

At the end of the class, discuss the following:

1. How well does Twitter support the class discussion process?
2. What are the objectives and measures of the class discussion process?

Source: Christin Gilbert / age fotostock / SuperStock.

3. What other educational processes can Twitter support? What are the objectives of these processes, and how does Twitter help achieve them?
4. Can in-class use of Twitter be used to integrate educational processes? These processes might include student assessment, student collaboration, technology use, and class discussion.

of capital. **Traditional capital** refers to investments into resources such as factories, machines, manufacturing equipment, and the like. **Human capital** is the investment in human knowledge and skills for future profit. By taking this class, you are investing in your own human capital. You are investing your money and time to obtain knowledge that you hope will differentiate you from other workers and ultimately give you a wage premium in the workforce.

Social capital is the investment in social relations with the expectation of returns in the marketplace.[5] When you attend a business function for the purpose of meeting people and reinforcing relationships, you are investing in your social capital. Similarly, when you join LinkedIn or contribute to Facebook, you are (or can be) investing in your social capital. Businesses invest in social capital for many reasons, and your contributions to your firm's social capital will be valued.

Building social capital is a process supported by social media IS. The social capital process is executed by people on behalf of their organizations, but it also pays dividends to the participating individuals. Most successful social capital processes share three objectives:[6]

1. Increase the number of relationships in a social network
2. Increase the strength of those relationships
3. Connect to those with more resources

As you build social capital, consider these three objectives and how social media IS can help you achieve those objectives. You gain social capital by adding more friends and by strengthening the relationships you have with existing friends. Further, you gain more social capital by adding friends and strengthening relationships with people who control resources that are important to you. Such calculations may seem cold, impersonal, and possibly even phony. When applied to the recreational use of social networking, they may be. But when you use social networking for professional purposes, keep in mind that social capital flows both ways. Professionals in other organizations seek out relationships with you as investments in their social capital.

How an Organization Can Use Social Media IS to Increase the Number of Relationships

Figure 10-15 shows the relationships of the Central Colorado State Athletic Department and its social media site. In this example, the department is using its social media site to promote its yearly alumni events in four different cities: City A to City D. The department wants to attract more alumni to these events with the overall objectives of raising funds and selling football tickets.

This diagram indicates how the department's relationship with four alumni can potentially lead to greater ticket sales. Alumni 1–4 in this example have a direct relationship with the Athletic Office social media site and have attended these events in the past. If the department can find a way to induce the four alumni to form a relationship with the events, they might spread the word of these events to their friends, Alumni 5–10, who might spread the word to their friends. If successful, the number of alumni with a relationship to the Athletic Department will increase rapidly.

Such relationship sales have been going on by word of mouth for centuries; what is new here is the use of social media IS to more rapidly increase relationships than in the past; social media in this context has been called "world of mouth" and "word of mouth on steroids."[7]

How an Organization Can Use Social Media IS to Increase the Strength of Relationships

To an organization, the **strength of a relationship** is the likelihood that the entity (person or other organization) in the relationship will do something that benefits the organization. An organization has a strong relationship with you if you buy its products, write positive reviews about it, post pictures of your use of its products, and so on.

---

[5] Nan Lin, *Social Capital: The Theory of Social Structure and Action* (Cambridge, UK: Cambridge University Press, 2002), Location 310 of the Kindle Edition.
[6] Henk Flap, "Social Capital in the Reproduction of Inequality," *Comparative Sociology of Family, Health, and Education*, Vol. 20 (1991), pp. 6179–6202.
[7] Erik Qualman, *Socialnomics: How Social Media Transforms the Way We Live and Do Business* (Hoboken, NJ: Wiley, 2009).

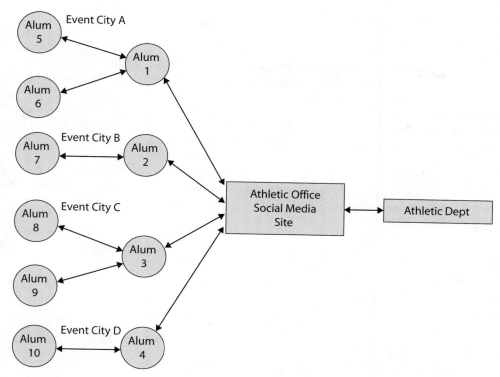

FIGURE 10-15
**Social Media Increasing
Number of Relationships**

In his autobiography, Benjamin Franklin provided a key insight.[8] He said that if you want to strengthen your relationship with someone in power, ask him or her to do you a favor. Before he invented the public library, he would ask powerful strangers to lend him their expensive books. In that same sense, organizations have learned that they can strengthen their relationships with you by asking you to do them a favor. When you provide that favor, it strengthens your relationship with the organization.

Each interaction strengthens relationships and hence increases social capital. The more you interact with a company, the stronger your commitment and allegiance. Businesses using social media should think of each Like, each pin, and each follow as a small positive step toward building a relationship. After many small connections, a relationship is nurtured.

How an Organization Can Use Social Media IS to Connect to Those with More Assets

The third objective of social capital is to connect with individuals or organizations with greater assets. The success of an organization's social capital process is thus partly a function of the social capital of those to whom it relates. The most visible measure is the number of relationships. Someone with 1,000 loyal Twitter followers is usually more valuable than someone with 10. But the calculation is more subtle than that; if those 1,000 followers are college students and the organization's product is adult diapers, the value of the relationship to the followers is low. A relationship with 10 Twitter followers who are in retirement homes would be more valuable.

This discussion brings us to the brink of social media use. Most organizations today (2014) ignore the value of entity assets and simply try to connect to more people with stronger relationships. This area is ripe for innovation. Data aggregators like ChoicePoint and Acxiom maintain detailed data about people worldwide. It would seem that such data could be used by information systems to calculate the potential value of a relationship to a particular individual. This possibility would enable organizations to better understand the value of their social networks as well as guide their behavior with regard to particular individuals.

Stay tuned; there are many ways to use social media to build social capital, and some ideas, maybe yours, will be very successful.

---

[8] Founding father of the United States. Author of *Poor Richard's Almanac*. Successful businessman; owner of a chain of print shops. Discoverer of groundbreaking principles in the theory of electricity. Inventor of bifocals, the potbelly stove, the lightning rod, and much more. Founder of the public library and the postal service. Darling of the French court and salons and, now, contributor to social network theory!

Q7. How Do Businesses Manage the Risks of Social Media?

Recently Dave Carroll, a singer and guitarist for a small touring band, was traveling from Chicago to Omaha, Nebraska, with his band. Having just boarded their United flight, they glanced out the window and saw to their horror that the ground crew loading the plane seemed to be playing catch with their instruments. When they arrived at their destination, Dave's $2500 Taylor guitar was in pieces. After trying to resolve the claim for months, Dave wrote and recorded his biggest hit—*United Breaks Guitars*, a humorous ballad that went viral on YouTube. After 500,000 views in 3 days, United contacted Dave to see how it could make things right.[9]

United has learned the hard way that social media has changed the way businesses communicate with their customers. This new type of communication comes with risks. In this question, we will consider management risks, risks from employee communication, and risks from nonemployee communication.

Management Risks

The most significant management risks are:

- Underestimation of labor costs
- Absence of dependable return on investment
- Customer privacy
- Dependence on social media application provider

One of the management challenges with social media applications is that their labor requirements are difficult to estimate. As with any new technology, few guidelines are available to estimate the time required to use them effectively.

Another challenge is to create useful measures of costs and benefits. The most traditional method of measuring costs and benefits is **return on investment (ROI)**, which is the amount earned by an investment as a percentage. For example, if a $200 investment returned $50, the ROI would be 50/200, or 25 percent. Unfortunately with social media, as with other new technology, the returns are not easy to quantify in dollars. The returns on a social media investment are typically hard to measure and may only unfold over many years. For example, a social media campaign may lead to positive word of mouth, stronger brand, buzz, or customer satisfaction, but none of these can be easily converted to a number. Also, the team that conducted the campaign may have learned lessons that can be used on upcoming projects—like how to estimate labor costs and manage such projects—but once again, these are hard to measure.

Another set of problems with social media are associated with customer privacy. One privacy problem is that many customers are naïve about privacy—they do not realize that if they did not buy the social media product, they are the product. This naiveté combined with a business desire to improve their processes using social media creates the perfect privacy storm. In fact, every time a business improves its customer-facing processes with social media data, the price is less privacy for the consumer. For example, if a hospital wants to improve collaboration among patients with a similar disease, this can only happen if the participants give up private data about their health. Businesses built on social media and businesses using this media must anticipate privacy concerns by users and privacy laws by governments that will restrict the use of social media data.

Although it is possible for organizations to develop their own social media capability, many organizations use social media application providers such as Facebook and Twitter. Those organizations are vulnerable to the success and policies of Facebook, Twitter, and others. Many social media providers are new companies with unproven business models; they may not survive. The risk for businesses relying on these platforms has been compared to building on rented property.

---

[9] "Singer's Revenge on United: A Hit Song," *UPI.com*, last modified July 9, 2009, www.upi.com/Odd_News/2009/07/09/Singers-revenge-on-United-A-hit-song/UPI-79301247160917/.

Employee Communication Risks

It seems like just about every week a professional athlete tweets something embarrassing. Sports franchises understand the marketing value of allowing their athletes to tweet to their fans, but this often turns into a public relations nightmare when the athlete communicates inappropriately.

The key to limiting employee risk for that sports franchise or any organization is to develop and publicize a **social media policy**, which is a statement that delineates employees' rights and responsibilities. The social media policy is a welcome opportunity for the business to inject some control or limits on behavior in a medium that provides the business few controls. You can find an index to 100 different policies at the Social Media Today Web site.[10] A short list of the attributes of a good social media policy is shown in Figure 10-16.

As shown in Figure 10-16, policies need to emphasize truth and honesty. As an experienced and wise business professional once said, "Nothing is more serviceable than the truth." It may not be convenient, but it is serviceable long term. Second, social media contributors and their employers should be transparent and above board. If you make a mistake, don't cover it up; instead, correct it, apologize, and make amends. Eric Qualman calls this being "flawsome." His point is that companies make mistakes but can use social media to show customers their true colors.

A third aspect of the policy is to specify a target metric for responding to customer complaints—how long on average will customers have to wait before they get a response. Customer expectations about social media response times are rapidly rising. More than half of Twitter users expect a response within 2 hours of tweeting about a customer service issue, while more than half of Facebook users expect a 24-hour response.[11] Policies must meet customer expectations.

User-Generated Content Risks

User-generated content, which simply means content contributed by nonemployee users, is the essence of social media relationships. As with any relationship, however, this content can be inappropriate or excessively negative in tone or otherwise problematic. Organizations need to determine how they will deal with such content before engaging in social media.

The major sources of user content problems are:

- Junk and crackpot contributions
- Unfavorable reviews
- Mutinous movements

Crackpots may use the site as a way of expressing passionately held views about unrelated topics, such as UFOs, government cover-ups, weird conspiracy theories, and so forth. Because of the possibility of such content, employees of the hosting business must regularly monitor the site and remove objectionable material immediately.

Disclose	Be timely—specify a response time goal. Be transparent—use your real name and employer. Be truthful—point out if you have a vested interest. Be yourself—stick to your expertise and write what you know.
Protect	Don't tell secrets. Don't slam the competition. Don't overshare.
Use Common Sense	Add value—make your contribution worthwhile. Keep it cool—don't inflame or respond to every criticism. Be flawsome—be upfront and quick with corrections.

FIGURE 10-16

Social Media IS Policy Attributes

[10] "Social Media Employee Policy Examples from over 100 Organizations," *Social Media Today*, last modified July 3, 2010, http://socialmediatoday.com/ralphpaglia/141903/social-media-employee-policy-examples-over-100-companies-and-organizations.
[11] Lisa Wirthman, "Taking Care of Business: Social Media Will Transform Customer Service," *Forbes*, last modified April 10, 2013, www.forbes.com/sites/capitalonespark/2013/04/10/taking-care-of-business-social-media-will-transform-customer-service/.

Unfavorable reviews are another risk. Research indicates that customers are sophisticated enough to know that few, if any, products are perfect. Most customers want to know the disadvantages of a product before purchasing it so they can determine if those disadvantages are important for their application. Customers expect both positive and negative comments; it is better to be perceived as honest and genuine than as old-fashioned and a hype machine. However, if every review is bad, if the product is rated 1 star out of 5, then the company is using social media to needlessly publish its problems. In this case, some action must be taken, as described next.

A **mutinous movement** is an extension of bad reviews where prosumers revolt and use an organization's site in damaging ways. An example of a mutinous movement was described in the opening vignette—a disgruntled alum was attempting to hijack the athletic booster Facebook page to organize a revolt against the athletic director.

The first task in managing social media is to know the sources of potential problems and monitor sites for problematic content. Once such content is found, however, organizations must have a plan for creating the organization's response. We consider those options next.

Responding to User Content Problems

Social media campaigns are like parties. While the party is ongoing, the host must know what to do with inappropriate behavior by a guest. The same applies to social media campaigns. What will it do with problematic content? Three possibilities are:

- Leave it
- Respond to it
- Delete it

If the problematic content represents reasonable criticism of the organization's products or services, the best response may be to leave it where it is. Such criticism indicates that the site is not just a shill for the organization but contains legitimate user content. Such criticism also serves as a free source of product reviews, which can be useful for the product development process.

A second response is to respond to the problematic content. This response is, however, dangerous. If the response could be construed, in any way, as patronizing or insulting to the content contributor, the response can enrage the user community and generate a strong backlash. Also, if the response appears defensive, it can become a strong public relations negative.

In most cases, responses are best reserved for when the problematic content has caused the organization to do something positive as a result. For example, suppose a user publishes that he or she was required to hold for customer support for 45 minutes. If the organization has done something to reduce wait times, then an effective response to the criticism is to recognize it as valid and state, nondefensively, what has been done to reduce wait times. If a reasonable, nondefensive response generates continued and unreasonable content from that same source, it is best for the organization to do nothing. "Never wrestle with a pig; you'll get dirty and the pig will enjoy it." Instead, allow the community to constrain the user. It will.

Deleting content should be reserved for contributions that are inappropriate because they are contributed by crackpots, because they have nothing to do with the site, or because they contain obscene or otherwise inappropriate content. However, deleting legitimate negative comments can result in a strong user backlash. As Heidi mentioned in the opening scenario, deleting Facebook contributions often appears arrogant and heavy-handed.

To wrap this up, most of the risks of using social media involve people: managers, employees, and customers. Because people use an IS by following procedures, procedures are essential in managing risk. While businesses have little impact on the social media procedures that their customers use, they can develop procedures for their own people that will guard customer privacy, guide employees' use, and govern user content issues. In the opening vignette, Heidi and the athletic director were operating without a procedure to respond to the inflammatory comment on the department's new Facebook alumni page. What do you think they should do? Regardless of your answer, the department needs procedures to follow.

Q8. 2024?

So much change is in the air: new Google apps, new uses of Twitter, widespread smartphone use, and moving apps to the cloud, just to name a few. Social media on mobile devices, sometimes referred to as **SoMo**, coupled with location-based marketing and wearable devices are sure to be in the news for the next 10 years.

One way to use SoMo may be location-based marketing. **Location-based marketing** integrates user location data into marketing activities. Imagine walking in your nearby downtown and receiving a tweet from one of your favorite restaurants for a half-priced dinner or a text message from a good friend who just received deep discounts to a movie starting in 10 minutes down the street. Businesses like restaurants, movie theaters, flower shops, hotels, and fresh-food outlets sell goods that expire, products that cannot be sold after a short time. Further, most of these businesses have already paid most of their costs for the product—there are few expenses for adding last-minute customers. Firms with this type of perishable inventory can use geolocation data and social media to help manage their inventory. Improving perishable inventory management with social media is similar to how Amazon.com revolutionized online inventory management.

SoMo will also promote the growing trend in wearable devices mentioned in Chapter 8. People want to use social media as they move about in the real world, so wearable devices that are sewn into clothes, added to eyeglasses, or worn as a watch will become more widespread.

Social media and privacy will also continue to clash, increasing the need for new options that preserve the features of social media but with better privacy. One early attempt is SnapChat; others can also be expected.

The business use of social media will also change as software tools to analyze social media data mature. New tools for crunching data from social media sources will allow businesses to spot useful patterns in their customers' communication in real time. One early example is the tracking of mobile customer social media use to estimate customer traffic during the Christmas holiday shopping season. If retailers know traffic is high, they can postpone discounting.

Social media is still in its infancy. Because of its low cost, ease of use, and flexibility, many firms will be experimenting with social media in the coming years. As we said in the beginning of the chapter, technique follows technology. Social media is a potentially disruptive technology. Only companies that can develop techniques for applying this technology to processes will reap the benefits. You will manage in very interesting and dynamic times. Your generation was the first to use these tools for personal use, and because of this experience you will be instrumental in helping firms use these apps to enhance their processes.

Ethics Guide

Ethics, Social Marketing, and Stretching the Truth

No one expects you to publish your ugliest picture on your Facebook page, but how far should you go to create a positive impression? If your hips and legs are not your best features, is it unethical to stand behind your sexy car in your photo? If you've been to one event with someone very popular in your crowd, is it unethical to publish photos that imply you meet as an everyday occurrence? Surely there is no obligation to publish pictures of yourself at boring events with unpopular people just to balance the scale for those photos in which you appear unrealistically attractive and overly popular.

As long as all of this occurs on a Facebook or Google+ account that you use for personal relationships, well, what goes around comes around. But in the following questions, consider the ethics of questionable social networking postings in the business arena.

DISCUSSION QUESTIONS

1. Suppose that a river rafting company starts a group on a social networking site for promoting rafting trips. Graham, a 15-year-old high school student who wants to be more grown-up than he is, posts a picture of a handsome 22-year-old male as a picture of himself. He also writes witty and clever comments on the site and claims to play the guitar and be an accomplished masseuse. Suppose someone decided to go on the rafting trip in part because of Graham's postings and was disappointed with the truth about Graham.
   a. Are Graham's actions ethical? Consider both the categorical imperative (page 20) and utilitarianism (page 40) perspectives.
   b. According to either ethical perspective, does the rafting company have an ethical responsibility to refund that person's fees?

2. Suppose you own and manage the rafting company in question 1.
   a. Is it unethical for you to encourage your employees to write positive reviews about your company? Use both the categorical imperative and utilitarianism perspectives.
   b. Does your assessment change if you ask your employees to use an email address other than the one they have at work? Use both the categorical imperative and utilitarianism perspectives.

3. Again, suppose you own and manage the rafting company and that you pay your employees a bonus for every client they bring to a rafting trip. Without specifying any particular technique, you encourage your employees to be creative in how they obtain clients. One employee invites his Facebook friends to a party at which he will show photos of prior rafting trips. On the way to the party, one of the friends has an automobile accident and dies. His spouse sues your company.
   a. Should your company be held accountable?
   b. Does it matter if you knew about the presentation? Would it matter if you had not encouraged your employees to be creative?

4. Suppose your rafting company has a Web site for customer reviews. In spite of your best efforts at camp cleanliness, on one trip (out of dozens), your staff accidentally served contaminated food and everyone became ill with food poisoning. One of those clients from that trip writes a poor review because of that experience. Is it ethical for you to delete that review from your site? Again, consider both the categorical and utilitarianism perspectives.

5. Instead of being the owner, suppose you were at one time employed by this rafting company and you were, undeservedly you think, terminated. To get even, you use Facebook to spread rumors to your friends (many of whom are river guides) about the safety of the company's trips.
   a. Are your actions legal?
   b. Are your actions ethical? Consider both the categorical imperative and utilitarianism perspectives.
   c. Do you see any ethical distinctions between this situation and that in question 4?
   d. Again, suppose that you were at one time employed by the rafting company and were undeservedly terminated. Using the company owner's name and other identifying data, you create a false Facebook account for her. You've known her for many years and have dozens of photos of her, some of which

were taken at parties and are unflattering and revealing. You post those photos along with critical comments that she made about clients or employees. Most of the comments were made when she was tired or frustrated, and they are hurtful but, because of her wit, also humorous. You send friend invitations to people she knows, many of whom are the target

of her biting and critical remarks. Are your actions ethical? Again, use both the categorical and utilitarianism perspectives.

6. Based on your answers in questions 1–5, formulate ethical principles for using social media for business purposes. Formulate ethical principles for creating or using user-generated content for business purposes.

Active Review

Use this Active Review to verify that you understand the material in the chapter. You can read the entire chapter and then perform the tasks in this review, or you can read the text material for just one question and perform the tasks in this review for that question before moving on to the next one.

Q1. What is social media, and why is it important to business?

Explain user-generated content and give an example. Describe the two activities of the social media process. Provide an example of how a business has used social media.

Q2. What are the objectives of the social media process?

Describe the unique wrinkle of social media. Explain the two objectives of users in the social media process. Describe the objectives of businesses and app providers. Explain the efficiency objective for social media.

Q3. What are the key components of a social media IS?

Describe the impact of the increasing use of mobile social media on advertising. Explain several of the key characteristics of social media software. Distinguish between content and connection data and give an example of each. Describe the result of informal social media procedures. Explain the characteristic of people that is both exciting and unnerving for businesses.

Q4. How do social media IS support social media activities?

Explain the concept of viral and why it is important to business. Describe the general rule about how often a business should describe its own products. Explain why understanding how customers search is useful for a business.

Q5. How can social media IS support business processes?

Give several examples of business processes supported by social media IS. Describe the promotion process, including its objectives. Explain the two important characteristics of social media promotions that involve customers. Describe the customer service process and its objectives. Explain crowdsourcing and listening processes and give examples of how businesses are using these processes. Describe several tips for running a successful social media promotion.

Q6. How can social media IS support the process of building social capital?

Explain capital and describe the three types of capital. Explain the possible benefits of social capital for business. Identify and explain the three objectives of the process of building social capital. Provide an example of how social media supports each of these three objectives.

Q7. How do businesses manage the risks of social media?

Explain several of the management risks of using social media. Describe the attributes of a good social media policy. Explain the sources of user content problems and the options for businesses in responding to user content problems.

Q8. 2024?

Explain SoMo. Describe how a business can use location-based marketing. Explain how businesses are using new tools on social media data.

Key Terms and Concepts

Using Your Knowledge

10-1. Visit Zillow at *www.zillow.com*. Enter the address of someone's home (your parents' perhaps) and obtain an appraisal of it. Check out the appraised values of the neighbors' homes. Do you think this site violates anyone's privacy? Why or why not? Find and describe features that demonstrate that this is a social media app. Explain why this site might be considered a threat by traditional real estate companies. How might real estate agents use this site to market their services? How can real estate brokers (those who own agencies) use this site to their advantage?

10-2. Suppose you are in charge of designing the university golf course's Facebook page. Describe three features that the golf course could put on its page (e.g., a link to tee time reservations). Explain what process would be improved at the golf course with each new feature and specify a measure you would use to assess this improvement.

10-3. Whereas the golf course deals directly with consumers, CBI, the bicycle wholesaler, deals with retailers that then sell to consumers. How does this change the way CBI uses social media? Specify processes at CBI that can be supported by social media and measures that will assess improvements.

10-4. Go to Wikipedia. Read the "About Wikipedia" page and the "Collaborative Writing" page. Make a diagram that shows the process of creating and updating a Wikipedia page. Is page creation and editing a process with an effectiveness goal or efficiency goal? What measures could be used to assess improvement in the process?

10-5. Search the Web using the words *Google My Maps* and follow the links to learn how to make your own maps. Then create a map of your own. Does My Maps have all the features of a social media app?

10-6. Visit Digg, Delicious, and Quora. Prepare a report or presentation to the class that explains the site, which social media characteristics are evident, and what personal or business processes the site can support.

10-7. Search the Web using the words *Office 365* and read about this Microsoft product. Which social media characteristics are evident? Do you think this approach will be successful for Microsoft?

10-8. Assess your own stock of social capital. What activities around campus would help you increase your social capital? What social media apps could you use to increase your social capital?

10-9. Become a prosumer. Find a cause or group on Facebook that you believe in and contribute in ways that you do not typically contribute. Does the organization value your help in an encouraging way? If you were in charge of the site, how would you reward prosumers?

10-10. Join LinkedIn if you have not done so already. Start a résumé and connect to people you know. Investigate job opportunities in your area of study. Locate organizations and research a few as you would if you had an upcoming job interview. Find graduates of your school in your speciality and ask them to connect with you. Use LinkedIn before your job interview by reading the résumés of people in your specialty.

Collaboration Exercise 10

Collaborate with a group of fellow students to answer the following questions. For this exercise, do not meet face to face. Your task will be easier if you coordinate your work with SharePoint, Office 365, Google Docs with Google+, or equivalent collaboration tools. (See Chapter 9 for a discussion of collaboration tools and processes.) Your answers should reflect the thinking of the entire group, not just that of one or two individuals.

With a group of classmates, propose and carry out a small marketing promotional initiative for an organization using social media. The organization may be a business, nonprofit, university program, student activity group, or other suitable entity. Run the promotion for several weeks.

Your criteria for success include usefulness to the client (i.e., how successful it is), thoroughness, and professionalism. To better understand how to promote your product or service, consult any introductory marketing textbook or online resource and search for *promotion* or *social media promotion*. You should also reread the keys to success for a social media campaign at the end of Q5 in this chapter before you begin. To better understand social media promotions, you might visit Mashable (*www.mashable.com*), a leading online social media site, or Technorati (*http://technorati.com*) to search the blogo-sphere for guidance on social media use.

To begin, your team should discuss and specify:

1. Your target audience (you may have more than one)
2. The benefit offered by your product/service
3. The objective of your promotional activity (e.g., pro-vide information, increase demand, differentiate, etc.)

4. Your initial design, message(s), or content
5. How success will be measured

At the end of your promotion, present to the class your plan, your experiences during the promotion, and what you would do differently next time.

CASE STUDY 10

Tourism Holdings Limited (thl)

Tourism Holdings Limited (thl) is a publicly listed New Zealand corporation that owns multiple brands and businesses in the tourism industry. Principal holdings of thl include:

- New Zealand tourist attractions such as Waitomo Black Water Rafting and Waitomo Glowworm Caves
- Kiwi Experience and Feejee Experience hop-on, hop-off tourist bus services
- Six brands of holiday rental vehicles
- Ci Munro, a van customization manufacturing facility

In 2009, thl earned $5 million in profit before interest and taxes on $170 million in revenue. It operates in New Zealand, Australia, and Fiji and has sales offices in Germany and the United Kingdom as well.

Thl originated as The Helicopter Line, a corporation that provided scenic helicopter flights over New Zealand. Over the years, thl sold the helicopter business and has since owned and operated numerous different tourism organizations and brands. Thl continues to frequently buy and sell tourism businesses. For the current list of businesses, visit *www.thlonline.com/THLBusinesses*.

According to Grant Webster, thl's CEO, "thl is a house of brands and not a branded house." Thus, in the holiday rental business, thl owns and operates six different van rental brands, which are differentiated on price.

Tourism Market

In 2008, an estimated 866 million international visitors toured the world. That number is expected to grow to more than 1.6 billion visitors by 2020, according to Tourism Business Magazine. In 2008, travel and tourism was the world's largest business sector, accounting for 230 million jobs and more than 10 percent of the world's GDP.[12]

Despite these long-term growth prospects, international tourism contracted recently following the financial crisis in the fall of 2008. As of June 2009, 1.15 million international travelers visited New Zealand annually,[13] a decrease of 5 percent from the year

before, and 5.5 million international travelers visited Australia, a decline of 2 percent.[14]

According to Webster, "While we believe the long-term prospects of tourism in our traditional markets of New Zealand, Australia, and Fiji will remain strong, thl's substantial growth opportunities will be achieved by expanding to other countries, possibly the United States, or Europe."

Investment in Information Systems

Thl considers information systems and technology as a core component of its business value and has invested in a variety of innovative information systems and Web 2.0 technologies. Webster, the CEO, speaks knowledgeably about information technologies, including SharePoint, OLAP, and data mining (discussed in Chapter 11).

Because of its acquisition of multiple brands and companies, thl accumulated a disparate set of information systems based on a variety of different technologies. These disparate technologies created excessive software maintenance activity and costs. To reduce costs and simplify IS management, thl converted its customer-facing Web sites to use Microsoft SharePoint. "Having a single development platform reduced our maintenance expenses and enabled us to focus management attention, development, and personnel training on a single set of technologies," according to Steve Pickering, Manager of Interactive Information Systems.

Thl uses SharePoint not for collaboration but rather as a development and hosting platform for sophisticated, highly interactive Web sites. You can find an example of such sophisticated capabilities at *www.kiwiexperience.com*. Click on "Pass map" and the Web site will display a map of New Zealand. Select a location for your tour, then select activities that interest you. The Web site will provide suggestions for where you can participate in each activity along your selected tour. Visit the site to get a sense of the interactivity and sophistication of processing.

Social media enables the tourism industry to disintermediate sales channels. According to the New Zealand Ministry of Tourism, the Internet was used by 49 percent of international travelers to research travel options in 2006. That percentage has increased dramatically, and it is likely well over 50 percent today.

---

[12] Tourism Business Magazine, November 2009, p. 20. Visit *www.tourismbusinessmag.co.nz/* for more information.

[13] "Tourism Research and Data," *New Zealand Ministry of Business, Innovation & Employment,* accessed September 19, 2013, www.med.govt.nz/sectors-industries/tourism/tourism-research-data.

[14] "Home," *Tourism Australia,* accessed September 19, 2013, www.tourism.australia.com.

As with all disintermediation, when thl sells directly to the consumer, it saves substantial distribution costs. To facilitate direct sales, thl actively uses Google AdWords and is a key consumer of Google Analytics. Thl is also experimenting with online chat, both voice and video. "A camper rental can cost $5,000 to $10,000 or more, and we believe our customers want a trusted relationship with a salesperson in order to commit," according to Webster. "We think that video online chat might give us that relationship with our customers."

Questions

10-11. This case implies that the frequent acquisition and disposition of tourism brands poses problems for information systems. Summarize what you think those problems might be. Consider all five components of an information system. To what extent does standardizing on a single development platform solve those problems? Which of the five components does such standardization help the most?

10-12. Visit *www.kiwiexperience.com* and click "Pass map." Select a variety of activities in the Adrenalin, Nature, and Kiwi Culture menus. Find a pass that would allow you to participate in all of your selected activities.

    a. Evaluate this user interface. Describe its strengths and weaknesses.

    b. Summarize the ways in which this site uses social media.

    c. Explain why this site is an example of a mashup.

10-13. Explore the social media links on the *kiwiexperience.com* home page.

    a. What are your initial reactions? Do the layout and concept invite you to participate and provide your own content?

    b. This Web site, and its use of social media, supports the promotion process for thl. What other thl processes do the Web site and social media support?

    c. Process improvement requires specific objectives and adequate measures. For example, one promotional objective might be to increase user interaction. The measure could be the number of clicks. What are two other possible promotional objectives for thl? Specify a measure for each.

    d. Will thl's current use of social media support the objectives and measures you specified in the previous item? How might it improve its use of social media so that it will better support your objectives for its promotion process?

I n a windowless office deep inside the corporate office of CBI, Ann, the manager of the accounting department, and Cody, an IT analyst, are looking intently at a monitor. Cody is showing Ann data about the CBI network traffic.

"Ann, we use this program to determine which computers are downloading music and video files," explains Cody.

Ann is curious: "What do we do when people abuse our system?"

"We let them know. Usually that takes care of it. But not with your man Shawn. We sent him our standard 'Don't abuse our system' emails, but nothing changed. Maybe it's time you do the supervisor thing and chat with him."

"Is he downloading illegally, or is it from iTunes or YouTube?"

"We don't look that closely. In either case, it slows our network."

Ann, not sure she likes where the conversation is headed, attempts to change the subject. "What else?"

With a mischievous glint, Cody shows Ann a screen that displays a line with each employee name and columns for popular applications like Facebook, Google, and Outlook. "We collect data on millions of packets of Internet traffic flowing in and out of CBI every day, and we sort them by IP address. This screen shows the IP address of each employee, their names, and how often they use each application."

As Ann struggles to find a measured response, Cody rambles on, "We track how often employees log in to Facebook. We also track when employees log into and out of the company network and what types of apps they use—email, video, the new ERP system. When they access email through our servers. Those kinds of things."

"I don't remember being told that someone is recording my keystrokes!"

Q1. What is business intelligence, and why is it important to business?

Q2. What are the objectives of the BI process?

Q3. What are the key components of a business intelligence IS?

Q4. How do BI information systems support BI activities?

Q5. How can BI information systems support business processes?

Q6. What is a Big Data BI system, and how is it used?

Q7. How do businesses manage the risks of business intelligence?

Q8. How does SAP do BI?

Q9. 2024?

"I thought HR put out a policy letter. A lot of companies are doing it. HR says this will help them someday determine who is productive and who is not."

"So if I don't send and receive email at night or on weekends someone is recording that? Do we have any reliable measures, or are we just guessing what the numbers might mean? Maybe people are using texting to get their job done faster than if they used email?"

"Hey that's a good point, I hadn't thought of that. I know Fred purchased like a terabyte of data from SPYIT to compare how people use our network to how employees at other companies use their networks. They have some pretty sophisticated statistics. I can't wait to see that data. I wish I knew how it works."

Undeterred by Ann's concerns, Cody carries on. "We've got other software that shows us how fast truck drivers are driving, how many insurance claims each employee makes, and when they swipe into and out of our buildings. It's a whole new game!"

Ann sighs. "But if we are going to be Big Brother and watch what everyone's doing, Big Brother has a lot to learn."

Chapter Preview

The Sales and Procurement operational processes described in Chapters 7 and 8 generate significant amounts of data. In addition, the dynamic processes associated with collaboration and social media in Chapters 9 and 10 can also spin off mountains of data. But these are just a few of the many processes generating data in an organization. Cody and Ann are examining another source of data—millions of packets of network traffic. All this data includes useful patterns, relationships, and insights, but it is hidden, like a needle in a haystack. Finding these useful patterns is the goal of business intelligence. This chapter considers business intelligence and the information systems that support it.

As a future business professional, your ability to analyze data will be a critical skill. According to Jim Goodnight, founder of SAS, "If you want to be successful in business, make sure you have some understanding of analytics and when to use them. People who can use analytics—such as data mining and forecasting—to turn raw data into better business decisions have never been in greater demand. With all the talk of "Big Data," organizations across industries need people who understand how to use analytics to make sense of it all. I encourage this year's graduates to learn about how and when analytics can support their decisions."[1]

In this chapter, we investigate how companies like CBI use BI systems to support their processes. Our approach is similar to the previous two chapters—we first examine the five components of a BI system, then the activities of BI, and finally the business processes that rely on BI. But we begin with BI—its importance to business and its objectives.

Q1. What Is Business Intelligence, and Why Is It Important to Business?

The quantity of data flooding the world is mind numbing. According to Google CEO Eric Schmidt, every week we create as much data as we did from the dawn of civilization to 2003.[2] Every day Facebook processes over 500 terabytes of data, and Twitter users create another 7. Google processes 24,000 terabytes of data, and Walmart collects more than 2,500 terabytes of customer transaction data every hour.[3]

[1] Eve Tahmincioglu, "CEO Advice for Grads: Travel, Learn, Follow Your Passion," *Today Money,* last modified June 5, 2012, www.today.com/money/ceo-advice-grads-travel-learn-follow-your-passion-813915.

[2] Eric Schmidt quoted in Klint Finley, "Was Eric Schmidt Wrong About the Historical Scale of the Internet?," *ReadWrite,* last modified February 7, 2011, http://readwrite.com/2011/02/07/are-we-really-creating-as-much#awesm=~obSZrnBnJCJKOy.

[3] Andrew McAfee and Erik Brynjolfsson, "Big Data: The Management Revolution," *Harvard Business Review,* last modified October 2012, http://hbr.org/2012/10/big-data-the-management-revolution; Thomas H. Davenport, Paul Barth, and Randy Bean, "How Big Data Is Different," *MIT Sloan Management Review* Fall 2012, http://sloanreview.mit.edu/article/how-big-data-is-different/; and Josh Constine, "How Big Is Facebook's Data? 2.5 Billion Pieces Of Content And 500+ Terabytes Ingested Every Day," *Techcrunch,* August 22, 2012 http://techcrunch.com/2012/08/22/how-big-is-facebooks-data-2-5-billion-pieces-of-content-and-500-terabytes-ingested-every-day/.

FIGURE 11-1
Five Sources of Data Growth

Health Care

Financial

Machine

Scientific

Communication

While these numbers are growing at rates that are hard to fathom, the main sources of data remain the same. These five sources of data are shown in Figure 11-1. The first source is financial—data from the billions of financial transactions that occur every day. Second, data is being generated by scientific advances such as mapping the human genome and global climate. A third source is our communications—every tweet, post, click, Like, email, comment, photo and search. Fourth, healthcare services like blood tests, MRIs, and hospital visits generate billions of records a day. But the fifth source of data may make the first four seem almost insignificant. There will soon be trillions of data-generating devices on the planet with us; hundreds of billions of mobile devices, RFID chips, and sensors are already here, and they will soon join forces with generations of new devices and comprise the "Internet of Things."[4] These devices will power the growth of data for many years to come.

As the amount of data has grown, so too has its stature in the world of business. Spending on the analysis of business data has tripled in the past 12 years. In 2011, venture capital firms alone invested $2.5 billion. Gartner, a leading IT research firm, flatly stated that business data analysis was the number one technology priority for businesses in 2012.[5] As *The Wall Street Journal* concluded, this is the "Next Big Thing."[6]

While many of us look for patterns some of the time, some will look for patterns most of the time. These data sleuths, these BI analysts, have a unique blend of statistical training and intense curiosity. This career field may find you, as Gartner forecasts a demand for 140,000 to 190,000 data specialists in the next 10 years. The job is sometimes referred to as *data scientist* and was hyped by *Harvard Business Review* as the sexiest job in the 21st century. Not only will BI analysts be needed, there is a need for 1.5 million managers who can work alongside them and turn insights from data into improved business processes.

Business intelligence is a process of acquiring, analyzing, and publishing data with an objective of discovering or revealing patterns in data that will inform a businessperson. This process is depicted in Figure 11-2. A **business intelligence system** is an information system that supports these three business intelligence activities. Often, databases in BI systems are quite large and are called Big Data applications; however, BI has long been employed on more

FIGURE 11-2
Main BI Process Activities and Roles

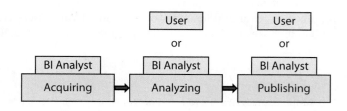

[4] Michael Chui, Markus Löffler, and Roger Roberts, "The Internet of Things," *McKinsey Quarterly,* last modified March 2010, www.mckinsey.com/insights/high_tech_telecoms_internet/the_internet_of_things.
[5] "Business Intelligence, Mobile and Cloud Top the Technology Priority List for CIOs in Asia: Gartner Executive Programs Survey," *Gartner Research,* last modified September 13, 2012, www.gartner.com/it/page.jsp?id=2159315.
[6] *The Wall Street Journal Online,* http://online.wsj.com/article/SB10001424127887323751104578147311334491922.html, accessed October 10, 2013.

FIGURE 11-3
Examples of BI

Company	Industry	Process	Objective
Target	Retail	Promote to new customers	Improve assessment of pregnancy
Netflix	Movie rental	Movie recommendation	Better prediction of next movie

routine-sized datasets. In this chapter, we first explain these more common, smaller BI systems and later explore how Big Data BI systems differ.

Examples of BI

BI systems are only valuable because they support business processes. BI systems support business processes just like Facebook supports your processes. Facebook has acquired data that you can analyze to improve your personal processes. You improve your personal processes when you use Facebook data to find out (a nerd might say analyze) what is happening with friends, discover revealing patterns in relationships among people, notice trends in people's lives, and predict how some dramas will unfold. In a similar fashion, you analyze Google's data to find Web sites and map locations and uncover trending topics. In much the same way, businesses analyze data to improve their processes—consider the BI examples listed in Figure 11-3.

Marketers at Target realized that the key to gaining new customers is to get them in the store when their family situation changes.[7] Target had learned that shopping habits get ingrained; family members shop for the same items at the same stores until they experience a significant change in situation. These situation changes are things like having a baby, getting a new job, or moving to a new city. These events upset ingrained buying patterns and allow the merchant a rare opportunity to get customers in the door. Seizing on this, Target developed a statistical analysis that could accurately assess when a potential customer became pregnant. Target would then mail the expectant mother discounts and coupons for vitamins, maternity clothing, and baby furniture.

Netflix, sitting on a billion customer movie reviews, used BI to improve its Movie Recommendation process. If Netflix is better than its competitors at the Movie Recommendation process, you will probably rent more from Netflix than from its competitors. Why would you go to a rental store or another cable or Web-based movie service if it cannot help you sift through thousands of movie choices and predict the ones you might like as successfully as Netflix?

While these are current examples of BI, also called *business analytics, predictive analytics, data science,* or simply *analytics,* businesses have been searching for patterns in data for a very long time. The term analytics dates back to the ninth century. BI systems used to analyze business data first became popular in the 1970s and were then called **decision support systems (DSS)**. A DSS is an information system used in support of decision making. It is still a term you may hear today when the supported process is decision making. We consider DSS to be a subset of BI.

To wrap this up, the business world is increasingly awash in data, and BI systems are growing in their capacity to help businesses identify important patterns in that data. To prepare you for a career that will frequently rely on BI, we start this chapter by considering the objectives of the BI process.

Q2. What Are the Objectives of the BI Process?

Like any process, the key to understanding the process is to understand its objectives. As shown in Figure 11-4, the objective of the BI process is to inform—an effectiveness objective—while staying within time and cost constraints—an efficiency objective.

The objective of most all Business Intelligence processes is to inform someone in the business. For example, a businessperson may be assessing a particular pattern or relationship, such as looking to see if sales are increasing or decreasing. In contrast, the BI process may also be used to browse data with a more undirected purpose such as asking "How are we doing?" or "What is new?"

---

[7] Charles Duhigg, "How Companies Learn Your Secrets," *The New York Times,* last modified February 16, 2012, www.nytimes.com/2012/02/19/magazine/shopping-habits.html?_r=2&hp=&pagewanted=all&.

FIGURE 11-4
BI Process Objectives

| **Effectiveness** |
| Informing—Assessment informing |
| Prediction informing |
| **Efficiency** |
| Time and cost |

Informing is a rather general term, so more often we use the specific terms **assessment** and **prediction**. Assessment, in business, means to be informed about current conditions, while prediction is to be informed about the likelihood of future events. Using previous examples, Cody and Ann at CBI are attempting to assess if the company's network is being misused, Target is trying to assess who is pregnant, and Netflix wants to predict the likelihood that you will enjoy the next movie. Assessment typically asks questions such as, "What action is needed?" "What is the problem?" "Where is the item?" or "Who is doing what?" With prediction, the questions become "What is the next best thing that can happen?" "What if we change this?" "What will happen next?" and "What are the chances they will react in a certain way?"

BI processes also pursue an efficiency objective: time and cost constraints. For example, Target specified a time and budget for its staff to develop its pregnancy prediction algorithm. While it may seem obvious that time and cost objectives should be met, usually they are not even well specified. It is difficult to nail down goals for time and cost because many BI projects are one-offs, unique projects not attempted before. One-offs are more difficult to assign specific cost and time goals than recurring events because there is no precedence to guide cost and time goals. Therefore, BI efficiency objectives often shift depending on progress toward the end result. For example, we can imagine a one-off BI project for Target—build a model to predict when a potential new customer is moving into an area close to one of its stores. The BI team may discover after 3 months and $300,000 that it has made limited but promising progress; if team members are given more time, they think they could double the accuracy of the model. Then after 6 more months and more cash, they claim that if they could buy a new dataset they are sure to have an even more useable model. And on it goes.

Now that we have explained business intelligence objectives, we turn to the main emphasis of this chapter: how BI information systems support business processes. Figure 11-5 depicts the relationship between BI IS, business intelligence activities, and business processes. Starting on the left, the five components of a BI IS are discussed next in Q3. Then the three BI activities—acquiring, analyzing, and publishing—are described in Q4. Finally, in Q5 we describe how BI IS support BI activities in actual business processes. As in Chapters 9 and 10, we display in Figure 11-5 those business processes as a rectangle, as a structured process would look; in reality, these dynamic processes can't be accurately represented using conventional diagramming.

FIGURE 11-5
BI IS Components and Business Processes

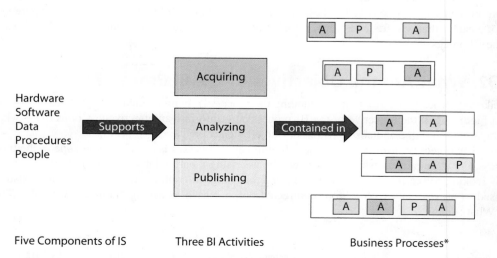

Five Components of IS · · · Three BI Activities · · · Business Processes*

* White space represents other activities in the business process

Q3. What Are the Key Components of a Business Intelligence IS?

As we have done in the previous two chapters, here we review the components of the information system. We expect that you will be better able to use these BI systems if you can see how they are different from other IS.

The Five Components of a BI Information System

Like any other successful information system, each of the five components of a BI system shown in Figure 11-6 must be individually effective for the system to be effective.

HARDWARE The key piece of hardware in a BI system is a BI server. A BI server is used by an analyst to analyze the data and produce the output. A BI server can deliver output in a variety of formats such as .docx, .xlsx, PDF, XML, dashboards, and many others. For example, at Netflix the BI server can push the results of the movie recommendation algorithm to a laptop or any mobile device. A BI server can also control access so that only authorized people can interact with different data elements or see published outputs.

One of the key features of a BI system is that it needs to grow as the database grows; it needs to be scalable. To achieve scalability, BI servers are modular; that is, servers can be added easily as the system grows. This need for scalability makes cloud computing attractive, as one of the cloud's best features is the ability to expand services.

SOFTWARE A variety of BI software supports each of the three activities in the BI process: acquiring, analyzing, and publishing. While some software products such as Excel can support several of the activities, very few support each of the steps. SAP, Oracle, and Microsoft offer a comprehensive suite of BI software products that support each of the activities for medium to large organizations.

In recent years as BI software has become easier to use, end users are doing more of the analyzing and publishing activities without the assistance of BI analysts. When users do BI analysis by themselves, it is called **self-service BI**. In addition to being easy to use, BI software needs to be compatible with other software because there are many different types of data to acquire, statistical analyses to run, and types of output to publish.

DATA Data can be collected for a BI system in two ways. First, the data may come from an **operational database** that contains the data from the operational processes in a company. Second, data may come from other sources that are then combined with operational process data. In either case, once the data are collected, they are prepared and stored in a **data warehouse**, a repository for the organization's BI data. BI data are kept in a data warehouse because a data warehouse is specially designed to make sorting and retrieving large volumes of data efficient. Operational databases, in contrast, are designed to make data inputs and updates efficient. In the BI world, operational databases are often referred to as **OLTP (online transactional processing)** systems, while the data warehouse is called **OLAP (online analytical processing)**.

PROCEDURES BI users and analysts follow a wide variety of procedures to acquire, analyze, and publish data. These methods of interaction depend on the activity and the analyst's knowledge

Five Components of IS	BI Information System
Hardware	Servers must be scalable, can provide control options, are often cloud based
Software	Differs by activity; analyze and publish software increasingly easier to use
Data	From operational sources and from external sources; data stored in a data warehouse
Procedures	Acquire activity requires technical training; analyze and publish activities increasingly designed for self-service BI
People	Informing differences based on differences in knowledge, education, and experience; differences promote need for collaboration

FIGURE 11-6

Five Components of BI Information Systems

and experience. For example, most of the procedures for acquiring and loading data into the warehouse are highly technical and require considerable training. While these "back end" structured procedures are always done by BI analysts, "front end" activities such as analysis and publishing are increasingly accomplished by trained end users following simple and intuitive procedures. In general, these front end BI procedures tend to be flexible and interactive, supporting users engaged in dynamic, nonroutine work.

PEOPLE There is no BI, no informing, without people. Two organizations could have very similar data, hardware, software, and procedures, but with different people, they can have vastly different results. One key difference is the knowledge people bring to the informing activity. If a rocket scientist and a high school student visit a vast public library looking for insights about recent advances in propulsion, the rocket scientist will quickly become more informed than the student. While we do not expect that college will make you a rocket scientist about every business topic, the conclusion is fairly clear—the business knowledge you develop at school will significantly affect your ability to use BI to be informed on the job; learn now to inform later.

There are two distinct types of people that use a BI system: end users and BI analysts. In the story at the beginning of the chapter, Ann is an example of a user and Cody is an analyst. Users interact with the output to find patterns in the data; BI systems are designed to help them become informed. Analysts often assist in this process by creating useful output and developing sound procedures for users to follow. However, analysts typically do not possess the business knowledge about the user's subject and must rely on the user for good questions to ask the data. The key is for users and analysts to collaborate effectively.

Key Attributes of BI Information Systems

The key aspects of BI systems include systems that are scalable. Typically, analysis begins with a small set of data, and if the analysis looks promising, the data is expanded. This need to scale makes cloud options particularly appealing. Second, BI software is increasingly easy to use, creating the opportunity for more self-service BI. Third, most BI applications depend on a data warehouse, so businesses must learn to acquire and store data in a different way from their traditional transactional database. Finally, informing is limited by user knowledge and collaboration skills.

Q4. How Do BI Information Systems Support BI Activities?

Business intelligence information systems support the three primary BI activities shown in Figure 11-7: acquiring, analyzing, and publishing data. Here we examine each with particular emphasis on the two types of analyzing called reporting and data mining.

FIGURE 11-7

Business Aspects of BI Activities

Acquiring
Four Subactivities:
Obtain data
Cleanse data
Organize and relate data
Catalog data
Analyzing
Two Types:
Reporting—examples: RFM, OLAP
Data mining—examples: regression, MBA
Publishing
Visualizations
Self-Serve, Digital Dashboard

Acquiring

The first step, acquiring data, means gaining access to data, extracting it, and putting it into a data warehouse. Although it is possible to analyze data in a transactional database, this course is not usually recommended. If the BI analyst makes an error, that error could cause a serious disruption in the company's operations. Also, operational data is structured for fast and reliable transaction processing. It is seldom structured in a way that readily supports BI analysis. Finally, BI analyses can require considerable processing; placing BI applications on operational servers can dramatically reduce system performance.

For these reasons, most organizations extract operational data for BI processing. For a small organization, the extraction may be as simple as a few SQL statements in Access. Larger organizations, however, typically create and staff a group of people who manage and run the data warehouse, which is a facility for managing an organization's BI data. This staff typically executes four sub-activities:

- Obtain data
- Cleanse data
- Organize and relate data
- Catalog data

Analysts obtain data for a data warehouse from several sources, as shown in Figure 11-8. Programs read production and other data and extract, clean, and prepare that data for BI analysis, the second BI activity. The prepared data are stored in a data warehouse using a data warehouse DBMS, which can be different from the organization's operational DBMS. For example, an organization might use Oracle for its operational database but use SQL Server for its data warehouse. Cleaning, organizing, and cataloging data can take considerable time and effort, but if not done well the analysis activity becomes an exercise in garbage in, garbage out.

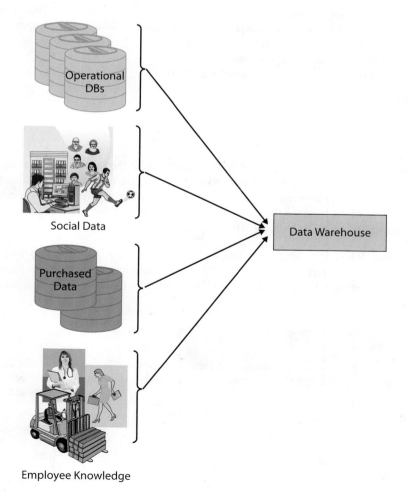

FIGURE 11-8

Obtain Subactivity: Sources of Data for a Data Warehouse

FIGURE 11-9
Purchased Data

- Name, address, phone
- Age
- Gender
- Ethnicity
- Religion
- Income
- Education
- Voter registration
- Home ownership
- Vehicles
- Magazine subscriptions
- Hobbies
- Catalog orders
- Marital status, life stage
- Height, weight, hair and eye color
- Spouse name, birth date
- Children's names and birth dates

As shown in Figure 11-8, data warehouses include data that are purchased from outside sources. The purchase of data about other companies is not unusual or particularly disconcerting from a privacy standpoint. However, companies might choose to buy personal consumer data (e.g., marital status) from data vendors such as Acxiom Corporation. Figure 11-9 lists some of the consumer data that can be readily purchased. An amazing (and, from a privacy standpoint, frightening) amount of data is available.

Analyzing

Once the data is acquired, it needs to be analyzed. It's one thing to have the notes, another to make music. **Analysis** methodically breaks a thing down to examine its details in order to discover or reveal its essential features. Analysis of a BI database breaks down the data to look for patterns in the details. Here we classify the two major types of BI analysis—reporting and data mining—whose differences are highlighted in Figure 11-10.

REPORTING **Reporting** applies simple operations to reveal patterns in the data. The analysis of the data is modest: Data are sorted and grouped, and simple totals and averages are calculated using operations such as sorting, grouping, and summing. The objective of the Reporting process is most often better assessment.

Reporting applications use four basic operations:

- Sorting
- Filtering
- Grouping
- Calculating

None of these operations is particularly sophisticated; they can all be accomplished using SQL and basic HTML or a simple report-writing tool. At times a single operation is the analysis activity; at other times these operations are combined like ingredients in a recipe to create a particular form of analysis for the end user. To whet your appetite, here we present two popular dishes—an RFM analysis and an OLAP slice and dice.

RFM Analysis **RFM** is used to analyze and rank customers according to their purchasing patterns. RFM considers how *recently* (R) a customer has ordered, how *frequently* (F) a customer ordered, and how much *money* (M) the customer has spent. The objective is to assess

FIGURE 11-10

Two Types of Analysis: Reporting and Data Mining

Informing Version	Common Type of Objective	Company in Figure 11-1	Common Analysis	Types
Reporting	Assessment	Target	Simple—summing, totaling	Noninteractive—RFM Interactive—OLAP
Data mining	Prediction	Netflix	Advanced statistics	Cluster Regression Market basket Decision tree Others

Customer	RFM Score
Philly Bikes	1 1 3
Airport Bikes	5 1 1
Ostseerad	5 4 5

FIGURE 11-11

Example of RFM Analysis from CBI

who the best customers are. For example, Best Buy found that 7 percent of its customers were responsible for 43 percent of its sales.[8]

To produce an RFM score as shown in Figure 11-11, the RFM reporting tool first sorts customer purchase records by the date of their most recent (R) purchase. In a common form of this analysis, the tool then divides the customers into five groups and gives customers in each group a score of 1 to 5. The 20 percent of the customers having the most recent orders are given an R score of 1, the 20 percent of the customers having the next most recent orders are given an R score of 2, and so forth, down to the last 20 percent, who are given an R score of 5.

The tool then re-sorts the customers on the basis of how frequently they order. The 20 percent of the customers who order most frequently are given an F score of 1, the next 20 percent of most frequently ordering customers are given a score of 2, and so forth, down to the least frequently ordering customers, who are given an F score of 5.

Finally, the tool sorts the customers again according to the amount spent on their orders. The 20 percent who have ordered the most expensive items are given an M score of 1, the next 20 percent are given an M score of 2, and so forth, down to the 20 percent who spend the least, who are given an M score of 5.

OLAP Slice and Dice Slicing and dicing uses the same basic analysis operations of sorting, grouping, filtering, and calculating, but, as the name implies, the operation is typically repeated. This analysis allows the user to execute these operations interactively; that is, the user or analyst can experiment with one operation, assess the output, and then go back and reanalyze the data. While it is a common way to analyze data, it also is frequently used by analysts to explore a new set of data. An initial exploration of data is always a good first step, as data doesn't talk to strangers.

Slicing and dicing is also referred to as OLAP cube slicing and dicing because the data that is sliced and diced is stored in an OLAP database structure called an info cube. Figure 11-12a shows a CBI info cube with three dimensions—customers, products, and year—and one measure—revenue. A **dimension** is a characteristic or attribute, and a **measure** is a data item of interest that can be

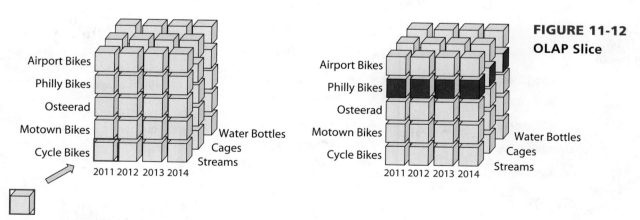

Revenue = $2344.56
for Cycle Bikes sales of Streams in 2011

(a) OLAP cube three dimensions with revenue measure

(b) OLAP cube sliced by Philly Bikes

FIGURE 11-12
OLAP Slice

---

[8] Dave Rich and Jeanne G. Harris, "Why Predictive Analytics Is a Game-Changer," *Forbes,* last modified April 1, 2010, www.forbes.com/2010/04/01/analytics-best-buy-technology-data-companies-10-accenture.html.

FIGURE 11-13
OLAP Dice

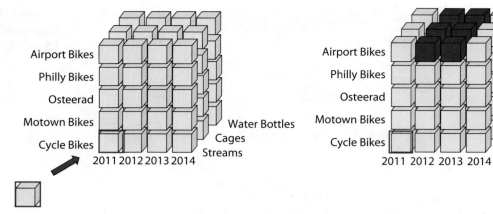

Revenue = $2344.56
for Cycle Bikes sales of Streams in 2011

(a) OLAP cube three dimensions
with revenue measure

(b) OLAP cube diced showing
Airport Bikes for 2012–13
for all three products

summed, averaged, or otherwise processed. At CBI there are other dimensions such as division, warehouse, and salesperson that are available for OLAP analysis, but including all of them in a graphic is not possible in a 3D world.

Slicing removes one dimension. Figure 11-12b shows how the customer Philly Bikes is selected, sliced out in red. A slice is like a filter, filtering out the other customers.

Dicing is similar to slicing except instead of a single row or column being sliced off, a smaller cube is sliced off. As shown in Figure 11-13, the original cube is diced to leave only 2 years—2012 and 2013—one customer—Airport Bikes—and all three products. The analyst here is investigating just a portion of the original data.

Slicing and dicing have two lesser-known siblings (ignored because their names don't rhyme)—drill down and roll up. When a **drill down** operation is done, one cube in the larger cube is isolated and its data analyzed. Figure 11-14a shows the original cube, then one small cube—Cycle Bikes sales of Streams in 2011—is expanded in Figure 11-14b to reveal the revenue by quarter for Cycle Bikes sales of Streams in 2011. A roll up operation is the opposite of drill down—details are combined as in the grouping operation.

The Appendix 11 tutorial uses SAP's popular OLAP analysis tool BO Explorer. In the tutorial, several of the reporting operations described here are demonstrated.

FIGURE 11-14
OLAP Drill Down

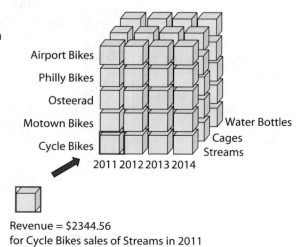

Revenue = $2344.56
for Cycle Bikes sales of Streams in 2011

(a) OLAP cube three dimensions
with revenue measure

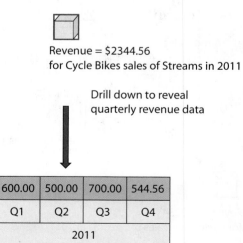

Revenue = $2344.56
for Cycle Bikes sales of Streams in 2011

Drill down to reveal
quarterly revenue data

600.00	500.00	700.00	544.56
Q1	Q2	Q3	Q4
2011			

(b) OLAP cube drill down on
Streams sold to Cycle Bikes
in 2011 by quarter

DATA MINING **Data mining** has the same activities as the Reporting activity. However, in data mining the statistics used are much more sophisticated and complex and the objective is better *prediction*. Prediction is fundamental, as life is lived by looking forward based on the understanding gained from looking backward. Data mining seeks to not only predict a particular event, it more often predicts the likelihood of various outcomes. For example, the data mining used by Netflix generates predictions about the likelihood that a customer will enjoy the recommended movie. Another example of the data mining activity predicts products that tend to be purchased together. In one famous example, data mining determined that customers who buy diapers are also likely to buy beer.

Data mining analysis has been applied to a wide variety of data. Online dating sites use data mining to predict compatible partners, cybersecurity applications look for digital signs to anticipate hacking, social media data mining predicts new customers for businesses, and Google Search uses data mining to predict links that will satisfy your search.

As shown in Figure 11-15, data mining resulted from a convergence of disciplines. Data mining emerged from statistics and mathematics and from artificial intelligence and machine-learning fields in computer science.

One reason CBI implemented the BI component of SAP was to conduct data mining. One example of the usefulness of data mining at CBI was that it improved the Outbound Delivery process. CBI outfitted its fleet of delivery trucks with sensors to track truck location and used the output of the Data Mining process to suggest smart routes to follow to avoid construction, traffic, and stoplights. In another application, CBI partnered with its retail customers to gain access to their sales data. The Data Mining process consolidates this customer data from the various retail outlets into a single data warehouse. Once combined, the data are mined with advanced statistical techniques to spot unusual buying patterns across the industry. These predictive buying patterns help CBI salespeople adjust future delivery dates and delivery options in order to save money for both the retailer and CBI.

Just like reporting, data mining has a variety of techniques. Here we present two examples to give you a better idea of how data mining is done.

Regression   One data mining analysis, which measures the effect of a set of variables on another variable, is called a **regression analysis**. A sample result for the bike company is:

$$\text{Net Sales Next Year} = \$3 \text{ million} + (20 \times \text{GDP growth}) + \text{Net Sales This Year}$$

Using this equation, analysts at CBI can create a prediction of next year's Net Sales. If the economy grows by 2 percent and sales this year were $10 million, then sales next year will be $3 + (20 \times .02) + 10 = \$13.4$ million.

As you will learn in your statistics classes, considerable skill is required to interpret the quality of such a model. The regression tool will create an equation, such as the one shown. Whether that equation is a good predictor of future Net Sales depends on statistical factors, such as t values, confidence intervals, and related statistical techniques.

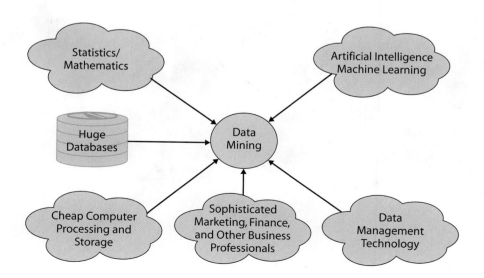

FIGURE 11-15

Convergent Disciplines for Data Mining

MBA Market Basket Analysis At CBI, Sue is well known as the best salesperson at **cross-selling** her customers, or selling her customers items in addition to those they request. Any of CBI's sales associates can fill a customer's order, but Sue is especially good at predicting which products a customer may also buy. She explains how she does it.

"It's simple," she says. "I just ask myself what is the next product they would want to buy. If a small bike shop starts to buy our more expensive touring bikes, I realize that their customers will soon want our more expensive bike tire pumps and handlebar tape."

A **market basket analysis (MBA),** also called an association analysis, predicts cross-selling opportunities. A market basket analysis shows the products that customers tend to buy together. For more details on MBA, see Application Exercise 11-2.

SUPERVISED AND UNSUPERVISED DATA MINING ANALYSIS Data mining analysis can be categorized as unsupervised and supervised. With **unsupervised data mining,** analysts do not create a model or hypothesis before running the analysis. Instead, they apply the data mining software to the data and observe the results. With this method, analysts create hypotheses *after the analysis* in order to explain the patterns found. Another term for unsupervised analysis is *data-driven analysis*. An example of unsupervised data mining is displayed in the opening vignette. Cody and Ann did not create a model that would assess misuse of the network; they jumped into the data without a hypothesis and are attempting to explain misuse after they analyze the data. MBA is also an example of unsupervised data mining. With **supervised data mining,** analysts develop a model *prior to the analysis* and apply statistical analyses to the data to estimate parameters of the model. Regression analysis is an example of supervised data mining.

Publishing

In the previous discussion, we illustrated the power and utility of reporting and data mining analysis. But for BI to be actionable, for it to inform, it must be published to the right user at the right time. In the Publishing activity, the results of the analysis activity are presented. A wide variety of presentations can be published, from simple text to charts and tables to more complex visualizations. Publishing options also include a variety of media. Some output is printed on paper; other output is generated in formats such as PDF files that can be printed or viewed electronically. Output can also be delivered to computer screens and smartphones.

A **visualization,** or simply viz, is an image or diagram that communicates a data pattern in a highly readable format. One classic viz is an electoral map that uses color to show the party of the candidate leading in the poll. An example is Figure 11-16, which shows counties and the concentration of Democrat and Republican voters. Other recent, well-known examples of visualizations include infographics and stock market displays that show rising stocks in one color

FIGURE 11-16
Electoral Map Visualization

Source: Chris Howard (http://www.SaltwaterWitch.com) based on U.S. census data and the 2012 election maps created by Mark Newman (http://www.personal.umich.edu/~mejn).

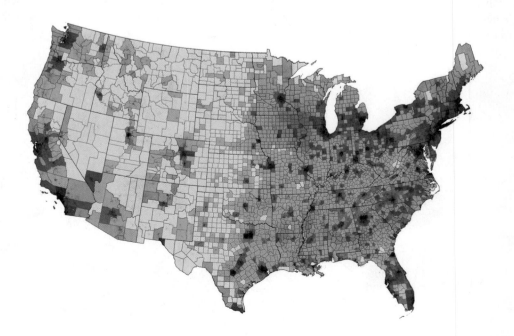

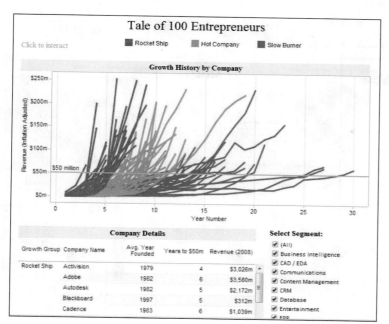

FIGURE 11-17

Example Tableau Visualization

Source: www.tableausoftware.com/
public/gallery/taleof100

and declining stocks in another. Increasingly, these vizs include options to filter the data, drill down on it, or interact with it in some other way. These advances in interactivity promote end user self-service and make it easier for users to inform themselves. As a result, expect demand for interactive visualizations to expand.

A very popular software choice for interactive visualizations is Tableau; a Tableau viz is shown in Figure 11-17.[9] That visualization shows the 100 largest software companies and their growth in sales up to the current year. Each line is color-coded for the speed of its growth; some companies were rocket ships, and others were slow burners. A user can click on a company line to drill down and see more details. On the right, notice the Select Segment filter, which allows the user to slice the 100-company set into particular segments like Business Intelligence or CRM. Tableau has also recently provided users the option to share their output by providing a clip of html code for a blog or Web site, much like YouTube provides a bit of code to embed a video on other sites. Using this feature, you can publish a viz about your fantasy sports team and post it on a blog where your friends could click on it and re-analyze the data and publish their own output. When you update your data on the Tableau server, all your friends' visualizations are updated.

One type of visualization is a **digital dashboard,** or simply dashboard, which is a viz customized for a particular user. Vendors such as Yahoo! and MSN provide common examples. Users of these services can define content they want—say, a local weather forecast, a list of stock prices, or a list of news sources—and the vendor constructs the display output customized for each user. Figure 11-18 shows an example of an SAP-generated dashboard. Dashboards are frequently used to monitor business processes and indicate abnormal conditions with clear signs such as red lights or gauges.

Q5. How Can BI Information Systems Support Business Processes?

Having considered the activities of a generic BI process and how BI information systems support these activities, here we consider specific business processes that rely on business intelligence IS. At the beginning of the chapter we gave two examples of processes that use BI systems: Target's New Customer Promotion process and Netflix's Movie Recommendation process. Here we expand on that list. Figure 11-19 lists a variety of the business processes supported by BI systems.

---

[9] Visit and interact with this viz at *http://blogs.wsj.com/venturecapital/2009/08/25/how-long-does-it-take-to-build-a-technology-empire/.*

FIGURE 11-18

Example SAP Dashboard

Source: www.sdn.sap.com/irj/scn/
index?rid=/library/uuid/40245c5e-767d-
2e10-e4b2-c779cf05d753

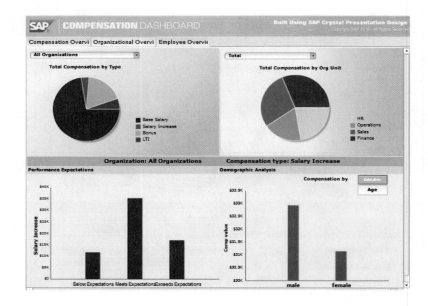

Supporting Existing Processes with BI Information Systems

To provide insight about the value of BI for business processes, we choose four of the processes in Figure 11-19 to present in more detail; these are shown in Figure 11-20. As you read, please notice the variety of processes supported by BI and the benefits that can result.

DECISION MAKING The **Decision Making process** is the selection of a choice among available options and can be done individually or in a group. It is one of the most frequently occurring processes in organizations. BI systems support the Decision Making process by acquiring data and providing analysis and publication software. One way to see the impact of BI on decision making is to examine the impact of Google Instant Search on your decision making. Google has acquired one of the largest databases ever created—links and keywords for billions of pages, stored in a database called an **index**. As you type keywords into the Google search box, the search string is analyzed and compared to the index and suggested terms are published for your decision. By using Instant Search, you save an average of 2.5 seconds per search, which amounts to a worldwide savings of 11 hours per second every second. What's more, the search is very accurate—using Google's predicted terms, you more often find what you seek.

KNOWLEDGE MANAGEMENT The **Knowledge Management (KM) process** in an organization creates value from intellectual capital and shares that knowledge with employees, managers, suppliers, customers, and others. For example, hospital employees can have a great deal of

FIGURE 11-19

Business Processes Supported by Business Intelligence IS

Business Processes Supported by BI Information System
Communication
Decision making
Knowledge management
Cybersecurity
Project management
Promotion
Branding
Product design
Next Best Offer
Sales
Health care and services
Fraud detection
Athlete assessment

Process	Example	Objective	Predict or Assess	Data Acquired
Decision Making	Google Instant Search	Faster, more accurate	Predict	Google's index of sites, keywords
Knowledge Management	Hospital billing	More correct billing	Assess	Data from prior bills
Next Best Offer (NBO)	Tesco	Increase redemption rates	Predict	Customer history, preferences, context
Online Sales	B2C site	Better conversion rate	Predict	Clicks, views, transactions

FIGURE 11-20

Example Processes Supported by BI Information Systems

knowledge about submitting insurance claims, but most of this knowledge is spread out among the employees, stored in the minds of healthcare professionals, and is not in data that can be analyzed. Without an effective KM process, hospital employees completing new insurance claims often fail to get it right the first time. Using BI, the hospital can acquire and store the knowledge of experienced employees. Later, this data can be analyzed as new claims are completed to improve the likelihood that claims are done right the first time. A hospital may decide to acquire and store knowledge about claim procedures in a wiki format. Another way to store knowledge data is an **expert system**, a rule-based system that acquires and stores human knowledge in the form of **if/then rules**. Such rules are statements that specify *if* a particular condition exists, *then* to take some action.

NEXT BEST OFFER (NBO) The **NBO process** is a targeted offer or proposed action for customers based on the data patterns in the customer's history and preferences, context, and attributes of the product or service.[10] The objective is to more accurately predict the percentage of customers who will accept the offer. An accurate prediction is essential. If you are too generous, too many customers accept and you lose money; if you are not generous enough, customers don't accept and you're stuck holding extra inventory. Businesses made NBOs for years before BI, but with BI, companies can more accurately predict the rate that offers will be accepted. For example, the UK retailer Tesco improved its NBO process by integrating BI data it has acquired about customer preferences. The result was redemption rates by its customers from 8 to 14 percent, which is four to seven times higher than traditional NBOs.

ONLINE SALES Retailers can improve their Online Sales process with BI. A key activity of the Online Sales process is acquiring customer data. This data might include which browser the visitor is using, the visitor's IP address, and whether the user eventually purchased from the site. Before BI, B2C businesses had to write their own code to acquire and analyze this type of data. Enter Google Analytics, mentioned in Chapter 8. Google Analytics is a powerful BI software for Web site owners to store and analyze site traffic data. This data includes the data mentioned earlier as well as where the customer came from (e.g., from a search engine or another site), the type of device being used, where the customer visited in the site, and the **conversion rate,** which is the ratio of the number of customers who eventually purchased divided by the number who visited. BI salespeople can analyze this type of data and predict useful changes to the site to increase conversion rates. One analysis technique is **A/B testing**, also called split testing. Using this technique, site developers build two identical pages, say two shopping cart pages. Page A shows a navigation menu across the top, whereas on Page B the same menu is on the left border of the screen. When visitors come to the site, they are randomly given either A or B, and the conversion rate for the two pages is analyzed to determine the better page.

---

[10] Thomas Davenport, *Enterprise Analytics* (New York: FT Press, 2013).

New Process	Example	Objective	Predict or Assess	Data Acquired
Airplane ETA	Airlines	More accurate arrival time	Predict	Prior arrivals GPS
Energy Conservation	Homes	Increase conservation	Assess	Electrical use

FIGURE 11-21

Examples of New Processes Supported by BI Information Systems

Supporting New Processes with BI Information Systems

As was our habit in previous chapters, we also examine new processes supported by BI information systems. These are processes that could not exist without modern BI. One example is the Player Assessment process for professional athletes, as depicted in the recent movie *Moneyball*. There are many examples of new processes. Here we consider two, as shown in Figure 11-21.

ETA ESTIMATION Airplane arrival time predictions are very important to airlines. Airlines need to be able to predict an accurate arrival time at the gate—if they get surprised by an early arrival, the plane sits there at the gate with hundreds of frustrated prisoners; if it is later than expected, the ground crew wastes time waiting for it and the airline cannot use that gate. In the old days, the process of estimating ETA was based on pilot estimates—pilots would use the airplane's radio and call in their estimated arrival time at the gate. Now PASSUR Aerospace provides a service called RightETA. PASSUR acquired data from years of airplane arrivals to each runway at all the major airports, including GPS location data, weather, winds, ground traffic congestion, and other magic ingredients. Analyzing the data, it continually creates an incredibly accurate prediction of an arrival time based on the current location of a plane. The savings is estimated to be several million dollars per year at major airports.

ENERGY CONSERVATION Public utilities are also using BI to help homeowners reduce energy consumption. In Dubuque, Iowa, 1,200 households volunteered for a pilot project sponsored by the city and its BI partner IBM. IBM designed energy meters that are placed on dishwashers, hair dryers, water heaters, and other devices in the house to show the energy cost for each device in real time. In the past, residents were given data on energy use only at the end of the month. Now the data is continuously published, and with better intelligence homeowners can reduce energy use and help Dubuque become a more sustainable city.

In this question, we wanted to highlight the central role of BI in a variety of business processes. We intentionally picked processes that use BI in new or particularly clever ways. When you work in an organization, you'll see other less flashy but helpful ways that BI supports processes.

Q6. What Is a Big Data BI System, and How Is It Used?

Earlier, we hinted that the size of databases that businesses are acquiring and analyzing is growing. In nearly all industries in the U.S. economy, companies with more than 1,000 employees are sitting on 200 terabytes of data.[11] Applying BI activities to large datasets is called Big Data, a $5 billion-a-year industry that is expected to exceed $50 billion by 2017.[12] Business is not the only source of growth for Big Data BI, as governments also use it to spot tax evasion and fight terrorism, healthcare agencies use it to better understand diseases, and scientists use it to analyze the human genome. Here we examine the characteristics of Big Data information systems, their techniques, and the business processes they support.

Big Data is a term used to describe data collections that are characterized by huge *volume*, rapid *velocity*, and great *variety*:

- Big Data datasets are at least a petabyte in size, and usually larger.
- Big Data is generated rapidly or accessed rapidly.
- Big Data has structured data, free-form text, log files, and possibly graphics, audio, and video.

[11] James Manyika et al., "Big Data: The Next Frontier for Innovation, Competition, and Productivity," *McKinsey Global Institute,* last modified May 2011, www.mckinsey.com/mgi/publications/big_data/index.asp.

[12] John Furrier, "Big Data Is Creating the Future—It's a $50 Billion Market," *Forbes,* last modified February 29, 2012, www.forbes.com/sites/siliconangle/2012/02/29/big-data-is-creating-the-future-its-a-50-billion-market/.

Volume refers to the size of the database, typically a petabyte or larger in size. The size of Big Data systems can be mind numbing—terabytes and petabytes. To appreciate the enormity of these sizes, consider these quantities in seconds, mega seconds, and tera seconds. A mega second, or 1,000,000 seconds, is 11 days. A giga second would be 32 years, a tera second 32,000 years, and a petasec 32 million years.

The velocity of the data is the rate at which the data is created or accessed. For Google's Instant Search to be useful, the search terms entered by a user must be applied to the data warehouse very quickly, and the response must also be rapid.

Finally, the variety of data addresses the diversity of the data. For example, in many large datasets it is common to define dates in different formats, to have different rules about missing data values, and to include free-form text and audio, video, and graphic data as well. This type of data is called unstructured data.

Compared to routine-size databases, Big Data IS differ not only in data but software too. BI software in Big Data applications often must divide the data and processing steps into many smaller tasks and assign those tasks to different servers. As a result, BI software must be adept at balancing the load it places on the hardware.

A little history on Big Data. About 10 years ago, Amazon.com determined that relational database technology wouldn't meet its needs, and it developed a nonrelational data store called Dynamo. Meanwhile, for many of the same reasons, Google developed a nonrelational data store called Bigtable. Facebook took concepts from both of the systems and developed a third nonrelational data store call Cassandra. In 2008, Facebook turned Cassandra over to the open source community. Such nonrelational databases have come to be called **NoSQL databases**, where NoSQL means nonrelational databases that support very high transaction rates processing relatively simple data structures replicated on many servers in the cloud. NoSQL is not the best term; NotRelationalDatabases would have been better, but the die has been cast.

MapReduce Technique

Because Big Data is huge, fast, and varied, it cannot be processed using traditional techniques. **MapReduce** is a technique for harnessing the power of thousands of computers working in parallel. The basic idea is that the Big Data collection is broken into pieces, and hundreds or thousands of independent processors search these pieces for something of interest. That process is referred to as the *Map* phase. In Figure 11-22, for example, a dataset having the logs of Google searches is broken into pieces, and each independent processor is instructed to search for and count search keywords. This figure, of course, shows just a small portion of the data; here you can see a portion of the keywords that begin with *H*.

As the processors finish, their results are combined in what is referred to as the *Reduce* phase. The result is a list of all the terms searched for on a given day and the count of each. The process is considerably more complex than described here, but this is the gist of the idea.

Hadoop is an open source program supported by the Apache Foundation[13] that implements MapReduce on potentially thousands of computers. Hadoop could drive the process of finding and counting the Google search terms, but Google uses its own proprietary version of MapReduce to do so instead.

Hadoop began as part of Cassandra, but the Apache Foundation split it off to become its own product. Hadoop is written in Java and originally ran on Linux; at this writing, Microsoft is reported to be implementing it on Windows Server as well. Amazon.com supports Hadoop as part of its EC3 cloud offering.

SAP HANA Technique

Recently, SAP introduced **SAP HANA,** its solution for Big Data. HANA is an in-memory database that is exceptionally fast. Traditional database systems as well as MapReduce systems keep data in secondary storage and access it via SQL statements. However, these trips to and from secondary storage slow down database operations. SAP built HANA to eliminate these trips, as it keeps everything it needs in memory.

In sum, Big Data systems use two techniques to cope with huge datasets. With MapReduce, it divides tasks to many servers; and with SAP HANA, it uses a solid state memory device.

---

[13] A nonprofit corporation that supports open source software projects, originally those for the Apache Web server, but today for a large number of additional major software projects.

FIGURE 11-22
MapReduce

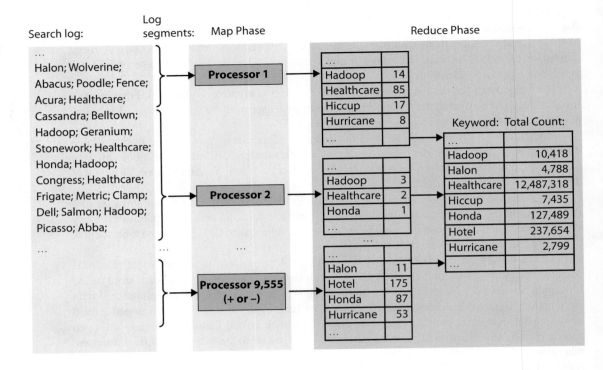

Processes Supported by Big Data BI IS

Like traditional BI IS, Big Data systems support a wide variety of business processes. Here we will briefly examine several of the processes, which are shown in Figure 11-23.

CONTINUOUS AUDITING The **Auditing process** is the official, unbiased examination of an organization's financial accounts. Traditionally, to execute an audit, the audit team would select a sample of financial transactions over a recent period of time and examine these transactions for unusual activity. With Big Data, this process no longer needs to sample a subset of transactions; it can examine every transaction. Not only can all the transactions be evaluated, the audit can happen in real time as the transactions are occurring, not at the end of a month or year. If discrepancies are occurring, a real-time assessment can identify them. In addition, with Big Data the analysis can be much more sophisticated; the number and variety of unusual patterns that can be evaluated are much greater than before.

COUNTERTERRORISM Most of the examples here are about business organizations, but government agencies also have processes that are supported by BI. Government agencies use BI like business organizations to bill citizens (taxation), analyze cyber security, predict revenues and costs, improve service, and quicken response. Governments also have unique processes that Big Data systems support such as law enforcement, polling, and counterterrorism. Counterterrorism

Processes	Example	Objective	Predict of Assess	Data Acquired
Continuous Auditing	Audit firm	Use more sophisticated analysis on all transactions as they occur	Assess	All transactions
Counterterrorism	Government	Accurately predict terror behavior	Predict	Government agency data on individuals
Cancer Treatment	Health	More successful treatment plan	Predict	DNA genome of patients and cancers

FIGURE 11-23
Business Processes Supported by Big Data BI

processes supported by Big Data technologies help connect data in information silos hoarded by different government agencies. The result is a faster and more complete analysis of data to spot patterns that predict possible terrorist activity.

CANCER TREATMENT Big Data can improve the treatment of some forms of cancer.[14] With Big Data, a patient who has recently been diagnosed with cancer can undergo DNA testing, and the patient's DNA data and cancer cell genome data can be collected and analyzed. This data can then be compared to the data from other patients who were previously diagnosed with a similar type of cancer. If near matches are found, successful treatment sequences can be used for the new patient. This will help doctors prescribe better treatments for their patients. Not only can the treatment process be improved, but treatment can be started earlier; the process of creating a genetic map of a patient used to take 2 days, but now with Big Data systems it can be done in 20 minutes.

Big Data is here to stay as more and more businesses learn how to use it to enhance their processes. We can also expect that today's Big Data will be tomorrow's Routine Data and tomorrow's Big Data will be hundreds and thousands of times larger. But while the size of the data will continue to grow, the fundamental lesson remains the same: information systems improve business processes. Size does not change the fundamental lesson, nor does it change the fundamental challenges; we describe these next.

Q7. How Do Businesses Manage the Risks of Business Intelligence?

Although the discussion in this chapter may have helped clarify the benefits of using a BI system, some of its problems may not be easy to see. Each of the BI components can have problems, and here we focus on the two most challenging: problems with data and problems with people.

Data Problems

Unfortunately, most operational and purchased data have problems that inhibit their usefulness for business intelligence. Figure 11-24 lists the major problem categories.

DIRTY DATA AND MISSING VALUES Problematic data are termed **dirty data**. Examples are a value of *B* for customer gender or *213* for customer age. These values can be problematic for BI purposes. In addition, purchased data often contain *missing* elements. Most data vendors state the percentage of missing values for each attribute in the data they sell. An organization buys such data because for some uses, some data are better than no data at all. This is especially true for data items whose values are difficult to obtain, such as the number of adults in a household, household income, dwelling type, and the education of the primary income earner. For BI applications, though, a few missing or erroneous data points can be worse than no data at all because they bias the analysis.

DATA NOT INTEGRATED—DATA SILOS Another problem is nonintegrated data. A particular BI analysis might require data from an ERP system, an e-commerce system, and a social networking application. Analysts might want to integrate that organizational data with purchased consumer data. Such a data collection will likely have relationships that are not represented in primary key/foreign key relationships. It is the function of personnel in the data warehouse to integrate such data somehow.

Nonintegrated data may also be the result of information silos within the organization. As shown in Figure 11-25, one silo may have BI data for Process 1, and another silo may have BI data for Process 2. With this situation, BI analysts and users must learn to use many different databases in order to do analysis. By consolidating BI data in one location, as shown at the bottom of Figure 11-25, each BI process can be more efficient.

Dirty data and missing values
Data not integrated—data silos
Wrong granularity

FIGURE 11-24

Common Data Problems in BI

---

[14] Derek Klobucher, "Big Data Can Save Lives—If Culture and Strategy Let It," *Forbes,* last modified February 21, 2013, www.forbes.com/sites/sap/2013/02/21/big-data-can-save-lives-if-culture-and-strategy-let-it/.

FIGURE 11-25
Integrating BI Data

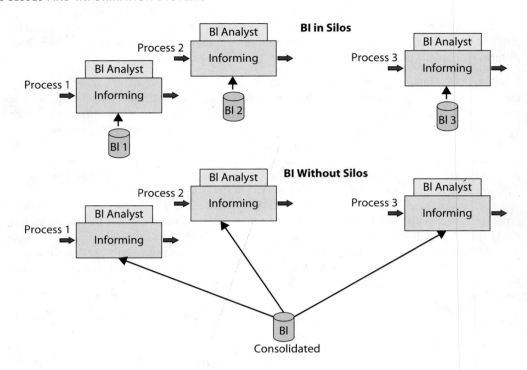

WRONG GRANULARITY Finally, data can also have the wrong **granularity**. Granularity is the level of detail of the data, and it can be too fine or too coarse. For the former, suppose we want to analyze the placement of graphics and controls on an order entry Web page. It is possible to capture the customers' clicking behavior in what is termed **clickstream data**. In the middle of the clickstream are data for clicks on the news, email, instant chat, and weather. Although all of that data may be useful for a study of consumer computer behavior, it will be overwhelming if all we want to know is how customers respond to an ad located differently on the screen. To proceed, the data analysts must throw away millions and millions of clicks. Data can also be too coarse. For example, a file of order totals cannot be used for a market basket analysis. For a market basket analysis, we need to know which items were purchased with which others. In general, it is better to have too fine a granularity than too coarse. If the granularity is too fine, the data can be made coarser by summing and grouping. If the granularity is too coarse, however, there is no way to separate the data into constituent parts.

People Problems

People problems fall into three categories: users, analysts, and leaders, as shown in Figure 11-26. Each group of people present unique challenges.

USERS User resistance is a common malady of all information systems, and BI is no exception. Users resist a BI system for a number of reasons—it may change their job, require knowledge the user does not have, or distract them from their primary work. A second problem is that an impressive visualization can be like putting lipstick on a pig; users may be entranced by the sophistication of the viz without realizing the underlying data is fairly meaningless.

A third type of user problem is that users may underestimate the cost of producing a BI report. It is difficult to identify accurately all the costs associated with a BI project. As a result, one or two users may consume too much of the BI analyst's time. They may believe that a particular dashboard or analysis is essential but may change their mind if accurate cost data were available.

Problems can also creep in when users do not understand the statistical operations done in the analysis activity. Some mistakes are unintentional and reflect a lack of understanding the data or the statistics and the assumptions behind them. But some mistakes may be intentional as users and analysts try to bend the analysis to support their conclusion. They decide before the analysis what the statistics should say, and they torture the data until it says what they want to hear.

ANALYSTS BI analysts also contribute their own share of problems. Analysts have a hard time saying, "Enough." Many BI projects have no obvious or convenient stopping point. Rather, the

Category	Output Problem
Users	User resistance, sophistication of viz may hide meaninglessness of results, underestimate cost of reports, unintentional and intentional mistakes
Analysts	No stopping point, asking wrong questions
Leaders	Unspecified scope, inadequate funding or staffing, limited statistical understanding, overselling results

FIGURE 11-26

BI People Problems: Users, Analysts, and Leaders

analyst might think, "Just one more week of experimenting with this data or one more run with this new model, and I'll have it." While engaged on the project, it is very hard to know if the project will turn out to be a resource black hole or an informational holy grail.

Another problem with BI systems is asking the wrong questions. Clearly some of the questions being asked at CBI in the opening scenario about worker productivity are not good questions. Oftentimes, the poor questions are due to a lack of understanding of the process by the analyst. While poor questions lead to poor results, every BI success involves valuable questions.

MIS InClass 11

I Know That, I Think

Set a lower and an upper bound for each of the following 10 questions. For example, if the question was "What is the age of President Obama?" you might think the answer is about 45, so you would set a lower bound of 40 and an upper bound of 50. Make your lower and upper bounds reasonable estimates, but make sure they are wide enough so you get 9 of the 10 questions correct. You are not allowed to use any help on this exercise. Once you have answered these questions, your instructor will tell you the correct answers.

Source: Sergejs Rahunoks/Fotolia

	Lower Bound	Upper Bound	Question
1.	_____	_____	What is the height of the Empire State Building?
2.	_____	_____	In what year was former President Reagan born?
3.	_____	_____	What is the length of the longest overland tunnel in the world?
4.	_____	_____	What is the current national circulation of *The Wall Street Journal*?
5.	_____	_____	What is the population of Australia?
6.	_____	_____	What is the distance between Atlanta and Dallas?
7.	_____	_____	How many books are in the Library of Congress?
8.	_____	_____	How many countries are there in the world?
9.	_____	_____	How many steps does the Washington Monument have?
10.	_____	_____	What year did Julius Caesar die?

As a class, discuss the following questions:

1. Why did you set your boundaries where you did?
2. What does your score on this exercise suggest?
3. Which Informing process (Reporting or Data Mining) would have improved your answers?

A wise person once said that questions are more important than answers. You will be rewarded in the future for asking good questions, so please take every opportunity to practice that skill while you are still in school.

LEADERS The last group of people we consider here are the leaders of the organization. Leaders may not provide adequate objectives to BI projects, they may inadequately fund them, and they may not adequately staff them. Another problem is that they may not understand the statistics used in the analysis or the assumptions that the analyst had to make, causing the leaders to misinterpret or overstate the results. Leaders can also contribute to BI pushback by overselling the potential of a BI system. BI will not often transform a business with a shocking finding. More often, BI confirms intuition and leads to steady improvements in processes, such as packing trucks more efficiently, rescheduling robot forklifts, and tweaking pricing algorithms.

To conclude, most of the risks of BI systems can be attributed to either data or people. While most of this chapter identified the virtues of using BI, knowing the risks may be more valuable to you. Being able to help your future business identify sources of difficulty will be greatly appreciated.

Q8. How Does SAP Do BI?

Like all ERP systems, SAP consolidates operational data in an OLTP database. Data from the OLTP or from other sources can be extracted and placed into the SAP OLAP database, which SAP calls a data warehouse, or Business Warehouse (BW). Once in the warehouse, the data is formed into information cubes like the one shown in Figure 11-12.

SAP offers a wide variety of applications to analyze data stored in information cubes. One popular set of SAP analysis tools is called **Business Objects (BOBJ)**. One BOBJ tool, Explorer, is used in the tutorial in Appendix 11. SAP also offers a number of other analysis packages; one of its most recent, Predictive Analysis, is also one of the most sophisticated.

A company that implements SAP can also choose to write program code to accomplish specific tasks that SAP does not provide. Approximately 95 percent of this program code is devoted to creating company-specific BI reports.

SAP and the other ERP vendors also make it possible to analyze data with software from other companies. One common method is to download data from SAP data warehouses into an Excel file and then use Excel to analyze the data. We provide data from CBI for analysis in Excel in Application Exercise 7-1 at the end of the textbook.

If Ann at CBI wants to analyze the financial transactions in the SAP database, she has three general options. As just mentioned, she can learn to download data to Excel and conduct the analysis herself. She could also analyze the data using software provided from SAP like BOBJ Explorer, or she could request from Cody and the IT department a specific report or dashboard that summarizes the data that she specifies.

Q9. 2024?

BI use will continue to expand as display technologies improve and Big Data matures. We believe three factors will affect this growth: mobile devices, unstructured data sources, and real-time use.

Mobile Devices

One trend that will affect BI is the trend in business toward mobile devices. BI was born in the era of laptop and desktop machines. As mobile devices grow in output sophistication and computing power, BI will increasingly be done on smartphones and tablets. For example, smartphones equipped with a cheap hardware appliance can evaluate blood samples in field clinics. The mobile device can conduct sophisticated statistical analysis of the blood and provide users interactive diagnostic tools if the blood sample has anomalies.

Not only will mobile devices be used to analyze and publish results, they will also create enormous volumes of location data for businesses and governments to acquire. By evaluating text messages and phone locations, BI researchers are already able to pinpoint flu outbreaks, the movement of political ideas, the loneliness of individuals, and the eating habits of users.[15] Another mobile

---

[15] Robert Hotz, "The Really Smart Phone," *Wall Street Journal*, April 23, 2011.

platform, drones, will also affect BI. Drones will provide businesses and governments new opportunities to acquire data on vehicle traffic, weather patterns, and agricultural production.

Unstructured Data

The recent trend of using unstructured data will continue and provide new opportunities. Current estimates suggest that only 5 percent of data used in BI is structured.[16] To demonstrate the potential of BI to use unstructured data, IBM built Watson, an autonomous BI system that could sift through 4 terabytes of data of structured and unstructured data to answer questions on the game show *Jeopardy!*[17] Watson proved to be very successful, defeating expert *Jeopardy!* contestants. Other Big Data systems will follow in Watson's footsteps—learning how to find patterns in unstructured data such as recorded conversations, written documents, videos of customer behavior, and images from drones. One Watson wannabe may be your next smartphone; it will use unstructured data to locate itself using visual cues, tell you what is in every building it sees, and share facts with you about every animal, tree, and person it sees or hears.

Real-Time Use

BI will also support rapid growth in real-time applications. Credit card companies will want to improve their ability to detect unusual card use on the spot and require you to personally verify the purchase on the telephone or in some other way before it will accept the charge. In medicine, smart scalpels will allow real-time analysis of cancer cells so surgeons can ensure that all the cancerous cells are removed during an operation.

Technology Backlash

As more data are collected on customers by credit card companies and social media sites, the usefulness of BI will continue to grow. This anticipated growth in data about individual financial and personal behavior may lead to a privacy backlash. **Privacy** is commonly defined as controlling how one's personal information is acquired and analyzed. In Chapter 10, we discussed privacy and social media conflicts; with BI, we can see that privacy concerns extend beyond social media and may affect many business processes that use customer data.

Earlier we discussed the benefits of BI for Target's New Customer process. However, after about a year of success for this program, a man in Minneapolis walked into a Target store and complained to the manager that his high school daughter got Target coupons for baby clothes and cribs. According to the father, his daughter was not pregnant and he did not appreciate Target's invasion of her privacy. The manager expressed regret at the obvious oversight. A few days later, the man called back and apologized. His daughter was, in fact, pregnant. Many people do not want organizations to know more about them, their likes and dislikes, than their parents and their friends.

That said, we all should be aware that we are walking, talking data generators as we use our mobile devices, shop online, participate in social media, and use credit cards and healthcare services. When employees at CBI use the network, they are generating data for Cody and Ann to analyze. Employee and customer data are sure to be very useful for a number of businesses. But exactly how this data will be used for business purposes and how it will be used legally versus illegally has yet to be worked out. Finding common ground between privacy and BI will be a constant challenge.

Privacy tensions will create a technology backlash, and so too will concerns about machines becoming smarter. Machine learning is similar to BI, except rather than people becoming informed, machines are informed; using this information, the machines learn and adapt. For example, Google used machine learning to create the world's best spell checker from the poor keyword spelling we provided.[18]

Machines work faster than humans, and they work 24/7. At some point, will machines know so much about us that we are incapable of understanding the results? What happens when, because of complexity, such BI machines can only communicate with other BI machines? What happens when machines can direct their own BI activities? There will be an accelerating positive feedback loop among the BI machines. Then what will they know about us? Is it important that at that date we will lack the capacity to know what the machines will know?

---

[16] Boris Evelson, "Data Discovery and Exploration: IBM Acquires Vivisimo," *Forrester,* last modified April 25, 2012, http://blogs.forrester.com/boris_evelson/12-04-25-data_discovery_and_exploration_ibm_acquires_vivisimo.

[17] Joab Jackson, "IBM Watson Vanquishes Human Jeopardy Foes," *PC World,* last modified February 16, 2011, www.pcworld.com/article/219893/ibm_watson_vanquishes_human_jeopardy_foes.html.

[18] "Clicking for Gold," *The Economist* Special Report, February 25, 2010.

Ethics Guide

Unseen Cyberazzi

A **data broker** or data aggregator is a company that acquires and purchases consumer and other data from public records, retailers, Internet cookie vendors, social media trackers, and other sources and uses it to create business intelligence that it sells to companies and the government. Two of the prominent data brokers are Datalogix and Acxiom Corporation.

Data brokers gather vast amounts of data. According to *The New York Times*, as of June 2012, Acxiom Corporation had used 23,000 servers to process data of 50 trillion transactions on 500 million consumers. It stores more than 15,000 data points on some consumers.

So, what does it do with all this data? If you buy pizza online on Friday nights, but only if you can get a substantial discount, a data broker (or the broker's customer) knows to send you a discount pizza coupon Friday morning. If you use a customer loyalty card at your local grocery store and regularly buy, say, large bags of potato chips, the data broker or its customer will send you coupons for more potato chips or for a second snack product that is frequently purchased by potato chip consumers.

Federal law provides strict limits on gathering and using medical and credit data. For other data, however, the possibilities are unlimited. In theory, data brokers enable you to view the data that is stored about you, but in practice it is difficult to learn how to request your data. Further, the process for doing so is torturous, and ultimately, the data that is released is limited to innocuous data such as your name, phone numbers, and current and former addresses. Without an easy means for viewing all of your data, it is impossible to verify its accuracy.

Of even greater concern, however, is the unknown processing of such data. What business intelligence techniques are employed by these companies? What are the accuracy and reliability of those techniques? If the data broker errs in predicting that you'll buy a pizza on Friday night, who cares? But if the data broker errs in predicting that you're a terrorist, it matters. Data brokers are silent on these questions.

DISCUSSION QUESTIONS

1. We've used Kant's categorical imperative as one criterion for assessing ethical behavior: Act as if you would have your behavior be a universal law. As a litmus test of this principle, we've said that if you're willing to publish your behavior on Facebook, then your behavior conforms to the categorical imperative.
   a. Consider the inverse of that litmus test. Is it true that if you're not willing to publish your behavior on Facebook, it is unethical? (You might find it easier to consider this question in a different but equivalent form: Your behavior is ethical if and only if you're willing to publish it on Facebook.)
   b. Considering your answer to question a, if data brokers are unwilling to say what data they are collecting and how they are processing it, is it reasonable to conclude their behavior is unethical? Explain your answer.
2. Using business intelligence applied to consumer purchasing data for targeted marketing seems innocuous enough. However, is it? Using both the categorical imperative (page 20) and utilitarianism (page 40) perspectives, assess the ethics of the following:
   a. Some people, whether from genetic factors, habit, lack of education, or other factors, are prone to overeating junk food. By focusing junk food sales offers at this market segment, data brokers or their customers are promoting obesity. Is their behavior ethical?
   b. Data brokers claim they can reliably infer ethnicity from consumer behavior data. Suppose they also determine that one ethnic group is more likely to attend college than others. Accordingly, they focus the marketing for college-prep materials, scholarships, and university admissions applications on this ethnic group. Over time, that group will be guided into positive (assuming you believe college is positive) decisions that other groups will not. Is this behavior different from ethnic profiling? Is it ethical?
3. Suppose a data broker correctly identifies that your grandmother is addicted to playing online hearts. From its business intelligence, it knows that frequent-hearts-players are strong prospects for online gambling. Accordingly, the data broker refers your grandmother's data to an online gambling vendor, one of its customers. Grandma gets hooked and loses all of her savings, including money earmarked for your college tuition.
   a. Is the data broker's behavior ethical?
   b. Assume the data broker says, "Look, it's not us, it's our customer, the online gambling vendor, that's

Source: Sergey Nivens/Shutterstock

causing the problem." Does the broker's posture absolve it of moral responsibility for Grandma's losses?

c. Is the online gambling vendor's behavior ethical?

d. Assume the online gambling vendor says, "Look, it's not us; it's Grandma. We provide fair and honest games. If Grandma likes to play games where the odds of winning are low, talk to Grandma." Assume in your answer that the gaming company has gone to great lengths to provide the elderly with an emotionally rewarding user experience for games with low winning odds. Does the vendor's posture absolve it of any moral responsibility for Grandma's losses?

e. Assuming your grandmother promised you tuition payments, is her behavior ethical?

4. If all of your behavior is ethical, then, according to the categorical imperative, you are willing to have your life story published on Facebook. Thus, you needn't be concerned about the data and business intelligence created about you. However, consider the following:

a. Suppose, as the most junior member of a club, you are required to purchase beer for your club's bimonthly beer fest. To obtain a substantial discount from the vendor, you use your customer loyalty card for these purchases. A data aggregator obtains your purchase history and classifies you as a heavy drinker. Unknown to you, the data aggregator informs your medical insurance company of its classification. Your insurance premiums increase and you never

know why. Using either the categorical imperative or utilitarianism, is there an ethical problem here?

b. Do you think something should be done to reduce the likelihood of situations like that in question a? If so, what?

c. Suppose you have a personal medical problem that you wish to keep private. Your condition requires you to purchase a particular set of off-the-shelf products from the pharmacy at your grocery store. A data aggregator observes your purchasing pattern, infers your problem, and sends you coupons and other promotional products that clearly identify your condition. Against your strongest wishes, your roommates become aware of your medical problem. Using either the categorical imperative or utilitarianism, is there an ethical problem here?

d. Do you think something should be done to reduce the likelihood of situations like that in question c? If so, what?

5. According to the Privacy Act of 1974, the U.S. Government is prohibited from storing many types of data about U.S. citizens. The act does not, however, prohibit it from purchasing business intelligence from data brokers. If the government purchases business intelligence that is based, in part, on data that it is prohibited from storing, is the government's behavior ethical? Use both the categorical imperative and utilitarianism perspectives in your answer.

Active Review

Use this Active Review to verify that you understand the material in the chapter. You can read the entire chapter and then perform the tasks in this review, or you can read the text material for just one question and perform the tasks in this review for that question before moving on to the next one.

Q1. What is business intelligence, and why is it important to business?

Describe the quantity of data in today's business environment and its five major sources. Explain the Business Intelligence process and its major activities. Describe how Target and Netflix are using BI.

Q2. What are the objectives of the BI process?

Describe the general effectiveness objective of the BI process and the two specific objectives. Explain the efficiency objective of the BI process.

Q3. What are the key components of a business intelligence IS?

Explain the functions of a BI server and its key feature. Describe how BI software has recently changed. Explain what is stored in a data warehouse and the difference between an OLTP and OLAP database. Describe how the procedures for the Acquiring activity differ from the Analyze and Publish activities. Explain how informing depends on people, and describe the two types of people that use a BI system.

Q4. How do BI information systems support BI activities?

Explain why operational data is typically not used for BI. Describe the sources of data in a data warehouse. Explain how the two types of analysis—reporting and data mining—differ. Describe the types of operations that are done with data in reporting. Explain the two examples of reporting. Describe in your own words slicing, dicing, drill down, and rollup. Explain regression and MBA analysis, and provide an example. Define *publishing* and *digital dashboards* and explain how dashboards are used with business processes.

Q5. How can BI information systems support business processes?

Name several business processes supported by BI information systems. Describe how the Google search engine supports your Decision Making process. Explain how if/then rules can store knowledge in a BI system that supports knowledge management. Describe the objective of the NBO process. Explain how Google Analytics supports the Online Sales process. Describe the two new processes supported by BI information systems.

Q6. What is a Big Data BI system, and how is it used?

Name the three ways that Big Data systems differ from routine data systems. Explain briefly the history of Big Data systems. Describe how MapReduce, Hadoop, and SAP HANA handle large datasets. State several processes supported by Big Data BI systems and include several new processes.

Q7. How do businesses manage the risks of business intelligence?

Describe the problems of dirty data and data with missing elements. Explain how nonintegrated data leads to problems. Define granularity and how granularity can be incorrect for BI use. Name the four BI problems associated with end users and give an example. Describe the two types of problems attributed to BI analysts. Explain how top management in an organization can create BI problems.

Q8. How does SAP do BI?

Describe two BI applications available with SAP. Explain the major use of SAP program code. Describe the three options for users to analyze SAP data.

Q9. 2024?

Name and describe the three factors that will affect BI growth in the next 10 years. Explain how mobile apps will affect BI. Give an example of unstructured data in BI and an example of a real-time application. Define *privacy* and explain how it will affect BI. Explain machine learning and how it is different from informing.

Key Terms and Concepts

A/B testing   345
Analysis   338
Assessment   334
Auditing process   348
Big Data   346
Business intelligence   332
Business intelligence system   332
Business Objects (BOBJ)   352
Clickstream data   350
Conversion rate   345
Cookie   358
Cross-selling   342
Data broker   354
Data mining   341
Data warehouse   335
Decision Making process   344
Decision support systems (DSS)   333

Digital dashboard   343
Dimension   339
Dirty data   349
Drill down   340
Expert system   345
Granularity   350
Hadoop   347
If/then rule   345
Index   344
Knowledge Management (KM)
   process   344
MapReduce   347
Market Basket Analysis (MBA)   342
Measure   339
Next Best Offer (NBO)
   process   345
NoSQL database   347

Online analytical processing
   (OLAP)   335
Online transactional processing
   (OLTP)   335
Operational database   335
Prediction   334
Privacy   353
Regression analysis   341
Reporting   338
RFM analysis   338
SAP HANA   347
Self-service BI   335
Slicing and dicing   339
Supervised data mining   342
Third-party cookie   358
Unsupervised data mining   342
Visualization   342

Using Your Knowledge

11-1. Reread the two examples at the beginning of the chapter that involved Target and Netflix. Specify the process that BI improves at each firm and a second process that BI could support. Explain the measures you would use to demonstrate how the BI example would improve the effectiveness or efficiency of the process.

11-2. Create a BPMN diagram of a Managerial process that can be supported by the Informing process. As in question 11-1, specify objectives and measures for that Managerial process and explain how the Informing process will improve those measures.

11-3. Reflect on the differences between reporting and data mining. What are their similarities and differences? How do their costs differ? What benefits does each offer? How would an organization choose between these two?

11-4. Suppose you are a member of the Audubon Society, and the board of the local chapter asks you to help it analyze its member data. The group wants to analyze the demographics of its membership against members' activity, including events attended, classes attended, volunteer activities, and donations. Describe two different reporting examples and one data mining example that it might develop.

11-5. You are the director of student activities at your university. Recently, some students have charged that your department misallocates its resources. They claim the allocation is based on outdated student preferences. Funds are given to activities that few students find attractive, and insufficient funds are allocated to new activities in which students do want to participate. Describe how you could use reporting and/or data mining to assess this claim.

11-6. In this chapter, we say that questions are more important than answers. Look at Figures 11-12, 11-13, and 11-14 and write down questions you have that might reveal patterns in the data shown in these figures.

11-7. Reread the opening scenario. CBI owns the computers, and workers should be productive with their time, but how did you react to the story? Do you think that CBI should know how employees use the network? Is it ethical to snoop on employee behavior? Assume that CBI wants to collect data on network misuse. Suggest measures that CBI could use to assess network misuse.

11-8. The following sayings about data and information are often used in business to convey an important idea. As you read these, select three and write down how they could be used to convey an idea from this chapter:

"If you want a green suit, turn on a green light."
"You don't fatten the pig by weighing it."
"Not everything that counts can be counted, and not everything that can be counted counts."
"Statistics are no substitute for judgment . . . and vice versa."
"Without data, you're just another person with an opinion."
"It ain't so much the things we know that get us in trouble, it's the things we know that just ain't so."

11-9. Go to Google Trends (*www.google.com/trends*) and enter the terms *Big Data, BigData,* and *Hadoop* to see how their popularity has grown recently.

Collaboration Exercise 11

Collaborate with a group of fellow students to answer the following questions. For this exercise do not meet face to face. Your task will be easier if you coordinate your work with SharePoint, Office 365, Google Docs with Google+, or equivalent collaboration tools. (See Chapter 9 for a discussion of collaboration tools and processes.) Your answers should reflect the thinking of the entire group, not just that of one or two individuals.

Mary Keeling owns and operates Carbon Creek Gardens, a retailer of trees, garden plants, perennial and annual flowers, and bulbs. "The Gardens," as her customers call it, also sells bags of soil, fertilizer, small garden tools, and garden sculptures.

Mary started the business 16 years ago when she bought a section of land that, because of water drainage, was unsuited for residential development. With hard work and perseverance, Mary has created a warm and inviting environment with a unique and carefully selected inventory of plants. The Gardens has become a favorite nursery for serious gardeners in her community.

"The problem," she says, "is that I've grown so large, I've lost track of my customers. The other day, I ran into Tootsie Swan at the grocery store, and I realized I hadn't seen her in ages. I said something like, 'Hi, Tootsie, I haven't seen you for a while,' and that statement unleashed an angry torrent from her. It turns out that she'd been in over a year ago and had wanted to return a plant. One of my part-time employees waited on her and had apparently insulted her, or at least didn't give her the service she wanted. So, she decided not to come back to The Gardens.

"Tootsie was one of my best customers. I'd lost her, and I didn't even know it! That really frustrates me. Is it inevitable that as I get bigger, I lose track of my customers? I don't think so.

"Somehow, I have to find out when regular customers aren't coming around. Had I known Tootsie had stopped shopping with us, I'd have called her to see what was going on. I need customers like her. I've got all sorts of data in my sales database. It seems like the insight I need is in there, but how do I get it out?" In this exercise, you will apply the knowledge of this chapter to Mary Keeling's problem.

1. Mary wants to know when she's lost a customer. One way to help her would be to produce a report, say in PDF format, showing the top 50 customers from the prior year. Mary could print that report or place it on a private section of her Web site so that she can download it from wherever she happens to be.

   Periodically—say, once a week—Mary could request a report that shows the top buyers for that week. That report could also be in PDF format, or it could just be produced onscreen. Mary could compare the two reports to determine who is missing. If she wonders whether a customer such as Tootsie has been ordering, she could request a query report on Tootsie's activities. Describe the advantages and disadvantages of this solution.

2. Describe the best possible application of an OLAP tool at Carbon Creek. Can it be used to solve the lost customer problem? Why or why not? What is the best way, if any, for Mary to use OLAP at Carbon Creek? If none, explain why.

3. Describe the best possible application of RFM analysis at Carbon Creek. Can it be used to solve the lost customer problem? Why or why not? What is the best way, if any, for Mary to use RFM at Carbon Creek? If none, explain why.

4. Describe the best possible application of market basket analysis at Carbon Creek. Can it be used to solve the lost customer problem? Why or why not? What is the best way, if any, for Mary to use market basket analysis at Carbon Creek? If none, explain why.

5. Which of the analysis options in this exercise will provide Mary the best value? If you owned Carbon Creek Gardens and were going to implement just one of these analysis options, which would you choose? Why?

CASE STUDY 11

Hadoop the Cookie Cutter

A **cookie** is data that a Web site stores on your computer to record something about its interaction with you. The cookie might contain data such as the date you last visited, whether you are currently signed in, or something else about your interaction with that site. Cookies can also contain a key value to one or more tables in a database that the server company maintains about your past interactions. In that case, when you access a site, the server uses the value of the cookie to look up your history. Such data could include your past purchases, portions of incomplete transactions, or the data and appearance you want for your Web page. Most of the time cookies ease your interaction with Web sites.

Cookie data includes the URL of the Web site of the cookie's owner. Thus, for example, when you go to Amazon, it asks your browser to place a cookie on your computer that includes its name, *www.amazon.com*. Your browser will do so unless you have turned cookies off.

A **third-party cookie** is a cookie created by a site other than the one you visited. Such cookies are generated in several ways, but the most common occurs when a Web page includes content from multiple sources. For example, Amazon designs its pages so that one or more sections contain ads provided by the ad-servicing company DoubleClick. When the browser constructs your Amazon page, it contacts DoubleClick to obtain the content for such sections (in this case, ads).

When it responds with the content, DoubleClick instructs your browser to store a DoubleClick cookie. That cookie is a third-party cookie. In general, third-party cookies do not contain the name or any value that identifies a particular user. Instead, they include the IP address to which the content was delivered.

On its own servers, when it creates the cookie, DoubleClick records that data in a log, and if you click on the ad, it will add that click to the log. This logging is repeated every time DoubleClick shows an ad. Cookies have an expiration date, but that date is set by the cookie creator, and they can last many years. So, over time, DoubleClick and any other third-party cookie owner will have a history of what they've shown, what ads have been clicked, and the intervals between interactions.

But the opportunity is even greater. DoubleClick has agreements not only with Amazon, but also with many others, such as Facebook. If Facebook includes any DoubleClick content on its site, DoubleClick will place another cookie on your computer. This cookie is different from the one that it placed via Amazon, but both cookies have your IP address and other data sufficient to associate the second cookie as originating from the same source as the first. So, DoubleClick now has a record of your ad response data on two sites. Over time, the cookie log will contain data to

show not only how you respond to ads, but also your pattern of visiting various Web sites on all those sites in which it places ads.

You might be surprised to learn how many third-party cookies you have. The browser Firefox has an optional feature called *Collusion* that tracks and graphs all the cookies on your computer. Figure 11-27 shows the cookies that were placed on my computer as I visited various Web sites. As you can see, in Figure 11-27a, when I started my computer and browser, there were no cookies. The cookies on my computer after I visited www.msn.com are shown in Figure 11-27b. At this point, there are already five third-party cookies tracking my behavior. After I visited www.yahoo.com and www.amazon.com as well, I had 12 third-party cookies, as shown in Figure 11-27c. Finally, Figure 11-27d shows the too-many-to-count third-party cookies on my machine after I visited the *Seattle Times*, Facebook, and LinkedIn as well. All of that is disturbing and bothersome, so I closed all of my browser sessions. Figure 11-27e shows that even after closing I was still being watched by third-party cookies.

Who are these companies that are gathering my browser behavior data? You can find out using Ghostery, another useful browser add-in feature (www.ghostery.com). Figure 11-28 shows the 10 third-party cookies installed by zulily.com when I visited its site. If you click on the name of the third-party cookie owner, it will display the popup shown in this figure. Click on the *What is . . .* and you can find out who that company is and what it does.

a. After Restart

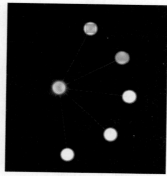

b. After MSN.com

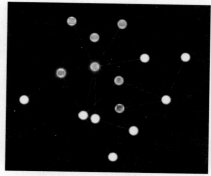

c. After Adding Yahoo! and Amazon

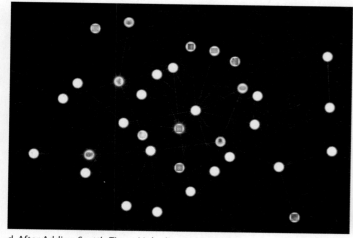

d. After Adding *Seattle Times*, LinkedIn, and Facebook

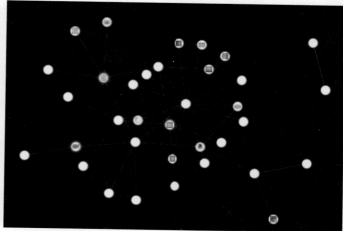

e. After Closing All Browser Windows

FIGURE 11-27
Third-Party Cookie Growth

Source: © Mozilla.

FIGURE 11-28
Ghostery® in Use

Third-party cookies generate incredible volumes of log data. For example, suppose a company, such as DoubleClick, shows 100 ads to a given computer in a day. If it is showing ads to 10 million computers (possible), that is a total of 1 billion log entries per day, or 365 billion a year. Truly this is Big Data.

Storage is essentially free, but how can they possibly process all that data? How do they parse the log to find entries just for your computer? How do they integrate data from different cookies on the same IP address? How do they analyze those entries to determine which ads you clicked on? How do they then characterize differences in ads to determine which characteristics matter most to you? The answer, as you learned in Q6, is to use parallel processing. Using a MapReduce algorithm, they distribute the work to thousands of processors that work in parallel. They then aggregate the results of these independent processors and then, possibly, move to a second phase of analysis where they do it again. Hadoop, the open source program that you learned about in Q6, is a favorite for this process. No wonder Amazon offers Hadoop MapReduce as part of EC3. It built it for itself, and now, given that it has it, why not lease it out?

Questions

11-10. Using your own words, explain how third-party cookies are created.

11-11. Suppose you are an ad-serving company, and you maintain a log of cookie data for ads you serve to Web pages for a particular vendor (say Amazon).
   a. How can you use this data to determine which are the best ads?
   b. How can you use this data to determine which are the best ad formats?
   c. How could you use records of past ads and ad clicks to determine which ads to send to a given IP address?

   d. How could you use this data to determine how well the technique you used in your answer to question c was working?
   e. How could you use this data to determine that a given IP address is used by more than one person?
   f. How does having this data give you a competitive advantage vis-à-vis other ad-serving companies?

11-12. Suppose you are an ad-serving company, and you have a log of cookie data for ads served to Web pages of all your customers (Amazon, Facebook, and so on).
   a. Describe, in general terms, how you can process the cookie data to associate log entries for a particular IP address.
   b. Explain how your answers to question 11-11 change, given that you have this additional data.
   c. Describe how you can use this log data to determine users who consistently seek the lowest price.
   d. Describe how you can use this log data to determine users who consistently seek the latest fashion.
   e. Explain why uses like those in c and d above are only possible with MapReduce or a similar technique.

11-13. As stated, third-party cookies usually do not contain, in themselves, data that identifies you as a particular person. However, Amazon, Facebook, and other first-party cookie vendors know who you are because you signed in. Only one of them needs to reveal your identity to the ad server, and your identity can then be correlated with your IP address. At that point, the ad server and potentially all of its clients know who you are. Are you concerned about the invasion of your privacy that third-party cookies enable? Explain your answer.

APPENDIX 11—SAP BUSINESS INTELLIGENCE TUTORIAL

This tutorial allows you to practice analyzing a large dataset using one of SAP's BI applications. This application, Business Objects Explorer, is a reporting analysis tool designed for non-IS professionals to analyze a dataset and publish simple graphical visualizations. As a reporting application, it supports most of the reporting operations discussed in the chapter: sort, filter, group, calculate, and graph.

This tutorial is not a process tutorial like the tutorials after Chapters 7 and 8. Instead, it shows how to do several of the basic reporting operations, then it asks you to use those reporting operations to answer a set of questions.

SAP provides several ways to interact with Business Objects Explorer. For this tutorial, we will use a public server.

1. Introduction

The example we will use is a very large dataset from a traditional manufacturing company. The 3 million records in the dataset include more than 40 measures such as revenue and profit as well as more than 10 dimensions such as year and customer group. Analysts use this data to analyze trends in revenue by year, to calculate profit from different product groups, and to obtain answers to other questions.

Go to *http://hanademo.testdrivesap.com/copa/#freeplay*.[1]
The following screen will appear:

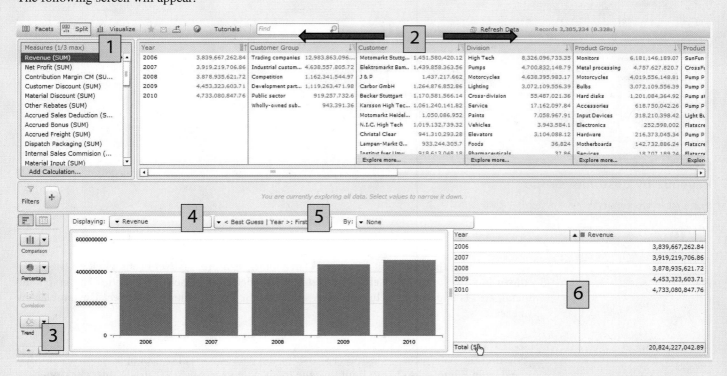

FIGURE 11A-1
Opening Screen in SAP Business Objects Explorer

Source: http://hanademo.testdrivesap.com/copa/#freeplay

---

[1] If SAP has moved the site, go online and search for *SAP Business Objects Explorer demos or tutorials* or *SAP HANA demo*. For SAP University Alliance Schools, you can also use Explorer with a dataset provided by UCC.

There are six areas highlighted in Figure 11A-1:

1. Measures
2. Dimensions
3. Graph options
4. Current Graph y-axis variable
5. Current Graph x-axis variable
6. Sort and detail section

Area 1 enables the analyst to select measures, data that can be summed, averaged, or processed. The default is the measure listed first, in this example, *Revenue*. The 10 dimension names are shown along the top of Area 2. Dimensions are characteristics or attributes; in this dataset these include Year, Customer Group, Customer, and Division. A slidebar at the bottom of this section reveals other dimensions; the default is the first dimension, *Year*. Area 3 offers a number of graphing options; the default is the bar chart. Drop-down boxes 4 and 5 allow the user to select measures and dimensions, and Area 6 enables the user to see details about the data on the graph and to sort the data.

From the bar chart in Figure 11A-1, you can see that revenues are up in recent years. If you need to know a detail such as how much revenue the company earned in any particular year, you can see that in the detail section on the lower right-hand side of the screen.

2. Display a Different Variable on the Graph

Currently the graph shows revenue by year. To see revenue by customer group, **click on the drop-down arrow to the left of Year in Area 5. Select Customer Group and click OK.** The graph and details area should look like Figure 11A-2. Notice that Customer Group is now the x-axis dimension and that the data in the sort and detail section has been updated.

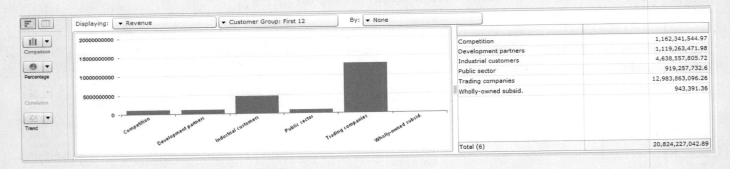

FIGURE 11A-2

Revenue by Customer Group

Source: http://hanademo.testdrivesap.com/copa/#freeplay

To change the other axis—Revenue—to another measure, say Net Profit, **click on the drop-down box in Area 4 and select the Net Profit check box. Deselect Revenue.** The graph and detail area is updated to include the new selection. Before continuing, **re-select Revenue** as the measure.

3. Filtering

Filtering the data means selecting a subset of the data to view. For example, one way to filter the data in Figure 11A-2 is to limit revenue to a single year, say 2010. To do this, **click on 2010 in the Year dimension** in Area 2. Explorer then filters the data and a new graph is displayed. Notice the button *Year 2010* appears between the Measures section and the Graph section as shown by the blue arrow in Figure 11A-3. To remove a filter, click on the x at the top right of the filter button.

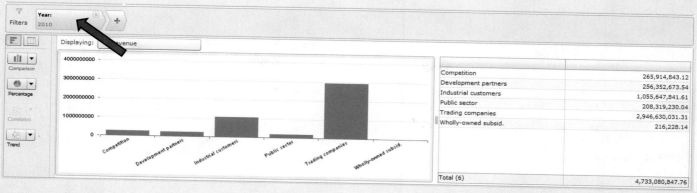

FIGURE 11A-3

2010 Filter for Revenue by Customer Group

Source: http://hanademo.testdrivesap.com/copa/#freeplay

4. Other Operations

A wide range of other reporting operations are also supported by Explorer.

- To show multiple measures, click on a second or third checkbox from the drop-down box in Area 4. Notice graphing options are now different. Experiment with different graph options (Area 3); selecting the down arrow to the right of the graph type icon reveals graphs available for that type.
- If you would like to sort the data, click on the arrows next to the column headings in Area 6 in the sort and detail section.
- You can create a new measure by clicking on Add Calculation at the bottom of the measures in Area 1.

Other analysis operations are available. To learn about them, search the web using *SAP BO Explorer tutorial* as key terms.

You Try It

To practice with the simple operations explained above, answer the following questions:

1. Create a Revenue by Year graph. What year has the lowest revenue? — **2006**
2. How much revenue was received in 2006? — **$3,839,667,262.84**
3. Create a Revenue by Customer Group graph. How much revenue was received from the lowest group? — **$943,391.36**
4. Filter the data in Question 3 by Year 2010. How much revenue was received from the lowest group in 2010? — **$216,228.14**
5. Apply a second filter, Country US. How much revenue was received from the lowest group in the US in 2010? — **$184,667.04**
6. Which division had the highest revenue in the US in 2010? — **Motorcycles**
7. Which division had the lowest net profit in the US in 2010? — **Pumps**

For more practice, write questions for other students and try to answer theirs.

For graphing practice, create a graph, then show a fellow student; try to make the graph the other student shows you.

PART 5

MIS MANAGEMENT PROCESSES

MIS, like all business endeavors, accomplishes work via processes. The typical IS department has processes for planning, developing, maintaining, and operating enterprise and interenterprise systems. The IS department is involved in the support of other departments and end users as well.

Most of these IS processes are beyond the scope of this book. However, in this last part and last chapter, we will consider three MIS management processes that are likely to involve you as a future business professional. They are processes for managing other business processes, processes for developing information systems, and processes for protecting IS.

You should know about the first two of these processes because you may be asked to participate. End users are the primary source of requirements for processes and systems development, and they are often called upon to provide feedback on processes and systems structures and features. You should know about IS security for three reasons. First, you need to know the major dimensions of IS security for your organization. This includes knowing the kinds of security safeguards that should be in place. Second, if those safeguards are not in place, you need to know how to argue effectively for their creation. Third, you will have responsibilities and roles to play in protecting the information systems that you use. As a business professional, you need to understand the rationale for those responsibilities and have sufficient knowledge to fulfill roles that you are assigned.

As Heidi was slogging across campus on her way to her dreaded 8:00 a.m. class in the business school, she saw an unusual scene as she got closer. Yellow crime scene tape blocked her entrance to the school, and seemingly every campus policeman was milling around the first floor holding a cup of coffee, eating donuts, and whispering.

Heidi saw a fellow prisoner of her 8 o'clock class, Cassie, who worked as a lab tech in the school. Heidi asked if she knew what was going on.

"Someone stole credit card information from students that used the lab machines."

As Cassie was spilling the beans, Jackie, the lab supervisor, walked by and Cassie asked, "Do the police know how it happened?"

"They think a student named Cassie stole credit card numbers," Jackie replied playfully.

"Actually, they think it might be some people who dressed up in maintenance outfits last month. They said the thieves got in through a window someone left open, then they somehow uploaded a root kit virus on the machines. When students used credit cards, that program copied the credit card numbers and sent them to some remote site."

Q1. What are the activities of business process management?

Q2. What are the activities of the systems development life cycle (SDLC) development process?

Q3. How can the scrum process overcome the problems of the SDLC?

Q4. What is information systems security?

Q5. How should you respond to security threats?

Q6. How should organizations respond to security threats?

Q7. How can technical and data safeguards protect against security threats?

Q8. How can human safeguards protect against security threats?

Q9. How should organizations respond to security incidents?

Cassie looked uncomfortable, "I've used the lab machines to pay my tuition bill with a credit card. Am I at risk?"

"I think you need to go introduce yourself to the police, Cassie. As I understand it, the thieves used the student credit cards and had items delivered to unoccupied appartments in town. Because they used a local address, the credit card companies were not suspcious.

"The police said some members of the group were acting like students and tried leaving several windows open before they found the right one that nobody noticed. They also put a keyboard logger on the lab supervisor's station and got the server login credentials. Once they got in through the window, they uploaded the virus on the server and waited for credit card information to start coming in.

"The police said these guys also planted some cameras to see door access codes and to observe police response times. They dressed up like maintenance men, but no one could give a description. They even found a department secretary who talked to them on the phone. Apparantly they asked the secretary about the electrical wiring, and she was very helpful."

Cassie headed back toward the dorms. "I guess I need to go look at my credit card account and see if anything weird was charged. But I guess I won't use the school's machines to check that out. Take notes for me in class, Heidi."

Every organization today needs to adapt to new technologies and new opportunities. Businesses that do not adapt cannot thrive, and they may not even be able to survive. Organizations can adapt by changing their strategy or, if the strategy remains the same, technology opportunities may require changes in processes or systems.

To help you help your organization adapt, we will consider several MIS management processes in this chapter: business process management, which is a process for managing other processes, and systems development, which is a process for creating and maintaining information systems. We discuss these processes in questions Q1 through Q3.

The balance of this chapter concerns IS security. You need only open your browser to today's news to see why IS security is so important. Living Social, Twitter, Pinterest, Microsoft, and other large organizations as well as the U.S. federal government suffered serious customer and client data breaches in 2013. Any organization for which you work is subject to the same security vulnerabilities and threats as they are. As you will see, you have important roles to play in implementing safeguards to protect your organization.

Chapter Preview

Q1. What Are the Activities of Business Process Management?

As we have stated repeatedly, business processes provide the key means by which businesses accomplish work. Because this is so, it is not surprising that businesses use a process to manage processes. The most important of such processes is known as *business process management (BPM)*. In this question, we will describe the primary activities of the BPM process. BPM and its principles are not only useful in large organizations with many processes but have also been applied to nonprofits, government agencies, and small organizations like the computer lab department at Heidi's school.

Figure 12-1 shows the four basic activities in **business process management (BPM)**, a cyclical process for systematically monitoring, modeling, creating, and implementing business processes. In Figure 12-1, note how the activities of monitor/model/create/implement repeat. As each activity is completed, it feeds into the next activity.

During the monitoring activity, managers evaluate process measures against their objectives and respond to changes in the business climate, as described below. Next, models and other forms of requirements for changes in the business process are developed. Components for implementing those requirements are then created, and the process changes are implemented. That implementation activity leads to the monitoring activity of the next cycle. Consider each activity in more detail.

FIGURE 12-1
Four Activities of the BPM Process

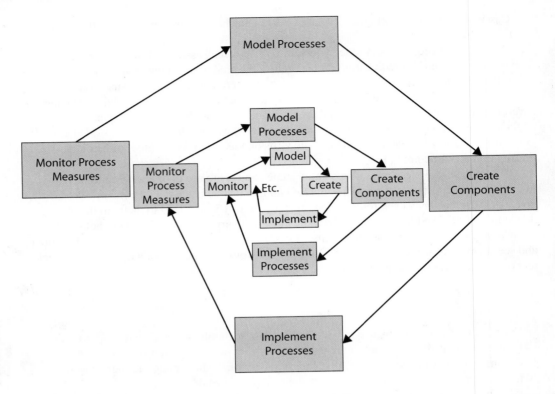

The BPM Monitoring Activity

Organizations are dynamic, and processes within organizations need to be adapted. The need for process change arises from two sources:

- The process does not consistently meet its objectives.
- Changes in the business environment.

Managers can learn that a process needs to be adapted in one of two ways. They can ignore the process and possible need for change until trouble ensues—the approach used by Heidi's school—or they can continually monitor the process and proactively make changes before problems occur.

Organizations that engage in process management take the latter approach. To do so, they create targets for process objectives and frequently, sometimes continuously, measure the process against those objectives.

MONITORING PROCESS PERFORMANCE BY ITS OBJECTIVES As you have learned, process objectives are either effective or efficient. Effectiveness assesses how well the process helps the organization achieve its strategy. For example, the shipping department of an organization that differentiates based on high-quality service will set high objectives for the percent of orders shipped on time, the percent of orders that are accurate, and the percent of orders that are delivered to the correct address. Measures of efficiency objectives determine how well the process uses its resources. For shipping, efficiency measures include the average cost of preparing a shipment, the number of trucks required to deliver shipments, the cost per item of packaging, and so forth. One of the objectives of the computer lab closing process is to keep the labs secure overnight, and the failure of this objective made the business school aware that it needed to change its process.

MONITORING FOR CHANGES IN THE PROCESS ENVIRONMENT Business processes need to be monitored against changes in technology. For example, 3D printing, mobile devices, and the cloud will require businesses to reassess their processes. A second source of change in a process's environment is the business itself. A substantial change in any of the following factors can signal a need to modify business processes:

- Market (e.g., new customer category, change in customer characteristics)
- Product lines

- Supply chain
- Company policy
- Company organization (e.g., merger or acquisition)
- Internationalization
- Business environment

The BPM Modeling Activity

At some point, either because a process is not meeting its performance objectives or because of changes in the business environment, processes will need to be changed. During the modeling activity, it is often necessary to document how the process currently works. To accomplish this, business users who have expertise and are involved in the process (this could be you!) adjust and evaluate those models. Usually teams build an as-is model that documents the current situation and then make adjustments to that model to solve process problems. A common way to construct an as-is model is with a BPMN document.

The BPM Create Components Activity

The third major BPM activity is to create process components. In this activity, the team designs changes to the business process at a depth sufficient for implementation. One component of the process may be an information system; if so, the systems development life cycle in Q2 may be used. In addition to IS components, procedures and training for activities that do not involve information systems need to be developed as well. At Heidi's school, new activities such as manually ensuring windows are locked were added to the closing process, and changes were made to the IS that maintained key codes for each lab door.

The BPM Implement Process Activity

Implementation activities make process changes operational. During this activity, process actors are trained on the activities they will perform and the IS procedures they will use. Activities to perform here are similar to implementation activities for the systems development life cycle (SDLC), and we will defer discussion of them to the SDLC discussion in Q2. For processes, however, note that if the new version of the business process involves considerable change for employees, there is likely to be resistance to the new system. The lab monitors at the school who now must execute a closing process that has twice as many activites are sure to be less than enthused. We discussed employee resistance to change in Chapters 5 through 8, and we won't repeat that discussion here. However, it is important to remember the need for addressing resistance to change.

The four activities of BPM are cyclical. Once a process change has been implemented, it is monitored. If it needs improvement, it is remodeled, and components are created and implemented. Many large firms label this ongoing cycle of process improvement a **continuous improvement process (CIP)**.

Q2. What Are the Activities of the Systems Development Life Cycle (SDLC) Development Process?

The second MIS management process, **systems development**, is the process of creating and maintaining an information system. As stated in Chapter 2, the relationship between a business process and an information system is many-to-many. A given business process may use one or more information systems, and a given information system may be used by more than one process. Because this is so, organizations can begin with BPM and, in the context of process management, create an IS. Or organizations can begin with an IS and back into the processes that will use it. In this question, we will assume the organization begins by developing the IS first.

Several processes are used to create information systems. The most common process is called the **systems development life cycle (SDLC)**. The SDLC process is composed of activities; some organizations define five activities, some seven, and some even more. The activities in these different versions are more or less the same; they are just grouped

Challenges of Information Systems Security

There are indeed many threats, but threats are just one reason security is difficult. Information security is a challenge for other reasons as well—attackers don't have to follow rules; data was designed to be copied and shared easily, not bottled up in a fortress; and firms like to use the newest but often insecure technology to build their applications. But perhaps the most challenging aspect of security is that businesses do not have the time to thoroughly test the security of their new systems before they are employed. To do so costs too much money and time. Understandably, most businesses have to operate on the principle "let's build this new money-making system, and if it works and we're still in business, we'll have the time and money to do security right."

To respond to these threats and challenges, organizations employ safeguards to reduce the likelihood of their occurrence and the severity of loss. Safeguards are, however, expensive to create and maintain. They also reduce work efficiency by making common tasks more difficult, adding labor expense. The goal of information security is to find an appropriate trade-off between the risk of loss and the cost of implementing safeguards. Before we consider how an organization balances risk and cost, consider you own situation.

Q5. How Should You Respond to Security Threats?

Your personal IS security goal should be to find an effective trade-off between the risk of loss and the cost of safeguards. However, few individuals take security as seriously as they should, and most fail to implement even low-cost safeguards.

Figure 12-15 lists recommended personal security safeguards. The first safeguard is to take security seriously. You cannot see the attempts that are being made, right now, to compromise your computer. Even though you are unaware of these threats, they are present, as you just learned.

When your security is compromised, the first indication you receive will be bogus charges on your credit card or messages from friends complaining about the disgusting email they just received from your email account.

If you decide to take computer security seriously, the single most important safeguard you can implement is to create and use strong passwords. A strong password does not contain any word, in any language, as part of the password. Use passwords with a mixture of upper- and lowercase letters and numbers and special characters.

In addition to using long, complex passwords, you should also use different passwords for different sites. That way, if one of your passwords is compromised, you do not lose control of all of your accounts.

Never send passwords, credit card data, or any other valuable data in email or IM. As stated numerous times in this text, most email and IM are not protected by encryption (see Q4), and you should assume that anything you write in email or IM could be posted on Facebook tomorrow.

Your browser automatically stores a history of your browsing activities and temporary files that contain sensitive data about where you've visited, what you've purchased, what your

---

• Take security seriously
• Create strong passwords
• Use multiple passwords
• Send no valuable data via email or IM
• Use https at trusted, reputable vendors
• Remove high-value assets from computers
• Clear browsing history, temporary files, and cookies (CCleaner or equivalent)
• Regularly update antivirus software
• Demonstrate security concern to your fellow workers
• Follow organizational security directives and guidelines
• Consider security for all business initiatives
• Use caution when using public machines

FIGURE 12-15

Personal Security Safeguards

account names and passwords are, and so forth. It also creates **cookies**, which are small files that your browser stores on your computer when you visit Web sites (see Case Study 9, page 299). Cookies enable you to access Web sites without having to sign in every time, and they speed up processing of some sites. Unfortunately, some cookies also contain sensitive security data. The best safeguard is to remove your browsing history, temporary files, and cookies from your computer and to set your browser to disable history and cookies.

CCleaner is a free, open source product that will do a more thorough job of removing all such data (*http://download.cnet.com/CCleaner/*) than browsers do. You should make a backup of your computer before using CCleaner, however. Removing and disabling cookies presents an excellent example of the trade-off between improved security and cost. Your security will be substantially improved, but your computer will be more difficult to use. You decide, but make a conscious decision; do not let ignorance of the vulnerability of such data make the decision for you.

Finally, don't use public machines such as the ones in hotels, coffee shops, Internet cafes, or airports for any communication you deem important. The malware running on these machines make them as unsanitary as the worst public bathroom.

Q6. How Should Organizations Respond to Security Threats?

In the previous question, we examined how you balance risk and cost. Now we will see how organizations accomplish this balance. In the case of organizations, a broader and more systematic approach needs to be taken. In this question, we examine three critical security fundamentals that are in place: security policy, risk management, and defense in layers. Then in Q7 and Q8 we discuss safeguards—the preventative measures used by organizations to reduce IS security risk.

Considering the first security fundamental, senior management must establish a company-wide security policy that states the organization's posture regarding data that it gathers about its customers, suppliers, partners, and employees. At a minimum, the policy should stipulate:

- What sensitive data the organization will store
- How it will process that data
- Whether data will be shared with other organizations
- How employees and others can obtain copies of data stored about them
- How employees and others can request changes to inaccurate data
- What employees can do with their own mobile devices at work
- What non-business-related activities employees can take with employee-owned equipment

Specific policy depends on whether the organization is governmental or nongovernmental, whether it is publically held or private, the organization's industry, the relationship of management to employees, and other factors. As a new hire, seek out your employer's security policy if it is not discussed with you in new employee training.

The second senior management security function is to manage risk. Risk cannot be eliminated, so *manage risk* means to proactively balance the trade-off between risk and cost. This trade-off varies from industry to industry and from organization to organization. Financial institutions are obvious targets for theft and must invest heavily in security safeguards. On the other hand, a bowling alley is unlikely to be much of a target, unless, of course, it stores credit card data on computers or mobile devices.

To make trade-off decisions, organizations need to create an inventory of the data they store and the threats to which that data is subject. Given this inventory, the organization needs to decide how much risk it wishes to take or, stated differently, which security safeguards it wishes to implement.

Before we dive into details of the technical, data, and human safeguards, we should reiterate the third security fundamental—defensive safeguards must be layered. No safeguard by itself is completely effective. It can impede some attacks, but by itself it can stop few. As a result, there is no master list of safeguards, no list that would ensure complete protection. Therefore, management must rely on a security defense that is layered. One way to organize the layers is to select safeguards from each of the categories: technical, data, and human.

Hardware	Software	Data	Procedures	People

Technical Safeguards	Data Safeguards	Human Safeguards
Identification and authorization	Data rights and responsibilities	Employees
Encryption	Passwords	Nonemployees
Firewalls	Encryption	Account admin
Malware protection	Backup and recovery	Backup and recovery
	Physical security	Security monitoring

FIGURE 12-16

Security Safeguards as They Relate to the Five Components

An easy way to remember information systems safeguards is to arrange them according to the five components of an information system, as shown in Figure 12-16. Some of the safeguards involve computer hardware and software. Some involve data; others involve procedures and people. We will consider technical, data, and human safeguards in the next three questions.

Q7. How Can Technical and Data Safeguards Protect Against Security Threats?

Technical safeguards involve the hardware and software components of an information system. Figure 12-17 lists primary technical safeguards. Consider each.

Identification and Authentication

Every information system today should require users to sign in with a user name and password. The user name *identifies* the user (the process of identification), and the password *authenticates* that user (the process of authentication). The process of **authentication** verifies the credentials of the individual seeking access to a computer resource.

Passwords have important weaknesses. In spite of repeated warnings, users often share their passwords, and many people choose ineffective, simple passwords. In fact, the 2011 Verizon report cited earlier states, "Absent, weak, and stolen credentials are careening out of control."[6] Because of these problems, some organizations choose to use smart cards and biometric authentication in addition to passwords.

A **smart card** is a plastic card similar to a credit card. Unlike credit, debit, and ATM cards, which have a magnetic strip, smart cards have a microchip. The microchip, which holds far more data than a magnetic strip, is loaded with identifying data. Users of smart cards are required to enter a personal identification number (PIN) to be authenticated.

Biometric authentication uses personal physical characteristics such as fingerprints, facial features, and retinal scans to authenticate users. Biometric authentication provides strong authentication, but the required equipment is expensive. Often, too, users resist biometric identification because they feel it is invasive. Note that authentication methods fall into three categories: what you know (password or PIN), what you have (smart card), and what you are (biometric).

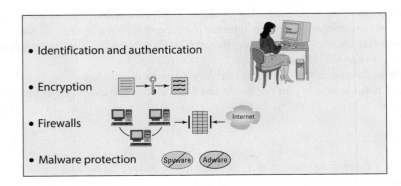

- Identification and authentication
- Encryption
- Firewalls
- Malware protection

FIGURE 12-17

Technical Safeguards

---

[6] *Verizon 2011 Data Breach Investigations Report,* accessed June 2012, www.verizonbusiness.com/resources/reports/rp_data-breach-investigations-report-2011_en_xg.pdf.

Encryption

Encryption is the process of transforming clear text into coded, unintelligible text for secure storage or communication. Commonly used methods are 3DES, RSA, and AES; search the Web for these terms if you want to know more about them.

A **key** is a number used to encrypt the data. It is called a *key* because it locks and unlocks a message, but it is a number used with an encryption algorithm and not a physical thing like the key to your apartment.

To encode a message, a computer program uses the encryption method with the key to convert a noncoded message into a coded message. The resulting coded message looks like gibberish.

Decoding (decrypting) a message is similar; a key is applied to the coded message to recover the original text. With **symmetric encryption**, the same key is used to encode and to decode. With **asymmetric encryption**, two keys are used; one key encodes the message, and the other key decodes the message. Symmetric encryption is simpler and much faster than asymmetric encryption.

A special version of asymmetric encryption, **public key/private key**, is used on the Internet. With this method, each site has a public key for encoding messages and a private key for decoding them. Before we explain how that works, consider the following analogy.

Suppose you send a friend an open combination lock (like you have on your gym locker). Suppose you are the only one who knows the combination to that lock. Now, suppose your friend puts something in a box and locks the lock. Now, neither your friend nor anyone else can open that box. The friend sends the locked box to you, and you apply the combination to open the box.

A public key is like the combination lock, and the private key is like the combination. Your friend uses the public key to code the message (lock the box), and you use the private key to decode the message (use the combination to open the lock). Now, suppose we have two generic computers, A and B. Suppose A wants to send an encrypted message to B. To do so, A sends B its public key (in our analogy, A sends B an open combination lock). Now B applies A's public key to the message and sends the resulting coded message back to A. At that point, neither B nor anyone other than A can decode that message. It is like the box with a locked combination lock. When A receives the coded message, A applies its private key (the combination in our analogy) to unlock or decrypt the message.

Again, public keys are like open combination locks. Computer A will send a lock to anyone who asks for one. But A never sends its private key (the combination) to anyone. Private keys stay private.

Most secure communication over the Internet uses a protocol called **https**. With https, data are encrypted using a protocol called the Secure Socket Layer (SSL), which is also known as Transport Layer Security (TLS). SSL/TLS uses a combination of public key/private key and symmetric encryption.

The basic idea is this: Symmetric encryption is fast and is preferred. But the two parties (say, you and a Web site) don't share a symmetric key. So, the two of you use asymmetric encryption to share the same symmetric key. Once you both have that key, you use symmetric encryption.

Figure 12-18 summarizes how SSL/TLS works when you communicate securely with a Web site:

1. Your computer obtains the public key of the Web site to which it will connect.
2. Your computer generates a key for symmetric encryption.
3. Your computer encodes that key using the Web site's public key. It sends the encrypted symmetric key to the Web site.
4. The Web site then decodes the symmetric key using its private key.
5. From that point forward, your computer and the Web site communicate using symmetric encryption.

Firewalls

A **firewall** is a computing device that prevents unauthorized access to parts of a network. Firewalls can prohibit outsiders from starting a session with any user behind the firewall. They can also disallow traffic from particular sites, such as known hacker addresses. They can prohibit traffic from legitimate, but unwanted, addresses, such as competitors' computers, and filter

1. Your computer obtains public key of Web site.

Web Site Public Key

You

2. Your computer generates key for symmetric encryption.

3. Your computer encrypts symmetric key using Web site's public key.

Web Site

Symmetric Key Encrypted Using Web Site's Public Key

4. Web site decodes your message using its private key. Obtains key for symmetric encryption.

Communications Using Symmetric Encryption

5. All communications between you and Web site use symmetric encryption.

FIGURE 12-18

The Essence of https (SSL or TLS)

outbound traffic as well. They can keep employees from accessing specific sites, such as competitors' sites, sites with pornographic material, or popular news sites. As a future manager, if you have particular sites with which you do not want your employees to communicate, you can ask your IS department to enforce that limit via the firewall.

Malware Protection

The next technical safeguard in our list in Figure 12-17 concerns malware. We defined the important terms in Chapter 4. To review, malware is viruses, worms, Trojan horses, spyware, and adware. In the opening vignette, spyware was installed on lab machines by the thieves.

- A virus is a computer program that replicates itself.
- The program code that causes unwanted or harmful activity is called the payload.
- A worm is a virus that propagates using the Internet or other computer network.
- Trojan horses are viruses that masquerade as useful programs or files.
- Spyware programs are installed on the user's computer without the user's knowledge or permission.
- Adware is similar to spyware, but it watches user activity and produces pop-up ads.

Figure 12-19 lists some of the symptoms of adware and spyware. Sometimes these symptoms develop slowly over time as more malware components are installed. Should these symptoms occur on your computer, remove the spyware or adware using anti-malware programs.

Fortunately, it is possible to avoid most malware using the following malware safeguards:

1. **Install antivirus and antispyware programs on your computer.** Your IS department will have a list of recommended (perhaps required) programs for this purpose. If you choose a program for yourself, choose one from a reputable vendor. Check reviews of anti-malware software on the Web before purchasing.
2. **Set up your anti-malware programs to scan your computer frequently.** You should scan your computer at least once a week and possibly more often. When you detect malware code, use the anti-malware software to remove it. If the code cannot be removed, contact your IS department or anti-malware vendor.
3. **Update malware definitions.** Malware definitions—patterns that exist in malware code—should be downloaded frequently. Anti-malware vendors update these definitions continuously, and you should install these updates as they become available.

- Slow system startup
- Sluggish system performance
- Many pop-up advertisements
- Suspicious browser homepage changes
- Suspicious changes to the taskbar and other system interfaces
- Unusual hard-disk activity

FIGURE 12-19

Spyware and Adware Symptoms

4. **Open email attachments only from known sources.** Also, even when opening attachments from known sources, do so with great care. With a properly configured firewall, email is the only outside-initiated traffic that can reach user computers. Most anti-malware programs check email attachments for malware code. However, all users should form the habit of *never* opening an email attachment from an unknown source.

5. **Promptly install software updates from legitimate sources.** Unfortunately, all programs are chock-full of security holes; vendors are fixing them as rapidly as they are discovered, but the practice is inexact. Install patches to the operating system and application programs promptly.

6. **Browse only in reputable Internet neighborhoods.** It is possible for some malware to install itself when you do nothing more than open a Web page. Don't go there!

7. **Don't use questionable discussion boards.** It is easy for hackers to install hidden malware on discussion board posts.

Data Safeguards

Data safeguards are outlined in Figure 12-20. One data safeguard is to define a specific data policy such as "We will not share identifying customer data with any other organization." Second, data administration and database administration(s) work together to specify user data rights and responsibilities. Third, those rights should be enforced by user accounts that are authenticated at least by passwords.

The organization should protect sensitive data by storing it in encrypted form. Such encryption uses one or more keys in ways similar to that described for data communication encryption.

One potential problem with stored data, however, is that the key might be lost or that disgruntled or terminated employees might destroy it. Because of this possibility, when data are encrypted, a trusted party should have a copy of the encryption key. This safety procedure is sometimes called **key escrow**.

Another data safeguard is to periodically create backup copies of database contents. The organization should store at least some of these backups off premises, possibly in a remote location. Additionally, IT personnel should periodically practice recovery to ensure that the backups are valid and that effective recovery procedures exist. Do not assume that just because a backup is made that the database is protected.

Physical security is another data safeguard. The computers that run the DBMS and all devices that store database data should reside in locked, controlled-access facilities. If not, they are subject not only to theft but also to damage. For better security, the organization should keep a log showing who entered the facility, when, and for what purpose. In the chapter-opening vignette, the locks on the computer labs are an example of physical security.

When organizations store databases in the cloud, all of the safeguards in Figure 12-20 should be part of the cloud service contract.

While these technical and data safeguards are essential, the most important safeguards wear shoes. Like most topics in this text, people play the most important role in security.

Q8. How Can Human Safeguards Protect Against Security Threats?

Human safeguards involve the people and procedure components of information systems. In general, human safeguards result when authorized users follow appropriate procedures for system use and recovery. Restricting access to authorized users requires effective authentication methods and careful user account management. In addition, appropriate security procedures

FIGURE 12-20
Data Safeguards

- Define data policies
- Data rights and responsibilities
- Rights enforced by user accounts authenticated by passwords
- Data encryption
- Backup and recovery procedures
- Physical security

must be designed as part of every information system, and users should be trained on the importance and use of those procedures. In this section, we will consider the development of human safeguards for employees, nonemployees, account administration, backup and recovery, and security monitoring.

Human Safeguards for Employees

Figure 12-21 lists more specific security considerations for employees. Consider each.

TRUST BUT VERIFY If motivated and trained about security, employees can make the security task much easier. The most important security safeguard for employees is to be less trusting of others using the system. More specifically, they should employ the Russian proverb "trust but verify." Employees should seek to verify that the people or Web sites they are communicating with are actually who they claim to be. People spend years learning who to trust and how to verify in the real world but throw this skill out the window when communicating online.

POSITION DEFINITIONS Effective human safeguards also include definitions of job tasks and responsibilities. In general, job descriptions should provide a separation of duties and authorities. For example, no single individual should be allowed to both approve expenses and write checks. Instead, one person should approve expenses, another pay them, and a third should account for

- Trust but verify

  "Who are you, really?"

- Position definition
  - Separate duties and authorities
  - Determine least privilege
  - Document position sensitivity

  "OK to pay this"

- Hiring and screening

  "Where did you last work?"

- Dissemination and enforcement
  - Responsibility
  - Accountability
  - Compliance

  "Let's talk security..."

- Termination
  - Friendly

  "Congratulations on your new job."

  - Unfriendly

  "We've closed your accounts. Good-bye."

FIGURE 12-21
Human Safeguards for Employees

the payment. Similarly, in inventory, no single person should be allowed to authorize an inventory withdrawal and also to remove the items from inventory. Given appropriate job descriptions, user accounts should be defined to give users the *least possible privilege* needed to perform their jobs.

HIRING AND SCREENING Security considerations should be part of the hiring process. Of course, if the position involves no sensitive data and no access to information systems, then screening for information systems security purposes will be minimal. When hiring for high-sensitivity positions, however, extensive interviews, references, and background investigations are appropriate. Note, too, that security screening applies not only to new employees but also to employees who are promoted into sensitive positions.

DISSEMINATION AND ENFORCEMENT Employees cannot be expected to follow security policies and procedures they do not know about. Therefore, employees need to be educated about the security policies, procedures, and responsibilities they will have.

Employee security training begins during new employee training with the explanation of general security policies and procedures. That general training must be amplified in accordance with the position's sensitivity and responsibilities. Promoted employees should receive security training that is appropriate to their new positions.

Enforcement consists of three interdependent factors: responsibility, accountability, and compliance. First, the company should clearly define the security *responsibilities* of each position. The design of the security program should be such that employees can be held *accountable* for security violations. Procedures should exist so that when critical data are lost, it is possible to determine how the loss occurred and who is accountable. Finally, the security program should encourage security *compliance.* Employee activities should regularly be monitored for compliance, and management should specify disciplinary action to be taken in light of noncompliance.

Management attitude is crucial—management needs to cultivate a culture of compliance. Culture starts with management behavior: Employee compliance is greater when management demonstrates, both in word and deed, a serious concern for security. If managers write passwords on staff bulletin boards, work on confidential documents on an unsecured wireless network, or ignore physical security procedures, then employee security attitudes and employee security compliance will suffer. Note, too, that effective security is a continuing management responsibility. Managers need to remind employees about security on a recurring basis, and perhaps the most effective reminders are stories of real-life security failures and their consequences. Stories, more than boring lists of do's and don'ts, have a bigger impact on the security behavior of employees.

TERMINATION Companies also must establish security policies and procedures for the termination of employees. Many employee terminations are friendly and occur as the result of promotion or retirement or when the employee resigns to take another position. Standard human resource policies should ensure that system administrators receive notification in advance of the employee's last day so they can remove accounts and passwords. The need to recover keys for encrypted data and any other special security requirements should be part of the employee's out-processing.

Unfriendly termination is more difficult because employees may be tempted to take malicious or harmful actions. In such a case, system administrators may need to remove user accounts and passwords prior to notifying the employee of his or her termination. Other actions may be needed to protect the company's data assets. A terminated sales employee, for example, may attempt to take the company's confidential customer and sales-prospect data for future use at another company.

The terminating employer should take steps to protect those data prior to the termination. The human resources department should be aware of the importance of giving IS administrators early notification of employee termination. No blanket policy exists; the information systems department must assess each case on an individual basis.

Human Safeguards for Nonemployee Personnel

Business requirements may necessitate opening information systems to nonemployee personnel—temporary personnel, vendors, partner personnel (employees of business partners), and the public. Although temporary personnel can be screened, to reduce costs the screening will be abbreviated from that for employees. In most cases, companies cannot screen either vendor or partner personnel. Of course, public users cannot be screened at all. Similar limitations pertain to security training and compliance testing. In the case of temporary, vendor, and partner personnel, the contracts that govern the activity should call for security measures appropriate to the sensitivity of the data and the IS resources involved. Companies should require vendors and partners to perform appropriate screening and security training. The contract also should mention specific security responsibilities that are particular to the work to be performed. Companies should provide accounts and passwords with the least privilege and remove those accounts as soon as possible.

Finally, note that the business relationship with the public, and with some partners, differs from that with temporary personnel and vendors. The public and some partners use the information system to receive a benefit. Consequently, safeguards need to protect such users from internal company security problems. A disgruntled employee who maliciously changes prices on a Web site potentially damages both public users and business partners. As one IT manager put it, "Rather than protecting ourselves from them, we need to protect them from us."

Account Administration

The administration of user accounts, passwords, and help-desk policies is another important human safeguard. Account management concerns the creation of new user accounts, the modification of existing account permissions, and the removal of unneeded accounts. Information system administrators perform all of these tasks, but account users have the responsibility to notify the administrators of the need for these actions. Account permissions as mentioned earlier should be based on the position definitions—a new hire should be given less access to files, apps, and menus than a trusted supervisor.

Passwords are the primary means of authentication. They are important not just for access to the user's computer but also for authentication to other networks and servers to which the user may have access. Because of the importance of passwords, the National Institute of Standards and Technology (NIST) recommends that employees be required to sign statements similar to those shown in Figure 12-22.

When an account is created, users should immediately change the password they are given to one of their own. In fact, well-constructed systems require the user to change the password on first use. Additionally, users should change passwords frequently thereafter. Some systems will require a password change every 3 months or perhaps more frequently. Users grumble at the nuisance of making such changes, but frequent password changes reduce not only the risk of password loss but also the extent of damage if an existing password is compromised.

In the past, help desks have been a serious security risk. A user who had forgotten his password would call the help desk and plead for the help desk representative to tell him his password or to reset the password to something else. "I can't get this report out without it!" was (and is) a common lament.

The problem for help desk representatives is, of course, that they have no way of determining that they are talking with the true user and not someone spoofing a true user who is launching a social engineering attack. But they are in a bind: If they do not help in some way, the help desk is perceived to be the "unhelpful desk."

To resolve such problems, many systems give the help desk representative a means of authenticating the user. Typically, the help desk information system has answers to questions that only the true user would know, such as the user's birthplace, mother's maiden name, or last four digits of an important account number.

Backup and Recovery Procedures

Backup procedures concern the creation of backup data to be used in the event of failure. Whereas operations personnel have the responsibility for backing up system databases and other systems data, departmental personnel have the need to back up data on their own computers.

> I hereby acknowledge personal receipt of the system password(s) associated with the user IDs listed below. I understand that I am responsible for protecting the password(s), will comply with all applicable system security standards, and will not divulge my password(s) to any person. I further understand that I must report to the Information Systems Security Officer any problem I encounter in the use of the password(s) or when I have reason to believe that the private nature of my password(s) has been compromised.

FIGURE 12-22
Sample Account Acknowledgement Form

Systems analysts should develop procedures for system recovery. First, how will the department manage its affairs when a critical system is unavailable? Customers will want to order and manufacturing will want to remove items from inventory even though a critical information system is unavailable. How will the department respond? Once the system is returned to service, how will records of business activities during the outage be entered into the system? How will service be resumed? The system developers should ask and answer these questions and others like them and develop procedures accordingly.

Security Monitoring

Security monitoring is the last of the human safeguards we will consider. Important monitoring functions are activity log analyses, security testing, and investigating and learning from security incidents.

Many information system programs produce *activity logs.* Firewalls produce logs of their activities, including lists of all dropped packets, infiltration attempts, and unauthorized access attempts from within the firewall. DBMS products produce logs of successful and failed log-ins.

Web servers produce voluminous logs of Web activities. The operating systems in personal computers can produce logs of log-ins and firewall activities. None of these logs add any value to an organization unless someone looks at them. Accordingly, an important security function is to analyze these logs for threat patterns, successful and unsuccessful attacks, and evidence of security vulnerabilities.

Today, most large organizations actively investigate their security vulnerabilities. When attacked or scanned, organizations then use IP traceback programs, such as Sam Spade, to determine who has attacked them. If you are technically minded, detail-oriented, and curious, a career as a security specialist in this field is almost as exciting as it appears on *CSI.* To learn more, check out Sam Spade, HotBot, or AppScan.

Security, like quality, is an ongoing process. There is no final state when technical, data, or human safeguards are complete and security is achieved. Instead, companies must monitor security on a continuing basis.

Q9. How Should Organizations Respond to Security Incidents?

When safeguards fail and an incident occurs, organizations need to execute an incident response plan. Figure 12-23 lists the major factors. First, every organization should have an incident response plan as part of the security program, and it should ensure employees know where to find it when an incident occurs. No organization should wait until some asset has been lost or compromised before deciding what to do. The plan should include how employees are to respond to security problems, whom they should contact, the reports they should make, and steps they can take to reduce further loss.

The plan should provide centralized reporting of all security incidents. Such reporting will enable an organization to determine if it is under systematic attack or whether an incident is isolated. Centralized reporting also allows the organization to learn about security threats, take consistent actions in response, and apply specialized expertise to all security problems.

When an incident does occur, speed is of the essence. Viruses and worms can spread very quickly across an organization's networks, and a fast response will help mitigate the consequences. Because of the need for speed, preparation pays. The incident response plan should identify critical personnel and their off-hours contact information. These personnel should be trained on where to go and what to do when they get there. Without adequate preparation, there is substantial risk that the actions of well-meaning people will make the problem worse.

FIGURE 12-23

Factors in Incident Response

- Have plan in place
- Centralized reporting
- Specific responses
  - Speed
  - Preparation pays
  - Don't make problem worse
- Practice

Also, the rumor mill will be alive with all sorts of nutty ideas about what to do. A cadre of well-informed, trained personnel will serve to dampen such rumors. Finally, organizations should periodically practice incident response. Without such practice, personnel will be poorly informed on the response plan, and the plan itself may have flaws that only become apparent during a drill.

MIS InClass 12

Phishing for Credit Cards, Identifying Numbers, and Bank Accounts

A phisher is an individual or organization that spoofs legitimate companies in an attempt to illegally capture personal data such as credit card numbers, email accounts, and driver's license numbers. Some phishers install malicious program code on users' computers as well.

Phishing is usually initiated via email. Phishers steal legitimate logos and trademarks and use official-sounding words in an attempt to fools users into revealing personal data or clicking a link. Phishers do not bother with laws about trademark use. They place names and logos like Visa, MasterCard, Discover, and American Express on their Web pages and use them as bait. In some cases, phishers copy the entire look and feel of a legitimate company's Web site.

In this exercise, you and a group of your fellow students will be asked to investigate phishing attacks. If you search the Web for *phishing*, be aware that your search may bring the attention of an active phisher. Therefore, do not give any data to any site that you visit as part of this exercise!

1. To learn phishing fundamentals, visit www.microsoft .com/security/online-privacy/phishing-symptoms.aspx. To see recent examples of phishing attacks, visit www.fraudwatchinternational.com/phishing-alerts.
   a. Using examples from these links, describe how phishing works.
   b. Explain why a link that appears to be legitimate, such as www.microsoft.mysite.com, may, in fact, be a link to a phisher's site.
   c. List five indicators of a phishing attack.
   d. Write an email that you could send to a nontechnical friend or relative that explains what phishing is and how your friend or relative can avoid it.
2. Suppose you received the email in Figure 12-24 and mistakenly clicked "See more details here." When you did so, you

Source: Brian A Jackson/Shutterstock.

were taken to the Web page shown in Figure 12-25. List every phishing symptom that you find in these figures and explain why it is a symptom.

3. Suppose you work for an organization that is being phished.
   a. How would you learn that your organization is being attacked?
   b. What steps should your organization take in response to the attack?
   c. What liability, if any, do you think your organization has for damages to customers that result from a phishing attack that carries your brand and trademarks?
4. Summarize why phishing is a serious problem for commerce today.
5. Describe actions that industry organizations, companies, governments, and individuals can take to help reduce phishing.

Your Order 1D: "17152492"
Order Date: "09/07/12"
Product Purchased: "Two First Class Tickets to Cozumel"
Your card type: "CREDIT"
Total Price: "$349.00"
Hello, when you purchased your tickets you provided an incorrect mailing address.
<u>See more details here</u>
Please follow the link and modify your mailing address or cancel your order. If you have questions, feel free to contact us <u>account@usefulbill.com</u>

FIGURE 12-24
Fake Phishing Email

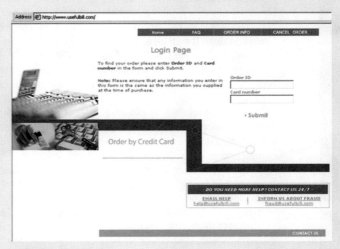

FIGURE 12-25
Fake Phishing Screen

Ethics Guide

Security Privacy

Some organizations have legal requirements to protect the customer data they collect and store, but the laws may be more limited than you think. The **Gramm-Leach-Bliley (GLB) Act**, passed by Congress in 1999, protects consumer financial data stored by financial institutions, which are defined as banks, securities firms, insurance companies, and organizations that provide financial advice, prepare tax returns, and provide similar financial services.

The Privacy Act of 1974 provides protections to individuals regarding records maintained by the U.S. government, and the privacy provisions of the Health Insurance Portability and Accountability Act (HIPAA) of 1996 give individuals the right to access their own health data created by doctors and other healthcare providers. HIPAA also sets rules and limits on who can read and receive your health information.

The law is stronger in other countries. In Australia, for example, the Privacy Principles of the Australian Privacy Act of 1988 govern not only government and healthcare data but also records maintained by businesses with revenues in excess of AU$3 million.

To understand the importance of the limitations, consider online retailers that routinely store customer credit card data. Do Dell, Amazon.com, the airlines, and other e-commerce businesses have a legal requirement to protect their customers' credit card data? Apparently not—at least not in the United States. The activities of such organizations are not governed by the GLB, the Privacy Act of 1974, or HIPAA.

Most consumers would say, however, that online retailers have an ethical requirement to protect a customer's credit card and other data, and most online retailers would agree. Or at least the retailers would agree that they have a strong business reason to protect that data. A substantial loss of credit card data by any large online retailer would have detrimental effects on both sales and brand reputation.

Data aggregators further complicate the risk to individuals because they develop a complete profile of households and individuals. And no federal law prohibits the U.S. government from buying information products from the data accumulators.

But let's bring the discussion closer to home. What requirements does your university have on the data it maintains about you? State law or university policy may govern those records, but no federal law does. Most universities consider it their responsibility to provide public access to graduation records. Anyone can determine when you graduated, your

degree, and your major. (Keep this service in mind when you write your résumé.)

Most professors endeavor to publish grades by student number and not by name, and there may be a state law that requires that separation. But what about your work? What about the papers you write, the answers you give on exams? What about the emails you send to your professor? These data are not protected by federal law, and they are probably not protected by state law. If your professor chooses to cite your work in research, she will be subject to copyright law but not privacy law. What you write is no longer your personal data; it belongs to the academic community. You can ask your professor what she intends to do with your coursework, emails, and office conversations, but none of that data is protected by law.

The bottom line: Be careful with your personal data. Large, reputable organizations are likely to endorse ethical privacy policy and to have strong and effective safeguards to effectuate that policy, but individuals and small organizations might not. If in doubt, ask.

DISCUSSION QUESTIONS

1. Using the categorical imperative (page 20) and utilitarianism (page 40) perspectives, assess the privacy ethics of the online retailer, the data aggregator, governments, and your professor. State assumptions you need to support your assessment, if any.

2. When you order from an online retailer, the data you provide is not protected by U.S. privacy law. Does this fact cause you to reconsider setting up an account with a stored credit card number? What is the advantage of storing the credit card number? Do you think the advantage is worth the risk? Are you more willing to take the risk with some companies than with others? Why or why not?

3. Suppose you are the treasurer of a student club and you store records of club members' payments in a database. In the past, members have disputed payment amounts; therefore, when you receive a payment, you scan an image of the check or credit card invoice and store the scanned image in a database.

   One day, you are using your computer in a local wireless coffee shop and a malicious student breaks into your computer over the wireless network and steals the club database. You know nothing about this until the next day, when a club member complains that a popular student Web site has published the names, bank names, and bank account numbers for everyone who has given you a check.

What liability do you have in this matter? Could you be classified as a financial institution because you are taking students' money? (You can find the GLB at *http:// business.ftc.gov/privacy-and-security/gramm-leach-bliley-act.*) If so, what liability do you have? If not, do you have any other liability? Does the coffee shop have a liability?

4. Suppose you are asked to fill out a study questionnaire that requires you to enter identifying data as well as answers to personal questions. You hesitate to provide the data, but the top part of the questionnaire states, "All responses will be strictly confidential." So, you fill out the questionnaire.

Unfortunately, the person who is conducting the study visits the same wireless coffee shop that you visited (in question 2), and the same malicious student breaks in and steals the study results. Your name and all of your responses appear on that same student Web site. Did the person conducting the study violate a law? Does the confidentiality assurance on the form increase that person's requirement to protect your data? Does your answer change if the person conducting the study is (a) a student, (b) a professor of music, or (c) a professor of computer security?

5. In truth, only a very talented and motivated hacker could steal databases from computers using a public wireless network. Such losses, although possible, are unlikely. However, any email you send or files you download can readily be sniffed at a public wireless facility. Knowing this, describe good practice for computer use at public wireless facilities.

6. Considering your answers to the above questions, state three to five general principles to guide your actions as you disseminate and store data.

Source: Max Krasnov/Shutterstock.

Active Review

Use this Active Review to verify that you understand the material in the chapter. You can read the entire chapter and then perform the tasks in this review, or you can read the text material for just one question and perform the tasks in this review for that question before moving on to the next one.

Q1. What are the activities of business process management?

Describe the need for business process management (BPM) and explain why it is a cycle. Name the four activities of the BPM process and summarize the tasks in each. Summarize two reasons that processes need to be changed and give an example of each.

Q2. What are the activities in the systems development life cycle (SDLC) development process?

Name five basic systems development activities. Describe tasks required for the definition, requirements, and create components activities. Explain the role of business analysts and IT analysts. Explain the tasks required to implement and maintain the system and assess the process. Describe four types of process/system conversion.

Q3. How can the scrum process overcome the problems of the SDLC?

Explain the three reasons that the SDLC is falling out of favor. In your own words, explain the meaning and importance of each of the principles in Figure 12-9. Explain how each of the scrum essential items in Figure 12-10 is implemented in the scrum process shown in Figure 12-11.

Q4. What is information systems security?

Define *information systems security* and explain why it is difficult to know the true size of the computer security problem. Describe threat, vulnerability, safeguard, and target, and give an example of each. List three types of threats and four types of security losses. Give different examples for the three rows of Figure 12-13. Summarize each of the elements in the cells of Figure 12-14. Explain why information security is difficult.

Q5. How should you respond to security threats?

Explain each of the elements in Figure 12-15. Summarize the characteristics of a strong password. Define *cookie* and explain why using a program like CCleaner is a good example of a computer security trade-off.

Q6. How should organizations respond to security threats?

Name and describe three security functions that senior management should address. Summarize the contents of a security policy. Explain what it means to manage risk. Summarize the steps that organizations should take when balancing risk and cost. Explain why safeguards should be layered.

Q7. How can technical and data safeguards protect against security threats?

Define *technical safeguard* and explain which of the five components are involved in such safeguards. Explain the use of identification and authentication, and describe three types of authentication. Describe symmetric and asymmetric encryption and explain how they are used for SSL/TLS. Define *firewall*. Name the five types of malware as defined in this text and briefly describe each. Describe the seven anti-malware techniques presented. Give examples of data safeguards.

Q8. How can human safeguards protect against security threats?

Name and describe the human safeguards for employees and nonemployee personnel. Summarize account administration safeguards. Describe backup and recovery options. Explain three security monitoring functions.

Q9. How should organizations respond to security incidents?

Summarize the actions that an organization should take when dealing with a security incident.

Key Terms and Concepts

Agile development   375
Asymmetric encryption   386
Authentication   385
Biometric authentication   385
Business analyst   371
Business process management
    (BPM)   367
Continuous improvement process
    (CIP)   369
Cookies   384
Cross-site scripting (XSS)   381
Denial of service (DOS)   382
Drive-by sniffers   381
Email spoofing   381
Encryption   386
Evil twin   381
Firewall   386

Gramm-Leach-Bliley (GLB) Act   394
Hacking   381
https   386
Human safeguards   388
Information systems security   378
IP spoofing   381
Key   386
Key escrow   388
Maintenance   374
Parallel installation   373
Phased installation   373
Phisher   381
Phishing   381
Pilot installation   373
Plunge installation   373
Pretexting   381
Public key/private key   386

Safeguard   379
Smart card   385
Sniffing   381
Social engineering   381
Spoofing   381
SQL injection attack   382
Stand-up   376
Symmetric encryption   386
System conversion   373
Systems development   369
Systems development life cycle
    (SDLC)   369
Target   379
Technical safeguards   385
Test plan   373
Threat   379
Vulnerability   379

Using Your Knowledge

12-1. Search Google or Bing for the phrase *what is a business analyst*. Investigate several of the links that you find and answer the following questions:
  a. What are the primary job responsibilities of a business analyst?
  b. What knowledge do business analysts need?
  c. What skills/personal traits do business analysts need?
  d. Would a career as a business analyst be interesting to you? Explain why or why not.

12-2. Reread the opening vignettes regarding CBI at the beginning of Chapters 7 and 8. Using that information as a background, generate a two- to three-page document that summarizes the security management activities that CBI should practice. Consider each of the vulnerabilities in Figure 12-14. As you write the document, keep in mind that CBI must strike a balance between comprehensive security management and cost. Explain what it means for CBI to manage risk. Describe the difference between not creating a security safeguard because CBI never thought about it and not creating a safeguard because of a risk management decision.

12-3. Consider the 12 categories of vulnerability in Figure 12-14. Describe the three most serious vulnerabilities to each of the following businesses:
  a. CBI
  b. Your university
  c. A neighborhood accounting firm

12-4. Describe a potential technical safeguard for each of the vulnerabilities you identified in your answer to question 12-3.

12-5. Describe a potential data safeguard for each of the vulnerabilities you identified in your answer to question 12-3. If no data safeguard is appropriate to a business, explain why.

12-6. Describe a potential human safeguard for each of the vulnerabilities you identified in your answer to question 12-3.

12-7. Describe how each of the organizations in question 12-3 should prepare for security incidents.

12-8. How likely are the vulnerabilities you identified in question 12-3? If you were the owner or a senior manager in these organizations, which of the items you described in questions 12-4 through 12-7 would you implement? Justify your answer.

Collaboration Exercise 12

Collaborate with a group of fellow students to answer the following questions. For this exercise do not meet face to face. Your task will be easier if you coordinate your work with SharePoint, Office 365, Google Docs with Google+, or equivalent collaboration tools. (See Chapter 9 for a discussion of collaboration tools and processes.) Your answers should reflect the thinking of the entire group, not just that of one or two individuals.

Opinions vary on whether cloud databases are more or less secure than in-house hosted databases. Some experts claim that cloud databases from reputable vendors such as Microsoft, Amazon, and Oracle are far more secure than in-house hosted ones. Others claim that the risk of mismanagement by a cloud vendor is too high; organizations should store critical and confidential data only in-house.

Working with your team, take a position on this issue by answering the following questions:

1. Search the Internet for *ISO 27001*. Explain the purpose of this standard.
2. Does compliance with ISO 27001 mean that a data center is secure? Does it mean that no security threat against compliant data centers will be successful? What does it mean?
3. Search the Internet for evidence that Microsoft Azure complies with ISO 27001. Summarize your findings.
4. Search the Internet for evidence that Amazon's EC2 complies with ISO 27001. Summarize your findings.

SAS 70 is an auditing standard that provides guidance for an auditor issuing a report about internal controls implemented by a cloud services provider. To assess the adequacy of data center controls, it is necessary to read and analyze the report that was prepared in accordance with SAS 70.

5. Search the Internet for evidence that Microsoft's auditors have issued a report in accordance with SAS 70. Summarize your findings.

6. Search the Internet for evidence that Amazon's auditors have issued a report in accordance with SAS 70. Summarize your findings.
7. Compare and contrast your answers to questions 3/4 and 5/6. Does your comparison cause you to believe that there are significant differences with regard to security and control between Azure and EC2?
8. Many small businesses operate with local servers running in broom closets or the like. Explain what using a cloud vendor that is compliant with these standards and statements means to such companies.
9. Suppose a publicly traded large organization operates its own Web farm and has certifications indicating that it has complied with ISO 27001 and has issued a statement of controls in accordance with SAS 70 that indicates controls are at least adequate. Is there any reason to believe that the organization's data assets on that Web farm are more or less secure than they would be if stored in Azure or EC2? Explain your answer.
10. Based on your answers to these questions, create a general statement as to the desirability, considering only data security, of storing data on Azure and EC2 as compared with storing it on servers managed in-house.

CASE STUDY 12

Will You Trust FIDO?

This text has stressed that the best protection users can provide themselves is strong passwords. The problem is that such passwords are easy to forget, no matter how clever the mnemonic for recalling them. Plus, some sites require users to regularly change their passwords, and people forget which password is current, especially for sites they seldom visit. As stated by David O'Connell, senior analyst at Nucleus Research, "Passwords are inconvenient, and people are careless with them. In a recent survey we conducted with enterprise users, we found that one-third of all people record passwords somewhere, whether on a sticky note or in a computer file."

Of course, when malicious code infects a computer, one of the first things it does is search for files that include the word *password* or some variant. And once the code has downloaded the password file, all of the user's sites and accounts are open. Even worse, because many users don't know their computer has been infiltrated until long after the attack, they don't know to change their passwords until it is too late.

Users sometimes avoid having multiple passwords by using one identity for multiple sites. Many Web sites, for example, offer to authenticate you using your Facebook or other common credentials. The site accepts your name and password and passes it over to Facebook for authentication. However tempting this might be to you, never do it because you have no way of telling what else

that site is doing with your Facebook credentials. It could be doing only what it says. Or it could be saving your credentials in a database, which may or may not be secure, or it could be selling your credentials to a criminal in Nigeria. You have no way of knowing what it's doing. In general, use your credentials only at the site for which they were created.

As of 2013, numerous alternatives to password authentication are under development. Some are biometric such as fingerprints or retinal scans; some rely on user behavior such as keystroke rhythm. It turns out that all of us have idiosyncrasies in the way we type that can be used to identify us. Voice can also be used to identify individuals; visit *www.porticusinc.com* to see one example.

Other alternatives to passwords include the picture password in Windows 8 in which the user makes three gestures over a photo. Still other options include naming the people in a group photo or providing facts about people in photos that only the user would know.

These authentication methods make fewer demands on users' memories, but they all suffer one defect: If the user's authentication is compromised once, it is compromised for all of the sites on which that authentication method is used.

To correct this defect, in 2012, Lenovo, PayPal, and other sponsoring organizations began development of a set of open standards and protocols known as FIDO, or Fast Identity OnLine. Since then, Google and other major organizations have joined the effort.

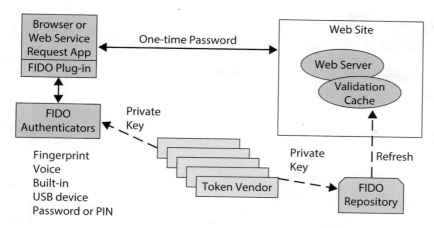

FIGURE 12-26
FIDO Schematic

Source: Based on *http://www*
.fidoalliance.org/how-it-works.html,
accessed May, 2013.

The standards are still under development, but the basic schematic, as of this writing, is shown in Figure 12-26. Users purchase an authenticating device, either as part of their mobile device or PC or as a separate USB device. The security of those devices can be improved by backing them up with a password or PIN. The user and the FIDO device are associated by the vendor of the device, shown as a Token Vendor in Figure 12-26. That vendor provides a secret value, like a private key, to the device and also to an independent third party called a FIDO Repository. The plan calls for many such repositories to exist; their purpose is to provide FIDO authenticating data to Web servers.

After a user has been authenticated, a plug-in to the user's browser will use the private key data to generate a one-time password (OTP; this means the password is used just for one session with a Web site) and send it to the Web site. There the Web server will pass the OTP to another FIDO application, the Validation Cache. The cache will, the first time it encounters an OTP from a user, contact a FIDO repository to obtain the user's private key data. It uses this data to validate the OTP. This contact with the FIDO repository need only be done once per user per Web site.

FIDO does not eliminate the need to send private data over the Internet, but it substantially reduces it. The private key data must be sent once to the user and once to each Web site the user visits. After that, only temporary OTP are exchanged between the user

and the Web site. Furthermore, the user's authentication data never leaves the user's device. Your password or PIN, for example, is never sent over a network.

Will you trust FIDO? Probably. The consortium is doing security business the right way: forming open standards and asking the community to find holes and problems long before the standard is implemented. It also has the support of major, well-funded organizations. Unless some fatal, non-fixable flaw is found in the FIDO scheme, you most likely will be using it within a few years.

Questions

12-9. Summarize the problems with passwords.

12-10. Explain why you should not use your Facebook credentials to authenticate yourself to non-Facebook Web sites.

12-11. Describe three authentication methods other than passwords.

12-12. Explain the advantages of FIDO to users and to Web sites.

12-13. Briefly describe how FIDO works.

12-14. Describe factors that will determine whether FIDO becomes an industry standard.

12-15. Is FIDO gaining popularity with users and vendors? Search the Web to find out.

Application Exercises

Please note all exercise files can be found on the following Web site: *www.pearsonhighered.com/kroenke*.

PART 1

Chapter 1

1-1. Figure AE-1 shows an Excel spreadsheet that the resort bicycle rental business, shown in Figure 1-15, page 19, uses to value and analyze its bicycle inventory. Examine this figure to understand the meaning of the data. Now use Excel to create a similar spreadsheet. Note the following:

- The top heading is in 20-point Calibri font. It is centered in the spreadsheet. Cells A1 through H1 have been merged.
- The second heading, *Bicycle Inventory Valuation*, is in 18-point Calibri, italics and red. It is centered in cells A2 through H2, which have been merged.
- The column headings are set in 11-point Calibri, bold. They are centered in their cells, and the text wraps in the cells.

  a. Make the first two rows of your spreadsheet similar to those in Figure AE-1. Choose your own colors for background and type, however.

  b. Place the current date so it is centered in cells C3, C4, and C5, which must be merged.

  c. Outline the cells as shown in the figure.

  d. Figure AE-1 uses the following formulas:

> **Cost of Current Inventory = Bike Cost × Number on Hand**
> **Revenue per Bike = Total Rental Revenue/Number on Hand**
> **Revenue as a Percent of Cost of Inventory = Total Rental Revenue/Cost of Current Inventory**

Please use these formulas in your spreadsheet, as shown in Figure AE-1.

  e. Format the cells in the columns as shown.

  f. Give three examples of decisions that the management of the bike rental agency might make from this data.

  g. What other calculation could you make from this data that would be useful to the bike rental management? Create a second version of this spreadsheet in your worksheet document that has this calculation.

1-2. In this exercise, you will learn how to create a query based on data that a user enters and how to use that query to create a data entry form.

  a. Download the Microsoft Access file **Ch01Ex02**. Open the file and familiarize yourself with the data in the Customer table.

Resort Bicycle Rental
Bicycle Inventory Valuation
Thursday, September 5, 2013

Make of Bike	Bike Cost	Number on Hand	Cost of Current Inventory	Number of Rentals	Total Rental Revenue	Revenue per Bike	Revenue as Percent of Cost of Inventory
Wonder Bike	325	12	$3,900	85	$6,375	$531	163.5%
Wonder Bike 2	385	4	$1,540	34	$4,570	$1,143	296.8%
Wonder Bike Supreme	475	8	$3,800	44	$5,200	$650	136.8%
LiteLift Pro	655	8	$5,240	25	$2,480	$310	47.3%
LiteLift Ladies	655	4	$2,620	40	$6,710	$1,678	256.1%
LiteLift Racer	795	3	$2,385	37	$5,900	$1,967	247.4%

FIGURE AE-1

b. Click *Create* in the Access ribbon and select *Query Design*. Select the *Customer* table as the basis for the query. Drag *CustomerName, CustomerEmail, DateOfLastRental, BikeLastRented, TotalNumberOfRentals*, and *TotalRentalRevenue* into the columns of the query results pane (the table at the bottom of the query design window).

c. In the *CustomerName* column, in the row labeled *Criteria*, place the following text:

[Enter Name of Customer:]

Type this exactly as shown, including the square brackets. This notation tells Access to ask you for a customer name to query.

d. In the ribbon, click the red exclamation mark labeled *Run*. Access will display a dialog box with the text "Enter Name of Customer:" (the text you entered in the query *Criteria* row). Enter the value *Scott, Rex* and click OK.

e. Save your query with the name *Parameter Query*.

f. Click the Home tab on the ribbon and click the *Design View* (upper left-hand button on the Home ribbon). Replace the text in the *Criteria* column of the *CustomerName* column with the following text. Type it exactly as shown:

Like "*" & [Enter part of Customer Name to search by:] & "*"

g. Run the query by clicking *Run* in the ribbon. Enter *Scott* when prompted *Enter part of Customer Name to search by*. Notice that the two customers who have the name Scott are displayed. If you have any problems, ensure that you have typed the phrase above *exactly* as shown into the *Criteria* row of the *CustomerName* column of your query.

h. Save your query again under the name *Parameter Query*. Close the query window.

i. Click *Create* in the Access ribbon. Under the Forms group, choose *Form Wizard* (if using an older version of Access you need to select the down arrow to the right of *More Forms*). In the dialog that opens, in the Tables/Queries box, click the down arrow. Select *Parameter Query*. Click the double chevron (>>) symbol and all of the columns in the query will move to the Selected Fields area.

j. Click *Next* two or three times (depending on your version of Access) until you come to the Finish option. In the box under *What title do you want for your form?* enter *Customer Query Form* and click *Finish*.

k. Enter *Scott* in the dialog box that appears and click OK. Access will open a form with the values for Scott, Rex. At the bottom of the form, click the right-facing arrow and the data for Scott, Bryan will appear.

l. Close the form. Select *Object Type* and *Forms* in the Access Navigation Pane. Double-click on Customer Query Form and enter the value *James*. Access will display data for all six customers having the value James in their name.

Chapter 2

2-1. The spreadsheet in Microsoft Excel file **Ch02Ex01** contains records of employee activity on special projects. Open this workbook and examine the data that you find in the three spreadsheets it contains. Assess the accuracy, relevancy, and sufficiency of this data to the following people and problems.

a. You manage the Denver plant, and you want to know how much time your employees are spending on special projects.

b. You manage the Reno plant, and you want to know how much time your employees are spending on special projects.

c. You manage the Quota Computation project in Chicago, and you want to know how much time your employees have spent on that project.

d. You manage the Quota Computation project for all three plants, and you want to know the total time employees have spent on your project.

e. You manage the Quota Computation project for all three plants, and you want to know the total labor cost for all employees on your project.

f. You manage the Quota Computation project for all three plants, and you want to know how the labor-hour total for your project compares with the labor-hour totals for the other special projects.

g. What conclusions can you make from this exercise?

2-2. The database in the Microsoft Access file **Ch02Ex02** contains the same records of employee activity on special projects as in Application Exercise 2-1. Before proceeding, open that database and view the records in the Employee Hours table.

a. Seven queries have been created that process this data in different ways. Using the criteria of accuracy, relevancy, and sufficiency, select the single query that is most appropriate for the information requirements in Application Exercise 2-1, parts a–f.

b. If a query contains the data but needs to be modified to make the data meaningful (sort, filter, add total row, etc.), describe the actions you should take on the current queries to easily find the information requested in Application Exercise 2-1, parts a–f.

c. If no current query meets the requirements for the information requested in Application Exercise 2-1, parts a–f, explain why. For these questions, design a query that will provide the desired information. If a query cannot be designed because the appropriate data is not in the database, describe the data that is needed to answer the question.

d. What conclusions can you make from this exercise?

e. Comparing your experiences on these two projects, what are the advantages and disadvantages of spreadsheets and databases?

PART 2

Chapter 3

3-1. Sometimes you will have data in one Office application and want to move it to another Office application without rekeying it. Often this occurs when data were created for one purpose but then are used for a second purpose. For example, Figure AE-2 presents a portion of an Excel spreadsheet that shows the assignment of computers to employees. Lucas, at Chuck's Bikes, might use such a spreadsheet to track who has which equipment.

Suppose that you (or Lucas) want to use this data to help you assess how to upgrade computers. Let's say, for example, that you want to upgrade all of the computers' operating systems to Windows 8. Furthermore, you want to first upgrade the computers that most need upgrading, but you have a limited budget. To address this situation, you would like to query the data in Figure AE-2 to find all computers that do not have Windows 8 and then select those with slower CPUs or smaller memory as candidates for upgrading. To do this, you need to move the data from Excel and into Access.

Once you have analyzed the data and determined the computers to upgrade, you want to produce a report. In that case, you may want to move the data from Access back to Excel or perhaps into Word. In this exercise, you will learn how to perform these tasks.

FIGURE AE-2

EmpLastName	EmpFirstName	Plant	Computer Brand	CPU (GHz)	Memory (	Disk (GB)	OS
Ashley	Jane	Denver	Dell	3	4	400	Windows 7
Davidson	Kaye	Denver	Dell	2	3	120	Vista
Ching	Kam Hoong	Denver	HP	2	3	100	Vista
Collins	Giovanni	Denver	Dell	1	1	80	Windows 8
Corning	Sandra	Denver	HP	1.2	1	120	Vista
Scott	Rex	Denver	HP	1.8	2	100	XP
Corovic	Jose	Denver	Dell	3	2	250	Windows 7
Lane	Brandon	Denver	Lenovo	2	1.512	250	Vista
Wei	Guang	Denver	IBM	2	1	120	Windows 7
Dixon	Eleanor	Denver	IBM	1	1.512	120	Vista
Lee	Brandon	Denver	Dell	0.5	2	80	XP
Duong	Linda	Denver	Dell	0.5	2	40	XP
Bosa	Victor	Denver	HP	1	2	30	Vista
Drew	Richard	Denver	HP	1	3	100	Windows 8
Adams	James	Denver	HP	1	1	80	XP
Lunden	Haley	Denver	Lenovo	2	0.512	80	Windows 7
Utran	Diem Thi	Denver	Dell	2	0.512	120	Windows 7
	Primary Contact:	Kaye Davidson					

a. To begin, download the Excel file **Ch03Ex01** into one of your directories. We will import the data in this file into Access, but before we do so, familiarize yourself with the data by opening it in Excel. Notice that there are three worksheets in this workbook. Close the Excel file.

b. Create a blank Access database. Name the database *Ch03Ex01_Answer*. Place it in some directory; it may be the same directory into which you have placed the Excel file, but it need not be. Close the default table that Access creates and delete it.

c. Now, we will import the data from the three worksheets in the Excel file **Ch03Ex01** into a single table in your Access database. In the ribbon, select *External Data* and *Excel* in the Import and Link group. Start the import. For the first worksheet (Denver), you should select *Import the source data into a new table in the current database*. Be sure to click *First Row Contains Column Headings* when Access presents your data. You can use the default Field types and let Access add the primary key. Name your table *Employees* and click *Finish*. There is no need to save your import script.

For the second and third worksheets, again click *External Data* and *Excel*, but this time select *Append a copy of the records to the table Employees*. Import all data.

d. Open the *Employee* table and examine the data. Notice that Access has erroneously imported a blank line and the Primary Contact data into rows at the end of each data set. This data is not part of the employee records, and you should delete it (in three places—once for each worksheet). The *Employee* table should have a total of 40 records.

e. Now, create a parameterized query on this data. Place all of the columns except *ID* into the query. In the *OS* column, set the criteria to select rows for which the value is not *Windows 8*. In the *CPU* (GHz) column, enter the criterion: *<=[Enter cutoff value for CPU]*. In the *Memory* (GB) column, enter the criterion: *<=[Enter cutoff value for Memory]*. Test your query. For example, run your query and enter a value of *2* for both CPU and memory. Verify that the correct rows are produced.

f. Use your query to find values of CPU and memory that give you as close to a maximum of 15 computers to upgrade as possible.

g. When you have found values of CPU and memory that give you 15, or nearly 15, computers to upgrade, leave your query open. Now, click *External data, Export group, More down arrow* and *Word* to create a Word document that contains the results of your query. Adjust the column widths of the created table so it fits on the page. Write a memo based on this table explaining that these are the computers you believe should be upgraded.

3-2.   Assume that you have been asked to create a spreadsheet to help make a local-versus-cloud decision for the servers on your organization's Web farm. Assume that you are considering the servers for a 5-year period, but you do not know exactly how many servers you will need. Initially, you know you will need five servers, but you might need as many as 50, depending on the success of your organization's e-commerce activity.

a. For the local-alternative calculations, set up your spreadsheet so you can enter the base price of the server hardware, the price of all software, and a maintenance expense that is some percentage of the hardware price. Assume that the percent you enter covers both hardware and software maintenance. Also assume that each server has a 3-year life, after which it has no value. Assume straight-line depreciation for computers used less than 3 years and that at the end of the 5 years you can sell the computers you have used for less than 3 years for their depreciated value. Also assume that your organization pays 2 percent interest on capital expenses. Assume the servers cost $5,000 each and the needed software costs $750. Assume that the maintenance expense varies from 2 to 7 percent.

b. For the cloud-alternative calculations, assume that the cloud vendor will lease the same computer hardware as you can purchase. The lease includes all the software you need as well as all maintenance. Set up your spreadsheet so you can enter various cloud costs, which vary according to the number of years of the lease (1, 2, or 3). Assume the cost of a 3-year lease is $285 per machine per month, a 2-year lease is $335 per machine per month, and a 1-year lease is $415 per machine per month. Also, the cloud vendor offers a 5 percent discount if you lease from 20 to 30 computers and a 10 percent discount if you lease from 31 to 50 computers.

c. Using your spreadsheet, compare the costs of local versus cloud under the following situations. (Assume you use either the local or cloud option. You cannot use the cloud for some and local for others.) Make assumptions, as necessary, and state those assumptions.

    (1) Your organization requires 20 servers for 5 years.

    (2) Your organization requires 20 servers for the first 2 years and 40 servers for the next 3 years.

    (3) Your organization requires 20 servers for the first 2 years, 40 servers for the next 2 years, and 50 servers for the last year.

    (4) Your organization requires 10 servers the first year, 20 servers the second year, 30 servers the third year, 40 servers the fourth year, and 50 servers the last year.

    (5) For the previous case, does the cheaper alternative change if the cost of the local servers is $4,000? If it is $8,000?

3-3. Numerous Web sites are available that will test your Internet data communications speed. A good one is available at www.speakeasy.net/speedtest/. (If that site is no longer active, Google or Bing "What is my Internet speed?" to find another speed-testing site. Use it.)

a. While connected to your university's network, go to Speakeasy and test your speed against servers in Seattle, New York City, and Atlanta. Compute your average upload and download speeds. Compare your speed to the speeds listed in Figure AE-3.

b. Go home or to a public wireless site and run the Speakeasy test again. Compute your average upload and download speeds. Compare your speed to those listed in Figure AE-3. If you are performing this test at home, are you getting the performance you are paying for?

c. Contact a friend or relative in another state. Ask him or her to run the Speakeasy test against those same three cities.

d. Compare the results in parts a, b, and c. What conclusion, if any, can you make from these tests?

Type	Topology	Transmission Line	Transmission Speed	Equipment Used	Protocol Commonly Used	Remarks
Local area network	Local area network	UTP or optical fiber	Common: 10/100/1000 Mbps Possible: 1 Gbps	Switch NIC UTP or optical	IEEE 802.3 (Ethernet)	Switches connect devices, multiple switches on all but small LANs.
	Local area network with wireless	UTP or optical for non-wireless connections	Up to 600 Mbps	Wireless access point Wireless NIC	IEEE 802.11n	Access point transforms wired LAN (802.3) to wireless LAN (802.11).
Connections to the Internet	DSL modem to ISP	DSL telephone	Personal: Upstream to 1 Mbps downstream to 40 Mbps (max 10 likely in most areas)	DSL modem DSL-capable telephone line	DSL	Can have computer and phone use simultaneously. Always connected.
	Cable modem to ISP	Cable TV lines to optical cable	Upstream to 1 Mbps Downstream 300 Kbps to 10 Mbps	Cable modem Cable TV cable	Cable	Capacity is shared with other sites; performance varies depending on others' use.
	WAN wireless	Wireless connection to WAN	500 Kbps to 1 Mbps	Wireless WAN modem	One of several wireless standards.	Sophisticated protocol enables several devices to use the same wireless frequency.

FIGURE AE-3

FIGURE AE-4

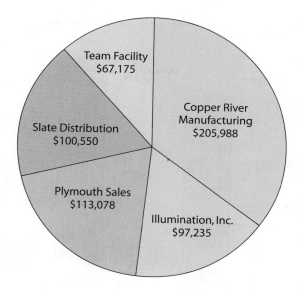

Team Facility
$67,175

Copper River
Manufacturing
$205,988

Slate Distribution
$100,550

Plymouth Sales
$113,078

Illumination, Inc.
$97,235

Chapter 4

4-1. A common scenario in business is to combine the processing of Microsoft Access and Excel. A typical scenario is for users to process relational data with Access, import some of the data into Excel, and use Excel's tools for creating professional-looking charts and graphs. You will do exactly that in this exercise.

Download the Access file **Ch04Ex01**. Open the database, and select *Database Tools/Relationships*. As you can see, there are three tables: *Product, Vendor Product Inventory*, and *Vendor*. Open each table individually to familiarize yourself with the data.

For this problem, we will define *Inventory Cost* as the product of *Industry Standard Cost* and *Quantity On Hand*. The query *Inventory Cost* computes these values for every item in inventory for every vendor. Open that query and view the data to be certain you understand this computation. Open the other queries as well so that you understand the data they produce.

  a. Sum this data by vendor and display it in a pie chart like that shown in Figure AE-4. Proceed as follows:

    (1) Open Excel and create a new spreadsheet.

    (2) Click *Data* on the ribbon and select *From Access* in the *Get External Data* group.

    (3) Navigate to the location in which you have stored the Access file **Ch04Ex01**.

    (4) Select the query that contains the data you need for this pie chart.

    (5) Import the data into a table.

    (6) Format the appropriate data as currency.

    (7) Select the range that contains the data, press the function key, and proceed from there to create the pie chart. Name the data and pie chart worksheets appropriately.

  b. Follow a similar procedure to create the bar chart shown in Figure AE-5. Place the data and the chart in separate worksheets and name them appropriately.

4-2. Suppose you are hired by an auto dealer to create a database of customers and their interests. Salespeople have been keeping data in a spreadsheet, and you have been asked to convert that data into a database. Because the dealer's data is so poorly structured, it will be a challenge, as you will see.

  a. Download the Excel file named **Ch04Ex02**. Open the spreadsheet and examine the data. It's a mess!

  b. Download the Access file with the same name, **Ch04Ex02**. Open the database, select *Database Tools*, and click *Relationships*. Examine the four tables and their relationships.

FIGURE AE-5

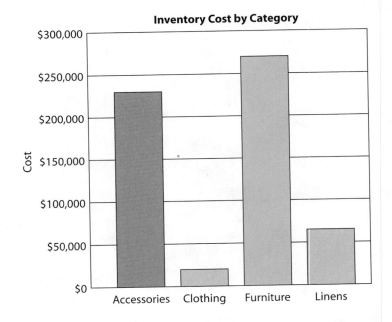

Inventory Cost by Category

c. Somehow, you have to transform the data in the spreadsheet into the table structure in the database. Because so little discipline was shown when creating the spreadsheet, this will be a labor-intensive task. To begin, import the spreadsheet data into a new table in the database; call that table *Sheet1* or some other name.

d. Copy the *Name* data in *Sheet1* onto the clipboard. Then open the *Customer* table and paste the column of name data into that table.

e. Unfortunately, the task becomes messy at this point. You can copy the *Car Interests* column into *Make or Model of Auto*, but then you will need to straighten out the values by hand. Phone numbers will need to be copied one at a time.

f. Open the *Customer* form and manually add any remaining data from the spreadsheet into each customer record. Connect the customer to his or her auto interests.

g. The data in the finished database has much more structure than that in the spreadsheet. Explain why that is both an advantage and a disadvantage. Under what circumstances is the database more appropriate? Less appropriate?

4-3. In this exercise, you will create a two-table database, define relationships, create a form and a report, and use them to enter data and view results.

a. Download the Excel file **Ch04Ex03**. Open the spreadsheet and review the data in the *Employee* and *Computer* worksheets.

b. Create a new Access database with the name *Ch04Ex03_Solution*. Close the table that Access automatically creates and delete it.

c. Import the data from the Excel spreadsheet into your database. Import the *Employee* worksheet into a table named *Employee*. Be sure to check *First Row Contains Column Headings*. Select *Choose my own primary key* and use the ID field as that key.

d. Import the *Computer* worksheet into a table named *Computer*. Check *First Row Contains Column Headings*, but let Access create the primary key.

e. Open the relationships window and add both *Employee* and *Computer* to the design space. Drag ID from *Employee* and drop it on *EmployeeID* in *Computer*. Check *Enforce Referential Integrity* and the two checkmarks below. Ensure that you know what these actions mean.

f. Open the Form Wizard dialog box (under *Create tab, Forms group, Form Wizard*), and add all of the columns for each of your tables to your form. Select *View your data by Employee*. Title your form *Employee* and your subform *Computer*.

g. Open the *Computer* subform and delete *EmployeeID* and *ComputerID*. These values are maintained by Access, and it is just a distraction to keep them. Your form should appear like the one shown in Figure AE-6.

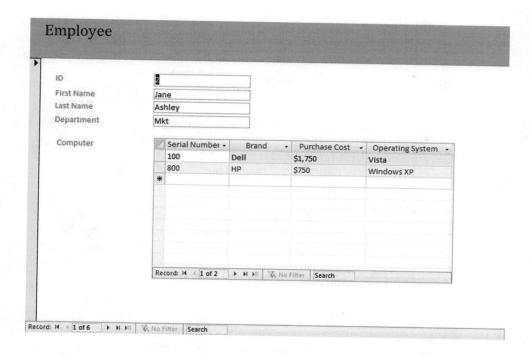

FIGURE AE-6

h. Use your form to add two new computers to *Jane Ashley*. Both computers are Dells, and both use Vista; one costs $750, and the second costs $1,400.

i. Delete the Lenovo computer for Rex Everest.

j. Use the Report Wizard (under *Create*) to create a report having all data from both the *Employee* and *Computer* tables. Play with the report design until you find a design you like. Correct the label alignment if you need to.

PART 3

Chapter 5

5-1. Assume that you have been hired to develop an Access database for a facilities reservation system at CBI's exercise facility. You have been given the following design for implementation:

FACILITY   (FacilityID, FacilityName, Description, StandardRentalFee)

RESERVATION (ReservationNumber, *FacilityID,* Date, StartTime, EndTime)

Where FacilityID and ReservationNumber are AutoNumber primary keys and RESERVATION FacilityID is a foreign key to FACILITY. Use the appropriate data types for the other columns.

a. Create these tables in Access.

b. Create the appropriate relationship in Access.

c. Import the data in the file **Ch05Ex01.txt** into the FACILITY table.

d. Create a reservation form for creating and viewing specific reservations.

e. Create a parameterized query for finding a reservation by value of ReservationNumber.

f. Create a report that shows all of the reservations for all facilities.

g. Create a parameterized report that shows all of the reservations for a particular date.

5-2. You are the manager of the pizza shop at Central Colorado State University where Sarah works. Recently, you provided your drivers with handheld GPS devices that display real-time traffic data. The owner of another franchise has asked you to give a presentation to the other franchise owners about the usefulness of the devices. To make your case, you collected data on 50 deliveries before and 50 deliveries after installing the devices at the end of June 2014. The data is located in the file **Ch05Ex02**.

In this spreadsheet, you have made two main sections. On the left is data from before the GPS devices were added, and on the right is data from after the GPS devices were added. There are four drivers, and each makes deliveries to four zones—A, B, C, and D. Zone A is composed of students in dorms at the campus; the other three zones are located in different geographic regions around the town. Also included in each of the two sections are time for delivery and the price of the delivery.

a. Format the labels at the top of each section using font size and color, fill color, and cell merging to make your spreadsheet look more professional.
b. Format the price data in currency format.
c. Calculate the average time and price before and after the GPS devices were used.
d. Calculate the average time and price before and after the GPS devices were used for zone A (dorm students).
e. How much time did the GPS devices save overall (all four zones combined)?
f. How much time did the GPS devices save per order for nonstudent deliveries?
g. If you are one of the managers considering adopting GPS devices, what factors might be different between your restaurant and the restaurant in this exercise that might affect your willingness to invest in GPS?

Chapter 6

6-1.   Central Colorado State is considering consolidating all purchasing functions into one central office. To assess the cost savings of such a move, the university collected data about the purchasing costs in three departments. These data are shown in the file **Ch06Ex01**.

The data show the number of orders and the total price of the orders for each of the three departments. The file also includes data on the monthly fixed costs of operating a purchasing office. Fixed costs include the cost of the purchasing agent(s) for that month; the estimated cost of the office space; and the approximate cost of other fixed costs, such as insurance and supervision. These three departments were chosen for data collection because they represent typical small, medium, and large purchasing offices.

a. If each purchasing agent costs the university $7,500 per month, calculate the total fixed cost for each of the offices.
b. Calculate the average fixed cost per order for each of the three departments.
c. Create a bar chart with appropriate labels and titles that shows the average fixed cost per order for each of the three departments.
d. The university estimates that it has 15 small, 5 medium, and 3 large departments. If each of these departments has the same number and price of orders as the three departments shown in the file, calculate the total number and total price for the entire university.
e. The university estimates that the fixed cost data for these other departments will be the same as the three departments shown in the file; that is, each small department will have the same data as the Athletics department, each medium department is like the Student Services department, and each large department is like the Bookstore. Calculate the total fixed costs for the entire university.
f. The university assumes that when purchasing is consolidated in one office, the average cost per order will be about the same as the Bookstore's average cost per order. Using the total number of orders for the university from part d and the average fixed cost per order of a large department from part b, how much will the university save if it consolidates purchasing in one location?

6-2.   Figure AE-7 is a sample bill of materials, a form that shows the components and parts used to construct a product. In this example, the product is a child's wagon. Such bills of materials are an essential part of manufacturing functional applications as well as ERP applications.

This particular example is a form produced using Microsoft Access. Producing such a form is a bit tricky, so this exercise will guide you through the steps required.

FIGURE AE-7

Ajax Toy Manufacturing Bill of Materials

You can then apply what you learn to produce a similar report. You can also use Access to experiment on extensions of this form.

a. Create a table named *PART* with columns *PartNumber, Level, Description, QuantityRequired*, and *PartOf*. *Description* and *Level* should be text, *PartNumber* should be AutoNumber, and *QuantityRequired* and *PartOf* should be numeric. Add the *PART* data shown in Figure AE-7 to your table.

b. Create a query that has all columns of *PART*. Restrict the view to rows having a value of 1 for *Level*. Name your query *qLevel1*.

c. Create two more queries that are restricted to rows having values of 2 or 3 for *Level*. Name your queries *qLevel2* and *qLevel3*, respectively.

d. Create a form that contains *PartNumber, Level,* and *Description* from *qLevel1*. You can use a wizard for this if you want. Name the form *Bill of Materials*.

e. Select the Subform/Subreport tool in the Controls section of the Design ribbon and create a subform in your form in part d. Set the data on this form to be all of the columns of *qLevel2*. After you have created the subform, ensure that the Link Child Fields property is set to *PartOf* and that the Link Master Fields property is set to *PartNumber*. (If using Access 2013, define the Form/Report fields as *PartNumber* and the Subform/subreport fields as *PartOf*.) Close the *Bill of Materials* form.

f. Open the subform created in part e and create a subform on it. Set the data on this subform to be all of the columns of *qLevel3*. After you have created the subform, ensure that the Link Child Fields property is set to *PartOf* and that the Link Master Fields property is set to *PartNumber*. (If using Access 2013, define the Form/Report fields as *PartNumber* and the Subform/subreport fields as *PartOf*.) Close the *Bill of Materials* form.

g. Open the *Bill of Materials* form. It should appear as in Figure AE-7. Open and close the form and add new data to the table. Using this form, add sample BOM data for a product of your own choosing.

h. Following the process similar to that just described, create a *Bill of Materials Report* that lists the data for all of your products.

i. **(Optional, challenging extension)** Each part in the BOM in Figure AE-7 can be used in at most one assembly (there is space to show just one *PartOf* value).

You can change your design to allow a part to be used in more than one assembly as follows: First, remove *PartOf* from PART. Next, create a second table that has two columns: *AssemblyPartNumber* and *ComponentPartNumber*. The first contains a part number of an assembly and the second a part number of a component. Every component of a part will have a row in this table. Extend the views described previously to use this second table and to produce a display similar to Figure AE-7.

Chapter 7

7-1. **SAP** Your firm, a small bike manufacturing outfit, is considering the possibility of adding a new item to its product line. This bike accessory is a 3rd Wheel, a trailer designed to carry children or, in a different configuration, goods and equipment (see Figure AE-8).

Your firm will procure and build the 3rd Wheel in-house if the labor costs for assembly are sufficiently less than the cost of procuring the 3rd Wheel already assembled. You are asked to estimate the labor cost of producing this new accessory. You have downloaded labor cost data from your ERP system into an Excel spreadsheet. This data file is **Ch07Ex01**. (To see how to download the data directly from SAP, see the end of this exercise.)

At the East plant there are four hourly wage rates for assembly workers and there are two possible unions that hourly pay is based upon—U001 and U002. To assemble the 3rd Wheel, the engineering department has developed several options. Each of the options requires a different set of hours for the pay rates, as shown below:

| | Labor Hours | | |
Pay Scale	Option A	Option B	Option C
0	5	3	7
1	3	4	2
2	2	2	1
3	2	1	2

a. Calculate the total labor cost for options A, B, and C for Union 001 and Union 002 using the minimum wage rate in each pay grade. Which option is lowest cost?

b. Calculate the total labor cost for options A, B, and C for Union 001 and Union 002 using the maximum wage rate in each pay grade. Which option is lowest cost?

FIGURE AE-8
3rd Wheel

Source: Jim West/Alamy Images.

FIGURE AE-9

Source: Copyright © SAP AG

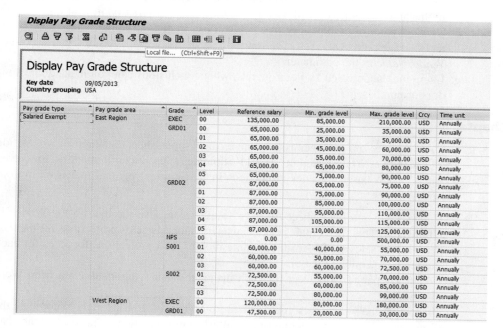

c. Create a chart with appropriate labels and titles that shows all six options in the previous two parts.

d. Another option for your firm is to outsource the payscale 0 work. If the bottom payscale work is removed, does the lowest cost option change?

e. The analysis in part d is a common one. This interactive analysis is also called "what-if" analysis. In part d you were asked, "What if payscale 0 work is outsourced?" If you expect to do "what-if" analysis on a spreadsheet, how does that change how you set up the original spreadsheet, its data, functions, and equations?

To download the data directly from SAP:[1]

(1) Log in to SAP as before.

(2) On the SAP Easy Access Screen, select:

> *Information Systems > General Report Selection > Human Resources > Personal Management > Compensation Management > Pay Structure > Display Pay Scale Structure*

(3) Enter *10* in Country Grouping (for USA), then click the *Execute* icon above Key date, as shown in Figure AE-9.

(4) On the Display Pay Scale Structure screen, click the *Local* file icon (ninth icon from left) and specify a file name and location for the file to be saved on the local machine, as shown in Figure AE-10.

(5) Open Excel. Navigate to the downloaded Excel file and open it. Inspect your spreadsheet. It should look like Figure AE-11.

FIGURE AE-10

Source: Copyright © SAP AG

Display Pay Grade Structure

Local file... (Ctrl+Shift+F9)

Display Pay Grade Structure

Key date 09/05/2013
Country grouping USA

Pay grade type	Pay grade area	Grade	Level	Reference salary	Min. grade level	Max. grade level	Crcy	Time unit
Salaried Exempt	East Region	EXEC	00	135,000.00	85,000.00	210,000.00	USD	Annually
		GRD01	00	65,000.00	25,000.00	35,000.00	USD	Annually
			01	65,000.00	35,000.00	50,000.00	USD	Annually
			02	65,000.00	45,000.00	60,000.00	USD	Annually
			03	65,000.00	55,000.00	70,000.00	USD	Annually
			04	65,000.00	65,000.00	80,000.00	USD	Annually
			05	65,000.00	75,000.00	90,000.00	USD	Annually
		GRD02	00	87,000.00	65,000.00	75,000.00	USD	Annually
			01	87,000.00	75,000.00	90,000.00	USD	Annually
			02	87,000.00	85,000.00	100,000.00	USD	Annually
			03	87,000.00	95,000.00	110,000.00	USD	Annually
			04	87,000.00	105,000.00	115,000.00	USD	Annually
			05	87,000.00	110,000.00	125,000.00	USD	Annually
		NPS	00	0.00	0.00	500,000.00	USD	Annually
		S001	01	60,000.00	40,000.00	55,000.00	USD	Annually
			02	60,000.00	50,000.00	70,000.00	USD	Annually
			03	60,000.00	60,000.00	72,500.00	USD	Annually
		S002	01	72,500.00	55,000.00	70,000.00	USD	Annually
			02	72,500.00	60,000.00	85,000.00	USD	Annually
			03	72,500.00	80,000.00	99,000.00	USD	Annually
	West Region	EXEC	00	120,000.00	80,000.00	180,000.00	USD	Annually
		GRD01	00	47,500.00	20,000.00	30,000.00	USD	Annually

[1] This example uses the Global Bike Inc SAP client set. See Appendix 7A for instructions on how to access this client set.

FIGURE AE-11

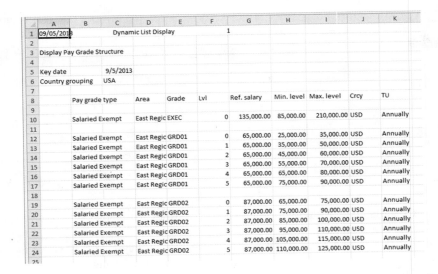

	A	B	C	D	E	F	G	H	I	J	K
1	09/05/2013			Dynamic List Display		1					
2											
3	Display Pay Grade Structure										
4											
5	Key date		9/5/2013								
6	Country grouping		USA								
7											
8		Pay grade type	Area	Grade	Lvl		Ref. salary	Min. level	Max. level	Crcy	TU
9											
10		Salaried Exempt	East Regic	EXEC	0		135,000.00	85,000.00	210,000.00	USD	Annually
11											
12		Salaried Exempt	East Regic	GRD01	0		65,000.00	25,000.00	35,000.00	USD	Annually
13		Salaried Exempt	East Regic	GRD01	1		65,000.00	35,000.00	50,000.00	USD	Annually
14		Salaried Exempt	East Regic	GRD01	2		65,000.00	45,000.00	60,000.00	USD	Annually
15		Salaried Exempt	East Regic	GRD01	3		65,000.00	55,000.00	70,000.00	USD	Annually
16		Salaried Exempt	East Regic	GRD01	4		65,000.00	65,000.00	80,000.00	USD	Annually
17		Salaried Exempt	East Regic	GRD01	5		65,000.00	75,000.00	90,000.00	USD	Annually
18											
19		Salaried Exempt	East Regic	GRD02	0		87,000.00	65,000.00	75,000.00	USD	Annually
20		Salaried Exempt	East Regic	GRD02	1		87,000.00	75,000.00	90,000.00	USD	Annually
21		Salaried Exempt	East Regic	GRD02	2		87,000.00	85,000.00	100,000.00	USD	Annually
22		Salaried Exempt	East Regic	GRD02	3		87,000.00	95,000.00	110,000.00	USD	Annually
23		Salaried Exempt	East Regic	GRD02	4		87,000.00	105,000.00	115,000.00	USD	Annually
24		Salaried Exempt	East Regic	GRD02	5		87,000.00	110,000.00	125,000.00	USD	Annually
25											

7-2. Assume that you have been given the task of compiling evaluations that your company's purchasing agents make of their e-commerce vendors. Each month, every purchasing agent evaluates all of the vendors that he or she has ordered from in the past month on three factors: price, quality, and responsiveness. Assume the ratings are from 1 to 5, with 5 being the best. Because your company has hundreds of vendors and dozens of purchasing agents, you decide to use Access to compile the results.

a. Create a database with three tables: VENDOR (*VendorNumber, Name, Contact*), PURCHASER (*EmpNumber, Name, Email*), and RATING (*EmpNumber, VendorNumber, Month, Year, PriceRating, QualityRating, ResponsivenessRating*). Assume that *VendorNumber* and *EmpNumber* are the keys of VENDOR and PURCHASER, respectively. Decide what you think is the appropriate key for RATING.

b. Create appropriate relationships.

c. Import the data in the Excel file **Ch07Ex02**. Note that the data for Vendor, Purchaser, and Rating are stored in three separate worksheets.

d. Create a query that shows the names of all vendors and their average scores.

e. Create a query that shows the names of all employees and their average scores. *Hint:* In this and in part f, you will need to use the *Group By* function in your query.

f. Create a parameterized query that you can use to obtain the minimum, maximum, and average ratings on each criterion for a particular vendor. Assume you will enter *VendorName* as the parameter.

g. Using the data created by your queries, what conclusions can you make about vendors or purchasers?

Chapter 8

8-1. Suppose your manager asks you to create a spreadsheet to compute a production schedule. Your schedule should stipulate a production quantity for seven products that is based on sales projections made by three regional managers in your company's three sales regions.

a. Create a separate worksheet for each sales region. Use the data in the Word file **Ch08Ex01**. This file contains each manager's monthly sales projections for the past year, actual sales results for those same months, and projections for sales for each month in the coming quarter.

b. Create a separate worksheet for each manager's data. Import the data from Word into Excel.

c. On each of the worksheets, use the data from the prior four quarters to compute the discrepancy between the actual sales and the sales projections. This discrepancy can be computed in several ways: You could calculate an overall average, or you could calculate an average per quarter or per month. You could also weight recent discrepancies more heavily than earlier ones. Choose a method that you think is most appropriate. Explain why you chose the method you did.

d. Modify your worksheets to use the discrepancy factors to compute an adjusted forecast for the coming quarter. Thus, each of your spreadsheets will show the raw forecast and the adjusted forecast for each month in the coming quarter.

e. Create a fourth worksheet that totals sales projections for all of the regions. Show both the unadjusted forecast and the adjusted forecast for each region and for the company overall. Show month and quarter totals.

f. Create a bar graph showing total monthly production. Display the unadjusted and adjusted forecasts using different-colored bars.

8-2. Do Application Exercise 5-1, if you have not already done so.

a. Add a Status column to the RESERVATION table, where Status can have values of *Not Confirmed*, *Confirmed*, or *Cancelled*. A reservation guarantees a customer a locker and access to all equipment. Explain why CBI might wish to track cancelled reservations.

b. Create a data entry form that would be appropriate to make a reservation at a facility.

c. Create a data entry form that would be appropriate to confirm a reservation at a facility.

d. Create a Daily Facility Use Report. Assume the report has a parameterized query to produce all reservations for a given date.

e. Input data and test your database. Use the Windows 7 Snipping Tool or some other tool to capture screen shots of your data entry screens and your report.

PART 4

Chapter 9

9-1. Suppose that you have been asked to assist in the managerial decision about how much to increase pay in the next year. Assume you are given a list of the departments in your company, along with the average salary for employees in that department for major companies in your industry. Additionally, you are given the names and salaries of 10 people in each of three departments in your company.

Assume you have been asked to create a spreadsheet that shows the names of the 10 employees in each department, their current salary, the difference between their current salary and the industry average salary for their department, and the percent their salary would need to be increased to meet the industry average. Your spreadsheet should also compute the average increase needed to meet the industry average for each department and the average increase, company-wide, to meet industry averages.

a. Use the data in the file **Ch09Ex01** and create the spreadsheet.

b. How can you use this analysis to contribute to the employee salary decision? Based on this data, what conclusions can you make?

c. Suppose other team members want to use your spreadsheet. Name three ways you can share it with them, and describe the advantages and disadvantages of each.

9-2. Suppose that you have been asked to assist in the managerial decision about how much to increase pay in the next year. Specifically, you are tasked to determine if there are significant salary differences among departments in your company.

You are given an Access database with a table of employee data with the following structure:

EMPLOYEE (Name, Department, Specialty, Salary)

where *Name* is the name of an employee who works in a department, *Department* is the department name, *Specialty* is the name of the employee's primary skill, and *Salary* is the employee's current salary. Assume that no two employees have the same name. You have been asked to answer the following queries:

(1) List the names, department, and salary of all employees earning more than $100,000.

(2) List the names and specialties of all employees in the Marketing department.

(3) Compute the average, maximum, and minimum salary of employees in your company.

(4) Compute the average, minimum, and maximum salary of employees in the Marketing department.

(5) Compute the average, minimum, and maximum salary of employees in the Information Systems department.

(6) *Extra credit:* Compute the average salary for employees in every department. Use *Group By.*

a. Design and run Access queries to obtain the answers to these questions, using the data in the file **Ch09Ex02**.

b. Explain how the data in your answer contributes to the salary increase decision.

c. Suppose other team members want to use your Access application. Name three ways you can share it with them, and describe the advantages and disadvantages of each.

Chapter 10

10-1. For the following exercises, tutorials and help are available from each social media platform and also by using a search engine.

a. Facebook: Create a Facebook page for a small local business, a student organization, or a team. Use a search engine to find instructions.

b. Twitter: Create an account and follow several of your classmates (and have them follow you). Tweet and send them a direct message. Make a tweet with a #hashtag, and then use Twitter's search function to find this tweet. Find your classmates' hashtag tweets. Find and follow popular accounts or accounts of individuals or organizations in an area of interest to you.

c. LinkedIn: Create an account and begin to fill out your profile. Create or extend the data in your profile (if you already had an account). Connect to your classmates. Add a photo. Find and follow companies, and explore the site and learn new options in Groups, Jobs, and Contacts.

d. Blogger: Create a blog about the use of social media in small business or another topic of interest to you. Embed a YouTube video in your blog. Follow other blogs.

10-2. 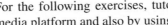 For the following exercises, tutorials and help are available from each social media platform and also by using a search engine.

a. Wikipedia: Create your own user account and log in. Go to your *User talk* page and click *Edit source.* You will be creating a page called *User talk:Yourusername.* Write a paragraph about social media. Find a classmate's user talk entry and edit his or her paragraph. Go back to your talk page and click *View History* to see how your page has been edited. Finally, find an entry on Wikipedia that you can contribute to and edit that page. Use a search engine and find instructions to play Wiki Races (an example is *http://wikibin.org/articles/wiki-races.html*).

b. Delicious, Digg, and StumbleUpon: Create accounts at these sites. Share your list of bookmarks in Delicious with a classmate.

c. Klout.com: Go to Klout.com or another social media monitoring site. Sign in with your Twitter account name and see the impact of your tweets. Read about how your clout is determined.

d. Google Drive: Create or use an existing Gmail account. Discover how to make a Google document, and share that document with your classmates. Edit the document simultaneously with classmates.

e. Tumblr and Pinterest: Create accounts on these platforms. Find three businesses that use them well and write a blog entry about what these organizations are doing right.

Chapter 11

11-1. OLAP cubes are very similar to Microsoft Excel pivot tables. For this exercise, assume that your organization's purchasing agents rate vendors similar to the situation described in Application Exercise 7-2.

a. Open the Excel file **Ch11Ex01**. The spreadsheet has the following column names: *VendorName, EmployeeName, Date, Year*, and *Rating*.

b. Under the *Insert* ribbon in Excel, click *Pivot Table*.

c. When asked to provide a data range, drag your mouse over the data you imported so as to select all of the data. Be sure to include the column headings. Excel will fill in the range values in the open dialog box. Place your pivot table in a separate spreadsheet.

d. Excel will create a field list on the right-hand side of your spreadsheet. Drag and drop the field named *VendorName* under the word "Rows" at the bottom of the field list. Drag and drop *EmployeeName* under the word "Columns." Now drag and drop the field named *Rating* under the word "Values." Voilà! You have a pivot table.

e. To see how the table works, drag and drop more fields onto the various sections of your pivot table. For example, drop *Year* on top of *Employee*. Then move *Year* below *Employee*. Now move *Year* below *Vendor*. All of this action is just like an OLAP cube, and, in fact, OLAP cubes are readily displayed in Excel pivot tables. The major difference is that OLAP cubes are usually based on thousands or more rows of data.

11-2. It is surprisingly easy to create a market basket report using table data in Access. To do so, however, you will need to enter SQL expressions into the Access query builder. Here you can just copy SQL statements to type them in. If you take a database class, you will learn how to code SQL statements like those you will use here.

a. Create an Access database with a table named *Order_Data* having columns *OrderNumber, ItemName*, and *Quantity*, with data types Number, Short Text, and Number, respectively. Define the key as the composite (*OrderNumber, ItemName*).

b. Import the data from the Excel file **Ch11Ex02** into the *Order_Data* table.

c. Now, to perform the market basket analysis, you will need to enter several SQL statements into Access. To do so, click the queries tab and select *Query Design* in Design view. Click *Close* when the Show Table dialog box appears. Right-click in the gray section above the grid. Select *SQL View*. Enter the following expression exactly as it appears here:

SELECT	**T1.ItemName as FirstItem,**
	T2.ItemName as SecondItem
FROM	**Order_Data T1, Order_Data T2**
WHERE	**T1.OrderNumber=**
	T2.OrderNumber
AND	**T1.ItemName<>**
	T2.ItemName;

Click the red exclamation point in the toolbar to run the query. Correct any typing mistakes and, once it works, save the query using the name *TwoItemBasket*.

d. Now enter a second SQL statement. Again, click the queries tab and select *Query Design* in Design view. Click *Close* when the Show Table dialog box appears. Right-click in the gray section above the grid. Select *SQL View*. Enter the following expression exactly as it appears here:

SELECT	**TwoItemBasket.FirstItem,**
	TwoItemBasket.SecondItem,
	Count(*) AS SupportCount
FROM	**TwoItemBasket**
GROUP BY	**TwoItemBasket.FirstItem,**
	TwoItemBasket.SecondItem;

Click *Run* and correct any typing mistakes and, once it works, save the query using the name *SupportCount*.

e. Examine the results of the second query and verify that the two query statements have correctly calculated the number of times that two items have appeared together. Explain further calculations you need to make to compute support.

f. Explain the calculations you need to make to compute lift. Although you can make those calculations using SQL, you need more SQL knowledge to do it, and we will skip that here.

g. Explain, in your own words, what the query in part c seems to be doing. What does the query in part d seem to be doing? Again, you will need to take a database class to learn how to code such expressions, but this exercise should give you a sense of the kinds of calculations that are possible with SQL.

PART 5

Chapter 12

12-1. Suppose you are given the task of keeping track of the number of labor hours invested in meetings for systems development projects. Assume your company uses the traditional systems-first process illustrated in Figure AE-12. Further assume that each SDLC step requires two types of meetings. *Working meetings* involve users, business analysts, systems analysts, programmers, and PQA test engineers. *Review meetings* involve all of those people, plus level-1 and level-2 managers of both user departments and the IS department.

a. Copy and paste the data in the Word file **Ch12Ex01_source1** into a spreadsheet.

b. Modify your spreadsheet to compute the total labor hours invested in each phase of a project. When a meeting occurs, assume you enter the project phase, the meeting type, the start time, the end time, and the number of each type of personnel attending. Your spreadsheet should calculate the number of labor hours and should add the meeting's hours to the totals for that phase and for the project overall.

c. Modify your spreadsheet to include the budgeted number (in the source data) of labor hours for each type of employee for each phase. This data is in **Ch12Ex01_source2**. In your spreadsheet, show the difference between the number of hours budgeted and the number actually consumed.

d. Change your spreadsheet to include the budgeted cost and actual cost of labor. Assume that you enter, once, the average labor cost for each type of employee, as stipulated in the source data.

FIGURE AE-12

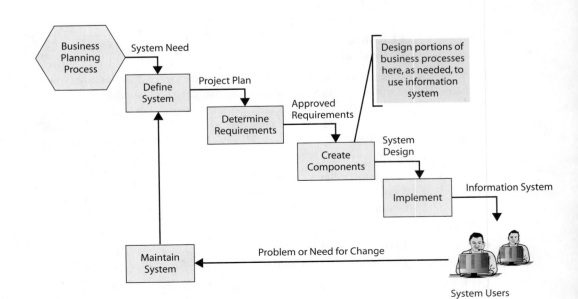

12-2. Use Access to develop a failure-tracking database application. Use the data in the Excel file **Ch12Ex02** for this exercise. The data includes columns for the following:

> *FailureNumber*
> *DateReported*
> *FailureDescription*
> *ReportedBy* (the name of the PQA engineer reporting the failure)
> *ReportedBy_email* (the email address of the PQA engineer reporting the failure)
> *FixedBy* (the name of the programmer who is assigned to fix the failure)
> *FixedBy_email* (the email address of the programmer assigned to fix the failure)
> *DateFailureFixed*
> *FixDescription*
> *DateFixVerified*
> *VerifiedBy* (the name of the PQA engineer verifying the fix)
> *VerifiedBy_email* (the email address of the PQA engineer verifying the fix)

a. The data in the spreadsheet are not normalized. Normalize the data by creating a *Failure* table, a *PQA Engineer* table, and a *Programmer* table. Add other appropriate columns to each table. Create appropriate relationships.
b. Create one or more forms that can be used to report a failure, to report a failure fix, and to report a failure verification. Create the form(s) so that the user can just pull down the name of a PQA engineer or programmer from the appropriate table to fill in the *ReportedBy*, *FixedBy*, and *VerifiedBy* fields.
c. Construct a report that shows all failures sorted by reporting PQA engineer and then by *Date Reported*.
d. Construct a report that shows only fixed and verified failures.
e. Construct a report that shows only fixed but unverified failures.

12-3. Suppose you have just been appointed manager of a help desk with an IS department. You have been there for just a week, and you are amazed to find only limited information to help you manage your employees. In fact, the only available data concerns the processing of particular issues, called *Tickets*. The following data are kept:

> **Ticket#, Date_Submitted, Date_Opened, Date_Closed, Type (new or repeat), Reporting_Employee_Name, Reporting_Employee_Division, Technician_Name, Problem_System, and Problem_Description**

You can find sample Ticket data in the Excel file **Ch12Ex03**.

As a manager, you need more data. Among your needs are data that will help you learn who are your best- and worst-performing technicians, how different systems compare in terms of number of problems reported and the time required to fix those problems, how different divisions compare in terms of problems reported and the time required to fix them, which technicians are the best and worst at solving problems with particular systems, and which technicians are best and worst at solving problems from particular divisions.

a. Using either Access or Excel or a combination of the two, produce the information listed previously from the data in the Excel file **Ch12Ex03**. In your answer, you may use queries, formulas, reports, forms, graphs, pivot tables, pivot charts, or any other type of Access or Excel display. Choose the best display for the type of data you are producing.
b. Explain how you would use these different types of data to manage your department.
c. Specify any additional data you would like to record to help you manage your department.
d. Use either Access or Excel or a combination to produce the data in part c.

12-4. Develop a spreadsheet model of the cost of a virus attack in an organization that has three types of computers: employee workstations, data servers, and Web servers. Assume that the number of computers affected by the virus depends on the severity of the virus. For the purposes of your model, assume that there are three levels of virus severity: *Low-severity* incidents affect fewer than 30 percent of the user workstations and none of the data or Web servers. *Medium-severity* incidents affect up to 70 percent of the user workstations, up to half of the Web servers, and none of the data servers. *High-severity* incidents can affect all organizational computers.

a. *Assumptions* for your model include:
  - 40 percent of incidents are low severity.
  - 35 percent of incidents are medium severity.
  - 25 percent of incidents are high severity.
  - Employees are able to remove viruses from their own workstations.
  - Trained technicians are required to repair servers.
  - The time to eliminate a virus from an infected computer depends on the computer type.
  - When employees remove the virus themselves, they are unproductive for twice the time require for the removal.

b. *Inputs* for your model include:
  - Severity level (low, medium, high)
  - Percentage of computers affected
  - The time it takes to remove the virus from each type of computer
  - Average employee hourly labor cost for virus removal
  - Average cost of a technician to remove a virus from servers
  - Total number of user computers, data servers, and Web servers affected by the virus

c. Run your simulation 10 times. Use the same inputs for each run, but draw a random number (assume a uniform distribution for all random numbers) to determine the severity level. Then draw random numbers to determine the percentage of computers of each type affected, using the constraints detailed earlier. For example, if the attack is of medium severity, draw a random number between 0 and 70 to indicate the percentage of infected user workstations and a random number between 0 and 50 to indicate the percentage of infected Web servers.

d. Calculate the following data and show the results for each run, and then calculate the average costs and hours for the 10 runs combined:
  - Total lost employee hours
  - Total dollar cost of lost employee hours
  - Total hours of technicians to fix the servers
  - Total cost of technician labor
  - Total overall cost

Glossary

10/100/1000 Ethernet. A type of Ethernet that conforms to the IEEE 802.3 protocol and allows for transmission at a rate of 10, 100, or 1,000 Mbps (megabits per second). **p. 68**

3D printing. Also called *additive manufacturing*; a process of depositing successive layers of material to manufacture objects. Just as current printers deposit ink in two dimensions, 3D printing deposits material in three dimensions, layering material in the third dimension as it dries. **p. 60**

A/B testing. Also called split testing; an analysis technique in which a Web site developer builds two identical pages with slight changes in design to determine the better conversion rate for each design. **p. 345**

ABAP. SAP's high-level application language that is used to enhance the functionality of SAP implementation. It is frequently used to format the data in reports. **p. 175**

Abstract reasoning. The ability to make and manipulate models. **p. 6**

Access. A popular personal and small workgroup DBMS product from Microsoft. **p. 94**

Access control. A way to specify limits on who can interact with an IS resource. **p. 164**

Activity. A task within a business process. **p. 27**

Actor. A person or computer who performs a subset of activities in a business process. **p. 28**

Additive manufacturing. Also called *3D printing*; a process of depositing successive layers of material to manufacture objects. Just as current printers deposit ink in two dimensions, additive manufacturing deposits material in three dimensions, layering material in the third dimension as it dries. **p. 60**

Agile development. A systems development process that conforms to specific principles designed to welcome change and deliver working versions of the product frequently. **p. 375**

Analysis. A method of breaking a thing down to examine its details in order to discover or reveal its essential features. **p. 338**

Android. A mobile operating system licensed by Google. **p. 54**

Application software. Programs that perform a business function. Some application programs are general purpose, such as Excel or Word. Others are specific to a business function, such as accounts payable. **p. 56**

ARM. A power-saving computer architecture that is designed for portable devices such as phones and tablets. **p. 55**

As-is diagram. A diagram that represents the current situation and processes. **p. 141**

Assessment. To look at something in order to be informed about current conditions. **p. 334**

Asymmetric encryption. An encryption method whereby different keys are used to encode and to decode the message; one key encodes the message, and the other key decodes the message. Symmetric encryption is simpler and much faster than asymmetric encryption. **p. 386**

Asynchronous communication. Information exchange that occurs when all members of a work team do not meet at the same time, such as those who work different shifts or in different locations. **p. 279**

Attribute. (1) A variable that provides properties for an html tag. Each attribute has a standard name. For example, the attribute for a hyperlink is *href*, and its value indicates which Web page is to be displayed when the user clicks the link. (2) Characteristics of an entity. Example attributes of *Order* would be *OrderNumber, OrderDate, SubTotal, Tax, Total*, and so forth. Example attributes of *Salesperson* would be *SalespersonName, Email, Phone*, and so forth. **p. 74**

Auction. Application that matches buyers and sellers by using an e-commerce version of a standard, competitive-bidding auction process. **p. 242**

Auditing process. The official, unbiased examination of an organization's financial accounts. **p. 348**

Augmented reality (AR). Technology that superimposes data or graphics onto a computer-generated display of the physical environment. **p. 202**

Authentication. The process whereby an information system verifies (validates) a user. **p. 385**

Automation. A system in which a computer does an activity or part of an activity that was once done by a person. **p. 137**

Big Data. Data collections that differ from relational databases by their huge volume, rapid velocity, and great variety. **p. 110**

Bigtable. A nonrelational data store developed by Google. **p. 110**

Bill of material (BOM). A structure or description that specifies the raw materials, quantities, and subassemblies to create a product. **p. 168**

Biometric authentication. The use of personal physical characteristics, such as fingerprints, facial features, and retinal scans, to verify users. **p. 385**

BlackBerry OS. One of the most successful early mobile operating systems that was used primarily by business users on BlackBerry devices. It is now losing market share to iOS and Android and may soon disappear from the market. **p. 54**

Bluetooth. A common wireless protocol designed for transmitting data over short distances, replacing cables. **p. 69**

Bottleneck. When a limited resource greatly reduces the output of an integrated series of activities or processes. **p. 140**

Bullwhip effect. Phenomenon in which the variability in the size and timing of orders increases at each stage up the supply chain, from customer to supplier. **p. 197**

Business analyst. Someone who is well versed in the Porter models, organizational strategy, and systems alignment theory such as COBIT and who also understands the proper role for technology. **p. 371**

Business intelligence. A process of acquiring, analyzing, and publishing data with an objective of discovering or revealing patterns in data that will inform a business person. **p. 332**

Business intelligence system. An information system that supports business processes by consolidating and analyzing data in a large database to help users create information. **p. 332**

Business Objects (BOBJ). SAP software that analyzes business intelligence data. Business Objects was an independent software firm until its acquisition by SAP. **p. 352**

Business process. A sequence of activities for accomplishing a function. **p. 27**

Business process management (BPM). A systematic process of modeling, creating, implementing, and assessing business processes. **p. 367**

Business Process Model and Notation (BPMN) Standard. A standard set of terms and graphical notations for documenting business processes. **p. 28**

Business-to-business (B2B). Sales between companies. **p. 228**

Business-to-consumer (B2C). Sales between a supplier and a retail customer (the consumer). **p. 228**

Business-to-government (B2G). Sales between companies and governmental organizations. **p. 242**

Buy-in. A term for selling a product or system for less than its true price. **p. 204**

Byte(s). (1) A character of data. (2) An 8-bit chunk. **p. 51**

Cable line. A type of WAN connection that provides high-speed data transmission using cable television lines. Because up to 500 user sites can share a cable line, performance varies depending on how many other users are sending and receiving data. **p. 69**

CAD (computer added design) software. General-purpose design software than can be used to create a three-dimensional data model for 3D printing or other types of models. **p. 60**

Capital. The investment of resources with the expectation of future returns in the marketplace. **p. 317**

Cassandra. A nonrelational data store created by Facebook that was based off the designs of Dynamo and Bigtable. **p. 110**

Categorical imperative. An ethical principle developed by the German philosopher Immanuel Kant. The categorical imperative states that one should behave only in a way that one would want the behavior to be a universal law. **p. 20**

Cause marketing. Using social media to promote social issues, hoping that this will result in profit for the business. **p. 314**

Central processing unit (CPU). The CPU selects instructions, processes them, performs arithmetic and logical comparisons, and stores results of operations in memory. **p. 50**

Charms. A new feature of Windows 8; icons that slide in from the right of the display. **p. 65**

Chrome. The visual overhead in a computer display; it is the windows, the menus, and other apparatus that drive the application. **p. 64**

Clearinghouse. Entity that provides goods and services at a stated price and arranges for the delivery of the goods, but never takes title to the goods. **p. 242**

Clickstream data. Web site data that describes a customer's clicking behavior. Such data includes everything the customer does at the Web site. **p. 350**

Client. A computer that provides word processing, spreadsheets, database access, and usually a network connection. **p. 50**

Closed source. Source code that is highly protected and only available to trusted employees and carefully vetted contractors. **p. 58**

Cloud. The elastic leasing of pooled computer resources over the Internet. **p. 75**

Collaboration. A dynamic process in which a group of people work together to achieve common objectives via communication and iteration. **p. 273**

Collaboration information system. An information system that supports collaboration; this system needs to support iteration and communication among team members. **p. 278**

Columns. Also called *fields*, or groups of bytes. A database table has multiple columns that are used to represent the attributes of an entity. Examples are *PartNumber*, *EmployeeName*, and *SalesDate*. **p. 91**

Commerce server. An application program that runs on a server-tier computer; it receives requests from users via the Web server, takes some action, and returns a response to the users via the Web server. **p. 72**

Competitive strategy. The strategy an organization chooses as the way it will succeed in its industry. According to Porter, there are four fundamental competitive strategies: cost leadership across an industry or within a particular industry segment and product differentiation across an industry or within a particular industry segment. **p. 14**

Computer-based information system. An information system that includes a computer. **p. 30**

Computer hardware. Electronic components and related gadgetry that input, process, output, store, and communicate data according to the instructions encoded in computer programs or software. **p. 30**

Configuration. The process of adapting ERP software to conform to customer requirements without changing program code. **p. 161**

Connection data. Data about relationships. **p. 309**

Content data. User-generated content and the responses to that content contributed by other users. **p. 309**

Context-sensitive chrome. Chrome provided by mobile applications that pops up in the display when appropriate. **p. 64**

Continuous improvement process (CIP). An ongoing cycle of process improvement; the process includes component creation, implementation, monitoring, and remodeling. **p. 369**

Control. A method used in a process to limit behavior. **p. 136**

Conversion rate. A measure of Web site traffic involving the ratio of the number of customers who eventually purchased divided by the number who visited. **p. 345**

Cookie(s). (1) Data that a Web site stores on your computer to record something about its interaction with you. (2) Small files that your browser stores on your computer when you visit Web sites. **p. 358**

Cooperation. A process where a group of people work together, all doing essentially the same type of work, to accomplish a job. **p. 273**

Cross-selling. The sale of related products; salespeople try to get customers who buy product *X* to also buy product *Y*. **p. 342**

Cross-site scripting (XSS). A technique used to compromise database data in which Web page scripting is injected into the server. **p. 381**

Crow's feet. Lines on an entity-relationship diagram that indicate a 1:N relationship between two entities. **p. 103**

Crow's-foot diagram. A type of entity-relationship diagram that uses a crow's foot symbol to designate a 1:N relationship. **p. 104**

Crowdsourcing. Outsourcing a task to a large number of users. **p. 315**

Culture. The day-to-day work habits and practices that workers take for granted. **p. 169**

Custom-developed software. Tailor-made software. **p. 57**

Customer relationship management (CRM). A system that integrates customer-facing processes and manages all the interactions with customers. **p. 238**

Customer service. the series of activities before, during, or after a sale with the goal of increasing customer satisfaction. **p. 314**

Customer service processes. Processes related to customer service; operational customer service processes include Track Orders, Customer Support, and Customer Support Training. **p. 132**

Customization. Writing new code to supplement an ERP system. **p. 161**

Dashboards. Easy to read, concise, up-to-the-minute displays of process KPIs. **p. 165**

Data. Recorded facts or figures. One of the five fundamental components of an information system. **p. 30**

Data broker. Also called a *data aggregator*; a company that acquires and purchases consumer and other data from public records, retailers, Internet cookie vendors, social media trackers, and other sources and uses it to create business intelligence that it sells to companies and the government. **p. 354**

Data integrity problem. In a database, the situation that exists when data items disagree with one another. An example is two different names for the same customer. **p. 105**

Data mining. A type of Informing process that uses sophisticated statistical analyses to uncover patterns in a large database of data in order to improve prediction. **p. 341**

Data model. A logical representation of the data in a database that describes the data and relationships that will be stored in the database. Akin to a blueprint. **p. 101**

Data warehouse. A facility that prepares, stores, and manages data specifically for reporting and data mining. **p. 335**

Database. A self-describing collection of integrated records. **p. 91**

Database administration (DBA). The management, development, operation, and maintenance of the database so as to achieve the organization's objectives. This staff function requires balancing conflicting goals: protecting the database while maximizing its availability for authorized use. In smaller organizations, this function usually is served by a single person. Larger organizations assign several people to an office of database administration. **p. 96**

Database application. Forms, reports, queries, and application programs for processing a database. A database can be processed by many different database applications. **p. 96**

Database application system. Applications, having the standard five components, that make database data more accessible and useful. Users employ a database application that consists of forms, formatted reports, queries, and application programs. Each of these, in turn, calls on the database management system (DBMS) to process the database tables. **p. 94**

Database management systems (DBMS). A program for creating, processing, and administering a database. A DBMS is a large and complex program that is licensed like an operating system. Microsoft Access and Oracle are example DBMS products. **p. 94**

Database tier. In the three-tier architecture, the tier that runs the DBMS and receives and processes SQL requests to retrieve and store data. **p. 72**

DB2. A popular, enterprise-class DBMS product from IBM. **p. 94**

Decision Making process. The selection of a choice among available options; can be done individually or in a groaup. **p. 344**

Decision support systems (DSS). An information system used in support of decision making. **p. 333**

Denial of service (DOS). A security problem in which users are not able to access an information system; can be caused by human errors, natural disaster, or malicious activity. **p. 382**

Desktop virtualization. A desktop operating system hosted by a server that can be accessed from any computer to which the user has access. **p. 56**

Digital dashboard. An electronic display that is customized for a particular user. Commonly provided by vendors like Yahoo! and MSN. **p. 343**

Digital subscriber line (DSL). A communications line that operates on the same lines as voice telephones, but does so in such a manner that its signals do not interfere with voice telephone service. **p. 69**

Dimension. A characteristic or attribute of data. **p. 339**

Direct interaction. Using content to drive application behavior, such as knowing that blue, underlined type can be used to navigate to a Web site. **p. 64**

Dirty data. Problematic data. Examples are a value of *B* for customer gender and a value of *213* for customer age. All these values are problematic when data mining. **p. 349**

Discussion forums. A form of asynchronous communication in which one group member posts an entry and other group members respond. A better form of group communication than e-mail, because it is more difficult for the discussion to go off track. **p. 281**

Disintermediation. Elimination of one or more middle layers in the supply chain. **p. 242**

Document library. A named collection of documents in SharePoint. **p. 288**

Dogfooding. The process of using a product or idea that you develop or promote. The term arose in the 1980s in the software industry when someone observed that their company wasn't using the product they developed. Or, "they weren't eating their own dog food." **p. 299**

Domain name. A worldwide-unique name that is affiliated with a public IP address. The process of changing a name into its IP address is called *resolving the domain name*. **p. 71**

Drill down. With an OLAP report, to further divide the data into more detail. **p. 340**

Drive-by sniffers. People who take computers with wireless connections through an area and search for unprotected wireless networks in an attempt to gain free Internet access or to gather unauthorized data. **p. 381**

Dual processor. A computer with two CPUs. **p. 50**

Dynamic processes. A process whose structure is fluid and dynamic. Contrast with structured processes. Collaboration is a dynamic process; SAP order entry is a structured process. **p. 33**

Dynamo. A nonrelational data store developed by Amazon.com. **p. 110**

E-commerce. A multifirm process of buying and selling goods and services using Internet technologies. **p. 241**

Effectiveness. A process objective that helps achieve organizational strategy. **p. 130**

Efficiency. A resource-oriented process objective; a process is efficient if it creates more output with the same inputs or the same output with fewer inputs. **p. 130**

Elastic. (1) The amount of resources leased in the cloud can be increased or decreased dynamically, programmatically, in a short span of time; organizations pay for just the resources that they use. (2) The number of servers can dynamically increase and decrease without disrupting performance. **p. 75**

Electronic exchange. Site that facilitates the matching of buyers and sellers; the business process is similar to that of a stock exchange. Sellers offer goods at a given price through the electronic exchange, and buyers make offers to purchase over the same exchange. Price matches result in transactions from which the exchange takes a commission. **p. 242**

Email spoofing. A synonym for *phishing*. A technique for obtaining unauthorized data that uses pretexting via e-mail. The *phisher* pretends to be a legitimate company and sends e-mail requests for confidential data, such as account numbers, Social Security numbers, account passwords, and so forth. Phishers direct traffic to their sites under the guise of a legitimate business. **p. 381**

Encryption. The process of transforming clear text into coded, unintelligible text for secure storage or communication. **p. 386**

Enterprise application integration (EAI). The integration of existing systems by providing layers of software that connect applications and their data together. **p. 155**

Enterprise DBMS. A product that processes large organizational and workgroup databases. These products support many users, perhaps thousands, and many different database applications. Such DBMS products support 24/7 operations and can manage databases that span dozens of different magnetic disks with hundreds of gigabytes or more of data. IBM's DB2, Microsoft's SQL Server, and Oracle's Oracle are examples of enterprise DBMS products. **p. 100**

Enterprise resource planning (ERP) system. A suite of software, a database, and a set of inherent processes for consolidating business operations into a single, consistent, information system. **p. 156**

Entity. In the E-R data model, a representation of some thing that users want to track. Some entities represent a physical object; others represent a logical construct or transaction. **p. 102**

Entity-relationship (E-R) data model. A popular technique for creating a data model whereby developers define the things that will be stored and identify the relationships among them. **p. 102**

Entity-relationship (E-R) diagrams. A type of diagram used by database designers to document entities and their relationships to each other. **p. 103**

Ethernet. Another name for the IEEE 802.3 protocol, Ethernet is a network protocol that operates at Layers 1 and 2 of the TCP/IP–OSI architecture. Ethernet, the world's most popular LAN protocol, is used on WANs as well. **p. 68**

Evil twin. A spoofed wireless access point that is similar to a legitimate access point; it is then used to eavesdrop on an unsuspecting user who mistakes the spoofed access point for the legitimate one. **p. 381**

Exabyte. 1,024 GB. **p. 51**

Executive support systems (ESS). Information systems that support strategic processes. **p. 130**

Experimentation. A careful and reasoned analysis of an opportunity, envisioning potential products or solutions or applications of technology, and then developing those ideas that seem to have the most promise, consistent with the resources you have. **p. 8**

Expert system. A rule-based system that acquires and stores human knowledge in the form of if/then rules. **p. 345**

Fields. Also called *columns*; groups of bytes in a database table. A database table has multiple columns that are used to represent the attributes of an entity. Examples are *PartNumber*, *EmployeeName*, and *SalesDate*. **p. 91**

File. A group of similar rows or records. In a database, sometimes called a *table*. **p. 91**

File server. A computer that stores files. **p. 283**

File Transfer Protocol (ftp). A Layer-5 protocol used to copy files from one computer to another. In interorganizational transaction processing, FTP enables users to exchange large files easily. **p. 71**

Finished goods inventory. Completed products awaiting delivery to customers. **p. 185**

Firewall. A computing device that prevents unauthorized access to parts of a network. **p. 386**

Five-component framework. The five fundamental components of an information system—computer hardware, software, data, procedures, and people—that are present in every information system, from the simplest to the most complex. **p. 30**

Five forces model. Model, proposed by Michael Porter, that assesses industry characteristics and profitability by means of five competitive forces—bargaining power of suppliers, threat of substitution, bargaining power of customers, rivalry among firms, and threat of new entrants. **p. 12**

Folksonomy. An emergent classification of content structure based on the processing of many user tags. **p. 309**

Foreign keys. A column or group of columns used to represent relationships. Values of the foreign key match values of the primary key in a different (foreign) table. **p. 93**

Form. Data entry forms are used to read, insert, modify, and delete database data. **p. 97**

Gap analysis. A study that highlights the differences between the business requirements that emerge from strategic planning and the capabilities of the ERP system. **p. 164**

Gigabyte (GB). 1,024 MB. **p. 51**

Google Drive. A free thin-client application for sharing documents, presentations, spreadsheets, drawings, and other data. **p. 284**

Gramm-Leach-Bliley (GLB) Act. Passed by Congress in 1999, this act protects consumer financial data stored by financial institutions, which are defined as banks, securities firms, insurance companies, and organizations that provide financial advice, prepare tax returns, and provide similar financial services. **p. 394**

Granularity. The level of detail in data. Customer name and account balance is large-granularity data. Customer name, balance, and the order details and payment history of every customer order is smaller granularity. **p. 350**

Hacking. Occurs when a person gains unauthorized access to a computer system. Although some people hack for the sheer joy of doing it, other hackers invade systems for the malicious purpose of stealing or modifying data. **p. 381**

Hadoop. An open-source program supported by the Apache Foundation that implements MapReduce on potentially thousands of computers. **p. 347**

Hashtag. A user-created tag that adds the prefix # to a word; this makes it easier to search for that term or keyword. **p. 309**

Horizontal-market application. Software that provides capabilities common across all organizations and industries; examples include word processors, graphics programs, spreadsheets, and presentation programs. **p. 56**

Host operating system. An operating system that runs one or more operating systems as applications. **p. 55**

href. The attribute for a hyperlink. **p. 74**

html (Hypertext Markup Language). A language that defines structure and layout of Web page content. An html tag is a notation used to define a data element for display or other purposes. **p. 73**

http (Hypertext Transport Protocol). A protocol used between browsers and Web servers. **p. 71**

https. A secure version of http. **p. 71**

Human capital. The investment in human knowledge and skills with the expectation of future returns in the marketplace. **p. 318**

Human resource processes. Organizational processes that assess the motivations and skills of employees; create job positions; investigate employee complaints; and staff, train, and evaluate personnel. **p. 133**

Human safeguards. Safeguards that result when authorized users follow appropriate procedures for system use and recovery. **p. 388**

Hyperlinks. A pointer to a Web page that contains the URL of a Web page. **p. 74**

Identifier. An attribute (or group of attributes) whose value is associated with one and only one entity instance. **p. 102**

IEEE 802.11 protocol. A protocol standard used for wireless LAN connections. **p. 68**

IEEE 802.3 protocol. A protocol standard used for wired LAN connections that specifies hardware characteristics, such as which wire carries which signals, and describes how messages are to be packaged and processed for wired transmission over the LAN. **p. 68**

If/then rule. A rule that specifies *if* a particular condition exists, *then* to take some action. **p. 345**

Inbound logistics processes. Processes that receive, store, and disseminate product input. **p. 132**

Index. A large database with links and keywords for billions of Web pages. **p. 344**

Industry-specific platform. An ERP system configuration that is appropriate for a particular industry, such as retail, manufacturing, or health care. **p. 173**

Information. (1) Knowledge derived from data, where *data* is defined as recorded facts or figures; (2) data presented in a meaningful context; (3) data processed by summing, ordering, averaging, grouping, comparing, or other similar operations; (4) a difference that makes a difference. **p. 35**

Information silo. An island of automation; information systems that work in isolation from one another. **p. 142**

Information system (IS). A group of components that interact to produce information. **p. 30**

Information systems security. The process of protecting information systems vulnerabilities from threats by creating appropriate safeguards. **p. 378**

Infrastructure as a service (IaaS). The cloud hosting of a bare server computer or disk drive. **p. 79**

Infrastructure processes. Essential supporting processes in the organization that enable day-to-day operations, such as processes in accounting, administration, quality assurance, and legal and financial areas. **p. 133**

Inherent processes. Process designs included in an ERP product that may be implemented by the organization. **p. 164**

Internal control. Systematically limiting the actions and behaviors of employees, processes, and systems within the organization to safeguard assets and to achieve objectives. **p. 188**

Internet. The collection of networks that is used to send e-mail or access a Web site. **p. 67**

Internet protocols and standards. Additions to TCP/IP that enable cloud-hosting vendors to provide processing capabilities in flexible yet standardized ways. **p. 75**

Internet service provider (ISP). An ISP provides users with Internet access. An ISP provides a user with a legitimate Internet address; it serves as the user's gateway to the Internet; and it passes communications back and forth between the user and the Internet. ISPs also pay for the Internet. They collect money from their customers and pay access fees and other charges on the users' behalf. **p. 69**

Interorganizational IS. Information systems that support processes and activities that span two or more independent organizations. **p. 241**

Invoice. An itemized bill. **p. 186**

iOS. The operating system used on the iPhone, iPad, and iPod Touch. **p. 54**

IP spoofing. A type of spoofing whereby an intruder uses another site's IP address as if it were that other site. **p. 381**

IT analysts. Also called *systems analysts*; Individuals with specialized training or education that enables them to support, maintain, and adapt a system after it has been implemented. **p. 163**

Iteration control. A collaboration tool that limits, and sometimes even directs, user activity. **p. 285**

Iteration management. A system that tracks changes to documents and provides features and functions to accommodate concurrent work; examples are Google Drive and Microsoft SkyDrive. **p. 284**

Just in time (JIT). A delivery method that synchronizes manufacturing and supply so that materials arrive just as the manufacturing process requires them. **p. 160**

Key. (1) A column or group of columns that identifies a unique row in a table. Also referred to as a Primary Key. (2) A number used to encrypt data. The encryption algorithm applies the key to the original message to produce the coded message. Decoding (decrypting) a message is similar; a key is applied to the coded message to recover the original text. **p. 92**

Key escrow. A control procedure whereby a trusted party is given a copy of a key used to encrypt database data. **p. 388**

Kilobyte (K). 1,024 bytes. **p. 51**

Knowledge Management (KM) process. A process in an organization that creates value from intellectual capital and shares that knowledge with employees, managers, suppliers, customers, and others. **p. 344**

KPI. Key performance indicators; quantities assigned to attributes that are used to measure the success of a process. **p. 135**

Lead time. The time required for a supplier to deliver an order. **p. 185**

Libraries. In version-control collaboration systems, shared directories that allow access to various documents by means of permissions. **p. 285**

License. Agreement that stipulates how a program can be used. Most specify the number of computers on which the program can be installed, some specify the number of users that can connect to and use the program remotely. Such agreements also stipulate limitations on the liability of the software vendor for the consequences of errors in the software. **p. 56**

Linkages. Process interactions across value chains. Linkages are important sources of efficiencies and are readily supported by information systems. **p. 16**

Linux. A version of Unix that was developed by the open source community. The open source community owns Linux, and there is no fee to use it. Linux is a popular operating system for Web servers. **p. 54**

Listening. Collecting and responding to customer-generated content on social media sites that is either positive or negative. **p. 316**

Local area network (LAN). A network that connects computers that reside in a single geographic location on the premises of the company that operates the LAN. The number of connected computers can range from two to several hundred. **p. 67**

Location-based marketing. The process of integrating customer location data into marketing activities. **p. 323**

Lost update problem. An issue in multiuser database processing in which two or more users try to make changes to the data but the database cannot make all those changes because it was not designed to process changes from multiple users. **p. 99**

Mac OS. An operating system developed by Apple Computer, Inc., for the Macintosh. The current version is Mac OS X Mountain Lion. Macintosh computers are used primarily by graphic artists and workers in the arts community. Mac OS was developed for the PowerPC, but as of 2006 runs on Intel processors as well. **p. 53**

Machine code. Code that has been compiled from source code and is ready to be processed by a computer. **p. 58**

Main memory. A set of cells in which each cell holds a byte of data or instruction; each cell has an address, and the CPU uses the addresses to identify particular data items. **p. 50**

Maintenance. In the context of information systems, (1) to fix the system to do what it was supposed to do in the first place or (2) to adapt the system to a change in requirements. **p. 374**

Management information systems (MIS). An information system that helps businesses achieve their goals and objectives. **p. 10**

Management (of MIS). The creation, monitoring, and adapting of processes, information systems, and information. **p. 10**

Managerial processes. Processes that concern resource use; includes planning, assessing, and analyzing the resources used by the company in pursuit of its strategy. **p. 130**

Manufacturing resource planning (MRPII). A manufacturing information system that schedules equipment and facilities and provides financial tracking of activities. **p. 159**

Many-to-many (N:M) relationship. Relationships involving two entity types in which an instance of one type can relate to many instances of the second type, and an instance of the second type can relate to many instances of the first. For example, the relationship between Student and Class is N:M. One student may enroll in many classes, and one class may have many students. Contrast with *one-to-many relationships*. **p. 104**

MapReduce. A technique used for harnessing the power of thousands of computers working in parallel. **p. 347**

Margin. The difference between the value that an activity generates and the cost of the activity. **p. 15**

Market Basket Analysis (MBA). An unsupervised data mining analysis that helps determine sales patterns. It shows the products that customers tend to buy together. **p. 342**

Mashup. The combining of output from two or more Web sites into a single user experience. **p. 310**

Master data. Also called *reference data*; data used in the organization that don't change with every transaction. **p. 162**

Material requirements planning (MRP). Software used to efficiently manage inventory, production, and labor. **p. 159**

Maximum cardinality. The maximum number of entities that can be involved in a relationship. Common examples of maximum cardinality are 1:N, N:M, and 1:1. **p. 104**

Measure(s). (1) Also called metrics or KPIs; quantities that are assigned to attributes; in the process context, measures help assess achievement of process objectives. (2) A data item of interest that can be summed, averaged, or otherwise processed. **p. 135**

Megabyte (MB). 1,024 KB. **p. 51**

Merchant company. In e-commerce, a company that takes title to the goods it sells. The company buys goods and resells them. **p. 241**

Metadata. Data that describe data. **p. 94**

Metrics. Also called measures or KPIs; quantities that are assigned to attributes; in the process context, measures help assess achievement of process objectives. **p. 135**

Microsoft Dynamics. A suite of ERP products licensed by Microsoft. The suite is composed of four ERP products, all obtained via acquisition: AX, Nav, GP, and SL. AX and Nav have the most capability, GP is smaller and easier to use. Although Dynamics has over 80,000 installations, the future of SL is particularly cloudy; Microsoft outsources the maintenance of the code to provide continuing support to existing customers. **p. 172**

Microsoft Lync. A communication tool that provides IM, audio and video conferencing, a shared whiteboard for team members to write on, and other shared facilities. **p. 281**

Microsoft SkyDrive. A collaboration tool that provides the ability to store and share Office documents and other files and offers free storage; also includes license-free Web application versions of Word, Excel, PowerPoint, and One Note. **p. 284**

Microsoft Windows. The most popular nonmobile client operating system for personal computers. **p. 52**

Minimum cardinality. The minimum number of entities that must be involved in a relationship. **p. 104**

Module. A suite of similar applications in an ERP system; examples include manufacturing and finance. **p. 173**

Moore's Law. A law, created by Gordon Moore, stating that the number of transistors per square inch on an integrated chip doubles every 18 months. Moore's prediction has proved generally accurate in the 40 years since it was made. Sometimes this law is stated that the performance of a computer doubles every 18 months. Although not strictly true, this version gives the gist of the idea. **p. 4**

Multiple instances. A separate ERP implementation for each country, business unit, or region. **p. 172**

Mutinous movement. An extension of bad reviews where prosumers revolt and use an organization's site in damaging ways. **p. 322**

MySQL. A popular open source DBMS product that is license-free for most applications. **p. 95**

Native applications. Applications that can run on just one operating system. **p. 59**

NetWeaver. The SAP application platform that connects SAP to hardware, third-party software, and output devices. NetWeaver provides an SOA interface that eases the integration of SAP with non-SAP applications. **p. 175**

Network. A collection of computers that communicate with one another over transmission lines. **p. 67**

Next Best Offer (NBO) process. A targeted offer or proposed action for customers based on the data patterns in the customer's history and preferences, context, and attributes of the product or service. **p. 345**

Nonmerchant company. An e-commerce company that arranges for the purchase and sale of goods without ever owning or taking title to those goods. **p. 241**

Normal forms. A classification of tables according to their characteristics and the kinds of problems they have. **p. 106**

Normalization. The process of converting poorly structured tables into two or more well-structured tables. **p. 105**

NoSQL databases. Nonrelational databases that support very high transaction rates processing relatively simple data structures replicated on many servers in the cloud. **p. 347**

NoSQL DBMS. A nonrelational database management system that supports very high transaction rates processing relatively simple, nonrelational data structures replicated on many servers in the cloud. **p. 110**

Object-oriented. Computer programming languages that are used to create difficult, complex applications; if used properly, they will result in high-performance code that is easy to alter when requirements change. **p. 60**

Object-relational database. A type of database that stores both object-oriented programming objects and relational data. Rarely used in commercial applications. **p. 93**

Objective. A goal that people in an organization have chosen to pursue. In the process context, managers develop and measure objectives for each process. Objectives fall into two categories: effectiveness and efficiency. **p. 130**

Off-the-shelf software. Generic application software that is used without customization. **p. 57**

Off-the-shelf with alterations software. Generic application software that is customized before use. **p. 57**

Office Web Apps. License-free Web application versions of Word, Excel, PowerPoint, and OneNote available on SkyDrive. **p. 284**

One-of-a-kind application. Software that is developed for a specific, unique need. **p. 57**

One-to-many (1:N) relationship. Relationships involving two entity types in which an instance of one type can relate to many instances of the second type, but an instance of the second type can relate to at most one instance of the first. For example, the relationship between *Department* and *Employee* is 1:N. A department may relate to many employees, but an employee relates to at most one department. **p. 103**

Online analytical processing (OLAP). An interactive type of reporting analysis that provides the ability to sum, count, average, and perform other simple arithmetic operations on groups of data. Such reports are interactive because users can change the format of the reports while viewing them. **p. 335**

Online transactional processing (OLTP). An operational process that uses an information system for the processing and reporting of day-to-day operational events. Order processing is a common OLTP example. **p. 335**

Operating system (OS). A computer program that controls the computer's resources. It manages the contents of main memory, processes keystrokes and mouse movements, sends signals to the display monitor, reads and writes disk files, and controls the processing of other programs. **p. 52**

Operational database. A data store that contains data produced and consumed by operational processes. **p. 335**

Operational processes. Common, routine, everyday business processes such as Procurement and Sales. **p. 129**

Oracle Database. A popular, enterprise-class DBMS product from Oracle Corporation. **p. 95**

Organizational data. Data about an organization, such as the location of its warehouses, the mailing addresses of the buildings, and the names of its financial accounts. **p. 162**

Ought-to-be diagram. A diagram of suggested improvements to a current process. **p. 141**

Outbound logistics processes. Processes that collect, store, and distribute products to buyers. **p. 132**

Parallel installation. A type of system conversion in which the new system runs in parallel with the old one for a while. Parallel installation is expensive because the organization incurs the costs of running both systems. **p. 373**

Parallel workflow. The condition that exists when two or more workers perform a task concurrently. A common example is concurrent review of a document. **p. 288**

PC virtualization. Using a personal computer to host several different operating systems. **p. 55**

People. As part of the five-component framework, one of the five fundamental components of an information system; includes those who operate and service the computers, those who maintain the data, those who support the networks, and those who use the system. **p. 30**

Personal computer (PC). A classic computing device that is used by an individual. **p. 50**

Personal DBMS. DBMS products designed for smaller, simpler database applications. Such products are used for personal or small workgroup applications that involve fewer than 100 users, and normally fewer than 15. Today, Microsoft Access is the only prominent personal DBMS. **p. 101**

Petabyte. 1,024 EB. **p. 51**

Phased installation. A type of system conversion in which the new system is installed in pieces across the organization(s). Once a given piece works, then the organization installs and tests another piece of the system, until the entire system has been installed. **p. 373**

Phisher. An individual or organization that spoofs legitimate companies in an attempt to illegally capture personal data, such as credit card numbers, e-mail accounts, and driver's license numbers. **p. 381**

Phishing. A technique for obtaining unauthorized data that uses pretexting via e-mail. The *phisher* pretends to be a legitimate company and sends an e-mail requesting confidential data, such as account numbers, Social Security numbers, account passwords, and so forth. **p. 381**

Pilot installation. A type of system conversion in which the organization implements the entire system on a limited portion of the business. The advantage of pilot implementation is that if the system fails, the failure is contained within a limited boundary. This reduces exposure of the business and also protects the new system from developing a negative reputation throughout the organization(s). **p. 373**

Platform as a service (PaaS). A category of cloud hosting in which vendors provide hosted computers, an operating system, and possibly a DBMS. **p. 78**

Plunge installation. A type of system conversion in which the organization shuts off the old system and starts the new system. If the new system fails, the organization is in trouble: Nothing can be done until either the new system is fixed or the old system is reinstalled. Because of the risk, organizations should avoid this conversion style if possible. Sometimes called *direct installation*. **p. 373**

Pooled. Physical hardware resources that are shared by many different organizations. **p. 75**

Posting. When the legal ownership of a material that has been sold is transferred from the seller to the buyer. **p. 234**

Power curve. A graph that shows the relationship of the power, or the utility that one gains from a software product, as a function of the time using that product. **p. 291**

Prediction. To look at something in order to be informed about the likelihood of future events. **p. 334**

Pretexting. A technique for gathering unauthorized information in which someone pretends to be someone else. A common scam involves a telephone caller who pretends to be from a credit card company and claims to be checking the validity of credit card numbers. Phishing is also a form of pretexting. **p. 381**

Primary activities. In Porter's value chain model, the fundamental activities that create value: inbound logistics, operations, outbound logistics, marketing/sales, and service. **p. 15**

Primary key. Also called a *key*; a column or group of columns that identifies a unique row in a table. **p. 92**

Privacy. Controlling how one's personal information is acquired and analyzed. **p. 353**

Private cloud. In-house hosting, delivered via Web service standards, that can be configured dynamically. **p. 78**

Procedures. Instructions for humans. One of the five fundamental components of an information system. **p. 30**

Process blueprint. In an ERP application, a comprehensive set of inherent processes for all organizational activities, each of which is documented with diagrams that use a set of standardized symbols. **p. 164**

Process improvement. A method used to help a process better achieve its objectives based on its measures. **p. 134**

Procurement. Obtaining goods and services. **p. 132 and 182**

Project data. Data that is part of the collaboration's work product, such as design documents. **p. 278**

Project management. The process of applying principles and techniques for planning, organizing, and monitoring temporary endeavors. **p. 286**

Project metadata. Data that is used to manage a project, such as schedules, tasks, budgets, and other managerial data. **p. 278**

Promotion. The process of sharing data about a product or service with the objective to improve awareness and sales. **p. 313**

Prosumer. A user who contributes to a Web site. **p. 317**

Protocol. A standardized means for coordinating an activity between two or more entities. **p. 67**

Public key/private key. A special version of asymmetric encryption that is popular on the Internet. With this method, each site has a public key for encoding messages and a private key for decoding them. **p. 386**

Pull data. Data that the device requests from the server. **p. 66**

Purchase order (PO). A written document requesting delivery of a specified quantity of a product or service in return for payment. **p. 184**

Purchase requisition (PR). An internal company document that issues a request for a purchase. When accepted, data from the purchase requisition is used in the purchase order. **p. 190**

Push data. Data that the server sends to or pushes onto a device. **p. 66**

Quad-processor. A computer with four CPUs. **p. 50**

Query. A request for data from a database. **p. 98**

R/3. One of the best-known versions of SAP. It was the first truly integrated system that was able to support most of organizations' major operational processes. **p. 175**

Radio-frequency identification (RFID). Computer chips that help identify and track items. As small as, and soon to be as cheap as, a postage stamp, RFID chips broadcast data to receivers that can display and record the broadcast data. **p. 202**

RAM (random access memory). Main memory consisting of cells that hold data or instructions. Each cell has an address that the CPU uses to read or write data. Memory locations can be read or written in any order, hence the term *random access*. RAM memory is almost always volatile. **p. 50**

Raw materials inventory. A repository of parts and subassemblies procured from suppliers that are used to produce products to be stored in the finished goods inventory. **p. 184**

Real-time price discount. A discounted price offered during a sales call. **p. 230**

Record. Also called a *row*, a group of columns in a database table. **p. 91**

Regression analysis. Supervised data mining analysis that estimates the values of parameters in a linear equation. Used to determine the relative influence of variables on an outcome and also to predict future values of that outcome. **p. 341**

Relation. The more formal name for a database table. **p. 93**

Relational database. A database that carries its data in the form of tables and that represents relationships using foreign keys. **p. 93**

Relationship. An association among entities or entity instances in an E-R model or an association among rows of a table in a relational database. **p. 103**

Report. A presentation of data in a structured or meaningful context. **p. 97**

Reporting. A process that uses simple statistical analysis to uncover patterns in a large database of data in order to improve assessment. **p. 338**

Repository. A collection of records, usually implemented as a database. **p. 29**

Request for proposals (RFP). A document that an organization posts to solicit bids from potential vendors. **p. 316**

Resources. The items, such as people, computers, and data and document collections, necessary to accomplish an activity. **p. 128**

Return on investment (ROI). A method of measuring costs and benefits based on the amount earned by an investment as a percentage. **p. 320**

Returns Management process. A process that manages the returns of faulty products for businesses. **p. 195**

RFM analysis. A type of reporting analysis that ranks customers according to the recency, frequency, and monetary value of their purchases. **p. 338**

Roaming. When users move their activities, especially long-running transactions, across devices. **p. 66**

Role. A subset of activities in a business process that is performed by a particular actor; resources are assigned to roles. **p. 28**

Roll up. To compile, total, and summarize data. For example, daily sales are "rolled up" into monthly sales. In accounting systems, transactions are "rolled up" into common accounting reports such as balance sheets and income statements. **p. 187**

Rows. Also called *records*, a group of columns in a database table. **p. 91**

Safeguard. Measure that individuals or organizations take to block a threat from obtaining an asset. **p. 379**

Sales. An operational outbound process comprised of three main activities—Sell, Ship, and Payment. **p. 227**

Sales process. An operational outbound process that records the sales order, ships the product, and bills the customer. **p. 132**

Salesforce.com. The preeminent cloud-based CRM vendor. **p. 244**

SAP AG. The world's most successful ERP vendor. SAP AG is the third largest software company in the world. The core business of SAP AG is selling licenses for its SAP software solutions and related services. In addition, it offers consulting, training, and other services for its software solutions. **p. 173**

SAP Business Suite. The new name for SAP's integrated software platform. The SAP Business Suite runs on NetWeaver. **p. 175**

SAP HANA. An in-memory database in SAP that is exceptionally fast. **p. 347**

Sarbanes-Oxley Act (SOX). A federal law requiring companies to exercise greater control over their financial processes. **p. 160**

Screen-sharing application. Applications that enable virtual meeting members to view the same whiteboard, application, or other display. **p. 281**

Self-efficacy. A person's belief that he or she can be successful at his or her job. **p. 169**

Self-service BI. When users do business intelligence analysis by themselves. **p. 335**

Sequential workflow. The condition that exists when two or more workers perform a task one at a time. A common example is the sequential review of a document. **p. 288**

Server(s). A computer that provides some type of service, such as hosting a database, running a blog, publishing a Web site, or selling goods. Server computers are faster, larger, and more powerful than client computers. **p. 50**

Server farm. A large collection of server computers that coordinates the activities of the servers, usually for commercial purposes. **p. 50**

Server tier. In the three-tier architecture, the tier that consists of computers that run Web servers to generate Web pages and other data in response to requests from browsers. Web servers also process application programs. **p. 72**

Server virtualization. A system in which a server computer hosts one or more other server computers. **p. 55**

Service. In SOA, a repeatable task that a business needs to perform. **p. 132**

Service-oriented architecture (SOA). The use of standard protocols to publish a menu of services that an application provides, the structure of data that it expects to receive, the structure of data that it will produce, and the ways in which services can be requested. **p. 78**

Showrooming. When someone visits a brick-and-mortar store to examine and evaluate products without the intention of buying them at the store. **p. 80**

Single instance. The use of one large ERP implementation to consolidate all the operations of an international firm. **p. 172**

Site license. A flat fee that authorizes the company to install a product, such as an operating system or application, on all of that company's computers or on all of the computers at a specific site. **p. 56**

Six Sigma. A popular strategy for process improvement that seeks to improve process outputs by removing causes of defects and minimizing variability in the process. **p. 141**

Slates. Also called *tablets*; computers that receive input via a touch screen rather than a keyboard or mouse. **p. 50**

Slicing and dicing. The repeated use of basic analysis operations such as sorting, grouping, filtering, and calculating. **p. 339**

Small office/home office (SOHO). A business office with usually fewer than 10 employees; often located in the business professional's home. **p. 68**

Smart card. A plastic card similar to a credit card that has a microchip loaded with identifying data; requires a PIN to be authenticated. **p. 385**

Smartphone. Cell phones with processing capability. **p. 50**

smtp (Simple Mail Transfer Protocol). A protocol used for e-mail transmissions. **p. 71**

Sniffing. A technique for intercepting computer communications. With wired networks, sniffing requires a physical connection to the network. With wireless networks, no such connection is required. **p. 381**

Social capital. The investment in social relations with expectation of future returns in the marketplace. **p. 318**

Social CRM. An information system that helps a company collect customer data from social media and share it among their customer facing processes. **p. 243**

Social engineering. A category of threats that involve manipulating a person or group to unknowingly release confidential information. **p. 381**

Social graph. A network of personal interdependencies, such as friendships, common interests, or kinship, on a social media application. **p. 309**

Social media. Any Web application that depends on user-generated content. **p. 304**

Social media information system. An information system that supports the two activities in the social media process: creating and sharing user-generated content. **p. 304**

Social media policy. A statement that delineates employees' rights and responsibilities when using social media for business purposes. **p. 321**

Software. As part of the five-component framework, one of the five fundamental components of an information system; includes computer programs used to record and process data. **p. 30**

Software as a service (SaaS). An organization that provides not only hardware infrastructure but also an operating system and application programs on top of that hardware. **p. 78**

SoMo. Social media on mobile devices. **p. 323**

Source code. Computer code as written by humans and that is understandable by humans. Source code must be translated into machine code before it can be processed. **p. 58**

Spoofing. When someone pretends to be someone else with the intent of obtaining unauthorized data. If you pretend to be your professor, you are spoofing your professor. **p. 381**

SQL injection attacks. A technique used to compromise database data in which SQL code is unknowingly processed by a Web page. **p. 382**

SQL Server. A popular enterprise-class DBMS product from Microsoft. **p. 94**

Stand-up. A component of the scrum process; a 15-minute meeting in which each team member states what he or she has done in the past day, what he or she will do in the coming day, and any factors that are blocking his or her progress. **p. 376**

Storage hardware. Computer components used to save data and programs. **p. 50**

Strategic processes. Business processes that seek to resolve issues that have a long-range impact on the organization. These processes have a broad scope and impact most of the firm. **p. 130**

Strength of a relationship. In the theory of social capital, the likelihood that a person or other organization in a relationship will do something that will benefit the organization. **p. 318**

Structured processes. Formally defined, standardized processes that support day-to-day operations such as accepting a return, placing an order, computing a sales commission, and so forth. **p. 33**

Structured Query Language (SQL). An international standard language for processing database data. **p. 95**

Substitute. In the five forces model, a competing product that performs the same or similar function as an industry's product by another means. **p. 12**

Supervised data mining. A form of data mining in which data miners develop a model prior to the analysis and apply statistical techniques to data to estimate values of the parameters of the model. **p. 342**

Supplier Evaluation process. A strategic process that determines the criteria for supplier selection and adds and removes suppliers from the list of approved suppliers. **p. 195**

Supplier Relationship Management (SRM) process. A process that automates, simplifies, and accelerates a variety of supply chain processes. SRM is a management process that helps companies reduce procurement costs, build collaborative supplier relationships, better manage supplier options, and improve time to market. **p. 195**

Supply chain management (SCM). The design, planning, execution, and integration of all supply chain processes. SCM uses a collection of tools, techniques, and management activities to help businesses develop integrated supply chains that support organizational strategy. **p. 196**

Support activities. In Porter's value chain model, the activities that contribute indirectly to value creation: procurement, technology, human resources, and the firm's infrastructure. **p. 15**

Surrogate key. Computer-generated unique identifier in the DBMS. **p. 111**

Swimlane. A long column in a BPMN diagram; each column contains all the activities for a particular role. **p. 28**

Switch. A special-purpose computer that receives and transmits data across a network. **p. 68**

Symbian. A mobile operating system that is popular on phones in Europe and the Far East. **p. 54**

Symmetric encryption. An encryption method whereby the same key is used to encode and to decode the message. **p. 386**

Synchronous communication. Information exchange that occurs when all members of a work team meet at the same time, such as face-to-face meetings or conference calls. **p. 279**

System. A group of components that interact to achieve some purpose. **p. 30**

System conversion. The process of converting business activity from the old system to the new. **p. 373**

Systems development. The process of creating and maintaining information systems. It is sometimes called *systems analysis and design*. **p. 369**

Systems development life cycle (SDLC). The classical process used to develop information systems. These basic tasks of systems development are combined into the following phases: system definition, requirements analysis, component design, implementation, and system maintenance (fix or enhance). **p. 369**

Systems thinking. The mental process of making one or more models of the components of a system and connecting the inputs and outputs among those components into a sensible whole, one that explains the phenomenon observed. **p. 7**

Table. Also called a *file*, a group of similar rows or records in a database. **p. 91**

Tablets. Also called *slates*; computers that receive input via a touch screen rather than a keyboard or mouse. **p. 50**

Tag. In markup languages such as html and XML, notation used to define a data element for display or other purposes. **p. 73**

Target. An asset that is desired by a threat. **p. 379**

TCP/IP (Transmission Control Protocol/Internet) Protocol architecture. A protocol architecture having four layers; forms the basis for the TCP/IP–OSI architecture used by the Internet. **p. 71**

Team survey. A form of asynchronous communication in which one team member creates a list of questions and other team members respond. Microsoft SharePoint has built-in survey capability. **p. 282**

Technical safeguard. Safeguard that involves the hardware and software components of an information system. **p. 385**

Technology development processes. A support activity in the value chain; includes designing, testing, and developing technology in support of the primary activities of an organization. **p. 133**

Terabyte (TB). 1,024 GB. **p. 51**

Test plan. A formal description of a system's response to use and misuse scenarios. **p. 373**

Thin–client applications. A software application that requires nothing more than a browser and can be run on many different operating systems. **p. 59**

Third-party cookie. A cookie created by a site other than the one you visited. **p. 358**

Threat. A challenge to information systems security. **p. 379**

Three-tier architecture. Architecture used by most e-commerce server applications. The tiers refer to three different classes of computers. The user tier consists of users' computers that have browsers that request and process Web pages. The server tier consists of computers that run Web servers and in the process generate Web pages and other data in response to requests from browsers. Web servers also process application programs. The third tier is the database tier, which runs the DBMS that processes the database. **p. 72**

Three-way match. The activity within the procurement process that ensures that the data on the invoice matches the data on the purchase order and the goods receipt. **p. 186**

Traditional capital. Investments into resources such as factories, machines, manufacturing equipment, and the like with the expectation of future returns in the market. **p. 318**

Train the trainer. Training sessions in which vendors train the organization's employees to become in-house trainers in order to improve training quality and reduce training expenses. **p. 163**

Transaction processing system (TPS). An information system that supports operational decision making. **p. 129**

Transactional data. Data related to events such as a purchase. **p. 162**

Unix. An operating system developed at Bell Labs in the 1970s. It has been the workhorse of the scientific and engineering communities since then. **p. 54**

Unsupervised data mining. A form of data mining whereby the analysts do not create a model or hypothesis before running the analysis. Instead, they apply the data mining technique to the data and observe the results. With this method, analysts create hypotheses after the analysis to explain the patterns found. **p. 342**

URL (Uniform Resource Locator). A document's address on the Web. URLs begin on the right with a top-level domain, and, moving left, include a domain name and then are followed by optional data that locates a document within that domain. **p. 71**

User experience (UX). A user interface and the way the user responds to the application. **p. 63**

User interface (UI). The presentation format of an application. **p. 63**

User-generated content. Publicly available content created by end users. **p. 321**

User tier. In the three-tier architecture, the tier that consists of computers that have browsers that request and process Web pages. **p. 72**

Utilitarianism. An ethics theory in which the morality of an act is determined by its outcome; acts are judged to be moral if they result in the greatest good to the greatest number or if they maximize happiness and reduce suffering; founders of the modern theory are Jeremy Bentham and John Stuart Mill. **p. 40**

Value. According to Porter, the amount of money that a customer is willing to pay for a resource, product, or service. **p. 15**

Value chain. A network of value-creating activities. **p. 15**

Version lock. Customizing software so heavily that the software cannot be upgraded when the ERP vendor upgrades their system to a new version. **p. 170**

Vertical-market application. Software that serves the needs of a specific industry. Examples of such programs are those used by dental offices to schedule appointments and bill patients, those used by auto mechanics to keep track of customer data and customers' automobile repairs, and those used by parts warehouses to track inventory, purchases, and sales. **p. 57**

Videoconferencing. A technology that combines a conference call with video cameras. **p. 281**

Viral. User-generated content, typically a video, that is shared and promoted by individuals on social media outlets in greater than expected volume. **p. 310**

Virtual machines (vm). In the process of virtualization, a hosted operating system. **p. 55**

Virtual meeting. A meeting in which participants do not meet in the same place and possibly not at the same time. **p. 281**

Visualization. The use of images, or diagrams, for communicating a message. Simple examples include bar charts and infographics. **p. 342**

Vulnerability. A weakness in an information system that provides an opportunity for threats to gain access to individual and organizational assets. **p. 379**

WAN wireless. A communications system that provides wireless connectivity to a wide area network. **p. 70**

Web. The Internet-based network of browsers and servers that process http or https. **p. 71**

Web 2.0. A loose grouping of capabilities, technologies, business models, and philosophies that characterize new and emerging business uses of the Internet. **p. 313**

Web farm. A facility that runs multiple Web servers. Work is distributed among the computers in a Web farm so as to maximize throughput. **p. 73**

Web page. A document encoded in html that is created, transmitted, and used using the World Wide Web. **p. 72**

Web server. A program that processes the http protocol and transmits Web pages on demand. Web servers also process application programs. **p. 72**

Web storefront. In e-commerce, a Web-based application that enables customers to enter and manage their orders. **p. 241**

Webinar. A virtual meeting in which attendees view each other on their computer screens. **p. 281**

Wide area network (WAN). A network that connects computers located at different geographic locations. **p. 67**

Windows RT. A version of Windows 8 designed for use on ARM devices. **p. 55**

Windows Server. A version of Windows that has been specially designed and configured for server use. **p. 55**

Wireless NIC (WNIC). Devices that enable wireless networks by communicating with wireless access points. Such devices can be cards that slide into the PCMA slot or they can be built-in, onboard devices. WNICs operate according to the 802.11 protocol. **p. 68**

Workflow. A process or procedure by which content is created, edited, used, and disposed. **p. 287**

Index